FOOD & WINE

MAGAZINE'S 2002 COOKBOOK

an entire year's recipes

FOOD & WINE

MAGAZINE'S 2002 COOKBOOK

an entire year's recipes

American Express Publishing Corporation
New York · FOOD & WINE BOOKS

FOOD & WINE MAGAZINE
EDITOR IN CHIEF Dana Cowin
CREATIVE DIRECTOR Stephen Scoble
EXECUTIVE FOOD EDITOR Tina Ujlaki

FOOD & WINE BOOKS
EDITOR IN CHIEF Judith Hill
ART DIRECTOR Perri DeFino
MANAGING EDITOR Miriam Harris
ASSOCIATE EDITOR Dana Speers
DESIGNER Elizabeth Rendfleisch
EDITORIAL ASSOCIATE Colleen McKinney
COPY EDITOR Lisa Leventer
PRODUCTION MANAGER Stuart Handelman

SENIOR VICE PRESIDENT, CHIEF MARKETING OFFICER Mark V. Stanich
VICE PRESIDENT, BRANDED PRODUCTS Bruce Rosner
OPERATIONS MANAGER Phil Black
BUSINESS MANAGER Doreen Camardi

---

cover photo: Keller & Keller (Orecchiette with Cauliflower, Anchovies and Pistachios, p. 122)
back photos:
top: Reed Davis (Garlicky Eggplant and Pepper Soup with Mint, p. 91)
center: William Meppem (Grilled Szechuan Chicken with Hoisin Barbecue Sauce, p. 199)
bottom: Quentin Bacon (Winter Apple Gratin, p. 370)

AMERICAN EXPRESS PUBLISHING CORPORATION
©2002 American Express Publishing Corporation

ISBN 0-916103-72-2   ISSN 1097-1564

Published by American Express Publishing Corporation
1120 Avenue of the Americas, New York, New York 10036

Manufactured in the United States of America

contents

182

396

381

foreword

Magazines hold a mirror up to our culture, reflecting our obsessions and our passions. Look at F&W and you can tell what was on people's plates, what was in their refrigerators and what kind of wine they were drinking. And so when we flip back through the past twelve months, it's clear that speed and convenience became even more of a priority for all of us. The magazine expanded its popular Fast column, providing recipes for some astonishingly flavorful food that can be prepared in under half an hour. To make it easier to find them, the Fast recipes are marked with a blue dot. Many other recipes are also marked with a user-friendly dot: red for make-ahead, green for healthy, orange for those from a Best New Chef.

In a world where people barely have time to throw dinner together, it's hard to imagine anyone would really want to make dessert. But we uncovered a latent passion for baking among our readers. Could it be that baking makes a house seem like a home? Calories are comfort? We added a dessert of the month (you must try Peggy Cullen's Chocolate Soufflé Sundae with Caramel and Bittersweet Chocolate Sauce, page 387) and lots of recipes for pies and cakes. We have to admit, we never got tired of testing the sweet recipes in our kitchens.

As the year 2001 concluded, many of us wanted the comfort that comes from being with friends and family. And our recipes reflect this desire too. So from our kitchen to yours, we wish you joy and solace in your gatherings around food and wine.

Dana Cowin
Editor in Chief
FOOD & WINE Magazine

Judith Hill
Editor in Chief
FOOD & WINE Books

1 hors d'oeuvres

Crispy Zucchini Chips

Crispy Zucchini Chips

4 SERVINGS

For the best results, use a mandoline to slice the zucchini and lemon.

- 4 cups pure olive oil
- 1 cup pastry flour

Kosher salt and freshly ground pepper

- 1 pound firm large zucchini, sliced into paper-thin rounds
- 1 lemon, sliced into ⅛-inch rounds
- 2 tablespoons finely chopped flat-leaf parsley
- 1 garlic clove, minced
- 15 large basil leaves

I. In a large, heavy saucepan, heat the pure olive oil to 350°. Set a wire rack over a large baking sheet and cover it with paper towels.

2. Put the pastry flour in a large resealable plastic bag and season it generously with salt and pepper. Add one-fourth of the zucchini and lemon slices to the bag and shake to coat them with flour. Remove the zucchini and lemon slices from the bag and shake off any excess flour. Add the floured slices to the hot oil and cook over high heat, turning once, until deep golden, about 2 minutes. Transfer to the paper towels to drain. Fry the remaining zucchini and lemon slices in 3 more batches, adjusting the heat as necessary to keep the oil temperature constant. Sprinkle the zucchini and lemon slices with the parsley and garlic.

3. Fry the basil leaves in the hot oil until crisp, 10 to 15 seconds. Transfer the fried leaves to paper towels to drain. Gently toss the fried basil leaves with the zucchini and lemon slices and serve at once.

—*Peggy Knickerbocker*

WINE A light Sauvignon Blanc with crisp acidity, such as the 1999 Mason or the 1999 Bernardus, both from California, will pair beautifully with these crisp zucchini chips and lemon slices.

Plantain Chips with Chicken and Mojito Mango Salsa

MAKES 4 DOZEN HORS D'OEUVRES ●●

Tortilla chips can be a good substitute for plantain chips.

- 1 tablespoon vegetable oil
- 2 skinless, boneless chicken breast halves (about 6 ounces each)

Salt and freshly ground pepper

- 1 large ripe mango, finely diced
- ¼ cup minced red onion
- 2 tablespoons Telluride Mojito (p. 396), without club soda
- 2 teaspoons minced jalapeño
- 1 teaspoon chopped fresh mint
- 1 teaspoon fresh lime juice
- 4 dozen large plantain chips

I. In a medium skillet, heat the oil until shimmering. Season the chicken with salt and pepper and cook over moderately high heat until browned on the bottom, about 4 minutes. Turn and cook over moderate heat until browned and cooked through, about 6 minutes longer. Transfer to a plate to cool completely.

2. Meanwhile, in a medium bowl, combine the mango with the onion, Telluride Mojito, jalapeño, mint and lime juice. Season with salt and pepper.

3. Arrange the plantain chips on a large tray. Halve the chicken breasts lengthwise, then thinly slice crosswise. Put a piece of chicken on each plantain chip, spoon the salsa on top and serve.

—*Grace Parisi*

Frico and Soppressata Chips

12 SERVINGS ●

Serving innovative bar snacks instead of fussy hors d'oeuvres will make your next cocktail party swing.

- ½ pound soppressata or other spiced salami, very thinly sliced
- 1 pound aged Gouda or Asiago, coarsely shredded

Optional seasonings: sesame seeds, finely chopped toasted pistachios, fennel pollen and Aleppo pepper flakes

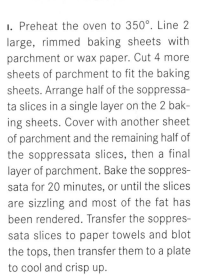

Plantain Chips with Chicken and Mojito Mango Salsa

I. Preheat the oven to 350°. Line 2 large, rimmed baking sheets with parchment or wax paper. Cut 4 more sheets of parchment to fit the baking sheets. Arrange half of the soppressata slices in a single layer on the 2 baking sheets. Cover with another sheet of parchment and the remaining half of the soppressata slices, then a final layer of parchment. Bake the soppressata for 20 minutes, or until the slices are sizzling and most of the fat has been rendered. Transfer the soppressata slices to paper towels and blot the tops, then transfer them to a plate to cool and crisp up.

2. Sprinkle 6 tablespoon-size mounds of the cheese in a large nonstick skillet. Top each mound with a pinch of the seasonings, if using. Cook the frico chips over moderately high heat until the cheese is lacy and slightly set. Using a thin, flexible metal spatula,

Sweet-and-Spicy Nut Mix

loosen and flip each frico and cook for 1 minute longer, or until crisp and golden. Transfer the frico chips to paper towels to drain, then transfer to a plate to cool and crisp up. Wipe out the skillet and repeat with the remaining cheese and seasonings.

—Grace Parisi

MAKE AHEAD The frico and soppressata chips can be stored in an airtight container for 1 day.

WINE A crisp nonvintage sparkling wine, such as the Green Point Brut from Australia or the Zardetto Prosecco di Conegliano Brut from Italy, would counterbalance the saltiness and seasonings of the cheese and sausage.

Sweet-and-Spicy Nut Mix

MAKES ABOUT 4 CUPS ●●

- ½ cup pecan halves
- ½ cup hazelnuts
- 3 tablespoons dark brown sugar
- 1½ tablespoons pure maple syrup
- 1 tablespoon unsalted butter, melted
- 1½ teaspoons kosher salt
- ¾ teaspoon cayenne pepper
- ½ teaspoon cinnamon
- ½ cup roasted whole cashews
- ½ cup roasted whole almonds
- 2 cups mini pretzel twists

1. Preheat the oven to 350°. Spread the pecan halves in a pie plate. Bake them for 10 minutes, or until lightly toasted; transfer to a plate. Spread the hazelnuts in the same pie plate. Bake them for 12 minutes, or until lightly toasted; transfer to a kitchen towel. Let the hazelnuts cool, then rub them together vigorously to remove the skins. Add the hazelnuts to the pecans. Leave the oven on.

2. In a medium bowl, mix the brown sugar with the maple syrup, melted butter, salt, cayenne and cinnamon. Add the pecans, hazelnuts, cashews, almonds and pretzels and toss until coated.

3. Spread the nut mix on a large, rimmed baking sheet and bake for 12 minutes, stirring occasionally. Let cool completely on the baking sheet, stirring occasionally to separate the nuts and pretzels. *—David Lebovitz*

Overnight Fennel and Jicama Pickles with Orange

12 SERVINGS ●

- ¼ cup rice vinegar
- 2 teaspoons kosher salt
- 1 teaspoon sugar
- Pinch of saffron, crumbled
- 1½ teaspoons crushed red pepper
- 2 tablespoons salt-packed capers, rinsed
- 3 juice oranges, zest julienned, juice squeezed and strained
- 1½ cups water
- 1 small jicama (1 pound), peeled and cut into 3-by-⅓-inch matchsticks
- 2 fennel bulbs (¾ pound each)— halved, cored and cut into ⅓-inch-thick wedges

1. In a medium bowl, stir the vinegar with the salt, sugar and saffron until the salt and sugar dissolve. Add the

FROM TOP: **Frico and Soppressata Chips (p. 11), Overnight Fennel and Jicama Pickles with Orange, and anchovies**

crushed red pepper, capers, orange zest and juice and water. In a deep glass or ceramic bowl, mix the jicama and fennel. Pour the brine over the vegetables. Press a sheet of plastic over the vegetables and top with a heavy pot lid or plate to keep them submerged in the brine. Refrigerate overnight.

2. Drain the pickles and reserve the brine. Arrange the pickles in a shallow bowl, drizzle them with some of the reserved brine and serve.

—*Grace Parisi*

ONE SERVING Calories 29 kcal, Total Fat 0.1 gm, Saturated Fat 0 gm, Protein 1 gm, Carbohydrates 7 gm

MAKE AHEAD The pickles can be refrigerated in the brine for 2 days.

Mushroom Pâté

MAKES 1 CUP ●●

This rich, rustic spread can be used to fill tea sandwiches, or it can be packed in a crock and served with toast.

- ¾ cup dried porcini mushrooms (¾ ounce)
- ⅔ cup boiling water
- 1 tablespoon olive oil
- 3 leeks, white and pale green parts only, coarsely chopped

Salt

- ¾ pound small white mushrooms, quartered
- 2 tablespoons Sercial Madeira

Freshly ground black pepper

1. In a small heatproof bowl, cover the dried porcini mushrooms with the boiling water; cover and let soften for 20 minutes.

2. Heat a large, heavy nonstick skillet. Add the olive oil, chopped leeks and salt and stir over moderate heat until the leeks begin to sizzle. Cover the skillet and cook the leeks, stirring frequently, until they haved softened, about 5 minutes.

3. Lift the porcini mushrooms from their soaking liquid and squeeze them dry. Place the porcini mushrooms in a

strainer and rinse them briefly to remove any grit, then pat them dry with paper towels. Coarsely chop the porcini mushrooms and add them to the leeks along with the white mushrooms. Pour in the Sercial Madeira and cook the mixture for 30 seconds. Carefully add the porcini mushroom soaking liquid, leaving behind any grit. Season the mushroom mixture with salt, cover and cook for 4 minutes. Uncover and cook, stirring, until the pan is dry and the mushrooms are browned, approximately 10 minutes longer.

4. Transfer the cooked mushrooms to a mortar or a food processor; pound to a coarse puree or process until coarsely chopped. Scrape half of the mushroom puree into a bowl. Pound or process the rest of the puree until fine. Stir the fine puree into the chunky one and season with salt and pepper. Transfer to a crock and serve warm or at room temperature.

—*Sally Schneider*

ONE-QUARTER CUP Calories 95 kcal, Total Fat 3.8 gm, Saturated Fat 0.5 gm

MAKE AHEAD The pâté can be refrigerated for 4 days.

Roasted Artichoke, Lemon and Garlic Dip

10 SERVINGS ●

You can substitute four 9-ounce packages of frozen artichoke hearts for the fresh whole artichokes called for below. Thaw the frozen hearts and squeeze them dry before using.

- 1 small lemon, halved
- 9 large artichokes (about 5½ pounds)
- 8 large unpeeled garlic cloves
- ¼ cup extra-virgin olive oil
- 2 thyme sprigs

Salt and freshly ground pepper

- 1 cup mayonnaise
- 4 tablespoons cream cheese, softened

- 3 tablespoons fine dry bread crumbs
- 2 teaspoons unsalted butter, melted

Crackers or bagel chips, for serving

1. Squeeze a lemon half into a large bowl of cold water and add the lemon half to the bowl. Working with 1 artichoke at a time, trim the stem to 1 inch and snap off all of the tough outer leaves. Using a sharp knife, cut off the top two-thirds of the artichoke. With a teaspoon, scoop out the furry choke. Peel the artichoke, removing all the dark green skin, and add it to the bowl of acidulated water. Repeat with the remaining artichokes.

2. Preheat the oven to 425°. Drain the artichokes and pat dry. Cut each artichoke into eighths. Quarter the remaining lemon half and remove the seeds. In the bowl, toss the artichokes with the lemon pieces, garlic, olive oil and thyme. Season with salt and pepper and spread on a large nonstick rimmed baking sheet. Bake the artichokes for about 40 minutes, stirring occasionally, until golden and tender. Let cool slightly and discard the thyme. Coarsely chop 8 of the roasted artichoke pieces and reserve. Reduce the oven temperature to 375°.

3. Peel the garlic; place in a food processor. Add the remaining roasted artichoke and lemon pieces; pulse until finely chopped. Add the mayonnaise and cream cheese and process until smooth. Season with salt and pepper. Add the reserved chopped artichokes and pulse just until combined. Spread the dip in an even layer in a small shallow baking dish.

4. In a small bowl, mix the bread crumbs and butter; sprinkle over the dip. Bake for 20 minutes, or until heated through and the topping is golden. Serve with crackers or bagel chips.

—*Grace Parisi*

MAKE AHEAD The artichoke dip can be prepared through Step 3 and refrigerated for up to 3 days.

hors d'oeuvres

Molded Fava Bean Puree with Dill

MAKES 4 CUPS ●●

The dried split fava beans are cooked until they become an ultra-creamy puree that can be molded. Serve the puree as a spread with warmed pita bread.

1½ cups dried split fava beans
     (9 ounces), picked over
     and rinsed
1   medium onion,
     finely chopped
¼   cup extra-virgin olive oil,
     plus more for drizzling
1   quart water
Salt and freshly ground
     pepper
½   cup chopped dill
¼   cup chopped scallions

1. In a medium saucepan, combine the fava beans with the onion, ¼ cup of olive oil and the water and bring to a boil over high heat. Reduce the heat to low and simmer, stirring occasionally, until the fava beans are falling apart, about 1 hour; as the beans thicken, toward the end of cooking, stir more frequently to prevent sticking.

2. Pass the bean mixture through a coarse sieve into a large bowl. Season with salt and pepper and stir in ¼ cup of the dill. Lightly oil a 4-cup soufflé dish or bowl and scrape in the fava bean puree; smooth the surface. Cover with plastic wrap and refrigerate until firm, at least 2 hours or overnight.

3. To unmold the fava bean puree, invert the soufflé dish onto a large plate and shake to release the puree. Drizzle the puree with olive oil and sprinkle with the remaining ¼ cup of dill and the chopped scallions.

—*Engin Akin*

ONE-QUARTER CUP Calories 89 kcal, Total Fat 3.6 gm, Saturated Fat 0.5 gm, Protein 4 gm, Carbohydrates 10 gm

MAKE AHEAD The molded fava bean puree can be refrigerated for 2 days.

Fava Bean Crostini

MAKES 2 DOZEN CROSTINI ●●

This garlicky, bright green fava puree is seasonal, delicious and—just as important—beautiful.

3½ pounds fresh fava beans,
     shelled (4 cups)
2   garlic cloves, smashed
2   teaspoons finely chopped thyme
2   teaspoons fresh lemon juice
1   teaspoon finely grated lemon zest
1   cup extra-virgin olive oil, plus
     more for drizzling
Salt and freshly ground pepper
Twenty-four ½-inch-thick slices of
     Italian bread
Lemon wedges, for serving

1. Preheat the broiler. Bring a medium saucepan of water to a boil. Add the shelled fava beans and cook until tender, approximately 5 minutes. Drain the fava beans and transfer them to a bowl of ice water to cool. Drain the beans, then peel and discard the tough outer skins.

2. In a food processor, puree the fava beans with the garlic, thyme, lemon juice and lemon zest. With the food processor running, add ¾ cup of the extra-virgin olive oil in a thin stream and process the mixture until it is smooth. Scrape the fava bean puree into a medium bowl and season with salt and pepper.

3. Brush the bread slices on both sides with the remaining ¼ cup of olive oil. Arrange the slices on a baking sheet and broil about 4 inches from the heat for 1 minute per side, or until golden and crisp.

4. Spread the toasted bread slices with the fava bean puree and arrange the crostini on a platter. Drizzle them with olive oil, sprinkle with salt and serve with lemon wedges.

—*Brandon Miller*

MAKE AHEAD The fava bean puree can be refrigerated for 2 days. Bring the puree to room temperature before proceeding.

Smoky Chickpea Dip

8 SERVINGS ●●●

A variation on hummus, minus the tahini, this creamy dip gets an unexpected kick from a smoky Spanish paprika called pimentón. It's a wonderful hors d'oeuvre when served with bread that has been brushed with olive oil and seasoned with salt, pepper and pimentón before grilling. You can use canned chickpeas in place of the dried ones called for here, but the texture and flavor won't be quite as interesting.

½   pound dried chickpeas, soaked
     overnight and drained
1   teaspoon cumin seeds
4   small garlic cloves, smashed
3   tablespoons fresh lemon juice
¼   teaspoon hot pimentón or
     other hot paprika
⅛   teaspoon cayenne pepper
2   tablespoons extra-virgin olive oil,
     plus more for drizzling
1   tablespoon extra-virgin olive oil
     with lemon (see Note)
Salt
2   tablespoons chopped cilantro
Grilled bread or pita, for serving

1. In a medium saucepan, cover the chickpeas with 3 inches of water and bring to a boil. Cover and simmer over moderate heat until just tender, about 1 hour and 15 minutes. Drain the chickpeas well and pat dry.

2. Meanwhile, in a small skillet, cook the cumin seeds over moderate heat, shaking the pan until they are lightly toasted, about 3 minutes. Transfer to a spice or coffee grinder and let cool, then grind to a fine powder.

3. In a food processor, combine the chickpeas with the garlic, lemon juice, cumin, pimentón and cayenne pepper and pulse until finely chopped. With the machine on, add the 2 tablespoons of extra-virgin olive oil and the lemon olive oil in a slow, steady stream and puree until the chickpea dip is very smooth. Season the dip with salt, then scrape it into a shallow bowl.

Smoky Chickpea Dip

Fava Bean Crostini

Drizzle with extra-virgin olive oil, sprinkle with the cilantro and serve with grilled bread or pita.

—*Randy Windham*

NOTE Bottles of lemon-flavored extra-virgin olive oil—made by crushing olives with lemons—are available at specialty markets and some large supermarkets. Medi Terranea's Agrumato Lemon Olive Oil is imported by Manicaretti (888-952-4005; www.manicaretti.com).

MAKE AHEAD The chickpea dip can be refrigerated overnight. Let return to room temperature, drizzle with olive oil and sprinkle with cilantro before serving.

WINE A fruity Sauvignon Blanc with fresh acidity will highlight the lemon and smoky paprika here. Try a light-bodied one with hints of tropical fruit, like the 2000 Grant Burge Kraft from Australia or the 2000 Delaire from South Africa.

Warm White Bean Bruschetta

MAKES 12 LARGE BRUSCHETTA ●

- 2 tablespoons pure olive oil
- ½ cup finely chopped onion
- 1 teaspoon finely chopped rosemary
- 1 cup dried small white beans, such as navy or Great Northern (½ pound), soaked overnight and drained
- 2 cups chicken stock or canned low-sodium broth
- 1 cup water
- 1 small carrot, cut into large chunks
- 1 bay leaf

Salt and freshly ground pepper

Twelve ½-inch-thick slices of Tuscan or peasant bread

Extra-virgin olive oil, for brushing and drizzling

- 1 large garlic clove, halved

Coarse sea salt

1. In a medium saucepan, heat the pure olive oil until shimmering. Add the onion and rosemary and cook over moderate heat, stirring occasionally, until the onion softens, about 5 minutes. Add the beans, stock, water, carrot and bay leaf and bring to a boil. Cover partially and simmer over moderately low heat until the beans are tender, about 45 minutes. Season the beans with salt and pepper and simmer for 10 minutes longer.

2. Drain the beans, reserving the cooking liquid. Discard the bay leaf. Transfer half of the beans to a food processor and puree until smooth. Add about ¼ cup of the reserved cooking liquid and process until creamy. Return the bean puree to the saucepan and stir in the remaining half of the beans; discard the remaining cooking liquid. Season with salt and pepper and keep warm.

3. Preheat a cast-iron grill pan or the broiler. Brush both sides of the bread with extra-virgin olive oil. Grill or broil until golden brown on both sides. Rub

Thick Herbed Yogurt

the toasts with the garlic clove, then spread with the bean puree. Arrange the bruschetta on a platter, drizzle with extra-virgin olive oil and sprinkle with sea salt. Serve right away.

—*Brandon Miller*

MAKE AHEAD The bean puree can be refrigerated for 1 week. Rewarm before serving.

Thick Herbed Yogurt

MAKES ABOUT 3 CUPS ●

Turkish yogurt is thick as clotted cream and just as rich. American yogurt that has been drained is a good approximation. The seasoned yogurt is marvelous with fresh pita bread.

- 4 cups plain whole milk yogurt (see Note after next recipe)
- 12 large scallions, finely chopped
- 2 jalapeños, seeded and minced
- 2 tablespoons white wine vinegar
- 2 garlic cloves, minced

Salt

- 1 pomegranate, seeded (1 cup)
- 2 tablespoons chopped dill
- 2 tablespoons chopped mint

Extra-virgin olive oil, for drizzling

1. Line a colander with cheesecloth or 2 sheets of damp paper towel. Set the colander over a bowl, add the yogurt and let drain in the refrigerator until thick, at least 4 hours or overnight.

2. In a bowl, mix the yogurt with the scallions, jalapeños, vinegar and garlic and season with salt. Transfer to a serving bowl. Sprinkle with the pomegranate seeds, dill and mint and drizzle generously with olive oil. Serve chilled or at room temperature. —*Engin Akin*

MAKE AHEAD The seasoned yogurt can be refrigerated overnight. Sprinkle with the toppings just before serving.

Eggplant and Toasted Almond Salad

MAKES 2 CUPS ● ●

The Turkish name for this creamy salad is *nazkatun,* which means "dainty women." Served with triangles of pita for scooping, it makes a perfect hors d'oeuvre. The yogurt needs to drain for at least four hours, so plan accordingly.

- 1½ cups plain whole milk yogurt (see Note)
- ½ cup whole almonds (2 ounces)

Two 1-pound eggplants

- 1½ tablespoons extra-virgin olive oil
- 1 garlic clove, minced
- 2 teaspoons fresh lemon juice

Salt

- 1 tablespoon chopped mint

1. Line a colander with cheesecloth or 2 sheets of damp paper towel. Set the colander over a bowl, add the yogurt and let drain in the refrigerator until thick, at least 4 hours or overnight.

2. Preheat the oven to 400°. Spread the almonds in a pie pan and toast for 8 minutes, or until browned; transfer to a plate to cool. Set aside 1 tablespoon of whole almonds; coarsely chop the rest.

3. Preheat the broiler. Put the eggplants on a rimmed baking sheet and pierce them in 3 places with a small knife. Broil the eggplants about 8 inches from the heat for 20 minutes, or until blackened on top and partially collapsed. Turn the eggplants over and broil for about 25 minutes, or until blackened and very soft. Let cool slightly, then discard the skins, stems and seeds.

4. Finely chop the eggplants and drain in a colander for 20 minutes. Transfer to a bowl, stir in the thickened yogurt, chopped almonds, olive oil, garlic and lemon juice and season with salt. Sprinkle the salad with mint, garnish with the reserved whole almonds and serve. —*Engin Akin*

ONE-QUARTER CUP Calories 119 kcal, Total Fat 7.8 gm, Saturated Fat 1.6 gm, Protein 4 gm, Carbohydrates 10 gm

NOTE Middle Eastern shops sell thick yogurt that has already been drained. You can skip Step 1 and substitute ¾ cup of store-bought thickened yogurt in Step 4.

MAKE AHEAD The eggplant salad can be refrigerated for up to 4 hours.

Gorgonzola and Walnut Terrine

10 SERVINGS, PLUS LEFTOVERS ● ●

- ¾ cup walnuts (3 ounces)
- 10 ounces Gorgonzola, preferably dolce, softened
- 6 ounces cream cheese, softened
- ½ pound fresh goat cheese, softened
- ½ cup minced chives

Freshly ground pepper

Toasted pumpernickel or baguette slices, for serving

1. Preheat the oven to 350°. Line a 4-cup soufflé dish, loaf pan or terrine with plastic wrap, allowing 4 inches of overhang on 2 sides.

2. Spread the walnuts in a pie plate and bake until lightly toasted, about 8 minutes. Let cool, then finely chop.

3. In a food processor, puree the Gorgonzola with two-thirds of the cream cheese until smooth.

4. In a bowl, blend the goat cheese with the remaining one-third of the

meze menu

fresh cranberry beans with tomatoes, onions and cinnamon (p. 302)

köfte with pistachios and tahini sauce (p. 25) | thick herbed yogurt (p. 16)

eggplant and toasted almond salad (p. 16) | circassian chicken (p. 189)

molded fava bean puree with dill (p. 14) | turkish tomato salad with fresh herbs (p. 69)

cream cheese and ¼ cup of the chives; season with pepper.

5. Sprinkle ⅓ cup of the walnuts in the bottom of the prepared dish. Spread half of the Gorgonzola mixture on top and sprinkle with half of the remaining walnuts and 2 tablespoons of the chives. Spread the goat cheese mixture on top, and sprinkle with the remaining walnuts and chives. Top with the remaining Gorgonzola mixture. Fold the plastic wrap over the top of the terrine and press lightly. Cover with more plastic wrap and refrigerate for at least 4 hours or up to 2 days.

6. To unmold the terrine, unwrap it and lift it out by the plastic wrap, then turn it out onto a platter. Slice it and let it return to room temperature before serving with toasts. —*Danielle Custer*
WINE A bright, tangy sparkling wine from California, such as the inexpensive Nonvintage Domaine Chandon Blanc de Noirs or the more complex 1996 "J," will cut the richness of the cheese and walnuts.

Gorgonzola and Walnut Terrine

Chicken Liver Pâté with Toast
MAKES ABOUT 1 CUP ●

- 4 tablespoons unsalted butter
- 1 medium onion, thinly sliced
- 1 garlic clove, coarsely chopped
- ½ pound chicken livers, trimmed
- Kosher salt
- Quatre-épices (see Note)
- ¼ cup Cognac or other brandy
- ½ baguette, cut crosswise into ¼-inch-thick slices
- Extra-virgin olive oil for brushing

1. In a large skillet, melt 2 tablespoons of the butter over moderate heat. Add the onion and garlic and cook, stirring occasionally, until lightly browned, about 10 minutes. Transfer to a food processor. Melt the remaining 2 tablespoons of butter in the same skillet. Add the livers, season with salt and ½ teaspoon of quatre-épices and cook over high heat until browned on the outside and pink inside, about 5 minutes. Transfer to the food processor.

2. Add the Cognac to the skillet and simmer over high heat until reduced by one-third, scraping up the browned bits from the bottom, about 3 minutes. Add the Cognac to the processor and puree until smooth. Season generously with salt and quatre-épices. Pack the pâté into a small bowl, press a piece of plastic directly on the pâté and refrigerate until firm, at least 2 hours or up to 3 days. Bring to room temperature before serving.

3. Preheat the oven to 350°. Brush the baguette slices on both sides with olive oil and arrange on a baking sheet. Sprinkle the bread liberally with salt and bake for 10 minutes, or until golden brown and crisp. Serve the pâté with the toast. —*Melissa Roberts*
NOTE Quatre-épices (four spices) is a French spice mixture. You can easily make your own by stirring together 2 teaspoons of freshly ground pepper, ½ teaspoon of ground cloves, ½ teaspoon of ground ginger and ½ teaspoon of freshly grated nutmeg.

Creamy Chicken Liver Mousse
12 SERVINGS, PLUS LEFTOVERS ●

The key to the rich texture of this chicken liver mousse is to let the livers come to room temperature and to blend the softened butter into them gradually when pureeing. This recipe must be refrigerated overnight in order to allow the flavors to develop, so plan accordingly.

- 1¼ pounds chicken livers, trimmed, at room temperature
- 8 large egg yolks, at room temperature
- 2 tablespoons brandy
- 2 tablespoons Calvados or other apple brandy
- 1 tablespoon salt
- 1½ teaspoons freshly ground white pepper
- ¾ teaspoon ground allspice
- Pinch of freshly grated nutmeg
- 3 sticks (¾ pound) unsalted butter, cut into tablespoons, at room temperature
- 2 cups heavy cream
- Toasted baguette slices, for serving
- Sweet-and-Sour Red-Onion Relish, for serving (recipe follows)

1. Preheat the oven to 275°. In a food processor, combine the livers, egg yolks, brandy, Calvados, salt, pepper, allspice and nutmeg and puree until smooth. With the machine on, blend in the softened butter, 1 tablespoon at a time, until all the butter is incorporated and the puree is creamy; if it looks curdled, wrap a hot kitchen towel around the processor bowl and puree until light and creamy.

2. Pass the puree through a fine strainer set over a large bowl and stir in the heavy cream until blended. Pour the puree into a 1½-quart enameled cast-iron terrine and set the terrine in a roasting pan. Pour enough boiling water into the roasting pan to reach halfway up the side of the terrine and bake for 1 hour and 10 minutes, or

Creamy Chicken Liver Mousse, with Sweet-and-Sour Red-Onion Relish

until the mousse is lightly browned on top and a toothpick inserted in the center comes out clean. Remove the terrine from the water bath and let cool, then cover with plastic wrap and aluminum foil and refrigerate overnight.

3. To unmold, dip the bottom of the terrine in a pan of hot water for 10 seconds, and run a paring knife around the edge of the mousse. Invert the mousse onto a long platter or rectangular plate. Cut it into ½-inch slices and transfer to plates. Serve with baguette toasts and the Sweet-and-Sour Red-Onion Relish.—*Scott Howell*

MAKE AHEAD The Creamy Chicken Liver Mousse can be refrigerated in its terrine for up to 1 week; place plastic wrap directly on its surface. Leftovers can be tightly wrapped in plastic and refrigerated for up to 5 days. Let stand at room temperature for 30 minutes before serving.

WINE The Nonvintage Deutz Brut or a fruity rosé sparkling wine, such as the Nonvintage Nicolas Feuillatte Brut Rosé, will contrast beautifully with this rich and creamy chicken liver mousse.

SWEET-AND-SOUR RED-ONION RELISH

MAKES ABOUT 1½ CUPS ●

There's no denying that Southerners love rich food, but this sweet and tart condiment helps keep the chicken liver mousse in check. The Campari adds a touch of bitterness.

  2 tablespoons unsalted butter
  2 large red onions (1½ pounds total), halved lengthwise and thinly sliced crosswise
  2 tablespoons sugar
  ½ cup golden raisins
  ½ cup red wine vinegar
  1 tablespoon Campari
Salt and freshly ground pepper

Melt the butter in a large saucepan. Add the onions, cover and cook over moderately low heat, stirring occasionally, until the onions are softened, about 15 minutes. Uncover, add the sugar and cook, stirring frequently, until very tender and lightly browned, 10 to 15 minutes. Stir in the raisins, vinegar and Campari and season with salt and pepper. Cook over moderately low heat until most of the liquid evaporates, about 10 minutes. Transfer the relish to a bowl and let cool completely. Serve at room temperature. —*S.H.*

MAKE AHEAD The relish can be refrigerated for up to 5 days.

Anchovy and Piquillo Pepper Bruschetta

6 SERVINGS ●

Six ½-inch-thick slices Tuscan bread
Extra-virgin olive oil
  1 large garlic clove, halved
One 8-ounce jar piquillo peppers, drained and cut into strips
  6 anchovies, rinsed and chopped
  12 caperberries, stemmed and sliced crosswise
Sea salt and freshly ground pepper

1. Preheat the broiler. Toast the bread until golden, then lightly brush with olive oil. Rub the toasted bread on 1 side with the garlic clove.

2. In a small bowl, toss the piquillos with the anchovies and caperberries. Spoon the topping on the toasted bread. Drizzle with olive oil, sprinkle with salt and pepper and serve.

—Emmanuel Kemiji

WINE Lustau's manzanilla sherry, from Spain, is light and dry, with high acidity and an almost salty tinge that complements the anchovies and a mineral earthiness that matches the peppers.

Crispy Bacon-Wrapped Stuffed Dates

8 SERVINGS ● ●

16 large Medjool dates, pitted

16 roasted almonds

Scant ¼ cup mild goat
   cheese, crumbled

8 slices of bacon (about 7 ounces),
   halved crosswise

1. Preheat the oven to 400°. Cut a lengthwise slit in the dates. Stuff each one with an almond and about ½ teaspoon of the goat cheese. Pinch the dates closed. Wrap each date securely in a piece of bacon and arrange the dates, seam side down, on a wire rack set on a baking sheet.

2. Bake the stuffed dates for about 20 minutes, or until the bacon is browned and crisp; turn each date after 10 minutes. Serve the stuffed dates warm or at room temperature.

—Jimmy Bradley

MAKE AHEAD The stuffed dates can be prepared through Step 1 and refrigerated for 1 day.

Marinated Fried Trout

6 SERVINGS ●

Light, tasty and colorful, this hors d'oeuvre, also known as *escavèche,* is a specialty of the Ardennes, the southern part of Belgium famous for its freshwater fish, game and wonderful smoked hams *(jambons d'Ardennes).* The trout has to marinate for two full days, so plan accordingly.

1½ cups tarragon vinegar

1 cup water

1½ tablespoons sugar

Salt

3 tablespoons vegetable oil

¾ pound skinless trout fillets

3 tablespoons unbleached
   all-purpose flour

Freshly ground pepper

½ Spanish or large Vidalia onion,
   sliced into ¼-inch-thick rings

1 large carrot, cut crosswise into
   ¼-inch-thick slices

½ red bell pepper, sliced lengthwise
   into ¼-inch strips

1 lemon, cut crosswise into ¼-inch-
   thick slices, ends discarded

6 bay leaves

1 tablespoon whole pink
   peppercorns

Herbed Fromage Blanc (recipe follows)

1. In a small saucepan, combine the tarragon vinegar with the water, sugar and 1 teaspoon of salt. Bring to a boil and simmer over moderate heat for 3 minutes.

2. Heat the oil in a large skillet. If necessary, cut the trout fillets into 6 pieces of equal size. Spread the flour in a pie plate and season with salt and pepper. Lightly flour the fillets, shaking off the excess. Fry the fillets in the hot oil over moderate heat until golden, about 2 minutes per side. Drain on paper towels.

3. Spread half the onion, carrot and bell pepper slices in a 1-quart glass or ceramic bowl or loaf pan. Set 3 trout fillets on top and cover with half the lemon slices, bay leaves and pink peppercorns. Repeat the layering with the remaining ingredients. Reheat the vinegar marinade and pour it over the fish; let cool completely. Cover with plastic wrap and refrigerate for at least 2 days and up to 1 week. Serve the trout at room temperature with the Herbed Fromage Blanc.

—Ruth Van Waerebeek

BEER The aromatic and vinegary flavors in the *escavèche* might overwhelm wine. Try beer. A full-flavored ale, such as Duvel, would be good.

MAKES 1 CUP ● ●

This dip is wonderful with crudités and brown country bread as well as with the Marinated Fried Trout.

1 cup fromage blanc or sour cream

1 tablespoon minced chives

1 tablespoon minced
   flat-leaf parsley

2 teaspoons olive oil

1 teaspoon minced tarragon

Salt and freshly ground pepper

In a bowl, blend the fromage blanc with the chives, parsley, olive oil and tarragon. Season with salt and pepper.

—R.V.W.

Smoky Tea-Cured Salmon with Ginger Butter

10 SERVINGS ●

This recipe is delicious and easy. Buy the Lapsang souchong tea in bulk at a Chinese market if you can; it's sure to be considerably less expensive than at a tea shop. The salmon must be left to cure in the refrigerator for two days, so plan accordingly.

1 cup Lapsang souchong
   tea leaves (2 ounces)

½ cup sugar

Kosher salt

Two 1-pound tail pieces of salmon
   fillet, with skin

1 stick (4 ounces) unsalted butter,
   at room temperature

3 tablespoons minced peeled
   fresh ginger

1 tablespoon minced chives

1 loaf of cocktail
   pumpernickel bread

1. Line a large glass baking dish with a double layer of plastic wrap, leaving 4 inches of overhang all around. In a small bowl, toss the tea with the sugar and ½ cup of kosher salt. Spread half of the curing mixture in the prepared dish. Set the salmon, skin side down, in the dish. Spread the remaining mixture over the fish and cover tightly with the overhanging plastic wrap. Set a plate on the salmon and top with a heavy can. Refrigerate the salmon for 2 days.

2. In a medium bowl, blend the butter with the ginger and chives and season with salt. Spread a thin layer of the ginger butter on each slice of pumpernickel bread, then cut the slices on the diagonal.

3. Rinse the salmon, removing as much of the curing mixture as possible; pat dry. Using a thin, sharp knife, cut the salmon crosswise into very thin slices. Place a small slice of salmon on each bread triangle and serve. —*Institute of Culinary Education, New York City*

MAKE AHEAD The rinsed and dried tea-cured salmon can be wrapped in plastic and refrigerated for 1 week.

Spicy Margarita Shrimp

MAKES 16 SKEWERS ●●

- ¼ cup Juicy Margarita (p. 396)
- 2 tablespoons vegetable oil
- 1 chipotle in adobo, seeded and minced
- Salt and freshly ground pepper
- 32 medium shrimp (about 1¼ pounds) shelled and deveined
- Lime wedges, for serving

I. Preheat the broiler. In a glass bowl, mix the Juicy Margarita, the vegetable oil and the chipotle in adobo. Season the mixture with salt and pepper, add the shrimp and toss to coat. Let the shrimp stand at room temperature for 15 minutes.

2. Drain the shrimp and arrange them on a baking sheet. Broil the shrimp as close to the heat as possible for 2 to 3 minutes, turning once, until they are opaque and cooked through. Put 2 shrimp on each of 16 skewers. Serve the Spicy Margarita Shrimp warm or at room temperature with lime wedges.

—*Grace Parisi*

FOUR SHRIMP Calories 87 kcal, Total Fat 2.1 gm, Saturated Fat 0.3 gm, Protein 14 gm, Carbohydrates 1 gm

Spicy Margarita Shrimp

Spice-Seared Shrimp

8 SERVINGS ●●

Here, shrimp in the shell is encrusted with sticky, spicy salt and then quickly stir-fried. The result is the best kind of finger food.

- 1 tablespoon coarse sea salt
- ½ tablespoon fennel seeds, lightly crushed
- ½ tablespoon coriander seeds, lightly crushed
- ½ tablespoon cumin seeds, lightly crushed
- ½ tablespoon crushed red pepper
- 1½ pounds small shrimp in their shells

Heat a large wok. Add the salt, the fennel, coriander and cumin seeds and the crushed red pepper and cook over high heat, stirring constantly, until the spices are lightly toasted, about 30 seconds. Add the shrimp and toss immediately with the spices. Cook, tossing constantly, until the shrimp are opaque and their shells are beginning to char, about 5 minutes. Transfer the shrimp and any toasted spices to a large bowl and serve.   —*Jamie Oliver*

WINE A Riesling is the ideal pick for the shrimp because it adeptly accents the salty and spicy flavors. Try the 1999 Chateau Ste. Michelle & Dr. Loosen Columbia Valley Eroica.

Spice-Seared Shrimp (p. 21)

Crispy Fried Shrimp with Green Herb Sauce

6 SERVINGS

Adding some ale to the batter for the shrimp guarantees that they will have an airy and delicious crust.

- ¾ cup unbleached all-purpose flour
- 1 teaspoon sugar

Salt

- ½ cup strong Belgian-style golden ale, such as Duvel
- 1 large egg, separated
- 2 tablespoons finely grated peeled fresh ginger
- 1 quart plus 1 tablespoon vegetable oil
- 24 large shrimp, shelled and deveined, tails left on

Green Herb Sauce (recipe follows)

1. In a medium bowl, mix the all-purpose flour with the sugar and 1 teaspoon of salt. Make a well in the center of the dry ingredients; stir in the golden ale, egg yolk, finely grated ginger and the 1 tablespoon of vegetable oil. Gradually stir the dry ingredients into the wet ingredients. Let the batter stand at room temperature for at least 20 minutes.

2. Meanwhile, in a large, heavy saucepan, heat the 1 quart of vegetable oil to 360°. In a small bowl, whisk the egg white with a pinch of salt until stiff peaks form. Gently fold the egg white into the room-temperature batter.

3. Dip the shrimp into the batter, one at a time, letting any excess batter drip back into the bowl. Cook the battered shrimp in batches so they're not crowded. Fry them over moderate heat until they are golden and crisp, 2 to 3 minutes a batch. Transfer each batch of the fried shrimp to paper towels to drain. Serve hot with the Green Herb Sauce.

—*Ruth Van Waerebeek*

BEER As everyone in Belgium knows, a potent ale, such as the country's famous Duvel, is fantastic with fried seafood.

Crispy Fried Shrimp with Green Herb Sauce

GREEN HERB SAUCE

MAKES ½ CUP ●

This simple but flavorful herb sauce is the perfect complement to the shrimp. It's also good as a salad dressing.

- 3 tablespoons minced flat-leaf parsley
- 3 tablespoons fresh lemon juice
- 3 tablespoons water
- 2 tablespoons vegetable oil
- 1½ tablespoons minced shallots
- 1½ tablespoons minced chives
- 1 teaspoon thyme leaves
- ½ teaspoon cayenne pepper

Salt

In a small bowl, mix the parsley with the fresh lemon juice, water, vegetable oil, minced shallots, chives, thyme leaves and cayenne. Season with salt.

—*R.V.W.*

MAKE AHEAD The sauce can be covered tightly and then refrigerated overnight.

Bloody Mary Cocktail Meatballs

MAKES ABOUT 2½ DOZEN

MEATBALLS ● ●

- ½ pound lean ground beef
- ½ pound ground pork
- 1 small tender celery rib with leaves, finely chopped
- 2 teaspoons prepared horseradish
- 1 large egg, lightly beaten
- 1 slice white sandwich bread— soaked in warm water, squeezed dry and crumbled into pieces
- ½ teaspoon hot sauce
- ½ teaspoon salt
- ¼ teaspoon freshly ground pepper
- 1 tablespoon vegetable oil
- ½ cup Three-Pepper Bloody Mary (p. 395)

1. In a bowl, combine the ground beef and pork with the chopped celery, horseradish, egg, crumbled bread, hot

Bloody Mary Cocktail Meatballs

sauce, salt and pepper and knead well. Roll the meat into 1-inch balls.

2. Heat the oil in a nonstick skillet until shimmering. Add the meatballs and cook over moderately high heat until browned all over, about 5 minutes. Add the Three-Pepper Bloody Mary and simmer over moderate heat until the liquid is reduced by half and the meatballs are glazed, about 2 minutes. Serve hot.　　—*Grace Parisi*

Köfte with Pistachios and Tahini Sauce

MAKES ABOUT 3 DOZEN KÖFTE

1½ cups (7 ounces) shelled
　　unsalted pistachios
¾ pound ground lamb
¾ pound ground beef
2 medium onions, grated
2 teaspoons ground cumin
1½ teaspoons kosher salt
1 teaspoon freshly ground
　　black pepper
½ teaspoon crushed red pepper
½ cup finely chopped
　　flat-leaf parsley
2 tablespoons pure olive oil
Tahini Sauce (recipe follows)

1. Preheat the oven to 350°. Spread the pistachios on a rimmed baking sheet and toast in the oven for about 8 minutes, or until lightly browned; let cool.

2. In a large bowl, combine the lamb, beef, pistachios, onions, cumin, salt, black pepper and crushed red pepper and mix with your hands. Refrigerate for at least 2 hours or overnight.

3. Lightly knead the parsley into the meat. Roll the meat into tablespoon-size balls. Heat 1 tablespoon of the oil in a large skillet. Add half of the meatballs and cook over moderate heat until browned all over, about 8 minutes; reduce the heat if the meatballs brown too quickly. Drain on paper towels. Repeat with the remaining 1 tablespoon of olive oil and meatballs. Serve the meatballs hot or at room temperature with the Tahini Sauce. —*Engin Akin*

Köfte with Pistachios and Tahini Sauce

TAHINI SAUCE

MAKES ABOUT 2 CUPS ●

For easy blending, bring the tahini paste to room temperature or warm it slightly in the microwave before adding the lemon juice; don't worry when it seizes up. Adding the water gives the sauce a creamy texture.

1 medium onion, thinly sliced
1 tablespoon ground cumin
1 teaspoon freshly
　　ground pepper
¼ cup plus 1 tablespoon
　　fresh lemon juice
½ cup tahini paste, at
　　room temperature
¼ cup water
Salt
Nigella seeds, for garnish (optional)

1. In a medium bowl, toss the onion with the cumin and pepper.

2. In a small bowl, using a whisk, work the lemon juice into the tahini. Gradually whisk in the water until smooth. Season with salt. Stir the sauce into the onion, then stir well and garnish with nigella seeds.　　—*E.A.*

MAKE AHEAD The sauce can be refrigerated overnight. Bring to room temperature before serving.

2 first courses

Spoonable Bloody Mary

hot or the gelatin will become grainy and lose its power to set the liquid.

2. Pour the juice into a glass measuring cup and stir in the remaining 2 1/2 cups of tomato juice and the vodka. Season with salt, pepper and the Worcestershire sauce, then pour into whiskey tumblers. Refrigerate until set, at least 6 hours or overnight.

3. In a blender, puree the chopped celery with the lemon juice. Strain the puree through a fine sieve and season with salt. Cover the celery juice and refrigerate.

4. In a medium bowl, whip the cream until soft peaks form. Add the hot sauce, season with salt and whip until firm. Cover and refrigerate.

5. Add 2 tablespoons of the celery juice to each glass of tomato jelly. Top with heaping teaspoons of the hot-pepper cream and the shredded basil. Serve with small spoons.

—*Massimo Bottura*

ONE SERVING Calories 86 kcal, Total Fat 2.9 gm, Saturated Fat 1.7 gm, Protein 2 gm, Carbohydrates 6 gm

MAKE AHEAD The jelly, celery juice and cream can be refrigerated separately for 2 days. Gently re-whip the cream before serving.

Celery and Olive Antipasto with Ricotta Salata

10 SERVINGS ●

15 large celery ribs, peeled and cut into 2-inch sticks

1/4 cup plus 2 tablespoons extra-virgin olive oil

3 1/2 tablespoons fresh lemon juice

Spoonable Bloody Marys

8 SERVINGS ●●●

In this recipe, the ever-popular drink is transformed into a jellied appetizer that is to be eaten with a spoon. A dollop of whipped cream flavored with salt and hot sauce, rather than sugar, is the final touch. The jelly needs to set for six hours or overnight, so plan accordingly.

2 1/4 teaspoons unflavored powdered gelatin (1 envelope)

3 1/2 cups tomato juice

1/2 cup vodka

Salt and freshly ground pepper

1/2 teaspoon Worcestershire sauce

5 celery ribs, peeled and coarsely chopped

2 tablespoons fresh lemon juice

1/4 cup heavy cream

1/2 teaspoon hot sauce

2 tablespoons finely shredded basil

1. In a small saucepan, sprinkle the powdered gelatin over 1 cup of the tomato juice and let stand until softened, about 5 minutes. Then set the saucepan over moderate heat and stir until the juice is warm and the gelatin has dissolved completely, about 4 minutes. Do not let the juice get too

Celery and Olive Antipasto with Ricotta Salata

Herb-Stuffed Zucchini Blossoms

Herb-Stuffed Zucchini Blossoms

4 SERVINGS ●

- 6 medium red Swiss chard leaves
- 1 cup stinging nettle leaves or spinach
- ¾ cup coarsely chopped flat-leaf parsley
- ¾ cup coarsely chopped sorrel
- ¾ cup finely chopped chives
- ¾ cup coarsely shredded zucchini
- ½ cup coarsely chopped lovage or celery leaves
- 2 teaspoons thyme leaves
- 1 garlic clove, minced
- 3 tablespoons freshly grated Pecorino
- 1 tablespoon fine dry bread crumbs
- 6 tablespoons extra-virgin olive oil

Salt and freshly ground pepper
- 24 large zucchini blossoms

1. Bring a medium saucepan of water to a boil. Halve the Swiss chard leaves lengthwise and remove the thick ribs and stems. Cut the ribs and stems into ¼-inch dice and transfer ¾ cup to a large bowl; discard the rest. Blanch the chard leaves in the boiling water until just wilted, about 10 seconds. Transfer the Swiss chard leaves to a bowl of ice water to cool, then drain and pat dry.

2. Bring the water in the saucepan back to a boil. Add the nettles and blanch for 1 minute (10 seconds if using spinach). Drain and refresh in ice water, then drain and squeeze dry. Coarsely chop the nettles or spinach and add to the chard stems, along with the parsley, sorrel, chives, zucchini, lovage or celery leaves, thyme leaves, garlic, Pecorino, bread crumbs and 4 tablespoons of the exra-virgin olive oil. Season with salt and pepper and gently toss.

3. Make a slit in the side of each zucchini blossom and snap off the pistils in the center. Spread the Swiss chard leaves on a work surface and pat completely dry. Spoon an equal amount of

---

- 3 jarred anchovy fillets, minced
- 3 garlic cloves, minced
- ¾ teaspoon finely grated lemon zest

Salt and freshly ground pepper
- ¾ cup Calamata olives (4 ounces), pitted and coarsely chopped
- 6 ounces ricotta salata, coarsely grated

1. Put the celery in a large bowl of ice water and refrigerate until curled and very crisp, at least 2 hours.

2. In a bowl, whisk the olive oil with the lemon juice, anchovies, garlic and lemon zest. Season with salt and pepper.

3. Drain the celery and pat dry. Return to the dry bowl and toss with the olives and dressing. Transfer the antipasto to a platter, scatter the ricotta salata over the top and serve. —*Marcia Kiesel*

MAKE AHEAD The drained celery and the dressing can be refrigerated separately overnight.

Stuffed Zucchini Flowers

4 SERVINGS ●●

- 2 tablespoons extra-virgin olive oil
- ¾ cup minced Vidalia onion
- 1 garlic clove, minced
- 1 medium zucchini, finely chopped

- 2 tablespoons minced parsley
- 1 tablespoon finely chopped basil
- 1 tablespoon finely chopped chervil
- ½ cup freshly grated Parmesan (about 2 ounces)

Salt and freshly ground pepper
- 8 large zucchini flowers
- 2 tablespoons water

1. Preheat the oven to 425°. Coat the bottom of a small baking dish with 1 teaspoon of olive oil. Heat 1 tablespoon of olive oil in a medium skillet. Add the onion and garlic, cover partially and cook over moderately low heat until softened. Add the zucchini and cook over moderate heat for 5 minutes, stirring frequently. Stir in the herbs, transfer to a bowl and let cool slightly. Stir in the Parmesan. Season with salt and pepper.

2. Carefully snap off the pistils in the flowers. Stuff each flower with 2 tablespoons of the filling and twist the petals to seal. Arrange the flowers in the baking dish and add the water. Bake for 9 minutes. Transfer to plates, drizzle with the remaining 2 teaspoons of oil and serve warm or at room temperature. —*Jean-Georges Vongerichten*

herb filling on each leaf. Press lightly and season with salt and pepper. Tightly roll up the Swiss chard leaves cigar-style. Stuff the chard rolls into 12 of the zucchini blossoms. Carefully fit the stuffed blossoms into the remaining 12 blossoms, overlapping the petals to seal.

4. Arrange the blossoms, seam side down, in a large skillet in a single layer. Add ½ cup of water and the remaining 2 tablespoons of olive oil and bring to a simmer. Cover tightly and cook over moderately high heat until just tender when pierced with a knife, about 10 minutes. Uncover and cook until the liquid is reduced to 3 tablespoons, about 2 minutes longer. Transfer the zucchini blossoms to plates or a platter and drizzle the pan juices on top.

—Frank Ruta

Feta with Black Olives

8 SERVINGS ● ●

1 pound feta, preferably French, cut into 1-inch pieces

½ pound pitted black olives (2 cups), such as Calamata

¼ cup extra-virgin olive oil

1 teaspoon finely grated lemon zest, plus fine strips for garnish

1 tablespoon torn oregano leaves

Coarse sea salt

Flat bread, crackers or pita, for serving

Arrange the feta and olives on a large plate and drizzle with the extra-virgin olive oil. Scatter the grated lemon zest and torn oregano leaves on top and sprinkle with coarse sea salt. Garnish the Feta with Black Olives with the lemon zest strips and serve with flat bread, crackers or pita. *—Vickie Gott*

Feta with Black Olives

Spring Pea and Fava Bean Crostini

4 SERVINGS ●

1½ tablespoons unsalted butter, softened

1 teaspoon minced chervil

1 teaspoon minced tarragon

1 teaspoon minced chives

½ teaspoon finely grated lemon zest

½ teaspoon fresh lemon juice

¼ teaspoon minced garlic

Salt and freshly ground pepper

2 pounds fava beans in their pods, shelled (2 cups)

1 tablespoon extra-virgin olive oil

¼ pound thin asparagus, cut into ½-inch lengths

¼ pound sugar snap peas

½ cup shelled fresh or frozen English peas (2½ ounces)

2 shallots, thinly sliced

3 tablespoons water

4 slices of country bread, toasted

1. In a small bowl, using a fork, blend the butter with the minced chervil, tarragon, chives, grated lemon zest, fresh lemon juice and minced garlic. Season with salt and pepper.

2. Blanch the fava beans in a medium saucepan of boiling water for 1 minute. Drain and let cool slightly, then peel the fava beans and discard the skins.

3. Heat the olive oil in a large skillet. Add the asparagus, snap peas, English peas (if fresh) and shallots and cook over moderate heat, stirring, about 4 minutes. Add the fava beans, English peas (if frozen) and water and cook until heated through, about 2 minutes. Remove from the heat and swirl in the herb butter. Season with salt and pepper.

4. Set a piece of toasted country bread in the center of each plate. Spoon the vegetables on top and serve. *—Eberhard Müller*

ONE SERVING Calories 271 kcal, Total Fat 9.2 gm, Saturated Fat 3.5 gm, Protein 11 gm, Carbohydrates 37 gm

Goat Cheese and Chive Fondue

12 SERVINGS ●

It's fun to serve this in a fondue pot, but you could also set it out in a warmed earthenware bowl or any container that will hold the heat.

- 1 cup heavy cream
- 11 ounces mild fresh goat cheese, cut into chunks
- 1 tablespoon finely snipped chives

Freshly ground pepper

Crudités, such as pear or fennel wedges and endive spears

Warm the cream in a heavy, medium saucepan until hot but not boiling. Gradually add the goat cheese, whisking until smooth. Remove from the heat, stir in the chives; season with pepper. Pour into a fondue pot and serve with crudités. —*Tom Douglas*

WINE The bubbles of an American sparkling wine will provide an attractive contrast to the creamy fondue. Look for a lighter-bodied example, such as the 1996 Argyle Brut from Oregon or the Nonvintage Roederer Estate Brut from California.

Parmigiano-Reggiano Three Ways

8 SERVINGS

This clever appetizer is composed of cheese crackers, cheese soufflés and a cheese sauce. It is important to buy the best Parmigiano-Reggiano you can find and grate it just before using it.

CRACKERS

- ½ cup freshly grated Parmigiano-Reggiano (about 1½ ounces)
- 1 tablespoon unsalted butter, softened
- 1½ teaspoons potato starch

SOUFFLÉS

- ¼ cup heavy cream
- 1½ cups fresh ricotta (¾ pound), at room temperature
- ¾ cup freshly grated Parmigiano-Reggiano (about 2 ounces)
- 6 large egg whites

Salt

SAUCE

- ¼ cup chicken stock, preferably homemade
- ¼ cup heavy cream
- ½ cup freshly grated Parmigiano-Reggiano (about 1½ ounces)

1. MAKE THE CRACKERS: Preheat the oven to 375°. In a bowl, using a wooden spoon, blend the Parmigiano-Reggiano with the butter and potato starch until crumbly. Sprinkle tablespoons of the mixture onto a large nonstick baking sheet and lightly press them into neat 2½-inch rounds spaced 2 inches apart. Bake for 3 minutes or until smooth, pale golden crackers form. Let the crackers cool on the baking sheet for about 30 seconds, then, using a spatula, carefully transfer them to a rack to cool and crisp. Leave the oven on.

2. MAKE THE SOUFFLÉS: Lightly butter eight ⅓- to ½-cup ramekins and set them on a baking sheet. In a large bowl, whip the heavy cream until soft peaks form. Blend in the ricotta and Parmigiano-Reggiano. In a large bowl, beat the egg whites with a pinch of salt, then whip them until firm peaks form. Using a spatula, stir one-third of the beaten whites into the ricotta mixture to loosen it, then fold in the remaining whites just until blended. Spoon the soufflé mixture into the prepared ramekins; run your thumb around the inside edges of the ramekins to clean them. Bake the soufflés in the center of the oven for approximately 20 minutes, or until they are puffed and slightly loose in the center.

3. MEANWHILE, MAKE THE SAUCE: In a small saucepan, bring the chicken stock to a boil. In another small saucepan, bring the heavy cream to a simmer over low heat. Add the Parmigiano-Reggiano to the cream and whisk to blend. Whisk in the hot chicken stock until smooth and remove from the heat.

4. When the soufflés are done, turn them out onto small plates; if they don't release easily, run a thin knife around the edge of the soufflés and try again. Pour the sauce around the soufflés, top each one with a Parmigiano cracker and serve at once.
—*Massimo Bottura*

MAKE AHEAD The crackers can be stored in an airtight container for up to 1 day. Recrisp them in a 350° oven for 30 seconds.

Portobello and Polenta Tamales

MAKES 6 TAMALES ●

Corn husks make perfect wrappers for grilled tamales. You can easily embellish the tamales by adding slices of grilled Italian sausage or, to be really decadent, a few disks of foie gras terrine.

- 6 large ears of corn
- 2 tablespoons olive oil
- 4 large portobello mushrooms, caps only, sliced ⅓ inch thick

Kosher salt and freshly ground pepper

- 2 garlic cloves, thinly sliced
- 1 tablespoon chopped flat-leaf parsley
- 1 quart water
- ½ cup instant polenta
- ¼ cup freshly grated Parmesan
- 1 tablespoon unsalted butter
- 3 ounces Monterey Jack, cut into twelve 2-by-¼-inch sticks

Vegetable oil, for the grill

Hot sauce or tomato salsa, for serving

1. Carefully remove the husks and silk from the ears of corn; make a cut slightly above the base of the corn, if necessary, to release the inner husks. Arrange the husks in 2 piles, the thick outer layers and the paler green, thinner ones. Cut the kernels from the cobs, stopping when you have 2 cups.

2. Heat the olive oil in a large saucepan. Add the mushrooms; season with salt and pepper. Cover and cook over moderate heat, stirring

Portobello and Polenta Tamales (p. 31)

Spring Vegetable Potpies (p. 34)

occasionally, until they begin to brown, about 8 minutes. Uncover, add the garlic and cook, stirring, until the garlic is fragrant and the mushrooms are browned, about 4 minutes. Season with salt and pepper and stir in the parsley. Transfer to a plate.

3. Add the water to the saucepan and bring to a boil. Add the corn and 1 teaspoon of salt. Cover and cook over moderate heat until tender, 4 minutes. Slowly whisk in the polenta over low heat until thickened, about 4 minutes. Remove from the heat. Stir in the Parmesan and butter. Season with salt and pepper.

4. To assemble the tamales, spread 2 outer husks on a work surface, overlapping them at their base ends by 3 inches. If necessary, lay 2 large knives along opposite edges of the husks to keep them open. Spread 1/3 cup of the polenta in the center of the husks to within 1/2 inch of the edge to form a 4-by-2-inch rectangle 1 inch thick. Press 2 sticks of cheese into the polenta and top each tamale with one-sixth of the mushrooms and garlic. Cover the mushrooms with 2 large inner husks, overlapping them at their base ends. Tie the ends with kitchen string. Repeat with the remaining husks and ingredients.

5. Light a grill. Lightly brush the grate with vegetable oil and grill the tamales, outer husk side down, over a medium-hot fire for about 4 minutes, or until nicely browned. Carefully flip the tamales and grill for 2 minutes longer. Invert onto plates and serve at once with hot sauce or tomato salsa.

—*Marcia Kiesel*

MAKE AHEAD The uncooked tamales can be refrigerated overnight.

WINE The sweet summer corn and creamy polenta will find an ideal partner in a big, buttery Chardonnay with some sweet, smoky oak. Choose a flavorful example from California, such as the 1999 Meridian Santa Barbara.

Spring Vegetable Potpies

6 SERVINGS ●

BROTH

- 1 tablespoon pure olive oil
- 1 medium red onion, coarsely chopped
- 1 teaspoon very finely chopped garlic
- 3 cups vegetable stock or low-sodium chicken broth
- 1/3 cup dry white wine
- 1 tablespoon chopped tarragon
- 1 tablespoon sherry vinegar
- 1 tablespoon honey
- 1 teaspoon very finely chopped thyme leaves

POTPIES

- 1 pound all-butter puff pastry dough, chilled
- 5 tablespoons unsalted butter
- 6 baby red or white potatoes, cut into 1/2-inch pieces
- 12 baby carrots, halved lengthwise
- 1 pound thin asparagus, cut into 1 1/2-inch lengths
- 12 small fresh morels, cut into 1-inch pieces (see Note)

Salt and freshly ground pepper

- 2 bunches of scallions (1/2 pound), cut into 1-inch lengths
- 6 medium kale leaves (about 1/2 pound), stems and inner ribs trimmed, leaves coarsely chopped
- 1 cup fresh or thawed frozen baby peas
- 1/4 cup snipped chives
- 1/4 cup finely chopped flat-leaf parsley
- 3 tablespoons all-purpose flour
- 3/4 cup heavy cream
- 2 teaspoons Dijon mustard
- 1 egg yolk mixed with 1 tablespoon heavy cream

1. MAKE THE BROTH: In a large saucepan, heat the pure olive oil until shimmering. Add the chopped onion and garlic and cook over moderately low heat, stirring frequently, until the onion is softened, about 3 minutes. Add the vegetable stock or chicken broth, dry white wine, chopped tarragon, sherry vinegar, honey and chopped thyme and bring to a boil over high heat. Reduce the heat to moderately low and simmer for 10 minutes. Strain the broth through a fine sieve, pressing hard on the onion to extract as much liquid as possible.

2. MAKE THE POTPIES: Preheat the oven to 400°. On a lightly floured surface, roll out the chilled puff pastry 1/8 inch thick. Using a 6-inch square cutter as a template, cut out 6 squares. Use a sharp knife to cut a 1-inch-long slit in the center of each square, then carefully transfer the puff pastry squares to a large baking sheet and refrigerate them until they are well chilled.

3. Melt 2 tablespoons of the butter in a large, deep skillet. Add the potatoes and carrots and cook over moderate heat until softened, about 10 minutes. Add the asparagus and morels, season with salt and pepper and cook over moderately high heat, stirring frequently, until the asparagus is crisp-tender, about 3 minutes. Add the scallions and cook, stirring, for 2 minutes. Add the kale and cook, stirring frequently, until wilted, about 2 minutes longer. Stir in the peas and cook just until heated through. Season the vegetables with salt and pepper and transfer to a large bowl. Stir in the snipped chives and chopped parsley.

4. Return the skillet to moderate heat and melt the remaining 3 tablespoons of butter. Add the flour and cook, stirring, until pale golden, about 1 minute. Whisk in the strained vegetable broth and cook over moderately high heat, whisking constantly, until thickened, about 2 minutes. Whisk in the cream and mustard and season with salt and pepper. Stir the vegetables into the sauce and let cool slightly.

5. Spoon the vegetable filling into six 1¼-cup ovenproof bowls. Lightly brush the rim of each bowl with the egg wash and carefully top each bowl with a puff pastry square. Gently press the pastry on the edges into the bowls to seal. There will be some overhang. Brush the pastry with the egg wash and set the bowls on a large, rimmed baking sheet. Bake the potpies for 30 minutes, or until the tops are golden brown and puffed and the filling is bubbling. Serve at once.

—*Christina Reid-Orchid*

NOTE One ounce of dried morels can be substituted if fresh morels are unavailable. Soak the dried mushrooms in 1 cup of boiling water until thoroughly softened; drain.

MAKE AHEAD The unbaked potpies can be refrigerated for 1 day. Bake for 40 minutes.

WINE A wine with a silky texture, such as a light Sémillon or Sauvignon Blanc–Sémillon blend, will echo the potpies' creamy vegetable filling and buttery crust. Consider the 1999 Leeuwin Estate Siblings Sauvignon Blanc–Semillon from Margaret River in Australia or the bargain 1999 Chateau Ste. Michelle Semillon Columbia Valley from Washington State.

Mini Goat Cheese Soufflés

MAKES 12 MINI SOUFFLÉS ● ●

The soufflés may collapse after you take them out of the oven, so serve them immediately. The soufflé mixture can also be made in larger ramekins (bake them a little longer) for a heartier serving.

- ⅓ **pound full-flavored, medium-firm goat cheese, such as Bûcheron, at room temperature**
- 2 **tablespoons milk**
- 1 **large egg yolk**
- **Freshly ground pepper**
- 3 **large egg whites, at room temperature**
- **Pinch of cream of tartar**

1. Preheat the oven to 400°. Lightly oil twelve ¼-cup ovenproof ramekins and arrange them on a small baking tray. Cut the rind off the cheese and discard. Crumble the cheese into a medium bowl. Beat the cheese with an electric mixer until fluffy. Add the milk, egg yolk and pepper and continue beating until the mixture is very thick and creamy.

2. Wash and dry the beaters. In a medium bowl, beat the egg whites with the cream of tartar until stiff peaks form. Stir one-fourth of the beaten whites into the cheese mixture to lighten it, then fold in the remaining whites. Spoon the soufflé mixture into the ramekins, mounding it in the center. Bake the soufflés for 11 to 12 minutes, or until puffed and golden. Serve at once.   —*Sally Schneider*

ONE SOUFFLÉ Calories 56 kcal, Total Fat 4.3 gm, Saturated Fat 2.8 gm

MAKE AHEAD The soufflé mixture can stand at room temperature for about 30 minutes before baking.

WINE Serve the soufflés with an amontillado sherry, such as Lustau Almacenista.

Double-Baked Three-Cheese Soufflés

MAKES 12 INDIVIDUAL SOUFFLÉS ●

Unlike a classic fragile soufflé, these individual soufflés are designed to fall and then puff brilliantly back to life with their second baking. This means that they can be made in advance, even the day before.

- 4 **tablespoons unsalted butter**
- ¼ **cup all-purpose flour**
- 1 **cup milk**
- 2½ **cups heavy cream**
- 4 **ounces mild goat cheese, crumbled (about 1 cup)**
- 10 **large egg yolks, lightly beaten**
- 2 **ounces Roquefort, crumbled (about ½ cup)**
- 1½ **cups freshly grated Gruyère (4 ounces)**
- **Salt and freshly ground white pepper**
- 8 **large egg whites**

1. Preheat the oven to 350°. Butter and flour twelve ⅓-cup ramekins. In a medium saucepan, melt the butter over moderate heat. Whisk in the flour until smooth. Gradually whisk in the milk and 1 cup of the heavy cream until smooth; bring to a boil, whisking

Mini Goat Cheese Soufflé

Double-Baked Three-Cheese Soufflé

French Scrambled Eggs with Truffle Oil

French Scrambled Eggs with Truffle Oil

6 SERVINGS ●

These creamy, custardlike scrambled eggs have a luxurious flavor.

- 12 large eggs
- ¼ cup plus 2 tablespoons mineral water
- 6 tablespoons cold unsalted butter, cut into small pieces

Sea salt and freshly ground pepper

- 2 teaspoons white truffle oil
- 1 tablespoon finely chopped chives
- 6 warmed brioche rolls, or 12 slices from a loaf of brioche, toasted

constantly, then reduce the heat to low and simmer, whisking, for 5 minutes. Remove from the heat and stir in the goat cheese. Scrape the sauce into a large bowl and let cool, stirring occasionally.

2. Beat the egg yolks into the sauce. Stir in the Roquefort and ½ cup of the Gruyère. Season with salt and pepper.

3. In a large stainless steel bowl, beat the egg whites with a pinch of salt until almost firm. Using a rubber spatula, fold one-third of the beaten whites into the cheese sauce, then fold in the remaining whites just until blended. Gently spoon the soufflé mixture into the prepared ramekins, filling them three-fourths full. Set the ramekins on a baking sheet. Run your thumb around the rim of each ramekin to clean the inside.

4. Bake the soufflés for 25 minutes, or until well risen and golden but not quite set in the center. Let cool, then invert onto a large heatproof platter or into individual gratin dishes.

5. Preheat the oven to 400°. Pour 2 tablespoons of the remaining heavy cream over each soufflé and sprinkle them with the remaining 1 cup of Gruyère. Bake the soufflés for 8 to 10 minutes, or until puffed and golden brown. If baking the soufflés on a platter, use a flat spatula to transfer them with their cream to plates, then serve.

—*Jeremiah Tower*

MAKE AHEAD The unmolded soufflés can be refrigerated overnight. Bring to room temperature before proceeding.

WINE A rich, mouth-filling white wine, such as the 1998 E. Guigal Condrieu, matches the texture of these light and creamy soufflés. Or try a silky red Burgundy, such as the 1997 Morey St-Denis Domaine Dujac.

In a bowl, whisk the eggs and water. Melt 2 tablespoons of the butter in a large stainless steel bowl set over a pot of simmering water. Add the eggs and cook over low heat, gently stirring with a heatproof rubber spatula and scraping the bottom of the bowl until the eggs just begin to set, about 5 minutes. Add the remaining butter to the eggs, 1 piece at a time, and cook, stirring and scraping the bottom and sides of the bowl, until the eggs are thick and cooked through but still soft, about 5 minutes longer. Season with salt and pepper; transfer to plates. Drizzle with the truffle oil, sprinkle with the chives and serve at once with the brioche. —*Peter Birmingham*

WINE The rich, ripe Chardonnay fruit and yeasty aroma of the 1996 Schramsberg Blanc de Blancs sparkling wine is a real friend to truffles. The wine's creaminess and balance also perfectly match the sumptuous eggs.

Fennel and Feta Cheese Frittata

4 SERVINGS ●

- 2 tablespoons extra-virgin olive oil
- 1 small onion, thinly sliced

Kosher salt

- 1 fennel bulb—halved, cored and coarsely chopped
- 1 teaspoon minced marjoram

Freshly ground pepper

- 8 large eggs
- 2 tablespoons unsalted butter
- ½ cup crumbled feta (about 2 ounces)
- 1 tablespoon coarsely chopped basil

1. Preheat the oven to 350°. Heat the oil in a 9-inch nonstick ovenproof skillet. Add the sliced onion, season with kosher salt and cook until softened, about 3 minutes. Add the chopped fennel and minced marjoram and season with salt. Cook over low heat, stirring occasionally, until the fennel is softened, about 5 minutes. Season the sautéed vegetables with pepper and transfer them to a plate.

2. In a medium bowl, whisk the eggs and season with salt and pepper. Melt the butter in the skillet and add the eggs. Spoon the sautéed vegetables evenly over the eggs and dot with the crumbled feta. Bake the frittata for about 12 minutes, or until the eggs are just set. Slide the frittata onto a large serving plate and sprinkle with the chopped basil. Let the frittata cool slightly, then cut into wedges and serve warm or at room temperature.

—*Stephanie Lyness*

Oven-Baked Asian Omelet

Oven-Baked Asian Omelet

4 SERVINGS ● ● ●

- 8 large eggs
- 6 large scallions, thinly sliced crosswise

Salt and freshly ground pepper

- 1 tablespoon canola oil
- 2 ounces smoked ham, finely chopped (½ cup)
- ¼ pound white mushrooms, thinly sliced
- 3 tablespoons soy sauce
- 3 ounces snow peas, thinly sliced lengthwise (1 cup)
- 3 ounces mung bean sprouts (1 cup)
- ¼ pound medium shrimp—shelled, deveined and halved crosswise
- 1 teaspoon rice vinegar
- ½ teaspoon Asian sesame oil

A few drops of Asian chili oil

- 2 tablespoons coarsely chopped cilantro

1. Preheat the oven to 425°. In a medium bowl, lightly beat the eggs with the scallions. Season with salt and pepper.

2. Heat the oil in a 9-inch nonstick ovenproof skillet. Add the chopped ham and cook over moderately high heat until lightly browned, about 1 minute. Add the mushrooms and cook until softened, about 2 minutes. Add

1 tablespoon of the soy sauce and simmer for 30 seconds. Add the snow peas and cook, stirring, for 30 seconds, then add the bean sprouts and cook, stirring, for 30 seconds. Season with salt and pepper. Push the shrimp into the vegetables and add the eggs, spreading them evenly. Bake the omelet in the oven for about 12 minutes, or until set in the center.

3. Meanwhile, in a small bowl, combine the remaining 2 tablespoons of soy sauce with the rice vinegar, sesame oil and chili oil. Remove the skillet from the oven, slide the omelet onto a serving plate and sprinkle with the cilantro. Cut the omelet into wedges and serve warm or at room temperature with the soy dipping sauce. —*Michael Roberts*

MAKE AHEAD The omelet and dipping sauce can be refrigerated overnight. Bring them to room temperature before serving.

Chilean Chorizo and Herb Tortilla

4 SERVINGS ●

In South America, flat omelets or frittatas are called tortillas; this one is made with spicy chorizo sausage, parsley and cilantro and sweet caramelized onion.

- 3 tablespoons extra-virgin olive oil
- 6 ounces chorizo, sliced into ¼-inch rounds
- 1 medium onion, thinly sliced

Salt and freshly ground pepper

- 8 large eggs, lightly beaten
- 2 tablespoons all-purpose flour
- ⅓ cup coarsely chopped flat-leaf parsley
- ⅓ cup coarsely chopped cilantro
- 1 scallion, finely chopped

1. In a large nonstick skillet, heat 1 tablespoon of oil until shimmering. Add the chorizo and cook over high heat until crisp and lightly browned on both sides, 2 to 3 minutes. Transfer the chorizo to a plate. Add the onion, season with salt and pepper and cook over moderate heat, stirring frequently, until softened and lightly browned, about 5 minutes. Add the onion to the chorizo.

2. In a large bowl, beat the eggs with the flour, parsley, cilantro and scallion and season with salt and pepper. Fold in the browned chorizo and onion. Heat 1 more tablespoon of the oil in the skillet. Add the egg mixture, spreading out the chorizo and onion. Cook the tortilla over moderate heat until just set around the edge, about 2 minutes. Using a spatula, lift the edge of the tortilla and tilt the pan to allow the uncooked eggs to seep underneath. Continue cooking until the bottom is golden and the top is still a bit runny, about 5 minutes longer.

3. Set a large flat plate over the skillet and invert the tortilla onto the plate. Heat the remaining 1 tablespoon of oil in the skillet. Slide the tortilla into the skillet and cook over moderate heat until the bottom is set and browned, about 2 minutes longer. Slide the tortilla onto a plate, cut into wedges and serve warm or at room temperature.

—*Ruth Van Waerebeek*

WINE A hearty red with fruit and spice will blend with the spicy sausage and sweet caramelized onions. Try a Chilean bottling made from the Carmenère grape, such as the 1999 Santa Rita Rapel Valley Reserva or the 1999 Vina Arboleda Caliterra Maipo Valley.

Chilled Asparagus with Crab Vinaigrette

Chilean Chorizo and Herb Tortilla

Chilled Asparagus with Crab Vinaigrette

8 SERVINGS ● ● ●

- 3 pounds medium asparagus
- ¼ cup canola oil
- 2 tablespoons Champagne vinegar
- ¼ pound lump crabmeat (1 cup)
- ½ red bell pepper, finely diced
- ½ yellow bell pepper, finely diced
- ½ small red onion, finely chopped
- 1 tablespoon chopped tarragon

Salt and freshly ground pepper

I. In a large, deep skillet of boiling salted water, cook the asparagus over high heat until crisp-tender, about 5 minutes. Drain the asparagus and refresh in a bowl of ice water. Drain and pat dry.

2. In a large bowl, mix the canola oil with the Champagne vinegar. Add the lump crabmeat, diced bell peppers, chopped onion and tarragon and season with salt and pepper. Transfer the cooked, chilled asparagus to a large, deep platter, spoon the crab vinaigrette over the top and serve.

—*Michael Kramer*

MAKE AHEAD The asparagus and vinaigrette can be refrigerated separately for 6 hours.

Peeky Toe Crab Napoleon

Peeky Toe Crab Napoleon

4 SERVINGS ● ● ●

At NoMI in Chicago, this best-selling dish is made with peeky toe crab and, surprisingly, bagel chips.

2 tablespoons crème fraîche
2 tablespoons finely diced red pepper
1½ teaspoons Dijon mustard
1 teaspoon finely grated lime zest
Salt and freshly ground pepper
10 ounces lump crabmeat, picked over
1 medium Hass avocado, diced
2 teaspoons extra-virgin olive oil, plus more for drizzling
1 teaspoon fresh lemon juice
12 whole plain bagel chips
½ small European cucumber, halved and thinly sliced
12 grape tomatoes, halved
1 teaspoon aged balsamic vinegar
4 chervil sprigs, for garnish

1. In a medium bowl, combine the crème fraîche with the red pepper, mustard and lime zest. Season with salt and pepper, then gently fold in the crabmeat. In a small bowl, toss the avocado with the oil and lemon juice.

2. Place 1 bagel chip on each of 4 plates. Spoon half of the crab onto the 4 bagel chips. Top each with another bagel chip, the remaining crab and a final chip. Arrange the cucumber slices, avocado and grape tomatoes on top. Drizzle olive oil and the balsamic vinegar on the plates, top with a chervil sprig and serve.

—*Sandro Gamba*

Lobster Salad with Potatoes, Corn and Tomatoes

8 SERVINGS ●

This salad can be made with heirloom tomatoes of different colors and sizes, depending on what's available at your local farmer's market. If you use small tomatoes, cut them in half instead of slicing them.

1½ pounds small red potatoes
Two 1-pound live lobsters
1½ cups fresh corn kernels (from 2 ears of corn)
¼ cup crème fraîche
¼ cup mayonnaise
1 tablespoon fresh lemon juice
Salt and freshly ground pepper
2 large tomatoes, thinly sliced
1 tablespoon snipped chives

Lobster Salad with Potatoes, Corn and Tomatoes

Flash-Cooked Shrimp Seviche with Popcorn

6 SERVINGS ● ●

In Ecuador, the most popular version of this delightful seviche-style salad is typically made with *conchas negras*—black clams—and Seville orange juice. It is often accompanied by popcorn or plantain chips.

- 1 pound medium shrimp
- 1 small red onion, very thinly sliced
- Salt
- 6 plum tomatoes, finely chopped
- 2 garlic cloves, minced
- 2 fresh cayenne chiles or jalapeños, seeded and minced
- 1 medium red bell pepper, finely chopped
- 1 medium green bell pepper, finely chopped
- ½ cup finely chopped cilantro
- ½ cup fresh orange juice
- ¼ cup fresh lime juice
- Freshly ground pepper
- Salted popcorn, for serving

1. In a medium saucepan of boiling salted water, cook the shrimp just until they begin to curl, about 1 minute. Drain and let cool slightly, then peel and devein. Cut the shrimp into ½-inch pieces.

2. In a heatproof bowl, toss the onion with 2 teaspoons of salt; let stand for 5 minutes. Add 1 cup of boiling water, let stand for 10 minutes and drain well.

3. In a large glass bowl, toss the onion with the tomatoes, garlic, chiles, red and green bell peppers, cilantro and orange and lime juices. Stir in the shrimp and season with salt and pepper. Cover with plastic wrap and refrigerate for 1 hour. Season the seviche with salt and pepper and serve chilled with a bowl of popcorn passed alongside. —*Maricel Presilla*

ONE SERVING Calories 118 kcal, Total Fat 1.6 gm, Saturated Fat 0.3 gm, Protein 14 gm, Carbohydrates 13 gm

MAKE AHEAD The seviche can be refrigerated for up to 2 hours.

1. In a large saucepan of boiling salted water, cook the potatoes until tender, about 20 minutes. Drain and let cool completely. Cut into chunks.

2. Bring a large pot of salted water to a boil. Add the lobsters, head first, cover and return the water to a boil. Uncover and boil the lobsters over high heat until the shells are bright red, 8 to 10 minutes. Using tongs, transfer the lobsters to a large bowl of ice water to cool; drain. Twist off the claws and tail and remove the meat. Add the claw meat to a large bowl. Remove the vein that runs the length of the tail. Cut the tail meat into ½-inch dice and add to the bowl with the claw meat.

3. In a medium saucepan of boiling salted water, cook the corn until crisp-tender, about 1 minute. Drain and refresh under cold water. Drain again and pat dry. Add the corn, diced potatoes, crème fraîche, mayonnaise and lemon juice to the lobsters, season with salt and pepper and mix well.

4. Arrange the sliced tomatoes on one side of 8 plates or a large platter and season with salt and pepper. Spoon the lobster salad next to the tomatoes, garnish with the chives and serve.

—*Michael Kramer*

MAKE AHEAD The lobster salad can be prepared through Step 3 and refrigerated for 2 days.

Flash-Cooked Shrimp
Seviche with Popcorn

Grilled Pancetta-Wrapped Shrimp with Fresh Herbs

8 SERVINGS

For the best results, marinate the shrimp overnight.

¼ cup dry white wine
¼ cup extra-virgin olive oil
1½ teaspoons Dijon mustard
1 tablespoon finely chopped flat-leaf parsley
1 tablespoon finely chopped basil
1 tablespoon coarsely chopped oregano
1 tablespoon thyme leaves
2 garlic cloves, smashed
⅓ pound thinly sliced pancetta
24 medium shrimp, shelled and deveined

1. In a shallow baking dish, whisk the wine with the olive oil and mustard. Add the herbs and garlic.

2. Wrap the pancetta tightly around the shrimp. Arrange the wrapped shrimp in the marinade in a single layer and chill for at least 2 hours.

3. Preheat a cast-iron grill pan or light a grill. Remove the shrimp from the herb marinade and grill it over high heat until browned outside and cooked through, 2 to 3 minutes per side. Transfer the shrimp to a large serving platter and serve at once.

—Joel Gott

Grilled Pancetta-Wrapped
Shrimp with Fresh Herbs

**Flash-Cooked Seviche with
Mushrooms and Avocado**

Flash-Cooked Seviche with Mushrooms and Avocado

4 SERVINGS ●

½ pound cleaned medium squid,
    cut crosswise into ¼-inch rings
¾ pound large shrimp,
    shelled and deveined
½ cup fresh lemon juice
3 tablespoons peanut oil
2 tablespoons finely chopped
    flat-leaf parsley
1 tablespoon finely
    chopped cilantro
1 large garlic clove, minced
1 jalapeño, seeded and minced
½ pound small white mushrooms,
    thinly sliced
Salt and freshly ground pepper
2 navel oranges
2 firm, ripe Hass avocados, peeled
    and cut into ½-inch wedges

I. Bring 2 medium saucepans of salted water to a strong boil. Add the squid to 1 saucepan and the shrimp to the other and boil until just cooked, about 1 minute for the squid and 3 minutes for the shrimp. Drain the squid and shrimp and immediately transfer to a bowl of ice water to cool. Drain again and pat dry.

2. In a large bowl, mix the lemon juice with the peanut oil, parsley, cilantro, garlic and jalapeño. Add the mushrooms, shrimp and squid. Season with salt and pepper and refrigerate until chilled, about 10 minutes.

3. Meanwhile, using a sharp knife, peel the oranges, removing all the bitter white pith. Working over a bowl, cut in between the membranes to release the sections. Squeeze the juice from the membranes over the chilled seviche.

4. Arrange the orange sections and avocado wedges around the edge of a platter. Using a slotted spoon, spread the seviche in the center. Spoon some of the marinade over the oranges and avocados and serve immediately.   —*Ruth Van Waerebeek*
BEER A bright, light Caribbean beer, such as Red Stripe from Jamaica or Banks Lager from Barbados, will contrast the spiciness and acidity here.

Ginger Shrimp with Sweet-Spicy Thai Dipping Sauce

10 SERVINGS ● ●

Here's a new take on the classic shrimp cocktail: ginger-pickled shrimp served with zesty Thai-style dipping sauce.

½ cup thinly sliced ginger
    (2½ ounces), lightly crushed
    with the side of a knife blade
½ cup rice vinegar
¼ cup sugar
6 dried red chiles, broken
    into several pieces
2 pounds large shrimp,
    shelled and deveined
4 cups small ice cubes
½ cup sweet Thai chili sauce
3 tablespoons fresh
    lime juice
2 tablespoons ketchup
1½ teaspoons Asian
    fish sauce
Celery sticks and cucumber spears,
    for serving

I. In a small saucepan, combine the ginger with the vinegar, sugar and chiles. Bring to a boil, stirring to dissolve the sugar. Transfer to a large bowl; let cool.

2. In a large pot of boiling salted water, simmer the shrimp until pink and cooked through, about 2 minutes. Drain the shrimp and add them to the ginger mixture. Stir in the ice cubes and refrigerate for at least 4 hours or overnight. Drain the shrimp and pat dry. Discard the ginger and chiles.

3. In a small bowl, mix the chili sauce with the lime juice, ketchup and fish sauce. Chill. Arrange the shrimp on a platter with the celery sticks and cucumber spears and serve with the sauce.   —*Grace Parisi*
MAKE AHEAD The marinating shrimp and the dipping sauce can be refrigerated separately overnight.

Scallops Wrapped in Kaffir Lime Leaves

4 SERVINGS ●

These scallops from the famed chef Jean-Georges Vongerichten are infused with citrusy flavor. Buy the lime leaves first, so you can gauge the size of scallops that will fit neatly inside. You might buy extra lime leaves for serving because the leaves that flavor the scallops as they cook lose their vibrant green color.

3 tablespoons unsalted butter
1 medium onion, halved and
    thinly sliced lengthwise
2 tablespoons water
½ cup chicken stock or
    canned low-sodium broth
Salt and freshly ground pepper
12 large kaffir lime leaves (see
    Asian Flavorings, p. 179)
12 sea scallops (10 to 12 ounces)
Cayenne pepper
1 tablespoon extra-virgin olive oil
Pinch of freshly grated nutmeg

I. Melt 2 tablespoons of the butter in a medium skillet. Add the onion and

Ginger Shrimp with Sweet-Spicy Thai Dipping Sauce

first courses

water and cover with a piece of moistened, crumpled parchment or wax paper. Cook over low heat, stirring once or twice, until the onion softens, about 10 minutes. Add the chicken stock, cover partially and simmer for 10 minutes. Season with salt and pepper and keep the onion warm.

2. Using a sharp paring knife, make a lengthwise slit in a lime leaf along the vein, without cutting through either end. Carefully slip a scallop into the slit. Repeat with the remaining scallops and lime leaves. Season the scallops with salt and cayenne.

3. In a large skillet, melt the remaining 1 tablespoon of butter in the olive oil.

Add the scallops and cook over high heat until golden on the bottom, about 2 minutes. Carefully turn the scallops and cook until opaque throughout, about 2 minutes longer.

4. Spoon the sauce in the center of warmed plates and arrange the scallops on top. Sprinkle with the nutmeg and serve. —*Jean-Georges Vongerichten*

MAKE AHEAD The lime leaf–wrapped scallops and the sauce can be refrigerated separately overnight.

WINE The delicate lime flavor in this dish finds echoes in a crisp Australian Riesling. Look for the 1998 Pikes Clare Valley or the 1998 Crabtree of Watervale Clare Valley.

Scallops Wrapped in Kaffir Lime Leaves

Seared Scallops with Fennel and Lemon Relish

4 SERVINGS ●●

¼ cup extra-virgin olive oil

1½ teaspoons finely grated lemon zest

1½ tablespoons fresh lemon juice

1 tablespoon chopped flat-leaf parsley

1 small shallot, very finely chopped

¼ cup diced fennel bulb

Large pinch of ground fennel

Salt and freshly ground pepper

1 pound large sea scallops

1 bunch of arugula, tough stems discarded

Lemon wedges, for serving

1. In a small bowl, whisk 3 tablespoons of the olive oil with the lemon zest, lemon juice, parsley, shallot, diced fennel bulb and ground fennel. Season with salt and pepper.

2. Heat the remaining 1 tablespoon of olive oil in a medium skillet. Season the scallops with salt and pepper and cook over moderately high heat until golden brown and opaque throughout, about 3 minutes per side.

3. Mound the arugula on plates and top with the scallops. Spoon the fennel and lemon relish on the scallops and serve with lemon wedges.

—*Joanne Weir*

ONE SERVING Calories 151 kcal, Total Fat 5.5 gm, Saturated Fat 0.7 gm, Protein 20 gm, Carbohydrates 5 gm

Scallops with Avocado and Spicy Tomato Sauce

4 SERVINGS ●

1 tablespoon extra-virgin olive oil

2 tablespoons finely diced red onion

1 tablespoon minced seeded jalapeño

4 plum tomatoes—3 coarsely chopped, 1 halved, seeded and finely diced

Coconut Cream Scallop Seviche

Seared Scallops with Fennel and Lemon Relish

1 tablespoon hot water

3½ teaspoons fresh lime juice

Salt and freshly ground pepper

½ Hass avocado, peeled and finely diced

1 tablespoon finely chopped cilantro

12 large sea scallops (1 pound)

1. Heat 1 teaspoon of the olive oil in an 8-inch skillet until shimmering. Add 1 tablespoon of the diced red onion and ½ tablespoon of the minced jalapeño and cook over moderately high heat, stirring constantly, until the onion is golden, about 4 minutes. Add the coarsely chopped tomatoes and the hot water and cook, stirring, until the tomatoes are just softened, about 3 minutes. Transfer the mixture to a blender or food processor and puree until smooth. Strain the sauce through a fine sieve set over a bowl, pressing on the solids. Stir in ½ teaspoon of the lime juice and season the tomato sauce with salt and pepper.

2. In a small bowl, gently toss the avocado with the tomato, cilantro and the remaining 1 tablespoon of red onion, ½ tablespoon of jalapeño and 3 teaspoons of lime juice. Season the salsa lightly with salt and pepper.

3. Heat the remaining 2 teaspoons of olive oil in a large, heavy skillet until shimmering. Season the scallops with salt and pepper and cook over high heat until the scallops are browned and crisp on the bottom, about 3 minutes. Turn the scallops and cook until just cooked through, about 2 minutes longer.

4. Spoon the tomato sauce into the center of 4 dinner plates and mound the avocado salsa in the center. Arrange 3 scallops around the mounds of avocado salsa and serve.

—*Toni Robertson*

ONE SERVING Calories 190 kcal, Total Fat 8.2 gm, Saturated Fat 1.1 gm, Protein 20 gm, Carbohydrates 9 gm

MAKE AHEAD The tomato sauce can be refrigerated for up to 1 day. Reheat gently before serving.

WINE The fruity and herbal character of a crisp Fumé Blanc or Sauvignon Blanc from California will balance the mild sweetness of the scallops with the acid in the avocado salsa and the tomato sauce. Consider the 1999 Cakebread Cellars Napa Valley Sauvignon Blanc or the 1998 Dry Creek Vineyard Sonoma County Fumé Blanc.

Coconut Cream Scallop Seviche

4 SERVINGS

In the Philippines, seviche is known as *kilaw*. At Chicago's Rambutan restaurant, reduced coconut milk is added to balance the dish's acidity.

½ cup fresh lime juice

¼ cup white wine vinegar

¼ cup mirin (sweet rice wine)

½ teaspoon finely grated fresh ginger

¼ teaspoon minced garlic

½ pound large sea scallops, horizontally sliced ⅓ inch thick

One 14-ounce can unsweetened coconut milk

½ cup diced red bell pepper

½ cup fresh pineapple, cut into small chunks

2   **tablespoons minced chives**
⅛   **teaspoon crushed red pepper**
Salt and freshly ground pepper

1. In a medium glass bowl, combine the lime juice, vinegar, mirin, ginger and garlic. Stir in the scallops and refrigerate for 30 minutes.

2. Meanwhile, in a medium saucepan, simmer the coconut milk over moderate heat, stirring occasionally, until reduced to ½ cup, about 20 minutes. Let cool completely, stirring occasionally.

3. Drain the scallops and return them to the bowl. Stir in the reduced coconut milk, red bell pepper, pineapple, chives and crushed red pepper and season with salt and pepper. Refrigerate the seviche for 1 hour. Let it stand at room temperature for 10 minutes and stir before serving. Serve with lime wedges.   —*Jennifer Aranas*

Rappie Pie

4 SERVINGS

This recipe is an adaptation of a very traditional Acadian dish also known as *pâte à la râpure* (grated pie).

2   **pounds russet potatoes, peeled**
1   **cup chicken stock, fish stock or bottled clam juice**
2   **medium onions, finely chopped**
Salt and freshly ground pepper
1   **teaspoon chopped thyme**
¼   **teaspoon cayenne pepper**
6   **tablespoons unsalted butter, softened**
1   **dozen cherrystone clams— shucked and coarsely chopped, clam liquid reserved**
½   **pound sea scallops, cut into 1-inch pieces**

1. Preheat the oven to 400°. Butter a medium glass or ceramic baking dish. Coarsely grate the potatoes and transfer to a coarse stainless-steel sieve. Using a spatula, press on the potatoes to extract as much liquid as possible.

2. In a skillet, cook the potatoes in the stock over moderate heat until thick, about 3 minutes. Remove from the heat and stir in half of the onions, a large pinch of salt, 1 teaspoon of pepper, ½ teaspoon of thyme and the cayenne.

3. Melt 2 tablespoons of the butter in a medium skillet. Add the remaining onions and ½ teaspoon of thyme and cook over low heat until the onions soften, about 8 minutes. Add the reserved clam liquid and boil over high heat until reduced by half, about 3 minutes. Remove from the heat and let cool, then stir in the clams and scallops and season with salt and pepper.

4. Spread half of the potatoes in a layer in the prepared baking dish. Spread the onions, clams and scallops on top, then cover with the remaining potatoes. Dot the top of the pie with the remaining 4 tablespoons of butter and bake for 45 minutes, until bubbling hot. Preheat the broiler. Broil for 3 minutes, or until browned and crisp on top. Let stand for 10 minutes before serving.

—*Charles Leary and Vaughn Perret*

Steamed Littlenecks with Zucchini and Red Peppers

4 SERVINGS ●●●

¼   **cup extra-virgin olive oil**
1   **small onion, chopped**
2   **red bell peppers, cut into ½-inch strips**
4   **garlic cloves, minced**
¾   **cup dry white wine**
¾   **cup water**
1   **teaspoon fennel seeds**
¼   **teaspoon crushed red pepper**
3   **dozen littleneck clams, scrubbed**
4   **small zucchini, cut into ½-inch strips**
¼   **cup chopped basil**

1. Heat the oil in a large enameled cast-iron casserole. Add the onion; cook over moderate heat until softened, 5 minutes. Add the bell peppers and garlic and cook, stirring, for 3 minutes. Stir in the wine, water, fennel and crushed pepper. Add the clams and zucchini, cover and cook over high heat, stirring occasionally, until the clams open, 7 minutes.

2. Using a slotted spoon, transfer the clams to shallow bowls. Season the clam broth with salt and pepper and spoon over the clams. Top with the chopped basil.   —*Jody Adams*

SERVE WITH Crusty French bread.

Manila Clams with Serrano Ham and Parsley Oil

8 SERVINGS ●

Manila clams are wonderfully dainty, but use larger ones, like cherrystones, for a heartier and more casual dish. Serve it with hunks of crusty French bread to soak up the flavorful broth.

PARSLEY OIL

2   **cups (packed) flat-leaf parsley leaves**
½   **cup extra-virgin olive oil**
Salt and freshly ground pepper

CLAMS

4   **plum tomatoes (1 pound), halved and cored**
3   **tablespoons extra-virgin olive oil**
3   **large garlic cloves, minced**
¼   **cup dry white wine**
3   **tablespoons fresh lemon juice**
Four 8-ounce bottles of clam juice
4   **dozen Manila or littleneck clams**
2   **ounces thinly sliced Serrano ham or prosciutto, julienned**
Salt and freshly ground pepper
2   **tablespoons coarsely chopped flat-leaf parsley**

1. **MAKE THE PARSLEY OIL:** In a food processor, process the parsley and olive oil to a puree. Let the puree stand at room temperature for at least 10 minutes or for up to 1 hour, then strain it through a coarse sieve. Season with salt and pepper.

2. **PREPARE THE CLAMS:** Put the tomatoes in a large nonstick skillet, cut side down, and cook over moderately high heat until charred, about

Steamed Littlenecks with Zucchini and Red Peppers

3 minutes. Transfer the tomatoes to a plate to cool slightly, then cut them lengthwise into ¼-inch wedges.

3. Heat the olive oil in a large saucepan. Add the garlic and cook over low heat until fragrant, about 2 minutes. Add the wine and lemon juice and boil over high heat until almost evaporated, about 4 minutes. Add the clam juice and bring to a boil. Add the clams, cover and cook until they begin to open, 3 to 4 minutes; using tongs, transfer the clams to a warm bowl as they open.

4. Add the tomatoes and ham to the clam broth and season with salt and pepper. Pour the broth over the clams and sprinkle with the chopped parsley. Serve the clams in warmed bowls and pass the parsley oil at the table.

—*Kevin Taylor*

MAKE AHEAD The parsley oil can be refrigerated for up to 3 days.

WINE A white wine with lively acidity will balance the bright lemon, tomato and ham flavors in this full-flavored shellfish dish. Consider one of these organic bottlings: the sparkling Nonvintage Toffoli Prosecco di Conegliano from the environs of Venice or the 1999 Frog's Leap Sauvignon Blanc from California.

Manila Clams with Serrano Ham and Parsley Oil

Mussels in Nasturtium Broth

Mussels with Saffron—Blood Orange Vinaigrette

Mussels with Saffron—Blood Orange Vinaigrette

4 SERVINGS ●

- 1 cup fresh blood orange juice (3 to 4 oranges)
- One 3-inch strip of blood orange zest
- 4 teaspoons Saffron Oil (recipe follows)
- Pinch each of salt and white pepper
- 1¼ pounds large mussels, debearded
- Coarse sea salt

I. In a small saucepan, boil the orange juice until reduced to ⅓ cup, about 12 minutes. Transfer to a bowl. Add the orange zest, Saffron Oil, salt and pepper and let stand for 1 hour.

2. Set a large cast-iron skillet over moderately high heat until very hot. Add the mussels and cook, shaking the pan occasionally, until they open, about 5 minutes. Transfer the mussels to a bowl and drizzle with some of the dressing. Sprinkle lightly with coarse salt and serve with the remaining dressing on the side.—*Sally Schneider*
ONE SERVING Calories 175 kcal, Total Fat 7.5 gm, Saturated Fat 1.1 gm

SAFFRON OIL

MAKES ½ CUP ●●

Use this intense oil on beans, tomatoes, potatoes, rice, pasta and seafood, and in vinaigrettes.

- ½ teaspoon coarsely crushed saffron threads
- ½ teaspoon hot water
- ¼ cup grapeseed oil
- ¼ cup extra-virgin olive oil

In a jar, mix the saffron and water and let stand for 10 minutes. In a small skillet, warm the oils together over low heat; add the oils to the jar and let cool. Cover the jar and shake well, then refrigerate the Saffron Oil for 2 days before using.   —*S.S.*
ONE TABLESPOON Calories 120 kcal, Total Fat 13.6 gm, Saturated Fat 1.6 gm

Wok-Roasted Mussels

4 SERVINGS ●

- 2 tablespoons grapeseed oil
- 12 garlic cloves, smashed
- 1 jalapeño, quartered lengthwise
- 2 pounds mussels, scrubbed and debearded
- 3 fresh bay leaves
- 1 teaspoon sea salt
- ½ teaspoon cracked black pepper
- ½ cup dry white wine

Set a wok over high heat for 7 minutes. Add the oil and heat until smoking. Add the garlic and jalapeño and stir-fry until lightly golden, about 2 minutes. Add the mussels and bay leaves, season with salt and pepper and cook, stirring occasionally, until the mussels open, about 6 minutes. Add the wine and boil until reduced by half, about 2 minutes. Spoon the mussels into bowls and serve.
—*Arnold Eric Wong*

Mussels in Nasturtium Broth

4 SERVINGS ●

At New York City restaurant Jean Georges, nasturtium blossoms add color and spice to mussel soup. The broth is made without cooking the flowers, so they keep all their spicy flavor.

- 1 cup water
- 4 tablespoons unsalted butter
- 1 small pinch of saffron threads
- 30 nasturtium flowers, plus more for garnish

1 tablespoon fresh lime juice

Sea salt

2 pounds mussels, scrubbed and debearded

½ cup dry white wine

I. In a small saucepan, bring the water, unsalted butter and saffron threads to a boil. Transfer the saffron water to a blender, add the 30 nasturtium flowers and fresh lime juice and blend until smooth. Strain the nasturtium broth through a fine sieve and season with salt.

2. In a large saucepan, combine the cleaned mussels and dry white wine. Cover and cook over high heat until the mussels open, about 5 minutes. Stir in the nasturtium broth. Spoon the mussels and broth into bowls, garnish with nasturtiums and serve.

—*Jean-Georges Vongerichten*

Coconut Curry Mussels

4 SERVINGS ●

One 1½-inch piece of fresh ginger, peeled

4 garlic cloves, halved

½ cup water

1 tablespoon extra-virgin olive oil

2 large Spanish onions, coarsely chopped

4 jalapeños—halved, seeded and thinly sliced

2 stalks lemongrass, inner white bulb only, thinly sliced crosswise

2 teaspoons ground cumin

1 teaspoon ground coriander

½ teaspoon turmeric

One 12-ounce can evaporated skim milk

½ cup unsweetened coconut milk

3 pounds mussels, scrubbed and debearded

2 tablespoons fresh lime juice

Kosher salt

⅓ cup coarsely chopped cilantro

Lime wedges, for serving

I. In a mini food processor, chop the ginger and garlic. Add the water and process until almost smooth.

2. Heat the oil in a large enameled cast-iron casserole. Add the onions, cover and cook over low heat, stirring occasionally, until softened, about 10 minutes. Add the jalapeños, lemongrass, cumin, coriander, turmeric and the garlic and ginger puree and cook, stirring, for 2 minutes. Stir in the evaporated milk and coconut milk and bring to a simmer. Remove from the heat and let stand for 30 minutes to 4 hours.

3. Bring the curry broth to a boil. Stir in the mussels, cover and cook over moderate heat just until the mussels open, about 7 minutes; discard any that don't open. Stir in the lime juice and season with salt. Spoon the mussels and their broth into shallow bowls, sprinkle with the cilantro and serve with lime wedges.—*Ann Chantal Altman*

ONE SERVING Calories 344 kcal, Total Fat 11.5 gm, Saturated Fat 4.7 gm, Protein 29 gm, Carbohydrates 31 gm

tips for buying and cooking with flowers

Do not eat flowers from florists or garden centers; use only organic ones. Double-check that any flower you want to eat is edible, even if it's just a garnish.

Remove pistils and stamens before eating flowers; consume only the petals.

To keep flowers fresh for a day or two, treat them like all flowers and stand them in a pitcher of water on the counter.

To keep flowers fresh for up to three days, keep them wrapped in damp paper towels in a resealable plastic bag in the refrigerator's vegetable crisper.

Steep small flowers, like lavender, honeysuckle and elderflowers, in milk or cream to flavor ice creams and custards, or use them to make flavored syrups.

Use larger flowers to hold fillings. In addition to zucchini blossoms, try tulips, hollyhocks, daylilies and gladioli.

Coconut Curry Mussels

first courses

Creamed Mussels on the Half Shell with Bacon and Leeks

12 SERVINGS ●

1 cup dry white wine
1 shallot, coarsely chopped
½ lemon, thickly sliced
10 thyme sprigs, plus ½ teaspoon minced thyme
5 whole peppercorns
1½ pounds medium mussels (about 60), scrubbed and debearded
3 thick slices of bacon, finely chopped
5 tablespoons unsalted butter
1 medium leek, white and tender green parts only, finely chopped
3 tablespoons heavy cream
Kosher salt and freshly ground pepper
⅔ cup coarse dry bread crumbs
1 tablespoon finely chopped flat-leaf parsley

I. In a large saucepan, combine the wine with the shallot, lemon slices, thyme sprigs and peppercorns and bring to a boil. Add the mussels, cover and cook over high heat, stirring occasionally, until most of the mussels open, about 5 minutes; remove from the heat. Pull the mussels out of the shells and discard half of each shell. Arrange the remaining shells on a baking sheet in a single layer and place a mussel in each shell. Strain the broth into a glass measuring cup, leaving any grit behind.

2. In a medium skillet, cook the bacon over moderately high heat, stirring, until browned, about 5 minutes. Transfer the bacon to a dish and pour all but 1 tablespoon of the fat from the skillet.

3. Melt 3 tablespoons of the butter in the skillet. Add the leek and cook over moderate heat, stirring occasionally, until softened, about 5 minutes. Add ½ cup of the mussel broth and cook until syrupy, about 15 minutes. Add the cream and simmer for a few minutes, until thickened. Stir in the bacon and

minced thyme and season with salt and pepper; let cool. Top each mussel with a scant teaspoon of the leek mixture.

4. Preheat the oven to 375°. Melt the remaining 2 tablespoons of butter in a small skillet. Add the bread crumbs and cook over moderate heat, stirring constantly, until golden and crisp, about 5 minutes. Stir in the parsley and ¼ teaspoon of salt. Sprinkle the crumbs over the mussels and bake in the upper third of the oven for about 5 minutes, or until hot and bubbling.
—*Tom Douglas*

MAKE AHEAD The mussels can be assembled and refrigerated overnight. Bake the mussels a few minutes extra if chilled.

Arctic Char Gravlax with Apple-Pecan Salad

6 SERVINGS

In this salad, gravlax is made with arctic char instead of the more common salmon for a silky, slightly sweet gravlax. The fish takes two days to cure, so plan accordingly.

GRAVLAX

3 cups kosher salt
1¼ cups packed light brown sugar
½ cup chopped fresh dill
3 tablespoons juniper berries, crushed
2 bay leaves
2 tablespoons black peppercorns
One 1-pound arctic char fillet, skin on

SALAD

1 cup pecan halves (4 ounces)
2 tablespoons Champagne or white wine vinegar
1 tablespoon honey
1 tablespoon Dijon mustard
¼ cup grapeseed oil
1 small garlic clove, minced
1½ teaspoons finely chopped thyme
Sea salt and freshly ground pepper
2 Granny Smith apples, cut into matchsticks
1 large Belgian endive—halved, cored and thinly sliced crosswise

I. MAKE THE GRAVLAX: In a bowl, mix the kosher salt with the light brown sugar, chopped fresh dill and crushed juniper berries. In a spice grinder, grind the bay leaves with the black peppercorns. Add to the salt cure and mix well. Spread half of the salt cure in a deep plate. Add the arctic char fillet, skin side down, and cover with the remaining salt. Cover the fish with plastic and refrigerate for 24 hours.

2. Remove the fish from the salt cure and soak it in ice water in the refrigerator for 3 hours. Drain the fish fillet and pat dry. Transfer the fish, skin side down, to a rack set on a baking sheet. Refrigerate the char fillet, uncovered, overnight.

3. MAKE THE SALAD: Preheat the oven to 350°. Spread the pecan halves in a pie plate and toast for 7 minutes, or until fragrant. Let cool. In a large bowl, whisk the Champagne or white wine vinegar with the honey and Dijon mustard. Add the grapeseed oil and whisk the vinaigrette until blended. Whisk in the minced garlic and chopped thyme and season with sea salt and pepper. Add the apples and Belgian endive and toss, then add the pecans and toss again.

4. Using a thin, sharp knife, thinly slice the gravlax on the diagonal off the skin. Mound the salad on plates, surround it with gravlax and serve.
—*Frank Mendoza*

ONE SERVING Calories 377 kcal, Total Fat 28.5 gm, Saturated Fat 2 gm, Protein 17 gm, Carbohydrates 15 gm

MAKE AHEAD The gravlax can be prepared through Step 2, then wrapped in plastic and refrigerated for 1 week.

WINE A lively German Riesling will blend with the flavors in the salad while cutting the richness of the fish. Two to look for: the 1999 Kesselstatt Bernkasteler Badstube Riesling Kabinett or the 1999 Dr. Fischer Ockfener Bockstein Riesling Kabinett.

Smoked Sturgeon with Deviled Eggs and Basil-Rose Mayonnaise

12 SERVINGS ●

This is a perfect opener for a dinner party because it can be made in advance. To give the mayonnaise a more intense flavor, you can grind the julienned rose petals with a pinch of salt before mixing them in.

- 12 large eggs
- ½ cup sour cream
- 1 teaspoon Dijon mustard
- ½ teaspoon curry powder

Hot sauce

Salt and freshly ground white pepper

- 1 cup mayonnaise
- ½ cup julienned basil leaves
- ¼ cup julienned organic rose petals, plus 2 tablespoons whole petals for garnish
- 2½ tablespoons fresh lemon juice
- ½ teaspoon finely grated lemon zest
- 1½ pounds thinly sliced smoked sturgeon or tuna

I. In a large saucepan, cover the eggs with water; bring to a boil. Reduce the heat to moderate and simmer for 14 minutes. Drain and transfer to a bowl of ice water. Let cool completely, then remove the shells. Cut a thin slice from the rounded ends so the eggs can stand upright. Slice 1 inch of egg white off the pointed ends, then carefully scoop out the yolks from the pointed ends and transfer to a large bowl.

2. Finely mash the yolks with a fork, then blend in the sour cream, mustard, curry powder and a few drops of hot sauce. Season with salt and white pepper. Spoon the filling into a sturdy resealable plastic bag and squeeze it into 1 corner. Then, using scissors, snip ½ inch from the corner of the bag and pipe the filling into the egg whites.

3. In a medium bowl, combine the mayonnaise with the basil and rose petals and the lemon juice and zest. Season with salt and white pepper.

4. Arrange the sliced sturgeon on 12 chilled salad plates. Set a deviled egg in the center of each plate and drizzle with the mayonnaise. Sprinkle with the whole rose petals and serve.

—*Jeremiah Tower*

MAKE AHEAD The stuffed deviled eggs and the mayonnaise can be refrigerated separately overnight.

WINE A light, refreshing, fruity-herbal white will complement the smoky sturgeon and stand up to the curry in the deviled eggs. A good choice would be the 1999 Vidal Blanc from Sakonnet Vineyards in Rhode Island. An easier-to-find alternative is the 1998 François Cotat Sancerre La Grande Côte from France.

Curried Lentils with Tomatoes and Yogurt Cucumbers

10 SERVINGS ● ●

To make this salad vegetarian, omit the bacon and substitute 2 tablespoons of vegetable oil for the bacon fat.

- 2 ounces lean thick-sliced bacon, cut crosswise into ⅓-inch strips (about ½ cup)
- 1 medium onion, minced
- 3 tablespoons minced fresh ginger
- 1 tablespoon curry powder
- 1 jalapeño, seeded and minced
- ½ teaspoon cinnamon
- 1 pound French green lentils, rinsed and picked over
- 2 cups water
- 2 cups chicken or vegetable stock or canned low-sodium broth

Salt and freshly ground pepper

- 1 large European cucumber— peeled, halved lengthwise, seeded and thinly sliced crosswise
- ¼ teaspoon ground cumin
- ¼ teaspoon ground coriander
- ½ cup buttermilk
- ¼ cup sour cream
- ½ teaspoon finely grated orange zest
- ¼ cup plus 2 tablespoons fresh orange juice
- 1 pint grape tomatoes, halved

I. In a large saucepan, cook the bacon over moderate heat, stirring often, until crisp, about 5 minutes. Drain the bacon on paper towels and set aside. Reserve 2 tablespoons of the bacon fat in the saucepan; discard the rest.

2. Add the onion to the bacon fat and cook over low heat, stirring occasionally, until softened, about 8 minutes. Add the ginger, curry powder, jalapeño and cinnamon and cook until fragrant, about 4 minutes. Stir in the lentils, water and stock and bring to a boil. Reduce the heat to low, cover and simmer until the lentils are tender and most of the liquid has been absorbed, about 35 minutes. Season with salt and pepper.

3. Meanwhile, in a medium bowl, sprinkle the cucumber slices with a large pinch of salt and let stand for 15 minutes. Drain and pat dry.

4. In a small skillet, toast the cumin and coriander over moderate heat until fragrant, about 40 seconds; transfer to a medium bowl and whisk in the the buttermilk, sour cream and orange zest. Stir in the cucumber slices and season the mixture with salt and pepper.

5. Transfer the lentils to a large shallow bowl. With a rubber spatula, gently stir in the orange juice and season with salt and pepper. Spoon the cucumber salad over the lentils. Sprinkle the bacon and tomatoes over the cucumbers and serve warm or at room temperature.

—*Danielle Custer*

Chickpea Salad with Four-Minute Eggs

4 SERVINGS ●

- 3 tablespoons fresh lemon juice
- 5 tablespoons extra-virgin olive oil

Salt and freshly ground pepper

One 19-ounce can of chickpeas, drained and rinsed

- ⅔ cup small green olives, pitted
- 10 small red radishes, quartered
- 2 cups flat-leaf parsley leaves

Ham Hock Salad with Pickled-Okra Sauce

3 scallions, white and light green
parts, finely chopped

4 large eggs, at room temperature

1 teaspoon white vinegar

1. In a medium bowl, whisk the lemon juice with 4 tablespoons of the extra-virgin olive oil and season with salt and pepper. In another medium bowl, lightly crush half of the chickpeas; mix in the whole chickpeas. Add half of the vinaigrette to the chickpeas and toss. Add the olives, radishes, parsley and scallions to the rest of the vinaigrette and toss. Spoon the chickpea salad onto 4 plates and top with the parsley salad.

2. Bring a medium saucepan of water to a boil. Add the eggs and boil over moderately high heat for 4 minutes. Drain, then rinse the eggs under cool water for 1 minute. Using the back of a spoon, gently crack the eggs all over and peel the shell off. Alternatively, poach the eggs: Fill a large skillet with enough water to reach two-thirds of the way up the side. Add the vinegar and bring to a simmer. One at a time, crack the eggs into the simmering water and poach until the whites are set but the yolks are still soft, 3 to 4 minutes.

3. Set an egg on each salad and drizzle with the remaining 1 tablespoon of olive oil. Sprinkle the salads with salt and pepper and serve immediately.

—*Gabrielle Hamilton*

Ham Hock Salad with Pickled-Okra Sauce

4 SERVINGS ●

4 pounds meaty ham hocks

2 cups chicken stock

2 cups plus 1 tablespoon water

½ medium onion

1 celery rib

8 black peppercorns

4 hard-cooked egg yolks, finely chopped

1 hard-cooked egg white, finely chopped

4 pickled okra, finely chopped, ¼ cup brine reserved

3 tablespoons vegetable oil

1 teaspoon Dijon mustard

2 tablespoons chopped chives

Salt and freshly ground pepper

2 medium Yukon Gold potatoes, peeled and sliced ¼ inch thick (about 12 slices)

1 tablespoon plus 1 teaspoon olive oil

3 tablespoons grated extra-sharp Cheddar

2 cups watercress leaves and small sprigs

2 teaspoons fresh lemon juice

1. Preheat the oven to 300°. In a large enameled cast-iron casserole, combine the ham hocks, stock, 2 cups of the water, the onion, celery and peppercorns and bring to a boil. Cover and braise in the oven for about 2 hours, or until the meat begins to fall off the bones. Remove the hocks and let cool, then remove the meat and shred it. Reserve 2 tablespoons of the braising liquid. Turn the oven up to 350°.

2. In a bowl, combine the egg yolks, egg white, pickled okra brine, 1 tablespoon of the braising liquid and the remaining 1 tablespoon of water. Whisk in the vegetable oil and Dijon mustard, then fold in the okra and chives. Season this gribiche sauce with salt and pepper.

3. On a lightly oiled baking sheet, toss the potato slices with 1 tablespoon of the olive oil and the cheese and season with salt and pepper. Spread in a single layer and bake for 20 minutes, or until tender and lightly browned. Keep warm.

4. In a small bowl, toss the watercress with the remaining 1 teaspoon of olive oil and the lemon juice. In a medium skillet, heat the remaining 1 tablespoon of braising liquid. Add the ham and stir until warmed through. Transfer to a medium bowl and fold in ¼ cup of the gribiche sauce. Pile ½ cup of the

ham in the center of each dinner plate. Arrange the watercress salad on one side and the potatoes on the other and serve.

—*Randy Lewis*

Mini Rib-Eye Tacos

8 SERVINGS ●

1 cup finely shredded green cabbage

½ tablespoon fresh lime juice

½ tablespoon finely chopped cilantro

Salt and freshly ground pepper

Eight 6-inch corn tortillas, cut into 4-inch rounds

¾ pound boneless rib eye, cut into ⅛-inch-thick slices (see Note)

3 tablespoons prepared green salsa

1. In a medium bowl, toss the cabbage with the lime juice and cilantro and season with salt and pepper.

2. Preheat a cast-iron griddle or grill pan. Heat the tortillas on the griddle until softened, about 10 seconds per side. Wrap in foil; keep warm. Adjust the burner under the grill pan to high and heat until the pan is extremely hot. Season the steak with salt and pepper and grill until browned, about 30 seconds. Turn and grill for 20 seconds longer.

3. Top the warm tortillas with the steak, cabbage slaw and green salsa. Fold the tacos in half and serve right away.

—*Mike Chelini*

NOTE Have your butcher slice the rib eye for you, or slice the meat ¼ inch thick and pound it to a ⅛-inch thickness.

WINE The Joel Gott 2000 Chardonnay pairs nicely with these spicy rib-eye tacos. Or try the 2000 Pavi Pinot Grigio; its crispness contrasts with the meatiness of the steak.

3 salads

Mixed Greens with Fresh Tomato Vinaigrette

8 SERVINGS ●●

- 2 large Belgian endives, cored, leaves separated
- 1 bunch of watercress, thick stems discarded
- 1 head of butter, baby Bibb or Boston lettuce, leaves torn
- 1 large bunch of arugula, thick stems discarded, or ¼ pound baby arugula
- ½ cup Fresh Tomato Vinaigrette (recipe follows)

Salt and freshly ground pepper

Combine the endives, watercress, lettuce and arugula in a large bowl. Add half of the dressing and gently toss to coat. Season with salt and pepper. Serve the salad on plates and drizzle with the remaining vinaigrette.

—*Stéphane Garnier*

FRESH TOMATO VINAIGRETTE

MAKES 1 CUP ●●●

Try this vinaigrette as a light sauce for pasta or grilled fish, chicken or steak.

- 3 tomatoes (¼ pound each)— 2 cut into large chunks and 1 peeled, seeded and chopped
- 1 garlic clove, smashed
- 1 tablespoon fresh lemon juice
- ¼ cup extra-virgin olive oil

Sea salt and freshly ground pepper

In a blender, puree the tomato chunks until smooth. Strain through a fine sieve, pressing hard on the solids. Rinse out the blender and return the tomato juice to it. Add the garlic and lemon juice and with the machine on, add the olive oil in a thin stream, blending until smooth. Add the chopped tomato and pulse just until chunky. Season with salt and pepper.

—*S.G.*

Mesclun Salad with Onion-Ginger Dressing

12 SERVINGS

The onion-ginger dressing is also wonderful served over grilled or roasted asparagus.

Four ¾-inch-thick slices of firm-textured white bread, torn into 1-inch pieces

- 3 tablespoons unsalted butter, melted
- 2 tablespoons finely chopped parsley

Salt

- 1 large sweet onion (10 ounces), cut crosswise into ½-inch-thick slices

Freshly ground pepper

Pure olive oil, for drizzling

- ⅔ cup extra-virgin olive oil
- ⅓ cup red wine vinegar
- 2 tablespoons minced shallots
- 1 tablespoon minced fresh ginger
- 1 garlic clove, minced
- 1½ pounds mesclun (24 loosely packed cups)

1. Preheat the oven to 350°. In a medium bowl, toss the bread with the butter and parsley and season with salt. Spread the croutons on a rimmed baking sheet and bake them for about 20 minutes, or until golden brown.

2. Season the onion slices with salt and pepper and lightly drizzle them with pure olive oil. In a large grill pan or skillet, char the onion slices over moderate heat until slightly softened and blackened in spots on both sides, about 18 minutes. Cut the charred onions into ½-inch dice.

Mesclun Salad with Onion-Ginger Dressing

greens & health

Researchers haven't yet analyzed the makeup of all baby greens; however, it's logical to assume that because plants develop vitamins, minerals and fiber as they grow, baby greens are less nutritious than mature greens. Even so, they are an excellent source of beta-carotene, vitamin C and folate, and a modest source of iron, calcium and potassium. They also contain compounds called phytochemicals that combat heart disease and other serious ailments. And in a few cases, baby greens proudly deliver nutrients that their older siblings might not. For instance, pea shoots contain a phytochemical called quercetin that fights cancer.

3. In a large bowl, whisk the extra-virgin olive oil with the red wine vinegar, minced shallots, ginger and garlic. Stir in the charred diced onions and season with salt and pepper. Add the mesclun to the dressing and toss well.
—*Scott Howell*

MAKE AHEAD The croutons can be stored at room temperature in an airtight container for up to 2 days. The dressing can be refrigerated for up to 2 days.

Baby Lettuce and Herb Salad with Shallot Vinaigrette

12 SERVINGS

- 2 pounds baby red beets or medium red beets
- ½ cup aged red wine vinegar
- 2 medium shallots, finely chopped
- Salt and freshly ground pepper
- ½ cup canola or grapeseed oil
- ½ cup extra-virgin olive oil
- 1 pound mixed baby salad greens
- 4 cups flat-leaf parsley leaves
- 2 cups basil leaves
- 1 cup tarragon leaves
- 1 pint cherry tomatoes, halved
- 2 bunches radishes, thinly sliced

1. In a medium saucepan, cover the beets with cold water and bring to a boil. Simmer over moderate heat until tender when pierced, about 20 minutes for baby beets and 40 minutes for medium beets. Drain, rinse in cold water and slip off the skins. Cut baby beets in half lengthwise; thinly slice medium beets crosswise. Let cool.

2. In a large bowl, combine the vinegar with the shallots and season with salt and pepper. Gradually whisk in the oils until emulsified. Add the greens, parsley, basil, tarragon, tomatoes and radishes to the bowl. Season with salt and pepper, toss gently and transfer to a platter. Sprinkle the beets on top and serve.
—*Brandon Miller*

MAKE AHEAD The whole cooked beets can be refrigerated overnight.

WINE The rich, round, powerful Nonvintage Veuve Clicquot Champagne has enough body and fruity-toasty flavors to stand up to the aromatic herbs in this salad.

Lettuce and Fresh Herb Salad with Pearl Onions

6 SERVINGS ● ●

- ½ pound pearl onions, root ends trimmed
- ¼ cup extra-virgin olive oil
- 1½ tablespoons Champagne vinegar
- Salt and freshly ground pepper
- ¾ pound assorted tender lettuces, such as oak leaf and Boston, torn into bite-size pieces (12 cups)
- 2 tablespoons minced chives
- 1 tablespoon minced tarragon
- 1 tablespoon minced basil

1. In a saucepan of boiling salted water, cook the onions until just tender, about 4 minutes. Drain and let cool, then peel.

2. In a bowl, mix the oil with the vinegar; season with salt and pepper. In a large salad bowl, toss the lettuces with the onions, chives, tarragon and basil. Add the vinaigrette, toss to coat and serve.
—*Murielle Andraud*

Tropical Spinach Salad with Warm Fruit Vinaigrette

6 SERVINGS ● ●

Tropical spinach is a vast family of greens that includes true spinach relatives as well as entirely different varieties.

- ¼ cup dried cranberries
- ¼ cup dried blueberries
- Boiling water
- ¼ cup walnut or olive oil
- 2 teaspoons curry powder
- 1 garlic clove, smashed
- 1 teaspoon honey
- 1 teaspoon salt
- ⅛ to ¼ teaspoon cayenne pepper
- ¼ cup fresh orange juice
- 8 cups tropical spinach leaves (3 ounces), washed and dried thoroughly

1. In a small saucepan, cover the dried cranberries and blueberries with boiling water and let them stand until softened, about 5 minutes. Drain the berries well.

2. Heat the walnut or olive oil in the same saucepan. Add the curry and smashed garlic clove and cook over low heat for 1 minute; discard the garlic. Add the honey, salt and cayenne, then whisk in the orange juice. Stir in the dried fruits and bring to a simmer. In a large bowl, toss the spinach with the hot dressing and serve at once.
—*Jack Staub*

baby greens

While parents calculate the age of their babies in weeks, farmers measure their babies—the leafy-green variety—in inches. Lee Jones at the Chef's Garden, a family farm in Huron, Ohio, that sells exclusively to restaurants, defines the stages of his greens this way: **micro,** 1 to 1¼ inches; **cotyledon,** 1¼ to 1¾ inches; **petite,** 1¾ to 2 inches; **ultra,** 2 to 3 inches; **baby,** 3 to 4 inches; **young,** 4 inches and up.

Tropical Spinach Salad
with Warm Fruit
Vinaigrette (p. 57)

Sprouts with Apples and
Nasturtium Leaves (p. 60)

salads

Watercress Salad

4 SERVINGS

Although it's designed to accompany Quail with Asian Spices (p. 205), this is a fine stand-alone salad that is fast and easy to make, at least if you omit the crunchy leeks (which you may not want to do; they're irresistible).

- 5 tablespoons vegetable oil
- 2 leeks, white parts only, sliced into very thin rings

Salt and freshly ground pepper

- 1½ tablespoons soy sauce
- 1 tablespoon sherry vinegar
- 1 tablespoon minced shallots
- 1½ tablespoons hazelnut, walnut or olive oil
- 1 bunch watercress (6 ounces), thick stems discarded
- 2 cups finely shredded red cabbage
- ¼ cup finely chopped chives, for garnish

1. Heat 2½ tablespoons of the vegetable oil in a large, heavy skillet. Add half the leeks, season with salt and pepper and cook over moderate heat until lightly browned, about 2 minutes; transfer to paper towels. Repeat with the remaining 2½ tablespoons of vegetable oil and the remaining leeks.

2. In a large bowl, whisk the soy sauce with the vinegar, shallots and a large pinch of salt. Slowly whisk in the hazelnut oil. Add the watercress and cabbage to the bowl along with half the fried leeks, season with salt and pepper and toss well. Garnish with the remaining fried leeks and the chives and serve.

—*Jean-Georges Vongerichten*

Sprouts with Apples and Nasturtium Leaves

4 SERVINGS ● ●

- ¼ pound mixed delicate sprouts, such as alfalfa, watercress and mustard seed (about 4 cups)
- 1 Granny Smith apple, finely julienned

- 1½ teaspoons toasted peanut or sesame oil
- 1½ teaspoons grapeseed oil

Fine sea salt

- 4 large nasturtium leaves
- ¼ cup sheep's milk or goat's milk yogurt

In a large bowl, toss the sprouts with the apple, peanut oil and grapeseed oil. Season with salt. Mound ½ cup of the sprout salad on each of 4 large plates. Top each mound with a nasturtium leaf and the remaining salad. Drizzle the yogurt around the plates and serve. —*Pierre Gagnaire*

Mâche and Blood Orange Salad

4 SERVINGS ● ●

- 1 teaspoon fennel seeds
- 2 blood oranges
- 1 lime plus 1 tablespoon fresh lime juice
- ½ cup fresh orange juice
- ¼ teaspoon sugar
- 1½ tablespoons grapeseed oil
- ½ tablespoon extra-virgin olive oil

Salt and freshly ground pepper

- 6 ounces mâche (8 cups)
- 1 Belgian endive—cored, halved lengthwise and sliced crosswise
- 1 ounce spicy sprouts, such as radish

1. In a small skillet, toast the fennel seeds until fragrant, about 1 minute. Transfer to a plate to cool.

2. Using a sharp knife, peel the blood oranges and the lime, removing all of the bitter white pith. Cut in between the membranes to release the orange and lime sections into separate bowls. Squeeze the juice from 1 of the orange membranes into a small saucepan. Discard the other membranes.

3. Add the lime juice, orange juice and sugar to the saucepan and simmer over low heat until reduced to 2 tablespoons, about 5 minutes. Add the juice to the lime sections. Let cool, then whisk in the oils and the fennel seeds. Season with salt and pepper.

4. In a large bowl, toss the mâche with the endive and sprouts. Add the dressing and toss to coat. Add the blood orange sections and toss again. Mound the salad on plates and serve.

—*Eberhard Müller*

ONE SERVING Calories 88 kcal, Total Fat 4.8 gm, Saturated Fat 0.5 gm, Protein 2 gm, Carbohydrates 11 gm

Citrus Salad with Arugula and Mint

4 SERVINGS ● ●

- 2 large navel oranges
- 2 Minneola, or Honeybell, tangelos
- 1 pink grapefruit
- 2 tablespoons extra-virgin olive oil

Salt and freshly ground pepper

- ¾ pound arugula, leaves torn into large pieces
- ¼ cup torn mint leaves
- 1 small red onion, thinly sliced

1. Using a sharp knife, peel the citrus fruits; be sure to remove all of the bitter white pith. Working over a strainer set in a bowl, cut in between the membranes to release the citrus sections into the strainer. Squeeze the juice from the membranes into the strainer.

2. Measure 2 tablespoons of the strained juice into a bowl; drink the rest. Whisk the olive oil into the juice; season with salt and pepper. Add the arugula, mint and red onion and toss. Add the fruit, toss gently and serve.

—*Grace Parisi*

ONE SERVING Calories 156 kcal, Total Fat 7.5 gm, Saturated Fat 1 gm, Protein 4 gm, Carbohydrates 22 gm

Arugula, Fresh Corn and Tomato Salad

8 SERVINGS ● ●

- ¼ cup Champagne vinegar or white wine vinegar
- ¼ cup minced shallots

Salt and freshly ground pepper

- 6 ears of white corn with small kernels, shucked

Mâche and Blood Orange Salad

½ cup extra-virgin olive oil

8 loosely packed cups arugula or peppercress (about ¾ pound)

3 pints cherry tomatoes, halved

8 fresh organic nasturtiums (see Note), gently torn into bite-size pieces (optional)

I. In a large bowl, mix the Champagne vinegar with the minced shallots and season the mixture with salt and pepper. Let the shallots stand in the vinegar for 10 minutes. Meanwhile, using a sharp, thin knife and working over another bowl, cut the kernels from the ears of white corn.

2. Whisk the olive oil into the Champagne vinegar and shallots until blended. Add the arugula and toss with the dressing. Add the cherry tomatoes and the corn kernels and toss gently. Transfer the salad to a large platter, scatter the nasturtiums on top and serve. —*Randy Windham*

NOTE When using flowers in a recipe, be sure that they are edible and organic (meaning they have not been sprayed with chemicals). Do not purchase flowers for cooking from florists or garden centers. Organic flowers are available at farmers' markets, specialty markets and some supermarkets.

Watermelon-Arugula Salad

Watermelon-Arugula Salad

4 SERVINGS ●●

⅓ cup very thinly sliced red onion

Ice cubes

½ pound peeled seedless watermelon flesh, cut into 1-inch dice (2 cups)

2 tablespoons balsamic vinegar

1 tablespoon extra-virgin olive oil

Salt and freshly ground pepper

Two 6-ounce bunches of arugula, tough stems discarded

¼ cup crumbled goat cheese

I. In a small bowl, cover the onion with cold water and ice cubes. Let stand for 30 minutes, then drain and pat dry.

2. In a medium bowl, toss the diced watermelon flesh with 1 tablespoon of the balsamic vinegar and leave the mixture to stand at room temperature for 10 minutes.

3. In another medium bowl, whisk the remaining 1 tablespoon of balsamic vinegar with the extra-virgin olive oil and season with salt and pepper. Add the arugula and onion and toss gently. Using a slotted spoon, scatter the watermelon over the salad and top with the crumbled goat cheese. —*Suki Hertz*

ONE SERVING Calories 127 kcal, Total Fat 7.1 gm, Saturated Fat 2.6 gm

Baby Spinach Salad with Goat Cheese and Dried Cherries

4 SERVINGS ●

- 1 teaspoon unsalted butter
- ⅓ cup sliced almonds
- 2 tablespoons extra-virgin olive oil
- 2 tablespoons balsamic vinegar

Salt and freshly ground pepper

One 10-ounce bag baby spinach

- ½ cup dried sour cherries
- 4 ounces mild goat cheese, crumbled

1. Melt the butter in a small skillet. Add the almonds and cook over moderately high heat, stirring constantly, until golden, about 3 minutes. Drain on paper towels and let cool completely.

2. In a small bowl, whisk the oil with the vinegar and season the vinaigrette with salt and pepper. In a large bowl, toss the spinach with the cherries and almonds. Add the vinaigrette and toss well. Add the goat cheese, toss the salad lightly and serve. —*Joanne Weir*

Ensalada Chilpancingo

6 SERVINGS

- 1 jalapeño—stemmed, seeded and coarsely chopped

Zest of 3 limes, finely grated

- ¼ cup sherry vinegar
- ½ teaspoon freshly ground pepper

Salt

- ½ cup extra-virgin olive oil

Vegetable oil, for frying (optional)

Four 5-inch yellow-corn tortillas, sliced into ¼-inch-wide strips

- 8 cups mixed greens
- 3 ounces queso fresco or ricotta salata, crumbled

1. In a blender or mini food processor, pulse the jalapeño with the lime zest, vinegar, pepper and 1½ teaspoons of salt until chopped. Blend in the oil.

2. In a medium saucepan, heat 2 inches of vegetable oil to 350°. Working in batches, fry the tortilla strips until crisp and golden, about 1 minute. Drain on paper towels and season with salt. Alternatively, preheat the oven to 400°. Spread the tortilla strips on a baking sheet and spray liberally with vegetable oil. Sprinkle the strips with salt and bake for 8 minutes, or until golden and crisp.

3. In a large bowl, toss the greens with the jalapeño vinaigrette. Mound the salad on plates, top with the crumbled cheese and tortilla strips and serve.

—*Generoso Bahena*

Palisades Market Caesar Salad

8 SERVINGS

- 1 cup mayonnaise
- 1 teaspoon Dijon mustard
- 1 garlic clove, minced
- ¼ cup freshly grated Parmesan
- 1 tablespoon red wine vinegar
- 1 tablespoon fresh lemon juice
- ¾ teaspoon Worcestershire sauce
- ¾ teaspoon Tabasco sauce

Salt and freshly ground pepper

- 2 pounds romaine lettuce, torn into bite-size pieces

Supercrisp Parmesan Croutons (recipe follows)

In a small bowl, whisk the mayonnaise with the mustard, garlic, Parmesan, vinegar, lemon juice, Worcestershire sauce and Tabasco. Season with salt and pepper. In a large bowl, toss the lettuce with the croutons and three-fourths of the dressing. Serve right away, passing the extra dressing at the table. —*Duncan Gott*

SUPERCRISP PARMESAN CROUTONS

MAKES ABOUT 4 CUPS ●

- 3 tablespoons unsalted butter
- 1 tablespoon extra-virgin olive oil
- 4 garlic cloves, very finely chopped

One ¾-pound loaf of focaccia or Italian bread, crusts removed, bread cut into ¾-inch dice

- ¼ cup freshly grated Parmesan

Pinch of sugar

Salt and freshly ground pepper

Preheat the oven to 300°. In a small skillet, melt the butter in the olive oil. Add the garlic and cook over moderately low heat until fragrant, about 2 minutes. Scrape the butter into a large bowl and toss with the diced bread. Add the Parmesan and sugar and season with salt and pepper. Spread the croutons on a large, rimmed baking sheet and bake for 45 minutes, stirring occasionally, until golden and crisp.

—*Joel Gott*

MAKE AHEAD The croutons can be stored in an airtight container for 3 days.

Warm Mushroom Salad with Parmesan and Arugula

4 SERVINGS ●●

This salad can be made with wild as well as cultivated mushrooms. The only requirement is that the dish be served warm so that the cheese begins to melt, wilting the arugula and exuding a lovely aroma.

- 2½ tablespoons extra-virgin olive oil
- 1 pound mixed mushrooms, cut into large pieces
- ¼ cup veal or chicken demiglace (see Note)

Sea salt

- 2 ounces Parmesan, shaved with a vegetable peeler
- 6 ounces young arugula (4 cups)

1. Heat 2 tablespoons of the oil in a large skillet. Add the mushrooms and cook over high heat, stirring, until tender and lightly browned, about 5 minutes. Add the demiglace and cook over moderate heat for 3 minutes, stirring occasionally. Season with salt. Mound the mushrooms on warmed plates and top with the Parmesan shavings.

2. In a bowl, toss the arugula with the remaining ½ tablespoon of olive oil and a pinch of salt. Pile the arugula on the mushrooms and serve.

—*Pierre Gagnaire*

NOTE Demiglace is available from Dean & DeLuca, 800-221-7714.

Bitter Greens with Cherry Beer Vinaigrette and Blue Cheese Toasts

6 SERVINGS

½ cup cherry-flavored beer, such as Boon Kriek

2 shallots, finely chopped

2 tablespoons dried cherries or cranberries, coarsely chopped

1 tablespoon honey

2 tablespoons red wine vinegar or raspberry vinegar

2 teaspoons Dijon mustard

½ cup canola oil

Salt and freshly ground pepper

1 tablespoon unsalted butter, softened

3 slices of firm white sandwich bread, crusts removed, bread cut in half to make triangles

¼ pound Roquefort or Gorgonzola

6 cups mixed bitter greens, such as radicchio, escarole and arugula

2 Belgian endives, cored and thinly sliced crosswise

1. Preheat the oven to 350°. In a small saucepan, combine the beer with the shallots, dried cherries and honey and bring to a boil over high heat. Reduce the heat to moderate and simmer, stirring occasionally, until the beer has reduced by half, about 5 minutes. Remove from the heat and let cool to lukewarm.

2. In a medium bowl, whisk the vinegar with the mustard. Whisk in the beer reduction, then gradually whisk in the canola oil. Season the cherry beer vinaigrette with salt and pepper.

3. Lightly butter the bread triangles on both sides and toast in the oven until golden. Depending on the consistency of the cheese, crumble or spread it on the toasts.

4. Add the greens and endives to the vinaigrette and toss to coat. Arrange the salad on plates, garnish each with a cheese toast and serve.

—*Ruth Van Waerebeek*

BEER Drink some of the cherry-flavored beer used in the vinaigrette to tone down the saltiness of the Roquefort.

Frisée Salad with Walnuts and Roquefort

4 SERVINGS

1 small shallot, minced

1 tablespoon balsamic vinegar

Salt and freshly ground pepper

3 tablespoons extra-virgin olive oil

1 teaspoon unsalted butter

¼ cup coarsely chopped walnuts

3 large Belgian endives, cored and cut crosswise 1 inch thick

1 head frisée (½ pound), torn into bite-size pieces

½ cup crumbled Roquefort (about 2 ounces)

1. In a large bowl, mix the shallot with the vinegar. Add a generous pinch each of salt and pepper and let stand for 5 minutes, then whisk in the olive oil.

2. Melt the butter in a small skillet. Add the walnuts and cook over moderately high heat, stirring, until golden and fragrant, about 5 minutes. Transfer the walnuts to paper towels, sprinkle with salt and let cool.

3. Add the endives and frisée to the dressing and toss well. Add the walnuts and cheese, toss again and serve.

—*Peggy Knickerbocker*

WINE A fruity, off-dry Riesling will play off the salty, tangy cheese and echo the sweet vinaigrette in this salad. Try the 1999 Washington Hills or the 1999 Kiona White Riesling, both from the Columbia Valley in Washington State.

Arugula and Pea Shoot Salad with Smoked Salmon

4 SERVINGS ●●

It's awfully hard to slice vegetables thinly and consistently using a knife. That's why chefs use a mandoline for perfect slices of celery root or other hard vegetables, as in this recipe. You

Arugula and Pea Shoot Salad with Smoked Salmon

don't need an expensive stainless-steel model; the plastic ones work very well.

2 tablespoons fresh lemon juice

2 teaspoons white truffle oil or extra-virgin olive oil

Salt and freshly ground pepper

½ pound celery root, peeled

¼ pound arugula (8 cups)

2 ounces pea shoots (2 packed cups)

¼ pound thinly sliced smoked salmon, cut into ¼-inch-wide strips

1. In a small bowl, mix the lemon juice with the truffle oil and season with salt and pepper. Set aside until ready to use.

2. Using a mandoline, slice the celery root very thinly. Stack the slices and cut them into very fine strips.

3. In a large bowl, toss the arugula with the pea shoots, celery root and smoked salmon. Add the dressing and toss well. Mound the salad on plates and serve.
—*Eberhard Müller*

ONE SERVING Calories 103 kcal, Total Fat 4 gm, Saturated Fat 0.6 gm, Protein 8 gm, Carbohydrates 11 gm

Artichoke Salad with Saffron Vinaigrette

2 SERVINGS

This recipe is from Manhattan's Bouley Bakery.

- 1 lemon, halved
- 3 large artichokes
- 2 tablespoons extra-virgin olive oil
- 2 slices of bacon, cut into 1-inch pieces
- 2 garlic cloves, thinly sliced
- 1 carrot, thinly sliced
- 1 medium onion, thinly sliced
- 2 cups dry Riesling
- 1 cup water
- 2 thyme sprigs
- 1 bay leaf

Salt and freshly ground pepper
Pinch of saffron threads

- ½ teaspoon sherry vinegar
- ½ teaspoon fresh lemon juice
- 1 head of Bibb lettuce, leaves separated

1. Squeeze the lemon juice into a bowl of cold water; add the lemon to the bowl. Using a sharp stainless-steel knife, cut off the artichoke stems and halve the artichokes crosswise. Discard the tops. Working with 1 artichoke at a time, pull off all the outer green leaves from the bottoms until you reach the yellow leaves. Trim off the tough outer skin. Scrape out the hairy choke with a teaspoon, then drop the artichoke hearts into the lemon water.

2. Heat ½ tablespoon of the oil in a medium saucepan. Add the bacon and cook over low heat, stirring until the fat begins to melt, about 4 minutes. Stir in the garlic, carrot and onion. Cover and cook over low heat until the vegetables are softened, about 8 minutes. Add the remaining 1½ tablespoons of oil and the artichoke hearts. Stir in the Riesling, water, thyme and bay leaf and bring to a boil. Season with salt and pepper and simmer over low heat until the artichoke hearts are tender, about 15 minutes.

3. Using a slotted spoon, transfer the artichoke hearts to a plate. Skim 1½ tablespoons of oil from the artichoke broth and put the oil in a small bowl. Crumble the saffron threads into the oil. Strain the artichoke broth. Pour ½ cup of the broth into the saucepan and boil over high heat until reduced by half, about 3 minutes. Discard any remaining artichoke broth.

4. Cut 1 artichoke heart in half and cut 1 of the halves into chunks. Transfer the artichoke chunks to a blender. Add the reduced broth and puree. With the machine on, slowly add the saffron oil and blend until smooth. Scrape the puree into a small bowl and stir in the sherry vinegar and lemon juice. Season with salt and pepper.

5. Thinly slice the remaining 2½ artichoke hearts. In a medium bowl, toss the Bibb lettuce with 1 tablespoon of the vinaigrette and arrange it on 2 plates. Top the lettuce with the sliced artichokes and drizzle with the remaining saffron vinaigrette and serve.

—Galen Zamarra

Warm Bacon and Egg Salad

4 SERVINGS ● ●

- 2 tablespoons extra-virgin olive oil
- 1 tablespoon balsamic vinegar
- 1 teaspoon sherry vinegar
- 1 tablespoon chopped basil
- 1 tablespoon chopped flat-leaf parsley

Salt and freshly ground pepper

- 12 cups packed mesclun (6 ounces)
- 1 tablespoon unsalted butter
- 2 slices of thick-cut lean bacon, cut crosswise into thin strips
- 2 large eggs, lightly beaten

1. In a large bowl, combine the oil, vinegars, basil and parsley. Season with salt and pepper. Add the mesclun and toss well.

2. Melt the butter in a nonstick skillet. Add the bacon; cook over moderately high heat until crisp, about 2 minutes. Quickly stir in the eggs and cook until barely scrambled, about 15 seconds. Remove from the heat to prevent overcooking. Spoon over the salad, toss and serve.

—Marc Vetri

Spinach and Avocado Salad

4 MAIN-COURSE SERVINGS ●

- ¾ pound thick-cut bacon
- 3 tablespoons sherry vinegar
- 1 tablespoon honey mustard

Kosher salt and freshly ground pepper

- ⅓ cup extra-virgin olive oil

Two 5-ounce bags of prewashed baby spinach

- 1 pint grape tomatoes, halved
- 3 large scallions, white and tender green parts, thinly sliced lengthwise
- 2 large Hass avocados, peeled and sliced into thin wedges

1. Preheat the oven to 500°. Arrange the bacon slices on a large, heavy, rimmed baking sheet. Roast for 15 minutes or until golden brown, turning the slices halfway through. Drain the bacon on paper towels and let cool, then cut the strips crosswise into 1-inch pieces.

2. In a small bowl, whisk the sherry vinegar with the honey mustard and season with salt and pepper. Whisk in the olive oil until emulsified.

3. In a large bowl, toss the spinach, tomatoes and scallions with the vinaigrette. Arrange the salad on plates, top with the sliced avocados and bacon and serve.

—Lily Barberio

Black-Eyed Pea and Arugula Salad

10 SERVINGS ● ●

- 4 ears of corn, shucked
- ⅓ cup extra-virgin olive oil, plus more for brushing

Salt and freshly ground pepper
Vegetable oil, for the grill

- 4 cups fresh or frozen black-eyed peas
- 3 tablespoons fresh lime juice

Spinach and Avocado Salad

1 tablespoon balsamic vinegar

2 red bell peppers, cut into
¼-inch dice

⅓ cup finely chopped red onion

⅓ cup finely chopped cilantro

2 jalapeños, seeded and minced

½ pound young arugula

1. Light a grill. Brush the ears of corn with extra-virgin olive oil and season with salt and pepper. Lightly brush the grill with the vegetable oil and grill the corn over a medium-hot fire, turning frequently, until lightly charred and almost tender, about 5 minutes. Let cool slightly. Over a bowl, cut the kernels from the cobs.

2. In a saucepan of boiling salted water, cook the black-eyed peas until tender, about 12 minutes. Drain and refresh under cold water. Drain again and pat dry.

3. In a large bowl, whisk the ⅓ cup of olive oil with the lime juice and balsamic vinegar. Season with salt and pepper. Add the grilled corn, black-eyed peas, red bell peppers, onion, cilantro and jalapeños and toss well. Season generously with salt and pepper. Cover and refrigerate for at least 1 hour or up to 4 hours. Toss the black-eyed pea salad with the arugula and transfer to a platter just before serving.
—*Danielle Custer*

**Black-Eyed Pea and
Arugula Salad**

Jalapeño Slaw

6 SERVINGS ● ● ●

⅓ cup pure olive oil

3½ tablespoons red wine vinegar

2 tablespoons chopped cilantro

1 teaspoon sugar

Salt and freshly ground pepper

1¼ pounds Savoy cabbage, finely
shredded (8 cups)

1 medium red onion, thinly sliced

1 fennel bulb, cored
and thinly sliced

2 large jalapeños, seeded and thinly
sliced lengthwise

In a large bowl, whisk the olive oil with the vinegar, cilantro and sugar and season with salt and pepper. Add the cabbage, onion, fennel and jalapeños to the dressing and toss well. Serve at once, or chill for 1 hour before serving.
—*Todd English*

Japanese Coleslaw with Sesame Seeds

8 SERVINGS ● ● ●

Dress this salad just before serving to keep the vegetables crisp.

2 tablespoons sesame seeds

1½ tablespoons fresh lemon juice

1½ tablespoons soy sauce

1½ tablespoons vegetable oil

1½ teaspoons Asian sesame oil

¼ small red cabbage, finely
shredded (2 cups)

¼ medium napa cabbage, finely
shredded (2 cups)

6 carrots, finely julienned (2 cups)

¼ pound daikon radish, peeled and
finely julienned (2 cups)

Salt and freshly ground pepper

1. In a small skillet, toast the sesame seeds, stirring occasionally, until lightly browned, about 2 minutes. In a small bowl, whisk the lemon juice with the soy sauce, vegetable oil and sesame oil.

2. In a large bowl, toss the red cabbage with the napa cabbage, carrots and daikon. Add the dressing, season with salt and pepper and toss to coat. Sprinkle with the sesame seeds and serve. —*Michael Kramer*

MAKE AHEAD The vegetables and soy dressing can be refrigerated separately for 2 days.

Red Cabbage Slaw with Lemon Dressing

6 TO 8 SERVINGS ●●

This crisp, refreshing cabbage and sprout slaw can be made with any variety of sprouts, from leafy sunflower, alfalfa and radish sprouts to sprouted lentils, chickpeas and beans.

- ⅓ cup raw sunflower seeds (1½ ounces)
- 2 teaspoons coarsely chopped jalapeño
- ¾ cup canola oil
- ⅓ cup fresh lemon juice
- ½ teaspoon salt
- ¼ teaspoon sugar
- ½ head of red cabbage, cored and cut into ¼-inch-wide strips (8 cups)
- 2 large carrots, coarsely shredded
- 4 ounces mixed sprouts, such as sunflower and radish (about 3 cups)

Freshly ground pepper

1. Preheat the oven to 350°. Spread the sunflower seeds on a baking sheet

looking for love?

Just open your refrigerator and pull out some celery. The stalks contain androsterone, a substance that apparently causes the body to release an irresistible scent that can't be consciously detected. Try some celery in a tangy slaw with soybeans to see if the theory holds.

and toast in the oven for about 8 minutes, or until fragrant. Let cool.

2. In a blender or food processor, combine the jalapeño, canola oil, lemon juice, salt and sugar and process until smooth.

3. In a large bowl, toss the cabbage with the carrots and sprouts. Add the dressing and the toasted sunflower seeds and toss to coat. Season with pepper, toss again and serve.

—*Ilene Rosen*

MAKE AHEAD The slaw can be refrigerated for up to 8 hours before serving.

Celery Slaw with Edamame

4 SERVINGS ●●

Edamame—that's the Japanese name for whole soybeans—may not be as commonplace as celery, but they are becoming more and more popular. Credit all the good news about soy's health benefits. The beans are available in the freezer section of many supermarkets and at Asian food markets.

- 4 large, tender celery ribs, plus 2 tablespoons coarsely chopped celery leaves
- 2 cups (6 ounces) frozen edamame (soybeans) in their pods
- 2 scallions, white and tender green parts, thinly sliced on the diagonal
- ¼ cup cilantro leaves
- 1 tablespoon torn mint leaves
- 1 tablespoon fresh lime juice
- 1 tablespoon canola oil

Sea salt

1. In a food processor or with a sharp knife, slice the celery as thinly as possible. Put the celery in a bowl of ice water and crisp for 15 minutes. Drain and pat dry. Wipe out the bowl and return the celery to it.

2. In a medium saucepan of boiling water, cook the soybeans for 5 minutes. Drain and refresh under cold water. Shell the soybeans and pat dry. Add the soybeans, scallions, cilantro,

mint and celery leaves to the celery and toss well.

3. In a bowl, whisk the lime juice with the oil. Pour the dressing over the vegetables, season with salt, toss and serve. —*Grace Parisi*

MAKE AHEAD The recipe can be prepared through Step 1 and refrigerated for 4 hours.

WINE A refreshing sparkling wine will balance the salty-sweetness of the celery and soybeans and point up the crisp texture of the celery. Look for a good nonvintage brut from France, such as the Deutz Brut Champagne Classic or the Laurent-Perrier Brut L.P.

Warm Brussels Sprout Slaw with Bacon

10 SERVINGS ●

- ¾ pound thick-sliced bacon, cut into ½-inch pieces
- 4 tablespoons unsalted butter
- 2 pounds Brussels sprouts, thinly sliced in a food processor

Salt and freshly ground pepper

- 2 Granny Smith apples—peeled, cored, coarsely shredded and squeezed dry
- 1 teaspoon thyme leaves

1. In a large skillet, cook the bacon over moderately high heat, stirring occasionally, until crisp, about 6 minutes. Drain on paper towels; reserve ¼ cup of fat.

2. In a large enameled cast-iron casserole, melt the butter in the bacon fat. Add the Brussels sprouts in batches and cook over high heat, stirring, until softened but still bright green, about 8 minutes. Season with salt and pepper. Add the apples and thyme; cook, stirring, until the apples are warmed through. Transfer the slaw to a platter, scatter the bacon on top and serve.

—*Grace Parisi*

MAKE AHEAD The cooked bacon and bacon fat and the uncooked sliced sprouts can be refrigerated overnight. Recrisp the bacon before serving.

Celery Slaw with Edamame

Sugar Snap Pea and Prosciutto Salad

Warm Fennel Salad

Sugar Snap Pea and Pea Shoot Salad

4 SERVINGS ● ●

½ pound sugar snap peas, trimmed and sliced lengthwise in thirds

3½ ounces pea shoots (4 cups)

3 tablespoons chopped tarragon

1½ tablespoons fresh lemon juice

Salt and freshly ground pepper

2½ tablespoons extra-virgin olive oil

In a bowl, toss the snap peas with the pea shoots and tarragon. Add the lemon juice and season with salt and pepper. Drizzle in the oil, toss well and serve. —*Melissa Clark*

Sugar Snap Pea and Prosciutto Salad

4 SERVINGS ●

¾ pound sugar snap peas

3 tablespoons extra-virgin olive oil

1 teaspoon finely grated lemon zest

1½ tablespoons fresh lemon juice

3 tablespoons finely chopped mint

3 ounces thinly sliced prosciutto, cut into thin strips

Salt and freshly ground pepper

1. Blanch the sugar snaps in a medium saucepan of boiling salted water until crisp-tender, about 1 minute. Drain and plunge into an ice bath. Pat the sugar snaps dry.

2. In a medium bowl, whisk the olive oil, lemon zest, lemon juice and mint. Add the sugar snaps and prosciutto, season with salt and pepper and toss. Arrange the salad on a platter and serve. —*Joanne Weir*

Mixed Tomato Salad with Green Tomato Vinaigrette

6 SERVINGS ● ●

Either mild or hot chiles are fine in the tangy dressing for this refreshing tomato salad; if you have more than one kind on hand, use a mixture of chiles.

1 underripe medium green tomato

¼ cup rice vinegar

Large pinch of sugar

6 tablespoons canola oil

Sea salt and freshly ground pepper

2 pounds assorted heirloom tomatoes, cut into wedges

1 pound assorted small tomatoes, larger tomatoes cut in half

2 tablespoons minced fresh chiles, such as jalapeño

1. Bring a small saucepan of water to a boil. Prepare a bowl of ice water.

2. Add the green tomato to the boiling water and cook until slightly softened and the skin is pale, about 7 minutes. Drain and transfer to the bowl of ice water and cool thoroughly, then drain again. Peel and core the green tomato and cut it into large chunks.

3. In a blender, combine the green tomato chunks with the vinegar and sugar and puree until the tomato is finely chopped. With the machine on, add the oil in a slow stream and blend until smooth. Season with salt and pepper.

4. Arrange all of the tomatoes on a large platter. Sprinkle with the chiles and season with salt and pepper. Drizzle the dressing all over the salad and serve. —*Ilene Rosen*

MAKE AHEAD The green tomato vinaigrette can be refrigerated for up to 3 days before serving.

Turkish Tomato Salad with Fresh Herbs

8 SERVINGS ●

Pomegranate molasses, which is a syrup made by boiling pomegranate juice with sugar and lemon juice, is a staple of Turkish cooking. It lends intense fruity and tangy flavors to this tomato, scallion and herb salad. Serve lots of bread for mopping up the wonderful tart dressing.

- 1½ cups (7 ounces) shelled unsalted pistachios or walnuts
- ½ cup pomegranate molasses
- ¼ cup extra-virgin olive oil
- Salt
- 2 pounds tomatoes, finely chopped, or cherry tomatoes, quartered
- 4 bunches of scallions (1 pound), finely chopped
- 2 cups chopped flat-leaf parsley (from two ¼-pound bunches)
- 1 cup chopped mint leaves (from one ¼-pound bunch)
- 1 medium cucumber—peeled, seeded and cut into ½-inch chunks
- 2 jalapeños, seeded and minced

I. Preheat the oven to 350°. Spread the pistachios on a rimmed baking sheet and toast in the oven for about 8 minutes, or until lightly browned; let the nuts cool.

2. In a small bowl, whisk the pomegranate molasses with the olive oil until blended. Season the dressing with salt.

3. In a large bowl, toss the chopped tomatoes or quartered cherry tomatoes with the scallions, parsley, mint, cucumber and jalapeños. Add the dressing and toss well. Season with salt. Spoon the salad onto a platter, sprinkle the pistachios over the top and serve. —*Engin Akin*

ONE CUP Calories 276 kcal, Total Fat 17.8 gm, Saturated Fat 2.3 gm, Protein 7 gm, Carbohydrates 25 gm

MAKE AHEAD The dressing can be made and the vegetables chopped 2 hours ahead. Toss just before serving.

Warm Fennel Salad

4 SERVINGS ●

- 2 fennel bulbs (2 pounds)—halved lengthwise, cored and sliced ¼ inch thick
- 2 tablespoons extra-virgin olive oil
- Salt and freshly ground pepper
- 3 ounces fresh goat cheese, in large chunks
- Lemon wedges, for serving

Preheat the oven to 425°. On a large, rimmed baking sheet, toss the fennel with the olive oil and season with salt and pepper. Bake for 30 minutes, or until the fennel is tender and browned around the edges. Transfer the fennel to a bowl. Add the chunks of goat cheese and toss with the fennel until melted slightly. Season with salt and pepper and serve with lemon wedges.

—*Charles Leary and Vaughn Perret*

Pomegranate-Fennel Salad

4 SERVINGS ●●

- 1 medium fennel bulb (about 1 pound), cored, and ¼ cup chopped feathery fronds reserved
- 2 medium navel oranges
- 12 Sicilian or other green olives, pitted and quartered
- ½ cup coarsely chopped parsley
- ¼ cup pomegranate seeds
- 1 tablespoon olive oil
- 1 tablespoon fresh lemon juice
- 1 tablespoon pomegranate or red wine vinegar
- 1 teaspoon honey
- ⅛ teaspoon cayenne pepper
- Salt

Pomegranate-Fennel Salad

1. Slice the fennel into thin julienne strips and add to a medium bowl.

2. Using a sharp knife, peel the oranges; remove all of the bitter white pith. Working over the bowl, cut in between the membranes to release the sections. Add the olives, parsley and pomegranate seeds to the bowl.

3. In a small jar, combine the olive oil, lemon juice, vinegar, honey, cayenne and salt and shake to blend. Pour the dressing over the salad. Add the chopped fennel fronds and toss gently. Serve at room temperature or chilled.

—*Suki Hertz*

ONE SERVING Calories 113 kcal, Total Fat 5.1 gm, Saturated Fat 0.8 gm

seed secrets

Break open the tough rind of a pomegranate and you'll find glistening clusters of translucent red seeds (known as arils), separated into groups by yellow-white membranes. To remove the pulp-covered arils, cut off the blossom end of the fruit and then score the rind four or six times. Submerge the pomegranate in a large bowl of water and break it into segments. Still working underwater, gently loosen the arils. The rind and membranes will float to the surface while the arils will drop to the bottom. A large pomegranate will yield about 1 cup of arils.

Sicilian Baked Onion Salad

4 SERVINGS ●●

This delicious baked onion salad is from the city of Siracusa. Most Sicilians bake the onions whole and then slice and dress them with the vinaigrette. Here, the onions are sliced first, then slowly baked so that each slice is richly caramelized and meltingly tender.

- 2 tablespoons extra-virgin olive oil, plus more for brushing
- 3 large onions (about 2 pounds)
- 2 tablespoons water
- 1 garlic clove, minced
- 1 tablespoon chopped flat-leaf parsley
- ½ teaspoon red or white wine vinegar
- ½ teaspoon salt
- ¼ teaspoon freshly ground black pepper
- ¼ teaspoon crushed red pepper

1. Preheat the oven to 300°. Brush a heavy baking sheet with extra-virgin olive oil. Cut the ends off the onions and discard. Leaving the outer onion skin intact, slice the onions crosswise ½ inch thick. Lay the onion slices on the prepared baking sheet and brush lightly with olive oil. Bake the onions for 1 hour, or until just tender. Turn the slices and bake for 30 minutes longer, or until deeply browned. Transfer the onions to a large, shallow serving dish and let cool to room temperature. Discard the onion skin and any dried-out rings.

2. In a small bowl, mix the remaining 2 tablespoons of extra-virgin olive oil with the water, minced garlic, chopped parsley, wine vinegar, salt, black pepper and crushed red pepper. Spoon the vinaigrette over the baked onions and serve. —*Paula Wolfert*

MAKE AHEAD The baked onions and vinaigrette can be refrigerated separately overnight. Bring both to room temperature before dressing and serving.

Grilled Vegetable Salad with Pesto Dressing

8 SERVINGS ●●

Any leftover pesto can be tossed with pasta, drizzled over chicken or steak or mixed with mayonnaise to make a sandwich spread.

- 2 medium zucchini, sliced crosswise ½ inch thick
- 2 yellow squash, sliced crosswise ½ inch thick
- 2 red bell peppers, quartered lengthwise
- 2 medium red onions, sliced crosswise ½ inch thick
- 1 medium eggplant, sliced crosswise ½ inch thick
- 1 cup extra-virgin olive oil

Salt and freshly ground pepper

- 1 tablespoon pine nuts
- 2 packed cups basil leaves
- 1 garlic clove, smashed
- 1 tablespoon fresh lemon juice
- 1 tablespoon water
- ¼ cup freshly grated Parmesan

1. Light a charcoal grill or preheat the broiler. Brush the zucchini, squash, peppers, onions and eggplant with ½ cup of the olive oil and season with salt and pepper. Grill the vegetables in batches, turning occasionally, until tender and browned, about 12 minutes for the zucchini, squash and peppers and 20 minutes for the eggplant and onions. Transfer the vegetables to a platter as they are cooked and let cool.

2. In a small skillet, toast the pine nuts until lightly browned, about 1 minute. In a food processor or blender, combine the basil with the garlic, lemon juice, water and pine nuts and pulse until finely chopped. With the machine on, slowly add the remaining ½ cup of olive oil and process until smooth. Add the Parmesan and pulse to blend. Season with salt and pepper. Drizzle the pesto dressing over the grilled vegetables and serve. —*Michael Kramer*

MAKE AHEAD The vegetables and dressing can be made 6 hours ahead.

Beet and Ginger Salad

4 SERVINGS ●

- 2 pounds medium beets
- ¼ cup sherry wine vinegar
- 1 tablespoon plus 1 teaspoon minced fresh ginger

Salt and freshly ground pepper
- 3 tablespoons vegetable oil
- 4 chives, cut into 2-inch lengths

1. Preheat the oven to 350°. Wash the beets and while still wet, wrap them individually in foil. Set them on a baking sheet and bake for 1 hour and 15 minutes, or until tender when pierced. Rub the skins off the warm beets with paper towels. Slice the beets crosswise ¼ inch thick, then stack the slices and cut them into ¼-inch strips.

2. In a medium bowl, mix the vinegar and ginger. Season with salt and pepper. Slowly whisk in the oil. Add the beets, toss to coat and let marinate for at least 30 minutes. Garnish with the chives and serve at room temperature.
—*Jean-Georges Vongerichten*

Two-Bean and Beet Salad with Feta

8 SERVINGS ●

- 2 pounds small golden or red beets, scrubbed
- 2 pounds mixed yellow wax and green beans
- ½ cup extra-virgin olive oil
- ¼ cup black currant vinegar or red wine vinegar
- 2 tablespoons minced chives

Salt
- ¼ pound feta, preferably Greek, crumbled (1 cup)

1. Preheat the oven to 375°. Arrange the beets in a baking dish and fill with ¼ inch of water. Cover with foil and bake for 45 minutes, or until tender. Let cool, then peel the beets and cut them into ½-inch-thick wedges.

2. In a very large pot of boiling salted water, cook the beans over high heat until crisp-tender, about 5 minutes.

Drain and refresh under cold water. Drain well and pat dry.

3. In a small bowl, whisk the olive oil with the vinegar until blended. In a large bowl, toss the beans with ½ cup of the vinaigrette and transfer to a platter. In the same large bowl, gently toss the beets and chives with the remaining ¼ cup of vinaigrette and spoon over the beans. Season with salt, sprinkle the feta on top and serve.
—*Randy Windham*

MAKE AHEAD The recipe can be prepared through Step 2. Refrigerate the beans and beets separately overnight. Let return to room temperature before proceeding.

Sliced Avocados with Black-Olive Vinaigrette

8 SERVINGS ●

- ¼ cup extra-virgin olive oil
- 4 teaspoons sherry vinegar
- 2 tablespoons black olive paste
- 2 teaspoons very finely chopped red onion
- 2 teaspoons very finely chopped fresh basil

Salt and freshly ground pepper
- 4 ripe Hass avocados

1. In a jar, combine the oil with the vinegar, olive paste, onion, basil and a generous pinch each of salt and pepper. Cover the jar tightly and shake until the vinaigrette is emulsified. Or

Two-Bean and Beet Salad with Feta

Ginger, Green Apple, Sweet Onion
and Coconut Salad

Spicy Bread and Tomato Salad

you can whisk the vinaigrette ingredients in a medium bowl.

2. Halve, pit and peel the avocados. Thinly slice them crosswise, keeping them intact. Using a spatula, transfer the avocado halves, cut side down, to a platter and gently press each of them to fan out the slices. Drizzle the vinaigrette on top of the avocados and serve.　　　　*—Jimmy Bradley*
MAKE AHEAD The vinaigrette can be refrigerated overnight.

Ginger, Green Apple, Sweet Onion and Coconut Salad

4 SERVINGS

Ginger adds a spicy bite to this refreshing salad.

> 2 Granny Smith apples (about 1 pound)—quartered lengthwise, cored and thinly sliced crosswise
> 1 small sweet onion, such as Vidalia, quartered lengthwise and thinly sliced crosswise

One 3-inch piece of ginger, peeled and cut into ⅛-by-2-inch matchsticks

> ½ cup finely grated peeled fresh coconut
> 3 tablespoons fresh lemon juice
> 2 tablespoons finely shredded basil

Salt and freshly ground pepper
Lemon Verbena Oil (recipe follows)

Toss the apples with the onion, ginger, coconut, lemon juice and basil. Season with salt and pepper. Add 3 tablespoons of Lemon Verbena Oil and toss; serve.

　　　　—Jean-Georges Vongerichten

WINE The tart and sweet flavors of this salad find a good match in a bright German Riesling that echoes the apple and lemon. Try the inexpensive 1999 Piesporter Michelsberg Riesling Kabinett or the 1999 "Dr. L" Dr. Loosen Riesling.

LEMON VERBENA OIL

MAKES ABOUT ½ CUP ●●

In addition to using this infused oil in salad dressing, you can drizzle it over steamed vegetables or sautéed fish or chicken.

> 1 cup lemon verbena leaves (about 3 ounces) or 2 stalks fresh lemongrass, tender inner white bulbs only, crushed
> ½ cup grapeseed oil

Pinch of salt

In a blender, combine the lemon verbena with the oil and blend for 2 minutes. Pour the oil into a jar and let stand for 1 hour, then strain, pressing

on the solids to extract as much oil as possible. Season with the salt.—*J.-G.V.*
MAKE AHEAD The Lemon Verbena Oil can be refrigerated for 1 week.

Watermelon Salad with Feta

4 SERVINGS ●

> ¼ cup extra-virgin olive oil
> 1½ tablespoons fresh lemon juice
> ½ teaspoon harissa or other hot sauce

Salt and freshly ground pepper

> 1½ pounds seedless watermelon, rind removed, fruit sliced ¼ inch thick
> ½ small red onion, thinly sliced
> ¼ cup coarsely chopped flat-leaf parsley
> ¼ cup pitted Moroccan or other oil-cured black olives, coarsely chopped
> 2 ounces feta, crumbled (about ½ cup)

In a small bowl, whisk the olive oil with the lemon juice and harissa and season with salt and pepper. Arrange the watermelon slices on a platter and sprinkle with the onion, parsley, olives and feta. Drizzle the dressing on top and serve.　　　　*—Melissa Clark*

Spicy Bread and Tomato Salad

4 SERVINGS ●●

This salad is made with whole wheat bread, which adds nuttiness, and it's got a warm, spice-infused dressing. Use a hearty bakery loaf rather than packaged sandwich bread.

> 12 thick slices of whole wheat bread, cut into ½-inch dice (about 15 cups)
> 2 tablespoons vegetable oil
> 1½ teaspoons mustard seeds
> 1 teaspoon cumin seeds
> 1 large onion, halved crosswise and sliced
> 2 jalapeños, seeded and finely chopped

Salt

> ½ teaspoon cayenne pepper

⅓ cup plain whole milk yogurt,
   stirred until smooth

2 medium tomatoes,
   finely chopped

1 medium European cucumber,
   peeled and cut into small dice

Juice of ½ lime

1. Preheat the oven to 375°. Spread the diced bread out on a baking sheet in a single layer and toast for 6 to 7 minutes, or until dry on the outside. Remove from the oven.

2. Heat the vegetable oil in a large skillet. Add the mustard seeds and cumin seeds and cook over moderate heat, stirring frequently, for 1 minute. Add the onion and jalapeños, season with salt and cook, stirring occasionally, until the onion is softened but not browned, about 8 minutes. Stir in the cayenne pepper and the yogurt. Add the toasted bread and stir gently to coat with the dressing. Stir in the tomatoes, cover and cook until the bread is softened, 4 to 5 minutes. Gently stir in the cucumber and lime juice and season with salt. Spoon the salad onto individual plates and serve.

—Suvir Saran

Red Lentil Salad with Feta and Beets

4 SERVINGS ●

4 small beets (¾ pound)

¼ cup grapeseed oil

1 tablespoon minced shallots

1 garlic clove, minced

½ teaspoon ground cumin

½ teaspoon ground fennel seeds

2 tablespoons balsamic vinegar

1 tablespoon fresh lemon juice

Pinch of cayenne pepper

Salt and freshly ground pepper

1 cup red lentils (7 ounces)

2 tablespoons chopped parsley

1 large bunch of arugula
   (6 ounces), leaves torn into
   bite-size pieces

2½ ounces feta, preferably French,
   crumbled (½ cup)

Red Lentil Salad with Feta and Beets

Salt-Baked Salmon Salad

1. Preheat the oven to 350°. Wrap the beets in foil and roast them for about 45 minutes, or until tender; let cool. Peel the beets and cut them into wedges.

2. In a medium skillet, heat the grapeseed oil until shimmering. Add the shallots and garlic and cook over moderately high heat until fragrant, about 1 minute. Add the cumin and fennel seeds and cook just until fragrant. Remove from the heat and whisk in the balsamic vinegar, lemon juice and cayenne. Season with salt and pepper and whisk until the vinaigrette is emulsified.

3. Bring a medium saucepan of lightly salted water to a boil. Add the lentils and cook just until tender, about 5 minutes. Drain the lentils and transfer to a bowl. Toss the lentils with half of the vinaigrette and let cool. Stir in the parsley.

4. Toss the arugula and beets with the remaining vinaigrette and season with salt and pepper. Mound the salad on dinner plates and spoon the lentils on top. Garnish with the feta and serve.

—*Toni Robertson*

ONE SERVING Calories 363 kcal, Total Fat 17.7 gm, Saturated Fat 4 gm, Protein 14 gm, Carbohydrates 38 gm **WINE** This salad calls for a fresh Pinot Grigio to provide a lively contrast. Try the 1999 Long Vineyards or the 1998 Swanson Napa Valley.

Salt-Baked Salmon Salad

4 SERVINGS ● ● ●

Kosher salt
One 1-pound salmon fillet, with skin
¼ cup extra-virgin olive oil
2 tablespoons balsamic vinegar
1½ teaspoons Dijon mustard
1 garlic clove, minced
Salt and freshly ground pepper
6 cups packed mesclun (3 ounces)
1 cup cherry tomatoes, halved
½ cup Calamata olives, pitted
and chopped
2 tablespoons chopped chives
2 tablespoons chopped basil

1. Preheat the oven to 400°. Spread a ¼-inch layer of kosher salt on a small rimmed baking sheet. Nestle the salmon in the salt, skin side down. Bake for 15 minutes, or until just cooked through. Using a spatula, lift the fillet from the skin and break it into bite-size pieces.

2. In a large bowl, whisk the oil with the vinegar, mustard and garlic; season with salt and pepper. Add the mesclun, tomatoes, olives, chives and basil and toss. Add the salmon; toss gently and serve.

—*Lance Dean Velasquez*

Crab and Endive Salad with Creamy Cognac Dressing

2 SERVINGS ● ●

¼ cup mayonnaise
¾ teaspoon Dijon mustard
1¼ teaspoons fresh lemon juice
1 teaspoon Cognac
½ tablespoon finely chopped
flat-leaf parsley
½ tablespoon snipped chives,
plus more for garnish
½ tablespoon coarsely
chopped tarragon
Kosher salt and freshly
ground pepper
Pinch of cayenne
½ teaspoon extra-virgin olive oil
1 celery rib, finely chopped
1 large Belgian endive, 6 outer
leaves reserved, the rest thinly
sliced crosswise
½ pound jumbo lump crabmeat,
picked over

1. In a small bowl, whisk the mayonnaise with the mustard, lemon juice, Cognac and fresh herbs. Season with salt and pepper and the cayenne.

2. Heat the olive oil in a small skillet. Add the celery and cook over moderately high heat until crisp-tender, about 1 minute. Spread the celery on a plate and refrigerate until chilled.

3. In a medium bowl, gently toss the sliced endive with the crabmeat, celery and Cognac dressing. Season with salt and pepper. Arrange 3 endive leaves on each plate. Spoon the crab salad in the center, garnish with chives and serve. —*Michael Romano*

Maine Lobster and Asparagus Salad with Curry Vinaigrette

6 SERVINGS

Curry oil adds an unusual twist to this succulent lobster salad. The recipe makes more oil than you'll need; drizzle the extra on sea bass or swordfish before grilling. The curry oil needs to stand overnight, so plan accordingly.

¼ cup Madras curry powder
2 tablespoons water
1 cup light olive oil
Three 1¼-pound lobsters
1 pound pencil-thin asparagus
2½ tablespoons Champagne vinegar
1 medium shallot, finely chopped
½ red bell pepper, very finely diced
Salt and freshly ground pepper
6 cups micro greens or mesclun
(about 6 ounces)
¼ cup cilantro leaves
¼ cup snipped chives

1. In a medium jar, stir the curry powder with the water to make a thick paste. Add the oil, cover tightly and shake to mix thoroughly. Let stand overnight. The next day, pour the curry oil into a clean jar, leaving all of the sediment behind.

2. In a large pot of boiling salted water, cook the lobsters until bright red all over, about 12 minutes. Plunge the lobsters into ice water, then drain. Twist off the claws, crack them and remove the meat. With kitchen scissors, slit the tail shells lengthwise and remove the meat. Discard the vein that runs the length of each tail. Slice the tails crosswise ¾ inch thick.

3. Bring a medium skillet of salted water to a boil. Add the asparagus and cook until crisp-tender, approximately

3 minutes. Plunge the asparagus into ice water, then drain and pat dry.

4. In a small bowl, pour the Champagne vinegar over the chopped shallot and let stand for 10 minutes. Whisk in 5 tablespoons of the curry oil until blended. Add the red bell pepper and season the curry vinaigrette with salt and pepper.

5. In a large bowl, toss the greens, cilantro and chives with half of the vinaigrette. Arrange the greens on a platter and surround with the asparagus. Top with the lobster, drizzle on the remaining vinaigrette and serve.

—*Melissa Kelly*

MAKE AHEAD The curry oil can be refrigerated for 1 month. The lobster meat can be refrigerated for 1 day.

WINE The sweet lobster and the curry vinaigrette in this salad call for a full-bodied, fruity Rhône-style white. Try the 1999 Andrew Murray Vineyards Enchanté Santa Barbara County, a blend of Roussanne, Marsanne and Viognier, or the 1998 Qupé Roussanne Edna Valley Alban Vineyard.

Shrimp, Avocado and Mango Salad

4 SERVINGS ●●

3 ½ tablespoons fresh lemon juice
⅓ cup extra-virgin olive oil
Salt and freshly ground pepper
¾ pound shelled and deveined large shrimp
2 ruby red grapefruits
1 Hass avocado, cut into ¼-inch dice
½ mango, cut into ¼-inch dice (¾ cup)
2 tablespoons chopped tarragon
2 tablespoons chopped cilantro
4 cups packed mesclun (2 ounces)

1. In a medium bowl, whisk 2 tablespoons of the lemon juice with the olive oil, 1 teaspoon of salt and ¼ teaspoon of pepper.

2. In a medium saucepan of boiling salted water, cook the shrimp until

opaque, about 3 minutes. Drain and refresh under cold water. Drain well and pat dry, then halve lengthwise.

3. Peel the grapefruits; remove all the bitter white pith. Working over a bowl, cut in between the membranes to release the sections. Drain the juice; reserve for another use. Add the shrimp, avocado, mango and herbs to the sections; toss gently with ¼ cup of the dressing and the remaining lemon juice. Season with salt and pepper. Toss the mesclun with the remaining dressing and mound on plates. Spoon the shrimp salad on top and serve.

—*Debra Ponzek*

Shrimp Salad with Watercress, Cannellini Beans and Mint

4 SERVINGS ●

1 pound large shrimp, shelled and deveined
5 ½ tablespoons extra-virgin olive oil
Salt and freshly ground pepper
¼ cup packed fresh mint leaves
2 tablespoons warm water
One 15-ounce can cannellini beans, drained and rinsed
1 tablespoon fresh lemon juice
1 bunch watercress (5 ounces), tough stems discarded
Lemon wedges, for serving

Shrimp Salad with Watercress, Cannellini Beans and Mint

1. Preheat the broiler and place a rack 6 inches from the heat. Toss the shrimp with 1 tablespoon of the oil; season with salt and pepper. Broil for 3 minutes, turning once, until opaque.

2. In a mini food processor, pulse the mint with the warm water. Add 4 tablespoons of the olive oil and puree until smooth.

3. In a medium bowl, toss the beans with the mint oil and shrimp and season with salt and pepper. In a large bowl, whisk the lemon juice with the remaining ½ tablespoon of olive oil. Add the watercress, season with salt and pepper and toss gently. Mound the watercress on large plates and spoon the shrimp salad on top. Serve with lemon wedges.   —*Joanne Weir*

Flash-Roasted Garlicky Calamari Salad

4 SERVINGS ●

- 1 pound cleaned small calamari, cut into ½-inch rings
- ¼ cup extra-virgin olive oil
- ½ teaspoon crushed red pepper
- Salt and freshly ground black pepper
- 2 garlic cloves, thinly sliced
- 1 tablespoon red wine vinegar
- ½ pound mixed baby greens

1. Preheat the oven to 450°. In a medium bowl, toss the calamari with 2 tablespoons of the olive oil and the crushed red pepper; season the calamari with salt and black pepper.

2. On a large, rimmed baking sheet, toss the garlic with the remaining 2 tablespoons of oil. Roast the garlic on the top shelf of the oven for about 4 minutes, or until lightly golden. Toss the calamari with the garlic and roast for about 3 minutes, until opaque and firm. Strain the calamari juices into a small bowl and whisk in the vinegar.

3. In a medium bowl, toss the greens with the dressing and season with salt and pepper. Mound the greens on plates, top with the calamari and serve.   —*Kate Heddings*

Mussel and Sea Bean Salad

4 SERVINGS ● ●

Sea beans, also known as marsh samphire and glasswort, grow in the shallow waters along the Pacific and Atlantic coasts. They have crisp, spiky cactuslike leaves and stems and a briny taste.

- 1 cup dry white wine
- 1 cup water
- 4 garlic cloves—3 smashed and 1 minced
- 2 tablespoons minced celery
- 2 tablespoons minced red bell pepper
- 1 small onion, thinly sliced
- 1 bay leaf
- 2 pounds mussels, scrubbed and debearded
- ½ pound sea beans (see Note), soaked in cool water for 30 minutes and drained, or thin green beans
- ¼ cup extra-virgin olive oil

Mussel and Sea Bean Salad

2 tablespoons white wine vinegar

2 teaspoons minced tarragon

½ teaspoon Dijon mustard

Salt and freshly ground pepper

2 cups shredded romaine lettuce

1. In a medium saucepan, combine the wine, water, smashed garlic, celery, red bell pepper, onion and bay leaf and bring to a boil. Cover and simmer for 3 minutes. Add the mussels, cover and cook over high heat for 3 to 5 minutes; remove the mussels to a bowl as they open. Strain the cooking liquid and return it to the pan. Remove the mussels from their shells and transfer to a bowl.

2. If using green beans, blanch them in the reserved mussel cooking liquid until bright green and tender, about 2 minutes. Remove the beans with a slotted spoon, pat dry and let cool completely. Cut the beans into 1½-inch lengths.

3. In a bowl, whisk the oil with the vinegar, tarragon, mustard and minced garlic. Season with salt and pepper.

4. Add the sea beans or green beans to the mussels and toss with 3 tablespoons of the vinaigrette. Season with salt and pepper. Toss the romaine with the remaining vinaigrette; mound on plates, top with the mussel salad and serve.

—*Charles Leary and Vaughn Perret*

NOTE Sea beans are available at Melissa's Specialty Produce, 800-468-7111.

Indian-Spiced Chicken Salad

4 SERVINGS ●

1 tablespoon coriander seeds

1½ teaspoons cumin seeds

½ teaspoon fennel seeds

½ teaspoon mustard seeds

¼ teaspoon fenugreek

5 tablespoons extra-virgin olive oil

2 tablespoons tawny port

2 garlic cloves, thinly sliced

Pinch of ground turmeric

Kosher salt and freshly ground pepper

Indian-Spiced Chicken Salad

4 skinless, boneless chicken breast
   halves (about 6 ounces each)
2 tablespoons fresh lemon juice
1 shallot, minced
¼ pound green beans
8 cups torn Boston lettuce leaves
1 large, ripe red papaya
   (1 pound)—peeled, seeded and
   cut into 1½-inch chunks
½ pint cherry tomatoes, halved
⅓ cup roasted cashews, chopped

1. In a small skillet, toast the coriander seeds, cumin seeds, fennel seeds, mustard seeds and fenugreek over moderate heat for 1 minute. Let cool completely, then coarsely grind.

2. In a large, shallow baking dish, mix 1 tablespoon plus 2 teaspoons of the ground spices with 2 tablespoons of the extra-virgin olive oil, the tawny port, sliced garlic, turmeric, ¼ teaspoon of kosher salt and ½ teaspoon of pepper. Add the chicken breasts and turn to coat thoroughly. Cover and refrigerate the chicken for 2 hours or overnight.

3. Mix the remaining ground spices with the lemon juice, shallot and the remaining 3 tablespoons of olive oil and season with salt and pepper.

4. In a saucepan of boiling salted water, cook the green beans for 3 minutes. Drain and refresh under cold water. Pat dry and cut into 2-inch lengths.

5. Light a grill or preheat a grill pan. Remove the chicken breasts from the marinade; discard the garlic. Grill the chicken over moderately high heat until cooked through, about 4 minutes per side. Let rest for 5 minutes, then cut into 1½-inch chunks.

6. In a large bowl, toss the lettuce with the papaya, tomatoes, green beans, chicken and the dressing. Sprinkle with the cashews and serve.

—*Marcia Kiesel*

VARIATION Yellow cherry tomatoes and yellow wax beans can stand in for red tomatoes and green beans.

Chicken and Rice Salad with Cranberry Vinaigrette

4 SERVINGS ●

¼ cup hazelnuts
¼ cup fresh cranberries
½ cup cranberry juice cocktail
1 tablespoon honey
1 teaspoon red wine vinegar
Sea salt and freshly ground pepper
1 tablespoon extra-virgin olive oil
Four 4-ounce skinless, boneless
   chicken breast halves
2 medium oranges
2 cups cooked rice
4 scallions, thinly sliced
⅓ cup chopped flat-leaf parsley
¼ cup dried cranberries

1. Preheat the oven to 350°. In a pie plate, toast the hazelnuts for 12 minutes, or until the nuts are fragrant and browned. Transfer the nuts to a kitchen towel and let cool completely, then rub the nuts together in the towel to remove the skins. Coarsely chop the hazelnuts. Increase the oven temperature to 425°.

2. In a small saucepan, simmer the fresh cranberries in the cranberry juice until the juice reduces by half, about 5 minutes. Transfer to a blender and let cool. Add the honey and red wine vinegar, season with salt and pepper and puree. With the machine on, blend in the olive oil.

3. Season the chicken breasts with salt and pepper and roast on a baking sheet for 10 minutes. Turn and roast for 10 minutes longer, or until just

Chicken and Rice Salad with Cranberry Vinaigrette

Beef Tenderloin Cobb Salad

cooked through. Let cool, then pull the meat into shreds and transfer to a large bowl.

4. Peel the oranges with a sharp knife; be sure to remove all the white pith. Working over a bowl, cut in between the membranes to release the sections. Dice the sections and add to the chicken. Reserve the juice for another use.

5. Add the rice, scallions, parsley, dried cranberries and vinaigrette to the chicken and toss. Mound the salad on plates, sprinkle with the hazelnuts and serve. —*Suki Hertz*

ONE SERVING Calories 386 kcal, Total Fat 9.9 gm, Saturated Fat 1.2 gm

WINE The sweetness of the dried cranberries and oranges calls for a fruity, tart and savory rosé, such as the 1999 Sanford Pinot Noir–Vin Gris from California or the 1999 Domaines Ott Rosé Clair de Noir Château de Selle from Provence.

Beef Tenderloin Cobb Salad

6 SERVINGS ●

½ cup chopped flat-leaf parsley
2 tablespoons extra-virgin olive oil
1 tablespoon sweet paprika
2 teaspoons ground cumin
5 garlic cloves, minced
Kosher salt and freshly ground pepper
2½ pounds trimmed beef tenderloin
½ cup mayonnaise
½ cup grated Parmesan
2 tablespoons Dijon mustard
2 tablespoons buttermilk
2 tablespoons fresh lemon juice
2 anchovy fillets, mashed
1 jalapeño, seeded and minced
1 tablespoon Worcestershire sauce
½ pound thickly sliced bacon
Two large heads of romaine lettuce, torn into bite-size pieces
2 large Hass avocados, cut into ½-inch dice
1½ cups Cornnuts
1 tablespoon pure olive oil
4 beefsteak tomatoes, cut into wedges
1 cup sunflower sprouts

1. In a large, shallow dish, combine the parsley, extra-virgin olive oil, paprika and cumin. Stir in half of the minced garlic, 1 tablespoon of kosher salt and 2 tablespoons of pepper. Add the meat and turn to coat thoroughly. Cover and refrigerate for 1 to 2 hours.

2. Preheat the oven to 400°. In a medium bowl, mix the mayonnaise with the grated Parmesan, Dijon mustard, buttermilk, lemon juice, mashed anchovies, minced jalapeño, Worcestershire sauce and the remaining minced garlic. Season the dressing with salt and pepper and refrigerate.

3. In a large skillet, cook the bacon over moderate heat until crisp, about 5 minutes. Drain and coarsely chop the bacon. In a large bowl, toss the romaine lettuce with the bacon, diced avocados and Cornnuts.

4. In a large ovenproof skillet, heat the pure olive oil until almost smoking. Remove the meat from the marinade and pat dry. Cook the beef tenderloin over moderately high heat until browned on 3 sides, about 3 minutes per side. Turn to brown on the last side and put the skillet in the oven. Roast the meat for about 25 minutes; an instant-read thermometer inserted in the thickest part should register 125° for medium rare. Transfer the tenderloin to a carving board and let stand for 10 minutes.

5. Toss the salad with half of the dressing. Mound on a large platter, surround with the tomato wedges and scatter the sprouts on top. Thinly slice the tenderloin, arrange on the salad and serve. Pass the extra dressing at the table. —*Todd English*

4 soups

Chilled Tomato Soup with Melon

2. Using a small melon baller, scoop a total of 20 balls from the cucumber and melons. Alternatively, cut the cucumber and melons into ½-inch dice. Pour the soup into bowls. Garnish with the melon and cucumber balls and the basil sprigs and serve.

—*Jean-Georges Vongerichten*

N O T E In winter, when most tomatoes are not very flavorful, plum tomatoes will still be good in this recipe.

M A K E   A H E A D The tomato soup can be refrigerated for 1 day.

W I N E The tomatoes and cucumber in this soup suggest a bright Spanish white, such as the 1999 De la Granja Rueda Basa Blanco, a blend of Sauvignon Blanc, Verdejo and Viura.

Cold Cucumber Soup with Mint

4 SERVINGS ● ●

½   large hothouse cucumber—peeled, seeded and cut into ¼-inch dice

8   small radishes, thinly sliced

1   garlic clove, minced

3   tablespoons chopped mint

3   tablespoons chopped dill

2   cups cold plain yogurt

1   cup cold low-fat milk

2   tablespoons fresh lemon juice

2   tablespoons extra-virgin olive oil

Salt and freshly ground pepper

In a small bowl, toss the cucumber, radishes, garlic and 2 tablespoons each of the mint and dill. In a medium bowl, whisk the yogurt with the milk, lemon juice and olive oil. Stir the vegetables into the yogurt and season with salt and pepper. Set the bowl over a larger bowl of ice water and stir occasionally until chilled, about 10 minutes. Ladle the soup into bowls, sprinkle with the remaining 1 tablespoon each of mint and dill and serve.

—*Joanne Weir*

O N E   S E R V I N G Calories 172 kcal, Total Fat 11.5 gm, Saturated Fat 3.9 gm, Protein 7 gm, Carbohydrates 11 gm

Chilled Tomato Soup with Melon

4 SERVINGS ● ●

The flavor of this smooth tomato soup is reminiscent of gazpacho—until you get to the melon garnish, which takes its inspiration from Asia. It's a surprising and beautiful dish.

2   pounds tomatoes, coarsely chopped (see Note)

¼   cup plus 1 tablespoon extra-virgin olive oil

6   basil leaves, plus small sprigs for garnish

2   garlic cloves, minced

2   tablespoons red wine vinegar

¼   teaspoon sugar

Salt and freshly ground pepper

½   European seedless cucumber, halved lengthwise

½   small melon, such as cantaloupe or honeydew, plus a wedge of seedless watermelon

I. In a medium saucepan, combine the tomatoes with the extra-virgin olive oil, basil leaves, minced garlic, red wine vinegar and sugar. Season with salt and pepper. Cook over low heat until hot but not boiling, about 10 minutes. Pass the soup through the fine disk of a food mill into a medium bowl to remove the tomato seeds and skin. Chill the soup in the refrigerator or quick-chill it by setting the bowl in a larger bowl of ice water.

Cold Cucumber Soup with Mint

Asparagus Vichyssoise

10 SERVINGS ● ● ● ●

This creamy soup is best the next day, after the flavors have blended; season it generously before serving.

- 2 pounds asparagus, tips reserved, stalks cut into 1-inch lengths
- 2 tablespoons unsalted butter
- 3 medium leeks, white and tender green parts only, thinly sliced
- ½ pound Yukon Gold potatoes, peeled and cut into 1-inch chunks
- 2½ cups chicken stock or canned low-sodium broth
- 2 cups water
- 1 large thyme sprig
- 1½ cups milk
- 1¼ teaspoons salt
- ¼ teaspoon freshly ground white pepper

Chive Oil, for serving (recipe follows)

1. In a saucepan of boiling salted water, blanch the asparagus tips until crisp-tender, about 1 minute. Drain the asparagus tips in a colander and refresh under cold water. Pat dry, halve the tips lengthwise and set aside.

2. Melt the butter in a large saucepan. Add the sliced leeks and cook over moderate heat, stirring, until softened, about 5 minutes. Add the asparagus stalks, potato chunks, chicken stock or broth, water and thyme sprig and bring to a boil. Reduce the heat to low, cover and simmer until the potatoes are tender, about 15 minutes.

3. Discard the thyme sprig. Working in batches, puree the soup in a blender, then transfer to a large bowl. Stir in the milk, salt and white pepper. Let the soup cool to room temperature, then refrigerate until chilled, at least 4 hours or overnight.

4. Ladle the soup into chilled bowls and drizzle with Chive Oil. Garnish with the asparagus tips and serve.

—*Danielle Custer*

MAKE AHEAD The Asparagus Vichyssoise can be refrigerated for up to 2 days.

WINE A crisp, herbal Sauvignon Blanc with sassy fruit will complement the vegetables and herbs in the soup; try one from California, such as the 1999 Caymus Vineyards or the 1999 Silverado Vineyards.

CHIVE OIL

MAKES ABOUT ⅓ CUP ● ● ●

- 1 large bunch of chives (1 ounce), minced
- ¼ cup extra-virgin olive oil

Salt

In a blender, puree the minced chives with the extra-virgin olive oil. Season with salt. Strain the Chive Oil through a fine sieve. Cover and refrigerate until ready to use. —*D.C.*

MAKE AHEAD The Chive Oil can be refrigerated for up to 5 days.

Asparagus Vichyssoise

Gazpacho with Grilled Seafood

Gazpacho with Grilled Seafood

6 SERVINGS ●

The soup needs to be refrigerated overnight, so plan accordingly.

- 1 pound cranberry beans, shelled (1 cup)
- Extra-virgin olive oil
- Salt and freshly ground pepper
- 5 cups tomato juice
- 1 large cucumber—peeled, halved, seeded and cut into ¼-inch dice
- 1 yellow pepper, cut into ¼-inch dice
- 1 medium sweet onion, cut into ¼-inch dice
- 1 medium fennel bulb, cored and cut into ¼-inch dice
- 1 large jalapeño, seeded and minced
- 1 large scallion, thinly sliced
- ¼ cup coarsely chopped cilantro
- ½ teaspoon finely grated lime zest
- ½ teaspoon finely grated lemon zest
- 2 tablespoons fresh lime juice
- 2 tablespoons fresh lemon juice
- ¾ pound sea scallops
- ¾ pound medium shrimp, shelled and deveined
- 6 large slices of peasant bread
- 1 large garlic clove

1. In a medium saucepan, cook the cranberry beans in boiling water until tender, about 12 minutes. Drain and transfer to a plate. Drizzle with olive oil and season with salt and pepper.

2. In a large bowl, combine the tomato juice with the cucumber, yellow pepper, onion, fennel, jalapeño, scallion and 2 tablespoons of the cilantro. Add the beans, cover and refrigerate overnight.

3. Stir the lime and lemon zest and juice into the soup. Season with salt and pepper and refrigerate for 1 to 2 hours.

4. Light a grill. Thread the scallops and shrimp on skewers, brush with olive oil and season with salt and pepper. Grill over a medium-hot fire until lightly charred, about 2 minutes per side.

Generously brush the bread with olive oil and grill over a medium-hot fire until lightly charred, about 1 minute per side. Rub the bread with the garlic.

5. Stir 2 tablespoons of cilantro into the soup. Serve the gazpacho with the seafood and bread.   —*Marcia Kiesel*

White Gazpacho with Shrimp

4 SERVINGS ● ● ●

6 slices of white sandwich bread, crusts discarded, bread torn into pieces

1 cup whole blanched almonds (6 ounces), chopped

¾ cup seedless green grapes

½ medium European cucumber— peeled, seeded and chopped

1 garlic clove, smashed

2½ cups cold water

½ cup extra-virgin olive oil

3 tablespoons sherry vinegar

Salt

Cayenne pepper

½ pound shelled and deveined medium shrimp

1 tomato, seeded and finely diced

2 tablespoons minced celery

2 tablespoons minced cilantro

1. Fill a large bowl with ice and water. In another bowl, combine the bread, almonds, grapes, cucumber and garlic with the water, oil and vinegar. Working in batches, puree in a blender, then strain through a fine sieve into a large bowl set in the ice bath. Stir the soup until chilled; season with salt and cayenne. Reserve the ice bath.

2. In a medium saucepan of boiling salted water, cook the shrimp until opaque, about 2 minutes. Drain and refresh in the ice bath until chilled. Drain well, pat dry and cut into quarters crosswise. Ladle the soup into chilled bowls. Garnish with the shrimp, tomato, celery and cilantro and serve.   —*Terrance Brennan*

MAKE AHEAD The soup and shrimp garnish can be refrigerated separately for up to 2 days.

Porcini Miso Broth

4 SERVINGS ● ●

This rich, earthy broth is a quick vegetarian alternative to meat stock. The dried porcini mushrooms, Madeira and miso give it a great deal of depth and body. It's wonderful on its own or as a soup with steamed or roasted baby root vegetables and a sprinkling of chopped fresh herbs. Among the many other delicious uses for the Porcini Miso Broth: to make gratins and pilafs and to sauce roasted or grilled veal or wild mushrooms.

1 cup dried porcini mushrooms (1 ounce)

6 cups hot water

1½ teaspoons unsalted butter

½ teaspoon vegetable oil

4 shallots, coarsely chopped

1 garlic clove, smashed

½ cup Madeira

1 bay leaf

1 tablespoon sweet white (shiro) miso

1 tablespoon red (aka) miso or country-style barley miso

1. In a medium bowl, soak the porcini mushrooms in the hot water until softened, about 20 minutes.

2. In a large saucepan, cook the butter over moderate heat until it smells like roasted nuts, about 3 minutes. Add the oil, shallots and garlic, cover and cook over low heat, stirring frequently, until the shallots are light golden,

Porcini Miso Broth

about 5 minutes. Add the Madeira and boil until reduced by half, about 3 minutes.

3. Add the porcini mushrooms to the saucepan and pour in their soaking liquid, stopping when you reach the grit at the bottom. Add the bay leaf and gently simmer the broth over low heat for 30 minutes. Remove from the heat and whisk in the white and red miso until well blended. Strain the broth through a fine sieve before serving or using. —*Sally Schneider*

ONE SERVING Calories 40 kcal, Total Fat 2.5 gm, Saturated Fat 1 gm, Carbohydrates 3 gm, Protein 1 gm

MAKE AHEAD The broth can be refrigerated for 3 days. Rewarm, being careful not to let the broth boil.

Light Vegetable Soup with Pistachio Pistou

8 SERVINGS ● ●

Adding a small dollop of pistou—the French version of pesto—to this light vegetarian soup gives it a nice, luxurious texture.

BROTH

- 2 quarts water
- ¼ cup tomato paste
- 3 large carrots, thickly sliced
- 3 medium onions, coarsely chopped

Two 2-inch wedges of green cabbage (about 6 ounces)

- 2 celery ribs, coarsely chopped

Trimmed stems from 1 fennel bulb

- 6 thyme sprigs
- 4 large garlic cloves, smashed

Salt

SOUP

- 2 medium carrots, thinly sliced
- 1 medium parsnip, cut into ¼-inch dice
- 1 large fennel bulb, stems trimmed, bulb halved, cored and thinly sliced lengthwise
- 1 medium onion, minced
- 1 small zucchini, cut into ¼-inch dice

- 4 plum tomatoes, cut into ½-inch dice

Salt and freshly ground pepper

Pistachio Pistou (recipe follows)

Shavings from one 2-ounce piece of Parmesan

1. MAKE THE BROTH: In a saucepan, whisk the water into the tomato paste. Add the carrots, onions, cabbage, celery, fennel stems, thyme and garlic. Season with salt and cook over low heat for 1 hour. Strain the broth into another large saucepan and discard the vegetables.

2. MAKE THE SOUP: Bring the broth to a boil. Add the thinly sliced carrots, diced parsnip, sliced fennel and minced onion. Reduce the heat to moderate, cover and simmer until the vegetables are tender, about 5 minutes. Add the zucchini and tomatoes, cover and simmer for 3 minutes longer. Season with salt and pepper.

3. Ladle the soup into shallow bowls and stir about ½ tablespoon of the Pistachio Pistou into each bowl. Top with the Parmesan shavings and serve.

—*Kevin Taylor*

MAKE AHEAD The soup can be refrigerated for up to 1 day.

WINE This light, earthy soup with a touch of richness calls for a wine with nutty and herbal flavors or one that is full and spicy. Two organic California choices: the 1999 Preston of Dry Creek Estate Sauvignon Blanc and the 1998 Mont St. John Madonna Estate Chardonnay.

PISTACHIO PISTOU

MAKES ABOUT ½ CUP ●

- ½ cup shelled unsalted pistachios (2 ounces)
- ¼ cup coarsely chopped basil
- 1 garlic clove, halved
- ¼ cup extra-virgin olive oil

Salt and freshly ground pepper

In a food processor, combine the unsalted pistachios with the basil and garlic and process to a paste. With the

machine on, slowly add the olive oil until incorporated. Scrape the pistou into a small bowl and season with salt and pepper. —*K.T.*

MAKE AHEAD The pistou can be refrigerated for up to 2 days.

Garden Tomato Soup with Cumin

8 SERVINGS ● ●

Prepared without the chicken stock, this fresh tomato soup becomes a delicious tomato sauce for pasta.

- ⅓ cup extra-virgin olive oil, plus more for drizzling
- 1 cup finely chopped sweet onion, such as Vidalia
- 4 large garlic cloves, smashed

Sea salt

- 1½ teaspoons ground cumin
- 7 pounds tomatoes, cored and coarsely chopped
- 2 cups chicken stock or canned low-sodium broth

Pinch of sugar

Freshly ground pepper

- ¼ cup coarsely chopped flat-leaf parsley
- ¼ cup coarsely chopped lovage or celery leaves, plus whole leaves for garnish

1. Heat ⅓ cup of the olive oil in a soup pot. Add the onion, garlic and a large pinch of salt and cook over low heat, stirring occasionally, until the onion is softened, about 5 minutes. Stir in the cumin and cook until fragrant, about 1 minute. Add the tomatoes and bring to a boil. Cook over moderate heat, stirring occasionally, until the tomatoes are soupy, about 20 minutes.

2. Pass the soup through a food mill or fine sieve, pressing hard on the solids to extract all the liquid. Return the soup to the pot. Add the chicken stock and sugar and season with salt and pepper. Simmer over moderate heat until reduced to 10 cups, about 25 minutes. Stir in the parsley and chopped lovage. Ladle the soup into

Light Vegetable Soup with Pistachio Pistou

Garden Tomato Soup with Cumin

Garlicky Eggplant and Pepper Soup with Mint

shallow bowls, garnish with the lovage leaves and drizzle with olive oil. Serve hot. —*Stéphane Garnier*

MAKE AHEAD The Garden Tomato Soup with Cumin can be refrigerated for 2 days. Reheat, garnish with the lovage leaves and drizzle with olive oil just before serving.

Tomato-Miso Soup

4 SERVINGS ● ●

1 tablespoon vegetable oil

½ pound shiitake mushrooms, stems discarded, caps thinly sliced

1 large garlic clove, minced

2 tablespoons tomato paste

4½ cups water

2 large tomatoes—peeled, seeded and coarsely chopped

½ cup light (shiro) miso

1 teaspoon soy sauce

¾ pound soft tofu, cut into 1-inch dice

2 large scallions, thinly sliced

4 small to medium radishes, thinly sliced

Heat the oil in a large saucepan. Add

the mushrooms and garlic and cook over moderate heat, stirring, until fragrant, about 1 minute. Cover and cook over low heat, stirring a few times, until the mushrooms are tender, about 6 minutes. Add the tomato paste and cook, stirring, for 1 minute. Pour in the water, stir well and bring to a boil. Add the tomatoes, cover and simmer over low heat for 5 minutes. Whisk in the miso and soy sauce and return to a simmer. Add the tofu and simmer for 2 minutes. Ladle into bowls, garnish with the scallions and radishes and serve.

—*Marcia Kiesel*

ONE SERVING Calories 203 kcal, Total Fat 7.1 gm, Saturated Fat 0.6 gm, Protein 8.2 gm, Carbohydrates 28 gm

Indian-Style Summer Squash Soup

6 SERVINGS ●

The secret ingredient in this somewhat spicy, Indian-inspired squash soup is buttermilk.

4 tablespoons unsalted butter

1 large onion, coarsely chopped

1 tablespoon finely chopped garlic

1 tablespoon Madras curry powder

2 pounds small summer squash or zucchini, cut into 1-inch rounds

3 cups chicken stock or canned low-sodium broth

1½ cups buttermilk

1 cup half-and-half

Salt and freshly ground pepper

¼ cup finely chopped cilantro

I. Melt the butter in a large saucepan. Stir in the onion and garlic, cover and cook over low heat, stirring occasionally, until softened, about 15 minutes. Add the curry powder and stir over moderate heat for 1 minute. Stir in the squash, add the stock and simmer over moderate heat until the squash is soft, about 25 minutes.

2. Puree the soup in batches in a blender or food processor. Pour into a saucepan and stir in the buttermilk and half-and-half. Season with salt and pepper and simmer just until heated through. Ladle the soup into shallow bowls, sprinkle with the cilantro and serve. —*Christina Reid-Orchid*

MAKE AHEAD The Indian-Style Summer Squash Soup can be refrigerated for 2 days. Add the cilantro just before serving.

Garlicky Eggplant and Pepper Soup with Mint

8 SERVINGS ●

This rustic soup becomes lusciously silky with a swirl of garlicky aioli. For an even more elegant version, puree the soup in batches and strain before serving with the aioli.

- 2 tablespoons extra-virgin olive oil, plus more for brushing
- 3 medium eggplants (about 3¾ pounds total), halved lengthwise
- 6 red bell peppers
- 2 medium onions, finely chopped

Salt

Cayenne pepper

- 5 cups rich chicken stock, preferably homemade (see Note)
- 3 garlic cloves, smashed
- 1 cup mayonnaise
- 2 teaspoons fresh lemon juice
- 2 tablespoons minced mint, plus more for garnish

1. Preheat the oven to 400°. Lightly brush a large, rimmed baking sheet with olive oil. Arrange the eggplants on the baking sheet, cut side down, and bake until just tender, about 20 minutes. Let cool slightly, then cut the eggplant halves lengthwise into thirds. Discard the eggplant skin and the very seedy portions, then cut the eggplants into ½-inch chunks.

2. Preheat the broiler. Lightly brush the red peppers with olive oil and set on a heavy baking sheet. Broil the red peppers 6 inches from the heat, turning the peppers occasionally, until lightly charred all over, about 15 minutes. Transfer to a bowl, cover with plastic wrap and let steam for 10 minutes. Peel, core and seed the peppers, then cut them into ¼-inch dice.

3. In a large saucepan, heat the 2 tablespoons of extra-virgin olive oil until shimmering. Add the onions and cook over moderately low heat, stirring occasionally, until softened, about 7 minutes. Gently stir in the eggplants and peppers and season with salt and cayenne. Add the stock and bring to a boil. Simmer over moderate heat until the flavors blend, about 10 minutes.

4. Meanwhile, in a mortar, pound the garlic cloves with ½ teaspoon of salt until smooth. Stir in the mayonnaise, fresh lemon juice and just a pinch of cayenne.

5. Stir the 2 tablespoons of mint into the soup and ladle into shallow bowls. Top with a dollop of aioli and a sprinkling of mint and serve.

—Randy Windham

NOTE This simple soup derives much of its flavor from chicken stock. If you don't have time to make your own, try one of the rich frozen stocks available at specialty markets.

MAKE AHEAD The recipe can be prepared ahead of time through Step 4. Refrigerate the soup and aioli separately overnight. Gently reheat the soup before serving.

Fresh Fennel Soup

4 SERVINGS ●

- 1 tablespoon unsalted butter
- 1 small onion, very finely chopped

Large pinch of ground fennel

- 1 garlic clove, very finely chopped
- 3 medium fennel bulbs, cored and cut into small pieces, feathery tops chopped
- 1 large red potato, peeled and diced
- 5 cups chicken stock or canned low-sodium broth
- ½ cup heavy cream

Salt and freshly ground pepper

1. Melt the butter in a large saucepan. Add the finely chopped onion and the ground fennel and cook over moderate heat until the onion softens, about 3 minutes. Add the garlic and cook for about 30 seconds, stirring constantly. Add the pieces of fennel bulb, potato and stock and bring to a boil; simmer until the fennel is tender, about 15 minutes.

2. Working in batches, puree the soup in a blender or food processor. Strain the soup into a clean saucepan, stir in the cream and season with salt and pepper. Serve the soup in bowls, sprinkled with the chopped fennel tops.

—Joanne Weir

Carrot and Star Anise Soup

4 SERVINGS ●

This gorgeous and fragrant soup with its mysterious and delicious flavors has long been an *amuse-bouche* at restaurant Guy Savoy, where it prepares the palate for more delights to come. It's adapted here to make larger servings that are ideal for the first course.

- 3 tablespoons unsalted butter
- 1 pound medium carrots, cut into 1-inch pieces
- 2 cups chicken stock or canned low-sodium broth
- 1 cup heavy cream

Sea salt and freshly ground white pepper

- 4 whole star anise pods

1. Melt the butter in a large saucepan. Add the carrots and cook over moderately low heat, stirring frequently, until lightly browned, about 5 minutes. Increase the heat to high, add the stock, cream and a pinch each of salt and white pepper and bring to a boil. Cover and cook over low heat until the carrots are very tender, about 50 minutes. Remove from the heat and add the star anise, cover and let infuse for 20 minutes.

2. Discard the star anise. Puree the soup in a blender until smooth. Season with salt and white pepper and serve.

—Guy Savoy

Carrot and Star Anise Soup (p. 91)

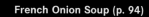
French Onion Soup (p. 94)

French Onion Soup

4 SERVINGS

Rich, flavorful beef broth, sweet cara-melized onions and a great melting cheese that hardens around the bowl into seductively crispy bits are a must for this classic.

- 2 tablespoons unsalted butter, plus softened butter for spreading
- 3 large onions (about 2 pounds), halved lengthwise and thinly sliced crosswise

Sea salt

- 2 tablespoons dry sherry
- 1 quart Rich Beef Stock (recipe follows)
- 1 bouquet garni, made with 1 bay leaf, 1 thyme sprig, 2 juniper berries and 2 flat-leaf parsley sprigs, tied in cheesecloth

Freshly ground pepper

Four ½-inch-thick slices sourdough bread, cut into 4-inch rounds

- 2 cups shredded Gruyère (about 6 ounces)

1. Melt the butter in a large enameled cast-iron casserole. Add the onions and a pinch of salt, cover and cook over moderate heat, stirring once or twice, until the onions soften, about 10 minutes. Uncover and cook over moderate heat, stirring frequently, until the onions are lightly browned, about 40 minutes.

2. Stir in the sherry. Add the stock and bouquet garni and bring to a boil. Cover and simmer over low heat until the soup has a deep flavor, about 30 minutes. Discard the bouquet garni and season the soup with salt and freshly ground pepper.

3. Preheat the oven to 350°. Butter the bread on both sides and place on a baking sheet. Toast for 15 minutes, turning the slices halfway through, until golden and crisp but not dried out. Raise the oven temperature to 425°.

4. Bring the soup to a simmer, ladle it into 4 deep ovenproof bowls and sprinkle with half of the cheese. Place a crouton in each bowl and sprinkle on the remaining cheese. Bake the bowls of soup on a baking sheet in the middle of the oven for 10 minutes, or until the cheese is bubbling. Serve hot.

—*Grace Parisi*

MAKE AHEAD The soup can be pre-pared through Step 3 up to 3 days ahead.

WINE A light, fruity Beaujolais will match the sweetness of the onions and the nuttiness of the Gruyère in this rich soup. Try the 1999 Joseph Drouhin Beaujolais-Villages or Moulin-à-Vent.

RICH BEEF STOCK

MAKES 1½ QUARTS ●

- 1 teaspoon vegetable oil
- 5 pounds meaty beef shanks, cut into 2-inch pieces
- 2 large carrots, cut into 2-inch lengths
- 2 celery ribs, cut into 2-inch lengths
- 1 large onion, quartered
- 4 quarts water

Sea salt

1. Preheat the oven to 450°. Heat the oil in a large roasting pan set over 2 burners. Add the shanks and cook over moderate heat until sizzling and lightly browned on 1 side, about 5 min-utes. Transfer to the oven and roast for 45 minutes, or until the meat and bones are browned. Add the vegeta-bles and roast for about 30 minutes longer, or until lightly browned.

2. Scrape everything into a stockpot. Set the roasting pan over high heat and add 1 cup of the water. Cook, scraping up the browned bits, until the pan is clean. Pour the pan juices into the stockpot along with the remaining 3 cups and 3 quarts of water and simmer over moderately high heat for 30 min-utes, skimming occasionally. Reduce the heat to moderately low, cover par-tially and simmer until the stock is rich-ly flavored and reduced to 2 quarts,

about 4 hours. Season with salt.

3. Strain the stock through a fine sieve set over a heatproof bowl. Refrigerate until cold, scrape off the fat and dis-card. Before using, boil the stock until reduced to 6 cups. —*G.P.*

MAKE AHEAD The stock can be refrigerated for 1 week or frozen for up to 2 months.

Wild Mushroom Broth with Parsnip Custard

10 SERVINGS ● ●

For a heartier version of this soup, add warm cooked wild rice to the broth.

- 3 pounds chicken wings

Kosher salt

- ½ cup dried porcini mushrooms (1 ounce)
- 1 cup boiling water
- 1 tablespoon vegetable oil
- 1 medium onion, thickly sliced
- 2 pounds whole oyster mushrooms, trimmed, stems coarsely chopped

Water

1½ tablespoons unsalted butter

Freshly ground pepper

Parsnip Custard (recipe follows)

1. Preheat the oven to 425°. Spread the chicken wings in a roasting pan and season with salt. Bake for about 45 minutes, or until deeply browned.

2. Meanwhile, put the porcini in a heatproof bowl with the boiling water and let soak until softened, about 20 minutes. Rub to loosen any grit, then lift them out. Let the soaking liquid stand for 5 minutes so the grit settles.

3. In a large saucepan, heat the oil until shimmering. Add the onion and cook over moderately high heat, stir-ring occasionally, until browned, about 5 minutes. Add the mushroom stems and cook until browned, about 5 min-utes. Add the porcini and their soaking liquid, leaving behind any grit. Stir in 3 quarts of water and bring to a boil.

4. Transfer the chicken wings to the saucepan. Set the roasting pan over

2 burners and cook over moderate heat until sizzling. Add 1 cup of water and bring to a simmer, scraping up the browned bits. Pour the pan juices into the saucepan and simmer over low heat, skimming occasionally, until reduced to 5 cups, about 2 hours. Strain the broth and skim off the fat.

5. In a large skillet, melt the butter over high heat. Add the oyster mushroom caps and season with salt and pepper. Reduce the heat to moderate, cover and cook, stirring occasionally, until softened and lightly browned, about 7 minutes. Uncover and cook, stirring, until well browned, about 4 minutes.

6. Bring the mushroom broth to a simmer and season with salt and pepper. Run a thin knife around the edge of each Parsnip Custard. Gently invert the custards, 1 at a time, onto a large spatula and transfer each to the center of a shallow bowl. Or, cut the large custard into 10 squares and place in the bowls. Ladle the broth around the custards, garnish with the mushrooms and serve. —*Marcia Kiesel*

MAKE AHEAD The broth and mushrooms can be refrigerated separately overnight. Reheat before serving.

PARSNIP CUSTARD
10 SERVINGS ●●

This creamy custard is also wonderful served on its own as a side dish.

- 1¼ pounds parsnips, peeled and cut crosswise into thick slices
- 3 large eggs, lightly beaten
- 1 cup milk
- ½ cup heavy cream
- 1¾ teaspoons kosher salt
- ¼ teaspoon freshly ground pepper

1. Preheat the oven to 325°. Lightly butter ten ¼-cup ramekins or an 8-by-12-inch glass baking dish. In a medium saucepan, steam the parsnips until very tender, about 25 minutes.

2. Transfer the parsnips to a food processor and puree. Strain the puree through a coarse sieve into a medium bowl. Whisk in the eggs, milk, cream, salt and pepper. Strain the custard through a fine sieve and pour it into the ramekins or the baking dish. Set the ramekins or the baking dish in a large roasting pan and carefully pour in enough hot water to reach halfway up the sides of the ramekins or the baking dish. Cover the pan loosely with foil. Bake for 45 minutes for the ramekins and 1 hour for the baking dish, or until the custards are just set. —*M.K.*

MAKE AHEAD The custards can be refrigerated overnight. Reheat in the ramekins or baking dish in a microwave oven on high until warmed through.

Vegetable Soup with Winter Squash Gnocchi
4 SERVINGS ●

GNOCCHI
- 1 cup Simple Squash Puree (recipe follows)
- ½ cup all-purpose flour
- 1 large egg, beaten
- 3 tablespoons grated Parmesan, plus shavings for garnish
- ¼ teaspoon ground nutmeg

Kosher salt

SOUP
- 1 tablespoon canola oil
- 2 leeks, white and tender green parts, finely chopped
- 1 small celery rib, finely chopped
- 4 cups chicken broth
- 1 plum tomato—peeled, seeded and finely diced
- 2 tablespoons minced parsley
- 1 teaspoon minced sage

Freshly ground pepper

1. MAKE THE GNOCCHI: In a medium bowl, combine the Simple Squash Puree with the flour, egg, Parmesan, nutmeg and ¾ teaspoon of salt and stir until smooth.

2. MAKE THE SOUP: Heat the oil in a large saucepan. Add the leeks and celery and cook over moderate heat, stirring occasionally, until the leeks are softened. Add the broth and tomato and bring to a boil.

3. Cut ½ inch off the corner of a sturdy plastic bag. Spoon the gnocchi dough into the bag. Gently squeeze the bag, cutting ½-inch lengths of dough into the simmering soup. Cook until the gnocchi rise to the surface; stir once and cook for 1 minute more. Add the parsley and sage and season with salt and pepper. Serve the soup with the shaved Parmesan.

—*Suki Hertz*

ONE SERVING Calories 248 kcal, Total Fat 10.4 gm, Saturated Fat 0.7 gm

SIMPLE SQUASH PUREE
MAKES 2 CUPS ●●

One 2-pound winter squash, halved

1. TO ROAST: Preheat the oven to 375°. Set the squash halves, cut side down, in a baking dish. Add ½ inch of water, cover tightly with foil and bake for about 1 hour, or until tender.

TO MICROWAVE: Set the squash halves, cut side down, in a microwave-safe baking dish. Add ½ inch of water, cover loosely with plastic and cook on high for 18 to 20 minutes, or until tender.

2. Transfer the squash, cut side down, to a rack and let drain until cool. Scoop out the flesh and pass through a strainer, ricer or food mill. —*S.H.*

ONE SERVING Calories 91 kcal, Total Fat 1.1 gm, Saturated Fat 0.2 gm

MAKE AHEAD The puree can be refrigerated for up to 3 days.

Velvety Onion Soup with Whipped Potato
8 SERVINGS

Superior ingredients, such as homemade chicken stock, are essential in this soup. Aged balsamic vinegar is worth the hefty price; only a few drops are used for each serving.

3 pounds chicken wings
Water
1 carrot, cut into 2-inch lengths
1 celery rib, cut into 2-inch lengths
Salt
3 tablespoons plus 2 teaspoons
extra-virgin olive oil
8 scallions, finely chopped
6 medium onions, coarsely
chopped
1 baking potato (½ pound), peeled
and cut into 1-inch pieces
1 garlic clove, halved
½ cup heavy cream
Aged balsamic vinegar, for drizzling
Cayenne pepper or paprika,
for sprinkling

1. In a large saucepan, cover the chicken wings with 10 cups of water. Add the carrot and celery and bring to a boil. Skim, add a few pinches of salt and simmer over low heat for 1½ hours. Strain the stock and skim off the fat. Measure out ½ cup of stock and set it aside.

2. Heat the 3 tablespoons of olive oil in a large saucepan. Add the scallions and cook over moderate heat until softened, about 3 minutes. Add the onions and cook over low heat, stirring occasionally, until softened, about 8 minutes. Add 2 quarts of the chicken stock and a pinch of salt and simmer over low heat until the onions and scallions are very soft, about 15 minutes. Working in batches, puree the soup in a blender until very smooth. Pour the soup into a clean saucepan and season with salt.

3. Heat the remaining 2 teaspoons of olive oil in a medium saucepan. Add the potato, garlic and a pinch of salt and cook over low heat, stirring, until the potato pieces are glazed, about 2 minutes. Add the reserved ½ cup of chicken stock and ½ cup of water and simmer over moderately low heat until most of the liquid has evaporated and the potato is tender, about 10 minutes.

4. Meanwhile, in a small bowl, whisk the heavy cream until soft peaks form. Pass the potato through a ricer into a medium bowl. Fold the whipped cream into the potato and season with salt.

5. Ladle the hot soup into warmed shallow bowls. Drizzle 8 drops of balsamic vinegar over each soup, then mound 2 tablespoons of the whipped potato in the center. Sprinkle with cayenne and serve at once.

—*Massimo Bottura*

MAKE AHEAD The soup can be prepared through Step 2 and refrigerated for up to 2 days.

WINE A big, full-bodied Chardonnay, such as the 1998 Gaja Langhe Gaia & Rey, will complement the richness of the onion soup. The Gaja Langhe Rossj-Bass Chardonnay is a less pricey alternative.

Creamy Garlic Soup

4 SERVINGS

By all means, try the peeled fresh garlic cloves from the produce section of your supermarket; they are every bit as good as the garlic heads you'll find there and infinitely easier to use.

7 tablespoons unsalted butter
2 heads of garlic, cloves separated
and peeled (about 6 ounces)
2 tablespoons all-purpose flour
4½ cups water
One 6-inch length of crustless
baguette, cut into ½-inch dice
4 large egg yolks
1 tablespoon Champagne vinegar
Salt and freshly ground pepper

1. Melt 3 tablespoons of the butter in a large saucepan. Add the garlic and cook over low heat until softened, about 10 minutes. Sprinkle the flour over the garlic and cook, stirring, until golden, about 4 minutes. Raise the heat to moderate and gradually add the water, stirring constantly, until it boils. Reduce the heat to moderately low, cover and simmer the soup until the garlic is very soft and falling apart, about 30 minutes.

2. In a large skillet, melt the remaining 4 tablespoons of butter over moderate heat. Add the bread and cook, stirring occasionally, until crisp and golden brown, about 10 minutes. Drain the croutons on paper towels.

Velvety Onion Soup with Whipped Potato

3. In a medium bowl, whisk the egg yolks with the vinegar. Gradually whisk 1 cup of the hot soup into the eggs. Reduce the heat to low. Add the eggs to the saucepan, stirring constantly until slightly thickened, about 5 minutes; do not let the soup boil or it will curdle. Season with salt and pepper and serve hot, with the croutons.

—Jean Calviac

Creamy Turnip Soup with Cheese Crisps

4 SERVINGS ●

This sweet, silky soup was inspired by the traditional turnip-laden Scotch broth and the delicate young root vegetables of Arran Island.

- 2 tablespoons extra-virgin olive oil
- 1 large Spanish onion, chopped
- 2 garlic cloves, chopped
- 1 pound small turnips, peeled and coarsely chopped
- ½ cup dry white wine
- 4 cups chicken stock or canned low-sodium broth, plus more for thinning the soup
- 2 tablespoons minced scallions
- ½ cup crème fraîche

Salt and freshly ground pepper
Cheese Crisps, for serving
   (recipe follows)

1. Heat the extra-virgin olive oil in a large saucepan until shimmering. Add the chopped onion and garlic and cook over moderately high heat, stirring occasionally, until softened, about 6 minutes. Add the turnips and cook, stirring frequently, until crisp-tender, about 5 minutes. Add the white wine and cook until almost evaporated, about 5 minutes. Add the 4 cups of chicken stock and bring to a boil. Reduce the heat to moderately low and simmer until the turnips are tender, about 25 minutes.

2. Working in batches, puree the soup in a blender or food processor, then strain it through a fine sieve. Return the soup to a clean saucepan, stir in

Creamy Turnip Soup with Cheese Crisps

the scallions and cook over moderate heat for 5 minutes. Whisk in the crème fraîche until fully incorporated; thin the soup with stock if necessary. Season with salt and pepper.

3. Ladle the soup into shallow bowls and serve with the Cheese Crisps.

—Bobby Flay

MAKE AHEAD The Creamy Turnip Soup can be refrigerated overnight. Gently reheat.

CHEESE CRISPS

MAKES ABOUT 16 CRISPS ● ●

Almost any freshly grated melting cheese can be used to make these crisps, but sharper cheeses are the best foil for the sweetness of the turnip soup.

- ½ cup freshly grated Parmesan
- ½ cup freshly grated Asiago
- 1 tablespoon all-purpose flour

Heat a large nonstick skillet. In a small bowl, toss the Parmesan and Asiago with the flour. Spoon level tablespoons of the cheese mixture at least 2 inches apart into the skillet. Flatten each mound of cheese into a 2½-inch round and cook the rounds over moderate heat until brown around the edges, about 2 minutes. Using a thin spatula, flip the cheese crisps and cook until golden brown. Transfer the crisps to a plate and let cool. *—B.F.*

MAKE AHEAD The cheese crisps can be stored in an airtight container for up to 2 days. Recrisp in a hot oven shortly before serving.

Winter Squash Soup with Porcini Cream

12 SERVINGS ●●

The whimsical presentation of this dish gives maximum dramatic effect with a minimum of last-minute effort. Both the soup and hollowed-out squash can be reheated in a microwave oven.

- ½ cup dried porcini (½ ounce)
- 1 cup boiling water
- Twelve 1- to 1¼-pound sweet dumpling squash
- Salt and freshly ground pepper
- 12 cups rich chicken or turkey stock, preferably homemade
- 5¼ pounds winter squash, such as butternut or pumpkin—peeled, seeded and cut into 1-inch dice
- 6 flat-leaf parsley sprigs, plus 2 tablespoons chopped flat-leaf parsley
- 4 small sage sprigs, plus more for garnish
- ½ cup heavy cream

1. In a medium heatproof bowl, soak the porcini in the boiling water until softened, about 20 minutes.

2. Meanwhile, preheat the oven to 350°. Using a sharp paring knife, carefully cut a 2-inch ring around the stems of each dumpling squash; remove and reserve. Scoop out and discard the seeds from inside the squash and those clinging to the tops. Season each squash with salt and pepper and replace the tops.

3. Set the squash on a baking sheet and bake for 30 minutes, or until just tender. Let cool slightly. Using a teaspoon, carefully scoop the flesh from each squash, leaving a ⅓-inch-thick shell. Replace the lids and reserve the flesh. Leave the oven on.

4. In a large saucepan, combine the stock with the butternut squash and the parsley and sage sprigs. Bring to a boil, then simmer over low heat until the squash is tender, about 20 minutes. Discard the parsley and sage sprigs. Working in batches, in a food processor, puree the squash with about ½ cup of the stock. Return the puree to the saucepan, add the reserved sweet dumpling squash flesh and stir to combine. Season with salt and pepper. Keep warm.

5. Rub the porcini to loosen any grit, discard any tough stems and transfer the mushrooms to a blender. Let the soaking liquid stand for 5 minutes, then slowly add ½ cup to the blender and puree. Scrape the puree into a bowl and season with salt and pepper.

6. In a medium bowl, whip the cream until firm. Fold in the mushroom puree and season with salt and pepper. Reheat the sweet dumpling squash in the oven, then transfer to plates and set the lids beside the squash. Stir the chopped parsley into the soup and ladle it into the squash. Spoon a dollop of porcini cream into each soup, garnish with the sage and serve. *—Jeremiah Tower*

MAKE AHEAD The components of this soup can be prepared through Step 5 and refrigerated separately overnight. The porcini cream can be made earlier in the day and refrigerated.

Tangy Sorrel and Potato Soup with Bacon

4 SERVINGS ●

Unlike most potato soups, this one is not pureed.

- 2 tablespoons unsalted butter
- ¼ pound French baguette, crusts removed, bread cut into ½-inch dice
- 2 ounces smoky bacon, cut into ¼-inch dice
- 1 medium onion, cut into ¼-inch dice
- ½ cup dry white wine
- 1½ quarts chicken stock or canned low-sodium broth
- 1 garlic clove, minced

Winter Squash Soup with Porcini Cream

½ pound Yukon Gold potatoes, peeled and cut into ¼-inch dice

Salt and freshly ground pepper

1½ tablespoons fresh lemon juice

¼ teaspoon finely grated lemon zest

3 tablespoons crème fraîche or heavy cream

½ pound sorrel, stems discarded, leaves coarsely chopped

1. Melt 1 tablespoon of the butter in a large skillet. Add the diced baguette and cook over moderately low heat until browned on the bottom, about 3 minutes. Stir the croutons and cook until crisp all over, about 2 minutes longer. Transfer to a plate to cool.

2. Melt the remaining 1 tablespoon of butter in a large saucepan. Add the bacon and cook over moderately low heat until lightly browned, about 4 minutes. Add the onion and cook until softened, about 7 minutes. Add the wine and simmer until almost evaporated, about 4 minutes. Add the stock and garlic and bring to a simmer. Add the potatoes, season with salt and pepper and cook until tender, about 10 minutes. Stir in the lemon juice and zest and the crème fraîche and simmer for 2 minutes. Remove from the heat and stir in the sorrel. Season with salt and pepper. Ladle the soup into bowls and serve; pass the croutons at the table. —Eberhard Müller

MAKE AHEAD The croutons can be made a day ahead. Store in an airtight container. The soup can be made without the sorrel and refrigerated overnight. Bring to a simmer and add the coarsely chopped sorrel just before serving.

Creamy Leek and Potato Soup

6 SERVINGS ● ●

2 tablespoons unsalted butter

4 large leeks, white and tender green parts only, thinly sliced

1 baking potato (½ pound), peeled and cut into 2-inch chunks

5 cups chicken stock or canned low-sodium broth

1 cup heavy cream

Salt and freshly ground pepper

Chervil or parsley sprigs, for garnish

Melt the butter in a large saucepan. Add the leeks and cook over low heat, stirring occasionally, until softened, about 8 minutes. Add the potato and chicken stock and bring to a boil. Cover partially and simmer over low heat until the potatoes are tender, about 15 minutes. Add the cream and simmer for 10 minutes longer. Working in batches, puree the soup in a blender, then return it to the pan. Season the soup with salt and pepper, garnish with chervil and serve.

—Murielle Andraud

MAKE AHEAD The soup can be refrigerated overnight.

WINE This creamy leek soup calls for a full, mellow wine that echoes its richness. Try the 1999 Château Bel Air Ouÿ from Bordeaux. A more widely available wine that matches the soup is a white Graves with a good proportion of Sémillon, such as the inexpensive 1997 Château Olivier Blanc.

Creamy Nettle and Potato Soup

6 SERVINGS ●

Nettles give a tangy flavor to this light, creamy soup. Because nettles are prickly, use gloves while working with them. You can substitute fresh spinach or a combination of parsley and sorrel.

6 tablespoons unsalted butter

4 medium shallots, coarsely chopped

4 celery ribs, coarsely chopped

1 large leek, white and tender green parts only, halved lengthwise and thinly sliced

1¼ pounds Yukon Gold potatoes, peeled and cut into ¼-inch dice

¼ cup dry white wine

1 tablespoon fresh lemon juice

4¼ cups water

Bouquet garni, made with 1 thyme sprig, 1 tarragon sprig and 1 bay leaf, tied with kitchen string

½ cup heavy cream

10 ounces nettles or spinach or 1 bunch (5 ounces) flat-leaf parsley and 1 bunch (4 ounces) sorrel, stems and tough ribs removed

Salt and freshly ground white pepper

1. Melt 4 tablespoons of the butter in a large, heavy saucepan. Add the shallots, celery, leek and potatoes, cover and cook over moderately low heat, stirring occasionally, until softened, about 8 minutes. Add the wine and lemon juice and cook over high heat until evaporated. Add 4 cups of the water and the bouquet garni and bring to a simmer. Cover and cook over moderately low heat until the vegetables are tender, about 15 minutes. Discard the bouquet garni.

2. Working in batches, puree the soup in a blender or food processor until smooth. Strain the soup into a clean saucepan through a fine sieve. Stir in the heavy cream.

3. Bring a medium saucepan of salted water to a boil. Add the nettles and

Creamy Leek and Potato Soup

soups

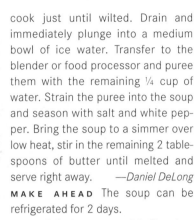

Creamy Nettle
and Potato Soup

cook just until wilted. Drain and immediately plunge into a medium bowl of ice water. Transfer to the blender or food processor and puree them with the remaining ¼ cup of water. Strain the puree into the soup and season with salt and white pepper. Bring the soup to a simmer over low heat, stir in the remaining 2 tablespoons of butter until melted and serve right away. —*Daniel DeLong*

MAKE AHEAD The soup can be refrigerated for 2 days.

WINE A lively, not-too-rich Chardonnay with no oak will highlight the creamy texture of this soup without overwhelming the delicate flavor. Choose a light bottling with notes of melon and apple, such as the 1999 Gallo of Sonoma or the 2000 Rosemount from South Eastern Australia.

Asian Coconut-Cabbage Soup with Lemongrass

4 SERVINGS ●

For a soup that's not strictly vegetarian but that has more Southeast Asian flavor, replace 3 tablespoons of the soy sauce with an equal amount of fish sauce.

About 14 cups water
- 6 ounces dried rice-stick noodles
- 1 tablespoon peanut oil or canola oil
- 1 teaspoon finely grated fresh ginger
- 2 stalks lemongrass—top third discarded, tough outer leaves trimmed, smashed lightly and cut into 2-inch lengths
- 1 pound sweet potatoes, peeled and cut into ½-inch dice
- 5 tablespoons soy sauce

Heaping ¼ teaspoon crushed red pepper

Salt
- 1 small head napa cabbage, sliced crosswise ⅓ inch thick (5 packed cups)
- 1 cup unsweetened coconut milk

Juice of 1 lime, plus lime wedges for serving
- 2½ cups small cilantro leaves and sprigs

1. Bring 8 cups of water to a boil. Remove from the heat, add the rice-stick noodles and let soak until the noodles are softened, about 5 minutes. Drain the noodles and transfer them to a large bowl.

2. Heat the peanut or canola oil in a large saucepan. Add the grated ginger and smashed lemongrass and cook over moderately low heat, stirring, until fragrant, about 2 minutes. Add the remaining 6 cups of water, cover and bring the mixture to a boil over high heat. Add the diced sweet potatoes, soy sauce and crushed red pepper and season to taste with salt. Lower the heat, cover the saucepan and simmer

Asian Coconut-Cabbage Soup with Lemongrass

until the sweet potatoes are tender, 7 to 10 minutes.

3. Add the cabbage and the unsweetened coconut milk and simmer, uncovered, for 5 minutes. Stir in the lime juice and the cilantro leaves. Add the softened rice-stick noodles, ladle the soup into bowls and serve with the lime wedges. —*Stephanie Lyness*

Winter Three-Grain Soup

Winter Three-Grain Soup

8 SERVINGS ● ●

This soup is filling, light and low in fat and calories. Most people who did not grow up eating grains tend to shy away from them. Here's one way to sneak them in.

- 3 medium leeks, white parts only, halved lengthwise and chopped
- 2 medium carrots, cut into ½-inch pieces
- 2 tablespoons extra-virgin olive oil
- 2 bay leaves
- ½ teaspoon thyme

Fine sea salt

One 14-ounce can peeled whole tomatoes, crushed, juices reserved

- 6 cups cold water
- 1 head of garlic, separated into peeled cloves
- ⅓ cup brown rice
- ⅓ cup dark green Puy lentils
- ⅓ cup wheat berries

Freshly ground pepper

1. In a 4-quart enameled cast-iron casserole, combine the chopped leeks, carrots, extra-virgin olive oil, bay leaves, thyme and 1 teaspoon of sea salt. Cover the casserole and cook the vegetables over low heat for 5 minutes, stirring a few times. Add the canned tomatoes with their juices, the water and garlic cloves and bring to a boil over moderate heat.

2. Add the brown rice, green lentils and wheat berries, cover and simmer over low heat until the grains are tender, 45 minutes to 1 hour. Thin with water if needed. Discard the bay leaves, season with salt and pepper and serve. —*Patricia Wells*

ONE CUP Calories 147 kcal, Total Fat 4 gm, Saturated Fat 0.6 gm, Protein 5 gm, Carbohydrates 24 gm

MAKE AHEAD The soup can be refrigerated for 2 days. Reheat gently and add a little water if necessary.

WINE Try a red Rhône like the Côtes-du-Rhône from Domaine Saint-Luc, where Ludovic Cornillon creates a gorgeous, full-bodied pure Syrah.

Quinoa Soup with Feta Cheese

6 SERVINGS

Simple, hearty soups made with protein-rich quinoa and peanuts are a staple of Ecuador's Andean region.

- 1¼ cups (7 ounces) quinoa
- 7 cups water
- ¼ cup unsalted dry-roasted peanuts
- 1 tablespoon unsalted butter
- 2 tablespoons Annatto Oil (p. 297)
- 1 medium onion, finely chopped
- 4 ounces feta, preferably French, or queso blanco, crumbled (about 1 cup)
- ½ teaspoon ground cumin
- 2½ cups whole milk
- 2 medium Yukon Gold potatoes, peeled and cut into 1-inch chunks

Salt

- 1 cup chicken stock or canned low-sodium broth
- ¼ cup heavy cream

Freshly ground pepper

Ají (p. 319), for serving

1. In a large saucepan, cover the quinoa with 6 cups of the water and bring to a boil. Simmer over moderate heat until just tender, about 20 minutes. Drain. Meanwhile, in a mini food processor, process the peanuts until finely ground; do not overprocess.

2. In a large saucepan, melt the butter in the Annatto Oil. Add the onion and cook over moderate heat, stirring, until softened, about 5 minutes. Add half of the feta and the cumin and cook, stirring, for 1 minute. Add the milk, potatoes and remaining 1 cup water and season generously with salt. Bring to a boil, then reduce the heat to low and simmer until the potatoes are softened, about 20 minutes.

3. Stir in the stock or broth, cream, quinoa, peanuts and remaining feta and simmer the soup for 5 minutes. Season the quinoa soup with salt and freshly ground pepper. Serve at once in warmed soup bowls, passing the Ají at the table. —*Maricel Presilla*

Spring Minestrone

4 SERVINGS ●●

- 2 tablespoons olive oil
- 1 leek, white and light green parts only, chopped
- 6 cups chicken stock or canned low-sodium broth
- 1 cup ditali or other small pasta

Salt

- 10 pencil-thin asparagus, cut into 1-inch lengths
- 1 small fennel bulb, cored and cut into ½-inch dice
- ¼ pound sugar snap peas, halved crosswise
- 1 cup coarsely chopped Swiss chard leaves

One 15-ounce can cannellini beans, drained and rinsed

- ½ pound thawed frozen peas
- 2 tablespoons chopped mint

Freshly ground pepper

- ½ cup freshly grated Parmesan

Heat the olive oil in a large saucepan. Add the chopped leek and cook over moderately high heat until softened, about 5 minutes. Add the chicken stock or broth and bring to a boil. Stir in the pasta and ½ teaspoon of salt and simmer for 5 minutes. Add the asparagus, diced fennel, sugar snap peas, Swiss chard and cannellini beans and simmer until the pasta is tender, about 5 minutes longer. Add

the thawed peas and chopped mint, season the soup with salt and pepper and simmer for 1 minute longer. Ladle the soup into bowls, sprinkle with grated Parmesan and serve.—*Joanne Weir*

ONE SERVING Calories 376 kcal, Total Fat 14 gm, Saturated Fat 3.7 gm, Protein 20 gm, Carbohydrates 50 gm

Creamy Chickpea Soup with Roasted Peppers

4 SERVINGS ●

- 1 tablespoon extra-virgin olive oil
- ½ pound kielbasa, halved lengthwise and cut crosswise ½ inch thick
- 1 medium onion, coarsely chopped
- 1 large garlic clove, minced
- 1 cup (about 8 ounces) drained roasted red or yellow peppers from a jar
- ½ teaspoon crushed red pepper
- 4 cups chicken stock or canned low-sodium broth
- 1 cup canned chickpeas, drained and rinsed
- ½ package (5 ounces) frozen chopped spinach
- ⅓ cup tubetti or other small pasta
- ½ cup prepared hummus

Salt and freshly ground black pepper

1. In a large saucepan, heat the olive oil until shimmering. Add the kielbasa, chopped onion, minced garlic, drained roasted peppers and crushed red pepper and cook over high heat, stirring frequently, until lightly browned, about 5 minutes. Add the chicken stock or broth, chickpeas and frozen chopped spinach and simmer the soup over moderate heat until the spinach is thawed, about 5 minutes.

2. Meanwhile, cook the pasta in a small pot of boiling salted water until barely al dente, about 6 minutes; drain. Add the pasta to the soup and stir in the hummus. Simmer until the pasta is al dente. Season the chickpea soup with salt and pepper and serve.

—*Grace Parisi*

Syrian Lentil Soup

4 SERVINGS ●●

- 2 tablespoons extra-virgin olive oil
- 1 large onion, chopped
- 1 medium carrot, chopped
- 1 medium celery rib with leaves, chopped
- 2 teaspoons ground cumin

Pinch of cinnamon

- ½ pound red or brown lentils
- 5 cups hot vegetable broth, chicken broth or water
- 1 small bunch Swiss chard (about 1 pound), stems discarded, leaves coarsely chopped
- 2 tablespoons fresh lemon juice

Salt and freshly ground pepper

Heat the extra-virgin olive oil in a large, heavy saucepan. Add the chopped onion, carrot and celery and cook over moderate heat until tender and slightly golden, about 8 minutes. Stir in the cumin and cinnamon and cook for 1 minute. Add the lentils and broth and bring to a boil. Reduce the heat, cover and simmer the soup until the lentils are tender, about 20 minutes. Stir in the chopped Swiss chard and simmer until tender. Add the fresh lemon juice, season with salt and pepper and serve. —*Joyce Goldstein*

Hearty Lentil Soup with Tomatoes

8 TO 10 SERVINGS ●

- 1 pound brown lentils, picked over
- 1 tablespoon extra-virgin olive oil
- ½ pound thickly sliced pancetta, cut into ¼-inch dice
- 1 small onion, finely chopped
- 1 medium carrot, finely chopped
- 1 celery rib, finely chopped
- 1 leek, white and tender green parts, finely chopped
- 2 garlic cloves, minced

1 teaspoon crushed red pepper
¾ pound plum tomatoes,
coarsely chopped
8 cups chicken stock or canned
low-sodium broth
1 bay leaf
Salt and freshly ground pepper
2 tablespoons finely chopped
flat-leaf parsley
Freshly grated Parmesan, for serving

1. Bring a large saucepan of water to a boil. Add the lentils and cook them over moderately high heat until they are barely tender, about 15 minutes; drain.

2. In a large soup pot, heat the extra-virgin olive oil until shimmering. Add the sliced pancetta and cook over moderately high heat, stirring frequently, until browned, about 5 minutes. Add the finely chopped onion, carrot, celery and leek and cook over moderate heat, stirring frequently, until softened, about 8 minutes. Add the minced garlic and crushed red pepper and cook for 1 minute. Add the chopped tomatoes and cook for 1 minute, then stir in the chicken stock or broth. Add the lentils, bay leaf, season with salt and freshly ground pepper and bring the soup to a boil. Simmer the soup over moderate heat until the lentils are tender but remain intact, about 20 minutes.

3. Just before serving, stir in the parsley and season with salt and pepper. Discard the bay leaf. Ladle the soup into warmed bowls and serve, passing the Parmesan at the table.

—*Don Pintabona*

MAKE AHEAD The Hearty Lentil Soup with Tomatoes can be refrigerated for 2 days.

WINE The earthy lentils and fresh tomatoes in this hearty country soup complement the rustic flavors and acidity of a red made from the Sangiovese grape. Look for a 1998 Chianti Classico, such as the Badia a Coltibuono or the Antinori Pèppoli.

Silky Chestnut Soup

2 TO 4 SERVINGS ●●

3 tablespoons canola oil
One 14-ounce vacuum-packed jar of
cooked and peeled chestnuts
(2½ cups)
1 medium onion, minced
1 medium leek, white and
tender green parts only,
halved lengthwise and sliced
¼ inch thick
2 teaspoons honey
4 cups chicken stock or canned
low-sodium broth
Salt and freshly ground pepper
2 teaspoons Cognac or brandy
1 tablespoon finely chopped
flat-leaf parsley

1. In a large saucepan, heat the canola oil until shimmering. Add 4 of the chestnuts and sauté over moderately high heat until lightly browned, about 5 minutes. Transfer the chestnuts to a plate and let cool.

2. Add the minced onion and sliced leek to the pan, cover and cook over moderate heat, stirring occasionally, until softened, about 5 minutes. Uncover and cook over moderately high heat, stirring frequently, until lightly browned, about 4 minutes. Add the honey and stir until melted. Stir in the remaining chestnuts and the chicken stock or broth, season with salt and freshly ground pepper and simmer the soup over moderate heat for 10 minutes.

3. Finely chop the sautéed chestnuts. Working in batches, puree the soup in a blender until smooth. Strain through a fine sieve. Season the soup with salt and pepper and stir in the Cognac or brandy. Ladle the soup into shallow bowls. Garnish with the chopped chestnuts and parsley and serve.

—*Alex Urena*

MAKE AHEAD The chestnut soup can be refrigerated overnight. Garnish with the sautéed chestnuts and parsley before serving.

Scallop Dumplings in Asian Broth

4 SERVINGS ●

DUMPLINGS

1 large egg white
1 tablespoon soy sauce
1 scallion, coarsely chopped
2 teaspoons minced fresh ginger
2 teaspoons vegetable oil
1½ teaspoons Asian sesame oil
1 teaspoon cornstarch
½ teaspoon kosher salt
¼ teaspoon freshly ground pepper
1 pound sea scallops, halved

BROTH

4½ cups canned low-sodium
chicken broth
Four 3-inch-long strips of lemon zest
3 large garlic cloves, smashed
2 teaspoons soy sauce
2 teaspoons minced fresh ginger
Salt and freshly ground pepper
16 snow peas, julienned
3 cups thinly sliced Savoy cabbage
Cilantro sprigs, sliced scallions, Asian
sesame oil and Asian hot sauce,
for garnish

Scallop Dumplings in Asian Broth

1. **MAKE THE DUMPLINGS:** In a food processor, blend the egg white with the soy sauce, scallion, ginger, vegetable oil, sesame oil, cornstarch, salt and pepper. Add all but 3 of the scallops and process to a coarse paste. Scrape the paste into a bowl. Cut the remaining scallops into ½-inch dice and fold them into the paste. Cover and refrigerate.

2. **MAKE THE BROTH:** In a large saucepan, combine the broth with the lemon zest, garlic, soy sauce, ginger and a pinch each of salt and pepper. Cover and simmer for 20 minutes. Remove from the heat and discard the lemon zest and garlic. Add the snow peas and cabbage and bring to a simmer.

3. Drop scant tablespoons of the scallop paste into the broth, then cover and simmer over low heat until the dumplings are just cooked through, about 2 minutes. Ladle into bowls, top with the garnishes and serve. —*Marcia Kiesel*

ONE SERVING Calories 218 kcal, Total Fat 7.2 gm, Saturated Fat 1.6 gm, Protein 27 gm, Carbohydrates 12 gm

Garlic and Egg Drop Soup with Crab

4 SERVINGS ●

¼ cup extra-virgin olive oil

4 slices of firm white bread, crusts removed, bread cut into 1-inch dice

4 garlic cloves, minced

¼ teaspoon crushed red pepper

6 cups chicken stock or canned low-sodium broth

2 large eggs, lightly beaten

¼ pound fresh lump crabmeat, picked over (¾ cup)

2 tablespoons minced cilantro or flat-leaf parsley

Salt and freshly ground pepper

In a large saucepan, heat 3 tablespoons of the olive oil. Add the bread in an even layer and cook over

moderately low heat, without turning, until browned on the bottom, about 4 minutes. Stir and cook for 1 minute longer. Push the croutons to the side. Add the remaining 1 tablespoon of olive oil to the pan. Add the garlic and crushed red pepper and cook until fragrant, about 1 minute. Stir the croutons with the flavored oil. Pour in the chicken stock and bring to a boil. Reduce the heat and simmer for 5 minutes. Whisk in the eggs. Remove from the heat and stir in the crabmeat and cilantro. Season with salt and pepper, ladle into bowls and serve.

—*Alex Lee*

Avocado-Lime Soup with Crab

4 SERVINGS ● ●

2 pounds ripe Hass avocados, peeled and cut into chunks

3 cups cold chicken stock or canned low-sodium broth

1 cup cold milk

3 tablespoons fresh lime juice

Salt and freshly ground black pepper

¼ pound jumbo lump crabmeat, picked over

2 tablespoons coarsely chopped cilantro

Pinch of cayenne pepper

In a blender or food processor, puree the avocados with the chicken stock until smooth. Add the milk and lime juice and puree until blended. Season with salt and black pepper. Ladle the soup into large bowls, garnish with the crabmeat, cilantro and cayenne and serve. —*Ruth Van Waerebeek*

MAKE AHEAD The soup can be refrigerated for 4 hours before serving.

WINE This thick, rich and silky soup calls for an equally creamy-textured big Chardonnay. Pick one with bright fruit to highlight the hints of lime in the soup, such as the 1999 Glazebrook Unoaked or the 2000 Omaka Springs Marlborough, both from New Zealand.

Fresh Corn Soup with Crab

4 TO 6 SERVINGS ● ●

A quick sauté of corn and a pinch of saffron flavor this 30-minute soup.

2 tablespoons unsalted butter

1 medium onion, chopped

1 medium carrot, chopped

1 celery rib, chopped

1 garlic clove, chopped

6 ears of corn, kernels cut off

1 bay leaf

Large pinch of saffron threads

4½ cups water

Salt and freshly ground pepper

½ pound lump crabmeat, picked over

¼ cup shredded basil

1. In a large skillet, melt the butter over moderate heat. Add the onion, carrot, celery and garlic and cook until just softened, about 5 minutes. Add the corn, bay leaf and saffron and cook for 5 minutes, stirring occasionally. Add the water and bring to a boil. Reduce the heat to moderately low and simmer for 15 minutes.

2. Discard the bay leaf. Transfer the soup to a blender and puree. Strain the soup through a fine sieve into a large bowl. Season with salt and pepper. Ladle the soup into bowls, top with the crabmeat and basil and serve.

—*Melissa Clark*

Shrimp and Corn Chowder with Garlic Croutons

4 SERVINGS ●

Twelve ½-inch-thick slices of Italian or French bread

1½ tablespoons extra-virgin olive oil

2 garlic cloves, 1 halved and 1 minced

1 teaspoon unsalted butter

2 slices bacon, finely diced

1 cup corn kernels

2 large scallions, thinly sliced crosswise

Scant ½ teaspoon crushed red pepper

3 tablespoons all-purpose flour

Fresh Corn Soup with Crab

heatproof measuring cup; discard the solids. Add water, if needed, to make 2 cups of liquid.

4. Wipe out the saucepan and melt the remaining 2 tablespoons of butter in it. Add the onion and celery and cook over moderate heat until softened, about 6 minutes. Stir in the tomato paste and cook the mixture until just glossy. Add the diluted clam juice and the reserved cooking liquid, leaving behind any grit. Bring to a boil and simmer for 20 minutes.

5. Add the cream and the reserved toasted bread cubes to the broth and simmer until the bread is softened, about 5 minutes. In a blender, puree the soup in batches until very smooth. Return the soup to the saucepan, season with salt and cayenne pepper and simmer until reduced to 8 cups, about 10 minutes.

6. Stir the mussels into the soup and bring to a simmer. Ladle into shallow bowls. Spread the toasts with the rouille and serve. —*Grace Parisi*

Curried Mussel and Butternut Squash Soup

NOTE Jarred piquillo peppers, from the Navarre region of Spain, are available at specialty food shops. Piquillos are richer in flavor than roasted red bell peppers and have a bit of heat. The best substitute is jarred roasted red peppers plus ¼ teaspoon of hot paprika.

MAKE AHEAD The rouille, mussels and soup can be refrigerated separately overnight. Store the toasts in an airtight container. Recrisp in a 325° oven if necessary.

Curried Mussel and Butternut Squash Soup

6 SERVINGS

In the Middle Ages, Flemish cities were at the crossroads of the Northern spice routes, and both brewers and cooks took advantage of exotic spices. You'll savor that influence in this curried soup.

- 2 tablespoons unsalted butter
- 2 shallots, finely chopped
- 1 leek, white and light green parts, sliced crosswise ½ inch thick
- 1 tablespoon curry powder
- One 2½-pound butternut squash— peeled, seeded and cut into ½-inch dice
- 2½ cups chicken stock or canned low-sodium broth
- 2 pounds mussels, scrubbed and debearded
- 1 cup dry white wine
- ½ cup water
- 2 thyme sprigs
- Freshly ground pepper
- Salt
- Cilantro leaves, for garnish

1. Melt the butter in a medium saucepan. Add the shallots and leek and cook over moderate heat, stirring occasionally, until softened, 3 to 4 minutes. Stir in the curry powder and cook until fragrant, about 1 minute. Add the butternut squash and stock, cover and simmer until the squash is very tender, 20 to 25 minutes.

Remove from the heat and let the soup cool to room temperature. Working in batches, puree the soup in a blender until smooth. Return the soup to the saucepan.

2. In another medium saucepan, combine the mussels with the white wine, water and thyme and season generously with pepper. Cover and bring to a boil over high heat. Steam the mussels for 3 to 5 minutes, shaking the pan occasionally; transfer the mussels to a bowl as they open. Remove the mussels from the shells and reserve 12 shells for garnish. Discard any unopened mussels.

3. Carefully pour the mussel cooking liquid into the soup, leaving behind any sand or grit. Reheat the soup and season with salt. Place 12 of the mussels in the reserved shells. Add the rest of the mussels to the soup to warm them. Ladle the soup into bowls, garnish with cilantro and the mussels in the shells and serve.

—*Ruth Van Waerebeek*

MAKE AHEAD The curried soup can be prepared through Step 1 and refrigerated overnight.

BEER Blanche de Bruges, light wheat beer from Belgium, is the ideal accompaniment to this soup.

Turkish Yogurt Soup with Chicken, Chickpeas and Rice

4 SERVINGS ●

- 1 cup water
- ½ cup basmati rice
- 4 cups chicken stock or canned low-sodium broth
- 1 pound skinless, boneless chicken thighs, cut into 1-inch pieces
- 1 cup full-fat plain yogurt
- 1 large egg yolk
- 2 tablespoons all-purpose flour
- One 15-ounce can chickpeas, drained and rinsed
- Salt and freshly ground pepper
- 2 tablespoons unsalted butter
- 2 teaspoons minced garlic

2 teaspoons sweet paprika

⅛ teaspoon cayenne pepper

3 tablespoons finely chopped mint

Lemon wedges, for serving

1. Bring the water to a boil in a medium saucepan. Add the rice, cover and cook over low heat until barely tender, about 15 minutes.

2. Meanwhile, in a medium saucepan, bring the stock to a simmer over moderately high heat. Add the chicken and simmer until cooked through, about 10 minutes. Using a slotted spoon, transfer the chicken to a plate. Skim any fat from the surface of the stock.

3. In a large saucepan, whisk the yogurt with the egg yolk and flour. Whisk in the stock and bring to a simmer over low heat, whisking occasionally. Stir in the chickpeas, rice and reserved chicken. Season with salt and pepper and keep warm over low heat.

4. Melt the butter in a small skillet. Add the garlic, paprika and cayenne and cook over moderate heat until fragrant, about 2 minutes. Ladle the soup into bowls and swirl in the garlic butter. Sprinkle with the mint and serve with lemon wedges. —*Joyce Goldstein*

Turkish Yogurt Soup with Chicken, Chickpeas and Rice

5 pasta

Fettuccine with Rosemary Butter

4 TO 6 SERVINGS ● ●

This quick and easy pasta is perfect for any day of the week. Serve it as is, with its boldly flavored herb sauce, or dress it up with crisp-fried pancetta, julienned prosciutto, chopped anchovies, cooked shrimp or chopped olives.

- 1 pound fettuccine
- 6 tablespoons unsalted butter
- ¼ cup rosemary leaves, finely chopped

Salt and freshly ground pepper

- ½ cup freshly grated Pecorino-Romano, for serving

1. In a large pot of boiling salted water, cook the fettuccine until al dente. Meanwhile, in a medium skillet, melt the butter over moderate heat until it begins to foam, about 1 minute. Reduce the heat to low, add the rosemary and cook until fragrant, about 2 minutes. Season the sauce with salt and pepper, remove from the heat and keep warm.

2. Drain the pasta, reserving ⅓ cup of the pasta cooking water. Add the pasta and the reserved water to the skillet and toss to coat with the sauce. Transfer the pasta to warmed bowls and serve immediately. Pass the freshly grated Pecorino at the table.

—*Barbara Lynch*

Linguine with Spring Herb Pesto and Wilted Greens

4 SERVINGS ●

Most pestos are made with garlic. This one isn't, so the flavor of the herbs and greens seems even brighter.

- 1 packed cup flat-leaf parsley leaves
- 1 packed cup basil leaves
- 1 tablespoon mint leaves
- 1 tablespoon tarragon
- 1 tablespoon sherry vinegar
- ⅓ cup plus 2 tablespoons extra-virgin olive oil

Salt and freshly ground pepper

- ¾ pound dried linguine
- ½ pound frisée, baby chicory or baby beet greens, torn into bite-size pieces
- ½ cup freshly grated Parmesan

1. In a blender or food processor, combine the parsley with the basil, mint, tarragon, sherry vinegar and ⅓ cup of olive oil. Blend until a coarse puree forms. Scrape the pesto into a bowl and season with salt and pepper.

2. Cook the linguine in a large pot of boiling salted water, stirring, until al dente. Reserve ¼ cup of the pasta cooking water, then drain the linguine and transfer it to a large warmed pasta bowl.

3. Return the pasta pot to moderately high heat. Add the remaining 2 tablespoons of olive oil and the frisée, season with salt and pepper and cook, stirring, until barely wilted, about 30 seconds. Add the frisée to the linguine along with 3 tablespoons of the reserved pasta cooking water. Using tongs, toss the pasta to evenly distribute the frisée. Add the pesto, season with salt and pepper and toss well. Add the remaining 1 tablespoon of pasta cooking water if the pasta seems dry. Sprinkle with the Parmesan, toss again and serve at once.

—*Eberhard Müller*

MAKE AHEAD The pesto can be prepared in advance and refrigerated overnight.

Linguine with Walnut-Parsley Pesto

4 SERVINGS ●

- 1 cup flat-leaf parsley leaves
- ½ cup basil leaves
- 2 small garlic cloves, minced
- ¼ cup toasted walnut pieces
- ¼ cup freshly grated Parmesan cheese
- ¼ cup extra-virgin olive oil
- ½ cup ricotta

Salt and freshly ground pepper

- ¾ pound linguine

1. In a mini food processor, pulse the parsley with the basil and garlic until chopped. Add the walnuts, Parmesan cheese and olive oil and process to a paste. Transfer the pesto to a large bowl, stir in the ricotta and season with salt and pepper.

2. Cook the linguine in a large pot of boiling salted water until al dente. Drain the pasta, reserving ½ cup of the cooking water. Toss the pasta with the pesto and the reserved cooking water, season with salt and pepper and serve.

—*Joanne Weir*

Trenette with Pesto and Haricots Verts

6 SERVINGS ●

This dish from Italy's Liguria region is traditionally made with pesto, potatoes, green beans and a thin, flat pasta called trenette—Italian for "ribbons"—that resembles linguine. This recipe omits the potatoes.

- ¾ cup pine nuts (about 3½ ounces)
- 2 garlic cloves
- 4½ cups loosely packed basil leaves
- 1 cup flat-leaf parsley leaves
- 1 stick (4 ounces) unsalted butter, softened
- 2 tablespoons extra-virgin olive oil
- ⅓ cup freshly grated Parmesan

Salt and freshly ground pepper

- 1 pound trenette or linguine
- ½ pound haricots verts, halved crosswise

1. Set a small skillet over moderately high heat. Add ¼ cup of the pine nuts and toast, stirring constantly, until golden, about 4 minutes. Transfer to a plate.

2. Meanwhile, in a food processor or blender, pulse the remaining ½ cup of pine nuts with the garlic until finely chopped. Add the basil, parsley, butter and olive oil and process until the basil is minced. Add the Parmesan and process to a thick puree. Season the pesto sauce with salt and pepper.

3. In a large pot of boiling salted water, cook the pasta until almost al dente. Add the haricots verts and cook for about 1 minute longer. Drain well.

4. In a warmed large bowl, toss the hot pasta and haricots verts with the pesto until well coated. Sprinkle with the toasted pine nuts and serve.

—*Barbara Lynch*

MAKE AHEAD The pesto sauce can be refrigerated for up to 2 days with plastic wrap pressed directly on the surface.

WINE The creamy, nutty pesto calls for a substantial, fresh, spicy white made from the Pigato grape. Try one from Liguria, such as the 1998 Terre Bianche Pigato or the 1998 Colle dei Bardellini Pigato La Torretta.

Tagliatelle with Lemon, Parmesan and Thyme

4 TO 6 SERVINGS ●

- 1 pound tagliatelle
- 1 cup freshly grated Parmesan
- 4 tablespoons unsalted butter
- 2 tablespoons chopped thyme

Finely grated zest of 2 lemons
Salt and freshly ground pepper

In a pot of boiling salted water, cook the tagliatelle until al dente. Drain the pasta, reserving ½ cup of the cooking water. Return the pasta to the pot. Add ½ cup of Parmesan and the butter, thyme, lemon zest and the reserved cooking water. Cook over moderate heat, tossing just until creamy. Season with salt and pepper and transfer to a bowl. Sprinkle with the remaining Parmesan and serve.

—*Kate Heddings*

Orzo with Tomatoes, Basil and Gorgonzola

4 FIRST-COURSE SERVINGS ●

Use just one pot and save time on cleanup.

- 3 tablespoons olive oil
- 1 cup orzo (6 ounces)
- ½ medium onion, finely chopped

Orzo with Tomatoes, Basil and Gorgonzola

- 3 garlic cloves, minced
- 1¼ cups chicken stock or canned low-sodium broth

Salt and freshly ground pepper

- 1 pint red and yellow cherry tomatoes, halved
- 12 basil leaves, coarsely chopped
- 2 ounces Gorgonzola, crumbled (⅓ cup)

1. Heat 2 tablespoons of olive oil in a medium saucepan. Add the orzo and cook over moderate heat, stirring with a wooden spoon, until lightly browned, about 3 minutes. Add the onion and cook, stirring, for 1 minute. Add half the garlic and cook, stirring, until fragrant, about 30 seconds. Add the stock and season with salt and pepper, then cover and simmer over low heat until the stock has been absorbed and the orzo is tender, about 12 minutes.

2. Meanwhile, in a bowl, toss the tomatoes with the remaining 1 tablespoon of olive oil, the remaining garlic and half of the basil. Season with salt and pepper.

3. Mound the orzo in the middle of plates or a platter. Spoon the tomatoes around the orzo, scatter the Gorgonzola and remaining basil over the top and serve. —*Michael Roberts*

Fettuccine with Lemon Basil Tomato Sauce

Fettuccine with Lemon Basil Tomato Sauce

4 SERVINGS ●●

- 1 pound beefsteak tomatoes, halved and coarsely grated
- ¼ small Vidalia onion, grated
- ¼ cup finely shredded lemon basil, plus sprigs for garnish
- 1 tablespoon fresh lemon juice
- 1 tablespoon extra-virgin olive oil
- 1 small garlic clove, minced
- ½ tablespoon balsamic vinegar
- ½ teaspoon chopped thyme

Salt and freshly ground pepper

- ¾ pound fettuccine
- 1 cup cherry and pear tomatoes, halved

Freshly grated Parmesan

1. In a large bowl, mix the grated tomatoes with the onion, shredded basil, lemon juice, oil, garlic, vinegar and thyme and season with salt and pepper. Let stand for 20 minutes.

2. Cook the fettuccine in a large pot of boiling salted water until al dente; drain. Add the fettuccine to the sauce and toss. Garnish with the tomatoes and basil sprigs. Serve with Parmesan.

—*Suki Hertz*

ONE SERVING Calories 390 kcal, Total Fat 5.6 mg, Saturated Fat 0.6 mg

Angel-Hair Pasta with Shallots and Pecorino

4 SERVINGS ●

- 4 medium tomatoes, finely chopped
- 5 tablespoons extra-virgin olive oil
- 1 tablespoon red wine vinegar
- 2 teaspoons balsamic vinegar
- 2 tablespoons finely chopped oregano

Finely grated zest of 1 lemon

- 2 medium bunches of arugula, large stems discarded (4 packed cups)
- 2 large shallots, thinly sliced

Salt

- ¾ pound angel-hair pasta
- ¼ cup freshly grated Pecorino, plus more for serving

Freshly ground pepper

1. Bring a large pot of salted water to a boil. In a large serving bowl, combine the tomatoes with 3 tablespoons of the olive oil and the red wine and balsamic vinegars. Stir in the oregano and lemon zest and set the arugula on top.

2. In a medium skillet, heat the remaining 2 tablespoons of olive oil. Add the shallots. Season with salt and cook over moderately high heat, stirring occasionally, until the shallots are browned, 3 to 5 minutes. Remove from the heat.

3. Cook the pasta in the boiling water until al dente. Drain and add to the serving bowl with the shallots and ¼ cup of Pecorino. Toss and season with salt and pepper. Serve with additional Pecorino. —*Stephanie Lyness*

Linguine with Saffron, Tomatoes and Herbs

8 SERVINGS

This pasta dish is made with a tasty vegetable stock that's simmered with saffron. The linguine cooks in the fragrant stock, which turns the pasta bright yellow.

- 1 pound cherry tomatoes, halved
- ¼ cup chopped pitted black olives, such as Gaeta (2 ounces)
- 2 tablespoons salted capers— soaked briefly, rinsed and coarsely chopped
- 2 anchovy fillets, mashed
- 1 celery rib, finely chopped
- 1 scallion, finely chopped
- 1 teaspoon minced thyme
- ¼ cup plus 1 tablespoon extra-virgin olive oil
- ¼ cup chopped basil
- ¼ cup chopped cilantro
- 2 tablespoons minced chives

Salt and freshly ground pepper

- 8 asparagus (about ½ pound), cut on the diagonal into 1-inch lengths
- 4 slices lean bacon (3 ounces), cut crosswise into ¼-inch matchsticks

basil varieties

CLOCKWISE FROM TOP: **Globe basil** has miniature leaves on a round plant. The flavor ranges from sweet to slightly spicy. Use the leaves whole. **Osmin Purple basil,** a small-leafed purple basil, has a sweet aroma and taste. **Genovese** is the classic Italian basil used in pesto. **Lime basil** has a distinctive lime flavor. **Armenian basil** is an unusual purple and green basil. **Licorice basil** has the aroma of anise and a flavor reminiscent of tarragon. The leaves have light purple veining and are attached to a lavender stem. **CENTER:** **Holy basil,** an aromatic herb with a clovelike taste, is traditionally used in Thai and Indian cuisine. The leaves are either green or green with reddish tips. Many of these basils, and others, are available from Johnny's Selected Seeds (207-437-4301; www.johnnyseeds.com) and Shepherd's Garden Seeds (860-482-3638; www.shepherdseeds.com).

- 1 cup dry white wine
- 4 quarts Vegetable Stock (recipe follows)
- ¼ teaspoon saffron threads
- 1½ pounds linguine

1. In a large, shallow serving bowl, combine the tomatoes with the olives, capers, anchovies, celery, scallion and thyme. Add 1 tablespoon oil and half of the basil, cilantro and chives and season with salt and pepper. Cover and set aside for up to 2 hours. ▸

2. In a large skillet of boiling salted water, cook the asparagus until almost tender, about 1 minute. Drain and refresh in cold water.

3. In the same skillet, cook the bacon over moderate heat until crisp, about 4 minutes. Add the wine and boil over high heat for 3 minutes. Stir in the asparagus and the remaining ¼ cup of olive oil and remove from the heat.

4. In a large pot, bring the stock to a boil with the saffron. Cover and simmer over low heat for 5 minutes. Salt the stock generously and return to a boil over high heat. Add the linguine and cook, stirring, until al dente. Drain the linguine and add it to the bowl with the tomatoes. Add the asparagus, season with salt and pepper and toss well. Sprinkle the linguine with the remaining half of the basil, cilantro and chives and serve at once. —*Massimo Bottura*

MAKE AHEAD The recipe can be prepared through Step 3 up to 2 hours ahead. Reheat the asparagus before adding it to the pasta.

VEGETABLE STOCK

MAKES ABOUT 5 QUARTS

- 5 quarts water
- ¼ cabbage
- 2 carrots
- 2 celery ribs
- 6 garlic cloves
- 1 medium onion
- 4 scallions
- ½ bunch of parsley
- 2 bay leaves
- 1 teaspoon whole peppercorns
- 4 thyme sprigs

Salt

Wash the vegetables, but leave them whole. In a stockpot, combine the water, cabbage, carrots, celery ribs, garlic cloves, onion, scallions, parsley, bay leaves, peppercorns and 4 thyme sprigs and bring to a boil. Skim off any foam that rises to the surface. Season with salt and simmer over low heat for 1¼ hours. Strain the stock. —*M.B.*

Orecchiette with Ricotta, Basil and Tomatoes

4 TO 6 SERVINGS ●

- 1 pound orecchiette
- 1 cup ricotta (about ½ pound), preferably fresh
- ½ cup packed basil leaves, coarsely chopped
- 1 small garlic clove, smashed
- 3 tablespoons extra-virgin olive oil

Salt and freshly ground pepper

- 2 pounds large tomatoes, seeded and coarsely chopped

1. In a large pot of boiling salted water, cook the orecchiette, stirring occasionally, until al dente.

2. Meanwhile, in a mini food processor, combine the ricotta with half of the chopped basil, the smashed garlic and 1 tablespoon of the extra-virgin olive oil. Season with salt and pepper and puree until smooth. Add the remaining basil and pulse just until chopped.

3. In a bowl, toss the tomatoes with the remaining 2 tablespoons of oil; season with salt and pepper. Drain the pasta and add it to the tomatoes. Stir in the basil ricotta and serve.

—*Kate Heddings*

Fettuccine with Quick Tomato Sauce and Hot Chili Oil

6 SERVINGS ●

Hot chili oil left over from this recipe can be used for making stir-fries and popping popcorn.

- ½ cup plus 3 tablespoons extra-virgin olive oil
- 1 dried spicy red chile
- 1 small dried chipotle chile
- 4 Szechuan peppercorns
- 3 black peppercorns, cracked
- 2 large garlic cloves, minced
- 1 medium sweet onion, such as Vidalia, finely chopped
- 3 large tomatoes, finely chopped
- 1 serrano or large jalapeño, very thinly sliced crosswise

- 1 teaspoon thyme leaves

Scant 1 teaspoon minced oregano

Salt and freshly ground pepper

- 1 pound dried egg fettuccine
- ½ cup coarsely chopped basil
- ¼ cup freshly grated Parmesan, plus more for serving

1. In a small saucepan, combine ½ cup of the extra-virgin olive oil with the dried red chile, the chipotle chile, Szechuan peppercorns and black peppercorns and bring to a simmer. Cook over very low heat for 15 minutes, then strain the hot chili oil into a jar.

2. In a large, deep skillet, heat the remaining 3 tablespoons of extra-virgin olive oil until shimmering. Add the minced garlic and cook over moderate heat, stirring, until fragrant but not browned, about 30 seconds. Add the chopped onion and cook, stirring frequently, until softened, about 5 minutes. Add the chopped tomatoes, sliced serrano or jalapeño, thyme and minced oregano, season with salt and pepper and bring to a simmer. Cook the tomato sauce over moderate heat until slightly thickened, about 5 minutes.

3. Meanwhile, in a large pot of boiling salted water, cook the fettuccine until al dente. Drain the pasta, shake it dry and return it to the pot. Add the tomato sauce, chopped basil, freshly grated Parmesan and ¼ cup of the hot chili oil and toss. Serve the fettuccine in bowls and pass grated Parmesan and the remaining hot chili oil at the table.

—*Larry Stone*

MAKE AHEAD The hot chili oil can be refrigerated for 2 months.

WINE Almost any lighter red goes well with the Fettuccine with Quick Tomato Sauce and Hot Chili Oil, which is slightly salty from the cheese and spicy from the oil. The 1999 J. L. Chave Selections Mon Coeur Côtes-du-Rhône from France, an especially good choice, also delivers a little acidity to balance the tomatoes.

Fettuccine with Quick Tomato Sauce and Hot Chili Oil

Spaghetti with Pancetta and Sun-Dried Tomatoes

¼ cup drained oil-packed sun-dried
   tomatoes, cut into strips
 2 tablespoons very finely
   chopped garlic
¼ cup shredded basil
Salt and freshly ground pepper
 1 pound spaghetti
Freshly grated Parmesan, for serving

Pasta Arrabbiata

4 SERVINGS ●

 ¾ pound pasta
 1 teaspoon extra-virgin olive oil
 4 thick-cut slices of bacon
 3 garlic cloves, smashed
 1 teaspoon crushed red pepper
One 35-ounce can diced tomatoes
Pinch of sugar
Kosher salt and freshly ground pepper
 1 tablespoon chopped fresh basil
 ½ cup freshly grated Parmesan

I. In a large pot of boiling salted water, cook the pasta until al dente; drain.
2. Meanwhile, heat the olive oil in a deep-sided medium skillet. Add the bacon and garlic and cook over moderately high heat until the garlic is golden and the bacon is lightly crisp, about 4 minutes. Add the red pepper

and cook, stirring, for 30 seconds. Add the tomatoes and their juices, the sugar and a pinch each of salt and pepper and cook over moderately high heat, stirring frequently, until the sauce is thick, about 15 minutes. Discard the bacon and stir in the basil.
3. Transfer the pasta to a warmed serving bowl and toss with the sauce. Sprinkle the cheese on top and serve.
—*Grace Parisi*

Spaghetti with Pancetta and Sun-Dried Tomatoes

4 SERVINGS ●

 ¼ cup extra-virgin olive oil
 ½ pound thickly sliced pancetta,
   cut crosswise into ¼-inch strips
 2 small red onions, sliced
   ¼ inch thick

I. Heat 2 tablespoons of the olive oil in a large skillet. Add the pancetta and cook over moderate heat until softened but not browned, about 3 minutes. Using a slotted spoon, transfer the pancetta to a plate.
2. Pour off all but 2 tablespoons of fat from the skillet. Add the remaining 2 tablespoons of olive oil and heat until shimmering. Add the onions and cook over moderately high heat until just beginning to brown, about 5 minutes. Add the pancetta and sun-dried tomatoes and cook over moderate heat for 5 minutes longer. Add the garlic and cook until fragrant, about 1 minute. Add the basil and season with salt and pepper.
3. Meanwhile, in a pot of boiling salted water, cook the spaghetti until al

dente. Drain the spaghetti, reserving ½ cup of the cooking water. Add the spaghetti to the skillet along with ¼ cup of the cooking water and toss over moderate heat until combined. Transfer to a bowl and serve, passing the Parmesan at the table.

—*Joyce Goldstein*

Pasta with Celery and Lemon

4 SERVINGS ●●

- 4 large celery ribs, peeled and cut into matchsticks, plus ¼ cup celery leaves for garnish
- ¾ pound thin linguine or spaghetti
- 3 tablespoons unsalted butter
- 1 tablespoon minced shallot
- 1 cup chicken stock

Large pinch of crushed red pepper

- ¼ cup freshly grated Parmesan
- ¼ cup chopped chives
- 2 teaspoons finely grated lemon zest

Salt and freshly ground pepper

1. In a large pot of boiling salted water, blanch the celery for 1 minute. Using a slotted spoon, transfer to a colander set in the sink and refresh under cold water. Bring the water back to a boil. Add the pasta and cook until just al dente.

2. Meanwhile, melt the butter in a large skillet. Add the minced shallot and cook over moderate heat until softened, about 2 minutes. Add the chicken stock, crushed red pepper and blanched celery and cook until the liquid is reduced by one-third, about 5 minutes.

3. Drain the pasta, reserving ¼ cup of the cooking water. Add the cooking water and grated Parmesan to the skillet and simmer for 2 minutes. Add the pasta, simmer for 1 minute and remove from the heat. Add the chives and lemon zest, season with salt and pepper and toss. Transfer the pasta to a large warmed bowl, sprinkle with the celery leaves and serve.

—*Rene Michelena*

Pasta with Bright Lights Swiss Chard

4 FIRST-COURSE SERVINGS ●

Bright Lights Swiss chard has ribs that are ruby red, Day-Glo orange, white, and shocking yellow—all in the same plant—but any variety of Swiss chard can be substituted.

- 1½ pounds Bright Lights Swiss chard
- ½ pound malloreddus pasta (see Note)
- 1 tablespoon unsalted butter
- 2½ tablespoons extra-virgin olive oil
- 3 large garlic cloves, thinly sliced
- 1 tablespoon fine lemon zest strips, cut with a zester

Salt and freshly ground pepper

- 3 ounces Gorgonzola, crumbled (½ packed cup)

1. Cut the chard stems crosswise ½ inch wide. Cut the leaves into ½-inch-wide strips. In a large saucepan of boiling water, cook the stems until almost tender, about 3 minutes. Using a slotted spoon, transfer the stems to a plate. Add the chard leaves to the boiling water and cook until tender, about 2 minutes. Drain the leaves and let cool, then coarsely chop.

2. Cook the malloreddus in a large pot of boiling salted water, stirring occasionally, until al dente; drain.

3. In a large skillet, melt the butter in 2 tablespoons of the olive oil. Add the garlic and lemon zest and cook over low heat until the garlic is golden, about 3 minutes. Add the chard and season with salt and pepper. Add the

Pasta with Bright Lights Swiss Chard

pasta to the skillet and toss until hot. Transfer the pasta to a large, warmed bowl, scatter the Gorgonzola on top and drizzle with the remaining ½ tablespoon of olive oil. Using 2 large spoons, toss briefly to melt the cheese slightly; serve at once.—*Marcia Kiesel*

NOTE Malloreddus is a small Sardinian ridged pasta that is often flavored with saffron. It can be white, bright yellow or tricolored, and it pairs beautifully with the multicolored chard. Malloreddus is available by mail order from Dean & DeLuca (800-999-0306; www.deandeluca.com).

VARIATION Farfalle, cavatappi and fusilli, with their folds and cavities, are also perfect for holding the chunks of vegetables and cheese. The chard can be replaced with lightly boiled watercress or grilled endive.

Pappardelle with Spinach and Feta

Rotelle with Caramelized Radicchio and Corn

4 SERVINGS ● ●

Rotelle is the preferred pasta for this simple main course because the sweet sautéed radicchio and corn kernels get cradled inside the wagon wheels.

- 1 cup fresh corn kernels (from 1 to 2 ears)
- 2 tablespoons extra-virgin olive oil
- 3 large shallots, thinly sliced
- 2 large garlic cloves, thinly sliced
- 1 large head of radicchio, coarsely chopped (4 packed cups)

Salt and freshly ground pepper

- ¾ pound rotelle or fusilli
- 1 tablespoon unsalted butter
- ⅓ cup freshly grated Pecorino, plus more for serving

1. Bring a large pot of salted water to a boil. Put the corn in a small sieve and blanch it in the boiling water for 2 minutes. Drain the corn and transfer it to a small bowl. Keep the pot of water at a simmer.

2. Heat the oil in a large skillet. Add the shallots and cook over moderately high heat, stirring, until softened, about

2 minutes. Add the corn and garlic and cook for 2 minutes. Add the radicchio and cook over low heat, stirring, until tender and beginning to brown, about 5 minutes. Season with salt and pepper. Remove from the heat.

3. Bring the water in the pot back to a boil. Add the pasta and cook, stirring, until al dente. Reserve ½ cup of the pasta cooking water and drain the rotelle. Return the rotelle to the pot and add the radicchio mixture, the reserved pasta cooking water, the butter and the ⅓ cup of Pecorino. Toss well and season with salt and pepper. Transfer the pasta to shallow bowls and serve, passing more Pecorino at the table. —*Stephanie Lyness*

Pappardelle with Spinach and Feta

4 SERVINGS ● ●

- ¾ pound dried pappardelle
- 2 pounds spinach, tough stems discarded, leaves washed but not dried
- 2 tablespoons extra-virgin olive oil
- 3 garlic cloves, thinly sliced

Pinch of crushed red pepper

Sea salt

- 2 ounces feta, crumbled (½ cup)
- 2 tablespoons finely chopped flat-leaf parsley

1. Cook the pappardelle in a large pot of boiling salted water until al dente. Drain the pasta in a colander set in the sink, reserving ¼ cup of the cooking water.

2. Meanwhile, in a large, deep skillet, cook the spinach leaves over high heat, stirring, until wilted, about 1 minute. Drain the spinach in a colander set over a bowl and press gently; reserve the liquid. Coarsely chop the spinach.

3. Wipe out the skillet and add the olive oil and garlic. Cook over moderate heat, stirring, until the garlic is lightly browned. Add the crushed red pepper and cook for 30 seconds. Add the spinach and a generous pinch of salt and cook, stirring until hot, about 1 minute.

4. Add the pasta to the skillet along with the reserved spinach liquid and pasta cooking water and season with

Pasta with Lemony Asparagus Sauce

Penne with Asparagus
and Artichokes

salt. Cook until the liquid has nearly evaporated and the spinach is silky, about 3 minutes. Stir in the feta and parsley and serve in deep bowls.

—*Grace Parisi*

ONE SERVING Calories 433 kcal, Total Fat 11.6 gm, Saturated Fat 3.3 gm, Protein 18 gm, Carbohydrates 65 gm

Pasta with Lemony Asparagus Sauce

4 SERVINGS ●

1½ pounds thin asparagus, tips cut into 1½-inch lengths, tips and stalks reserved separately

⅓ cup extra-virgin olive oil

1½ teaspoons finely grated lemon zest

Fine sea salt

¾ pound gemelli pasta

¾ cup freshly grated Parmesan (2 ounces)

Freshly ground pepper

I. In a large pot of boiling salted water, cook the asparagus stalks until tender, about 3 minutes. Transfer the stalks to a food processor. Add the olive oil, lemon zest and ½ teaspoon of salt and blend until smooth.

2. Add the asparagus tips to the boiling water and cook until tender, about 3 minutes. Transfer the tips to a colander and rinse under cold water; drain and pat dry.

3. Add the pasta to the boiling water and cook, stirring, for half of the recommended time. Drain, reserving 1½ cups of the pasta cooking water; return the pasta to the pot.

4. Add ¼ cup of the reserved pasta water to the asparagus mixture in the processor and blend. Add the sauce and 1 cup of the reserved pasta water to the pasta and simmer over high heat, stirring often, until the pasta is al dente. Stir in the asparagus tips and Parmesan and cook for 1 minute. Add the remaining ¼ cup of pasta water if the sauce seems too thick. Season with salt and pepper and serve.

—*Joshua Eisen*

WINE A Riesling will work beautifully with this somewhat difficult-to-match dish. Try the 1999 Robert Weil Riesling Kabinett Halbtrocken or the 1999 Hogue Johannisberg Riesling.

Penne with Asparagus and Artichokes

4 SERVINGS ●

4 teaspoons pine nuts

1½ pounds asparagus, cut into 1½-inch lengths

2 teaspoons extra-virgin olive oil

Salt and freshly ground pepper

24 baby artichokes (about 2 pounds)— outer leaves discarded, bottoms trimmed, artichokes quartered and rubbed with a lemon half

1½ cups low-sodium nonfat chicken broth

3 tablespoons fresh lemon juice

2 garlic cloves, thinly sliced

½ pound penne

¾ cup frozen baby peas, thawed

⅓ cup freshly grated Parmesan

3 tablespoons coarsely chopped flat-leaf parsley

1. Preheat the oven to 350°. Spread the pine nuts in a pie plate and bake for about 6 minutes, or until lightly toasted. Transfer to a plate. Increase the oven temperature to 450°.

2. In a bowl, toss the asparagus with 1 teaspoon of extra-virgin olive oil, 1½ teaspoons of salt and ¼ teaspoon of pepper. Spread the asparagus on a rimmed baking sheet and roast for 15 minutes, or until browned, shifting the pan every 5 minutes so the asparagus cooks evenly.

3. Meanwhile, in a large nonstick skillet, heat the remaining 1 teaspoon of extra-virgin olive oil. Add the baby artichokes, cut side down, and cook over moderate heat until just golden brown, about 5 minutes. Add the chicken broth, lemon juice and sliced garlic, cover and cook over low heat until the artichokes are just tender, about 8 minutes.

4. In a large pot of boiling salted water, cook the penne until al dente. Drain the pasta well and return it to the pot. Add the asparagus, artichokes, peas, grated Parmesan and chopped parsley and toss well. Transfer the pasta to warmed bowls; sprinkle with the toasted pine nuts and serve.

—*Ann Chantal Altman*

ONE SERVING Calories 368 kcal, Total Fat 8 gm, Saturated Fat 2.3 gm, Protein 20 gm, Carbohydrates 56 gm

Mediterranean Pasta with Broccoli

4 SERVINGS ●●

- 1½ **pounds broccoli, stalks peeled and sliced crosswise, florets broken into small pieces**
- ¾ **pound elbow macaroni**
- ¼ **cup extra-virgin olive oil**
- ½ **cup coarsely chopped walnuts**
- 3 **large garlic cloves, minced**
- 4 **oil-packed anchovy fillets, drained**
- ¼ **cup finely grated Parmigiano-Reggiano**

Salt and freshly ground pepper

1. Bring a large pot of salted water to a boil. Add the broccoli stalks and cook for 3 minutes, then add the pasta and cook, stirring occasionally, for 5 minutes. Add the broccoli florets and continue cooking until the pasta is al dente. Drain the pasta and broccoli and return them to the pot.

2. Meanwhile, heat the extra-virgin olive oil in a large, heavy skillet. Add the walnuts and cook over moderate heat, stirring, for 2 minutes. Add the garlic and anchovies and cook until the anchovies break down, about 2 minutes longer. Add the drained pasta and broccoli and toss well. Sprinkle with the Parmigiano, season with salt and pepper and serve.

—*Clifford A. Wright*

Fettuccine with Spicy Broccoli

4 SERVINGS ●

- 2 **tablespoons pine nuts**
- ¾ **pound dried fettuccine**
- 3 **tablespoons extra-virgin olive oil**
- 1½ **pounds broccoli, cut into 2-inch-wide florets with 3-inch stems**
- 4 **large garlic cloves, thinly sliced**
- ½ **teaspoon crushed red pepper**

Salt and freshly ground black pepper

- ½ **tablespoon unsalted butter**
- ½ **cup freshly grated Pecorino, plus more for serving**

1. In a large skillet, toast the pine nuts over moderate heat, shaking the pan occasionally, until the nuts are golden, about 2 minutes. Transfer to a plate.

2. In a large pot of boiling salted water, cook the pasta until al dente. Reserve

Mediterranean Pasta with Broccoli

½ cup of the pasta cooking water and drain the fettuccine.

3. Meanwhile, heat 2 tablespoons of the extra-virgin olive oil in the skillet and add the broccoli. Cover and cook over moderate heat until browned on the bottom, about 5 minutes. Stir the broccoli, then add the remaining 1 tablespoon of olive oil, the garlic and the crushed red pepper. Season the broccoli with salt and pepper and cook, stirring gently, until the garlic is fragrant, about 1 minute. Turn off the heat and cover.

4. Transfer the fettuccine to a warmed bowl and toss with the butter. Add the broccoli and the pasta cooking water and toss well. Sprinkle with the toasted pine nuts and the Pecorino and serve, passing more cheese at the table. —*Marcia Kiesel*

Orecchiette with Cauliflower, Anchovies and Pistachios

Orecchiette with Cauliflower, Anchovies and Pistachios

6 SERVINGS ● ●

Pasta dishes sampled in Sicily served as the inspiration for this nutty and earthy orecchiette.

- ½ **cup unsalted pistachios**
- 1 **head cauliflower, cut into small florets**
- 1 **stick (4 ounces) unsalted butter, cut into tablespoons**
- 5 **oil-packed anchovy fillets, drained and minced**
- 1½ **cups chicken stock or canned low-sodium broth**
- 1 **pound orecchiette**
- ½ **cup coarsely chopped flat-leaf parsley**
- ½ **cup freshly grated Parmesan**
- 1 **teaspoon crushed red pepper**

Salt and freshly ground pepper

1. Preheat the oven to 350°. Spread the pistachios in a pie plate and bake for about 5 minutes, or until lightly toasted. Let cool, then coarsely chop.

2. In a medium saucepan of boiling water, blanch the cauliflower florets for 1 minute. Drain and set aside.

3. In a large, deep skillet, cook the butter over moderate heat until golden brown, about 4 minutes. Add the cauliflower and cook over moderately high heat until golden. Add the anchovies and cook, stirring, for 2 minutes. Stir in the stock and cook until the cauliflower is tender, about 3 minutes.

4. Meanwhile, in a large pot of boiling salted water, cook the orecchiette until al dente. Drain the pasta and add it to the skillet. Stir in the parsley, Parmesan and crushed red pepper and season with salt and pepper. Transfer to a warmed bowl, sprinkle with the chopped pistachios and serve.

—*Barbara Lynch*

WINE Highlight the saltiness of the anchovies and Parmesan in this pasta with a young, very dry and fragrant rosé that has a slightly bitter edge. Try the 1999 Tasca d'Almerita Regaleali Rosato from Sicily or the delicious 1999 Mastroberardino Irpinia Rosato Lacrimarosa.

Pasta with Mushrooms and Mascarpone

6 SERVINGS ● ●

Campanelle is a festive pasta shaped like bellflowers. Medium pasta shells are a fine substitute.

- 4 **tablespoons unsalted butter**
- ¼ **cup coarse fresh bread crumbs**
- 1 **pound campanelle pasta**
- 1 **pound assorted stemmed mushrooms, such as cremini, shiitakes and chanterelles, thickly sliced**

Salt and freshly ground pepper

- ¼ **cup heavy cream**
- 1 **cup mascarpone (½ pound), at room temperature**
- 2 **tablespoons snipped chives**

1. Melt ½ tablespoon of the butter in a large, deep skillet. When the foam subsides, add the bread crumbs and cook over moderately high heat, stirring, until golden and crisp, 4 to 5 minutes. Transfer the bread crumbs to a plate and wipe out the skillet with a paper towel.

2. In a large pot of boiling salted water, cook the pasta until just barely al dente. Drain the pasta, reserving 1½ cups of the pasta cooking water.

3. Meanwhile, melt the remaining 3½ tablespoons of butter in the skillet. Add the mushrooms, season with salt and pepper and cook over high heat, stirring, until tender and lightly browned, about 5 minutes. Add the cream and cook over moderate heat, scraping up any browned bits from the bottom of the pan, until almost evaporated, about 2 minutes. Stir in the mascarpone and ¾ cup of the reserved pasta cooking water and cook until a creamy sauce forms.

4. Add the pasta to the sauce and toss gently over moderate heat until fully coated and cooked through, about 3

Pasta with Mushrooms and Mascarpone

minutes; add the remaining ¾ cup of pasta cooking water as needed to keep the pasta moist. Transfer to a large, warmed bowl, sprinkle with the toasted bread crumbs and chives and serve. —*Barbara Lynch*

WINE Contrast the earthiness of the mushrooms in this dish with a rich but medium-bodied red wine that has lots of fruit. A Dolcetto d'Alba, such as the 1999 Giacosa Falletto or the 1999 Ceretto Rossana, would be ideal.

Pennette with Zucchini, Ricotta Salata and Fresh Herbs

4 SERVINGS ●

- ¼ cup extra-virgin olive oil
- 3 small zucchini, sliced into ¼-inch rounds
- 1 garlic clove, minced

Salt and freshly ground pepper

- ½ pound ricotta salata, crumbled (about 2 cups)
- ¼ cup finely chopped basil
- 2 tablespoons snipped chives
- 1 tablespoon finely chopped mint
- 2 teaspoons finely chopped oregano
- 1 pint grape tomatoes, halved lengthwise
- ½ pound pennette or other pasta

1. Heat 1 tablespoon of the olive oil in a large, deep skillet. Add the zucchini and garlic and cook over moderately high heat, stirring frequently, until the garlic is golden and the zucchini crisp-tender, about 5 minutes. Season the zucchini with salt and pepper.

2. In a large bowl, mix the ricotta salata with the basil, chives, mint, oregano and the remaining 3 tablespoons of olive oil. Stir in the tomatoes.

3. Cook the pasta in a large pot of boiling salted water until al dente. Drain the pasta, reserving 3 tablespoons of the cooking water. Add the pasta, zucchini and reserved cooking water to the ricotta and season with salt and pepper. Toss well and serve.

—*Joanne Weir*

Fettuccine with Grated Beets and Cheese

6 SERVINGS ●

- 3 tablespoons poppy seeds
- 6 tablespoons unsalted butter
- 1½ pounds beets, peeled and finely grated in a food processor

Salt and freshly ground pepper

- 1 pound fresh or dried fettuccine
- ⅔ cup freshly grated Parmigiano-Reggiano
- 1 teaspoon balsamic vinegar
- ¼ cup minced chives, for garnish

1. In a large, heavy saucepan, toast the poppy seeds over high heat, stirring, until they smell slightly nutty, about 2 minutes. Transfer to a small bowl. Add 5 tablespoons of the butter to the saucepan and cook over moderate heat until beginning to brown, about 5 minutes. Stir in the beets and season with salt and pepper. Reduce the heat to low, cover and cook until tender, about 10 minutes.

2. Meanwhile, in a large pot of boiling salted water, cook the pasta until al dente. Drain and transfer to a large warmed serving bowl. Toss the pasta with the remaining 1 tablespoon of butter and the grated cheese; season with salt and pepper. Stir in the beets and sprinkle the pasta with the toasted poppy seeds. Add the balsamic vinegar to the fettuccine, garnish with chives, season again with salt and pepper and serve. —*Melissa Clark*

Farfalle with Savoy Cabbage, Pancetta and Mozzarella

4 SERVINGS

- ¼ cup extra-virgin olive oil
- ¼ pound thinly sliced pancetta
- 3 tablespoons pine nuts
- 2 teaspoons chopped thyme leaves
- 1 garlic clove, minced
- 1 head of Savoy cabbage (about 1¾ pounds)— quartered, cored and cut crosswise into ½-inch ribbons

Salt and freshly ground pepper

TOP: **Fettuccine with Grated Beets and Cheese**
CENTER: **Farfalle with Savoy Cabbage, Pancetta and Mozzarella**
BOTTOM: **Farfalle with Pancetta and Peas**

½ cup water
¼ cup freshly grated Parmesan
1 pound farfalle
7 ounces fresh mozzarella, preferably buffalo, cut into ½-inch dice

1. Heat 1 tablespoon of the olive oil in a large, deep nonstick skillet. Add the pancetta and cook over moderate heat, turning once, until golden, about 5 minutes. Transfer the pancetta to a cutting board and coarsely chop. Strain the fat through a fine sieve; wipe out the skillet and pour the fat back in.

2. Add the pine nuts to the skillet and cook over moderate heat, stirring, until golden, about 3 minutes. Using a slotted spoon, transfer the nuts to a plate. Add the thyme and garlic to the skillet and cook, stirring, until fragrant, about 1 minute. Add the cabbage and toss to coat with fat. Cover the skillet and cook over moderately low heat until the cabbage is wilted, about 3 minutes. Season with salt and pepper. Add the water and Parmesan, cover and cook until the cabbage is tender, about 10 minutes.

3. Meanwhile, cook the farfalle in boiling salted water until al dente. Drain the pasta and shake dry, then return it to the pot. Add the cabbage, mozzarella, pancetta, pine nuts and the remaining 3 tablespoons of olive oil and toss until the cheese is slightly melted. Season with salt and pepper. Transfer to a bowl and serve.

—*Jamie Oliver*

Farfalle with Pancetta and Peas

6 SERVINGS ●

1 pound farfalle
3 tablespoons extra-virgin olive oil
6 ounces thickly sliced pancetta, cut into 1-by-¼-inch matchsticks
1 large Spanish onion, chopped
4 large garlic cloves, thinly sliced

Four-Cheese Macaroni and Cheese

1 pound tomatoes, coarsely chopped
½ teaspoon crushed red pepper
¾ cup frozen baby peas, thawed
Salt and freshly ground pepper
¼ cup shredded mint leaves
¾ cup fresh ricotta
Freshly grated Parmesan, for serving

1. In a large pot of boiling salted water, cook the farfalle until al dente. Drain the pasta and reserve 1 cup of the cooking water.

2. In a large, deep skillet, heat the olive oil until shimmering. Add the pancetta and cook over moderately high heat until browned, about 5 minutes. Using a slotted spoon, transfer the pancetta to a plate. Add the onion to the skillet and cook over moderate heat, stirring frequently, until softened, about 5 minutes. Add the garlic and cook until it begins to brown, 6 to 7 minutes. Add the tomatoes and crushed red pepper and cook for 2 minutes. Stir in the peas and season with salt and pepper.

3. Add the farfalle to the skillet along with ½ cup of the reserved cooking water and toss over moderate heat until coated with the sauce. Stir in the pancetta and mint. Transfer the pasta to bowls and dollop the ricotta on top. Serve at once, passing the Parmesan at the table. —*Don Pintabona*

WINE Either a red or white with good acidity will blend with the tomatoes, creamy ricotta, and salty pancetta here. Look for a fruity, light and lively Zinfandel, such as the 1998 Steele Clear Lake Catfish Vineyard from California. Or try a fresh, clean, spicy Pinot Grigio, such as the 2000 Santa Margherita Alto Adige from Italy.

Four-Cheese Macaroni and Cheese

6 SERVINGS ●

1 pound orecchiette or rigatoni
2 cups milk
6 tablespoons unsalted butter
1 medium onion, finely chopped
3 tablespoons all-purpose flour
6 ounces Taleggio cheese, rind discarded, cheese finely chopped
¼ pound Italian Fontina, shredded

Soba Noodle Salad with Smoked Duck

5. Preheat the boiler. Broil the macaroni and cheese for 2 minutes, or until browned. Let stand for about 5 minutes before serving. —*Don Pintabona*

MAKE AHEAD The macaroni and cheese can be assembled and refrigerated for 1 day. Bake at 350° for 40 minutes before broiling.

Soba Noodle Salad with Smoked Duck

4 SERVINGS ●

- ¾ pound soba noodles
- 7 tablespoons peanut oil
- 5 tablespoons soy sauce
- 2 tablespoons rice vinegar
- 2 teaspoons Asian sesame oil
- 2 garlic cloves, minced
- Dash of hot sauce
- ½ pound smoked duck or chicken, cut into thick matchsticks
- ⅓ cup chopped chives
- 2 scallions, white and light green parts only, sliced

1. In a large pot of boiling salted water, cook the soba noodles until al dente. Drain and transfer to a large bowl. Toss the cooked noodles with 1 tablespoon of the peanut oil.

2. In a large bowl, whisk the soy sauce together with the rice vinegar, sesame oil, garlic and hot sauce. Slowly whisk in the remaining 6 tablespoons of peanut oil. Add the noodles to the dressing, and toss to coat. Add the duck and chives, garnish with the scallions and serve at room temperature. —*Melissa Clark*

Crispy Saffron Noodle Cake

6 SIDE-DISH SERVINGS ●

- ⅛ teaspoon saffron threads, finely crushed
- 1 teaspoon hot water
- 2 tablespoons unsalted butter
- 1 garlic clove, halved
- ⅓ cup freshly grated Parmesan
- ½ pound egg linguine
- 12 coriander seeds, coarsely ground
- Salt and freshly ground pepper

1. Preheat the oven to 475°. In a small bowl, mix the crushed saffron threads with the water and let stand for at least 10 minutes.

- 3 ounces Robiola cheese, rind removed
- Salt and freshly ground pepper
- 2 ounces Gorgonzola Dolce Latte, crumbled
- ⅓ cup coarse dry bread crumbs

1. Preheat the oven to 350°. In a large pot of boiling salted water, cook the orecchiette until al dente; drain.

2. Meanwhile, in a small saucepan, bring the milk to a simmer, then remove from the heat.

3. In a large saucepan, melt 4 tablespoons of the butter. Add the onion and cook over moderate heat, stirring, until softened, about 5 minutes. Add the flour and cook, stirring, for 1 minute. Slowly pour in the milk, whisking constantly until smooth. Bring to a simmer and cook over low heat for 3 minutes, whisking often. Stir in the Taleggio, Fontina and Robiola until melted. Remove the pan from the heat and stir in the orecchiette. Season with salt and pepper.

4. Transfer the pasta to a buttered 4-quart baking dish. Top with the Gorgonzola, then the bread crumbs. Dot with 2 tablespoons of butter and bake for about 25 minutes, or until bubbling.

Crispy Saffron Noodle Cake

2. Melt the butter in a small saucepan. Add the saffron liquid, remove from the heat and let stand for 10 minutes.

3. Rub a 10-inch ovenproof nonstick skillet with the garlic. Brush the skillet with 1 teaspoon of the saffron butter. Sprinkle with 2 tablespoons of the Parmesan.

4. In a large pot of boiling salted water, cook the noodles until al dente. Drain and rinse; pat dry. Toss the noodles with the remaining saffron butter and season with the coriander and salt and pepper. Spread the noodles in the skillet, pressing lightly. Sprinkle with the remaining Parmesan and bake for 30 minutes, or until golden and crisp. Invert the noodle cake onto a work surface, cut into wedges and serve.

—*Sally Schneider*

ONE SERVING Calories 206 kcal, Total Fat 7.4 gm, Saturated Fat 3.9 gm

Asian Noodles with Fresh and Pickled Greens

6 TO 8 SERVINGS ● ●

- 1 **pound dried rice noodles (about ¼ inch wide)**
- ½ **pound package frozen edamame (soy beans) or 1 heaping cup shelled beans**
- ⅔ **cup chopped rinsed pickled mustard greens or rinsed sauerkraut**
- 2 **tablespoons coarsely chopped fermented black beans**
- ⅓ **cup plus 2 tablespoons vegetable oil**
- ¼ **cup water**
- 3 **tablespoons rice vinegar**
- 1 **tablespoon Dijon mustard**
- ¼ **pound young mustard greens, stemmed and chopped (2 packed cups)**

Salt and freshly ground pepper

1. Soak the noodles in cold water until pliable, about 10 minutes.

2. In a medium saucepan of boiling salted water, cook the edamame until tender, 5 to 6 minutes. Drain and rinse

Asian Noodles with Fresh and Pickled Greens

under cold water, then pat dry. Shell the edamame if necessary and transfer to a large bowl.

3. In a large saucepan of boiling salted water, cook the noodles, stirring, until tender, about 3 minutes. Drain, rinse under cold water and pat dry. Add the noodles to the edamame along with the pickled greens and fermented beans, and toss with 2 tablespoons of the oil.

4. In a bowl, whisk the water with the rice vinegar, mustard and the remaining ⅓ cup of oil. Add to the noodles and toss. Add the fresh mustard greens, season with salt and pepper and serve. —*Ilene Rosen*

MAKE AHEAD The dish can stand at room temperature for up to 2 hours.

WINE A light but highly acidic and fruity Sauvignon Blanc will point up the peppery greens and balance the tangy dressing. Try the 2000 Geyser Peak or the 1999 Meridian from California.

Stir-Fried Rice Noodles with Kohlrabi and Basil

4 SERVINGS ●●

The star of this dish is the turnip-like vegetable kohlrabi; it's sliced and sautéed until browned, which enhances its sweetness and adds a light crispness. The rice noodles can be found at Asian markets.

  8 cups water
10 ounces dried rice noodles (about ⅓ inch wide)
  5 tablespoons soy sauce
  1 tablespoon dry white wine
  1 tablespoon sugar
  ½ teaspoon Chinese chili oil
  3 tablespoons peanut oil
  1 pound kohlrabi—peeled, halved and thinly sliced
  1 red bell pepper, thinly sliced
1½ tablespoons minced garlic
  2 large eggs, lightly beaten
  1 cup mung bean sprouts
  2 scallions, sliced on the diagonal
  1 cup chopped basil

1. Bring the water to a boil. Remove from the heat, add the rice noodles and let soak until the noodles are tender, about 7 minutes. Drain well.

2. In a small bowl, stir together the soy sauce, white wine, sugar and chili oil.

3. In a large skillet or a wok with a handle, heat the peanut oil. Add the kohlrabi and cook over moderately high heat until browned, about 3 minutes. Stir and cook for 1 minute. Add the red pepper and garlic and stir-fry until the garlic is fragrant, about 2 minutes. Add the eggs; stir-fry until just set, about 30 seconds.

4. Add the rice noodles, bean sprouts, scallions, basil and the soy sauce mixture. Cook over moderately low heat, tossing gently, until the noodles are heated through and coated with sauce, about 1 minute. Transfer the noodles to plates or bowls and serve at once. —*Stephanie Lyness*

Pasta with Anchovies and Pan-Toasted Bread Crumbs

4 FIRST-COURSE SERVINGS ●

Like many Sicilian pastas, this traditional dish from Siracusa is sprinkled with toasted bread crumbs instead of grated cheese.

10 oil-packed anchovy fillets, drained
Milk, for soaking
  ½ cup coarse fresh bread crumbs
  ⅓ cup extra-virgin olive oil
  1 garlic clove, smashed
  ¼ teaspoon crushed red pepper
  ½ pound spaghettini
  2 tablespoons coarsely chopped flat-leaf parsley

1. In a bowl, cover the anchovies with milk and soak for 10 minutes. Drain well and finely chop. In a small dry skillet, lightly toast the bread crumbs over moderate heat until golden brown, about 4 minutes. Transfer the bread crumbs to a plate and let cool.

2. Heat the olive oil in a large skillet. Add the garlic and cook over moderate heat until golden, about 2 minutes.

Stir-Fried Rice Noodles with Kohlrabi and Basil

Remove from the heat and discard the garlic. Add the crushed red pepper and anchovies to the garlic oil and mash the anchovies against the side of the pan with a wooden spoon until a smooth puree forms. Cook the anchovy sauce over moderately low heat for 1 minute, then remove from the heat.

3. In a large pot of boiling salted water, cook the pasta until just al dente. Drain the pasta, reserving 3 tablespoons of the pasta cooking water.

4. Add the pasta water to the anchovy sauce and warm over moderately low heat. Add the pasta and toss to coat. Transfer the pasta to a warmed serving bowl, toss with the bread crumbs and parsley and serve. —*Paula Wolfert*

WINE The anchovies in this pasta have a particular affinity with refreshing, fruity and slightly chilled rosés. Look for a good Sicilian example, such as the 1999 Regaleali Rosato, or try a California bottling, such as the 1999 Swanson Rosato Napa Valley.

Spicy Linguine with Halibut and Tomato

4 SERVINGS ●●

- 1 pound white fish fillets, such as halibut or cod, cut into ¼-inch strips
- ¼ cup extra-virgin olive oil
- ¼ cup finely chopped basil
- 4 garlic cloves, 1 crushed and 3 minced
- 2 small dried red chiles
- 1 small onion, finely chopped
- 1 pound plum tomatoes—peeled, seeded and chopped
- 1 cup dry white wine

Salt and freshly ground pepper

- ¾ pound linguine

1. Toss the fish with 2 tablespoons of olive oil and the basil. In a large enameled cast-iron casserole, combine the remaining 2 tablespoons of olive oil with the crushed garlic and dried chiles. Cook over moderately high heat, stirring frequently, until the garlic turns golden brown. Discard the garlic and chiles.

2. Add the minced garlic and onion to the casserole and cook, stirring occasionally, until softened, about 4 minutes. Stir in the tomatoes and wine, reduce the heat to moderate and simmer for 15 minutes. Raise the heat to moderately high, add the fish, and cook, stirring, until opaque, about 5 minutes. Season with salt and pepper.

3. Meanwhile, cook the linguine in a large pot of boiling salted water until al dente; drain. Add the pasta to the fish sauce, toss well and serve.

—*Clifford A. Wright*

Linguine with Tuna, Garlic and Olive Oil

6 SERVINGS ●●

This is one of those quick dishes you can make with what you probably have on hand. It's healthy as it is with all that parsley (an excellent source of vitamins A and C), but you can boost your greens by adding a vegetable

Spicy Linguine with Halibut and Tomato

such as broccoli or rapini to the pasta cooking water about three minutes before the pasta is done. Drain the pasta and greens together, then return them to the pot, pour the sauce on top and continue as directed.

- 1 pound linguine
- 4 large garlic cloves, minced
- ¼ cup extra-virgin olive oil

One 6-ounce can of Italian tuna packed in olive oil, drained and flaked

- ¾ cup minced flat-leaf parsley
- ½ teaspoon crushed red pepper

Salt and freshly ground pepper

1. Cook the linguine in a large pot of boiling salted water, stirring occasionally, until al dente. Reserve 1 cup of the pasta cooking water, then drain the pasta and return it to the pot.

2. Meanwhile, in a small saucepan, cook the minced garlic in the extra-virgin olive oil over low heat until lightly browned, about 10 minutes. Add ½ cup of the reserved linguine cooking water and the flaked tuna, chopped parsley and crushed red pepper and cook over moderate heat for 2 minutes.

3. Pour the tuna sauce into the pot with the linguine, add the remaining ½ cup of pasta cooking water and simmer over high heat, tossing, until the sauce is mostly absorbed, about 2 minutes. Season with salt and pepper and serve. —*Nancy Harmon Jenkins*

ONE SERVING Calories 434 kcal, Total Fat 15.3 gm, Saturated Fat 2.2 gm, Protein 16 gm, Carbohydrates 58 gm

WINE The garlicky sauce, meaty tuna

Spicy Scallops with Capellini

cook over moderately high heat, turning once, until browned on both sides and pink in the center, about 6 minutes. Transfer to a plate. When cool enough to handle, cut the tuna into 1-inch pieces.

2. In a large pot of boiling salted water, cook the linguine until al dente; drain.

3. Meanwhile, heat the remaining ¼ cup plus 2 tablespoons of olive oil in a large, deep skillet. Add the onions, cover and cook over moderate heat, stirring occasionally, until softened, about 8 minutes. Add the lemon zest and garlic and cook over moderately high heat, stirring, until fragrant, about 3 minutes. Add the lemon juice, olives, capers and tuna and stir until heated through, about 2 minutes. Add the linguine to the skillet and toss. Season with salt and pepper, sprinkle with the parsley and serve.

—Joyce Goldstein

Spicy Scallops with Capellini

4 SERVINGS ●

This simple and delicious recipe is based on Chilean pil-pil sauce. Dried hot red chiles are mandatory, as are garlic and olive oil; the sauce invariably accompanies seafood. In Chile the recipe is served in individual earthenware dishes and eaten with bread to scoop up the sauce.

- 1 pound scallops, quartered if large
- 6 tablespoons extra-virgin olive oil
- ¼ cup dry white wine
- 2 tablespoons finely chopped flat-leaf parsley
- 1 tablespoon minced garlic
- 1 small dried chipotle chile with seeds, stemmed and finely chopped

Fine sea salt
- ½ pound capellini

1. Preheat the oven to 400°. Bring a large pot of salted water to a boil. In a large glass or ceramic baking dish, toss the scallops with the extra-virgin olive oil, wine, parsley, garlic and

and spicy crushed red pepper in this recipe all point to a tart but assertive white, such as a Tocai Friulano from Italy, as a perfect flavor foil. Among the top choices to look for are the 1998 Ronco del Gnemiz and the 1998 Schiopetto.

Linguine with Fresh Tuna, Olives and Capers

4 SERVINGS ● ●

- 1 pound albacore or ahi tuna steak, about ¾ inch thick

Salt and freshly ground pepper
- ½ cup extra-virgin olive oil
- 1 pound linguine
- 2 medium red onions, halved lengthwise and thinly sliced crosswise
- 3 tablespoons finely grated lemon zest
- 2 tablespoons very finely chopped garlic
- ¼ cup fresh lemon juice
- 12 Calamata olives (2 ounces), pitted and coarsely chopped
- 2 tablespoons capers, drained and coarsely chopped
- 2 tablespoons chopped flat-leaf parsley

1. Season the tuna with salt and pepper. Heat 2 tablespoons of the olive oil in a large skillet. Add the tuna and chipotle. Season with salt and bake for about 15 minutes, or until the oil is sizzling and the scallops are firm.

2. Add the capellini to the boiling water and cook until just al dente, about 3 minutes. Drain the pasta and transfer to a serving bowl. Add the scallops and their juices to the pasta, toss well and serve immediately.

—*Ruth Van Waerebeek*

WINE Tame the hot chile peppers and garlic in this dish with a refreshingly fruity off-dry Riesling. Look for the 2000 Hogue Cellars from Washington State or the 2000 Bonny Doon Vineyard Pacific Rim from California.

Spaghettini with Shrimp, Olives and Tomatoes

6 SERVINGS ● ●

This easy and flavorful variation on pasta with shrimp and garlic is perfect for a quick midweek meal. Buy the shrimp already shelled and deveined to make the recipe even faster.

- 1 pound spaghettini
- 3 tablespoons extra-virgin olive oil
- ¼ teaspoon crushed red pepper
- 3 garlic cloves, minced
- 2 large plum tomatoes, cut into ¼-inch dice

Salt

- 1 pound medium shrimp, shelled and deveined, tails left on
- ½ cup oil-cured black olives, pitted and coarsely chopped

Freshly ground pepper

- ½ cup flat-leaf parsley, finely chopped

1. In a large pot of boiling salted water, cook the pasta until al dente. Reserve ½ cup of the pasta cooking water. Drain the spaghettini and return it to the pot.

2. Meanwhile, heat the olive oil in a medium skillet. Add the crushed red pepper and cook over low heat, stirring, for 2 minutes. Add the garlic and cook until fragrant, about 2 minutes. Stir in the tomatoes and cook over

moderate heat for 3 minutes. Season with salt. Add the shrimp and cook until they turn pink and begin to curl, about 3 minutes. Stir in the olives and reserved pasta cooking water and cook until the sauce thickens slightly, about 2 minutes. Season with salt and pepper. Toss the pasta with the sauce and parsley to coat, transfer to a warmed bowl and serve.

—*Barbara Lynch*

WINE The 1999 San Felice Belcaro, a lemony Tuscan Sauvignon Blanc, pairs well with the olives and tomatoes in this dish.

Pecorino Ravioli with Orange Zest

4 SERVINGS ●

If you're not inclined to make pasta, you can buy gyoza wrappers from your local Asian market for these potent Pecorino ravioli; lightly moisten the edges of the wrappers before folding them over the cheese in Step 3.

- 1 cup plus 2 tablespoons all-purpose flour
- 3 large egg yolks, lightly beaten
- 1 large egg, lightly beaten
- ½ tablespoon milk
- 1 teaspoon extra-virgin olive oil

One 6-ounce piece of Pecorino, preferably Sardinian or Pecorino Romano, cut into twenty-four 1½-by-1-by-⅛-inch rectangles, plus more for grating

Salt

- 4 tablespoons unsalted butter
- 1¼ teaspoons finely grated orange zest

Freshly ground pepper

1. In a food processor, pulse the flour a few times. Add the lightly beaten egg yolks and whole egg, the milk and the extra-virgin olive oil and process the ingredients until they form a dough. Scrape the dough out onto a work surface and knead until smooth, about 2 minutes. Flatten the ravioli dough into a disk, wrap in plastic and let stand at

room temperature for at least 30 minutes or for up to 2 hours.

2. Cut the dough into 4 equal pieces; work with 1 piece at a time and keep the rest wrapped. Flatten the dough with your hands and run it through successively narrower settings on a pasta machine until you reach the thinnest. Cut the pasta sheet into six 3½-inch squares. Transfer the squares to a lightly floured baking sheet and cover with plastic wrap. Repeat with the remaining pasta dough.

3. Lay a pasta square on the work surface. Set a piece of cheese ⅓ inch from the bottom edge; fold the top of the square over the cheese to make a neat rectangle. Press lightly all around the filling to release any air. Repeat with the remaining pasta and cheese. Using a fluted pastry cutter, trim the ravioli edges to seal them. Transfer the ravioli to a lightly floured baking sheet, cover with plastic wrap and refrigerate for up to 3 hours.

4. Bring a large saucepan of water to a boil. Salt the water generously, add the Pecorino ravioli and boil just until al dente.

5. Meanwhile, melt the butter in a large skillet and add the orange zest. In a colander, drain the ravioli, allowing a little of the cooking water to remain so they don't stick. Add the ravioli to the skillet and gently toss with the butter to coat. Transfer the ravioli to shallow bowls. Season with pepper and garnish with a little grated Pecorino. Serve at once.

—*FOOD & WINE Test Kitchen*

MAKE AHEAD The uncooked ravioli can be frozen for up to 1 month.

WINE Two disparate elements—the salty, sharp Pecorino filling and the fruity orange zest garnish—balance the big flavors of the 1997 Robert Craig Cabernet Sauvignon, the 1997 Dunn Vineyards Cabernet Sauvignon and the 1999 Howell Mountain Vineyards Zinfandel.

Shrimp and Fennel Ravioli

4 SERVINGS ●

RAVIOLI

- 1 tablespoon unsalted butter
- ½ small fennel bulb—halved, cored and coarsely chopped, fronds chopped for garnish
- 1 medium leek, white and tender green parts only, finely chopped

Salt and freshly ground pepper

- 12 medium shrimp, shelled and deveined, 8 shrimp cut into ¼-inch dice
- 24 round gyoza skins
- 1 egg white, lightly beaten

SAUCE

- 3 tablespoons dry white wine
- 2 tablespoons minced shallots
- ¼ teaspoon finely grated fresh ginger
- ½ cup low-sodium nonfat chicken broth
- 1½ teaspoons soy sauce
- 1½ teaspoons cornstarch dissolved in 1 tablespoon cold water

Salt and freshly ground pepper

- ¼ cup snipped chives

1. MAKE THE RAVIOLI: Melt the butter in a small saucepan. Add the fennel and leek, cover and cook over low heat, stirring occasionally, until softened but not browned, about 15 minutes. Season generously with salt and pepper. Transfer to a bowl and let cool completely, then stir in the raw diced shrimp.

2. Lay the gyoza skins side by side on a work surface. Spoon 1 rounded tablespoon of shrimp filling into the center of 12 of the skins, then lightly brush the edges with the beaten egg white. Top with the remaining 12 skins; push out any air pockets and press to seal at the edges. Transfer the ravioli to a lightly floured baking sheet, cover and refrigerate.

3. MAKE THE SAUCE: In a small saucepan, cook the white wine and minced shallots over moderately high heat until reduced by half, about 2 minutes. Scrape the mixture into a blender and add the ginger. With the machine on, slowly add the chicken broth and blend until smooth. Return to the saucepan. Add the soy sauce and bring to a boil. Stir in the cornstarch slurry and simmer for 1 minute, stirring constantly. Season with salt and pepper.

4. In a large pot of boiling salted water, cook the ravioli until they float to the surface and the shrimp filling turns pink, about 3 minutes. Transfer the ravioli to warmed plates with a slotted spoon.

5. Add the remaining 4 shrimp to the boiling water. Cook just until pink, about 1 minute. Garnish the ravioli with the shrimp. Spoon the sauce on top, sprinkle with the fennel fronds and chives and serve.

—*Ann Chantal Altman*

ONE SERVING Calories 192 kcal, Total Fat 4.1 gm, Saturated Fat 2.1 gm, Protein 11 gm, Carbohydrates 28 gm

Pasta with Mussels and Tomatoes

4 SERVINGS ● ● ●

- 5 tablespoons extra-virgin olive oil
- 1 medium onion, minced
- 1 large garlic clove, thinly sliced
- 1½ cups dry white wine
- 1 pound plum tomatoes, peeled and chopped
- ½ teaspoon crushed red pepper
- 2 pounds mussels, scrubbed and debearded

Salt and freshly ground pepper

- ¾ pound spaghettini
- ¼ cup chopped flat-leaf parsley

1. Heat 3 tablespoons of the olive oil in a large, deep skillet until shimmering. Add the onion and garlic and cook over moderate heat until fragrant and softened, about 6 minutes. Increase the heat to moderately high, add the wine and boil until reduced to ½ cup, about 12 minutes. Add the tomatoes,

Shrimp and Fennel Ravioli

crushed red pepper and mussels. Cover and cook until the mussels open, about 5 minutes. Transfer the mussels with a slotted spoon to a large warmed bowl. Season the sauce with salt and pepper, cover and remove the skillet from the heat.

2. Meanwhile, in a large pot of boiling salted water, cook the pasta until al dente. Drain the pasta, reserving ½ cup of the cooking water.

3. Add the pasta and the water to the sauce and toss over low heat for 1 minute. Add the pasta and the sauce to the mussels and toss. Sprinkle with the parsley, drizzle with the remaining 2 tablespoons of olive oil and serve.

—*George Germon and Johanne Killeen*

Orecchiette with Broccoli Rabe and Chicken

4 SERVINGS ●

- 2 pounds broccoli rabe, thick stems discarded
- 1¼ pounds skinless, boneless chicken thighs, trimmed of all visible fat and sliced ½ inch thick

Salt and freshly ground pepper

- 2 tablespoons plus 2 teaspoons extra-virgin olive oil
- 2 cups orecchiette
- 6 garlic cloves, thinly sliced
- ½ teaspoon crushed red pepper
- ¾ cup low-sodium nonfat chicken broth
- ¼ cup freshly grated Parmesan

1. In a large pot of boiling salted water, blanch the broccoli rabe for 3 minutes. Transfer to a large bowl of ice water and let cool. Drain the broccoli rabe well and coarsely chop.

2. Season the chicken with 1 teaspoon of salt and ½ teaspoon of pepper. In a large, deep skillet, heat 1 tablespoon of the olive oil until shimmering. Add half the chicken and cook over moderately high heat until deep brown all over, about 8 minutes. Transfer the chicken to a plate and repeat with another tablespoon of olive oil and the remaining chicken.

3. In a large pot of boiling salted water, cook the orecchiette until al dente. Heat the remaining 2 teaspoons of olive oil in the skillet. Add the garlic and crushed red pepper and cook over moderate heat, stirring constantly, until the garlic is golden. Add the chicken broth and scrape up any browned bits from the bottom of the pan. Return the chicken to the pan and cook until the broth is reduced by two-thirds, about 5 minutes. Add the broccoli rabe and cook until heated through, 1 minute.

4. Meanwhile, drain the pasta. Add it to the chicken and broccoli rabe and toss well. Transfer to warmed plates, sprinkle with the Parmesan and serve.

—*Ann Chantal Altman*

ONE SERVING Calories 484 kcal, Total Fat 17.4 gm, Saturated Fat 3.8 gm, Protein 41 gm, Carbohydrates 42 gm

Pappardelle with Pork, Walnuts and Olives

4 SERVINGS ●

3 tablespoons extra-virgin olive oil
1 small onion, minced
1 celery rib, minced
3 garlic cloves, minced
3 ounces thinly sliced pancetta, cut into narrow strips
⅓ cup finely chopped mint
1 pound pork tenderloin, cut into ½-inch dice
½ cup walnuts, coarsely chopped
½ cup coarsely chopped pitted Calamata olives
Salt and freshly ground pepper
½ cup dry white wine
¾ pound pappardelle or fettuccine
½ cup freshly grated Pecorino Romano

1. Heat the oil in a skillet. Add the minced onion, celery, garlic, pancetta and 3 tablespoons of the mint. Cook over moderately high heat, stirring, until the pancetta is slightly crisp, about 6 minutes.

2. Push the onion mixture to the side of the skillet. Add the pork and cook until browned, about 5 minutes. Stir in the walnuts and olives and season with salt and pepper; cook for 1 minute. Add the wine; simmer over moderate heat until reduced to 2 tablespoons, about 5 minutes.

3. In a large pot of boiling salted water, cook the pasta until al dente; drain well. Add the pasta to the skillet and toss with the sauce over moderately high heat for 1 minute. Serve the pasta in bowls, sprinkled with the remaining 2 tablespoons of mint and the cheese.

—*Clifford A. Wright*

Rigatoni with Spicy Sausage and Cannellini Beans

6 SERVINGS ●

Pork and white beans are classic partners in Tuscany. This recipe adds a twist: spicy sausage. For a mellower version of this pasta, try sweet Italian sausage instead.

2 tablespoons extra-virgin olive oil
4 garlic cloves, minced
1 large onion, coarsely chopped
1 pound hot Italian sausage, casings removed
1 cup dry red wine
One 28-ounce can peeled Italian tomatoes, drained and coarsely chopped, liquid reserved
½ teaspoon crushed red pepper
Salt and freshly ground pepper
1 pound rigatoni
One 19-ounce can cannellini beans, drained and rinsed
½ cup freshly grated Parmesan, plus more for serving
2 tablespoons coarsely chopped basil, plus leaves for garnish
2 tablespoons unsalted butter, cut into small pieces

1. In a large, deep skillet, heat the extra-virgin olive oil until shimmering. Add the minced garlic and cook over moderate heat, stirring, until golden, about 1 minute. Add the chopped onion and sausage; break the meat up with a wooden spoon and cook until it just loses its pink color, about 7 minutes. Add the red wine and cook over high heat until reduced by half, about 10 minutes. Stir in the chopped tomatoes, their liquid and the crushed red pepper and season with salt and freshly ground pepper. Cook over moderate heat until slightly thickened, about 30 minutes.

2. Meanwhile, in a large pot of boiling salted water, cook the rigatoni until al dente. Drain well, reserving ½ cup of the pasta cooking water.

3. Add the rigatoni to the sauce and gently stir in the beans, ½ cup of Parmesan, the chopped basil and the butter. Cook, stirring gently, until heated through, about 3 minutes. Add some of the reserved pasta cooking water if the pasta looks dry. Transfer to warmed bowls, garnish with basil leaves and serve. Pass additional Parmesan at the table.

—*Barbara Lynch*

WINE The berry fruit and peppery notes in a rich Syrah play off both the spicy sausage and the acidity of the tomatoes in the sauce. Pick a good example from Tuscany, such as the 1997 Isole e Olena or the more available 1997 Castello Banfi Sant'Antimo Colvecchio.

Pappardelle with Tangy Veal Ragù

Pappardelle with Tangy Veal Ragù

6 SERVINGS ● ●

Balsamic vinegar and red wine add a tangy bite to the hearty veal ragù. Have your butcher tie the veal shanks once around the center so they will hold together while browning.

Four 1-pound veal shanks, about
    2½ inches thick, tied
Salt and freshly ground pepper
All-purpose flour, for dredging
  ¼ cup extra-virgin olive oil
  4 garlic cloves, minced
  3 medium carrots, finely chopped
  2 celery ribs, finely chopped
  1 medium onion, finely chopped
  2 cups dry red wine
  ¾ cup balsamic vinegar
One 35-ounce can peeled Italian
    tomatoes, drained and coarsely
    chopped, liquid reserved
  2 cups beef stock or canned
    low-sodium broth
  1 fresh rosemary sprig about
    6 inches long, plus more
    rosemary sprigs for garnish
  ¼ cup finely chopped basil
  2 cups water
  1 pound pappardelle
Freshly grated Parmesan, for serving

1. Season the veal shanks with salt and pepper and dredge them in flour, shaking off the excess. In a large enameled cast-iron casserole, heat the olive oil until shimmering. Add the veal shanks and cook over high heat, turning, until browned all over, about 15 minutes. Transfer the veal shanks to a plate.

2. Add the garlic, carrots, celery and onion to the casserole and cook over moderate heat, stirring frequently, until lightly browned, about 5 minutes. Add the wine and balsamic vinegar and cook over high heat, stirring occasionally, until the liquid has reduced to a thick syrup, about 25 minutes.

3. Return the veal shanks to the casserole and add the tomatoes and their liquid, the beef broth, 1 rosemary sprig, 2 tablespoons of the basil and the water. Season with salt and pepper and bring to a boil. Cover partially and cook over low heat, stirring occasionally, until the veal is very tender, about 2½ hours.

4. Transfer the veal to a plate and let cool slightly. Discard the bones. Cut the meat into 1-inch pieces.

5. Strain the sauce through a fine sieve, pressing on the solids to extract as much liquid as possible; discard the solids. Rinse the casserole and return the sauce to it. Boil the sauce over high heat until reduced to 2½ cups, 8 to 10 minutes. Stir in the veal and the remaining 2 tablespoons of basil and season with salt and pepper. Keep the veal ragù warm over low heat.

6. In a large pot of boiling salted water, cook the pappardelle until al dente. Drain thoroughly and return to the pot. Add the veal ragù and toss gently. Transfer to a warmed large bowl, sprinkle with Parmesan and garnish with rosemary sprigs. Serve immediately, passing more Parmesan at the table.

—*Barbara Lynch*

MAKE AHEAD The veal ragù can be prepared through Step 5 and refrigerated for 3 days or frozen for 1 month.
WINE The succulent, tangy flavors in this dish go well with the bright ripe fruit and medium body and tannin of wines made from the Sagrantino grape. Try the fairly expensive 1996 Arnaldo Caprai Sagrantino di Montefalco or the less expensive 1996 Antonelli Sagrantino di Montefalco.

Penne with Spoon-Dropped Baby Meatballs in Green Sauce

4 SERVINGS ●

 10 ounces baby spinach,
    rinsed but not dried
  ¼ cup mascarpone
  3 tablespoons heavy cream
  4 garlic cloves, lightly crushed
Salt and freshly ground pepper
  1 small onion, quartered
  1 large egg
  1 teaspoon finely chopped
    rosemary
  ¾ pound lean ground beef
  6 tablespoons freshly grated
    Parmigiano-Reggiano
  3 tablespoons extra-virgin olive oil
  ½ cup dry white wine
  2 large egg yolks
  ¾ pound penne

1. Put the damp spinach in a large saucepan and cook over high heat until wilted, about 3 minutes. Transfer the spinach to a strainer and drain. In a food processor, combine the spinach with the mascarpone, 1 tablespoon of the heavy cream and 1 garlic clove and puree for 30 seconds. Transfer the spinach mixture to a bowl and season with salt and pepper.

2. Wipe out the bowl of the food processor. Add the onion quarters and 2 more garlic cloves and process until finely chopped. Add the whole egg and the rosemary and process for 30 seconds longer. Add the ground beef and ¼ cup of the Parmigiano. Season the meatball mixture with salt and pepper and process until blended.

3. In a large skillet, cook the remaining 1 garlic clove in 1 tablespoon of the olive oil over moderately high heat until the garlic begins to sizzle. Drop rounded teaspoons of the meat mixture into the pan and cook until sizzling, shaking the pan for even browning. Add the wine and the remaining 2 tablespoons of cream and cook for 3 minutes longer, stirring gently. Reduce the heat to low and add the spinach puree. Cover and cook until the sauce thickens slightly, about 10 minutes. In a bowl, beat the egg yolks with the remaining 2 tablespoons of grated Parmigiano and 2 tablespoons of olive oil and season with pepper.

4. Meanwhile, in a large pot of boiling salted water, cook the pasta until al

dente, then drain and transfer to a bowl. Toss the pasta with the egg yolk mixture, the green sauce and the meatballs and serve immediately.
—*Clifford A. Wright*

Spaghetti with Ground Lamb and Spinach

6 SERVINGS ●

2 tablespoons extra-virgin olive oil

1 small onion, chopped

3 large garlic cloves, finely chopped

1½ pounds ground lamb

⅓ cup tomato paste

¾ cup dry red wine

½ teaspoon dried oregano

Salt and freshly ground pepper

1¼ pounds baby spinach, chopped

3 tablespoons finely chopped mint

1 pound spaghetti

⅓ cup freshly grated Pecorino Romano, for sprinkling

1. In a large casserole, heat the olive oil over moderately high heat. Add the onion and garlic and cook, stirring, until translucent, about 5 minutes. Add the lamb and cook, stirring, until the meat is lightly browned, about 10 minutes. Stir in the tomato paste, wine and oregano; season with salt and pepper. Cover and simmer over low heat for 10 minutes. Add the spinach and mint and cook, covered, for 10 minutes longer.

2. Meanwhile, in a large pot of boiling salted water, cook the pasta until al dente. Drain the pasta, reserving ¼ cup of the cooking liquid. Toss the pasta with the cooking liquid and the ground lamb sauce. Serve at once with the Pecorino. —*Clifford A. Wright*

Roasted Carrot and Butternut Squash Cannelloni

4 FIRST-COURSE SERVINGS ●

You can use any good-quality white or green fresh pasta sheets for this vegetable-rich cannelloni. Look for the thinnest sheets possible and trim them to size with a sharp knife.

Roasted Carrot and Butternut Squash Cannelloni

3 large carrots, cut into 1-inch pieces

¾ pound butternut squash, peeled and cut into 1-inch dice (2 cups)

4 garlic cloves

1 teaspoon thyme leaves

2 tablespoons extra-virgin olive oil

Salt and freshly ground pepper

6 tablespoons freshly grated Parmesan (1½ ounces)

Pinch of freshly grated nutmeg

½ pound chanterelle mushrooms, thickly sliced if large

One ¾-pound bunch of Swiss chard, leaves only, coarsely chopped

1 cup chicken stock or canned low-sodium broth

1 tablespoon unsalted butter

24 small sage leaves

Eight 4-inch-square store-bought fresh pasta sheets (4 ounces)

1. Preheat the oven to 400°. On a large, rimmed nonstick baking sheet, toss the carrots and squash with the garlic, thyme and 1 tablespoon of the olive oil. Season with salt and pepper. Roast the vegetables for about 20 minutes, tossing once or twice, until golden and tender. Turn the oven down to 350°.

2. Transfer the garlic to a small bowl and mash with the back of a fork. Scrape the remaining vegetables into a medium bowl and coarsely mash them. Stir ¼ cup of the Parmesan and the nutmeg into the mashed vegetables. Season with salt and pepper.

3. In a large skillet, heat the remaining 1 tablespoon of oil until shimmering. Add the mushrooms, season with salt and pepper and cook over moderately high heat, stirring frequently, until softened, about 5 minutes. Add the Swiss chard and chicken stock and cook, stirring frequently, until the greens are tender and the liquid in the pan has reduced to a few tablespoons, about 10 minutes. Stir in the mashed garlic and season with salt and pepper. Keep warm.

4. Melt the butter in a small skillet. Add half of the sage leaves and cook over moderately high heat, stirring, until crisp, about 2 minutes. Drain on paper towels and sprinkle with salt. Repeat with the remaining sage leaves.

5. Bring a medium saucepan of salted water to a boil. Add the pasta sheets and cook until tender, about 4 minutes. Drain and shake off any excess water. Lay each sheet on a work surface and pat dry. Spoon 2½ tablespoons of the mashed carrots and squash into the center of each pasta sheet. Roll the pasta around the filling to form logs. Place the cannelloni, seam side down, in a small baking dish. Brush lightly with water and sprinkle with the remaining 2 tablespoons of Parmesan.

6. Bake the cannelloni for about 5 minutes, or until golden and heated through. Spoon the warm chanterelle mushrooms and Swiss chard in the center of large plates and top with the cannelloni. Garnish the cannelloni with the crisp sage leaves and serve.

—*Toni Robertson*

ONE SERVING Calories 256 kcal, Total Fat 13.3 gm, Saturated Fat 4.4 gm, Protein 9 gm, Carbohydrates 29 gm

MAKE AHEAD The Roasted Carrot and Butternut Squash Cannelloni can be prepared through Step 3 and refrigerated overnight.

Tuscan-Style Lasagna

8 SERVINGS ●●

A typical Tuscan style ragù, the sauce in this recipe consists mainly of simmered meats with only a touch of tomato and is used with a creamy white sauce to bind this rich lasagna.

- 2 tablespoons olive oil
- 5 garlic cloves, minced
- 3 medium carrots, minced
- 2 celery ribs, minced
- 1 medium onion, minced
- ⅓ pound chicken livers, trimmed and coarsely chopped (optional)
- 2 tablespoons coarsely chopped sage
- 1 pound ground veal
- 1 pound ground lean pork
- 1 pound ground lean lamb

Salt and freshly ground pepper

- 2 cups dry red wine
- 2 cups beef stock or canned low-sodium broth

One 14½-ounce can whole tomatoes, drained and coarsely chopped

- 2 tablespoons coarsely chopped basil
- ½ cup heavy cream
- 24 flat 8-by-3-inch lasagna noodles (about 1¼ pounds)
- 4 cups of White Sauce (recipe follows), at room temperature
- ¾ cup freshly grated Parmesan

1. In a large saucepan, heat the oil until shimmering. Add the garlic and cook over moderate heat until lightly browned, about 1 minute. Add the carrots, celery and onion and cook, stirring, until softened, about 10 minutes. Stir in the chicken livers and sage and cook, stirring occasionally, just until the livers lose their pink color, about 3 minutes. Add the ground veal, pork and lamb and season with salt and pepper. Break up the meat with a wooden spoon and cook over high heat until no trace of pink remains, about 8 minutes. Pour in the wine and cook over high heat, stirring, until reduced by half, about 15 minutes.

2. Stir in the beef stock, tomatoes and basil and season with salt and pepper. Cover partially and simmer the ragù over moderately low heat, stirring occasionally, until the liquid has reduced by half, about 45 minutes. Uncover, add the cream and cook for 10 minutes longer. Remove the ragù from the heat and skim off the fat, using a ladle.

3. Meanwhile, in a large pot of boiling salted water, cook the lasagna noodles until al dente. Drain and rinse under cold water, then pat dry and spread out on 2 clean kitchen towels.

4. Preheat the oven to 350°. Spread 1 cup of the ragù in a 9-by-13-inch glass baking dish and top with a layer made of 4 noodles. Spread 1⅓ cups of the ragù over the noodles and dollop with scant tablespoons from ⅔ cup of the White Sauce, then sprinkle with 2 tablespoons of the Parmesan. Repeat to make 4 more layers. Top with the remaining lasagna noodles, White Sauce and Parmesan. Reserve any remaining ragù for passing tableside.

5. Bake the lasagna for 35 minutes, or until heated through. Preheat the broiler. Broil the lasagna until the top is bubbling and golden, about 1 minute. Let the lasagna stand for 10 minutes before serving.   —*Barbara Lynch* ▶

MAKE AHEAD The Tuscan-Style Lasagna can be assembled and refrigerated for 1 day. Bring to room temperature before baking.

WINE The acidity and tannin of a Chianti Classico will cut the richness of the sauce. Look for a full-bodied example from the superlative 1997 vintage, such as the Fattoria di Felsina Berardenga Riserva or the less expensive La Castellina Riserva.

WHITE SAUCE

MAKES ABOUT 4 CUPS ●

- 1 stick (4 ounces) unsalted butter
- ½ cup all-purpose flour
- 4 cups milk

Salt and freshly ground pepper
Pinch of freshly grated nutmeg

Melt the butter in a large saucepan. Whisk in the flour and cook over moderately high heat, whisking constantly, until golden brown, 2 to 3 minutes. Slowly whisk in the milk and cook over moderate heat, whisking frequently, until the sauce is thickened, about 15 minutes. Remove the sauce from the heat and season with salt, pepper and the nutmeg. Use at once.   —*B.L.*

Gnocchi with Sweet Peas, Tomatoes and Sage Brown Butter

Here's proof that the simplest dishes can be the most delicious.

4 SERVINGS ●

- 3 medium baking potatoes (about 1⅔ pounds)
- 1 large egg
- ⅓ teaspoon freshly grated nutmeg

Kosher salt

- ¾ cup all-purpose flour, plus more for dusting
- 4 tablespoons unsalted butter
- 12 large sage leaves
- 2 tablespoons chopped flat-leaf parsley

Finely grated zest of 1 lemon

- 1 cup fresh or thawed frozen baby peas, blanched if fresh
- 1 pint yellow cherry tomatoes, halved lengthwise

Freshly ground black pepper

- ½ cup freshly grated Parmesan

1. Preheat the oven to 450°. Pierce the potatoes all over with a fork and bake for 1 hour, or until tender. Let cool slightly, then halve lengthwise and scoop out the flesh. Pass the potatoes through a ricer or food mill into a large bowl. Measure out 2 cups and let cool slightly. Save any remaining potatoes for another use.

2. In a medium bowl, using a handheld mixer, beat the potatoes at low speed with the egg, nutmeg and ½ teaspoon of salt just until combined. Mix in the flour until a soft dough forms.

3. Line a baking sheet with wax paper and dust it with flour. On a lightly floured surface, gently knead the dough for 1 minute, until smooth. Quarter the dough and roll each quarter into a ½-inch-thick rope; cut the ropes into 1-inch pieces and transfer to the baking sheet. Hold a fork with the tines pointing slightly downward and gently roll each piece of dough against the tines to make slight grooves.

4. Bring a large saucepan of salted water to a boil. Add the gnocchi and cover. When the water returns to a boil, uncover, stir gently and boil for about 1 minute, or until tender. Using a slotted spoon, lift the gnocchi into a strainer to drain.

5. Melt the butter in a large, deep skillet. Add the sage and parsley and cook over moderately high heat until the sage is crisp and the butter starts to brown, about 3 minutes. Add the gnocchi and lemon zest and toss well. Add the peas, tomatoes and a generous pinch of salt and pepper and cook, tossing, until heated through, about 2 minutes. Add the Parmesan and toss to combine. Transfer the gnocchi to bowls and serve.   —*Craig Stoll*

Gnocchi with Sweet Peas, Tomatoes and Sage Brown Butter

6 fish
shellfish

basil & health

Like most leafy greens, basil is a good source of **folic acid, vitamin C and the minerals potassium, calcium and iron**—but only if eaten by the cupful. A normal serving of one tablespoon of chopped basil has only minimal benefits; for instance, it provides only 1 percent of the recommended daily intake of vitamin A. Basil contributes to healthy eating mainly because it gives lots of flavor to recipes without fat or salt. And it may have some positive psychological effects: Paul Schulick, a research herbalist at New Chapter (a company that makes herbal products), suggests using the kind called **holy basil to counter depression and stress.** Steep two or three leaves of fresh holy basil in eight ounces of hot water for three minutes. Strain and drink.

Grilled Trout with Summer Salad and Basil Oil

4 SERVINGS ●
   4 ears of corn
Olive oil, for brushing
   4 medium zucchini, halved
      lengthwise and seeded
   8 scallions
   ½ cup cherry tomatoes, halved
   ½ cup thinly shredded basil leaves
   1 tablespoon fresh lemon juice
   2 tablespoons plus 2 teaspoons
      Basil Oil (recipe follows)
Salt and freshly ground pepper
   4 trout fillets (6 ounces each)

1. Light a grill. Brush the corn with oil and grill over a medium-low fire, turning, often, for about 20 minutes, or until tender; let cool slightly. In a large bowl, cut the kernels from the cobs.

2. Brush the zucchini and scallions with olive oil and grill, turning, until lightly charred, about 4 minutes for the scallions and 6 for the zucchini. Slice the zucchini on the diagonal ½ inch thick and coarsely chop the scallions;

add to the corn. Add the tomatoes, basil, lemon juice and 2 tablespoons of the Basil Oil and season with salt and pepper.

3. Brush the trout with olive oil and season with salt and pepper. Grill over a medium-hot fire for 3 minutes per side, or until lightly charred and just cooked through. Drizzle the trout with the remaining 2 teaspoons of the Basil Oil and serve with the salad.

—Suki Hertz

ONE SERVING Calories 292 kcal, Total Fat 14.7 gm, Saturated Fat 2.7 gm

BASIL OIL

MAKES ABOUT ⅓ CUP ●
   2 packed cups basil leaves
   ½ cup extra-virgin olive oil

Prepare a bowl of ice water. In a small saucepan of boiling water, blanch the basil for 15 seconds. Drain and add the basil to the ice water; squeeze dry. In a blender, puree the basil with the olive oil. Scrape into a bowl, cover and refrigerate overnight. Bring the Basil Oil to room temperature and strain.

—S.H.

MAKE AHEAD The Basil Oil can be refrigerated for up to 5 days.

Red Snapper with Carrot Confit and Baked Lemon

4 SERVINGS

The slow-cooked, meltingly tender whole carrots are flavored with orange and olive oil. Baked lemon is a quick, simple and amazingly flavorful garnish.

   1 cup fresh orange juice
   ½ cup extra-virgin olive oil
   1 teaspoon finely grated
      orange zest
   1 teaspoon cumin seeds
   1 teaspoon minced garlic
Salt
   1 pound medium carrots
   1 teaspoon fresh lemon juice
   2 lemons, ends removed and
      halved crosswise
   4 teaspoons sugar

Four 6-ounce red snapper fillets,
   with skin
Freshly ground pepper
   2 tablespoons coarsely chopped
      cilantro, for garnish

1. Preheat the oven to 450°. In a medium skillet, combine the orange juice with ¼ cup of the olive oil, the orange zest, cumin seeds, garlic and a generous pinch of salt and simmer over moderate heat for 3 minutes. Reduce the heat to low and add the carrots, then cover and cook until the carrots are very tender but still hold their shape, about 45 minutes. Transfer the carrots to a plate and keep warm. Increase the heat to high and simmer the sauce until reduced to a syrupy glaze, about 3 minutes. Remove the skillet from the heat and stir the lemon juice and 1 tablespoon of olive oil into the orange sauce.

2. Stand the lemon halves on their ends in a small ovenproof dish. Sprinkle each with 1 teaspoon of sugar and bake for about 20 minutes, or until the sugar is melted and the lemon pulp is soft. Remove the dish from the oven and cover with foil to keep warm. Increase the oven temperature to 500°.

3. Season the snapper with salt and pepper. Heat the remaining 3 tablespoons of oil in a large nonstick ovenproof skillet. Add the fish, skin side down, and cook over high heat until browned on the bottom, about 2 minutes. Transfer the skillet to the oven and roast the fillets for 6 to 8 minutes, or until they are opaque. Arrange the fillets, skin side up, on plates with the carrots alongside. Drizzle the orange sauce on the fish and garnish with the cilantro and baked lemon halves.

—Jean-Georges Vongerichten

WINE Highlight the citrus and cumin here with a lively, fragrant and tart Riesling from Australia. Try the 1999 Leeuwin Estate Margaret River or the 1999 Wolf Blass Eden-Clare Valleys Gold Label.

Indonesian Baked Fish

4 SERVINGS ●●

1 tablespoon minced garlic
1½ teaspoons salt
1 teaspoon freshly ground pepper
Four 6- to 8-ounce red snapper
  fillets, skinned
½ cup soy sauce
3 tablespoons fresh lemon juice
2 tablespoons brown sugar
½ teaspoon crushed red pepper
Vegetable oil, for brushing
2 tablespoons unsalted
  butter, melted

1. Preheat the broiler and position a rack 6 inches from the heat.

2. In a small bowl, mash the garlic with the salt and pepper until a paste forms. Rub the snapper fillets with the garlic paste.

3. In a saucepan, combine the soy sauce, lemon juice, brown sugar and crushed red pepper. Bring to a boil over high heat, stirring, until the sugar dissolves.

4. Brush a baking sheet with oil. Arrange the fillets on the baking sheet and pour half of the sauce over them. Broil for 8 minutes, or until the fillets are firm to the touch and opaque. Transfer the fish to a platter or plates. Drizzle with the remaining sauce and the melted butter. —*Joyce Goldstein*

SERVE WITH Steamed rice.

Sautéed Snapper with Provençal Artichoke Stew

4 SERVINGS ●

1 lemon, halved
4 large artichokes
Salt
1 Valencia orange
2 garlic cloves, thinly sliced
½ pound thin green beans
6 tablespoons extra-virgin olive oil
3 celery ribs, thinly sliced
2 medium carrots, thinly sliced
1 medium onion, halved lengthwise
  and thinly sliced crosswise
1 leek, white and tender green
  parts, halved lengthwise and
  thinly sliced crosswise
Freshly ground pepper
2 cups water
1 cup dry white wine
Bouquet garni: 1 bay leaf, 2 thyme
  sprigs and 3 parsley sprigs
Four 6-ounce red snapper fillets,
  halved crosswise
2 medium tomatoes—peeled,
  seeded and chopped
2 tablespoons finely shredded basil

1. Squeeze the lemon juice into a large bowl of water and add the lemon. Snap off the outer leaves of an artichoke and trim the stem to ½ inch. Using a sharp knife, cut off the top two-thirds of the leaves, then peel the base and stem. Drop the artichoke into the acidulated water and repeat with the rest.

2. Bring a medium saucepan half-filled with water to a boil and add a large pinch of salt. Add the artichokes, cover and cook over moderate heat until tender, about 15 minutes; drain and let cool. Quarter the artichokes and scoop out the furry chokes with a spoon.

3. Using a sharp knife, peel the orange, removing all of the bitter white pith. Working over a bowl, cut in between the membranes to release the sections. Discard any seeds.

4. In a medium saucepan of boiling salted water, cook the sliced garlic until tender, about 5 minutes. Using a slotted spoon, transfer the garlic to a small bowl. Add the green beans to the saucepan and boil until they are crisp-tender, about 3 minutes; drain.

5. Heat 2 tablespoons of the olive oil in a large skillet. Add the celery, carrots, onion and leek and cook them over

**Sautéed Snapper with
Provençal Artichoke Stew**

moderate heat until just softened, about 10 minutes. Season with salt and pepper, then add the water, wine and bouquet garni. Cook the vegetables until the carrots are tender and the broth is slightly reduced, about 15 minutes. Remove from the heat. Add the artichokes, green beans and garlic to the skillet and keep warm.

6. Heat 2 tablespoons of the oil in a large nonstick skillet. Season the snapper with salt and pepper and add the fillets to the skillet, skin side up.

world of oil

The best-known high-quality, estate-bottled extra-virgin olive oils are from Tuscany and Umbria, but excellent oils from elsewhere in Italy and around the globe are increasingly visible in American stores, often at better prices.

ITALY Puglia (the heel of Italy's boot) produces more than half of the country's olive oil, much of it first-rate. Sicilian and Calabrian oils are round and fruity; central Italian oils are spicier.

SPAIN Andalusian oil, from the South, is made from a blend of olives, including the intensely grassy Picual. The strong flavors aren't popular with American consumers, but Nuñez de Prado and Columela brands are gentler. In Catalonia, Arbequina olives produce an exceptional oil with a rich, nutty flavor that's more agreeable to the American palate.

GREECE With its deliciously buttery aroma and fruity flavor, Greek oil is an excellent buy in 5- or 10-liter containers at Greek and Middle Eastern markets. Brands such as Biolea, Morea and Greek Gourmet are fairly easy to find.

WHERE'S NEXT California oils are the (pricey) up-and-comers. As with California wine, there isn't a typical flavor profile, since there haven't been centuries to establish one. Meanwhile, large new plantations in South Africa, Australia and New Zealand are starting to bear fruit.

Cook over high heat until golden, about 4 minutes per side. Transfer the fillets to a large, deep platter.

7. Add the vegetables from the large skillet along with the tomatoes, orange sections and basil to the large nonstick skillet and cook over high heat until the tomatoes are just heated through, about 1 minute. Discard the bouquet garni. Ladle the vegetables over the fish, drizzle with the remaining 2 tablespoons of olive oil and serve. —*Carrie Nahabedian*

MAKE AHEAD The stew can be prepared through Step 5 early in the day and kept at room temperature.

Spicy Snapper and Shrimp Stew
4 SERVINGS ●●

Everything in this seafood stew cooks together in one pan, making the cleanup as easy as the cooking.

- 2 tablespoons extra-virgin olive oil
- 4 large garlic cloves, minced
- 1 large red bell pepper, cut into ¼-inch dice
- 1 small onion, finely chopped
- One 14-ounce can crushed tomatoes
- ½ teaspoon crushed red pepper
- ½ teaspoon dried thyme
- ¼ teaspoon saffron threads, crushed
- 1 pound snapper, cod or halibut fillet, cut into 2-inch chunks
- ½ pound medium shrimp, shelled and deveined

Salt and freshly ground pepper
Steamed rice, for serving

Heat the olive oil in a large saucepan. Add the garlic, bell pepper and onion, cover and cook over moderately low heat until softened, about 8 minutes. Add the tomatoes, crushed red pepper, thyme and saffron, cover and simmer for 5 minutes. Add the snapper and shrimp, cover and simmer until the seafood is just cooked through, about 5 minutes. Season with salt and pepper. Serve in bowls at once with the rice. —*Michael Roberts*

Whole Jerked Red Snapper
4 SERVINGS ●

Although many pair Jamaica's fiery jerk seasoning with chicken and pork, it's also great with fish, especially whole red snapper.

- 4 whole 1- to 1½-pound red snappers, cleaned
- 1 Scotch bonnet chile, seeded and coarsely chopped
- 4 large scallions, coarsely chopped
- 3 garlic cloves
- 1 small shallot, coarsely chopped
- One ½-inch piece of peeled fresh ginger, coarsely chopped
- 1 teaspoon chopped thyme
- 1½ teaspoons kosher salt
- 1 teaspoon brown sugar
- ½ teaspoon ground allspice
- ½ teaspoon freshly ground pepper
- ¼ teaspoon ground cinnamon
- 2 tablespoons vegetable oil, plus more for the grill
- 1 tablespoon dark rum
- 1 tablespoon fresh lime juice
- 1 tablespoon water
- 2 teaspoons soy sauce

1. Make 3 crosswise slashes down to the bone on each side of each fish. In a food processor, process the Scotch bonnet chile, scallions, garlic, shallot, ginger, thyme, salt, brown sugar, allspice, pepper and cinnamon until a coarse paste forms. Add 2 tablespoons of vegetable oil, the dark rum, lime juice, water and soy sauce and puree.

2. Arrange the snappers in a shallow dish. Stuff the cavities and slashes with the seasoning paste; refrigerate for 1 hour.

3. Light a grill. If using fish baskets, lightly brush with oil and place the fish inside. If using a fish grate, preheat it and lightly brush with oil. Grill the fish over a medium-hot fire until cooked through, 8 minutes per side. Serve at once. —*Steven Raichlen*

Roasted Cod with Steamer Clams and Pistachio Sauce

remaining cilantro mixture. Pour the sauce over the fish and serve at once.

—*Nancy Harmon Jenkins*

ONE SERVING Calories 280 kcal, Total Fat 11.6 gm, Saturated Fat 1.8 gm, Protein 40 gm, Carbohydrates 2 gm

WINE A fruity wine with good acidity, such as the off-dry 1999 Wente Riesling Arroyo Seco Monterey County, complements the Asian flavors here.

Roasted Cod with Steamer Clams and Pistachio Sauce

4 SERVINGS ●

Clam broth and pistachios make a simple sauce with complex flavors.

- 30 steamer clams (about 2 pounds), scrubbed
- 8 large fingerling potatoes (about 10 ounces), cut into ¼-inch rounds

Salt

- ¾ cup chopped chives
- ⅓ cup plus 3 tablespoons olive oil
- ⅓ cup shelled roasted salted pistachios, finely ground
- 3 tablespoons plus 1 teaspoon unsalted butter
- ¼ teaspoon fresh lemon juice

Freshly ground pepper

Four 6-ounce skinless cod fillets

All-purpose flour, for dusting

1. In a large skillet, bring ¼ inch of water to a boil. Add the clams, cover and cook until opened, about 3 minutes. Remove the clams. Strain the cooking liquid through a fine sieve into a medium bowl. When the clams are cool enough to handle, remove them from their shells and pull off the brown outer membrane. Rinse each clam in the cooking liquid, then strain the cooking liquid again through a fine sieve to remove any sand or grit.

2. Put the potatoes in a saucepan of cold salted water and bring to a boil. Simmer until just tender, about 5 minutes; drain.

3. In a blender, puree the chopped chives with ⅓ cup of the olive oil until

Oven-Steamed Fish with Ginger and Olive Oil

6 SERVINGS ●

Olive oil may seem out of place in a Chinese-inspired recipe, but the flavor is lovely with the soy sauce and black vinegar.

- ¼ cup finely chopped cilantro
- 2 garlic cloves, minced
- 2 large scallions, minced
- 1 tablespoon minced peeled fresh ginger

Finely grated zest of 1 lemon

- 1½ teaspoons kosher salt
- ½ teaspoon pepper

One 4½-pound whole red snapper, cleaned

- 2 tablespoons fresh lemon juice
- ¼ cup extra-virgin olive oil
- 1½ teaspoons soy sauce
- 1 teaspoon Chinese black vinegar or balsamic vinegar

1. Preheat the oven to 425°. In a small bowl, combine the cilantro with the garlic, scallions, ginger, lemon zest, salt and pepper. On a sturdy baking sheet, spread a sheet of heavy-duty aluminum foil large enough to wrap loosely around the fish. Sprinkle one-third of the cilantro mixture lengthwise down the center of the foil. Set the fish on the mixture and sprinkle another third on top. Drizzle the lemon juice over the fish and fold up the foil sides and ends, forming a loose but well-sealed packet. Bake the fish for 40 minutes, or until cooked through.

2. Meanwhile, in a small saucepan, combine the olive oil with the soy sauce and vinegar and warm over moderate heat.

3. Carefully open the fish packet and pour off the juices. Transfer the fish to a large platter and sprinkle with the

the mixture is a smooth puree. Using a small spatula, press the puree through a fine sieve into a small bowl. Season with salt.

4. In a small saucepan, combine the ground pistachios with ½ cup of the reserved clam cooking liquid and bring to a boil. Remove from the heat and whisk in 3 tablespoons of the butter. Stir in the lemon juice and season the sauce with salt and pepper. Keep the pistachio sauce warm.

5. Season the cod with salt and pepper and dust with flour. Heat the remaining 3 tablespoons of olive oil in a large skillet over moderately high heat. Add the cod, skinned side up, and cook until golden, about 4 minutes. Turn the cod and cook for 3 to 4 minutes longer, or until just opaque throughout. Transfer the cod to a plate and keep warm.

6. In a medium-size skillet, heat 2 tablespoons more of the reserved

clam cooking liquid. Add the clams, potatoes and the remaining 1 teaspoon of butter and simmer just until heated through. Pour the pistachio sauce onto plates. Divide the clams and potatoes among the plates and set the cod on top. Drizzle the plates with the chive oil and serve.—*Anita Lo*

Broiled Striped Bass with Ginger-Scallion Oil

4 SERVINGS

    4 **scallions, thinly sliced**
    2 **tablespoons minced fresh ginger**
    1 **garlic clove, minced**
Pinch of crushed red pepper
  ¼ **cup vegetable oil**
    2 **tablespoons fresh lemon juice**
    1 **teaspoon soy sauce**
    1 **teaspoon kosher salt**
Four 5-ounce skinless striped bass fillets (about 1 inch thick)

1. In a bowl, combine the scallions, ginger, garlic and red pepper. In a saucepan, heat the oil until shimmering. Pour the hot oil over the scallion mixture and stir in the lemon juice, soy sauce and salt.

2. Preheat the broiler. Brush the striped bass fillets on both sides with some of the scallion oil. Arrange on a broiler pan skinned side down; broil until just cooked through, about 5 minutes. Transfer the fillets to plates; spoon some scallion oil on top.

—*Alex Lee*

SERVE WITH Stir-Fried Asparagus (p. 288).

WINE Seek out an Alsatian Pinot Gris, such as the 1997 Domaine Ostertag Fronholz.

Miso-Glazed Chilean Sea Bass

4 SERVINGS ●

The marinade here is also wonderful for other oily fish, such as salmon. Vary it as suggested in the Note (next page) for red meats. The fish is best marinated for at least 12 hours, so plan accordingly.

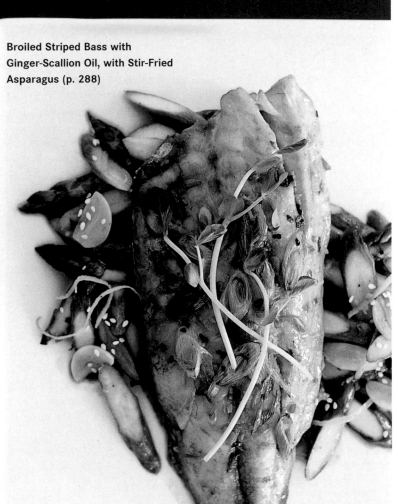

Broiled Striped Bass with Ginger-Scallion Oil, with Stir-Fried Asparagus (p. 288)

1 cup sweet white (shiro) miso
3 tablespoons dark brown sugar
¼ cup sake
¼ cup mirin or medium-dry sherry
Four 6-ounce skinless Chilean
    sea bass fillets
1 teaspoon extra-virgin olive oil

1. In a small saucepan, mix the sweet white miso with the dark brown sugar, sake and mirin or sherry and bring to a simmer over moderate heat. Reduce the heat to low and cook for 2 minutes, stirring occasionally. Transfer the marinade to a small bowl and let cool completely.

2. Spread one-third of the miso marinade in a glass baking dish just large enough to hold the fish in a single layer. Add the fish fillets, skinned side down, and spread the remaining marinade on top. Cover with plastic wrap and refrigerate for at least 12 and up to 24 hours.

3. Light a grill or preheat the broiler. Scrape the marinade from the sea bass and pat the fillets dry with paper towels.

4. Brush the fish with the olive oil. Grill the fish 6 inches from the heat for about 8 minutes, turning once, until just cooked through. Alternatively, arrange the fillets on a broiler pan, skinned side up, and broil 3 inches from the heat for 4 minutes. Turn the fillets and broil for 2 minutes longer, or until just cooked through. Serve hot.

—*Sally Schneider*

ONE SERVING Calories 190 kcal, Total Fat 4.6 gm, Saturated Fat 1 gm, Carbohydrates 4 gm, Protein 31 gm

NOTE For a version of this marinade that is delicious with red meats—especially beef and lamb—simply replace half of the white miso with red miso or country-style barley miso. Use the marinade as directed in the recipe and grill or broil the meat to the desired doneness.

SERVE WITH Steamed or braised baby bok choy.

Miso-Glazed Chilean Sea Bass

Foil-Baked Sea Bass with Spinach

4 SERVINGS ●

  4 tablespoons unsalted butter,
    cut into small pieces, plus
    1½ tablespoons softened
    butter for brushing
One 5-ounce bag prewashed
    baby spinach
Salt and freshly ground pepper
  1 medium shallot, minced
Four 8-ounce skinless sea bass fillets
¼ cup dry white wine

1. Preheat the oven to 425°. Tear off four 18-inch lengths of foil. Generously brush the softened butter over an 8-inch square in the center of each foil sheet. Mound the baby spinach in the center of the sheets and season with salt and pepper. Sprinkle with the shallot. Season both sides of each sea bass fillet with salt and pepper and set the fillets on the spinach. Scatter the pieces of butter over the fish. Pull the sides of the foil up around the fish and drizzle the fillets with the wine. Fold the edges of the foil to make sealed packets.

2. Arrange the packets on a baking sheet and bake for about 12 minutes, or until the fish is cooked through. Transfer 1 of the packets to a medium bowl. Carefully make a small tear in the side of the packet and pour the

Foil-Baked Sea Bass with Spinach

juices into the bowl. Repeat with the 3 remaining packets. Using a spatula, transfer the fish and spinach to shallow soup plates, pour the cooking juices over the fish and serve.

—*Kate Heddings*

SERVE WITH Steamed rice or boiled new potatoes.

Sea Bass with Fennel, Tomato and Orange

4 SERVINGS ●●

  1 tablespoon extra-virgin olive oil
  1 large fennel bulb—halved,
    cored and thinly sliced—plus 1
    tablespoon minced fennel fronds
  1 onion, halved and thinly sliced
  1 tender celery rib, thinly sliced
  1 cup chopped drained canned
    tomatoes, plus ½ cup strained
    tomato juices
¼ cup dry white wine
  1 teaspoon finely grated
    orange zest
Pinch of saffron threads, crumbled
Pinch of crushed red pepper
Sea salt
Four 6-ounce skinless sea bass fillets
  2 tablespoons finely chopped
    flat-leaf parsley

Sea Bass with Fennel,
Tomato and Orange

Steamed Sea Bass with Tamarind Sauce

4 SERVINGS

One 2½-inch block of tamarind
pulp (5 ounces)

3¼ cups water

2 tablespoons cumin seeds

1 tablespoon coriander seeds

¼ cup unsweetened coconut milk

¼ cup unsalted dry-roasted peanuts

3 tablespoons minced
peeled ginger

2 teaspoons harissa

4 tablespoons plus 1 teaspoon
unsalted butter

3 pounds non-oily white fish bones,
rinsed and cut into large pieces

5 scallions, thinly sliced

1 garlic clove, crushed

24 pearl onions, blanched
and peeled

Four 6-ounce sea bass fillets

Salt and freshly ground pepper

1 teaspoon fresh lime juice

2 tablespoons finely
shredded mint leaves

1. In a small saucepan, cover the tamarind pulp with 1¼ cups of water and bring to a simmer. Remove the saucepan from the heat and let stand, stirring occasionally, until the tamarind pulp is softened and broken down, about 15 minutes. Pass the tamarind through a fine sieve, pressing hard to extract as much pulp as possible. Discard the fibers and seeds in the sieve.

2. In a small skillet, toast the cumin and coriander seeds over moderate heat until fragrant, about 3 minutes. Transfer the spices to a plate to cool, then grind them finely in a spice grinder. In a blender, combine the

1. In a large, deep skillet, heat 2 teaspoons of the oil. Add the fennel slices, onion and celery, cover and cook over moderate heat, stirring occasionally, until softened, about 10 minutes. Uncover and cook, stirring, until the vegetables are lightly browned, about 5 minutes. Add the tomatoes, wine, ¾ teaspoon of the orange zest, the saffron and red pepper and cook over high heat until the liquid has evaporated, about 5 minutes.

2. Add the tomato juices, season with salt and bring to a simmer. Arrange the fish fillets in the sauce in a single layer and season with salt. Cover and cook over moderate heat until the fish is opaque throughout, 8 to 10 minutes.

3. Mix the parsley with the fennel fronds and the remaining 1 teaspoon olive oil and ¼ teaspoon orange zest; season with salt. Spoon the fish and sauce onto warmed plates, sprinkle with the parsley mixture and serve.

—*Grace Parisi*

ONE SERVING Calories 254 kcal, Total Fat 7.1 gm, Saturated Fat 1.4 gm, Protein 34 gm, Carbohydrates 13 gm

Sea Bass with Edamame-Rye Crust

ground spices with the coconut milk, peanuts, ginger, harissa and all but 1 tablespoon of the tamarind puree and blend to make a smooth, aromatic puree.

3. Melt 2 tablespoons of the butter in a large saucepan. Add the fish bones and cook over moderate heat until the fish on the bones is opaque, about 10 minutes. Add the scallions and garlic and cook until softened, about 3 minutes. Stir in 6 tablespoons of the aromatic puree (see Note). Add the remaining 2 cups of water and bring to a boil, then reduce the heat to low and simmer for 20 minutes. Strain the stock into a small saucepan and boil until reduced to 1 cup, about 10 minutes. Cover the stock and keep warm.

4. In a medium saucepan of boiling salted water, simmer the pearl onions over moderate heat until they are tender, about 6 minutes. Drain the pearl onions and return them to the saucepan. Add 1 teaspoon of butter, shake the pan to coat the onions and keep them warm.

5. Season the fish fillets with salt and pepper and set them, skin side up, on a heatproof plate that fits snugly in a large, deep skillet. Put 3 balls of crumpled foil in the skillet, add 1 inch of water and bring to a boil. Carefully set the plate on the foil balls, cover the skillet and steam the fish over high heat until the flesh flakes easily, about 8 minutes.

6. In a blender, mix the fish stock with the lime juice, the reserved 1 tablespoon of tamarind puree and the remaining 2 tablespoons of butter and blend until frothy. Season with salt and pepper and blend again. Set the fillets in soup plates and pour the tamarind sauce around them. Stir the mint into the pearl onions, arrange around the fish and serve.

—*Jean-Georges Vongerichten*

N O T E The remaining aromatic puree can be refrigerated for 1 week and used to marinate seafood or chicken.

M A K E A H E A D The recipe can be prepared through Step 3 and refrigerated for 2 days.

W I N E An inexpensive white with good acidity and a hint of sweetness perfectly complements the sweet, sour and spicy sauce. Try an off-dry 1999 Riesling or Chenin Blanc from Hogue Cellars in Washington State.

Sea Bass with Edamame-Rye Crust

4 SERVINGS ●

- 1 **cup coarsely chopped chives, plus 2 tablespoons finely chopped**
- ⅓ **cup grapeseed or canola oil**

Sea salt

- 1½ **pounds Yukon Gold potatoes, peeled and cut into 2-inch chunks**
- 5 **tablespoons unsalted butter**
- ⅔ **cup half-and-half**
- ⅔ **cup shelled fresh or frozen soybeans (edamame)**
- ½ **cup coarse, dry rye-bread crumbs**

Four 6-ounce black sea bass fillets

Cayenne pepper

1. Blend the coarsely chopped chives with the oil and a generous pinch of salt at high speed until smooth. Transfer the chive oil to a jar.

2. In a large saucepan, cover the potatoes with cold water and bring to a boil. Salt the water and simmer the potatoes until tender, about 20 minutes. Drain thoroughly. Pass the potatoes through a ricer or the fine disk of a food mill back into the saucepan.

3. In a small saucepan, melt 2 tablespoons of the butter in the half-and-half. Add to the potatoes, season with salt and stir until smooth. Stir in all but 2 tablespoons of the chive oil and keep warm over very low heat.

4. Bring a small saucepan of salted water to a boil. Add the soybeans and boil over high heat for 5 minutes. Drain and let cool, then finely chop.

5. Melt 2 tablespoons of the butter in a small skillet. Add the chopped soybeans and cook over moderately high heat until sizzling, about 2 minutes. Stir in the bread crumbs and the 2 tablespoons of finely chopped chives and season with salt.

6. Season the fish on both sides with salt and cayenne. In a large nonstick skillet, melt the remaining 1 tablespoon of butter over moderately high heat. Add the fish, skin side up, and cook until golden brown, about 5 minutes. Turn the fish and cook for 1 minute longer, or until just cooked through. Turn the fish again and spoon the soybean crust on top of each fillet, pressing lightly to adhere.

7. Mound the mashed potatoes in the center of each plate and set the fish on top. Drizzle the remaining chive oil around the fish and serve.

—*Wylie Dufresne*

Nut-Crusted Sea Bass with Mushroom Vinaigrette

4 SERVINGS

- 4 **hazelnuts**
- 4 **almonds**
- 2 **tablespoons coriander seeds**
- 2 **tablespoons sesame seeds**
- 1 **tablespoon whole peppercorns**
- 5 **tablespoons unsalted butter**
- ½ **pound mushrooms, thinly sliced**
- 1 **cup water**
- 1 **tablespoon honey**
- 1 **tablespoon fresh lemon juice**
- 1 **tablespoon sherry vinegar**
- 1 **tablespoon soy sauce**

All-purpose flour

- ½ **cup heavy cream**

Four 6-ounce black sea bass fillets, with skin, each fillet cut crosswise into thirds

Salt

Vegetable oil

1. In a small dry skillet, combine the hazelnuts, almonds, coriander and sesame seeds and peppercorns. Toast the mixture over moderately low heat, stirring, until fragrant and lightly browned, about 4 minutes; transfer the nuts and spices to a plate and let cool completely. Coarsely chop the nuts. In a spice grinder, combine the nuts with the spices and grind to a coarse powder.

2. Melt 1 tablespoon of the butter in a large skillet. Add the sliced mushrooms and cook over moderately high heat, stirring occasionally, until they are nicely browned, about 8 minutes. Add the water, honey, lemon juice, vinegar and soy sauce and bring to a boil over high heat. Reduce the heat to low and simmer the mixture until the liquid has reduced to 3 tablespoons, about 20 minutes. Strain the mixture through a coarse sieve set over a small saucepan, pressing hard on the mushrooms to extract as much of the reduction as possible.

3. In a small skillet, cook the remaining 4 tablespoons of butter over moderate heat until browned and nutty-smelling, about 4 minutes. Gradually whisk the browned butter into the reduction; set the mushroom vinaigrette aside.

4. Spread the nut-and-spice powder on one large plate and spread some flour on another. Pour the heavy cream into a shallow bowl. Season the pieces of fish with salt and coat them with the nut-and-spice powder. Then dip each piece in the cream and coat in the flour, shaking off the excess.

5. In a large skillet, heat ¼ inch of oil until shimmering. Add half of the sea bass fillets, skin side down, and cook over moderate heat until browned and just cooked through, 3 to 4 minutes per side. Transfer the cooked fillets to a warmed platter. Repeat with the remaining fish, adding more oil to the skillet if necessary.

6. Rewarm the mushroom vinaigrette over moderately low heat, whisking constantly; do not let it boil. Season with salt, drizzle it over the fish and serve. —*Jean-Georges Vongerichten*
MAKE AHEAD You can make the

mushroom vinaigrette early in the day and keep it covered at room temperature. The spice powder can also be made ahead of time and stored in a jar for up to 2 days.
SERVE WITH Fragrant rice or steamed new potatoes.
WINE The toasted nuts in the spice crust and the slightly sweet vinaigrette tune the choice to a medium-bodied, round Chardonnay. Pick a subtle but reasonably priced white Burgundy with hints of lemon and nuts, such as the 1998 Joseph Drouhin St-Aubin or the 1999 Olivier Leflaive St-Aubin En Remilly.

Indian-Spiced Roasted Striped Bass

4 SERVINGS ●

- 2 teaspoons coriander seeds
- 2 teaspoons fennel seeds
- 1 teaspoon cumin seeds
- 2 teaspoons kosher salt
- 1 teaspoon freshly ground pepper
- 1 stalk fresh lemongrass, inner bulb only, minced (optional)
- 2 teaspoons finely chopped garlic
- 4 whole striped bass (1½ pounds each), pan-dressed

Olive oil spray

- 4 rosemary sprigs
- 12 thin lemon slices, cut in half, plus lemon wedges for serving

1. Preheat the oven to 500°. In a skillet, toast the coriander, fennel and cumin seeds over high heat, stirring, until the spices are lightly browned, about 2 minutes. Transfer to a plate and let cool. Scrape the spices into a spice grinder, add the salt and pepper and grind to a powder. Transfer to a small bowl and stir in the lemongrass and garlic.

2. Using a sharp knife, make three ½-inch-deep diagonal slits in both sides of each fish. Spray with olive oil on both sides of the fish. Rub the cavities with half of the spice mixture and

tuck a rosemary sprig in each one. Rub the remaining spices onto the skin and into the slits. Tuck a lemon slice into each slit and let the fish marinate at room temperature for 30 minutes.

3. Transfer the fish to a large, rimmed nonstick baking sheet and spray lightly with olive oil on both sides. Bake for 20 minutes, or until the flesh flakes with a fork. Serve 1 fish per person, with lemon wedges. —*Toni Robertson*
ONE SERVING Calories 300 kcal, Total Fat 7.7 gm, Saturated Fat 1.6 gm, Protein 52 gm, Carbohydrates 3 gm
WINE A smooth Chardonnay without much oak will round out the slightly sour and pungent herbs and spices that flavor the fish. Try the inexpensive 1998 Mark West Russian River Valley or the 1998 Cuvaison Napa Valley.

Grilled Halibut with Sauce Vierge

4 SERVINGS ●

- ¼ teaspoon coriander seeds
- ¼ cup extra-virgin olive oil
- 1 tablespoon fresh lemon juice
- 1 tablespoon finely chopped basil
- 1 tablespoon finely chopped cilantro
- 1 large plum tomato—peeled, seeded and diced

Salt and freshly ground pepper

Four 6-ounce skinless halibut fillets, about 1¼ inches thick

- 2 tablespoons pure olive oil

1. Light a grill or preheat a grill pan. In a small skillet, toast the coriander seeds over moderately high heat until fragrant, about 20 seconds. Transfer the coriander seeds to a plate and let cool completely. Grind the coriander seeds to a fine powder in a spice grinder and transfer them to a small bowl. Whisk in the extra-virgin olive oil, lemon juice, basil, cilantro and tomato. Season the sauce with salt and pepper.

2. Rub the halibut fillets all over with the pure olive oil. Season the halibut fillets with salt and pepper and grill them over a moderately hot fire until lightly charred and just cooked through, about 4 minutes per side. Transfer the halibut fillets to a serving platter, spoon the sauce on top and serve immediately.　*—Glenn Monk*

SERVE WITH Sweet pea risotto, boiled new potatoes or wild rice.

WINE The crisp, clean and almost spicy flavor of Mission Hill Winery's 1998 Private Reserve Pinot Blanc is an ideal match for grilled halibut and other firm, white-fleshed fish.

Halibut with Swiss Chard, Leek and Pepper Stew

Halibut with Swiss Chard, Leek and Pepper Stew

4 SERVINGS ●

- 1 tablespoon extra-virgin olive oil
- 1 large Spanish onion, chopped
- 1 large leek, white and tender green parts, halved lengthwise and sliced crosswise ¼ inch thick
- 4 large garlic cloves, thinly sliced
- ½ cup dry white wine
- ½ medium butternut squash, peeled and cut into ¾-inch dice
- ½ pound Swiss chard, stems discarded, leaves torn into large pieces
- 1 red bell pepper, cut into ¾-inch dice
- 1 yellow bell pepper, cut into ¾-inch dice
- ½ teaspoon fennel seeds
- ½ teaspoon dried thyme
- ¼ teaspoon crushed red pepper

Salt and freshly ground pepper

Four 6-ounce skinless halibut fillets

- ½ cup shredded basil leaves

1. Preheat the oven to 425°. Heat the olive oil in a large enameled cast-iron casserole. Add the onion, leek and garlic, cover and cook over low heat, stirring occasionally, until softened, about 10 minutes. Add the wine and cook until almost evaporated, about 3 minutes. Add the squash, chard, bell peppers, fennel seeds, thyme and crushed red pepper. Season the vegetables generously with salt and pepper, cover and cook over low heat, stirring occasionally, until the squash is tender, about 15 minutes.

2. Spread half of the vegetable stew in an 8-by-11-inch glass or ceramic baking dish. Season the halibut with salt and pepper and nestle the fillets in the stew; cover with the remaining vegetables. Bake for about 15 minutes, or until the halibut is just cooked through. Sprinkle with the basil and serve.　*—Ann Chantal Altman*

ONE SERVING Calories 334 kcal, Total Fat 7.9 gm, Saturated Fat 1.1 gm, Protein 39 gm, Carbohydrates 26 gm

Mediterranean-Style Halibut

4 SERVINGS ●●

- 2 medium zucchini, thinly sliced

Salt

- 2 tablespoons sun-dried tomato oil from the jar
- ⅓ cup oil-packed sun-dried tomatoes, drained and coarsely chopped
- ½ cup oil-cured black olives (about 3 ounces), pitted and coarsely chopped
- ¼ cup coarsely chopped cilantro

Freshly ground pepper

Four 6-ounce skinless halibut fillets

1. Preheat the oven to 400°. In a medium bowl, toss the zucchini with ¾ teaspoon of salt and let stand for 10 minutes. Rinse, drain and gently squeeze any excess moisture from the zucchini; pat dry with paper towels. Arrange four 18-inch-long pieces of foil on a work surface and lightly brush the center of each with a little of the sun-dried tomato oil.

2. In a small bowl, combine the sun-dried tomatoes and the rest of the tomato oil with the olives and cilantro and season with pepper. Make a bed of overlapping zucchini slices approximately the size of the fish fillets in the center of each piece of foil. Sprinkle half of the sun-dried tomato mixture over the zucchini, top with the fish fillets and sprinkle with the remaining sun-dried tomato mixture. Fold up the foil and seal the packets.

3. Set the foil packets on a large baking sheet and bake for about 15 minutes, or until the halibut is cooked through and the zucchini is tender. ▶

Transfer the foil packets to plates and serve, letting each diner open up their packet at the table (warn them to be careful of the steam).

—Ruth Van Waerebeek

WINE The sweetness of sun-dried tomatoes and the saltiness of olives tune the choice to either a light red, such as the 1999 Sangiovese del Umbria La Carraia, or a white with good acidity, such as the 1999 Icardi Cortese L'Aurora.

Halibut with Curried Okra and Corn

4 SERVINGS ●●

- 3 tablespoons extra-virgin olive oil
- 1 tablespoon curry powder
- 2 scallions, white and light green parts only, thinly sliced
- 1 garlic clove, minced

Salt and freshly ground pepper

- 1 pound okra, sliced ¼ inch thick
- 1 pint cherry tomatoes, halved
- 2 large ears of corn, kernels cut off
- 1½ pounds halibut fillets
- 2 tablespoons water
- 3 tablespoons chopped celery leaves
- 2 tablespoons minced chives

Hot sauce, for serving (optional)

1. Heat the extra-virgin olive oil in a large skillet. Add the curry powder, sliced scallions and minced garlic and season with salt and pepper. Cook over moderately high heat until fragrant, about 2 minutes. Add the sliced okra and cook for 3 minutes. Add the cherry tomatoes and cook until softened, about 4 minutes. Stir in the corn and cook for 2 minutes.

2. Set the halibut fillets on the vegetables and season with salt and pepper. Add the water to the skillet, cover and cook the fish and vegetables over moderate heat for 8 minutes, or until the halibut is cooked through. Transfer to plates, garnish with the celery leaves and chives and serve with hot sauce.
—Melissa Clark

Steamed Halibut with Cumin and Avocado

4 SERVINGS ●●

This Mexican-inspired recipe is easy enough to make on a weeknight yet elegant enough for company.

- 1 teaspoon cumin seeds
- 1 tablespoon extra-virgin olive oil
- 1 tablespoon thinly sliced shallot
- ½ cup bottled clam juice
- 2 firm, ripe avocados (9 ounces each)—halved, pitted and sliced lengthwise into ¼-inch-thick pieces
- 2 teaspoons fresh lemon juice
- ½ cup cilantro leaves, plus sprigs for garnish

Salt and freshly ground pepper

Four 6-ounce halibut fillets, about 1 inch thick

- 2 medium tomatoes—peeled, seeded and coarsely chopped

1. In a small skillet, toast the cumin over moderate heat until fragrant, about 30 seconds. Transfer to a plate to cool.

2. Heat the olive oil in a small skillet. Add the shallot and cook over moderate heat until softened, about 2 minutes. Add the clam juice and simmer for 3 minutes; transfer to a blender. Add an avocado half, the lemon juice and cilantro leaves and blend until

smooth. Scrape the sauce into a small saucepan and season with salt and pepper.

3. Season the halibut fillets with salt and pepper and sprinkle the cumin seeds on both sides, pressing to adhere. Add 3 inches of water to a steamer and bring to a boil over high heat. Transfer the fish to the steamer basket, cover and cook over moderate heat for 2 minutes. Uncover and spoon some of the tomatoes on top of each fillet. Cover and steam until the fish is just opaque throughout, about 3 minutes more.

4. Gently reheat the avocado sauce, but do not boil. Transfer the fish to plates and pour the sauce alongside. Garnish with the remaining avocado slices and cilantro sprigs and serve at once.
—Michael Roberts

Sautéed Monkfish with Leeks and Shiitakes

4 SERVINGS

Sweet, mild spring leeks meet succulent monkfish in this delicious dish.

- 4 tablespoons unsalted butter
- ½ pound shiitake mushrooms, stems discarded, caps cut into ¼-inch dice

Salt and freshly ground pepper

- ¼ cup dry white wine, such as Riesling
- 2 pounds slender leeks, white and tender green parts only, halved lengthwise and cut crosswise on the diagonal into ½-inch-thick pieces
- 1 cup chicken stock or canned low-sodium broth
- 1½ pounds trimmed monkfish fillet, cut crosswise into ½-inch-thick medallions

Unbleached all-purpose flour, for dredging

- 1 tablespoon vegetable oil
- 2 tablespoons minced chives or a combination of chives and garlic chives

Sautéed Monkfish with Leeks and Shiitakes

1. Melt 1 tablespoon of the butter in a very large skillet. When the butter starts to brown, quickly add the diced shiitake mushroom caps. Season the mushrooms with salt and ground pepper to taste and cook over moderate heat, stirring, until softened, about 3 minutes. Add the dry white wine and cook just until it evaporates, about 1 minute. Transfer the sautéed shiitake mushrooms to a bowl and then wipe out the skillet.

2. In a medium enameled cast-iron casserole, melt 2 tablespoons of the butter. Add the leeks, season with salt and pepper and cook over moderate heat, stirring, until softened, about 1 minute. Add the chicken stock or broth and bring to a boil. Cover and cook over moderate heat for 3 minutes. Stir well, cover and cook for 3 minutes longer.

3. Season the monkfish medallions with salt and pepper and lightly dredge them in flour; shake off the excess flour. In the very large skillet, heat the vegetable oil until almost smoking. Add the monkfish medallions and cook them over moderately high heat until they are browned on the bottom, about 3 minutes. Turn the medallions, reduce the heat to moderate and cook until just opaque throughout, about 3 minutes.

4. Bring the stewed leeks to a boil. Stir in the shiitake mushrooms and season with salt and pepper. Remove from the heat and stir in the minced chives and the remaining 1 tablespoon of butter. Spoon the leek stew onto plates, set the monkfish medallions on top and serve at once.

—*Eberhard Müller*

ONE SERVING Calories 396 kcal, Total Fat 19.5 gm, Saturated Fat 8.5 gm, Protein 29 gm, Carbohydrates 27 gm

MAKE AHEAD The leek and shiitake stew can be prepared through Step 2 and refrigerated overnight. Reheat gently while you prepare the fish.

Creamy Monkfish and Mussel Stew

4 SERVINGS

This classic Flemish seafood stew is called *waterzooi*. Thinly slicing the vegetables on a mandoline makes easy work of cutting them into thin matchsticks.

- 1 stick (4 ounces) unsalted butter
- 1 pound non-oily fish bones
- 4 shallots, thinly sliced
- 1 celery rib, chopped
- 1 carrot, coarsely chopped, plus 2 carrots halved crosswise and cut into matchsticks
- 6 thyme sprigs
- 2 teaspoons coarse salt
- 1 teaspoon peppercorns
- 4 cups cold water
- ¾ cup dry white wine
- ¾ pound celery root, peeled and cut into matchsticks
- 2 leeks, white and tender green parts, cut into 1½-inch-long matchsticks

Salt and freshly ground pepper

- 1 cup heavy cream
- 2 tablespoons plus 2 teaspoons cornstarch dissolved in ¼ cup cold water
- 2½ pounds monkfish fillet, cut into 1½-inch pieces
- 1 pound mussels, scrubbed and debearded

1. In a large saucepan, melt 4 tablespoons of the butter over moderate heat. Add the fish bones, shallots, celery, chopped carrot, thyme, salt and peppercorns and cook over low heat for 10 minutes. Add the water and wine and simmer for 30 minutes.

2. Meanwhile, in a large skillet, melt the remaining 4 tablespoons of butter over moderate heat. Add the celery root, leeks and carrot matchsticks, cover and cook, stirring often, until softened, about 5 minutes. Season with salt and pepper and set aside.

3. Strain the fish stock into a large saucepan. Whisk in the heavy cream and the dissolved cornstarch and bring to a simmer, whisking until thickened. Season with salt and pepper. Add the monkfish and the reserved vegetables and set the mussels on top. Cover and cook until the mussels open, 8 to 10 minutes. Serve in soup plates or bowls. —*Van Gogh's Table*

MAKE AHEAD The Creamy Monkfish and Mussel Stew can be prepared through Step 2 up to 2 days ahead. Strain the fish stock into a glass or ceramic bowl before refrigerating.

WINE The lean and meaty monkfish and mussels and the rich broth suggest a round and creamy Chardonnay. Opt for a lighter French Burgundy that isn't too powerful or oaky, such as the 1999 Antonin Rodet Château de Rully Blanc or the 1999 Domaine de La Folie Rully Blanc Clos St-Jacques.

Swordfish Tagine

4 SERVINGS ●●

- ½ cup flat-leaf parsley leaves
- ¼ cup cilantro leaves
- 2 garlic cloves, smashed
- 2 tablespoons fresh lemon juice
- ½ jalapeño, seeded
- 1 tablespoon pimentón or other paprika
- 8 saffron threads

Salt and freshly ground pepper

- ⅔ cup extra-virgin olive oil

One 2-pound swordfish steak, 1 inch thick

- 1 cup pitted green olives, quartered, for garnish

Lemon slices, for garnish

1. Preheat the oven to 350°. In a food processor, combine the parsley, cilantro, garlic, lemon juice, jalapeño, pimentón, saffron, 1 teaspoon of salt and ¼ teaspoon of pepper; process until chopped. With the machine on, slowly add the olive oil and process until emulsified.

2. Season the swordfish with salt and pepper. In a glass baking dish, pour the marinade over the fish; turn to

Mesquite Grilled Swordfish
with Charred Tomato Salsa

coat. Bake the fish for 18 to 20 minutes, or until just cooked through. Transfer to a platter, spoon the marinade on top and garnish with the olives and lemon slices.

—*Tamara Murphy*

SERVE WITH Couscous.

Mesquite Grilled Swordfish with Charred Tomato Salsa

4 SERVINGS ●

This dish gets its distinctive smoky flavor from the mesquite chips and the flame-charred salsa, which also offers the heat of red chiles. The swordfish supply seems to be returning after concern about dwindling numbers, which is why most chefs have ended their voluntary embargo of this rich and tasty fish.

- 1 cup mesquite wood chips
- 3 tablespoons fresh lime juice
- 3 tablespoons extra-virgin olive oil
- 1 garlic clove, minced

Four ¾-inch-thick swordfish steaks
(about 6 ounces each)

Salt and freshly ground pepper

Vegetable oil, for the grill

Charred Tomato Salsa
(recipe follows)

1. Soak the wood chips in water for 1 hour; drain. Meanwhile, in a large, shallow baking dish, combine the lime juice with the extra-virgin olive oil and garlic. Add the swordfish steaks, season with salt and pepper; turn to coat. Refrigerate for 20 minutes.

2. Light a grill. If using charcoal, scatter the wood chips over the coals. If using a gas grill, place the chips in the smoker box or on a 12-inch square of foil; fold the foil into a 6-inch square and poke 12 holes in the top. Place the package near the flames and heat until smoking. Lightly brush the grate with vegetable oil. Grill the swordfish until just cooked through, about 4 minutes per side. Spoon some Charred Tomato Salsa on each steak and serve.

—*Steven Raichlen*

WINE The velvety texture of the swordfish and the tart, smoky flavors of the salsa suggest a rich, fruity Sauvignon Blanc with brisk acidity and smoky overtones. Try the 1999 Inama Sauvignon Veneto Vulcaia Fumé from Italy or the expensive 1998 Château Smith Haut Lafitte Blanc from France.

CHARRED TOMATO SALSA

MAKES ABOUT 1 CUP ● ●

- 1 cup mesquite wood chips
- 3 dried red chiles, such as
  de árbol or cayenne

Vegetable oil, for the grill

- 1 large ripe tomato
- 1 garlic clove
- ½ small onion, halved
- ½ canned chipotle chile in adobo, seeded, with 2 teaspoons of sauce from the can
- 2 tablespoons chopped cilantro
- ½ tablespoon fresh lime juice

Salt and freshly ground pepper

1. Soak the wood chips in water for 1 hour and drain. Meanwhile, in a small heatproof bowl, cover the dried red chiles with boiling water and let stand until softened, about 30 minutes. Drain well. Discard the stems and seeds and finely chop the chiles.

2. Light a grill. If using charcoal, scatter the wood chips over the coals. If using a gas grill, place the chips in the smoker box or on a 12-inch square of foil; fold the foil into a 6-inch square and poke 12 holes in the top. Place the package near the flames and heat until smoking.

3. Lightly brush the grate with oil. Place the tomato, stem side down, in the center of the grill. Cover and cook, turning occasionally, until softened and charred all over, about 10 minutes. Meanwhile, thread the garlic clove and onion onto a skewer. Place the skewer at the edge of the fire, where it is cooler. Cover and cook, turning, until lightly browned and just softened, about 8 minutes.

Swordfish with
Sweet Onions
and Red Plums

4. Core and peel the tomato. In a blender, combine the tomato with the reconstituted chiles, grilled garlic and onion, chipotle and adobo sauce, cilantro and lime juice; puree until smooth. Scrape the salsa into a bowl and season with salt and pepper.

—*S.R.*

MAKE AHEAD The salsa can be refrigerated overnight. Remove it from the refrigerator about an hour before serving so it has time to come to room temperature.

Swordfish with Sweet Onions and Red Plums

4 SERVINGS ● ●

- ¼ cup extra-virgin olive oil
- 2 sweet onions, such as Vidalia or Walla Walla, very thinly sliced
- 2 garlic cloves, smashed
- 2 rosemary sprigs
- 1½ tablespoons red wine vinegar
- 2 teaspoons honey

Sea salt and freshly ground pepper

- 6 firm red plums—halved, pitted and cut into wedges
- 1½ pounds swordfish
  (1½ inches thick)

1. Light a grill or preheat the broiler. In a large skillet, heat 3 tablespoons of the olive oil over high heat. Add the onions, garlic, rosemary, vinegar and honey and cook until the onions soften, about 4 minutes. Season with salt and pepper. Cover and cook over low heat until the onions are very tender, about 10 minutes. Add the plums to the skillet, cover and cook until the plums are tender, about 8 minutes. Discard the rosemary sprigs.

2. Meanwhile, brush the swordfish with the remaining 1 tablespoon of olive oil and season with salt and pepper. Grill the fish until it is just cooked through, about 5 minutes per side. Spoon the onions and plums onto a platter, top with the swordfish and serve. —*Melissa Clark*

Roast Salmon with Lime Salsa

4 SERVINGS ●●

The vibrant flavors in this roast salmon with fresh lime salsa will energize you So will the protein: It allegedly increases levels of a brain chemical called tyrosine, making you feel alert.

- 2 large limes
- ⅓ cup very thinly sliced red onion
- 2 tablespoons chopped cilantro
- 1 small jalapeño—halved, seeded and very thinly sliced crosswise
- 2 tablespoons canola oil

Pinch of sugar

Sea salt

Four 6-ounce center-cut skinless salmon fillets

Freshly ground pepper

1. Preheat the oven to 425°. Using a sharp knife, carefully peel the limes; be sure to remove all of the bitter white pith. Working over a bowl, cut in between the membranes to release the lime sections into the bowl. Cut each section crosswise into quarters. Return the limes to the bowl and stir in the onion, cilantro and jalapeño. Add 1 tablespoon of the oil, the sugar and a pinch of salt and toss well.

2. Heat the remaining 1 tablespoon of oil in an ovenproof skillet until shimmering. Season the fillets on both sides with salt and pepper and add to the skillet, skinned side up. Cook over moderately high heat until golden brown on the bottom, about 2 minutes. Transfer the skillet to the oven and roast the salmon for 5 minutes, or until just cooked through. Transfer to 4 dinner plates, spoon the salsa on top and serve. —*Grace Parisi*

WINE Salmon generally pairs well with red; here the tangy lime and sweet red onion salsa tune the choice to a bright fruity Burgundy or Pinot Noir. Two excellent choices: the 1998 Louis Jadot Chorey-lès-Beaune from France and the 1998 Coldstream Hills Yarra Valley Pinot Noir from Australia.

Salmon in Galangal-Tomato Compote

4 SERVINGS

- ⅓ cup coriander seeds
- 1½ tablespoons mace blades
- 1 teaspoon cardamom seeds
- 1 star anise pod
- 1 whole clove

Cayenne pepper

- 1¾ pounds tomatoes—peeled, cored and halved crosswise
- 2½ tablespoons extra-virgin olive oil
- 4 garlic cloves, lightly smashed
- 2 tablespoons unsalted butter
- 1 large onion, finely chopped
- 2 tablespoons minced peeled galangal (see Asian Flavorings, p. 179)
- 1 teaspoon finely grated lemon zest
- 1 tablespoon light brown sugar
- 2 tablespoons rice vinegar
- 1 cup water
- ½ large mango, peeled and cut into ½-inch dice
- 10 large basil leaves, plus shredded basil for garnish
- 2 teaspoons fresh lemon juice

Salt

Four 6-ounce skinless salmon fillets

1. In a medium skillet, combine the coriander seeds, mace blades, cardamom seeds, star anise and whole clove and toast over moderately high heat, shaking the skillet frequently, until fragrant, about 2 minutes. Transfer the spices to a plate to cool. Finely grind the spices with ½ teaspoon of cayenne.

2. Scoop the seeds and pulp from the tomatoes and put in a strainer set over a bowl; press on the seeds and pulp to extract all the juice. Cut the tomato flesh into ½-inch pieces and add them to the juice.

3. Heat 1½ tablespoons of the olive oil in a small skillet. Add the garlic and cook over moderately low heat, stirring occasionally, until golden, about 5 minutes.

4. Melt the butter in a large, deep skillet. Add the onion and cook over moderately high heat, stirring frequently, until softened, 4 to 5 minutes. Add the garlic, 2 tablespoons of the ground spices and the galangal, lemon zest and brown sugar and cook, stirring, for 2 minutes. Add the rice vinegar and cook until evaporated, about 30 seconds. Add the tomatoes, water, mango and whole basil leaves and simmer over low heat for 40 minutes. Stir in the lemon juice and season with salt and cayenne; keep warm.

5. Season the salmon with salt and cayenne. Heat the remaining 1 tablespoon of oil in a large skillet. Add the salmon and cook over moderately high heat until browned on the bottom, 3 minutes. Turn and cook until browned on the second side, 2 to 3 minutes.

6. Pour the tomato compote into a strainer set over a bowl. Mound the compote in warmed soup plates, top with the salmon fillets and spoon the strained tomato broth around. Garnish with the shredded basil and serve.

—*Jean-Georges Vongerichten*

MAKE AHEAD The tomato compote can be prepared through Step 4 up to

Roast Salmon with Lime Salsa

4 hours before serving. Reheat the compote before proceeding with the recipe.

WINE A tart, fresh-tasting Sauvignon Blanc will balance the acidity of the tomatoes and the lemony and sweet flavors in the compote. Look for the 1998 Alderbrook Dry Creek Valley from California or the 2000 Mulderbosch Sauvignon Blanc Stellenbosch from South Africa.

Pan-Seared Salmon with Mediterranean Salad

4 SERVINGS ●

- 1 small fennel bulb, cored and thinly sliced
- 1 Belgian endive, cut crosswise into 1-inch-thick slices
- 1 small head of radicchio, torn into bite-size pieces
- ¼ cup flat-leaf parsley leaves
- ¼ cup pitted Calamata olives, coarsely chopped
- 3½ tablespoons extra-virgin olive oil
- 2 tablespoons fresh lemon juice
- 1 garlic clove, minced

Salt and freshly ground pepper

Four 6-ounce skinless salmon fillets

Lemon wedges, for serving

1. In a medium bowl, toss the sliced fennel, endive, radicchio, parsley and chopped olives. In a small bowl, whisk 3 tablespoons of the extra-virgin olive oil with the lemon juice and garlic. Toss 3½ tablespoons of the dressing with the salad and season with salt and pepper.

2. Heat the remaining ½ tablespoon of olive oil in a medium nonstick skillet. Season the salmon with salt and pepper. Add the fillets to the pan and cook over high heat until browned, about 2 minutes per side.

3. Mound the salad on plates and top with the salmon. Drizzle the remaining dressing on the fish and serve with lemon wedges.   —*Joanne Weir*

Seared Salmon with Pearl Onions and Chanterelles

4 SERVINGS

- 1 stick (4 ounces) unsalted butter
- 1 large carrot, finely chopped
- 1 large Granny Smith apple, peeled and finely chopped
- 2 large shallots, finely chopped
- 2 garlic cloves, minced
- 1 bottle dry red wine
- 1½ cups ruby port
- ⅓ cup dried porcini mushrooms
- ½ cup chicken demiglace (see Note)
- 6 parsley sprigs plus 1 tablespoon minced parsley
- 4 whole black peppercorns
- 3 thyme sprigs
- 1 bay leaf
- 1 cup small pearl onions, peeled and root ends trimmed

Salt and freshly ground pepper

- 2 tablespoons dry white wine
- ½ pound small chanterelle mushrooms
- 2 pounds center-cut salmon fillet with skin, at room temperature
- 2 tablespoons pure olive oil

1. In a large skillet, melt 2 tablespoons of the butter over moderate heat. Add the chopped carrot, apple, shallots and half of the minced garlic and cook, stirring occasionally, until browned, about 10 minutes. Add the red wine, ruby port and porcini mushrooms and simmer until the liquid reduces to ½ cup, about 20 minutes. Stir in the chicken demiglace, parsley sprigs, black peppercorns, thyme sprigs and bay leaf and simmer until reduced to ½ cup, about 15 minutes longer. Strain the sauce into a small saucepan.

2. In another small saucepan, melt 2 tablespoons of the butter over moderately low heat. Add the peeled pearl onions, season with salt and freshly ground pepper and cook, stirring, until softened, about 7 minutes. Add the

white wine and simmer over moderately high heat until the pan is nearly dry, about 1 minute.

3. In a medium skillet, melt 2 tablespoons of the butter over high heat. Add the chanterelle mushrooms and the remaining half of the minced garlic, season with salt and freshly ground pepper and cook, stirring, until the mushrooms are nicely browned and tender, about 4 minutes. Remove the skillet from the heat. Stir in the pearl onions and minced parsley and cover to keep warm.

4. Using a sharp knife, score the salmon skin in a diamond pattern, making the cuts 1 inch apart. Cut the salmon fillet into 4 equal portions and season them with salt.

5. Heat the olive oil in a large nonstick skillet. Add the salmon, skin side down, and cook over high heat until the skin is crisp, about 5 minutes. Turn and cook for 1 minute longer.

6. Bring the sauce to a simmer. Remove from the heat and whisk in the remaining 2 tablespoons of butter; season with salt and pepper. Set the salmon fillets on plates. Drizzle the sauce around them, spoon the mushrooms and onions on top and serve.

—*Joshua Eisen*

NOTE F&W's favorite brands of demiglace are D'Artagnan (800-327-8246) and Perfect Addition (949-640-0220).

MAKE AHEAD The sauce can be refrigerated for a week.

WINE Serve the fillet with either the 1999 Domaine Jean-Marc Bouley Volnay or the 1998 Domaine Drouhin Pinot Noir.

Chilled Salmon with Endive and Asparagus Salad

4 SERVINGS ●●●

You can cook the asparagus in salted water, then remove it and add the salmon fillets and white wine to the same skillet, so there's one less pot to wash.

Kosher salt

1 pound medium asparagus

1 cup dry white wine

Four 6-ounce skinless salmon fillets

¼ cup balsamic vinegar

2 tablespoons Dijon mustard

¼ cup plus 1 tablespoon
   extra-virgin olive oil

Freshly ground pepper

½ lemon

3 Belgian endives, cored
   and cut crosswise into
   ½-inch-thick slices

2 tablespoons minced chives

1. Add 3 inches of water and 2 teaspoons of salt to a large skillet and bring to a boil. Add the asparagus and cook until barely tender, about 4 minutes. Line a large plate with paper towels and, using a slotted spoon, transfer the asparagus to the plate and refrigerate. Keep the water boiling.

2. Add the white wine to the water in the skillet and return to a boil. Add the skinless salmon fillets and simmer the fish over low heat until just cooked through, about 7 minutes. Transfer the poached salmon fillets to a plate and refrigerate.

3. Meanwhile, in a small bowl, mix the balsamic vinegar with the Dijon mustard. Whisk in the extra-virgin olive oil and season with salt and pepper. In a large bowl, squeeze the juice from the lemon half over the sliced Belgian endives and toss well.

4. Arrange the asparagus on plates or a large platter. Add 1 tablespoon of the dressing to the endives and toss well. Spoon the endives over the bottom of the asparagus. Set the salmon next to the asparagus and drizzle the remaining dressing around the plate. Garnish with the chives and serve.

—*Michael Roberts*

MAKE AHEAD The asparagus, salmon and dressing can be prepared 1 day ahead of time and refrigerated overnight. Whisk the dressing before proceeding.

Seared Salmon with
Pearl Onions and Chanterelles

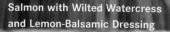

Salmon with Wilted Watercress and Lemon-Balsamic Dressing

Salmon with Wilted Watercress and Lemon-Balsamic Dressing

4 SERVINGS ● ●

- 2 tablespoons plus 2 teaspoons balsamic vinegar
- 2 tablespoons plus 2 teaspoons extra-virgin olive oil
- 4 teaspoons fresh lemon juice
- 4 small garlic cloves, minced
- 2 teaspoons finely grated lemon zest

Salt and freshly ground pepper
Four 6-ounce salmon fillets, skinned
- 1 pound watercress, large stems removed

I. In a bowl, mix the vinegar with the olive oil, lemon juice, garlic and lemon zest. Season with salt and pepper.

2. In a large, deep skillet, bring 1 inch of water to a boil. Lightly oil a steamer rack and set it in the skillet. Carefully add the fillets in a single layer. Cover and steam over moderate heat for 5 minutes. Strew the watercress over the salmon, cover and steam for 1 minute. Transfer to plates. Spoon the dressing over the salmon and serve.

—*Marcia Kiesel*

ONE SERVING Calories 324 kcal, Total Fat 17.3 gm, Saturated Fat 3.3 gm, Protein 39 gm, Carbohydrates 4 gm

Braised Salmon with Roasted Almonds

4 SERVINGS ● ●

- ¼ cup whole roasted almonds
- 3 tablespoons extra-virgin olive oil, plus more for drizzling
- ¼ cup minced onion
- ¼ cup minced cilantro
- 2 large garlic cloves, minced
- 2 anchovy fillets, drained and mashed
- ⅛ teaspoon cayenne pepper

Salt and freshly ground pepper
Four 6-ounce skinless salmon fillets
- ¾ pound linguine

I. In a mini food processor, finely grind the almonds. In a large skillet, heat 3 tablespoons of the olive oil. Stir in the almonds, the onion, cilantro, garlic, anchovies and cayenne and season with salt and pepper. Add the salmon to the skillet and spoon some of the almond mixture on top. Season the salmon with salt and pepper and drizzle with a little olive oil. Cover the salmon and cook over moderate heat for 5 minutes. Reduce the heat to moderately low and cook until the salmon is just opaque throughout, 8 to 10 minutes longer.

2. Meanwhile, in a large pot of boiling salted water, cook the linguine until al dente; drain and transfer to a serving platter. Spoon the almond sauce and salmon on top and serve at once.

—*Clifford A. Wright*

Fragrant Five-Spice Salmon with Savoy Cabbage

4 SERVINGS

- ¼ cup extra-virgin olive oil
- 1 tablespoon minced fresh ginger
- 1 large garlic clove, finely chopped
- 2 teaspoons five-spice powder

Four 6-ounce skinless salmon fillets
- 1 tablespoon unsalted butter
- ¼ pound sliced bacon (4 slices), cut into 1-inch pieces
- ½ cup chicken stock or canned low-sodium broth

One 1½-pound head of Savoy cabbage, cored and finely shredded
Salt and freshly ground white pepper

I. In a shallow dish, mix 3 tablespoons of the oil with the ginger, garlic and five-spice powder. Add the salmon and coat with the marinade. Cover the fish and refrigerate for at least 1 hour or for up to 4 hours.

2. Meanwhile, melt the butter in a large saucepan. Add the bacon and cook over moderately low heat until the bacon is lightly browned, about 4 minutes. Pour off all but 2 tablespoons of the fat from the pan. Add the stock and bring to a boil, then stir in the cabbage. Cover and cook over low heat, stirring a few times, until the cabbage is crisp-tender, about 5 minutes. Season with salt and white pepper, cover and keep warm.

3. In a large skillet, heat the remaining 1 tablespoon of olive oil. Season both sides of the fillets with salt and

MENU

FIRST COURSE
manila clams with serrano ham and parsley oil (p. 46)

1999 FROG'S LEAP
SAUVIGNON BLANC

light vegetable soup with pistachio pistou (p. 88)

1998 MONT ST. JOHN
MADONNA ESTATE CHARDONNAY

MAIN COURSE
olive oil poached salmon with chanterelles and asparagus

three onion risotto (p. 308)

1998 MONT ST. JOHN
MADONNA ESTATE PINOT NOIR

DESSERT
roast pineapple splits with macadamia brittle (p. 375)

1997 LOLONIS EUGENIA
LATE HARVEST SAUVIGNON BLANC

pepper. When the oil is almost smoking, add the fish, skinned side up, and cook over moderately high heat until browned, about 4 minutes. Reduce the heat to moderate and turn the fillets. Cook until browned on the other side and barely opaque in the center, about 3 minutes. Spoon the cabbage onto 4 plates, top with the salmon and serve immediately. —*Glenn Monk*

SERVE WITH Whipped sweet potatoes and sautéed apples.

WINE Pair the salmon with the 1998 Blue Mountain Pinot Gris. This wine's hints of pear, apricot and lychee stand up remarkably well to the spiciness of this dish.

Olive Oil Poached Salmon with Chanterelles and Asparagus

8 SERVINGS

Poaching salmon in olive oil makes it even richer. This technique also works especially well with white-fleshed fish, such as striped bass or halibut.

- 3 cups chicken stock or canned low-sodium broth
- 1 pound chanterelles or other wild mushrooms, stems trimmed and reserved, large mushrooms halved
- 1 tablespoon extra-virgin olive oil

Salt and freshly ground pepper

- 2 garlic cloves, minced
- 24 thin asparagus (about 1 pound)
- 8 skinless center-cut salmon fillets (4 ounces each)
- 2 cups pure olive oil
- 1 teaspoon thyme
- 4 tablespoons cold unsalted butter, cut into tablespoons

Three Onion Risotto (p. 308)

1. Heat the chicken stock in a medium saucepan. Add the chanterelle trimmings, cover and simmer over low heat for 10 minutes. Strain the broth and discard the trimmings.

2. In a large skillet, heat the extra-virgin olive oil until shimmering. Add the chanterelles, season lightly with salt and pepper and cook over moderately high heat, stirring, until dry and golden brown, about 8 minutes. Add the garlic and cook, stirring frequently, until fragrant, about 3 minutes. Transfer the chanterelles to a plate; add the broth to the skillet and boil

Fragrant Five-Spice Salmon with Savoy Cabbage

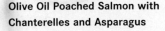

Olive Oil Poached Salmon with Chanterelles and Asparagus

until reduced to 1 cup, about 10 minutes. Return the chanterelles to the skillet.

3. In a large saucepan of boiling salted water, cook the asparagus until almost tender, about 2 minutes. Remove from the heat and cover.

4. Season the salmon with salt and pepper. In a large, deep skillet, heat the pure olive oil until shimmering. Add the salmon and cook over moderate heat for 3 minutes. Carefully turn the fillets and simmer until just cooked through, about 3 minutes longer.

5. Bring the chanterelles to a boil and remove from the heat. Add the thyme and whisk in the butter, 1 tablespoon at a time. Season with salt and pepper. Spoon the sauce into warmed shallow bowls. Set a salmon fillet in each bowl, spoon the Three Onion Risotto beside it and garnish with the asparagus.

—Kevin Taylor

MAKE AHEAD The chanterelle sauce can be made early in the day and rewarmed before serving.

WINE An intense, complex red with sweet fruit and some oak will play off the intense, complex flavors of the salmon, chanterelles and risotto. Two organic wines to try are the 1997 Domaine Canet Valette Saint-Chinian Maghani and the 1998 Mont St. John Madonna Estate Pinot Noir.

Roasted Salmon with Warm Lentil Salad

4 SERVINGS ●

- ¾ cup Puy lentils, rinsed and picked over
- 1 medium carrot, cut into ¼-inch dice
- 1 small onion, cut into ¼-inch dice
- 1 bay leaf
- 2 garlic cloves, minced

Salt

- 1 red bell pepper
- 1 yellow bell pepper
- 1 teaspoon lemon zest
- ½ teaspoon orange zest
- 3 tablespoons fresh lemon juice
- 3 tablespoons fresh orange juice
- 2 tablespoons extra-virgin olive oil
- 2 teaspoons sherry vinegar
- ¼ cup mint leaves, shredded

Freshly ground pepper

Four 4-ounce skinless salmon fillets

Lemon slices or wedges, for serving

1. Preheat the broiler. In a medium saucepan, combine the lentils with the carrot, onion, bay leaf, 1 teaspoon of the garlic and 1 teaspoon of salt. Add enough cold water to reach 2 inches above the lentils. Bring to a boil. Reduce the heat to moderately low and simmer until the lentils are tender but still hold their shape, about 25 minutes. Drain well. Transfer to a bowl and discard the bay leaf; keep warm.

2. Meanwhile, halve the bell peppers lengthwise and remove the cores. Arrange the peppers on a baking sheet, cut side down, and broil for 8 minutes, or until the skin blisters and begins to char. Transfer the bell peppers to a bowl, cover with plastic wrap and let steam for 5 minutes. Peel the peppers and cut them into ⅛-inch dice; transfer to a bowl. Decrease the oven temperature to 425°.

3. In a small bowl, combine the lemon and orange zests with the lemon and orange juices. Add the remaining garlic, then slowly whisk in the olive oil. Pour the dressing over the lentils and toss gently. Stir in the diced peppers, sherry vinegar and 3 tablespoons of the mint. Season with salt and pepper.

4. Season the salmon with salt and pepper and set it on a baking sheet, skinned side down. Roast for 12 to 15 minutes, or until just cooked through. Transfer the salmon to plates and spoon the lentil salad alongside. Garnish with the remaining mint and serve with lemon slices.

—Ann Chantal Altman

ONE SERVING Calories 426 kcal, Total Fat 18.8 gm, Saturated Fat 3.3 gm, Protein 32 gm, Carbohydrates 33 gm

Salmon with Brown Butter Béarnaise

4 SERVINGS

Classic béarnaise—a thick, egg- and butter-rich sauce—is lightened here for the modern palate.

One 1¼-pound center-cut salmon fillet, skinned

Fine sea salt or kosher salt

- 2 medium chicken drumsticks
- 2 large garlic cloves, unpeeled
- 1 tablespoon pure olive oil, plus more for drizzling

Freshly ground pepper

- ½ pound salmon bones
- 2½ cups chicken stock or canned low-sodium broth
- 4 tablespoons unsalted butter
- 1 large shallot, minced
- ¼ teaspoon crushed white peppercorns
- ¾ cup dry white wine
- ⅓ cup sherry vinegar
- 1 tarragon sprig plus 1 tablespoon chopped tarragon

1. Sprinkle the salmon fillet with 1 teaspoon of salt. Cover the salmon and refrigerate for 1½ hours.

2. Cut the fish crosswise into 8 even slices about ¾ inch thick. Lay 2 of the salmon slices on their sides, matching the wide inner section with the thin belly section so they fit together. Tie the pieces together with kitchen string around the circumference to hold them together. Repeat with the remaining salmon pieces; cover and refrigerate.

3. Preheat the oven to 375°. In a small baking dish, drizzle the chicken and garlic cloves with oil. Season with salt and pepper, cover with foil and bake for 30 minutes, or until the garlic is softened. Reduce the oven temperature to 325°.

4. In a medium saucepan, heat the olive oil. Add the salmon bones, season with salt and pepper and cook over moderate heat, stirring, until the bones turn opaque, about 4 minutes.

Grilled Salmon with Fennel Butter

Add the roasted chicken and garlic with any accumulated juices, then pour in the stock. Bring to a boil. Simmer over low heat, skimming until reduced by half, about 40 minutes. Strain the reduction.

5. In a small saucepan, melt 2 tablespoons of the butter. Add the shallot and white peppercorns and cook over low heat until softened, about 5 minutes. Add the white wine, vinegar and tarragon sprig and boil over moderate heat until almost evaporated, about 12 minutes. Add the reduction and simmer over low heat until reduced to ⅔ cup, about 10 minutes; let the sauce stand off the heat for 1 minute.

6. In a small skillet, melt the remaining 2 tablespoons of butter until nutty brown. Whisk the brown butter into the reduced sauce, season with salt and pepper and stir in the chopped tarragon.

7. Set an 18-by-12-inch piece of parchment paper on a rimmed baking sheet and arrange the salmon on the paper. Cover the fish with another piece of parchment, fold the ends neatly under on all sides and press well to seal. Bake the fillets for about 12 minutes, or until the salmon is barely cooked through.

8. Reheat the tarragon sauce over moderate heat, whisking constantly; do not boil. Set each salmon fillet on a plate, spoon the sauce on top and serve.   —*Laurent Gras*

WINE Pinot Noir, a classic match with salmon, provides an attractive, fruity contrast to the sauce's sweet, winy flavors. Look for the 1998 Marimar Torres Russian River Valley Don Miguel Vineyard or the 1998 Wild Horse Central Coast.

Grilled Salmon with Fennel Butter

12 SERVINGS

Grilling a whole salmon is a Seattle tradition, particularly for special occasions. If you don't plan to eat the skin, ask your fishmonger to leave the scales on; the fish will be less likely to stick to the grill.

One 6- to 7-pound salmon—cleaned, rinsed and patted dry, head and tail removed

Sea salt

1   **medium onion, thinly sliced**

1   **lemon, thinly sliced**

½   **cup fennel fronds**

Pure olive oil, for brushing

Fennel Butter (recipe follows)

1. Light a grill. Season the salmon inside and out with salt. Stuff the cavity with the onion, lemon and fennel fronds. Using cotton string, tie the salmon in 4 places. Make 4 incisions in the thickest part of each side of the fish, cutting down to the bone. Brush the salmon generously with olive oil and oil the grate.

2. Set the salmon over a medium-hot fire. Cover and grill with the vents open for 15 minutes, or until the skin is browned on the bottom. Using 2 metal spatulas, loosen the salmon from the grate and carefully turn over. Cover and grill for about 20 minutes longer, or until just cooked through and an instant-read thermometer inserted in the thickest part of the fish registers 135° to 140°. Transfer the salmon to a platter and let rest for 5 minutes. Remove the strings and serve with Fennel Butter.   —*Tom Douglas*

WINE A Chardonnay with rich fruit and good body and texture will stand up to the smoky grilled flavors of the salmon and echo the sweetness of the fennel butter. Pick a rich, round one without too much oak, such as the 1999 Chateau Ste. Michelle Cold Creek Vineyard or the bargain 1999 Hogue Columbia Valley Vineyard, from Washington State.

FENNEL BUTTER

MAKES ¾ CUP ● ●

1½   **sticks (6 ounces) unsalted butter, at room temperature**

2   **tablespoons chopped fennel fronds**

2   **tablespoons fresh orange juice**

2   **teaspoons finely grated orange zest**

1   **teaspoon honey**

Salt and freshly ground pepper

Combine all of the ingredients in a food processor and blend until smooth. Scrape the butter into a bowl and serve.   —*T.D.*

MAKE AHEAD The fennel butter can be refrigerated for 3 days or frozen for 2 weeks.

Smoked Salmon Hash with Dill Vinaigrette

4 SERVINGS

This deliciously crisp hash, made with Scotland's finest cold-smoked salmon, is wonderful on its own or served with poached eggs for brunch.

½   **pound center-cut Scottish cold-smoked salmon in 1 piece**

1   **red bell pepper**

3   **tablespoons minced dill**

1 tablespoon plus 1 teaspoon fresh lemon juice

1 tablespoon minced shallot

¼ cup plus 2 teaspoons extra-virgin olive oil

Salt and freshly ground pepper

¾ pound Yukon Gold potatoes, cut into ¼-inch dice

1 tablespoon drained prepared horseradish

4 poached eggs, for serving

2 tablespoons salmon caviar

1. Cut the salmon crosswise into 1-inch strips. In a medium saucepan of boiling water, poach the salmon until just cooked through, about 2 minutes. Drain on paper towels and break into large flakes.

2. Roast the bell pepper over a low gas flame or under the broiler, turning occasionally, until lightly charred all over, about 15 minutes. Transfer to a bowl, cover with plastic wrap and let steam for 15 minutes. Peel, core and seed the pepper. Cut into ¼-inch dice.

3. In a mini food processor, puree 1 tablespoon of the dill with the lemon juice and shallot. In a slow, steady stream, add 2 tablespoons plus 2 teaspoons of the olive oil and process until emulsified. Season with salt and pepper.

4. In a saucepan fitted with a steamer basket, bring 1 inch of water to a boil. Add the potatoes and cook until just tender, about 4 minutes. In a medium bowl, toss the potatoes with the roasted bell pepper, flaked salmon, horseradish and the remaining 2 tablespoons of dill. Season with pepper.

5. Heat a large cast-iron skillet. Add the remaining 2 tablespoons of olive oil and heat until shimmering. Add the hash mixture in an even layer and fry over moderately high heat until golden and crisp on the bottom, about 3 minutes. Scrape up the hash and turn; continue frying until golden and crisp all over, about 8 minutes longer. Season with salt and pepper and transfer to plates. Top the hash with the poached eggs, drizzle with the vinaigrette and garnish with the salmon caviar. Serve at once.   —*Bobby Flay*

Chile-Ginger Marinated Tuna Steaks

6 SERVINGS ● ●

The spicy Asian-flavored marinade is also delicious for flank steak. Palm sugar can replace the brown sugar to make a richer, more syrupy marinade.

½ cup (packed) light brown sugar

¼ cup vegetable oil

¼ cup coarsely chopped peeled fresh ginger

¼ cup finely chopped shallots

2 tablespoons Asian chile-garlic sauce (available at Asian markets)

Six 1-inch-thick tuna steaks (about ½ pound each)

Salt and freshly ground pepper

1. In a food processor or blender, combine the sugar, oil, ginger, shallots and chile-garlic sauce and process until a coarse puree forms.

2. Arrange the tuna steaks in a 13-by-9-inch glass baking dish. Pour the marinade over the steaks and turn to coat. Cover with plastic wrap and refrigerate for 2 hours, turning once.

3. Light a grill or preheat the broiler. Season the tuna steaks on both sides with salt and pepper. Grill the steaks, turning once, for about 4 minutes per side for medium rare. Slice the tuna steaks across the grain and serve warm, at room temperature or chilled.

—*Ilene Rosen*

MAKE AHEAD The grilled tuna can be refrigerated overnight.

WINE A rich, fruity rosé with good acidity will best complement the sweet and spicy accents of the tuna. Choose the 1999 La Palma from Chile or the 1999 Domaine Saint-André de Figuière Vieilles Vignes from Provence.

Smoked Salmon Hash with Dill Vinaigrette

Seared Tuna Salad with Piment d'Espelette

4 SERVINGS ●

½ cup plus 2 tablespoons
extra-virgin olive oil
2 red bell peppers,
very thinly sliced
1 medium onion,
very thinly sliced
5 garlic cloves, sliced paper thin
1½ teaspoons thyme leaves
½ cup water
Kosher salt
Piment d'Espelette
Four 6-ounce tuna steaks, 1 inch thick
1 small head of frisée, torn
into bite-size pieces
2 tablespoons finely chopped
flat-leaf parsley
1 tablespoon sherry vinegar

1. Heat ½ cup of the extra-virgin olive oil in a large skillet. Add the sliced red bell peppers, onion, garlic and thyme leaves and cook over moderate heat until crisp-tender, about 5 minutes. Add the water and cook over moderately low heat until the vegetables are very soft and the liquid has evaporated, about 25 minutes. Season the vegetables with salt and ½ teaspoon of piment d'Espelette, then transfer to a bowl to cool.

2. Rub the tuna steaks with the remaining 2 tablespoons of extra-virgin olive oil and season generously with salt and ½ teaspoon of piment d'Espelette. Heat a large, heavy skillet. Add the tuna steaks and cook over high heat, turning once, until browned on the outside and medium rare on the inside, about 4 minutes. Transfer the tuna steaks to a cutting board and slice ½ inch thick.

3. Add the frisée, parsley and vinegar to the peppers, season with salt and piment d'Espelette and toss. Mound the salad on plates and top with the tuna. Sprinkle with salt and piment d'Espelette and serve.

—*Gerald Hirigoyen*

Smoked Fish Jambalaya

4 SERVINGS

¼ cup extra-virgin olive oil
1 cup minced onion
1 cup minced green bell pepper
1 cup minced celery
4 bay leaves
3 whole cloves
2 tablespoons minced garlic
2 teaspoons chopped thyme
1 teaspoon kosher salt
1 teaspoon cayenne pepper
1 teaspoon freshly ground pepper
1 teaspoon filé powder (see Note)
½ teaspoon ground cumin
½ pound sea scallops, halved
½ pound skinless, boneless
smoked white fish fillets,
cut into 2-inch chunks
2 cups long-grain rice
2 cups bottled clam juice
2 cups water
1 tablespoon Worcestershire sauce

1. Preheat the oven to 375°. Heat the extra-virgin olive oil in a large enameled cast-iron casserole. Add the minced onion, green bell pepper and celery and cook over moderate heat, stirring occasionally, until softened, about 8 minutes. Add the bay leaves, cloves, minced garlic, chopped thyme, kosher salt, cayenne pepper, black pepper, filé powder and cumin and cook, stirring, until fragrant, about 3 minutes. Stir in the scallops, smoked fish and rice. Add the clam juice, water and Worcestershire sauce, cover and bring to a simmer.

2. Bake the jambalaya for 25 minutes, or until all of the liquid has been absorbed. Let the jambalaya stand, covered, for 10 minutes. Pick out the bay leaves and cloves before serving, if desired.

—*Charles Leary and Vaughn Perret*

NOTE Filé powder is made from ground dried sassafras leaves. It acts as a thickener for stews and soups and is an integral ingredient in Creole cooking.

Scallops with Mushrooms and Whiskey Sauce

4 SERVINGS ●

1 pound mushrooms, quartered
1 tablespoon fresh lemon juice
2½ tablespoons unsalted butter
Salt and freshly ground pepper
1½ pounds bay scallops
4 scallions, thinly sliced crosswise
⅓ cup whiskey
¼ cup heavy cream

1. Toss the mushrooms with the lemon juice. In a skillet, melt 1 tablespoon of the butter. Add the mushrooms, season with salt and pepper and cook over moderately high heat until they start to brown, about 2 minutes. Reduce the heat to moderate and cook until the mushrooms are deeply browned, about 6 minutes. Transfer to a large plate.

2. Add 1 tablespoon of the butter to the skillet and melt over high heat. Add the scallops to the pan in an even layer and season with salt and pepper. Cook the scallops undisturbed until they start to brown and some juices are exuded, about 2 minutes. Stir briefly, then transfer the scallops and any accumulated juices to a bowl.

3. Add the remaining ½ tablespoon of butter and the scallions to the skillet. Cook over moderately low heat, stirring, for 1 minute. Add the whiskey and carefully ignite it with a long match. When the flames die down, add the cream, mushrooms and any juices from the scallops. Simmer the sauce until slightly reduced. Add the scallops to the sauce, season with salt and pepper and serve. —*Marcia Kiesel*

Sea Scallops and Leeks with Chive Noodles

4 SERVINGS

½ pound medium egg noodles
6 tablespoons unsalted butter
3 leeks, white and light green parts,
thinly sliced crosswise
2 tablespoons minced fresh ginger

½ cup dry white wine
1½ pounds large sea scallops
Salt and freshly ground pepper
¼ cup heavy cream
Pinch of ground mace
¼ cup finely snipped chives

1. Cook the egg noodles in a large pot of boiling salted water, stirring often, until al dente; drain.

2. Meanwhile, in a large, deep skillet, melt 3 tablespoons of the butter over low heat. Add the leeks and cook, stirring, until tender, about 8 minutes. Add the ginger and cook over moderate heat for 2 minutes. Pour in the wine and bring to a simmer. Season the scallops with salt and pepper and add them to the skillet. Cover and cook over low heat for 2 minutes. Turn the scallops, cover and simmer until just cooked through, about 2 minutes. Transfer the scallops to a plate and keep warm.

3. Add the cream and mace to the skillet and bring to a simmer. Add the egg noodles and the remaining 3 tablespoons of butter and toss to coat. Season with salt and pepper. Add the scallops and 3 tablespoons of the chives and toss again. Mound the egg noodles and scallops on plates, sprinkle with the remaining chives and serve. —*Joshua Eisen*

WINE Pair this dish with either the 1999 Olivier Leflaive Frères Les Narvaux Meursault or the 1998 Chateau Montelena Napa Valley Chardonnay.

Sautéed Seafood with Spicy Romesco Sauce

4 SERVINGS

3 red bell peppers
1 ancho chile—stemmed, seeded and torn into large pieces
3 tablespoons extra-virgin olive oil
One 1-inch-thick slice of country white bread, crust discarded, bread toasted and torn into 1-inch pieces
⅓ cup sliced blanched almonds

2 garlic cloves, minced
Salt
½ cup cherry tomatoes, halved
2 teaspoons sherry vinegar
¼ cup water
Freshly ground pepper
½ pound medium shrimp, shelled and deveined, tails left on
½ pound large sea scallops
¾ pound cleaned squid, bodies cut into ¼-inch rings, large tentacles halved
½ cup coarsely chopped flat-leaf parsley or cilantro

1. Roast the bell peppers directly over a gas flame or under the broiler, turning, until blackened or charred all over. Transfer to a bowl, cover with plastic wrap and let steam for 10 minutes, then peel and remove the cores.

2. Meanwhile, in a small bowl, cover the ancho chile with hot water and let stand for 15 minutes. Drain the chile and pat dry.

3. In a large skillet, heat 2 tablespoons of the olive oil until shimmering. Add the ancho chile and cook over moderate heat, stirring, for 2 minutes.

4. In a food processor, combine the bread with the almonds and garlic. Season with salt and process until the mixture resembles fine bread crumbs. Add the ancho and its oil, the peppers, tomatoes and vinegar and puree. With the machine on, add the water. Scrape into a bowl and season with salt and pepper.

5. Heat the remaining 1 tablespoon of olive oil in the skillet. Add the shrimp and scallops, season with salt and pepper and cook over moderate heat for 1 minute, then turn and cook for 30 seconds longer. Add 1 cup of the romesco sauce and bring to a simmer; if the sauce seems too thick, add 2 tablespoons of water to loosen it. Add the squid and cook just until it turns opaque, about 2 minutes. Remove from the heat, season with salt and stir in the parsley. Transfer to a platter and serve. Pass the remaining romesco sauce at the table or refrigerate for another use. —*Ann Chantal Altman*

ONE SERVING Calories 375 kcal, Total Fat 16.8 gm, Saturated Fat 2.3 gm, Protein 34 gm, Carbohydrates 22 gm

Fresh Crab Salad with Lime Zest

4 SERVINGS ●●●

A variation of this crab salad is part of a luxurious dish served at Pic, a restaurant in Valence, France. Fresh crabmeat is such a delicacy that the crab salad deserves to stand alone.

3 tablespoons mayonnaise
1½ teaspoons finely grated lime zest
1 teaspoon fresh lime juice
1 pound fresh lump crabmeat, picked over
Salt and freshly ground pepper
Lettuce leaves, for garnish
Lime wedges, for garnish

Simple Shellfish Spice Mix

MAKES ABOUT 2 TABLESPOONS ●●●

Dust this spice mix on such shellfish as shrimp or scallops as well as on white-flesh finfish, or thin boneless chicken breasts or pork chops; then sauté, broil or grill.

1 tablespoon plus 1 teaspoon fennel seeds
3 whole cloves
½ bay leaf
1 teaspoon chopped rosemary

In a small skillet, combine the fennel seeds with the cloves and bay leaf. Cook over moderate heat, shaking the skillet, until the spices are fragrant, about 1 minute. Transfer the toasted spices to a spice grinder and let cool completely. Add the rosemary and grind to a medium-fine powder. —*Gray Kunz*

MAKE AHEAD The shellfish spice mix can be stored in an airtight container for up to 5 days.

In a medium bowl, mix the mayonnaise with the lime zest and lime juice. Gently fold in the crabmeat and season with salt and pepper. Arrange lettuce leaves on a platter or plates and mound the crab salad on top. Garnish with lime wedges and serve.

—*Patricia Wells*

ONE SERVING Calories 191 kcal, Total Fat 10.2 gm, Saturated Fat 1.5 gm, Protein 23 gm, Carbohydrates 1 gm

MAKE AHEAD The Fresh Crab Salad with Lime Zest can be prepared in advance and refrigerated for 4 hours. Shortly before serving, mound the salad on the lettuce. Serve cold or just lightly chilled.

WINE Crab is marvelous with a chilled dry Sauvignon Blanc from the Loire. The tartness sets off shellfish to perfection. Try a Quincy, perhaps from Domaine Mardon.

Soft-Shell Crabs with Wilted Arugula

4 SERVINGS ●

- ½ cup all-purpose flour
- Salt and freshly ground pepper
- 8 medium soft-shell crabs, cleaned
- 2 tablespoons unsalted butter
- ¼ cup extra-virgin olive oil
- 6 ounces baby arugula (8 loosely packed cups)
- 2 ounces thinly sliced Serrano ham or prosciutto
- Lemon wedges, for serving

I. Season the flour with salt and pepper; dredge the crabs in the flour, tapping off any excess. In a large skillet, melt 1 tablespoon of the butter in 1 tablespoon of the oil. Add 4 of the crabs to the skillet and cook over moderately high heat until golden, about 3 minutes per side. Transfer the crabs to a low oven and keep warm. Repeat with another tablespoon each of the butter and oil and the remaining crabs.

2. Wipe out the skillet. Add the remaining 2 tablespoons of oil and heat until shimmering. Add the arugula and season lightly with salt. Remove from the heat and toss quickly to barely wilt the arugula. Arrange the ham slices on plates and top with the crabs. Mound the arugula alongside and serve with lemon wedges. —*Melissa Clark*

Soft-Shell Crabs with Fennel and Mesclun Salad

4 SERVINGS

A sophisticated vinaigrette using Pernod adds more fennel flavor to the fennel salad. Soaking the crabs in heavily seasoned milk is far more effective than adding salt to the flour coating.

- 1 cup milk
- Kosher salt and freshly ground pepper
- 8 medium soft-shell crabs (1½ pounds)
- 1 fennel bulb (about 1¼ pounds), trimmed and cored, fronds reserved
- 3 tablespoons fresh lemon juice

Fresh Crab Salad with Lime Zest

3 tablespoons extra-virgin
olive oil

1 tablespoon Pernod or other
anise-flavored liqueur

1 tablespoon fresh lime juice

½ teaspoon sugar

6 tablespoons vegetable oil

All-purpose flour, for dredging

¼ pound mesclun (8 cups)

1. Preheat the oven to 400°. Pour the milk into a large shallow dish and season with 2 teaspoons of salt and ½ teaspoon of pepper. Put the crabs in the milk and let marinate for about 10 minutes.

2. Slice the fennel very thinly on a mandoline. Transfer the fennel to a bowl and sprinkle generously with salt. Toss with 1½ tablespoons of the lemon juice and refrigerate until ready to use.

3. In a small bowl, mix the remaining 1½ tablespoons of lemon juice with the extra-virgin olive oil, Pernod, lime juice and sugar. Season with salt and pepper.

4. Heat 3 tablespoons of the vegetable oil in a large skillet. One by one, lift 4 of the crabs out of the milk and dredge them in flour, shaking off the excess. When the oil is almost smoking, fry the crabs over moderately high heat, top shell side down, until browned and crisp on the bottom, about 3 minutes. Turn the crabs and cook until crisp on the second side, about 2 minutes longer. Transfer the crabs to a rimmed baking sheet. Discard the oil and carefully wipe the skillet clean. Heat the remaining 3 tablespoons of vegetable oil in the pan. Flour and fry the remaining crabs, then transfer them to the baking sheet. Keep the crabs hot in the oven while you prepare the fennel salad.

5. Squeeze the fennel dry. In a large bowl, combine the mesclun with the fennel and toss with the vinaigrette. Mound the salad on plates, top each salad with 2 crabs and serve.

—Eberhard Müller

MAKE AHEAD The vinaigrette can be refrigerated overnight.

Soft-Shell Crabs with Farro Salad

4 SERVINGS ●

½ cup unsweetened pineapple juice

2 fresh hot red chiles, seeded
and minced

4½ teaspoons minced fresh ginger

2 tablespoons chopped cilantro

2 tablespoons thick coconut cream,
spooned from the top of a chilled
can of unsweetened coconut milk

¼ cup olive oil

4 jumbo soft-shell crabs
(about 3 ounces each)

1 cup farro

½ cucumber—peeled, seeded and
finely diced

½ red bell pepper, finely diced

1 Hass avocado, finely diced

6 slices smoked bacon

5 tablespoons fresh lime juice

2 tablespoons chopped basil

Salt and freshly ground pepper

Four 1½-inch-thick slices of red or
yellow watermelon, peeled

Turbinado or granulated brown sugar

1 teaspoon unsalted butter

2 tablespoons vegetable oil

Soft-Shell Crabs with Farro Salad

1. In a small saucepan, boil the pineapple juice until reduced to 2 tablespoons, about 15 minutes. Transfer to a large bowl. Stir in the minced red chiles, 2 teaspoons of the ginger, the cilantro, coconut cream and 1 tablespoon of the olive oil. Add the crabs and refrigerate.

2. In a medium saucepan of boiling salted water, cook the farro until just tender, about 15 minutes; drain. Transfer the farro to a large bowl and add the cucumber, bell pepper and avocado.

3. In a medium skillet, cook the bacon over moderate heat until lightly crisp. Pour off all but 2 tablespoons of the bacon fat from the skillet. Cut the cooked bacon into thin strips and add it to the farro. In a small bowl, combine the lime juice with the remaining 3 tablespoons of olive oil, the remaining 2½ teaspoons of ginger and the basil and season generously with salt and pepper. Pour the dressing over the farro and toss.

4. Heat the reserved bacon fat in the skillet until almost smoking. Coat the watermelon with turbinado sugar. Add the butter to the skillet, then add the watermelon and cook over high heat until well browned, about 2 minutes per side.

5. In a large skillet, heat the vegetable oil over moderately high heat. Remove the crabs from the marinade and season with salt and pepper; sauté until cooked through, about 3 minutes per side. Spoon the salad onto plates, set the crabs on top and garnish with the caramelized watermelon. Serve at once. —*E. Michael Reidt*

Shrimp Salad with Lime Zest

6 TO 8 SERVINGS ● ●

A surprise ingredient is used to lighten the shrimp salad—whipped cream.

- 1 cup kosher salt
- 6 cups cold water
- 2½ pounds medium shrimp, shelled and deveined
- 3 tablespoons heavy cream
- ½ cup mayonnaise
- 1½ tablespoons fresh lime juice
- 1½ teaspoons finely grated lime zest
- ¼ cup finely diced celery
- 2 tablespoons finely chopped dill
- 1 tablespoon thinly sliced garlic chives

Table salt and freshly ground pepper

1. Bring a large saucepan of salted water to a boil. Prepare a bowl of ice water.

2. In a large bowl, dissolve the kosher salt in the water. Add the shrimp and let stand for 30 seconds, then rinse well. Add the shrimp to the boiling water and cook until firm and pink, 2 to 3 minutes. Drain the shrimp and

Shrimp Salad with Lime Zest

Garlicky Shrimp with Lemon

1. Melt the butter in a large skillet. Add the minced garlic and cook over low heat until the garlic is golden, about 2 minutes. Add the shrimp, season lightly with salt and pepper and cook over moderate heat, turning often, until the shrimp are almost cooked through, about 4 minutes. Transfer the shrimp to a plate.

2. Add the white wine to the skillet and simmer over moderate heat for 2 minutes. Add the lemon juice and simmer for 2 minutes longer. Return the shrimp and their juices to the skillet and cook, stirring, for 1 minute. Season the shrimp with salt and pepper and garnish with parsley. Serve at once, with bread. —*Murielle Andraud*

WINE Play off the citrus and garlic notes of the shrimp with an herby Sauvignon Blanc–based wine from the Bordeaux appellation Entre-Deux-Mers, such as the 2000 Château Marjosse Blanc. Or try the readily available 2000 Château Bonnet Blanc.

Madras Shrimp Curry

4 SERVINGS ●

    3   tablespoons canola oil
    1   medium onion, coarsely chopped
    1   tablespoon grated peeled
        fresh ginger
1½   teaspoons minced garlic
1½   tablespoons Madras curry powder
    1   cup unsweetened coconut milk
    1   cup chicken stock or canned
        low-sodium chicken broth
1½   pounds shelled and deveined
        medium shrimp
Salt
Cayenne pepper
    2   tablespoons finely chopped mint
  ½   teaspoon finely grated lemon zest
Steamed rice, for serving

1. Heat the oil in a large, deep skillet until shimmering. Add the onion and cook over moderate heat, stirring occasionally, until softened and just beginning to brown, about 7 minutes. Add the ginger, garlic and curry and

transfer to the ice water to cool. Drain again and pat dry.

3. In a bowl, beat the cream until stiff. Whisk in the mayonnaise, lime juice and zest, and stir in the celery, dill and chives. Add the shrimp and toss well. Season with table salt and pepper and serve. —*Ilene Rosen*

MAKE AHEAD The shrimp salad can be refrigerated for up to 5 hours.

WINE Highlight the sweet shrimp and the tangy dressing with a light, citrusy Riesling from Washington State, such as the 1999 Eroica from Chateau Ste. Michelle Dr. Loosen or the bargain 1999 Hogue Cellars Johannisberg Riesling.

Garlicky Shrimp with Lemon

6 SERVINGS ●

Try to find Mayan head-on shrimp from Ecuador; their rich taste and orange color make this easy preparation sublime. They are available by mail order from Wild Edibles, 212-687-4255.

    6   tablespoons unsalted butter
    3   garlic cloves, minced
  24   large shrimp (4 pounds),
        shelled and deveined
Sea salt and freshly ground pepper
  ¼   cup plus 2 tablespoons dry
        white wine
    3   tablespoons fresh lemon juice
Coarsely chopped parsley, for garnish
Crusty baguettes, for serving

Shrimp in Pomegranate Curry

pomegranate pantry

Pomegranate juice is great as a mixer or served straight up. It is available bottled, in health food stores, or you can make your own by cutting a pomegranate in half and using a citrus juicer; a large fruit will yield about half a cup.
Pomegranate molasses (also called pomegranate essence) is a concentrated juice sold in Middle Eastern markets that's often used in sauces, marinades and glazes. The word *molasses* refers to its syrupy texture, not its taste. You can make pomegranate syrup as a substitute by reducing 4 cups of pomegranate juice to about ¾ cup and adding a little sugar.
Pomegranate vinegar, made from Champagne vinegar with a touch of pomegranate molasses or concentrated juice, brightens sauces and vinaigrettes.

cook, stirring, until fragrant, about 2 minutes. Add the coconut milk and stock and simmer over moderate heat until reduced by one-third and thickened, about 8 minutes.

2. Add the shrimp, season with salt and cayenne and simmer over moderate heat until the shrimp are pink and cooked through, about 5 minutes. Stir in the mint and lemon zest and serve in deep bowls over steamed rice.

—*Joyce Goldstein*

Shrimp in Pomegranate Curry

4 SERVINGS ● ●

¼ cup pomegranate molasses
½ cup water
3 tablespoons vegetable oil
1 large onion, finely chopped
2 teaspoons hot curry powder
1 tablespoon minced garlic
4 canned tomatoes, seeded and finely chopped
Salt and freshly ground pepper
1 pound large shrimp, shelled and deveined, tails left on
½ cup finely chopped cilantro

1. In a small jar, mix the pomegranate molasses with the water.

2. Heat 2 tablespoons of the vegetable oil in a small saucepan. Add the chopped onion and hot curry powder and cook over moderately high heat, stirring often, until the onion is softened, 3 to 5 minutes. Add the minced garlic and cook for 1 minute. Stir in the pomegranate mixture and chopped tomatoes and season with salt and pepper. Cover and cook, stirring often, until the onion is very soft, about 15 minutes.

3. Meanwhile, in a large skillet, heat the remaining 1 tablespoon of vegetable oil. Season the shrimp with salt and pepper, add them to the skillet and stir-fry over moderately high heat until firm to the touch and just cooked through, about 2 minutes. Stir in the cilantro.

4. Spoon the shrimp onto plates, pour the pomegranate curry sauce on top and serve immediately. —*Suki Hertz*

ONE SERVING Calories 314 kcal, Total Fat 13 gm, Saturated Fat 1.2 gm

Shrimp and Baby Beets with Sherry Vinegar

4 SERVINGS ●

This would make a terrific lunch or supper paired with the Tabbouleh with Mint, Cilantro and Chives on page 312.

20 baby beets (1¼ pounds), preferably a mixture of white, golden and red, greens trimmed
Salt
2 tablespoons unsalted butter
¼ cup plus 1 tablespoon chicken stock, canned low-sodium broth or water

Zucchini-Wrapped Shrimp
with Bacon

Coddled Shrimp with
Corn and Asparagus Risotto

Asian Coconut-
Milk Shrimp

¾ pound medium shrimp—shelled,
deveined and butterflied
Freshly ground pepper
2 tablespoons sherry vinegar
1 tablespoon capers
1 tablespoon minced chives
1 tablespoon minced parsley

1. Put each color of beet into a separate small saucepan and cover with water. Bring to a boil, salt the water and simmer over low heat until tender, about 20 minutes. Drain and peel the beets.

2. In a medium skillet, melt the butter in ¼ cup of the chicken stock. Add the shrimp, season with salt and pepper and cook over moderate heat, stirring, for 2 minutes. Using a slotted spoon, transfer the shrimp to a plate and cover loosely with foil.

3. Add the sherry vinegar and the beets to the skillet and bring to a simmer over moderate heat. Stir in the capers, chives, parsley, shrimp and the remaining 1 tablespoon of stock and season with salt and pepper. Serve at once.   —*Eberhard Müller*

ONE SERVING Calories 186 kcal, Total Fat 7.7 gm, Saturated Fat 4.1 gm, Protein 17 gm, Carbohydrates 12 gm

MAKE AHEAD The cooked beets can be refrigerated overnight. Bring to room temperature before proceeding.

Zucchini-Wrapped Shrimp with Bacon

4 SERVINGS

This recipe has you thinly slice zucchini lengthwise. For a different look, simply cut the zucchini crosswise into ⅓-inch-thick coins. Or, for more flavor, wrap a sprig of thyme around each shrimp as you thread it onto the skewer.

3 tablespoons coarsely
chopped basil
2 tablespoons extra-virgin olive oil,
plus more for brushing
1 large garlic clove, minced
Salt and freshly ground pepper
1½ pounds medium shrimp,
shelled and deveined
4 medium zucchini (5 to 6 ounces),
halved lengthwise, then cut
lengthwise into ¼-inch-thick
slices
¾ pound slab bacon, sliced ¼ inch
thick and cut crosswise into
1½-inch squares

1. In a bowl, combine the basil with 2 tablespoons of the extra-virgin olive oil and the garlic. Season lightly with salt and pepper. Add the shrimp and turn to coat.

2. In a shallow bowl, generously brush the zucchini slices on both sides with olive oil and season with salt and pepper; let stand for 5 minutes to soften.

3. In a skillet, cook the bacon over moderate heat until lightly browned, about 2 minutes per side. Drain.

4. Working at the tip of a 12-inch skewer, pierce the very end of a zucchini slice. Swing the zucchini to the side and skewer a shrimp, then loop the zucchini slice around the shrimp and pierce the zucchini slice to secure it around the shrimp. Add another shrimp, wrap the rest of the zucchini slice around it and secure it on the skewer. Add a bacon square. Repeat the threading, using 2 more zucchini slices, 4 more shrimp and 2 more bacon squares. Thread the remaining ingredients to make 8 skewers.

5. Light a grill or preheat a grill pan. Oil the grill and grill 4 skewers at a time over high heat for about 2 minutes per side, or just until the shrimp are cooked through and the zucchini are still crunchy. Serve hot.—*Marcia Kiesel*

Coddled Shrimp with Corn and Asparagus Risotto

4 SERVINGS ●

Not a true, long-stirred risotto, this shortcut version is still nicely creamy.

- 2 tablespoons unsalted butter
- 2 cups corn kernels (from 4 to 5 ears of corn)
- 1 cup chicken stock or canned low-sodium broth
- ¼ cup long-grain rice
- 1 teaspoon chopped summer savory or thyme

Salt and freshly ground pepper

- ½ pound medium asparagus, sliced into thin rounds
- 6 tablespoons heavy cream
- ¼ teaspoon Old Bay spice (optional)
- 1 pound medium shrimp, shelled and deveined
- ¼ cup minced chives, plus long snipped chives for garnish

1. Melt 1 tablespoon of the butter in a small saucepan. Add the corn, ¾ cup

of chicken stock, the rice and summer savory and season with salt and pepper. Cover and cook over moderate heat for 4 minutes. Add the asparagus and cook until the rice is tender, about 8 minutes. Add 2 tablespoons of heavy cream and cook over high heat until the mixture starts to hold together, about 1 minute. Mound the "risotto" in the center of plates or a platter and keep warm.

2. Meanwhile, in a medium saucepan, heat the remaining ¼ cup of stock, ¼ cup of cream, 1 tablespoon of butter and the Old Bay spice over low heat for about 1 minute. Season with salt and pepper. Add the shrimp, cover and cook for 3 minutes. Using a slotted spoon, transfer the shrimp to the plates with the risotto. Bring the liquid left in the pan to a boil and cook until slightly thickened, about 1 minute. Remove the pan from the heat and add the minced chives. Pour the cooking liquid over the shrimp, garnish with the long chives and serve immediately.   —*Michael Roberts*

Asian Coconut-Milk Shrimp

4 SERVINGS ●

- 1½ teaspoons canola oil
- 1 medium shallot, very finely chopped
- 1 small jalapeño, seeded and finely chopped
- 1½ teaspoons finely grated lime zest
- ¾ cup unsweetened coconut milk
- ½ teaspoon sugar

Salt

- 1½ pounds shelled and deveined medium shrimp
- 2 tablespoons finely chopped cilantro

Steamed rice, for serving

- ¼ cup dry-roasted unsalted peanuts, chopped

In a large skillet, heat the canola oil. When it begins to shimmer, add the chopped shallot; cook over moderate

Crispy Cream of Wheat Coating

MAKES 1 CUP ● ● ●

This recipe proves that Cream of Wheat isn't only baby food. The coating produces an incredibly crispy cornmeal-like crust for seafood. Use it for shrimp, white-flesh fish fillets such as flounder, or oily fish such as salmon; then pan-fry or deep-fry them in vegetable oil.

- 1 cup Cream of Wheat cereal (not instant)
- 2 teaspoons kosher salt
- 1 teaspoon cayenne pepper
- 1 teaspoon freshly ground white pepper

In a small bowl, mix the Cream of Wheat with the salt, cayenne and white pepper.

—*Gray Kunz*

MAKE AHEAD The coating can be stored at room temperature in an airtight container for up to 1 week.

heat until softened, about 1 minute. Stir in the jalapeño and lime zest, then pour in the coconut milk. Add the sugar, season generously with salt and bring to a simmer. Add the shrimp and cook, stirring frequently, until opaque, about 5 minutes. Stir in the chopped cilantro. Spoon the shrimp and sauce over steamed rice, sprinkle with the peanuts and serve.

—*Kate Heddings*

Avocado and Lobster Salad

4 SERVINGS ●

The marriage of lobster and avocado makes for one delicious dish. What's more, avocados contain phenylalanine, which may raise levels of endorphins in the brain and create a natural high.

Two 1½-pound lobsters

- 3 tablespoons rice vinegar
- ½ teaspoon soy sauce
- ¼ teaspoon finely grated fresh ginger

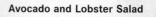
Avocado and Lobster Salad

Pinch of sugar

3 tablespoons canola oil

Salt and freshly ground pepper

1 bunch of watercress (6 ounces), large stems discarded

1 Hass avocado, peeled and cut into chunks

1. In a large pot of boiling water, cook the lobsters until they turn bright red, about 13 minutes. Drain and let cool. Twist off the tails and claws. Crack the claws and remove the meat; cut into large pieces. Using kitchen scissors, slit the tail shells lengthwise up the center and remove the tail meat. Remove the black intestinal vein and discard. Cut the tail meat into 1-inch medallions. Cover and refrigerate the lobster meat.

2. In a large bowl, combine the vinegar with the soy sauce, ginger and sugar. Whisk in the oil until emulsified, then season with salt and pepper. Add the watercress and lobster and toss gently, then add the avocado and toss just until dressed. Serve chilled.

—*Grace Parisi*

MAKE AHEAD You can shell the lobster a day ahead and keep it tightly wrapped in the refrigerator overnight.

WINE A Chardonnay-rich sparkling wine with brisk acidity will echo the sweetness of the lobster and balance the salty soy and peppery watercress flavors. The 1994 Domaine Carneros Le Rêve and the 1997 Iron Horse Vineyard Blanc de Blancs fit the bill.

Couscous with Clams

4 SERVINGS ●

2 cups water

1 tablespoon unsalted butter

Salt

One 10-ounce package of couscous

5 tablespoons extra-virgin olive oil

2 garlic cloves, thinly sliced

½ teaspoon crushed red pepper

¾ cup dry white wine

3 pounds Manila clams or cockles, rinsed

1 cup drained roasted red peppers from a jar, cut into thin strips

1 cup drained canned white beans

2 large scallions, thinly sliced

1. In a medium saucepan, bring the water to a boil with the butter and a generous pinch of salt. Stir in the couscous, cover the pan and remove from the heat.

2. In a large, deep skillet, heat ¼ cup of the olive oil until shimmering. Add the garlic and cook over high heat, stirring, until lightly browned, about 1 minute. Stir in the crushed red pepper and the wine and boil until the wine is reduced by half, about 5 minutes. Add the clams and bring to a boil. Cover the skillet, lower the heat to moderate and cook, stirring occasionally, until the clams open, about 3 minutes. Add the red peppers, beans and scallions and cook just until heated through, about 1 minute.

3. Fluff the couscous with a fork and spoon it into 4 deep bowls. Spoon the clams, peppers and beans over the couscous. Stir the remaining 1 tablespoon of olive oil into the broth, spoon it over the clams and serve.

—*Grace Parisi*

Mussel and Chickpea Stew

4 SERVINGS ●

2½ cups water

¾ cup dry white wine

2 bay leaves

4 pounds mussels, scrubbed and debearded

1 tablespoon extra-virgin olive oil

1 large leek, white and 3 inches of green, halved lengthwise and cut crosswise into ⅓-inch-thick slices

1 small celery rib, cut crosswise into ¼-inch-thick slices

1 small poblano or red Anaheim chile—halved, seeded and cut crosswise into ¼-inch-thick slices

½ small onion, coarsely chopped

Salt and freshly ground pepper

4 large garlic cloves, minced

¼ teaspoon loosely packed saffron threads, crumbled

Pinch of ground allspice

1 cup canned Italian tomatoes, chopped, with their juices

1 medium red potato (3 ounces), peeled and cut into ¼-inch dice

One 15-ounce can chickpeas, drained and rinsed

1. Set a colander in a large heatproof bowl in the sink. In a large saucepan, combine the water with ½ cup of the white wine and the bay leaves and bring to a boil. Add the mussels, cover and steam, shaking the pan a few times, until the mussels open, 4 to 5 minutes. Drain the mussels in the colander; reserve the cooking liquid. Remove the mussels from their shells and put them in a bowl. Cover with plastic wrap.

2. Heat the extra-virgin olive oil in a large saucepan. Add the sliced leek, celery, poblano or Anaheim chile and onion and season with salt and pepper. Cover and cook the leek mixture over low heat, stirring often, until softened, about 8 minutes. Add the minced garlic, crushed saffron and allspice, cover and cook until fragrant, about 5 minutes. Add the chopped tomatoes and cook over moderate heat, stirring, until the juices have evaporated and the tomatoes start to brown, about 4 minutes. Add the remaining ¼ cup of white wine. Slowly pour in the reserved mussel cooking liquid, stopping before you reach the grit.

3. Add the potato and chickpeas to the saucepan and bring to a boil. Cover and cook over low heat for 25 minutes. Season with salt and pepper. Just before serving, add the mussels and reheat them gently in the stew.

—*Marcia Kiesel*

ONE SERVING Calories 320 kcal, Total Fat 8.2 gm, Saturated Fat 1.1 gm, Protein 25 gm, Carbohydrates 35 gm

SERVE WITH Crusty bread.

7 chicken
other birds

spice guide

Black peppercorns are the sun-dried unripe fruits of the *Piper nigrum* plant.

Cinnamon is the bark of an evergreen tree in the laurel family.

Cloves are the unopened flower buds of the evergreen clove tree.

Coriander seeds come from the cilantro plant.

Cumin seeds are produced by a hot-climate plant native to the Nile valley.

Curry powder is a mixture of whole native Indian spices that may contain as few as two ingredients, or as many as ten, that are dry-roasted and ground.

Sesame seeds, which come in brown, white and black varieties, burst out of the ripe seed capsules of the small annual sesame plant.

White peppercorns are ripe red berries of the *Piper nigrum* plant that are soaked in water until the outer skin can be rubbed off.

Star anise is the brown fruit of a small evergreen tree native to China; when the anise ripens, it opens into a star shape.

Spicy Chicken Salad

4 SERVINGS ●●

- 1 tablespoon pure mild chile powder, preferably ancho
- 2 teaspoons ground cumin
- 1 teaspoon ground coriander

Salt

Four 6-ounce skinless, boneless chicken breast halves, pounded ⅓ inch thick

Olive oil cooking spray

- 10 ounces spinach, stems discarded, leaves torn into large pieces
- 1 pint grape tomatoes, halved
- 4 scallions, thinly sliced
- 1 Hass avocado—halved, pitted, peeled and cut into thin wedges
- 6 radishes, thinly sliced
- ½ cup plus 2 tablespoons plain nonfat yogurt (5 ounces)
- 1 tablespoon extra-virgin olive oil

Spicy Chicken Salad

- 1 tablespoon fresh lemon juice
- 1 garlic clove, minced

Freshly ground pepper

1. Preheat the broiler. In a small bowl, combine the chile powder with the cumin, coriander and ½ teaspoon of salt. Coat the chicken breasts with the spices. Lightly coat a broiler pan with olive oil cooking spray, then set the chicken breasts on it. Broil the chicken for about 4 minutes per side, or until cooked through. Transfer the chicken to a cutting board and let cool, then slice on the diagonal into ⅓-inch strips.

2. In a large bowl, toss the spinach with the tomatoes, scallions, avocado and radishes. In a small bowl, whisk the yogurt with the olive oil, lemon juice and garlic and season with salt and pepper. Pour the dressing over the salad, add the chicken and toss well, then serve. —*Ann Chantal Altman*

ONE SERVING Calories 387 kcal, Total Fat 16.6 gm, Saturated Fat 3 gm, Protein 46 gm, Carbohydrates 15 gm

Chicken Salad with Farro and Olives

6 SERVINGS

This salad, with its olive oil and lemon juice dressing, lends itself to endless variations. You can substitute one cup of grapes for the olives, basmati rice or barley for the farro and blanched almonds for the hazelnuts. Chickpeas or chopped pickles would make good additions to the basic salad, but don't pile on too many ingredients; you want the flavors to stay in balance.

- 1 cup farro (see Note)
- 2 cups water
- ⅓ cup hazelnuts (1½ ounces)
- ¾ cup fresh baby peas or thawed frozen peas (¼ pound)
- ¾ teaspoon coriander seeds
- 1 garlic clove, smashed
- 1 teaspoon finely grated lemon zest
- 1 teaspoon coarse sea salt
- ¼ teaspoon curry powder
- ¼ cup extra-virgin olive oil
- 2 tablespoons fresh lemon juice
- ¾ pound roasted chicken breast, skinned and cut into ½-inch dice (2 cups)
- ⅓ cup thinly sliced celery
- 3 radishes, thinly sliced
- 1 tablespoon coarsely chopped flat-leaf parsley
- 1 tablespoon chervil leaves or coarsely chopped chives

Freshly ground pepper

- ⅓ cup green olives, pitted and halved lengthwise

Radicchio leaves, for serving (optional)

1. Preheat the oven to 350°. In a small saucepan, cover the farro with the water and bring to a boil. Cover and cook over low heat until tender, 18 to 20 minutes. Drain the farro and transfer it to a large bowl to cool slightly.

2. Meanwhile, spread the hazelnuts in a pie plate and toast in the oven for about 14 minutes, or until lightly browned and fragrant. Let cool, then transfer the nuts to a kitchen towel and rub off the skins. Coarsely chop the nuts.

3. If using fresh peas, cook them in a medium saucepan of boiling water until tender, about 5 minutes; drain.

4. In a small skillet, toast the coriander seeds over moderate heat until fragrant and lightly browned, about 3 minutes. Transfer to a mortar and coarsely grind. Add the smashed garlic clove, lemon zest, sea salt and

curry powder to the mortar and pound to a paste. Add the extra-virgin olive oil and lemon juice and stir until combined.

5. Stir half of the dressing into the farro and let stand until cooled to room temperature. Add the chicken, peas, celery, radishes, parsley, chervil and the remaining dressing. Season the salad with pepper and toss to mix. Just before serving, add the olives and hazelnuts. Mound the chicken salad on the radicchio leaves and serve.

—*Nancy Harmon Jenkins*

ONE SERVING Calories 352 kcal, Total Fat 17.5 gm, Saturated Fat 2.3 gm, Protein 25 gm, Carbohydrates 27 gm

NOTE Farro, an ancient Italian wheat-like grain, has started reappearing on menus in Italy and is a recent arrival to America.

Chicken Salad with Farro and Olives

Thai-Style Chicken in Lettuce Leaves

4 SERVINGS ●

- 3 tablespoons rice vinegar
- ¼ cup sugar
- 4 teaspoons minced garlic
- 2 teaspoons crushed red pepper
- ¼ cup soy sauce
- 2 teaspoons finely grated fresh ginger
- 1½ teaspoons Asian sesame oil

Four 6-ounce skinless, boneless chicken breast halves, pounded to a ½-inch thickness

- 1 European cucumber, peeled and cut into ¼-inch dice
- 1 cup mung bean sprouts
- ¼ cup mint leaves
- ¼ cup cilantro leaves
- 2 tablespoons chopped roasted peanuts
- 1 head of leaf lettuce
- 2 tablespoons water

1. In a small saucepan, mix the rice vinegar with the sugar and cook over moderate heat, stirring, until the sugar dissolves. Add 1 teaspoon of the minced garlic and the crushed red pepper and let cool.

2. In a large bowl, mix 2 tablespoons of the sweet seasoned vinegar with the remaining 3 teaspoons of garlic and the soy sauce, ginger and sesame oil. Set aside 2 tablespoons of this soy marinade. Add the chicken to the remaining marinade in the bowl and refrigerate for at least 1 hour or overnight.

3. Light a grill or preheat the broiler and position a rack 6 inches from the heat. Remove the chicken from the marinade and let it drain, then grill or broil for about 2 minutes per side, until browned and cooked through. Transfer the chicken to a cutting board and let rest for 5 minutes. Cut the chicken crosswise into ½-inch strips and mound in a bowl.

4. In a medium bowl, toss the diced cucumber with the remaining sweet

asian flavorings

Galangal The rhizome of a plant in the ginger family, galangal has translucent golden skin and a sharp, peppery flavor.

Ginger This knobby, golden beige, smooth rhizome adds a clean, aromatic taste and spicy bite to foods when it's sliced, minced or grated.

Kaffir lime leaves Often used in much the same way as bay leaves—added whole to dishes and then discarded—these glossy dark green leaves have a distinct lemon-lime flavor.

Lemongrass This tropical grass has an inimitable lemon flavor that is released when its tender inner bulb is crushed or chopped.

Tamarind The sour pulp and seeds of this large pod are pressed into soft blocks that must be soaked and strained before using. The concentrate can be used straight from the container.

seasoned vinegar. Put the bean sprouts, mint, cilantro and peanuts in separate bowls. Arrange the lettuce leaves in a basket. Add the water to the reserved 2 tablespoons of soy marinade. Let guests wrap the chicken and garnishes in lettuce leaves and pass the soy marinade and cucumber salad separately. —*Grace Parisi*

ONE SERVING Calories 346 kcal, Total Fat 9 gm, Saturated Fat 1.9 gm, Protein 44 gm, Carbohydrates 21 gm

Sautéed Chicken Paillards with Greek Salad

4 SERVINGS ●

- 4 skinless, boneless chicken cutlets (6 ounces each), about ½ inch thick
- ¼ cup plus 1 tablespoon extra-virgin olive oil
- ¼ teaspoon crumbled dried oregano
- Salt and freshly ground pepper
- 1 tablespoon fresh lemon juice
- ¼ pound feta cheese, crumbled
- 1 cup cherry tomatoes, halved
- 1 kirby cucumber or ½ unwaxed cucumber, cut into ½-inch dice
- 1 large scallion, thinly sliced
- 12 arugula leaves, torn into pieces
- 12 mint leaves, torn into pieces

1. Rub the chicken with 1 tablespoon of the olive oil and the oregano and season with salt and pepper.

2. In a large bowl, mix 2 tablespoons of the olive oil with the lemon juice and season with salt and pepper. Add the feta, tomatoes, cucumber, scallion, arugula and mint. Season the salad with salt and pepper and toss well.

3. In each of 2 large skillets, heat 1 tablespoon of olive oil until shimmering. Add the chicken cutlets and cook over high heat until golden on the bottom, about 5 minutes. Turn the chicken and cook just until done, about 2 minutes longer. Transfer the chicken cutlets to plates, spoon the salad on top or alongside and serve.

—*Grace Parisi*

Cashew Chicken with Bok Choy

4 SERVINGS ● ●

- ¼ cup chicken stock or canned low-sodium broth
- ¼ cup dry sherry
- ¼ cup soy sauce
- 1 teaspoon cornstarch
- 2 tablespoons canola oil
- ¾ cup raw cashews
- 5 scallions, white and green parts separated and thinly sliced crosswise
- 1 teaspoon minced peeled fresh ginger
- 1 garlic clove, minced
- ½ teaspoon Szechuan peppercorns
- 1¼ pounds chicken tenderloins
- Salt and freshly ground pepper
- 1 pound bok choy, longer ribs halved crosswise
- Steamed rice, for serving

1. In a small bowl, use a fork to blend the chicken stock with the sherry, soy sauce and cornstarch.

2. Heat 1 tablespoon of the oil in a large skillet. Add the cashews and cook over moderate heat, stirring, until lightly browned, about 1 minute. Using a slotted spoon, transfer the nuts to a plate.

3. Heat the remaining 1 tablespoon of canola oil in the skillet. Add the white part of the scallions, the minced ginger, garlic and Szechuan peppercorns and cook, stirring, for 1 minute. Add the sauce and arrange the chicken tenderloins in a single layer in the skillet; season with salt and pepper. Arrange the bok choy in a layer over the chicken. Cover and cook until the chicken is cooked through and the bok choy is tender, 5 to 7 minutes. Transfer the chicken, bok choy and sauce to bowls. Garnish with the scallion greens and cashews and serve with rice.

—*Michael Roberts*

Thai Basil and Chile Chicken

4 SERVINGS ● ●

- 3 tablespoons fresh lime juice
- 2 tablespoons soy sauce
- 1½ teaspoons sugar
- 1 teaspoon Asian fish sauce
- 2 tablespoons peanut oil
- 1 pound skinless, boneless chicken breasts, cut into strips or chunks
- 3 garlic cloves, minced
- 8 scallions, cut into ½-inch lengths
- 4 plum tomatoes, chopped
- 1 Thai or bird chile, minced
- 1 cup coarsely chopped Thai basil
- Steamed rice, for serving

1. In a bowl, combine the lime juice with the soy sauce, sugar and fish sauce.

2. Heat 1 tablespoon of the oil in a large skillet or wok. Add the chicken and garlic and stir-fry over high heat for 3 minutes; transfer to a plate. Add the remaining 1 tablespoon of oil and the scallions to the skillet and stir-fry for 2 minutes. Add the tomatoes and chile and stir-fry for 2 minutes. Stir in the chicken and the lime juice mixture and simmer for 30 seconds. Remove from the heat and stir in the Thai basil.

—*Suki Hertz*

ONE SERVING Calories 227 kcal, Total Fat 8.9 mg, Saturated Fat 1.4 mg

SERVE WITH Rice.

Chicken and Papaya Stir-Fry

4 SERVINGS ● ●

- 2 teaspoons soy sauce
- 2 teaspoons dry white wine
- 1 teaspoon cornstarch
- 1 pound skinless, boneless chicken breast halves, cut into 1½-inch pieces
- 1 tablespoon vegetable oil
- 1 small onion, thickly sliced
- 2 teaspoons minced fresh ginger
- 1 large garlic clove, minced
- 1 poblano or red Anaheim chile, seeded and thickly sliced
- ¼ teaspoon crushed red pepper
- 1 tablespoon soy sauce
- ½ cup fresh orange juice
- Two ½-pound ripe papayas— peeled, seeded and cut into 3-by-½-inch strips
- 1 tablespoon fresh lemon juice
- Salt and freshly ground pepper
- 1 large scallion, thinly sliced

1. In a medium bowl, combine the soy sauce with the wine and cornstarch. Add the chicken and turn to coat.

2. Heat the oil in a wok or large skillet over moderately high heat. Add the onion, ginger and garlic and stir-fry for 30 seconds. Add the chicken and stir-fry for 5 minutes. Add the poblano

Cashew Chicken with Bok Choy

Thai Basil and Chile Chicken

Chicken and Papaya Stir-Fry

and crushed red pepper and continue stir-frying until the chicken is cooked through and the poblano softens, about 3 minutes. Add the soy sauce and stir-fry for 30 seconds. Using a slotted spoon, transfer the chicken to a plate.

3. Add the orange juice to the wok and boil until slightly thickened, about 3 minutes. Return the chicken to the wok, add the papaya strips and stir-fry until hot, about 1 minute. Add the lemon juice, season with salt and pepper and transfer to a platter. Garnish with the scallion slices and serve.

—*Marcia Kiesel*

ONE SERVING Calories 272 kcal, Total Fat 5.3 gm, Saturated Fat 0.7 gm, Protein 29 gm, Carbohydrates 28 gm

Lemon-Rosemary Chicken Under a Skillet

4 SERVINGS

This recipe is a twist on the Italian classic *pollo al mattone*—chicken cooked under a brick. Here a cast-iron skillet presses the chicken onto the grill to give it beautiful grill marks and incredibly crisp skin.

Four 8- to 10-ounce chicken breast halves, on the bone

1 teaspoon kosher salt

1 teaspoon coarsely ground pepper

3 garlic cloves, minced

2 tablespoons chopped rosemary

¼ cup extra-virgin olive oil

¼ cup fresh lemon juice

Vegetable oil, for the grill

Lemon wedges, for serving

1. In a shallow glass or ceramic baking dish, sprinkle both sides of the chicken with the salt, pepper, garlic and rosemary and rub the seasonings in thoroughly. Pour the olive oil and lemon juice over the chicken and refrigerate for 1 hour, turning every 15 minutes.

2. Light a grill. Lightly brush the grate with oil and arrange the chicken breasts on the grate, skin side down, with the breast tips facing in the same direction at a 45° angle to the bars of the grate. Set a large cast-iron skillet on top of the breasts and grill over a medium-hot fire for 8 minutes; rotate the chicken breasts a quarter turn after 4 minutes to make attractive crosshatched grill marks. Flip the chicken breasts and repeat, grilling them until they are cooked through, about 8 minutes longer. Serve with lemon wedges.   —*Steven Raichlen*

WINE The chicken's grilled, lemony flavors call for a rich Chardonnay with smoky, lemony echoes, such as the 1998 Edna Valley Vineyard Paragon.

Lemongrass Chicken

4 SERVINGS

This is a good place to start experimenting with fresh spices: The pungent paste is easy to make, though it needs a couple of hours to fully flavor the chicken. It can also be used on salmon and scallops.

- 2 stalks fresh lemongrass, tender white inner bulbs only, smashed and coarsely chopped
- 2 large shallots, coarsely chopped (¼ pound)
- 2 garlic cloves, coarsely chopped
- 1 Thai chile, chopped
- 1 tablespoon Asian fish sauce
- 4 boneless chicken breast halves, with skin (about 7 ounces each)
- 1 tablespoon vegetable oil

Salt and freshly ground pepper

1. In a food processor, combine the lemongrass with the shallots, garlic, chile and fish sauce and pulse to a coarse paste. Set the chicken breasts on a plate, skin side down. Spread the paste on the fleshy side of the chicken, cover and refrigerate for at least 2 hours. Bring the chicken to room temperature before cooking.

2. Preheat the oven to 450°. Transfer the chicken, skin side down, to paper towels. Heat the oil in a large nonstick ovenproof skillet. Add the chicken, skin side down, season with salt and pepper and cook over moderately high heat until lightly browned on the bottom, about 5 minutes. Transfer the skillet to the oven and roast the chicken for 7 minutes, or until it is deep golden on the bottom. Carefully turn the chicken, season with salt and

pepper and roast for 5 minutes longer, or until cooked through. Set the chicken breasts on a platter or plates and serve.   —*Jean-Georges Vongerichten*

MAKE AHEAD The lemongrass paste can be refrigerated for 2 days.

WINE The hot chile, tangy fish sauce and aromatic lemongrass suggest a Chardonnay with no oak. Try a bright New Zealand example, such as the 2000 Brancott Vineyards Gisborne or the 1999 Babich Hawke's Bay Fernhill Vineyard.

Grilled Chicken with Arugula and Orange Salsa Verde

4 SERVINGS ●

One 4-ounce bunch of arugula, coarsely chopped
- 2 tablespoons snipped chives
- 2 tablespoons capers, drained and rinsed
- 1 garlic clove, minced
- 2 teaspoons finely grated orange zest
- ¼ cup extra-virgin olive oil, plus more for brushing
- 3 tablespoons fresh orange juice
- 1 tablespoon white wine vinegar

Salt and freshly ground pepper
Four 6-ounce boneless chicken breast halves, with skin
Orange sections, for garnish

1. In a mini food processor, pulse the arugula with the snipped chives, capers, garlic and orange zest until the arugula is finely chopped. Add ¼ cup of the olive oil, the orange juice and vinegar and pulse to a coarse puree. Transfer the salsa to a bowl and season with salt and pepper.

2. Light a grill or heat a grill pan. Lightly brush the chicken with olive oil and season with salt and pepper. Grill the chicken over moderate heat, turning occasionally, until nicely browned and cooked through, about 12 minutes. Transfer the chicken to plates and top with the salsa. Garnish with the orange sections and serve.   —*Joanne Weir*

MENU

HORS D'OEUVRES
feta with black olives (p. 30)
grilled pancetta-wrapped shrimp (p. 41)
mini rib-eye tacos (p. 53)

MAIN COURSE
grilled chicken breasts with verjus and tarragon butter
palisades market caesar salad (p. 62)
greek fries (p. 306)

DESSERTS
gingersnaps (p. 351)
lemon coconut bars (p. 345)
coffee toffee crunch cake (p. 329)

Grilled Chicken Breasts with Verjus and Tarragon Butter

8 SERVINGS

Verjus is the tart, unfermented juice of unripe grapes. If it's unavailable, Sauvignon Blanc may be substituted.

- ¾ cup verjus
- ¼ cup plus 2 tablespoons finely chopped tarragon

Salt and freshly ground pepper
- 8 skinless, boneless chicken breast halves (6 ounces each)
- 1 stick (4 ounces) unsalted butter, melted

1. In a large resealable plastic bag, combine the verjus with ¼ cup of the tarragon, 1 tablespoon of salt and 1 teaspoon of pepper. Add the chicken and seal the bag. Refrigerate for 3 hours, turning the bag once or twice.

2. Preheat the oven to 250°. Preheat a cast-iron grill pan or light a grill and brush lightly with oil. Remove the chicken from the marinade, scraping off as much tarragon as possible. Grill the chicken over high heat until browned but not cooked through, about 2 minutes per side.

3. Arrange the chicken breasts in a 9-by-13-inch baking dish. Add the remaining 2 tablespoons of tarragon to the butter and pour the mixture over

Grilled Chicken Breasts with Verjus and Tarragon Butter, with Palisades Market Caesar Salad (p. 62) and Greek Fries (p. 306)

the chicken. Bake for 20 minutes, or until cooked through. Slice, drizzle the tarragon butter on top and serve.

—*Cary Gott*

WINE A spicy red with plenty of fruit will pair beautifully with the buttery grilled chicken. Try the 2000 Joel Gott Zinfandel or the lush 1998 Joseph Phelps Insignia.

Mustard-Baked Chicken with a Pretzel Crust

6 SERVINGS ●●

For a crisp topping, it's essential to use thick, hard pretzels, such as the sourdough or handmade versions.

- ½ **pound hard pretzels, coarsely crushed (4 cups)**
- ½ **cup canola oil**
- ½ **cup whole-grain mustard**
- 2 **tablespoons Dijon mustard**
- ¼ **cup water**
- 3 **tablespoons red wine vinegar**

Salt and freshly ground pepper

- 6 **large skinless, boneless chicken breast halves**

I. Preheat the oven to 400°. In a food processor, pulse the pretzels until coarsely ground; you should have coarse chunks and fine crumbs. Transfer to a large, shallow bowl.

2. Wipe out the food processor. Add the oil, mustards, water and vinegar and process until smooth. Season the dressing with salt and pepper.

3. Pour half the dressing into a large, shallow bowl, add the chicken breasts and turn to coat. Dredge the chicken in the pretzel crumbs and transfer to a rack set over a rimmed baking sheet. Bake in the upper third of the oven for 20 to 25 minutes, or until cooked through. Slice the chicken and serve warm or at room temperature with the remaining mustard dressing.

—*Ilene Rosen*

MAKE AHEAD The baked chicken and dressing can be kept at room temperature for up to 2 hours.

WINE The chicken's crunchy coating

and tart-and-creamy mustard dressing suggest a tart, lighter red with direct, fruity flavors. Look for a Pinot Noir from Oregon, such as the 1999 Lange or the 1998 Oak Knoll Vintage Reserve.

Amazon Fried Chicken Breasts with Cilantro Sauce

4 SERVINGS ●●

- 2 **cups cilantro leaves**
- 2 **garlic cloves**
- 1 **jalapeño, seeded**
- 2 **tablespoons distilled white vinegar**
- 2 **tablespoons water**
- 1 **cup mayonnaise**
- 2 **large eggs**
- ½ **cup all-purpose flour**
- ¼ **teaspoon salt**
- ¼ **teaspoon freshly ground pepper**

One 5½-ounce bag of potato chips, finely crushed

Four 6-ounce skinless, boneless chicken breast halves, pounded ½ inch thick

- 2 **tablespoons vegetable oil**

I. In a blender, combine the cilantro leaves, garlic cloves, jalapeño, white vinegar and water and puree. Transfer to a bowl and whisk in the mayonnaise. Cover the cilantro sauce and refrigerate.

2. In a shallow bowl, lightly beat the eggs. In another shallow bowl, combine the flour, salt and pepper. Spread the potato chips in a third bowl. Lightly coat the chicken with the flour, shaking off any excess, then dip in the beaten eggs. Coat the chicken with the potato chips.

3. Heat the oil in a large nonstick skillet until shimmering. Add the chicken and cook over moderately high heat until golden and cooked through, about 5 minutes per side. Transfer to plates. Serve at once with the cilantro sauce. —*Michael Cordúa*

SERVE WITH Tomato salad.

Amazon Fried Chicken Breasts with Cilantro Sauce

Glazed Chicken Breasts with Coffee BBQ Sauce

6 SERVINGS

Coffee adds smokiness and depth to this barbecue sauce. The sauce is wonderful with pork and lamb as well as chicken.

- 2 **tablespoons unsalted butter**
- 2 **large shallots, very finely chopped**
- 8 **medium garlic cloves, very finely chopped**
- ½ **habanero or Scotch bonnet chile, seeded and minced**
- 2 **teaspoons ground coriander**
- 2 **teaspoons ground cumin**
- 1 **tablespoon tomato paste**
- ½ **cup dry sherry**
- 2 **cups chicken stock or canned low-sodium broth**
- ¼ **cup strong brewed coffee**
- 2 **tablespoons unsulphured molasses**
- 3 **tablespoons honey**

Salt and freshly ground pepper

- 6 **chicken breast halves, on the bone (about 10 ounces each)**

I. Melt the butter in a saucepan. Add the shallots, garlic and habanero and cook over moderately low heat, stirring frequently, until the shallots soften and begin to brown, about 8 minutes. Add the coriander and cumin and cook for 30 seconds. Add the tomato paste and cook over moderately high heat, stirring, until glossy, about 1 minute. Pour in the sherry and simmer over moderately low heat until slightly syrupy, about 7 minutes. Stir in the stock, coffee and molasses and simmer for 1 hour, until reduced to 1½ cups. Stir in the honey. Season with salt and pepper.

2. Preheat the broiler. Position a rack 8 to 10 inches from the heat source. Season the chicken breasts with salt and pepper and broil for about 25 minutes, turning occasionally, until golden and almost cooked through. Brush the chicken with ½ cup of the sauce and broil for about 5 minutes longer, turning frequently, until the chicken is cooked through. Transfer the chicken to a platter and pass the remaining barbecue sauce at the table.

—*Frank Mendoza*

ONE SERVING Calories 440 kcal, Total Fat 17 gm, Saturated Fat 6.3 gm, Protein 49 gm, Carbohydrates 20 gm

MAKE AHEAD The barbecue sauce can be refrigerated for 2 weeks.

WINE The 1997 Steele Syrah Sonoma Valley Parmelee-Hill is an excellent choice, as is the 1998 Ridge Zinfandel Sonoma Station, for the rich, sweet, spicy, bitter barbecue sauce.

Glazed Chicken Breasts with Coffee BBQ Sauce

Chicken Stuffed with Red Peppers and Basil

8 SERVINGS ●●

Roast and peel the bell peppers yourself or use a jarred brand.

- **3** red or yellow bell peppers, or a mixture
- **3** tablespoons extra-virgin olive oil
- **8** skinless, boneless chicken breast halves (about 6 ounces each)

Salt and freshly ground pepper

- **½** cup freshly grated Parmesan cheese
- **24** basil leaves

I. Preheat the oven to 450°. Rub the bell peppers with 1 tablespoon of the olive oil and put them on a baking sheet. Roast the peppers for about 40 minutes, turning occasionally, until charred and very soft. Transfer the peppers to a bowl to cool, then core, seed and peel. Cut the peppers into 1-by-3-inch strips.

2. Using a sharp, thin knife, cut a horizontal pocket in each chicken breast half. Season the pockets with salt and pepper and sprinkle 1 tablespoon of the Parmesan in each. Tuck the basil leaves and roasted peppers into the pockets. Press the chicken breasts lightly to close.

3. Heat 1 tablespoon of the olive oil in each of 2 medium skillets. Season the chicken breasts with salt and pepper, add 4 to each skillet and cook over moderately high heat until browned on both sides, 7 to 8 minutes. Serve the chicken warm or at room temperature.

—*Stéphane Garnier*

MAKE AHEAD The Chicken Stuffed with Red Peppers and Basil can be prepared through Step 2 and refrigerated overnight. Return the chicken to room temperature before cooking.

WINE A fruity, fragrant red Chinon with fresh acidity and up-front fruit flavors will stand up to the sweet pepper and salty Parmesan stuffing. Try the 1998 Charles Joguet Clos de la Dioterie or the 1997 Marc Brédif.

MENU

FIRST COURSE
summer tomato pissaladière (p. 282)

garden tomato soup with cumin (p. 88)

MAIN COURSE
chicken stuffed with red peppers and basil

heirloom tomato and eggplant gratin (p. 294)

SALAD
mixed greens with fresh tomato vinaigrette (p. 56)

DESSERT
vanilla ice cream with green-tomato jam (p. 321)

Chicken Stuffed with Red Peppers and Basil, with Heirloom Tomato and Eggplant Gratin (p. 294)

Zuleta's Rice Torta

6 SERVINGS ●

This rich, comforting casserole falls somewhere between lasagna and risotto. It is best accompanied with Ají, an Ecuadoran condiment, but can also be served with brown sugar.

⅓ cup raisins
Four ¾-pound chicken breast
    halves, on the bone
6 tablespoons unsalted butter,
    cut into tablespoons
6 tablespoons all-purpose flour
1 quart milk
Salt and freshly ground pepper
Pinch of freshly grated nutmeg
2 tablespoons vegetable oil
1 medium onion, coarsely grated
1 medium tomato—peeled,
    seeded and coarsely chopped
1 tablespoon Worcestershire sauce
½ teaspoon minced rosemary
2 large eggs, separated
4 cups cooked long-grain rice,
    at room temperature
2 cups grated mild Cheddar
Ají (p. 319) and brown sugar,
    for serving

1. In a small bowl, cover the raisins with hot water and let stand for 10 minutes. Drain well.

2. In a large saucepan, cover the chicken with water and bring to a boil. Reduce the heat to low and simmer until just cooked through, about 25 minutes. Transfer to a large plate and let cool slightly. Pull the meat from the bones and tear it into thin shreds.

3. Meanwhile, melt the butter in a medium saucepan. Stir in the flour and cook over moderate heat until golden, 1 minute. Gradually whisk in the milk until smooth. Bring to a boil over moderately high heat, whisking constantly until thickened. Simmer the white sauce over low heat for 25 minutes, whisking often. Season with salt, pepper and the nutmeg. Cover and remove from the heat.

4. Preheat the oven to 350°. Butter a 9-by-13-inch glass baking dish. In a large skillet, heat the vegetable oil. Add the onion and tomato and cook over moderately low heat, stirring occasionally, until the onion is softened, about 8 minutes. Stir in the shredded chicken, Worcestershire sauce and rosemary; season with salt and pepper.

5. Stir the egg yolks into the white sauce. In a medium stainless-steel bowl, beat the egg whites until stiff. In a large bowl, combine the rice with the white sauce, raisins and cheese and season with salt and pepper. Fold in the beaten egg whites. Spread half of the rice in the prepared baking dish, cover with the chicken sauce and spread the remaining rice on top.

6. Bake the torta for about 40 minutes, or until piping hot throughout. Preheat the broiler. Broil the torta for 2 minutes, or until browned. Let stand for 5 minutes; serve the torta with Ají and brown sugar.

—Hacienda Zuleta, Ecuador

MAKE AHEAD The recipe can be prepared through Step 5 and refrigerated overnight. Bring to room temperature before baking.

Creole Chicken and Ham Fried Rice

4 TO 6 SERVINGS ●

This fried rice, studded with sautéed chicken and smoky ham, is softer and moister than the Asian version. Any kind of long- or medium-grain white rice, especially leftover, works nicely.

3 tablespoons canola oil
1 pound skinless, boneless
    chicken thighs, cut into
    1-inch pieces
Salt and freshly ground black pepper
1 large red bell pepper, thinly sliced
4 large scallions, thickly sliced
½ pound smoked ham, cut into
    ½-inch dice
1 teaspoon sweet paprika
Pinch of cayenne pepper
3 cups cooked white rice
½ pound medium shrimp,
    shelled and deveined
½ cup water
Hot sauce, for serving

1. In a large nonstick skillet, heat 1 tablespoon of oil until shimmering. Season the chicken with salt and black pepper and cook over high heat, stirring, until browned all over, 6 to 7 minutes. Transfer to a plate.

2. Heat another tablespoon of oil in the skillet. Add the red pepper and half of the scallions and season with salt and pepper. Stir-fry the vegetables over high heat until crisp-tender and lightly browned, about 5 minutes. Add the ham, paprika and cayenne and stir-fry for 30 seconds.

3. Add the remaining 1 tablespoon of oil to the skillet along with the chicken, rice, shrimp and water and cook over moderate heat, stirring, until the shrimp are pink and the chicken is cooked through, about 5 minutes. Remove from the heat, cover tightly and let stand for 2 minutes to allow the flavors to blend. Transfer the fried rice to a bowl, garnish with the remaining scallions and serve with hot sauce.

—Ruth Van Waerebeek

WINE A soft and fruity Chenin Blanc will contrast with the smoky and lightly spicy flavors of this dish. Two good examples: the 2000 Baron Herzog Clarksburg from California and the 2000 Simonsig Stellenbosch from South Africa.

Couscous with Curried Chicken and Chickpeas

4 SERVINGS ●

2 tablespoons extra-virgin
    olive oil
1¼ pounds skinless, boneless
    chicken thighs, cut into
    1-inch pieces
Salt and freshly ground pepper
1 medium onion, chopped
2 teaspoons Madras curry powder

Creole Chicken and Ham Fried Rice

Couscous with Curried
Chicken and Chickpeas

½ tablespoon extra-virgin olive oil
1 large Spanish onion, thinly sliced
2 tablespoons pomegranate
  molasses (see Note)
2½ teaspoons light brown sugar
Pinch of saffron threads
½ teaspoon freshly ground
  cumin seeds
Seeds from ½ pomegranate
½ cup coarsely chopped cilantro

½ teaspoon ground cinnamon
Pinch of cayenne pepper
3 cups chicken stock or canned
  low-sodium broth
1 red bell pepper, diced
2 small zucchini, diced
One 15-ounce can chickpeas,
  drained and rinsed
1½ cups water
1 cup couscous
½ cup chopped cilantro,
  plus whole sprigs for garnish

1. In a large skillet, heat the extra-virgin olive oil until shimmering. Season the chicken with salt and pepper and cook over moderately high heat, stirring, until golden, about 5 minutes. Add the onion, curry, cinnamon, cayenne and ¼ teaspoon of pepper. Cook, stirring, until fragrant, about 1 minute. Add the chicken stock or broth and simmer until reduced by one-third, about 10 minutes. Add the diced red pepper and zucchini and

simmer until tender, about 10 minutes. Add the chickpeas and cook for 1 minute longer. Season the curried chicken with salt.

2. Meanwhile, in a small saucepan, bring the water to a boil. Add the couscous and ½ teaspoon of salt, cover and let stand for 10 minutes. Fluff the couscous with a fork, then add the chopped cilantro and toss. Transfer the curry to a serving bowl, garnish with the cilantro sprigs and serve with the couscous. —*Joanne Weir*

Chicken with Walnut-Pomegranate Sauce

4 SERVINGS ●●
½ cup walnuts (2 ounces)
Eight 4-ounce skinless chicken thighs
  on the bone, visible fat trimmed
Salt and freshly ground pepper
Olive oil cooking spray
1¼ cups low-sodium nonfat
  chicken broth

1. In a food processor, finely grind the walnuts; do not grind to a paste.

2. Season the chicken with salt and pepper. Lightly grease a large nonstick skillet with olive oil cooking spray, and heat. Add the chicken and cook over moderate heat until browned, about 5 minutes per side. Transfer to a plate.

3. Add the chicken broth to the skillet and bring to a boil over high heat, scraping up any browned bits on the bottom. Remove from the heat.

4. Heat the olive oil in a large enameled cast-iron casserole. Add the onion, cover and cook over low heat, stirring occasionally, until softened and just starting to brown, about 20 minutes. Uncover and cook, stirring, until browned, about 10 minutes. Add the ground walnuts, pomegranate molasses, brown sugar, saffron, cumin and the chicken broth and bring to a boil. Simmer over low heat for 15 minutes. Add the chicken thighs, cover and simmer until cooked through and tender, about 15 minutes.

5. Transfer the chicken to a plate and simmer the sauce over moderate heat until slightly thickened, about 2 minutes. Return the chicken to the sauce, turn to coat and season with salt and pepper. Transfer the chicken to plates; spoon the sauce on top. Sprinkle with the pomegranate seeds and cilantro and serve.   —*Ann Chantal Altman*

ONE SERVING Calories 366 kcal, Total Fat 17.4 gm, Saturated Fat 2.6 gm, Protein 31 gm, Carbohydrates 22 gm

NOTE Pomegranate molasses is available at Middle Eastern groceries.

Vietnamese Grilled Chicken and Eggplant

2 SERVINGS ●

- 2 garlic cloves
- 1½ teaspoons sugar
- Pinch of crushed red pepper
- Salt and freshly ground pepper
- ¼ cup fresh lime juice
- 2 tablespoons chopped cilantro
- 2 tablespoons water
- 1 tablespoon fish sauce
- 1 scallion, white and light green part only, thinly sliced
- 4 Asian eggplants, halved lengthwise
- 3 tablespoons vegetable oil
- 4 boneless chicken thighs (about 1¼ pounds)

I. Light a grill or preheat the broiler. In a mortar, mash the garlic with the sugar, crushed red pepper and a large pinch each of salt and pepper until a paste forms. Stir in the lime juice and cilantro. Transfer half of the mixture to a medium bowl and stir in the water, fish sauce and scallion to make a dipping sauce.

2. Brush the eggplants with 1½ tablespoons of the oil and season with salt and pepper. Season the chicken with salt and pepper. Stir the remaining 1½ tablespoons of oil into the remaining garlic-lime mixture and spread it all over the chicken. Grill or broil the chicken and eggplants, turning once, until cooked through, about 5 minutes for the eggplants and 12 minutes for the chicken. Transfer to a platter and serve at once with the dipping sauce.

—*Melissa Clark*

Garlic-Cilantro Chicken Thighs with Miso

4 SERVINGS ●

- 2 large garlic cloves, thinly sliced
- 1 tablespoon plus 1 teaspoon dark (red) miso
- ¼ cup plus 2 tablespoons chicken stock or canned low-sodium broth
- 3 tablespoons rice or cider vinegar
- ½ teaspoon Worcestershire sauce
- 8 chicken thighs (about 1½ pounds)
- ¼ cup dry white wine
- 2 tablespoons chopped cilantro
- 1 scallion, thinly sliced

I. Place an oven rack in the middle of the oven and preheat the broiler. In a small bowl, mix the garlic with the miso. Stir in the chicken stock, vinegar and Worcestershire sauce.

2. Put the chicken in a baking dish, skin side down, and pour on the miso sauce. Set the dish on the rack and broil for 15 minutes. Turn the thighs and broil for about 10 minutes longer, or until the skin is crisp and the chicken is cooked through. Transfer to a platter and skim the fat off the sauce.

Spiced Chicken Tacos with Crispy Skins

3. Add the wine to the baking dish and broil until the wine sizzles. Stir well and pour the sauce over the chicken. Sprinkle with the cilantro and scallion and serve at once. —*Michael Roberts*

Spiced Chicken Tacos with Crispy Skins

12 SERVINGS ●

Let guests make their own meals with an assortment of taco fixings. To add a terrific flavor boost to chicken tacos, turn the skin into super-crisp cracklings.

- 2 large ancho chiles
- 1½ cups boiling water
- 8 garlic cloves, halved
- 2 tablespoons cider vinegar
- 2 teaspoons ground cumin
- 1½ teaspoons ground cinnamon
- 1½ teaspoons ground allspice
- 1 teaspoon cayenne pepper
- Kosher salt
- 12 whole chicken legs, trimmed of excess fat and loose skin
- Freshly ground pepper
- 24 warmed stone-ground corn tortillas, for serving

1. Preheat the oven to 350°. In a medium heatproof bowl, cover the ancho chiles with the boiling water and let soak until softened, about 20 minutes. Drain the anchos and reserve the soaking liquid. Stem, seed and coarsely chop the anchos.

2. In a food processor, pulse the anchos with the garlic, vinegar, cumin, cinnamon, allspice, cayenne and 1 teaspoon of salt until a coarse paste forms. Add the reserved ancho soaking liquid and process until smooth.

3. Arrange the chicken legs in a shallow roasting pan, skin side up. Pour the ancho sauce on the chicken and toss to coat. Roast the chicken legs in the upper third of the oven for 1½ hours, or until the meat is cooked through and the skin is crisp. Using tongs, lift the crisp skin off each leg in

1 piece and transfer it to a baking sheet. Flatten each piece of skin with your hands. Season the chicken skin with salt and pepper, then bake for 2 to 3 minutes, or until very crisp.

4. Transfer the chicken legs to a large plate. Remove the meat from the bones. Shred the chicken and spread it in a medium roasting pan. Pour the roasting juices into a glass measuring cup and skim the fat from the surface. Pour the juices over the chicken and season with salt and pepper.

5. Preheat the broiler. Broil the shredded chicken for about 4 minutes, stirring a few times, until the chicken begins to crisp at the edges. Transfer the chicken and sauce to a warmed serving bowl. Arrange the crisp chicken skin in another bowl and serve with the warmed tortillas. —*Marcia Kiesel*

MAKE AHEAD The recipe can be prepared through Step 4 and refrigerated for 1 day. Crisp the skin in a 400° oven for 5 minutes. Bring the chicken to room temperature before broiling.

SERVE WITH Diced avocados, shredded iceberg and romaine lettuces, lime wedges, shredded Jack cheese, finely shredded Asiago cheese and crumbled soft goat cheese.

WINE The sweet and hot spices in this dish call for a simple, direct, fruity wine. Look for a fresh, inexpensive rosé with good acidity, such as Château Routas Rouvière Rosé from Provence or Preston of Dry Creek Le Petit Faux Rosé Dry Creek Valley.

Crispy Spiced Fried Chicken

4 TO 6 SERVINGS

Poultry contains vitamin B_1, which allegedly counteracts anger, but the chipotle chiles and cayenne pepper in the crispy crust will do a slow burn even if you don't.

- 4 pounds chicken wings, legs and thighs, trimmed of excess fat
- 2 cups buttermilk or plain nonfat yogurt

- 2½ tablespoons kosher salt
- 2 tablespoons plus 2 teaspoons ground chipotle powder
- 2 cups all-purpose flour
- ½ teaspoon cayenne pepper
- Peanut oil, for frying

1. Rinse the chicken and pat dry. Cut the wings in half and discard the wing tips. In a bowl, mix the buttermilk with 1 tablespoon of the kosher salt and 2 teaspoons of the chipotle powder. Add the chicken, turn to coat and let stand at room temperature for 20 minutes.

2. In a resealable plastic bag, mix the flour with the remaining 2 tablespoons of chipotle powder, the cayenne and the remaining 1½ tablespoons of kosher salt. Seal the bag and shake to blend.

3. In a large, heavy skillet, heat ¾ inch of peanut oil to 360°. Working in 2 batches, shake the buttermilk off the chicken, put the chicken in the bag with the flour mixture and shake to coat well. Add the chicken to the hot oil and fry over moderate heat, turning once or twice, until golden and crisp, about 20 minutes; lower the heat if necessary so the chicken doesn't brown too quickly. Drain the chicken on a rack lined with paper towels and serve immediately. —*Grace Parisi*

MAKE AHEAD The recipe can be prepared through Step 1 and refrigerated for 8 hours.

Circassian Chicken

4 SERVINGS ●

This version of a classic Turkish dish is a chicken salad with a creamy walnut sauce.

- One 3-pound chicken
- 2½ quarts plus 1 cup water
- 1 small onion, halved
- 1 carrot, halved
- 2 whole cloves
- Salt
- 4 thin slices of white sandwich bread (3 ounces), crusts removed
- 3 cups walnuts (¾ pound), chopped

2 teaspoons ground coriander

2 garlic cloves, minced

1 teaspoon freshly ground black pepper

2½ teaspoons crushed red pepper

2 tablespoons French walnut oil

1. In a large pot, cover the chicken with 2½ quarts of the water. Add the onion, carrot, cloves and a large pinch of salt and bring to a boil. Reduce the heat to low, skim the broth and simmer until the chicken is cooked through, about 1 hour and 15 minutes.

2. Transfer the chicken to a platter and let cool slightly. Skim the fat from the broth and measure 1 cup; reserve the remaining broth for another use. Remove the meat from the chicken and discard the skin and bones. Cut the chicken meat into bite-size pieces and transfer to a medium bowl.

3. In a shallow bowl, soak the bread in the remaining 1 cup of water until softened, then squeeze dry. In a food processor, combine 2½ cups of the walnuts with the reserved 1 cup of broth, the bread, coriander, minced garlic, black pepper and 1½ teaspoons of crushed red pepper; process to a coarse puree and add to the chicken. Finely grind the remaining ½ cup of walnuts in the food processor and stir into the chicken. Season the chicken salad with salt and transfer to a serving bowl.

4. In a small saucepan, warm the walnut oil over low heat. Add the remaining 1 teaspoon of crushed red pepper and cook for 1 minute. Drizzle the hot oil over the chicken salad and serve at room temperature. —*Engin Akin*

MAKE AHEAD The chicken salad can be refrigerated overnight. Drizzle on the hot oil just before serving.

Chicken with Ale and Juniper Berries

4 SERVINGS

One 4-pound chicken, cut into 8 pieces

Salt and freshly ground pepper

4 tablespoons cold unsalted butter, 3 tablespoons cut into small dice

1 tablespoon vegetable oil

3 shallots, minced

½ cup plus 2 tablespoons dark ale, such as Maredsous Abbey Ale

1½ tablespoons juniper berries, coarsely crushed

1 teaspoon pink peppercorns, coarsely crushed

2 tablespoons finely chopped flat-leaf parsley

1. Season the chicken generously with salt and pepper. In a large skillet, melt the 1 tablespoon of uncut butter in the oil. Add the chicken in batches and cook over moderately high heat until browned, about 5 minutes per side; remove to a plate. Reduce the heat to moderate, add the shallots and cook, stirring occasionally, until softened, about 1 minute. Add ½ cup of the dark ale and bring to a boil, scraping up the browned bits from the bottom. Return the chicken to the skillet, cover and simmer for 15 minutes. Turn and baste the chicken with the pan juices, then cover and simmer until cooked through, about 15 minutes longer.

2. Remove the chicken from the skillet and keep warm. Boil the pan juices over high heat until syrupy, about 5 minutes. Reduce the heat to moderate. Add the crushed juniper berries, pink peppercorns and the remaining 2 tablespoons of ale, then whisk in the remaining 3 tablespoons of cold butter, a few pieces at a time. Season with salt and pepper. Remove from the heat. Return the chicken to the skillet and spoon the sauce over it to coat. Serve the chicken on a platter or dinner plates, sprinkled with the parsley.

—*Ruth Van Waerebeek*

BEER The best beverage here is more of the same ale that's in the dish.

Sautéed Chicken with Green Olives and Cilantro

4 SERVINGS

North African in spirit, this dish is easy enough for weeknight cooking but impressive enough to serve to guests. Note the sauté-and-roast technique used to prepare the chicken, which results in crisp skin and juicy meat.

menu

hors d'oeuvres **crispy fried shrimp with green herb sauce (p. 23)**

marinated fried trout (p. 20) | DUVEL ALE

first course **curried mussel and butternut squash soup (p. 108)** | BLANCHE DE BRUGES

main course **chicken with ale and juniper berries | buttermilk mashed potatoes (p. 307)**

sautéed endives with apples and currants (p. 288) | MAREDSOUS ABBEY ALE

salad **bitter greens with cherry beer vinaigrette and blue cheese toasts (p. 63)** | BOON KRIEK

dessert **flemish sugar tart (p. 342)** | BOON FRAMBOISE

Chicken with Ale and Juniper Berries, with Buttermilk Mashed Potatoes (p. 307) and Sautéed Endives wih Apples and Currants (p. 288)

Sautéed Chicken with Green Olives and Cilantro

¼ cup extra-virgin olive oil

¼ cup minced onion

2 teaspoons minced fresh ginger

2 teaspoons minced garlic

One 2-inch cinnamon stick

3 saffron threads

2 cups chicken stock or canned low-sodium broth

Salt and freshly ground pepper

One 3½-pound chicken, cut into 8 pieces

2 tablespoons minced green olives

2 teaspoons fresh lemon juice

1 tablespoon coarsely chopped cilantro, plus more for garnish

1. Preheat the oven to 500°. Heat 1 tablespoon of the olive oil in a small saucepan. Add the onion, ginger, garlic, cinnamon and saffron and cook over moderate heat until the onion softens, about 5 minutes. Add the chicken stock and season with salt and pepper. Increase the heat to high and simmer, stirring occasionally, until the liquid reduces by three-quarters and becomes syrupy, about 20 minutes. Remove from the heat.

2. Season the chicken with salt and pepper. Heat 2 tablespoons of the olive oil in a large ovenproof skillet.

Add the chicken, skin side down, and cook over moderately high heat until lightly browned, 5 to 8 minutes. Turn the chicken and cook for 2 minutes. Turn the pieces skin side down and roast in the oven for about 25 minutes, or until the juices run clear when a thigh is pierced.

3. Remove the cinnamon stick from the sauce. Add the olives and the remaining 1 tablespoon of olive oil and season with pepper. Rewarm the sauce over low heat for 1 minute. Remove from the heat and stir in the lemon juice and the 1 tablespoon of chopped cilantro. Arrange the chicken on plates and spoon the sauce around it. Garnish with cilantro and serve.

—*Jean-Georges Vongerichten*

WINE Contrast the strong, sweet, spicy and salty notes in the relish with a fruity, medium-weight Zinfandel. Look for the 1997 Eberle Paso Robles Sauret Vineyard or the 1998 Ridge Sonoma Station.

Chicken with Olives and Preserved Lemon

4 SERVINGS ●●

2 teaspoons fennel seeds

2 teaspoons coriander seeds

2 teaspoons cumin seeds

One 3½-pound chicken, cut into 8 pieces

Salt and freshly ground pepper

2 tablespoons extra-virgin olive oil

1 large onion, thinly sliced

1 medium fennel bulb—halved, cored and thinly sliced lengthwise

4 large garlic cloves, thinly sliced

One 28-ounce can peeled Italian tomatoes, drained and coarsely chopped

1 cup Moroccan green olives, pitted and halved

1 cup dry white wine

1½ cups chicken stock

2 small preserved lemons— quartered, pulp scraped out, peel finely julienned

¼ cup chopped cilantro

Chicken with Olives and Preserved Lemon

1. In a small skillet, combine the 3 seeds and cook over moderate heat, shaking the pan, until fragrant, about 2 minutes. Remove, let cool, then grind in a spice grinder.

2. Season the chicken with salt and pepper. In a large enameled cast-iron casserole, heat the oil. Put in the chicken and brown well over moderate heat, about 10 minutes. Remove the chicken. Add the onion and fennel bulb to the casserole and brown lightly over moderate heat, stirring occasionally, about 10 minutes. Add the garlic and ground spices and cook until fragrant, about 2 minutes.

3. Stir in the tomatoes, olives and wine and bring to a boil. Return the chicken to the casserole. Add the stock and preserved lemons and season with salt and pepper. Bring to a simmer, then cover and cook over low heat until the chicken is tender and cooked through, about 25 minutes. Transfer the chicken to a platter and keep warm.

4. Boil the sauce to thicken, about 12 minutes. Season with salt and pepper; pour over the chicken. Sprinkle with cilantro.   —*Johnathan Sundstrom*
MAKE AHEAD The dish can be refrigerated for 2 days.
SERVE WITH Couscous sprinkled with pine nuts and dried currants.

Chicken in Paprika Cream Sauce
6 SERVINGS ●

In Austria this dish is traditionally served to celebrate anniversaries. You can make it with all white meat if you prefer (use six breast halves).

- 2 teaspoons caraway seeds
- 1 red bell pepper
- Three ½-pound skinless, boneless chicken breast halves, each cut crosswise into 3 pieces
- 3 whole chicken legs, cut into drumsticks and thighs
- Salt and freshly ground pepper
- 2 tablespoons sweet Hungarian paprika
- All-purpose flour, for dusting
- 3 tablespoons peanut oil
- 2 medium onions, thinly sliced
- 3 large garlic cloves, minced
- 1 medium tomato—peeled, seeded and chopped
- 2 tablespoons minced marjoram
- 1 tablespoon tomato paste
- 1 teaspoon minced thyme
- 1 bay leaf
- ½ cup dry white wine
- 1½ cups chicken stock or canned low-sodium broth
- ¼ cup plus 2 tablespoons crème fraîche
- 2 tablespoons minced parsley

1. In a small skillet, toast the caraway seeds over moderate heat until fragrant, about 1 minute. Transfer the seeds to a spice grinder and let cool completely, then grind to a powder.

2. Roast the red pepper directly over an open flame or in the broiler, turning, until charred all over. Put the pepper in a bowl, cover with plastic and let steam for 10 minutes. Discard the skin, stem and seeds and cut the pepper into ¼-inch strips.

3. Season the chicken with salt and pepper and dust with 1 tablespoon of the paprika. Lightly dust the chicken with flour. Heat the oil in a large enameled cast-iron casserole. Add the chicken in batches and cook over moderately high heat until browned, about 2 minutes per side. Transfer to a large plate.

4. Add the onions and garlic to the casserole and cook over moderate heat, stirring, until softened, about 5 minutes. Add the ground caraway and the remaining 1 tablespoon of paprika and cook, stirring, until fragrant, about 2 minutes. Add the tomato, marjoram, tomato paste, thyme and bay leaf and cook, stirring, for 1 minute. Stir in the wine and simmer for 1 minute. Add the stock, season with salt and pepper and bring to a simmer.

5. Return the chicken to the casserole along with any accumulated juices. Cover and simmer over low heat until the breast pieces are cooked through; start checking after 10 minutes. Transfer the breast pieces to a plate. Continue simmering until the drumsticks and thighs are cooked through and tender, about 15 minutes longer. Transfer the drumsticks and thighs to the plate.

6. Add ¼ cup of the crème fraîche to the sauce and simmer for 5 minutes. Discard the bay leaf. Working in batches, transfer the hot sauce to a blender; add half of the roasted pepper strips to the sauce and puree. Return the chicken to the casserole and pour the sauce on top. Bring to a simmer and season with salt and pepper. Transfer the chicken to a serving bowl. Stir the remaining 2 tablespoons of crème fraîche and drizzle over the chicken, then garnish with the remaining half of the pepper strips, sprinkle with the parsley and serve.   —*Wolfgang Puck*
MAKE AHEAD The dish can be refrigerated overnight. Reheat gently.
SERVE WITH Rice or spaetzle.
WINE The smooth, creamy sauce will flatter the ripe fruit and soft texture of an Austrian Riesling. Try the 2000 Zull Schrattenthal Innere Bergen or the 2000 Schloss Gobelsburg Zöbinger Heiligenstein.

Brazilian Chicken Stew

4 SERVINGS ●

This delectable chicken-and-coconut stew simmers only briefly. It's done in 20 minutes.

- ⅓ cup peeled and thinly sliced ginger (3 ounces)
- 4 garlic cloves, chopped
- 2 jalapeños, seeded and chopped
- 2 tablespoons fresh lemon juice
- 1 tablespoon sweet paprika
- 2 tablespoons water
- ¼ cup vegetable oil
- 3 medium onions, coarsely chopped
- 2 cups drained canned plum tomatoes, coarsely chopped, juices reserved
- ½ cup unsweetened coconut milk
- ½ cup dry-roasted peanuts, finely chopped
- ¼ cup shredded unsweetened coconut, plus more for garnish
- ¼ cup chopped cilantro, plus more for garnish

Brazilian Chicken Stew

- 3 cups chicken stock or canned low-sodium broth
- Salt and freshly ground pepper
- 2 pounds skinless, boneless chicken thighs, cut into 1½-inch pieces
- Steamed rice and lemon wedges, for serving

1. In a food processor, pulse the sliced ginger with the chopped garlic cloves, chopped jalapeños, fresh lemon juice and sweet paprika until the ginger, garlic and jalapeños are very finely chopped. Add the water and process the mixture to a paste.

2. In a large saucepan, heat 2 tablespoons of the vegetable oil until it's shimmering. Add the coarsely chopped onions and cook over moderate heat until they're softened, about 8 minutes. Add the paste from Step 1 and cook until it begins to brown, about 3 minutes. Add half of the coarsely chopped tomatoes along with the coconut milk, peanuts, ¼ cup of the shredded coconut and 2 tablespoons of the chopped cilantro and cook until slightly thickened, about 5 minutes.

3. Scrape the sauce into a food processor or blender and puree. Return the sauce to the saucepan. Add the stock and the remaining tomatoes and 2 tablespoons of cilantro and bring to a boil. Season with salt and pepper and simmer over moderate heat until reduced to 5 cups, about 20 minutes. Keep warm.

4. Meanwhile, in a large nonstick skillet, heat the remaining 2 tablespoons of oil until shimmering. Season the chicken with salt and pepper and sauté over moderately high heat until golden and cooked through, about 10 minutes.

5. Add the chicken; season with salt and pepper. Spoon into bowls and garnish with coconut and cilantro. Serve with steamed rice and lemon wedges.
—*Joyce Goldstein*

Chicken, Shrimp and Andouille Gumbo

12 SERVINGS ●

To achieve the ultimate flavor for this authentic recipe, use the smokiest andouille sausage you can find. One excellent brand to try: Applegate Farms' Jugtown Mountain Smokehouse (800-587-5858).

- ⅔ cup plus 1 tablespoon vegetable oil
- 2 pounds medium shrimp, shelled and deveined, shells reserved
- 2 pounds chicken wings
- Salt and freshly ground pepper
- 2 tablespoons tomato paste
- 4 quarts chicken stock or low-sodium broth
- 3 bay leaves
- 6 whole chicken legs
- 1 cup all-purpose flour
- 8 large garlic cloves, finely chopped
- 6 large scallions, white and green parts thinly sliced separately
- 4 medium celery ribs, cut into ½-inch dice
- 2 large Spanish onions, coarsely chopped
- 2 medium green peppers, cut into ½-inch dice
- 1 pound smoked andouille sausage, half finely chopped, half sliced into ¼-inch rounds
- 2 teaspoons dried thyme
- 1 teaspoon cayenne pepper
- 1 pound okra, stems trimmed, cut into ½-inch rounds
- 3 tablespoons filé powder (see Note)

1. In a large, heavy stockpot, heat 1 tablespoon of the vegetable oil. Add the reserved shrimp shells and chicken wings, season with salt and pepper and cook over moderately high heat, stirring occasionally, until the chicken wings are browned, about 10 minutes. Add 1 tablespoon of the tomato paste and cook, stirring, until glossy, about 2

Chicken, Shrimp and
Andouille Gumbo

minutes. Slowly pour in the stock, stirring with a wooden spoon to release any browned bits on the bottom of the pot. Add the bay leaves and bring to a boil. Skim the surface of the stock, reduce the heat to low and simmer for 1½ hours, skimming occasionally.

2. Add the chicken legs to the stock and simmer until they are cooked through, about 40 minutes. Strain the stock into a heatproof bowl and transfer the chicken legs to a large plate. When the legs are cool enough to handle, remove the meat and discard the skin and bones. Tear the meat into 2-inch pieces and set aside. Skim the fat from the surface of the stock and reserve the stock.

3. In a large enameled cast-iron casserole, stir the remaining ⅔ cup of vegetable oil with the flour until smooth. Cook the oil and flour over moderately low heat, stirring constantly, until a deep brown roux forms, about 25 minutes. Add the garlic, scallion whites, celery, onions, green peppers and finely chopped andouille sausage. Cook over low heat, stirring occasionally, until the vegetables soften, about 15 minutes. Add the thyme, cayenne, 1 teaspoon of salt and ¼ teaspoon of pepper and cook, stirring, for 2 minutes. Add the remaining 1 tablespoon of tomato paste and cook, stirring, for 1 minute. Gradually whisk in the reserved stock. Simmer over low heat for 1 hour, skimming occasionally.

4. Add the okra and simmer until just tender, about 8 minutes. Add the reserved shredded chicken and the andouille rounds and simmer for 10 minutes. Season the gumbo with salt and pepper. Add the shrimp and simmer for 1 minute. Turn off the heat and let the gumbo stand for a few minutes. Stir in the filé powder and scallion greens and serve hot. —*Marcia Kiesel*
NOTE Filé powder is made from ground dried sassafras leaves. It acts as a thickener for stews and should be added at the very end to avoid over-thickening. It's available in the spice section of most supermarkets.
MAKE AHEAD The Chicken, Shrimp and Andouille Gumbo can be prepared through Step 3 up to 3 days ahead and refrigerated. Reheat gently and proceed.
SERVE WITH White rice.
WINE OR BEER Cool this spicy gumbo with an inexpensive, tangy, fruity white wine, such as the 1999 Eno Friulia Pinot Grigio, or a light Latin-American beer, such as Cerveza-Aguila.

Simple Roasted Chicken

2 TO 3 SERVINGS

- 1 tablespoon unsalted butter, softened
- One 2½- to 3-pound chicken—neck, wing tips and gizzard reserved
- ½ teaspoon sweet paprika
- Salt and freshly ground pepper
- 1 carrot, cut into 1-inch pieces
- 1 celery rib, cut into 1-inch pieces
- 1 onion, coarsely chopped
- 5 unpeeled garlic cloves
- 1 cup dry white wine

I. Preheat the oven to 425°. Rub the butter all over the chicken and set it in a medium cast-iron skillet. In a small bowl, mix the sweet paprika with ½ teaspoon each of salt and pepper and sprinkle all over the chicken. Scatter the carrot, celery, chopped onion, garlic cloves and reserved neck, wing tips and gizzard around the chicken and cook over high heat until sizzling, about 2 minutes.

2. Transfer the skillet to the oven and roast the chicken for 50 minutes, or until the skin is golden brown and crisp and an instant-read thermometer inserted in the thickest part of the thigh registers 170°. Transfer the chicken to a cutting board and let rest for about 10 minutes.

3. Add the white wine to the skillet and cook over high heat, stirring, until reduced to ½ cup, about 5 minutes. Strain the pan juices into a bowl and skim off any fat.

4. Carve the roasted chicken and serve with the pan juices. If serving with the Farro with Shiitake Mushrooms, spoon the farro onto plates and arrange the carved chicken on top. —*Dan Barber*
SERVE WITH Farro with Shiitake Mushrooms (p. 312).

Garlicky Roast Chicken

4 SERVINGS

Here's the perfect chicken recipe for garlic-lovers.

- 3 tablespoons unsalted butter, softened
- One 3½-pound chicken
- Salt and freshly ground pepper
- 2 heads of garlic, cloves separated but not peeled
- 3 tablespoons water

I. Preheat the oven to 400°. Rub the butter all over the chicken and inside the cavity. Season the chicken skin and cavity with salt and pepper. Put half of the garlic in the cavity. Tie the legs together.

2. Spread the remaining garlic cloves in the center of a medium roasting pan and set the chicken on top. Pour the water into the pan and roast the chicken for 1 hour, basting occasionally; the bird is done if the juices run clear when an inner thigh is pierced. Transfer the chicken to a cutting board, cover loosely with foil and let rest for 10 minutes. Discard the string. Carve the chicken and serve it with the roasted garlic cloves from the pan.

—*Jean Calviac*
WINE The garlic flavors of this roast chicken suggest a light-bodied, juicy red. Try one from the local appellation of Buzet, made from Cabernet Sauvignon, Merlot and Cabernet Franc. Two bargain examples: the 1996 Baron d'Ardeuil and the 1996 Château de Gueyze.

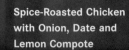

Spice-Roasted Chicken
with Onion, Date and
Lemon Compote

Spice-Roasted Chicken with Onion, Date and Lemon Compote

4 SERVINGS

A curry spice blend gives chicken exotic flavor and a gorgeous golden color.

Kosher salt

½ **cup sugar**

Water

**One 3½-pound chicken,
    rinsed and patted dry**

2 **tablespoons cumin seeds**

1 **cinnamon stick, broken into
    small pieces**

1 **tablespoon ground ginger**

1 **tablespoon curry powder**

1 **tablespoon grapeseed oil**

5 **tablespoons unsalted butter**

4 **pitted dates**

2 **medium onions, cut into
    ½-inch dice**

Finely grated zest of 4 lemons

Freshly ground pepper

1. In a deep bowl just large enough to hold the chicken, stir ½ cup of salt and the sugar into 1 quart of cold water until completely dissolved. Add the chicken to the brine, breast down, and refrigerate it for 1½ hours. Drain the chicken and pat thoroughly dry.

2. Meanwhile, in a small dry skillet, toast the cumin seeds and cinnamon over moderate heat until fragrant, about 1 minute. Transfer to a spice grinder and grind to a coarse powder. Mix the powder with the ginger and curry powder.

3. Preheat the oven to 450°. Season the chicken inside and out with the spice mix and tie the legs together. Heat the oil in a large ovenproof skillet. Add 1 tablespoon of the butter and melt over moderately high heat. Add the chicken on its side and cook until browned, about 5 minutes; turn and brown the second side. Turn the chicken breast side up and roast it in the oven for 55 minutes, or until the juices in the cavity run clear.

4. Meanwhile, bring a small saucepan of water to a boil over high heat. Add the dates and simmer over moderate heat for 1 minute, then drain. Peel the dates and cut them into ¼-inch dice.

5. Melt the remaining 4 tablespoons of butter in a large skillet. Add the onions and ¼ cup of water, cover and cook over low heat until the onions are very tender, about 25 minutes. Add the lemon zest and diced dates and season with salt and pepper.

6. Transfer the chicken to a carving board and let rest for 10 minutes. Serve the chicken with the warm compote.   —*Jean-Georges Vongerichten*

MAKE AHEAD The compote can be refrigerated for 3 days. Reheat gently before serving.

WINE An intensely fragrant Viognier with lots of body will echo the exotic spices and highlight the fruitiness of the compote. Pick an elegant French bottling, such as the 1999 Cave Yves Cuilleron Condrieu or the bargain 1999 Georges Duboeuf Viognier.

Lemon and Rosemary Chicken

4 SERVINGS ●

One 3½-pound organic chicken

**Sea salt and freshly ground
    white pepper**

1 **small lemon, preferably
    organic, quartered**

8 **thyme sprigs plus ½ teaspoon
    thyme leaves**

4 **medium Yukon Gold potatoes
    (¼ pound each), scrubbed
    and quartered**

4 **large carrots,
    quartered lengthwise**

4 **medium onions, quartered**

1 **large head of garlic, cloves
    separated but not peeled**

6 **bay leaves**

4 **rosemary sprigs**

½ **teaspoon oregano**

¾ **cup water**

**Lemon and Garlic Puree
    (recipe follows)**

1. Preheat the oven to 425°. Generously season the cavity of the chicken with salt and pepper. Add the quartered lemon and the thyme sprigs to the chicken cavity. Season the outside of the chicken all over with salt and pepper.

2. In a large roasting pan, arrange the potatoes, carrots and onions cut side down in a single layer. Scatter the garlic cloves, thyme leaves, bay leaves, rosemary and oregano over the vegetables and season with salt and pepper. Set the chicken on the vegetables and pour ½ cup of water into the pan.

3. Roast the chicken and vegetables for about 1 hour and 15 minutes, or until the chicken juices run clear from the cavity and the vegetables are tender; rotate the pan once or twice for even cooking and add ¼ cup of water if the vegetables seem dry.

4. Transfer the chicken to a carving board, cover loosely with foil and let rest for 10 minutes. Arrange the vegetables on a large, warmed platter. Remove the garlic cloves from their

Lemon and Rosemary Chicken

¼ teaspoon crumbled dried sage
Kosher salt and freshly ground pepper
3¼ cups chicken stock or canned
low-sodium broth
One 3½-pound chicken,
rinsed and patted dry
6 medium carrots,
sliced ¼ inch thick

I. Preheat the oven to 450°. Spread the bread slices directly on the racks in the oven and toast for about 3 minutes, or until dry and lightly browned, turning halfway through; let cool. Tear the slices into ½-inch pieces and transfer to a large bowl.

2. In a skillet, cook the pancetta over moderate heat, turning once, until crisp, about 5 minutes. Chop the pancetta and add to the bowl with the bread.

3. Add the onion, celery and minced garlic to the skillet and cook, stirring frequently, until softened, about 5 minutes. Add the kale, rosemary, sage and a generous pinch each of salt and pepper and cook over moderate heat until the kale is wilted, about 3 minutes. Scrape the vegetables into the bowl with the bread.

4. Add 2 cups of the broth to the skillet and boil over high heat, scraping up any browned bits, until reduced to 1 cup, about 15 minutes. Pour the broth over the bread and toss; let stand, tossing occasionally, until the stuffing is cool and evenly moistened, about 10 minutes. Season with salt and pepper.

5. Using your fingertips, loosen the chicken skin: Begin at the tip of each breast and work your way up the breast and down the thighs. Tuck the sliced garlic under the skin. Loosely pack 1½ cups of the bread stuffing into the cavity, mounding it slightly around the opening.

6. Set the chicken on a rack in a roasting pan and season very generously with salt and pepper. Roast the chicken for 30 minutes, or until the skin is

skin and carve the chicken. Arrange the chicken and garlic on the platter. Remove the lemon quarters from the cavity and squeeze the juice all over the chicken. Serve with the Lemon and Garlic Puree. —*Patricia Wells*
ONE SERVING Calories 557 kcal, Total Fat 19.3 gm, Saturated Fat 5.3 gm, Protein 44 gm, Carbohydrates 52 gm
WINE A sublime, simple chicken always calls out for a good glass of Beaujolais-Villages, preferably a Saint-Amour.

LEMON AND GARLIC PUREE

MAKES ABOUT 1¾ CUPS ●
This intensely flavored puree is delicious with lamb and fish as well as roast chicken.

4 whole garlic heads, separated into unpeeled cloves
2 cups 1% milk
1 small thin-skinned organic lemon, thinly sliced, ends and seeds discarded
Fine sea salt

In a small saucepan, simmer the garlic cloves in the milk over low heat until the garlic is soft, about 30 minutes. Strain the garlic, reserving the milk.

When cool enough to handle, peel the garlic cloves and put them in a food processor. Add the reserved milk and the lemon slices and puree. Season with salt. —*P.W.*
ONE TABLESPOON Calories 15 kcal, Total Fat 0.2 gm, Saturated Fat 0.1 gm, Protein 1 gm, Carbohydrates 3 gm
MAKE AHEAD The Lemon and Garlic Puree can be refrigerated for 2 days. Bring to room temperature before serving.

Roasted Chicken with Kale and Pancetta Stuffing

4 SERVINGS
Roasting this stuffed chicken at 450° makes the skin extra crispy.

½ pound sliced white peasant bread, crust removed
¼ pound thinly sliced pancetta
1 medium onion, finely chopped
1 small celery rib, finely chopped
4 garlic cloves, 2 minced and 2 thickly sliced
½ pound kale, thick stems discarded, leaves coarsely chopped
2 teaspoons finely chopped rosemary

Roasted Chicken with Kale and Pancetta Stuffing

Roast Chicken with Chicken Livers

lightly golden. Spread the carrots in the pan and roast the chicken for 1 hour longer, until it is deep golden and the juices run clear when a thigh is pierced. Transfer the chicken and carrots to a platter.

7. Meanwhile, spoon the remaining stuffing into a small baking dish and drizzle with ¼ cup of the chicken stock. Bake the stuffing for about 15 minutes, or until hot and crisp on top.

8. Strain the chicken pan juices into a small saucepan. Set the roasting pan over high heat, add the remaining 1 cup of stock and bring to a boil, scraping up any browned bits. Strain the stock into the saucepan and boil until reduced to ¾ cup, about 15 minutes. Spoon off any fat and season the sauce with salt and pepper. Transfer to a gravy boat and serve with the chicken and stuffing. —*Grace Parisi*

MAKE AHEAD The recipe can be prepared through Step 4 and refrigerated for 1 day.

WINE The salty, rich stuffing suggests a round, fruity Chardonnay, like the

bargain 1999 Rosemount. Or, consider a smooth and fruity Spanish red Rioja, like the 1993 Faustino Martinez Faustino I Gran Reserva or the inexpensive 1997 Montecillo Crianza.

Roast Chicken with Chicken Livers

4 SERVINGS

Roast chicken is dressed up with a rich braised garlic and peppercorn sauce and juicy seared chicken livers.

One 3¾- to 4-pound chicken

- 1   teaspoon coarsely chopped thyme

Salt

- ½   cup extra-virgin olive oil
- 20   garlic cloves, peeled
- 2   teaspoons coarsely crushed black peppercorns
- ¼   pound chicken livers, trimmed and cut into 1-inch pieces

Freshly ground pepper

- 2   tablespoons chopped Gaeta olives
- 1   tablespoon minced flat-leaf parsley

1. Preheat the oven to 350°. Set the chicken in a roasting pan just large enough to hold it. Sprinkle the thyme in the cavity and season the bird inside and out with salt. Tie the legs together. Pour the olive oil over the chicken and scatter the garlic cloves and peppercorns in the pan.

2. Roast the chicken for about 20 minutes, or until the garlic is soft and golden. Transfer the garlic to a coarse sieve set over a small saucepan. Roast the chicken for about 1 hour longer, or until the juices in the cavity run clear. Tip the chicken in the pan to drain the juices, then transfer the bird to a carving board and cover loosely with foil. Skim the fat from the pan juices and reserve 1 tablespoon. Press the garlic through the sieve into the saucepan and pour in the pan juices with the peppercorns.

3. In a medium skillet, heat the 1 tablespoon of reserved fat just until smoking. Add the chicken livers, season with salt and freshly ground pepper and cook over high heat until browned on both sides and pink in the center, about 1 minute. Add the livers to the pan sauce and bring the sauce to a simmer. Season with salt and remove from the heat.

4. Carve the chicken and arrange on plates. Spoon the sauce on top, garnish with the olives and parsley and serve.   —*FOOD & WINE Test Kitchen*

WINE The voluptuous 1997 Dunn Vineyards Cabernet Sauvignon and the 1999 Howell Mountain Vineyards Old Vines Zinfandel balance the luxurious flavors of the garlic and peppercorn sauce.

Grilled Szechuan Chicken with Hoisin Barbecue Sauce

4 SERVINGS

Roasting a whole bird on the grill over indirect heat results in crackling crisp skin and moist, tender meat. Toasting the peppercorns in a skillet adds a surprising depth of flavor.

1½ tablespoons Szechuan peppercorns
 1 teaspoon black peppercorns
 1 teaspoon kosher salt
 1 teaspoon finely grated fresh ginger
 1 garlic clove, minced
 1 tablespoon Asian sesame oil
One 4-pound chicken, rinsed and patted dry
Vegetable oil, for the grill
Hoisin Barbecue Sauce (recipe follows)
Grilled scallions and onion slices, for serving

I. In a small skillet, toast the Szechuan and black peppercorns over moderate heat until fragrant, about 1 minute. Transfer to a bowl and let cool.

2. In a spice grinder, grind the peppercorns. Transfer to a bowl and mix with the salt, ginger, garlic and sesame oil until a coarse paste forms. Spread half of the paste under the chicken's skin and rub the rest all over the skin. Tie the legs together with kitchen string.

3. Light a grill and set it up for indirect grilling. If using charcoal, when the fire is medium hot, rake the coals into two piles on opposite sides of the grill. Place a foil drip pan in the center of the grill. If using a gas grill, light the front and rear or outside burners.

4. Lightly brush the grate with vegetable oil. Set the chicken on the grill, breast side up, over the drip pan, away from the heat. Cover and grill until the skin is crisp and an instant-read thermometer inserted into the inner thigh registers 165°, about 1½ hours. Transfer to a cutting board and let stand for 5 minutes before carving. Serve with the Hoisin Barbecue Sauce and the grilled scallions and onions.

—*Steven Raichlen*

WINE The forward fruit of a dry or an off-dry Riesling will accentuate the spices and provide a bright contrast to the sweet, smoky nuances in this dish. Two good examples: the 1999 Dr. Loosen Riesling QbA Mosel-Saar-Ruwer from Germany and the 2000 Giesen Riesling Canterbury from New Zealand.

HOISIN BARBECUE SAUCE

MAKES ABOUT 1 CUP ●●

Like ketchup in an American barbecue sauce, the Chinese condiment hoisin provides a satisfying contrast of sweet, salty and aromatic flavors.

 2 teaspoons vegetable oil
 2 garlic cloves, minced
 ½ cup hoisin sauce

Grilled Szechuan Chicken with Hoisin Barbecue Sauce

1 tablespoon light soy sauce

3 tablespoons sake or dry sherry

1 tablespoon ketchup

1 tablespoon rice vinegar

½ teaspoon Asian sesame oil

Heat the vegetable oil in a small saucepan and cook the garlic over moderately low heat until fragrant, about 2 minutes. Add the hoisin sauce, soy sauce, sake, ketchup and rice vinegar and simmer over moderately low heat, stirring, until thickened, about 3 minutes. Remove from the heat and stir in the sesame oil. Let cool and serve. —*S.R.*

MAKE AHEAD The hoisin barbecue sauce can be refrigerated for 2 days.

Poached Chicken with Grainy Mustard Sauce

4 SERVINGS ●

This is essentially a pot-au-feu with chicken instead of beef. You can cook the chicken with additional vegetables, such as cabbage, turnips, parsnips and rutabagas; simply add them to the pot halfway through and cook until tender. Strain and save the leftover broth for enjoying on its own, with chopped fresh herbs, or for making soups or stews.

CHICKEN

One 4-pound organic chicken

2 medium onions, quartered

4 carrots, cut into thirds

2 large leeks, white and tender green parts—halved, rinsed and cut into thirds

4 celery ribs, cut into thirds

Two 1-pound celery roots, peeled and quartered

8 thyme sprigs

1 teaspoon peppercorns

1 tablespoon coarse salt

MUSTARD SAUCE

2 tablespoons unsalted butter

2 tablespoons all-purpose flour

½ cup heavy cream

1½ tablespoons grainy mustard

Salt and freshly ground pepper

I. PREPARE THE CHICKEN: Put all of the ingredients in a large saucepan. Add enough water to just cover the chicken and bring to a boil. Gently simmer the chicken, turning it once, until cooked through, about 1 hour. Transfer the chicken to a platter and let cool slightly.

2. MAKE THE MUSTARD SAUCE: In a medium saucepan, melt the butter over moderate heat. Whisk in the flour until blended. Gradually whisk in 1 cup of the chicken poaching liquid until smooth and bring to a simmer, whisking. Stir in the cream and mustard and season with salt and pepper; keep the sauce warm.

3. Carve the chicken and surround it with the vegetables. Spoon a little of the poaching liquid over the chicken and vegetables to moisten them and serve with the mustard sauce.

—*Van Gogh's Table*

MAKE AHEAD The Poached Chicken with Grainy Mustard Sauce can be prepared up to 2 days ahead.

SERVE WITH Rice pilaf.

WINE Try a fruity, zesty light red Burgundy or a fresh and intense Alsace Pinot Blanc here. Either will point up the mustard sauce without overwhelming the chicken. Look for the 1999 Maison Leroy Bourgogne Rouge or the 1999 Bergheim Marcel Deiss Pinot Blanc.

Black Bean Stew with Sherry Creamed Corn

4 SERVINGS ●

1 tablespoon extra-virgin olive oil

1 medium onion, coarsely chopped

2 large garlic cloves, minced

½ teaspoon ground cumin

¼ teaspoon cayenne pepper

Pinch of cinnamon

1 tablespoon tomato paste

1 cup chicken stock, canned low-sodium broth or water

Two 15½-ounce cans black beans, drained and rinsed

1 pound smoked chicken, turkey or pork sausage, sliced into ¼-inch rounds

2 cups corn kernels

1 cup heavy cream

2 tablespoons medium-dry sherry

4 small scallions, thinly sliced

Salt and freshly ground black pepper

I. Heat the olive oil in a large saucepan. Add the onion, garlic, cumin, cayenne and cinnamon, cover and cook over moderate heat, stirring a few times, until the onion softens, about 5 minutes. Add the tomato paste and stir until shiny, about 1 minute. Add the stock, black beans and sausage and bring to a simmer. Cover and cook over low heat for 10 minutes.

2. Meanwhile, in a medium saucepan, simmer the corn in the cream over low heat, stirring occasionally, until thickened, about 10 minutes. Add the sherry and scallions and simmer for 3 minutes longer. Season with salt and pepper.

3. Ladle the stew into bowls, spoon the corn on top and serve.

—*Marcia Kiesel*

Parmesan-Crusted Turkey Tenderloins

4 SERVINGS ●

¼ cup plus 2 tablespoons all-purpose flour

¼ cup plus 1 tablespoon freshly grated Parmesan

2 tablespoons finely chopped flat-leaf parsley

2 large garlic cloves, minced

¼ teaspoon salt

¼ teaspoon freshly ground pepper

2 large eggs

1½ pounds turkey tenderloin, cut crosswise into 4 equal pieces

2 tablespoons unsalted butter

2 tablespoons pure olive oil

1 lemon, quartered, for serving

I. On a large plate, mix the flour with the Parmesan, parsley, garlic, salt and pepper. In a shallow bowl, beat the eggs to mix. Gently pound the pieces of turkey ⅓ inch thick. Dip the turkey pieces in the egg, then roll in the flour mixture, patting off the excess.

2. In a large skillet, melt 1 tablespoon of the butter in 1 tablespoon of the olive oil. Add 2 of the turkey pieces and cook over moderately high heat until browned and just cooked, about 3 minutes per side; reduce the heat to moderate when the skillet gets too hot. Transfer the turkey to dinner plates. Repeat with the remaining 1 tablespoon of butter, 1 tablespoon of olive oil and 2 pieces of turkey. Serve with the lemon quarters.

—*Michael Roberts*

Sautéed Turkey Scaloppine

4 SERVINGS ●

Olive oil cooking spray
Four 4-ounce turkey cutlets,
      pounded ¼ inch thick
Salt and freshly ground pepper
  1 tablespoon unsalted butter
  4 bunches scallions, white and light
      green parts, thinly sliced (2 cups)
1¾ cups low-sodium nonfat
      chicken broth
  1 tablespoon veal demiglace
      (see Note p. 259)
  1 bay leaf
  ⅓ cup plus 1 tablespoon
      dry Marsala
  1 tablespoon all-purpose flour
  2 tablespoons snipped chives

1. Grease a large nonstick skillet with olive oil cooking spray and set the pan over moderately high heat. Season the turkey cutlets with salt and pepper. Add 2 cutlets to the skillet and cook, turning once, until golden brown, about 3 minutes. Transfer to a plate and repeat with the remaining cutlets.

2. Melt the butter in the skillet. Add the scallions and cook until softened, about 3 minutes. Add 1½ cups of the chicken broth, the demiglace, bay leaf and ⅓ cup of the Marsala and simmer

for 8 minutes. In a small bowl, whisk the remaining ¼ cup of chicken broth into the flour until smooth. Stir the slurry into the sauce and simmer for 3 minutes. Discard the bay leaf.

3. In a blender, puree 1 cup of the sauce until smooth. Stir the puree into the remaining sauce in the skillet and season with salt and pepper.

4. Warm the turkey cutlets in the sauce over low heat. Stir in the remaining 1 tablespoon of Marsala. Transfer the turkey to plates and spoon the sauce on top. Garnish with the chives and serve.

—*Ann Chantal Altman*

ONE SERVING Calories 168 kcal, Total Fat 1.2 gm, Saturated Fat 0.3 gm, Protein 25 gm, Carbohydrates 46 gm
SERVE WITH Hazelnut-Cranberry Wild Rice (p. 310) or brown rice.

Turkey Sausages with Apricots and Sage

4 SERVINGS ●

  1 tablespoon olive oil
  8 turkey or pork sausages
      (1½ pounds)
  1 tablespoon unsalted butter
  4 ripe apricots (½ pound)—halved,
      pitted and cut lengthwise into
      eighths
  2 tablespoons balsamic vinegar
  1 tablespoon coarsely
      chopped sage
  2 teaspoons light brown sugar
Salt and freshly ground pepper
  1 tablespoon coarsely chopped
      flat-leaf parsley

1. Heat the olive oil in a large skillet. Add the sausages and brown well over moderately high heat. Reduce the heat to low, cover and cook them through, about 10 minutes. Transfer the sausages to a plate and keep warm.

2. Melt the butter in the same skillet. Add the apricots, balsamic vinegar, sage and brown sugar and season with salt and pepper. Cook over moderately low heat until the apricots begin to

soften, 3 to 4 minutes. Stir in the parsley. Transfer the sausages to plates or a platter, pour the apricots and pan juices over them and serve at once.

—*Michael Roberts*

Guinea Hen with Herbed-Bread Stuffing

4 SERVINGS

  3 tablespoons extra-virgin olive oil
  3 chicken livers (¼ pound),
      trimmed
Salt and freshly ground pepper
  1 onion, finely chopped
  4 garlic cloves, minced
  2 ounces pancetta or prosciutto,
      finely diced (⅓ cup)
Three ¼-inch-thick slices of peasant
      bread (2 ounces), toasted and cut
      into ¼-inch dice
  3 tablespoons minced parsley
  2 teaspoons minced sage
  2 teaspoons minced rosemary
  2 teaspoons minced thyme
  ¾ cup chicken stock or
      low-sodium broth

Guinea Hen with
Herbed-Bread Stuffing

One 3 ¾-pound guinea hen
    or chicken
2 tablespoons unsalted
    butter, melted
¼ cup dry white wine

1. Preheat the oven to 450°. Set a rack in a flameproof roasting pan just large enough to hold the hen. Heat 1 tablespoon of the olive oil in a medium skillet. Add the chicken livers, season with salt and pepper and cook over moderately high heat, turning, until browned but still pink inside, about 5 minutes. Transfer to a plate and let cool; finely chop.

2. Add the onion, garlic and 1 tablespoon of the olive oil to the skillet and cook over moderately low heat, stirring, until the onion softens, about 4 minutes. Add the pancetta or prosciutto and cook, stirring, for 3 minutes. Scrape the mixture into a medium bowl. Add the diced toast, chicken livers, parsley, sage, rosemary and thyme and toss well.

3. Add ¼ cup of the stock and the remaining 1 tablespoon of olive oil to the skillet and simmer, scraping up any browned bits from the bottom; pour over the stuffing and toss. Season with salt and pepper and let cool.

4. Season the cavity of the guinea hen with salt and pepper. Starting from the cavity end, carefully separate the skin from the breast meat, then slide your fingers along the thighs and legs to free the skin. Gently push the stuffing under the skin, working it down around the legs and thighs and evenly covering the breast meat. Tie the legs together. Transfer the hen to the roasting pan. Brush the skin with some of the melted butter and season with salt and pepper.

5. Roast the guinea hen for 20 minutes, then baste with the remaining melted butter. Reduce the oven temperature to 350° and continue roasting the bird for 30 minutes, or until an instant-read thermometer inserted in

an inner thigh registers 170°. Transfer the guinea hen to a platter.

6. Remove the rack from the roasting pan. Pour off as much of the fat as possible. Set the pan over high heat, add the wine and bring to a boil, scraping up any browned bits from the bottom. Add the remaining ½ cup of stock and any accumulated hen juices and simmer until the sauce is flavorful. Skim off the fat, season with salt and pepper and transfer to a gravy boat. Carve the hen and serve with the pan sauce.   —*Joshua Eisen*

SERVE WITH Roasted fennel, carrots or parsnips.

WINE Partner the stuffed guinea hen with either the 1999 Castello di Ama Chianti Classico or the 1997 Silverado Vineyards Sangiovese.

Guinea Hen with Fall Fruits

4 SERVINGS

This recipe results in a gorgeous, burnished-brown hen. The secret is roasting the bird with some fruit in the pan, which sweetens the juices; basting the bird with those juices deeply caramelizes the skin.

2½ tablespoons unsalted butter,
    softened
One 3½-pound guinea hen
Salt and freshly ground pepper
4 plums, halved and pitted
2 cups seedless grapes
Sage sprigs, for garnish (optional)

1. Preheat the oven to 400°. Rub the butter all over the hen and inside the cavity. Season the skin and cavity with salt and pepper. Add 2 plum halves and 1 cup of the grapes to the cavity. Tie the legs together.

2. Set the hen in a medium roasting pan and roast for 15 minutes. Baste the bird, then roast for another 30 minutes. Scatter the remaining 6 plum halves and 1 cup of grapes around the hen and baste the bird with the pan juices. Continue to roast for about 20 minutes, basting 2 more times; the

hen is done when an instant-read thermometer inserted in an inner thigh registers 170°.

3. Transfer the hen to a platter, cover loosely with foil and let rest for 10 minutes. Discard the string. Spoon the fruit from the cavity around the bird. Add the fruit from the pan and any juices to the platter, garnish with sage sprigs and serve.   —*Jean Calviac*

SERVE WITH Chicken Liver Pâté with Toast (p. 18).

WINE A spicy red with hints of plum and some tannin will highlight the deep flavors in this dish. Two good choices from the Gascony region: the 1998 Château Lagrezette Cahors or the more powerful 1996 Château Bouscasse Madiran.

Spice-Rubbed Turkey with Sage Gravy

12 SERVINGS

This turkey is flavored with sage butter and a seasoned salt mixture, then refrigerated overnight before roasting to ensure a crisp skin.

10 tablespoons unsalted butter,
     6 at room temperature and
     4 melted
¼   cup plus 2 tablespoons
     minced sage
Kosher salt and freshly ground pepper
1½ teaspoons coriander seeds
One 15-pound turkey—cavity fat
     removed, neck and wing tips
     reserved for Rich Turkey Stock
     (recipe follows) and gizzard
     reserved for gravy
2   large shallots, halved
½   orange, quartered
¾   cup plus 1 tablespoon
     all-purpose flour
2   quarts Rich Turkey Stock
     (recipe follows)

1. In a bowl, mash the 6 tablespoons of softened butter with ¼ cup of sage and season with salt and pepper. In a small skillet, toast the coriander seeds over moderate heat until fragrant,

Spice-Rubbed Turkey with Sage Gravy, with Sweet-and-Sour Beets (p. 298) and Brown Butter Kale (p. 287)

about 1 minute. Transfer to a spice grinder and let cool, then grind to a powder. In a small bowl, mix the ground coriander with 1½ tablespoons of salt and ½ tablespoon of pepper.

2. Starting from the cavity end of the turkey, carefully use your fingers to separate the skin from the breast meat. Gently rub the sage butter under the skin, evenly coating the breast. Sprinkle the turkey inside and out with the seasoned salt. Refrigerate the turkey, uncovered, overnight. Bring the turkey to room temperature before roasting (allow 3 hours).

3. Preheat the oven to 350°. Put the shallots and orange in the turkey cavity and tie the legs together. Set the turkey and gizzard on a rack in a roasting pan. Brush the melted butter on the turkey and roast it for about 2½ hours, basting every 30 minutes. Halfway through roasting, rotate the turkey for even cooking. Cover the breast loosely with foil during the last hour of roasting. The bird is done when an instant-read thermometer inserted in an inner thigh registers 165°.

4. Transfer the turkey to a carving board and let rest for at least 30 minutes. Cut the gizzard into ¼-inch dice. Pour the pan juices into a measuring cup. Spoon off ½ cup plus 3 tablespoons of the fat, add it to the roasting pan and set the pan over 2 burners on moderate heat. Stir the flour into the fat until blended, then gradually whisk in the Rich Turkey Stock, scraping up the browned bits on the bottom of the pan. Simmer over low heat until no floury taste remains, about 20 minutes. Add the reserved pan juices, the gizzard and the remaining 2 tablespoons of sage and season with salt and pepper. Carve the turkey, arrange on a platter and serve with the gravy and the Wild Mushroom Stuffing.

—*Tom Douglas*

SERVE WITH Wild Mushroom Stuffing (p. 268).

WINE A low-tannin Pinot Noir won't overwhelm the mild turkey. Try the 1998 Panther Creek Reserve from Oregon or the 1999 Acacia Winery Carneros from California.

RICH TURKEY STOCK
MAKES ABOUT 3 QUARTS ●●

7 pounds turkey parts, such as wings, thighs and drumsticks

14 cups water

Reserved turkey neck and wing tips (optional)

1 large onion, thickly sliced

1 large carrot, thickly sliced

1 large celery rib, thickly sliced

2 garlic cloves, sliced

1 teaspoon kosher salt

Freshly ground pepper

I. Preheat the oven to 400°. In a large roasting pan, roast the turkey parts for about 1 hour, turning occasionally, until well browned; transfer the roasted turkey parts to a large pot.

2. Set the roasting pan over 2 burners. Add 3 cups of water and boil, scraping up the browned bits from the bottom of the pan. Add the liquid to the pot.

3. Add the neck and wing tips to the pot along with the onion, carrot, celery, garlic, salt, several pinches of pepper and the remaining 11 cups of water. Bring to a boil. Reduce the heat to moderately low, cover partially and simmer the stock for about 2½ hours. Strain the stock and skim the fat before using. —*T.D.*

MAKE AHEAD The stock can be refrigerated for 3 days or frozen for 1 month.

Maple-Glazed Turkey with Bourbon-Pecan Gravy

15 SERVINGS

The turkey needs to marinate overnight, so plan accordingly.

One 18- to 20-pound turkey—neck
    and giblets reserved for
    another use
1½ cups Kentucky bourbon
½ cup fresh orange juice
⅓ cup pure maple syrup
1 tablespoon chopped thyme
Kosher salt and freshly ground pepper
1 stick (4 ounces) unsalted
    butter, softened
Water
¾ cup all-purpose flour
4 cups Rich Turkey Stock (p. 203)
½ pound pecans (about 2 cups),
    lightly toasted and chopped

I. Using your fingers, carefully loosen the skin over the turkey breast and thighs; try not to tear the skin. Set a large oven roasting bag in a very large bowl. Put the turkey in the bag, cavity end up.

2. In a bowl, mix the bourbon with the orange juice, maple syrup, chopped thyme and 1½ teaspoons each of salt and pepper. Slowly pour the bourbon mixture under the turkey skin and press to distribute it evenly over the breast and thighs. Wrap the turkey tightly in the bag and seal with a twist tie. Refrigerate the turkey overnight. Bring the turkey to room temperature before roasting.

3. Preheat the oven to 325°. Remove the marinated turkey from the bag and set it in a large roasting pan. Pour the marinade into a large measuring cup. Rub 6 tablespoons of the softened butter under the breast skin and rub the remaining 2 tablespoons over the skin. Tie the turkey legs together with twine.

4. Pour ½ cup of the reserved marinade into the roasting pan and roast the turkey for 30 minutes. Baste the turkey with the pan juices and add 1 cup of water to the pan. Roast the turkey for 1 hour longer, basting it with the pan juices every half hour. Add the remaining marinade to the pan. Cover the turkey loosely with aluminum foil and roast for about 2 hours longer, or until an instant-read thermometer inserted in the thickest part of the thigh registers 165°.

5. Carefully transfer the turkey to a carving board, allowing the juices in the cavity to run into the pan. Cover the turkey loosely with foil and let it rest for 30 minutes.

6. Pour the pan juices into a bowl and skim the fat; reserve 6 tablespoons of the fat. In a large saucepan, mix the fat with the flour to form a paste. In a medium saucepan, warm the Rich Turkey Stock and slowly whisk it into the flour paste. Bring to a boil over moderate heat, whisking constantly. Whisk in the reserved pan juices and simmer over low heat, whisking frequently, until thickened and flavorful, about 25 minutes. Season with salt and pepper and stir in the pecans; transfer to a large gravy boat. Carve the turkey, arrange on a platter and serve with the pecan gravy.

—*Marcia Kiesel*

Braised Turkey with Honey-Mustard Cranberry Sauce

4 SERVINGS ●●

3 tablespoons canola oil
4 turkey drumsticks (10 to
    12 ounces each), skinned
Salt and freshly ground pepper
2 leeks, white and light green parts
    only, coarsely chopped
3 carrots, 1 coarsely chopped and
    2 sliced ½ inch thick
2 celery ribs, coarsely chopped
2 cups dry white wine
3 cups chicken stock or canned
    low-sodium broth
1½ cups cranberries (6 ounces)
3 thyme sprigs
2 medium turnips (¾ pound),
    peeled and cut into eighths
Honey-Mustard Cranberry Sauce, for
    serving (recipe follows)

I. Preheat the oven to 325°. Heat the oil in a large enameled cast-iron casserole. Season the turkey drumsticks with salt and pepper and brown them on all sides over moderately high heat, about 10 minutes. Transfer to a plate.

2. Add the leeks, chopped carrot and celery to the casserole and cook over moderate heat until softened, about 4 minutes. Add the white wine and boil until reduced by half, about 5 minutes. Add the chicken stock, cranberries and thyme and bring to a simmer. Add the turkey drumsticks and their juices. Cover and braise in the oven for 30 minutes. Turn the turkey drumsticks and add the turnips and sliced carrots. Cover and braise for about 1 hour longer, or until the turkey and vegetables are very tender.

3. Using a slotted spoon, transfer the turkey, sliced carrots and turnips to a large plate. Strain the sauce through a coarse sieve set over a large bowl, pressing on the solids to extract as much liquid as possible. Return the sauce to the casserole and boil until reduced to 2½ cups, about 15 minutes.

4. Remove the turkey meat from the

bones. Return the turkey and vegetables to the casserole, cover and cook over low heat until warmed through. Season with salt and pepper and serve with Honey-Mustard Cranberry Sauce.

—*Suki Hertz*

ONE SERVING Calories 428 kcal, Total Fat 13.8 gm, Saturated Fat 1.8 gm

MAKE AHEAD The braised turkey can be refrigerated for 2 days.

SERVE WITH Boiled potatoes, egg noodles or wild rice.

WINE Point up the fruity flavors in this hearty stew with a lively Beaujolais that has notes of cherries and cranberries. Pick a medium-weight example, such as the 2000 Georges Duboeuf Flower Label Regnié or the 2000 Louis Jadot Beaujolais-Villages.

HONEY-MUSTARD CRANBERRY SAUCE

MAKES ABOUT 1 CUP ●●●

- 2 cups cranberries (½ pound)
- ½ cup water
- ½ cup orange-blossom honey
- 1 tablespoon grainy mustard

In a large saucepan, combine the cranberries, water and honey and bring to a boil over high heat. Reduce the heat to moderate and simmer for 10 minutes, stirring occasionally. Remove from the heat and stir in the mustard. Serve the sauce warm or cool. —*S.H.*

ONE TABLESPOON Calories 37 kcal, Total Fat 0.1 gm, Saturated Fat 0 gm

MAKE AHEAD The sauce can be refrigerated for 5 days.

Quail with Asian Spices

4 SERVINGS

The quail absorb all the flavors of this intense Chinese-style marinade. You could also use chicken or other birds.

- 1 cup soy sauce
- 1 cup water
- 4 shallots, minced
- ¼ cup rice vinegar
- 2 tablespoons five-spice powder
- 2 tablespoons light brown sugar
- 1 tablespoon minced fresh ginger
- 1 tablespoon minced garlic
- 1 tablespoon coarsely cracked black peppercorns

Six 3-ounce partially boned quail
- ¼ cup vegetable oil

1. In a medium saucepan, combine the soy sauce with the water, shallots, rice vinegar, five-spice powder, brown sugar, ginger, garlic and peppercorns. Simmer over moderately high heat for 3 minutes, stirring occasionally. Cool to room temperature, then strain the sauce into a large bowl. Add the quail and turn to coat. Cover with plastic wrap and refrigerate for at least 3 hours or overnight. Bring to room temperature before proceeding.

2. Remove the quail from the marinade and pat dry. Heat the oil in a large skillet. Add the quail and cook over high heat until the skin is browned and the meat is rare, about 3 minutes per side. Cut the quail in half lengthwise and serve hot.

—*Jean-Georges Vongerichten*

SERVE WITH Watercress Salad (p. 60).

WINE A Pinot Noir works well with Asian spices because it generally has low tannin and plenty of fruit. Try fruity Oregon bottlings, such as the 1998 Bethel Heights Wädenswil or the 1998 Argyle Reserve.

Spiced Duck Breasts with Port and Olives

4 SERVINGS

- 8 juniper berries
- 4 whole cloves
- 2 teaspoons whole black peppercorns
- 2 teaspoons coriander seeds
- 1 star anise pod
- ¼ teaspoon cinnamon
- ⅛ teaspoon ground cardamom
- 2 small bay leaves
- 1 tablespoon kosher salt
- 1½ teaspoons finely grated orange zest

berries & health

In the battle against heart disease, researchers are investigating the potential of cranberries. Like other brightly colored fruits and vegetables, these berries are packed with antioxidants and may have some of the same heart-healthy benefits as red wine. Such studies augment new research into the use of cranberries as a remedy for urinary tract infections. Scientists now believe that the condensed tannins in cranberries, rather than the acids, deserve the credit for fending off bacteria, and they're looking at whether these tannins can also fight the bacteria behind gum disease and stomach ulcers. Cranberries are well-known as a vitamin C source: An 8-ounce glass of cranberry juice cocktail has a full day's requirement.

- 4 boneless Pekin duck breast halves (about 6 ounces each)
- 1 tablespoon extra-virgin olive oil
- 1 large bunch of thyme, plus 3 thyme sprigs
- ½ cup ruby port
- ¼ cup dry red wine
- 1 tablespoon vegetable oil
- 2 large shallots, minced
- 1 cup chicken stock or low-sodium broth
- ½ cup Calamata olives, pitted and chopped
- 2 tablespoons finely chopped parsley
- 1 tablespoon finely chopped mint

1. In a spice mill or mortar, combine the juniper berries, cloves, peppercorns, coriander, star anise, cinnamon, cardamom and 1 bay leaf and grind to a powder. Stir in the salt and orange zest.

2. Using a sharp knife, score the duck skin in a diamond pattern, making the cuts ½ inch apart. Using your fingers,

rub the duck breasts with the olive oil and then with the spice mixture. Set 2 of the breasts skin side down on a plate and top each with half of the bunch of thyme. Cover each breast with another duck breast, skin side up. Wrap each pair of duck breasts in plastic and let stand for at least 1 hour or refrigerate overnight. Bring the duck to room temperature before cooking if chilled.

3. In a small saucepan, bring the port and red wine to a boil and continue cooking until reduced by half, about 5 minutes.

4. Heat the vegetable oil in a large skillet. Remove the plastic from the duck breasts and discard the thyme. Add the breasts, skin side down, to the skillet and cook over moderately low heat until the duck skin is deeply browned, about 8 minutes. Pour off all but 1 tablespoon of the fat from the skillet. Turn the breasts and cook for 2 more minutes for medium rare. Transfer the duck to a warmed platter and cover loosely with foil.

5. Add the shallots to the skillet and cook, stirring, until softened, about 3 minutes. Add the chicken stock or broth, reduced port and red wine and the remaining bay leaf and 3 thyme sprigs. Add any accumulated duck juices and boil over moderate heat, scraping up the browned bits from the bottom. Simmer until reduced to ⅔ cup, about 10 minutes. Strain the sauce into a small saucepan. Stir in the olives, parsley and mint and bring to a simmer. Slice the duck breasts crosswise and serve with the sauce.

—*Joshua Eisen*

MAKE AHEAD The spice rub can be stored for 1 week in an airtight jar. Add the orange zest before using.

WINE With this duck a red is in order. Perhaps the 1998 Paul Jaboulet-Aîné Domaine Raymond Roure Crozes-Hermitage or, from Australia, the 1999 Clarendon Hills Moritz Shiraz.

Smoked Duck Breasts with Raspberry-Port Sauce

4 SERVINGS ●

You can use fresh duck breasts in place of the smoked breasts called for below; cook them a little longer.

- 2 tablespoons unsalted butter
- 1 shallot, minced
- ¼ cup ruby port
- ¼ cup dry white wine
- 2 tablespoons seedless raspberry preserves
- 1 tablespoon raspberry vinegar
- 1 tablespoon Dijon mustard
- ½ cup raspberries

Salt and freshly ground pepper

Two ¾-pound smoked duck breasts

- 1 teaspoon vegetable oil

1. Melt 1 tablespoon of the butter in a medium saucepan. Add the shallot and cook over moderate heat, stirring frequently, until softened, about 2 minutes. Add the port and white wine and cook over moderate heat until the sauce is reduced to 2 tablespoons, about 7 minutes. Add the raspberry preserves, vinegar and mustard and whisk over low heat until smooth. Add the raspberries and cook, whisking gently to break up the berries. Whisk in the remaining 1 tablespoon of butter and season with salt and pepper; keep the sauce warm.

2. Using a thin, sharp knife, make a crisscross pattern in the duck skin. Heat the oil in a large skillet. Add the duck breasts, skin side down, and cook over moderate heat until the skin is browned and crisp, 4 to 5 minutes; pour off the rendered fat as it accumulates in the pan. Turn the duck breasts and cook until the bottom is browned, about 2 minutes. Turn the duck again and cook over moderately low heat until most of the fat has been rendered, about 5 minutes longer; don't let the skin burn.

3. Transfer the duck breasts to a cutting board and let them rest for 5 minutes. Thinly slice the duck on the diagonal and arrange on plates. Spoon the raspberry-port sauce all around the duck and serve.

—*Ruth Van Waerebeek*

WINE The intensely fruity, berry-sweet sauce served with the duck breasts suggests a rich Merlot-based red with echoes of bright raspberry. Look for the 1998 Swanson Merlot Napa Valley or the bargain 1998 Château de Rougerie from Bordeaux.

Thyme-Braised Duck Legs with Chanterelles and Potatoes

4 SERVINGS ●

- ½ cup dried porcini mushrooms (about ½ ounce)
- 2 cups boiling water
- 24 pearl onions (about ½ pound)
- 1 tablespoon pure olive oil
- 4 large duck legs (about 1 pound each), skin and excess fat trimmed

Salt and freshly ground pepper

- 2 ounces pancetta, finely diced
- 3 large shallots, finely chopped
- 1 large garlic clove, finely chopped
- ½ pound chanterelles, stems trimmed, mushrooms halved if large
- 12 small red potatoes (about ¾ pound), scrubbed
- 8 large thyme sprigs
- 1½ cups chicken stock or canned low-sodium broth
- 1 cup full-bodied red wine, such as Pinot Noir

1. Preheat the oven to 325°. In a small bowl, soak the dried porcini in 1 cup of the boiling water until the porcini are softened, about 20 minutes. Using your fingers, rub any grit off the mushrooms in the soaking liquid. Drain the mushrooms, reserving the soaking liquid; squeeze any excess liquid from the mushrooms and coarsely chop them. Slowly pour the porcini mushroom soaking liquid into a cup, stopping before you reach the grit at the bottom.

2. In a medium bowl, soak the pearl onions in the remaining 1 cup of boiling water for 1 minute. Drain the pearl onions, then trim and peel them.

3. In a large enameled cast-iron skillet or medium casserole, heat the olive oil until shimmering. Season the duck legs with salt and pepper. Add the duck legs to the skillet and cook over moderate heat until deeply browned, about 5 minutes per side. Transfer the duck legs to a plate. Add the pearl onions to the skillet and cook over low heat, stirring once or twice, until the onions are richly browned all over, about 10 minutes. Transfer the onions to a plate.

4. Pour off all but 1 tablespoon of fat from the skillet and add the pancetta. Cook over low heat, stirring, until the pancetta is lightly browned, about 4 minutes. Add the shallots, garlic and chanterelles to the skillet and cook, stirring occasionally, until the chanterelles soften, about 5 minutes. Add the potatoes, thyme, chicken stock, wine and the reserved porcinis and porcini liquid and bring to a simmer. Submerge the duck legs in the sauce, cover and bake for 1 hour. Stir in the pearl onions, then cover and bake for 30 minutes longer, or until the duck is very tender.

5. Using a large spoon, skim the fat from the sauce and discard the thyme sprigs. Season the sauce with salt and pepper. Serve the braised duck hot.

—*Glenn Monk*

MAKE AHEAD The duck stew can be refrigerated for 2 days. Reheat gently before serving.

SERVE WITH Warm crusty bread and a tossed green salad.

WINE The rich and earthy notes of braised duck, pancetta, chanterelles and porcini mushrooms are echoed by a Pinot Noir. In British Columbia 1998 was a great year for this grape, and Quails' Gate Estate's 1998 Limited Release Pinot Noir is one of the best.

Thyme-Braised Duck Legs with Chanterelles and Potatoes

8 pork
veal

Pork Chops with Mustard-Caper Sauce

4 SERVINGS ●

1 tablespoon extra-virgin olive oil
Four 9-ounce pork loin chops
(1¼ inches thick)
Salt and freshly ground pepper
1½ cups chicken stock or canned
low-sodium broth
⅓ cup drained capers
½ teaspoon finely
chopped rosemary
2 tablespoons Dijon mustard
2 tablespoons unsalted butter

1. In a large skillet, heat the olive oil until shimmering. Season the pork with salt and pepper, add them to the skillet and cook over moderately high heat until they are well browned, about 5 minutes per side. Transfer the pork chops to a large plate and cover loosely with foil.

2. Add the stock, capers and chopped rosemary to the skillet and boil until reduced to ¾ cup, about 5 minutes. Return the pork chops to the pan and simmer until cooked through, about 3 minutes. Transfer the pork chops to 4 plates. Whisk the mustard and butter into the sauce and season with salt and pepper. Pour the mustard-caper sauce over the chops and serve.

—Joanne Weir

Pork Chops with Green Peppercorn Sauce

4 SERVINGS ●

The complexly flavored white wine sauce that accompanies the pork chops includes pungent green peppercorns. They contrast nicely with the sweetness of the currants.

1 tablespoon unsalted butter
1 tablespoon extra-virgin
olive oil
Four 10-ounce pork loin chops,
cut ¾ inch thick
Salt and freshly ground pepper
1 large shallot, minced
½ cup dry white wine
½ cup heavy cream
2 tablespoons
dried currants
1 teaspoon brined green
peppercorns, drained
and crushed
1 tablespoon finely chopped
flat-leaf parsley

1. In a large, deep skillet, melt the butter in the olive oil. Season the pork chops with salt and pepper and add them to the skillet. Cook the chops over moderately high heat, turning once, until browned, about 6 minutes total cooking time. Transfer the pork chops to a large plate.

2. Add the shallot to the skillet and cook over moderate heat, stirring frequently, until softened, about 3 minutes. Add the white wine; scrape up the browned bits from the bottom of the pan and cook until the pan juices are reduced to 2 tablespoons, about 5 minutes. Add the heavy cream, currants and green peppercorns and bring the sauce to a simmer.

3. Return the pork chops to the skillet along with any accumulated juices. Cover the skillet tightly and simmer the pork chops over moderately low heat until cooked through, about 5 minutes. Transfer the chops to a platter. Stir the parsley into the sauce and season with salt and pepper. Pour over the chops and serve at once.

—Ruth Van Waerebeek

WINE A highly acidic light red will stand up to the briny peppercorns in the sauce, without overwhelming the mild pork chops. Two good options to try with this dish—both Italian Barberas: the 1997 Vicara Barbera del Monferrato and the 1999 Bruno Giacosa Barbera d'Alba.

Pork Chops, Corn and Mascarpone Macaroni and Cheese

4 SERVINGS ●
PORK CHOPS

10 cups water
½ cup kosher salt
⅓ cup sugar
10 thyme sprigs
3 rosemary sprigs
1 head of garlic, halved crosswise
1 tablespoon black peppercorns
1 teaspoon crushed red pepper
2 oranges, halved crosswise
Four 12-ounce center-cut pork chops,
about 1½-inches thick
MACARONI AND CHEESE
2 tablespoons unsalted butter
3 tablespoons all-purpose flour
2¼ cups milk
½ cup freshly grated extra-sharp
white Cheddar
¼ cup mascarpone

Bourbon-Mustard Brine

MAKES ABOUT 2½ CUPS ● ● ●
The bourbon in this brine infuses meat with a woody, smoky flavor. The mustard adds sharpness and tang. The paprika softens these strong flavors.

1 cup bourbon
½ cup Dijon mustard
½ cup wildflower honey
1 tablespoon plus
1 teaspoon paprika
¼ cup kosher salt

In a medium bowl, mix the bourbon with the Dijon mustard, the wildflower honey, paprika and kosher salt. Stir until the salt is dissolved; refrigerate until ready to use.

—Gray Kunz

MAKE AHEAD The bourbon-mustard brine can be refrigerated in a covered jar for up to 1 week.

SERVING SUGGESTION This recipe makes enough brine for four 10-ounce pork rib or loin chops cut about 1¼ inches thick. Marinate the chops for 5 hours, then pat dry and sauté until cooked through. The brine also works for chicken or game.

¼ cup freshly grated Parmesan

Salt and freshly ground pepper

Freshly grated nutmeg

½ pound penne

CORN

2 tablespoons unsalted butter

8 ears of white corn,
   kernels removed

½ cup chicken stock

Salt and freshly ground pepper

White-truffle oil

1. BRINE THE PORK CHOPS: In a large saucepan, combine the water with the salt, sugar, thyme, rosemary, garlic, peppercorns and crushed red pepper. Squeeze the juice from the orange halves into the brine and add the oranges. Bring to a simmer over moderately high heat, stirring to dissolve the salt and sugar. Transfer to a large bowl and let cool completely. Add the pork chops and refrigerate, covered, for 12 hours.

2. MAKE THE MACARONI AND CHEESE: Melt the butter in a medium saucepan. Stir in the flour until a paste forms. Gradually whisk in the milk until smooth; bring to a boil over moderately high heat, whisking constantly. Reduce the heat to low and simmer for 10 minutes, whisking often. Remove from the heat. Stir in the Cheddar, mascarpone and 2 tablespoons of the Parmesan. Season with salt, pepper and nutmeg and transfer to a large bowl.

3. Meanwhile, in a large saucepan of boiling salted water, cook the penne until al dente; drain. Stir the penne into the cheese sauce. Spoon the penne into four 1-cup gratin dishes and sprinkle with the remaining 2 tablespoons of Parmesan.

4. MAKE THE CORN: Melt the butter in a large skillet. Add the corn and cook over moderately high heat, stirring, for 2 minutes. Add the stock and simmer until the corn is just tender, about 2 minutes longer. Season with salt and pepper.

Pork Chops, Corn and Mascarpone Macaroni and Cheese

5. Shortly before serving, preheat the oven to 400°. Bake the macaroni and cheese for about 12 minutes, or until bubbling. Turn on the broiler and broil the macaroni and cheese for about 1 minute, or until lightly browned. Keep warm. Meanwhile, light a grill or heat a grill pan. Remove the chops from the brine and pat dry. Brush the grill with oil. Grill the chops over a medium-hot fire for 6 minutes per side, or until browned and just cooked through. Reheat the corn. Set the chops on plates, spoon the corn alongside and drizzle with truffle oil. Place a dish of macaroni and cheese on each plate and serve. —*Kelly Courtney*

Honey-Thyme Pork Chops with Mashed Sweet Potatoes

6 SERVINGS

3 pounds sweet potatoes

Six ¾-pound pork rib chops,
   cut 1 inch thick

Olive oil, for brushing

Salt and freshly ground pepper

½ cup honey

¼ cup thyme leaves

¾ cup heavy cream, warmed

4 tablespoons melted butter

1. Preheat the oven to 375°. Put the potatoes in a baking pan and bake them for 45 minutes, or until tender.

2. Light a grill or preheat a grill pan. Brush the chops with olive oil and season with salt and pepper. Grill over high heat until lightly charred, about 3 minutes per side. Transfer to a rimmed baking sheet. Brush the chops with the honey and sprinkle with the thyme.

3. When the sweet potatoes are done, raise the oven to 450°. Roast the pork chops for 10 minutes, basting once with the pan juices, until glazed and only slightly pink in the center.

4. Peel the potatoes and pass them through a food mill set over a large bowl. Whisk in the cream and melted butter; season with salt and pepper.

5. Transfer the chops to a platter and top with the pan juices. Serve at once, with the mashed sweet potatoes.

—*Don Pintabona*

WINE The sweet elements here call for an aromatic Viognier or a spicy Gewürztraminer.

MENU

HORS D'OEUVRES
spice-seared shrimp (p. 21)
smashed zucchini with garlic, chiles and mint (p. 319)
moroccan chickpea flat breads (p. 266)

FIRST COURSE
farfalle with savoy cabbage, pancetta and mozzarella (p. 124)

1999 CHATEAU STE. MICHELLE & DR. LOOSEN COLUMBIA VALLEY EROICA RIESLING

MAIN COURSE
pork chops with roasted parsnips, pears and potatoes
spinach with porcini and rosemary (p. 286)

1998 PEGASUS BAY WAIPARA PINOT NOIR

DESSERTS
chocolate pots (p. 385)
orange and polenta biscuits (p. 348)

Pork Chops with Roasted Parsnips, Pears and Potatoes

8 SERVINGS

These succulent pork chops marinate in a fragrant mixture of rosemary, olive oil, garlic and lemon zest for at least one hour before being roasted, so plan accordingly.

¾ **cup plus 2 tablespoons extra-virgin olive oil**
12 **garlic cloves, lightly smashed**
4 **large rosemary sprigs, cut into 2-inch lengths**
Zest of 3 lemons, removed with a vegetable peeler
Freshly ground pepper
Eight 8- to 10-ounce pork rib chops, ¾ to 1 inch thick
6 **parsnips, quartered lengthwise**
6 **firm but ripe Bartlett pears, quartered lengthwise and cored**
3 **pounds Yukon Gold potatoes, cut into ⅓-inch-thick slices**
Kosher salt
Minted Bread Vinaigrette (recipe follows)

1. In a large roasting pan, mix ¾ cup of the olive oil with the smashed garlic, rosemary sprigs, lemon zest and ½ teaspoon of freshly ground pepper. Arrange the pork chops in the pan in a single layer and turn to coat. Marinate the chops for 1 hour at room temperature or for up to 12 hours in the refrigerator; return to room temperature before roasting.

2. Preheat the oven to 425° and position the racks in the top and bottom of the oven. Remove the pork chops from the marinade; scrape off the rosemary, lemon and garlic and let the marinade drip back into the roasting pan. Transfer the chops to a platter.

3. Add the quartered parsnips, quartered pears and sliced potatoes to the roasting pan, season with salt and toss to coat with the marinade. Spread the pears and vegetables on 2 large, rimmed baking sheets. Roast for about 40 minutes, stirring occasionally, until the vegetables are tender; shift the baking sheets from top to bottom and turn them front to back halfway through roasting.

4. Meanwhile, heat 1 tablespoon of the olive oil in each of 2 large skillets. Season the pork chops with salt, add them to the skillets and cook over high heat until golden brown on both sides, about 5 minutes total. Set 4 pork chops on the vegetables on each baking sheet and roast for about 5 minutes for slightly pink meat. Transfer the pork chops and vegetables to a large platter or to individual plates and serve with the Minted Bread Vinaigrette.

—*Jamie Oliver*

WINE The rich roasted vegetables and sweet pears that accompany the pork chops point to a light red wine from New Zealand. Consider a Pinot Noir, such as the 1998 Pegasus Bay Waipara or the 1998 Solstone Estate Marlborough.

MINTED BREAD VINAIGRETTE

MAKES ABOUT 1 CUP ●

Bread sauce is usually served with roast turkey and pork, but you'll find this is also good with lamb, chicken and fish.

Leaves from one 2½-ounce bunch of mint
Two 1-ounce slices of white sandwich bread, crusts trimmed, bread cut into ¼-inch dice
¾ **cup extra-virgin olive oil**
2 **teaspoons Dijon mustard**
2 **teaspoons red wine vinegar**
Salt and freshly ground pepper

1. In a mini food processor, pulse the mint leaves until coarsely chopped. Add the diced bread and pulse until finely chopped.

2. Transfer the mint and bread mixture to a bowl and stir in the extra-virgin olive oil, Dijon mustard and red wine vinegar. Season the vinaigrette to taste with salt and pepper. —*J.O.*

Pork Chops with Roasted Parsnips, Pears and Potatoes, with Minted Bread Vinaigrette (in bowl) and Spinach with Porcini and Rosemary (p. 286)

Soppressata-Wrapped Pork

6 SERVINGS ●

Pork tenderloin is usually too lean to grill. But marinating it, wrapping it in thinly sliced soppressata and then skewering it with rosemary branches allows the meat to get basted with the soppressata's delectable fat and flavored from within by the rosemary. Long, thick rosemary branches for skewering are available at most large supermarkets. The pork needs to marinate overnight, so start a day ahead.

- ¼ cup plus 2 tablespoons
  dry white wine
- ¼ cup plus 2 tablespoons
  extra-virgin olive oil
- 2¼ pounds pork tenderloin, cut
  into eighteen 3-inch lengths
- Salt and freshly ground pepper
- ½ pound very thinly
  sliced soppressata
- 6 large rosemary branches

- 2 large red onions, cut into
  2-inch wedges
- Vegetable oil, for the grill

I. In a large bowl, mix the wine with the olive oil. Add the pork and turn to coat. Cover and refrigerate overnight.

2. Drain the pork and discard the marinade. Lightly season the pork with salt and season generously with pepper. Overlap 2 slices of soppressata on a work surface; put a length of pork in the center and roll it up in the soppressata. Repeat with the remaining soppressata and pork.

3. Strip 2 inches of leaves from the thick end of the rosemary branches. Using a sharp paring knife, whittle the ends to points. Thread 2 onion wedges onto each branch followed by 1 pork bundle; repeat twice.

4. Light a grill. Lightly brush the grate with vegetable oil. Grill the skewers over a medium-low fire, turning until the pork and onions are cooked through and the soppressata is crisp, about 12 minutes. Serve at once.

—*Marcia Kiesel*

MAKE AHEAD The pork bundles can be assembled earlier in the day and refrigerated before grilling.

WINE The spicy soppressata suggests a soft, dry red with smoky overtones and some spice to match. Consider the 1999 Vigna Nirane Dolcetto d'Alba or the 1999 Giacomo Conterno Dolcetto d'Alba.

Pork Medallions with Onion Marmalade

8 SERVINGS

Cooking the onions in butter and sugar gives a beautiful sheen to this rich, tangy marmalade.

- 6 tablespoons unsalted butter
- 2 medium white onions,
  finely chopped
- ⅔ cup sugar
- ¾ cup plus ⅓ cup dry red wine
- ¾ cup raspberry vinegar
- Salt

- Eight 4-ounce pork loin medallions
- Freshly ground pepper
- 1 teaspoon minced rosemary
- 8 very thin slices of pancetta
  (2 ounces)
- 2 tablespoons pure olive oil
- 8 garlic cloves
- ¼ cup balsamic vinegar
- 1½ cups beef stock or canned
  low-sodium broth

I. Melt the butter in a large saucepan. Add the chopped onions and sugar, cover and cook over low heat, stirring occasionally, until the onions are caramelized, about 30 minutes. Add ¾ cup of the red wine and the raspberry vinegar and boil until the liquid is syrupy, about 8 minutes. Season the onions with salt.

2. Meanwhile, season the pork with salt and pepper and sprinkle with the rosemary. Top each medallion with a slice of pancetta and, using kitchen string, tie up like a package. Heat the olive oil with the garlic in a large skillet. Add the pork medallions, pancetta side down, and cook over moderately high heat until browned on the bottom, about 3 minutes. Reduce the heat to moderate, turn the medallions and cook until just cooked through and browned on the second side, about 3 minutes longer. Transfer the medallions to a warmed platter and cover loosely with foil. Discard the garlic.

3. Add the remaining ⅓ cup of red wine and the balsamic vinegar to the skillet and boil over moderate heat, scraping up the browned bits on the bottom, until reduced by half, about 2 minutes. Add the stock and simmer until reduced to ⅔ cup, about 5 minutes. Stir in any juices from the pork and season with salt and pepper.

4. Remove the string, set the pork medallions on plates and spoon the onion marmalade alongside. Pour the sauce over the medallions and serve.

—*Massimo Bottura*

MAKE AHEAD The onion marmalade

can be refrigerated for 3 days. Bring to room temperature before serving.

WINE Look for a bright, fruity-spicy Italian red that won't overwhelm the mild pork, such as a medium-bodied Dolcetto d'Alba with soft tannins. Two good ones are the 1999 Bruno Giacosa Dolcetto d'Alba Falletto and the 1998 Fratelli Pecchenino Dolcetto di Dogliani Sirì d'Jermu.

Pork Tenderloin with Bell Peppers and Chipotles

4 SERVINGS ●

1½ tablespoons extra-virgin olive oil
1¾ pounds pork tenderloins, trimmed
Salt and freshly ground pepper
 1 large onion, halved lengthwise and thinly sliced crosswise
 1 cup water
 2 chipotle chiles in adobo, seeded and coarsely chopped, ½ teaspoon adobo reserved
 1 red bell pepper, thinly sliced
 1 yellow bell pepper, thinly sliced
 1 green bell pepper, thinly sliced

ı. Heat the extra-virgin olive oil in a large skillet. Season the tenderloins with salt and pepper and brown them in the skillet over moderately high heat, about 4 minutes per side. Transfer to a plate. Add the onion to the skillet and season with salt and pepper. Cover and cook over low heat until softened, about 10 minutes.

2. Return the tenderloins to the skillet and add the water and the chipotles and adobo. Cover and simmer over low heat for 5 minutes. Turn the tenderloins over and scatter all of the bell peppers on top. Cover and simmer until the meat is slightly pink inside, about 5 minutes longer. Transfer the meat to a carving board and cover loosely with foil.

3. Stir the pepper mixture and boil over high heat until the juices thicken slightly, about 5 minutes. Season with salt and pepper. Pour the peppers into

a shallow serving dish. Slice the pork tenderloins ½ inch thick, arrange them on the peppers and serve.

—Patricia Wells

ONE SERVING Calories 355 kcal, Total Fat 14 gm, Saturated Fat 3.4 gm, Protein 40 gm, Carbohydrates 14 gm
SERVE WITH Steamed brown rice.
WINE This powerful dish demands a powerful wine. Look for a fine bottle from Languedoc-Roussillon, such as a Corbières from Château les Palais, a rustic wine with a certain elegance.

Pork with Spicy Cucumber Salad

4 SERVINGS ●

One 14-ounce can unsweetened coconut milk
 1 tablespoon plus 1 teaspoon fish sauce
 1 teaspoon ground coriander
 1 teaspoon curry powder
 ⅓ cup plus 1 tablespoon light brown sugar
Two ¾-pound pork tenderloins
 ⅓ cup white vinegar
Salt
 2 Thai, or bird, chiles or serrano chiles, seeded and minced
 1 tablespoon vegetable oil
 1 shallot, minced
 ⅔ cup creamy peanut butter
1½ teaspoons Thai red curry paste
 2 tablespoons boiling water, if needed
1½ tablespoons fresh lime juice
 3 small cucumbers—peeled, halved lengthwise, seeded and thinly sliced
 ¼ cup finely chopped cilantro
 2 tablespoons finely chopped basil
 ⅓ cup chopped salted peanuts

ı. In a large bowl, mix ½ cup of the coconut milk with 1 tablespoon of the fish sauce, the coriander, curry powder and 1 tablespoon of brown sugar. Add the pork and let stand, turning occasionally, for 10 minutes.

2. In a small saucepan, combine the vinegar with the remaining ⅓ cup of

Pork Medallions with Onion Marmalade

brown sugar and ½ teaspoon salt. Simmer over moderate heat, stirring, just until the sugar dissolves. Add the chiles. Pour the dressing into a medium bowl and let cool.

3. Light a grill or preheat a cast-iron grill pan. Grill the pork over moderate heat until browned all over and firm to the touch, about 15 minutes for medium. Transfer to a cutting board, cover loosely with foil and let stand for 10 minutes.

4. Meanwhile, heat the oil in a medium skillet. Add the shallot and cook over moderate heat until softened, about 2 minutes. Add the peanut butter, red curry paste and the remaining 1¼ cups of coconut milk and 1 teaspoon of fish sauce. Simmer over low heat until slightly thickened, about 2 minutes. If the sauce breaks, whisk in the boiling water. Add the lime juice and season with salt.

5. Add the sliced cucumbers to the dressing and toss, then add the cilantro and basil. Mound the cucumber salad in the center of a large platter. Thinly slice the pork and arrange around the cucumber salad. Sprinkle with the salted peanuts and serve the peanut sauce on the side.

—Melissa Clark

Lemon-Glazed Roast
Pork with Sage, with
Duet of Cauliflower (p. 297)

Pork Tenderloin Stuffed with Apples and Dried Fruit

4 SERVINGS ●

½ cup coarsely chopped mixed
   dried fruit, such as golden raisins,
   cranberries, apricots and prunes
¼ cup full-bodied dry red wine
1 teaspoon unsalted butter
1 Granny Smith apple—peeled,
   cored and thinly sliced
¼ cup finely chopped onion
3 tablespoons water
Salt and freshly ground pepper
One 1-pound pork tenderloin
1 teaspoon vegetable oil
½ cup chicken stock or canned
   low-sodium broth

1. In a small bowl, mix the dried fruit with the wine. Melt the butter in a large ovenproof skillet. Add the apple and cook over moderate heat for 3 minutes. Add the onion and cook, stirring, until softened, about 7 minutes. Add the water as the pan dries out.

2. Drain the dried fruit, reserving the wine. Stir the dried fruit into the apple and onion in the skillet and season with salt and pepper. Transfer to a plate to cool. Coarsely chop ½ cup of the fruit mixture and reserve it for making the sauce. Wipe out the skillet.

3. Preheat the oven to 425°. Insert a sharpening steel or the handle of a wooden spoon into the thick end of the tenderloin. Carefully push the steel through the tenderloin and roll the meat to widen the hole slightly. Stuff the tenderloin with the fruit mixture and seal the ends with toothpicks.

4. Heat the oil in the skillet. Season the meat with salt and pepper and brown it in the skillet over high heat, turning, for about 6 minutes. Transfer the skillet to the oven and roast the meat for 10 minutes. Transfer the meat to a cutting board and let rest for 5 minutes.

5. Add the reserved wine to the skillet and cook over high heat, scraping up any browned bits, until syrupy, about 2 minutes. Add the stock and cook until reduced by half, about 5 minutes. Stir in the reserved ½ cup of the fruit mixture and season with salt and pepper. Slice the tenderloin crosswise ½ inch thick and serve with the sauce.
—*Grace Parisi*

ONE SERVING Calories 244 kcal, Total Fat 7.4 gm, Saturated Fat 2.5 gm, Protein 25 gm, Carbohydrates 19 gm

Lemon-Glazed Roast Pork with Sage

4 SERVINGS

Bespectacled and mustachioed Prosper Montagné was one of the most influential chefs of the 20th century. His suckling pig recipe was the inspiration for this pork roast.

One 2-pound pork loin, boned and
   bones reserved
8 sage leaves, plus 2 large sprigs
2 tablespoons pure olive oil, plus
   more for rubbing
Fine sea salt or kosher salt
4 lemons, zest removed in long,
   wide strips, plus 1 cup fresh
   lemon juice
3 tablespoons sugar
Freshly ground pepper
4 cups chicken stock or canned
   low-sodium broth

1. Using a paring knife, make 8 incisions all over the pork roast. Roll up the sage leaves and press each one into an incision. Rub the roast all over with olive oil and lightly sprinkle with salt. Let marinate at room temperature for up to 2 hours.

2. In a small saucepan, simmer the lemon zest, juice and sugar over low heat, stirring, until reduced to ¼ cup, about 20 minutes; strain the syrup.

3. Heat 1 tablespoon of the olive oil in a medium saucepan. Add the pork bones, season with salt and pepper and brown over low heat for 10 minutes; discard the fat. Add 2 cups of the stock and simmer until reduced by half, about 30 minutes. Add the remaining 2 cups of stock and simmer until reduced to 1 cup, about 30 minutes. Add the sage sprigs and simmer until reduced to ½ cup, about 20 more minutes; strain.

4. Preheat the oven to 300°. Heat the remaining 1 tablespoon of oil in an ovenproof skillet. Add the pork, fat side down, and brown over moderate heat for about 10 minutes; discard the fat. Turn the pork fat side up and roast for 30 minutes; baste twice with the lemon syrup. Roast for about 15 minutes, basting with the pan juices, until an instant-read thermometer inserted in the center registers 145°. Let the roast rest for 10 minutes.

5. Reheat the sauce; season with salt and pepper. Carve the roast and serve with the pan sauce.   —*Laurent Gras*

MAKE AHEAD The recipe can be made through Step 3 and refrigerated for 1 day.

SERVE WITH Duet of Cauliflower (p. 297).

Star Anise Pork

6 SERVINGS

½ cup chicken stock or canned
   low-sodium broth
¼ cup dry sherry
¼ cup soy sauce
2 tablespoons light brown sugar
2 whole star anise pods, crushed
2 garlic cloves, minced
¼ teaspoon Chinese
   five-spice powder
One 3-pound boneless pork shoulder,
   tied, or 6 pork loin chops, cut
   1¼ inches thick (¾ pound each)
Salt and freshly ground pepper
1 tablespoon extra-virgin
   olive oil
2 tablespoons coarsely chopped
   cilantro (optional)

1. In a small bowl, mix the stock with the sherry, soy, brown sugar, star anise, garlic and five-spice powder.

2. TO MAKE STAR ANISE PORK SHOULDER: Season the pork with

salt and pepper. Heat the extra-virgin olive oil in a large enameled cast-iron casserole. Add the pork and cook over moderate heat, turning occasionally, until browned all over, about 15 minutes. Add the sauce mixture and bring to a boil, scraping up any browned bits from the bottom of the casserole. Cover the casserole tightly and cook the pork over low heat for about 3 hours, turning the roast every 30 minutes, until very tender. Remove the

pork and boil the sauce until it is reduced to 1 cup, about 5 minutes. Discard the strings. Pull the pork into long shreds and return to the casserole. Garnish with the cilantro and serve.

TO MAKE STAR ANISE PORK CHOPS: Pour the sauce mixture into a large resealable plastic bag. Add the chops and marinate in the refrigerator for at least 2 hours or for up to 8 hours. Drain the chops, pat dry and

season with salt and pepper. Heat the oil in a large skillet. Add the pork chops and cook over moderately high heat, turning occasionally, until browned and cooked through, about 12 minutes. Serve the pork chops.

—*Rori Trovato*

SERVE WITH Pasta or rice.

WINE Salty, pungent Chinese-style pork will taste even better when paired with a Gewürztraminer's sweet fruit and rich texture.

Star Anise Pork

Pork Roast with a Walnut-Parmesan Crust

6 TO 8 SERVINGS

Toasted nuts, Parmesan and mixed herbs make a savory stuffing and crisp topping for roast pork. Baked butternut squash wedges would make a sweet accompaniment.

- ¾ **cup walnut halves (about 3 ounces)**
- 2 **tablespoons unsalted butter**
- 1 **medium onion, minced**
- ¼ **cup toasted fine bread crumbs**
- 2 **tablespoons finely chopped flat-leaf parsley**
- 2 **teaspoons finely chopped sage**
- ¼ **cup freshly grated Parmesan**

Salt and freshly ground pepper

One 3-pound boneless pork shoulder roast, butterflied

- 1 **tablespoon extra-virgin olive oil**

Water

- ¼ **cup dry red wine**
- ½ **cup chicken stock or canned low-sodium broth**
- 1 **teaspoon all-purpose flour**

1. Preheat the oven to 325°. Spread the walnuts in a pie plate and toast for about 10 minutes, or until golden. Let cool, then coarsely grind the nuts. Leave the oven on.

2. Melt the butter in a medium skillet. Add the onion and cook over moderately high heat until softened and lightly browned, about 5 minutes. Add the ground walnuts, bread crumbs, parsley and sage and let cool. Stir in the Parmesan and season with salt and pepper.

3. Spread the pork roast open and season with salt and pepper. Spread half of the walnut mixture on the pork, then roll up the roast and tie it at 1-inch intervals with cotton string.

4. In a sturdy roasting pan, heat the extra-virgin olive oil until shimmering. Season the pork roast with salt and pepper and cook over moderately high heat until browned all over, 10 to 12 minutes. Add ½ cup of water to the

Pork Roast with a
Walnut-Parmesan Crust

pan. Roast the pork for about 2 hours, basting occasionally and adding ¼ cup of water to the pan each time you baste. The meat is done when an instant-read thermometer inserted in the center of the roast registers 160°. Transfer the pork to a baking sheet and let stand for 10 minutes. Pour any pan juices into a measuring cup and skim off the fat.

5. Preheat the broiler. Discard the strings from the pork roast. Press the remaining ground walnut mixture onto the pork roast and broil 10 inches from the heat for about 5 minutes, or until the nut crust is golden and crisp. Let the pork stand while you make the sauce.

6. Set the roasting pan over high heat. Add the red wine and boil until reduced by half, scraping up any browned bits from the bottom of the pan. Add the chicken stock and any reserved pan juices and boil until reduced by one-third. Whisk the flour into 2 tablespoons of water, then

whisk the slurry into the sauce in the roasting pan and bring to a boil. Cook until the sauce is slightly thickened and no floury taste remains. Strain the sauce into a gravy boat and season with salt and pepper.

7. Carve the pork into thick slices and serve with the sauce.

—*FOOD & WINE Test Kitchen*

MAKE AHEAD The Pork Roast with a Walnut-Parmesan Crust can be prepared through Step 3 and refrigerated overnight.

WINE The 1997 Robert Craig Cabernet Sauvignon and the 1992 Howell Mountain Vineyards Cabernet Sauvignon have enough fruit to pair with the juicy pork.

Pork and Winter Squash Stew

4 SERVINGS ● ●

1½ pounds pork tenderloin, trimmed and cut into 1-inch pieces
Salt and freshly ground pepper
2 tablespoons extra-virgin olive oil
1¾ cups low-sodium nonfat chicken broth
2 large onions, coarsely chopped
4 garlic cloves, minced
1 tablespoon ground cumin
¼ teaspoon crushed red pepper
2 bay leaves
⅔ cup dry white wine
One 28-ounce can crushed tomatoes
1 medium butternut squash, peeled and cut into 1-inch chunks (3 cups)
½ cup coarsely chopped cilantro
Couscous, for serving

1. Preheat the oven to 350°. Season the pork with salt and pepper. In a large enameled cast-iron casserole, heat ½ tablespoon of the olive oil until shimmering. Add half of the pork and cook over moderately high heat, stirring occasionally, until browned on all sides, about 5 minutes. Transfer the pork to a plate. Repeat with another ½ tablespoon of olive oil and the remaining pork.

2. Meanwhile, in a small saucepan, boil the chicken broth until reduced to 1 cup, about 10 minutes.

3. Add the remaining 1 tablespoon of oil to the casserole. Add the onions and cook, stirring, until softened, about 5 minutes. Stir in the garlic, cumin, crushed red pepper and bay leaves and cook over moderate heat for 1 minute. Add the white wine and boil until reduced by half. Stir in the crushed tomatoes, reduced chicken broth and the pork. Bring to a simmer, cover, then transfer to the oven and bake for 1 hour.

4. Return the casserole to the top of the stove and add the butternut squash to the stew; cook over moderate heat until the squash is tender, about 20 minutes.

5. Discard the bay leaves from the stew. Stir in half of the cilantro and sprinkle the rest on top. Spoon the Pork and Winter Squash Stew on plates and serve with couscous.

—*Ann Chantal Altman*

ONE SERVING Calories 434 kcal, Total Fat 14.8 gm, Saturated Fat 3.4 gm, Protein 43 gm, Carbohydrates 33 gm

Cider-Basted Baby Back Ribs with Lemon Barbecue Sauce

4 SERVINGS

No American barbecue is complete without ribs. Perfection means ribs that are tender, sweet and spicy—just the sort of ribs you get when you coat baby backs with a homemade rub, baste them with apple cider, grill them with plenty of hickory smoke and serve them with a sweet and tangy barbecue sauce. The ribs need to marinate for at least four hours, so plan accordingly.

1 tablespoon plus 2 teaspoons light brown sugar
1 tablespoon plus 1 teaspoon sweet paprika
1 tablespoon kosher salt
2 teaspoons minced garlic
1 teaspoon freshly ground pepper
2 racks baby back pork ribs (about 4 pounds)
2 cups hickory chips
2 cups apple cider
Vegetable oil, for the grill
Lemon Barbecue Sauce (recipe follows)

1. In a small bowl, combine the brown sugar with the paprika, salt, garlic and pepper. Rub the seasonings all over the ribs, cover and refrigerate for at least 4 hours or for up to 8 hours.

2. Soak the hickory chips in 1 cup of the cider for 30 minutes, then drain. Light a grill and set it up for indirect grilling. If using charcoal, when the fire is medium hot, rake the coals into two piles on opposite sides of the grill. Place a foil drip pan in the center of the grill. If using a gas grill, light the front and rear or outside burners.

3. Scatter the wood chips over the charcoal. If using a gas grill, place the chips in the smoker box or on a 12-inch square of foil; fold the foil into a 6-inch square and poke 12 holes in the top. Place the package near the flames and heat until smoking. Cover the grill and adjust the vents until the temperature registers 325°.

4. Pour the remaining 1 cup of apple cider into a spray bottle. Spray both sides of the ribs with the cider. Lightly brush the grate with oil. Set the ribs, bone side down, on the grill directly over the drip pan or between the 2 burners of a gas grill. Cover and cook for 35 minutes, spraying the ribs with cider twice. Turn the ribs and add more hot coals to the fire if needed, letting the coals burn uncovered for about 10 minutes. Cover and grill the ribs until very tender, spraying with cider two more times, about 40 minutes longer. Lightly brush both sides of the ribs with the Lemon Barbecue Sauce and move them directly over the fire. Grill until deeply browned, about 2 minutes per side. ▸

**Cider-Basted Baby Back Ribs
with Lemon Barbecue Sauce**

5. Serve the ribs with the remaining barbecue sauce. —*Steven Raichlen*
BEER Chilled beer is the best accompaniment for a tangy-sweet barbecue sauce and a refreshing contrast to these richly flavored ribs. Go for a lager-style bottling, such as Dos Equis from Mexico or Lone Star from Texas.

LEMON BARBECUE SAUCE
MAKES ABOUT 1½ CUPS ● ●

- 1 cup ketchup
- ¼ cup light brown sugar
- 1 teaspoon finely grated lemon zest
- 3 tablespoons fresh lemon juice
- 1 tablespoon molasses
- ½ tablespoon Worcestershire sauce
- 1 teaspoon dry mustard
- ¼ teaspoon freshly ground pepper

Combine all of the ingredients in a small saucepan and bring to a boil. Simmer the barbecue sauce over moderate heat until thickened, about 4 minutes. Let cool, then refrigerate.

—*S.R.*

MAKE AHEAD The sauce can be refrigerated for 1 week.

Sausage-and-Herb-Stuffed Tomatoes
4 SERVINGS ●

Serve these tomatoes as a first course or side dish, or double the recipe and turn them into a main course with rice.

- 4 medium tomatoes
- Salt
- ½ cup milk
- One 2-inch piece of crustless baguette, torn into ½-inch pieces
- 3 tablespoons extra-virgin olive oil
- 1 medium onion, finely chopped
- 1 garlic clove, finely chopped
- ½ pound sweet Italian sausage, casings removed
- 1 cup shredded romaine lettuce
- ¼ cup chopped parsley
- 2 tablespoons chopped basil
- 2 large eggs, lightly beaten
- ¼ teaspoon freshly ground pepper

1. Preheat the oven to 400°. Cut the top third off each tomato and reserve. Scoop out the seeds and flesh from the tomatoes, leaving thin but sturdy walls. Sprinkle the tomato shells with ½ teaspoon of salt and turn them upside down on a rack to drain for 30 minutes.

2. Meanwhile, warm the milk in a small saucepan. Remove from the heat and add the bread. In a medium skillet, heat 2 tablespoons of the extra-virgin olive oil. Add the chopped onion and cook over moderate heat until softened, about 5 minutes. Add the chopped garlic and cook until fragrant, about 1 minute. Add the sausage and cook, breaking up the pieces with a wooden spoon, until browned and no longer pink inside, about 8 minutes. Add the shredded Romaine lettuce and cook until wilted, about 1 minute. Remove the mixture from the heat and let cool.

3. Remove the bread from the milk and squeeze dry. Add the bread, chopped parsley, basil and eggs to the sausage mixture and stir to combine. Season with 1 teaspoon of salt and the pepper.

4. Set the drained tomato shells in a gratin dish and fill with the stuffing, mounding it slightly. Set the tomato lids on top. Drizzle the remaining 1 tablespoon of olive oil over the tomatoes and bake for about 20 minutes, or until the tomatoes begin to collapse and wrinkle. Serve hot or at room temperature. —*Jean Calviac*

MAKE AHEAD The stuffed tomatoes, cooked or uncooked, can be refrigerated overnight.

WINE A medium-bodied, inexpensive red with good fruit and herb and spice flavors will complement the herby sausage filling. Choose the 1998 Moulin Lagrezette, a Merlot-Malbec blend from Cahors, or a Merlot, such as the 1998 Chiroulet Côtes de Gascogne Rouge.

Franks and Beans Cassoulet
6 SERVINGS ●

- 2 tablespoons pure olive oil
- 4 garlic cloves, minced
- 2 celery ribs, finely chopped
- 1 medium onion, minced
- 1 pound navy or Great Northern beans, picked over and rinsed
- 8 cups chicken stock or canned low-sodium broth
- 4 medium tomatoes, seeded and coarsely chopped
- ½ cup ketchup
- ¼ cup light brown sugar
- 3 tablespoons white vinegar
- 2 tablespoons Dijon mustard
- 2 tablespoons chopped basil
- 1½ tablespoons minced rosemary
- 2 teaspoons ground cumin
- 1 teaspoon sweet paprika
- Salt and freshly ground pepper
- 1 tablespoon unsalted butter, plus more for spreading
- ½ pound each knockwurst and weisswurst, halved lengthwise
- ½ pound Italian sausage, cooked and halved lengthwise
- Six ½-inch-thick slices of Italian bread, crusts removed
- 1½ ounces sharp Cheddar, grated

1. Heat the olive oil in a large saucepan. Add the garlic, celery and onion and cook over low heat, stirring, until softened, about 8 minutes. Add the beans and stock and bring to a boil. Reduce the heat to low, cover partially and simmer until the beans are almost tender, 45 minutes to 1 hour. Stir in the tomatoes, ketchup, brown sugar, vinegar, mustard, basil, rosemary, cumin and paprika. Simmer over moderately low heat until the beans are very tender and the sauce is thick, about 30 minutes longer. Season with salt and pepper.

2. Preheat the oven to 350°. Melt the tablespoon of butter in a large, deep ovenproof skillet. Add the sausages and brown over moderately high heat, about 1 minute per side. Transfer to a

menu SEE PHOTO ON OVERLEAF

hors d'oeuvres **creamy chicken liver mousse (p. 18)** | **sweet-and-sour red-onion relish (p. 19)**

NONVINTAGE DEUTZ BRUT

first course **mesclun salad with onion-ginger dressing (p. 56)**

main course **barbecued fresh ham** | **ancho-fig compote (p. 225)**

sweet potato gratin with prunes (p. 307) | **creamed collard greens with parmesan crumbs (p. 288)**

nana's skillet corn bread (p. 267) | **angel biscuits (p. 267)**

1999 HOGUE CELLARS CHENIN BLANC | 1997 WYNN'S SHIRAZ

dessert **carrot cake with lemon mascarpone frosting (p. 328)**

1995 BERINGER LATE-HARVEST NIGHTINGALE

plate and pour off any excess oil from the skillet. Add the beans to the pan, then nestle the sausages in the beans. Butter the bread on both sides and season with salt and pepper. Set the bread on the beans and sprinkle the Cheddar over the bread. Bake in the center of the oven for about 20 minutes, or until the cheese is browned and the bread is crisp. Serve at once.

—*Todd English*

WINE The bright berry fruit and strong acidity of a lively, medium-bodied Zinfandel will highlight the spiciness of the sausages and contrast with the earthiness of the beans. Two good choices: the 1999 Joel Gott and the 1998 Francis Coppola Diamond Series.

Barbecued Fresh Ham
12 SERVINGS, PLUS LEFTOVERS

The tangy sauce for this recipe is inspired by both the tomato- and vinegar-based barbecue sauces from the western and eastern parts of Tennessee. The ham is marinated in the barbecue sauce overnight, so plan accordingly.

One 28-ounce can whole
  tomatoes, coarsely chopped,
  with their liquid
2 cups white vinegar
2 cups water
2½ tablespoons honey
2½ tablespoons
  unsulphured molasses
1½ tablespoons tomato paste
8 garlic cloves
4 dried chipotle chiles,
  stems discarded
2 tablespoons kosher salt
1½ tablespoons coriander seeds
1 tablespoon cumin seeds
½ tablespoon whole
  black peppercorns
1 bay leaf
One 10-pound fresh ham, bone-in
Salt and freshly ground pepper
1 cup chicken stock or canned
  low-sodium broth
Ancho-Fig Compote, for serving
  (recipe follows)

1. In a large saucepan, combine the tomatoes and their liquid with the vinegar, water, honey, molasses, tomato paste, garlic, chipotles, kosher salt, coriander, cumin, peppercorns and bay leaf and simmer over low heat for 2¾ hours, stirring occasionally. Let cool. Remove the bay leaf.

2. Working in batches, puree the sauce in a blender. Refrigerate ½ cup of the sauce. Put the ham in a deep bowl or pot and pour the rest of the sauce over it. Turn the ham to coat it, then cover with plastic wrap and refrigerate overnight. Bring the ham to room temperature before proceeding.

3. Preheat the oven to 400°. Transfer the ham to a roasting pan; reserve the marinade. Add ½ cup of water to the roasting pan. Season the ham with salt and pepper, brush it with some of the reserved marinade and roast for 30 minutes. Reduce the oven temperature to 300°. Cover the ham loosely with foil and roast for about 4 hours longer, basting it with marinade every 15 minutes and adding a few tablespoons of water to the pan when it seems dry. The ham is done when an instant-read thermometer inserted into the thickest part registers 145°. Discard the remaining marinade.

4. Transfer the ham to a carving board and let stand for 20 minutes. Pour the juices from the roasting pan into a bowl and skim off the fat. Return the juices to the roasting pan and set it over moderately high heat. Add the chicken stock and bring to a simmer, scraping up any browned bits from the bottom of the pan with a wooden spoon. Stir in the reserved ½ cup of sauce and bring to a boil. Pour the barbecue sauce into a warmed gravy boat.

5. Carve the ham and serve with the barbecue jus and the Ancho-Fig Compote.

—*Scott Howell*

MAKE AHEAD The pureed barbecue sauce can be refrigerated for 1 week.

WINE The salty, pungent ham suggests a red or white that has good fruit and no strong oak flavors. Try a soft, off-dry Chenin Blanc from Washington State, such as the 1999 Hogue Cellars, or a bright, fruity-spicy Australian Shiraz, such as the 1997 Wynn's. ▶

FROM FAR END OF TABLE: Creamed Collard Greens with Parmesan Crumbs (p. 288); Barbecued Fresh Ham (p. 223); Ancho-Fig Compote (p. 225); Sweet Potato Gratin with Prunes (p. 307); Nana's Skillet Corn Bread (p. 267)

ANCHO-FIG COMPOTE

MAKES ABOUT 3 CUPS ●

This sweet-hot compote is marvelous with the pungent ham. Also try it with Creamy Chicken Liver Mousse (p. 18).

- 1 small ancho chile
- 2 tablespoons extra-virgin olive oil
- 1 medium onion, thinly sliced
- 1 pound moist dried figs, cut into ¾-inch pieces
- 1½ cups water
- ½ cup cider vinegar
- 1 tablespoon fresh thyme leaves

1. Soak the ancho in hot water until softened, about 10 minutes. Drain and pat dry; discard the stem and seeds. Slice the chile into thin strips.

2. Heat the oil in a medium saucepan. Add the ancho and onion, cover and cook over moderately low heat until the onion softens, about 4 minutes. Add the figs and cook for 5 minutes, then add the water, vinegar and thyme and simmer for 30 minutes, or until the figs are tender and the compote has thickened. —*S.H.*

ONE SERVING Calories 126 kcal, Total Fat 2.8 gm, Saturated Fat 0.4 gm, Protein 1 gm, Carbohydrates 27 gm

MAKE AHEAD The Ancho-Fig Compote can be made ahead and refrigerated for up to 5 days.

Spiced Smoked Ham with Mango-Cranberry Chutney

10 TO 12 SERVINGS ●

Choose a smoked ham with a substantial layer of exterior fat. Use only half of the spice rub if the fat layer is less than ⅛ inch thick.

One 10- to 12-pound smoked ham, bone-in

- 2 cups sparkling apple cider
- ½ cup dry sherry

Water

- 2 tablespoons coriander seeds
- 1½ tablespoons cumin seeds
- 1 tablespoon fennel seeds
- 2 teaspoons cardamom pods, seeds only

Spiced Smoked Ham with Mango-Cranberry Chutney

- 1 tablespoon light brown sugar
- 1 teaspoon salt
- ¼ teaspoon cayenne pepper

Mango-Cranberry Chutney (recipe follows)

1. Preheat the oven to 350°. Remove the rind from the ham and trim the fat to a ½-inch layer. Using a sharp knife, score the fat in a crosshatch pattern without cutting into the meat.

2. Set the ham in a large roasting pan, fat side up; add the cider and sherry and cover loosely with foil. Bake for 4 hours, basting with the pan juices every half hour; add water if the pan looks dry. The ham is done when it is golden and an instant-read thermometer inserted in the thickest part registers 150°. Transfer to a sturdy, rimmed baking sheet.

3. In a medium skillet, toast the coriander, cumin, fennel and cardamom seeds over moderate heat until they are fragrant, about 2 minutes. Transfer to a spice grinder and let cool completely, then coarsely grind. Mix in the sugar, salt and cayenne. Sprinkle the spice mixture over the ham, lightly pressing it into the crosshatched fat. Bake the ham for about 20 minutes, until the crust is golden. Transfer the ham to a cutting board and let stand for 15 minutes.

4. Set the roasting pan over high heat until sizzling. Add 1 cup of water and simmer, scraping up the browned bits, until reduced to ¼ cup. Pour the pan juices into a bowl and skim off the fat. Carve the ham into thin slices and arrange on a platter. Serve with the pan juices and the Mango-Cranberry Chutney. —*Grace Parisi*

MAKE AHEAD The ham can be baked 3 hours ahead. Serve at room temperature with rewarmed pan juices. ▶

MANGO-CRANBERRY CHUTNEY
MAKES ABOUT 4½ CUPS ● ●

- 1 tablespoon peanut oil
- 1 small Vidalia or other sweet onion, chopped
- Pinch of salt
- 1 teaspoon curry powder
- 1 cinnamon stick, broken in half
- 1 cup granulated sugar
- 1 cup packed light brown sugar
- ½ cup cider vinegar
- 2 large underripe mangoes, peeled and cut into ¾-inch dice
- 1 pound cranberries
- 1 teaspoon mustard seeds

1. Heat 1 teaspoon of the peanut oil in a large saucepan. Add the chopped onion and salt and cook over moderately low heat, stirring, until the onion softens, about 8 minutes. Add the curry and cinnamon stick and cook for 1 minute. Stir in the sugars and cider vinegar and bring to a boil. Add the diced mangoes and cook, stirring occasionally, until softened, 35 to 40 minutes. Add the cranberries and cook over moderate heat for 40 minutes, crushing them against the sides of the pan.

2. Heat the remaining 2 teaspoons of peanut oil in a small skillet. Add the mustard seeds and cook until they begin to pop, then stir into the chutney. Transfer to a bowl and let cool.

—*G.P.*

MAKE AHEAD The Mango-Cranberry Chutney can be refrigerated for up to 2 weeks.

Ham in Cider Sauce
4 SERVINGS ●

- 2 tablespoons unsalted butter
- Four ½-pound slices of smoked ham, cut ¼ inch thick
- 2 shallots, finely chopped
- ⅔ cup hard cider
- Freshly ground pepper
- Snipped chives

1. Melt 1 tablespoon of butter in a large skillet. Add 2 ham slices and cook over moderately high heat, turning once, until lightly browned, about 4 minutes. Transfer the cooked slices to a platter and repeat with the remaining butter and ham.

2. Add the shallots to the skillet and cook over moderate heat, stirring occasionally, until lightly browned. Add the cider and bring to a simmer over high heat, scraping up any browned bits. Return the ham slices to the skillet and cook until warmed through. Transfer the ham to a platter and season with pepper. Boil the sauce until reduced to ¼ cup, about 2 minutes longer. Pour the sauce over the ham, sprinkle with snipped chives and serve.

—*Jane Sigal*

Crisp Veal-and-Pork Patties
6 SERVINGS ●

- 2 large kaiser rolls (3 ounces each), cut into 1-inch pieces
- 2 cups milk
- ¾ pound ground pork
- ¾ pound ground veal
- 2 large eggs, lightly beaten
- 1 large onion, finely chopped
- 4 garlic cloves, minced
- 2 tablespoons finely chopped parsley
- 2 teaspoons marjoram or thyme
- 2 tablespoons Dijon mustard
- 2 teaspoons sweet Hungarian paprika
- Salt and freshly ground pepper
- 3 cups fresh bread crumbs
- 2 tablespoons unsalted butter
- 2 tablespoons vegetable oil

1. In a large bowl, soak the rolls in the milk until softened, about 10 minutes. Squeeze out the milk and return the rolls to the bowl. Add the pork and veal and mix well with your hands. Add the eggs, onion, garlic, parsley, marjoram, mustard and paprika and carefully mix until smooth. Season with salt and pepper.

2. Divide the mixture into 12 portions and form them into flat ovals. Spread the bread crumbs in a shallow bowl and thoroughly coat the patties on both sides.

3. In a large skillet, melt the butter in the oil over moderately high heat. Working in batches, fry the patties until golden brown and firm, about 5 minutes per side. Reduce the heat to moderate if the pan gets too hot. Serve warm. —*Wolfgang Puck*

MAKE AHEAD The pork patties can be formed early in the day and refrigerated.

WINE A simple red will blend well with the creamy, mild flavors of this dish. Opt for the easy-to-drink Austrian 1999 Zull Schrattenthal Blauer Portugieser Weinviertel or the bargain 1999 Calina Maule Valley Merlot from Chile.

Veal Milanese on Tossed Herb Salad
4 SERVINGS

- ½ pound mesclun
- 1 small bunch of arugula, stemmed and torn into bite-size pieces
- 1 small fennel bulb—quartered, cored and very thinly sliced
- ½ cup torn basil
- ¼ cup tarragon leaves
- ¼ cup spearmint leaves
- ¼ cup extra-virgin olive oil
- 1½ tablespoons fresh lemon juice
- Sea salt and freshly ground pepper
- ⅔ cup all-purpose flour
- 3 large eggs
- 3 cups fresh bread crumbs
- ½ cup freshly grated Parmesan
- 2 tablespoons thyme leaves
- 1½ pounds veal scaloppine, pounded ⅛ inch thick
- 4 tablespoons unsalted butter
- ½ cup pure olive oil
- Lemon wedges, for serving

1. In a large bowl, toss the mesclun with the arugula, fennel, basil, tarragon and spearmint, cover and refrigerate.

In a small bowl, whisk the extra-virgin olive oil with the lemon juice and season with salt and pepper.

2. In a soup plate, mix the flour with 1 teaspoon of salt and ½ teaspoon of pepper. In another soup plate, beat the eggs. In a medium bowl, mix the bread crumbs with the Parmesan and thyme.

3. Heat a large skillet. Dredge a piece of veal in the flour and shake off the excess. Dip the veal in the beaten eggs and then in the Parmesan crumbs, patting the crumbs on firmly. Repeat with 2 more pieces of veal. In the skillet, melt 1 tablespoon of the butter in 2 tablespoons of pure olive oil. Add the breaded veal and cook over moderately high heat until golden on the bottom, about 2 minutes. Turn and cook for 2 minutes more. Transfer to a baking sheet and keep warm. Repeat with the remaining veal, adding more butter and olive oil to the pan as necessary.

4. Add the dressing to the salad and toss to coat. Mound the salad on plates. Top with the scaloppine and serve with lemon wedges.

—*Joshua Eisen*

WINE Serve the veal with either the 1999 Pascal Jolivet Pouilly-Fumé or the 2001 Babich Marlborough Sauvignon Blanc.

Veal with Tomato and Basil

4 SERVINGS ● ●

Eight 2-ounce veal scaloppine, pounded ¼ inch thick

Salt and freshly ground pepper

Olive oil cooking spray

4 medium plum tomatoes—peeled, seeded and finely chopped

1¾ cups low-sodium nonfat chicken broth

2 tablespoons veal demiglace (see Note)

¼ cup balsamic vinegar

2 tablespoons crème fraîche

½ cup packed basil leaves, finely chopped

MENU

FIRST COURSE
creamy leek and potato soup
(p. 99)

1997 CHÂTEAU OLIVIER BLANC

FISH COURSE
garlicky shrimp with
lemon (p. 170)

2000 CHÂTEAU BONNET BLANC

MAIN COURSE
pan-seared veal medallions
with french morels

1998 CHÂTEAU TROPLONG-MONDOT

SALAD
lettuce and fresh herb salad
with pearl onions (p. 57)

DESSERTS
silky chocolate cake (p. 331)

1998 MAS AMIEL MAURY

crème caramel (p. 381)

1996 CHÂTEAU TIRECUL LA
GRAVIÈRE MONBAZILLAC

---

1. Season the veal with salt and pepper. Grease a large nonstick skillet with olive oil cooking spray, and heat. Add as many scaloppine as will fit in a single layer and cook over moderately high heat until lightly browned, about 30 seconds per side; transfer to a plate. Repeat with the remaining veal.

2. Add half the tomatoes to the skillet. Cook over moderately high heat for 2 minutes. Stir in the broth and demiglace and cook for 5 minutes. Add the vinegar; cook 5 minutes longer, stirring occasionally. Whisk in the crème fraîche and cook until reduced by one-third, about 7 minutes. Season with salt and pepper.

3. Add the veal and ¼ cup of the basil to the skillet and cook over low heat until the meat is warmed through and

---

basted with the sauce. Transfer the scaloppine to a platter or plates and pour the sauce on top. Sprinkle with the remaining tomatoes and basil and serve.   —*Ann Chantal Altman*

ONE SERVING Calories 178 kcal, Total Fat 5.2 gm, Saturated Fat 2.2 gm, Protein 26 gm, Carbohydrates 5 gm

NOTE Veal demiglace is available at specialty food shops.

Pan-Seared Veal Medallions with French Morels

6 SERVINGS

Tender French morels add an intense and smoky flavor to the veal sauce.

2 ounces small dried French morels (2 cups)

2 cups boiling water

Twelve 3-ounce veal medallions (½ inch thick), from the eye round

Salt and freshly ground pepper

2 tablespoons unsalted butter

1 tablespoon vegetable oil

3 shallots, minced

½ cup dry white wine

½ cup chicken stock or canned low-sodium broth

½ cup crème fraîche

1 tablespoon fresh lemon juice

Long snipped chives, for garnish

Steamed new potatoes, thickly sliced, for serving

1. Soak the morels in the boiling water until softened, about 30 minutes. Remove and rinse under running water, rubbing to loosen any grit. Let the soaking liquid stand.

2. Season the veal with salt and pepper. In a very large skillet, melt 1 tablespoon of the butter in the oil. Add the veal and cook over high heat until browned on the bottom, 2 to 3 minutes. Turn and cook until browned on the bottom and the meat is just pink inside, about 3 minutes. Transfer to a warmed platter and cover loosely with foil.

3. Melt the remaining 1 tablespoon of butter in the same skillet. Add the

---

**Pan-Seared Veal Medallions
with French Morels**

Veal Medallions with Fig
and Almond Cream Sauce

Veal Medallions with Fig and Almond Cream Sauce

4 SERVINGS ●

In this recipe, succulent veal gets the Mediterranean treatment with fresh figs and almonds.

1½ **pounds boneless**
    veal loin, sliced into
    8 medallions
Salt and freshly ground pepper
  4 **tablespoons unsalted butter**
  ¾ **cup dry Marsala**
  ⅓ **cup blanched**
    whole almonds
  ¾ **cup heavy cream**
  4 **ripe green figs, trimmed and**
    coarsely chopped (see Note)
  1 **teaspoon fresh lemon juice**
  2 **tablespoons finely**
    chopped mint, plus
    a few sprigs for garnish

1. Season the veal medallions generously with salt and pepper. Melt the butter in a large, heavy skillet. Add the veal medallions in a single layer and cook over moderate heat, about 6 minutes. Transfer the veal medallions to a plate, cover loosely with foil and keep warm.

2. Pour off all but 1 tablespoon of fat from the skillet. Add the Marsala and blanched almonds and boil over moderately high heat until the Marsala is syrupy, about 5 minutes. Reduce the heat to moderately low, add the heavy cream and chopped figs and cook for 4 minutes, stirring occasionally. Stir in the lemon juice, season with salt and pepper and cook the sauce for 2 minutes longer. Pour in any accumulated juices from the meat and stir in the chopped mint.

3. Arrange the veal medallions on a serving platter and spoon the fig sauce on top. Garnish the veal with mint sprigs and serve immediately.

—*Clifford A. Wright*

NOTE If you prefer your sauce without fig skins, scoop the flesh out of the fruit and discard the skins.

minced shallots and cook over low heat, stirring, until softened, about 5 minutes. Add the white wine and boil, scraping up any browned bits from the bottom, until almost evaporated, about 4 minutes. Add the morels and their soaking liquid, leaving any grit behind. Cover and simmer over low heat until the morels are softened, about 5 minutes. Add the chicken stock or broth and any accumulated veal juices and simmer over moderately high heat until reduced by half, about 5 minutes. Add the crème fraîche and simmer the sauce until thickened, about 4 minutes. Add the lemon juice and season with salt and pepper to taste.

4. Return the veal medallions to the skillet and simmer for 1 minute, turning once. Transfer the veal and sauce to a platter or plates. Garnish with long snipped chives and serve with steamed new potatoes.

—*Murielle Andraud*

WINE A full, plummy Merlot-based wine with a supple texture, rich fruit and hints of herbs and earth will stand up to this rich veal dish. Besides such hard-to-find 1999 *garagiste* wines (most of which will hit the shelves in 2002) as the Château de Valandraud, try a St-Émilion with a similar character, like the 1998 Château Troplong-Mondot, or the lighter and less expensive 1998 Château Plaisance.

Pan-Fried Veal Chops with Mushrooms and Cilantro

Pan-Fried Veal Chops with Mushrooms and Cilantro

4 SERVINGS ●

- 4 veal loin chops (about 2½ pounds)
- Salt and freshly ground pepper
- 1 teaspoon vegetable oil
- ½ cup dry Marsala wine
- ¼ cup extra-virgin olive oil
- 4 garlic cloves, finely chopped
- 1 pound cremini mushrooms, caps and stems sliced
- ½ cup finely chopped cilantro

1. Season the veal with salt and pepper. In a skillet, heat the oil until smoking. Add the chops and cook over high heat, turning once, until browned, about 8 minutes. Reduce the heat to moderate and cook, turning once, until just cooked through, about 20 minutes for medium rare. Transfer to a platter; keep warm. Pour the Marsala into the skillet and cook for 1 minute, scraping up any browned bits. Remove from the heat.
2. Meanwhile, in another skillet, heat the olive oil. Add the garlic and cook over moderate heat, stirring, until golden, about 2 minutes. Add the mushrooms, season with salt and pepper and cook, stirring, until almost all of the liquid has evaporated and the mushrooms are golden, about 15 minutes.
3. Add the Marsala from the first skillet and simmer until nearly evaporated, about 5 minutes. Stir in the cilantro and any accumulated meat juices from the platter; season with salt and pepper. Spoon the mushroom sauce over the chops and serve.
—*Clifford A. Wright*

Roasted Veal Chops with Mushrooms and Madeira

2 SERVINGS

- 1 cup rich beef stock or canned double-strength broth
- ½ cup water
- 4 baby turnips, peeled
- 4 baby carrots, peeled
- 4 pearl onions, peeled
- 2 garlic cloves, peeled
- 2 veal rib chops (¾ pound each), cut 1¼ inches thick
- Salt and freshly ground white pepper
- Pinch of ground cloves
- Pinch of freshly grated nutmeg
- 3 tablespoons unsalted butter, cut into tablespoons
- ½ pound oyster mushrooms, quartered
- ¼ pound shiitake mushrooms, caps quartered
- ½ cup Madeira
- 2 tablespoons coarsely chopped flat-leaf parsley

1. In a small saucepan, bring the stock and water to a boil. Add the turnips, carrots, pearl onions and garlic, reduce the heat to low and cover. Simmer until the vegetables are tender, transferring them to a plate as they are done, 8 to 10 minutes. Reserve the garlic cloves and the broth.
2. Preheat the oven to 400°. Season the veal chops with salt, white pepper and the cloves and nutmeg. Melt 1 tablespoon of the butter in a large skillet. Add the chops and pearl onions and cook over moderately high heat, turning once, until the chops and onions are nicely browned, about 8 minutes. Return the onions to the plate with the other vegetables and transfer the chops to a rimmed baking sheet. Roast in the oven until pink in the center, about 10 minutes.
3. Meanwhile, melt 1 tablespoon of the butter in the skillet. Add the mushrooms, season with salt and white pepper and cook over moderate heat, without stirring, until browned on the bottom, about 4 minutes. Stir in ¼ cup of the Madeira, cover and cook over low heat until tender, about 4 minutes. Add the remaining ¼ cup of Madeira and cook over moderately high heat for 2 minutes longer.
4. Transfer the veal chops to dinner plates and keep warm. Pour any veal roasting juices into the mushrooms. Add the vegetables and the reserved broth and garlic and simmer over low heat until warmed through, about 1 minute. Remove from the heat, and swirl in the remaining 1 tablespoon of butter and season with salt and white pepper. Pour the sauce and vegetables over the veal chops, sprinkle with the chopped parsley and serve.
—*Galen Zamarra*

Braised Veal Shank with Marjoram

6 SERVINGS ●

- 2½ to 3 pounds of boneless veal shank or shoulder, cut into 3-by-2-inch pieces
- Salt and freshly ground pepper
- 2 tablespoons vegetable oil
- 1 tablespoon unsalted butter
- 1 large onion, finely chopped
- 3 tablespoons all-purpose flour
- 2 cups dry white wine
- 3 cups chicken stock or canned low-sodium broth

Roasted Veal Chops with Mushrooms and Madeira

1 small celery rib, finely chopped
3 tablespoons marjoram
1 bay leaf
2 whole cloves
1 cup heavy cream
2 to 3 tablespoons fresh lemon juice

1. Season the veal with salt and pepper. Heat the oil in a large enameled cast-iron casserole. Working in batches, cook the veal over moderately high heat until browned on all sides, 5 to 7 minutes. Transfer to a plate and pour off the oil.

2. Melt the butter in the saucepan. Add the onion and cook over moderate heat, stirring often, until softened, about 5 minutes. Return the veal to the pan, sprinkle with the flour and stir for 2 minutes. Add the wine and bring to a boil, scraping up any browned bits from the bottom of the pan. Add the stock, celery, marjoram, bay leaf and cloves and season with salt and pepper. Reduce the heat to low, cover and simmer gently until the veal is very tender, about 1½ hours.

3. Using a slotted spoon, transfer the veal to a large, deep serving platter and cover loosely with foil. Simmer the veal cooking liquid until reduced to 4 cups, about 10 minutes. Add the cream and boil until reduced by one-third. Season the sauce with salt, pepper and lemon juice, strain it over the veal and serve. —*Wolfgang Puck*

MAKE AHEAD The Braised Veal Shank with Marjoram can be made up to 2 days ahead and reheated.

SERVE WITH Steamed carrots and broccoli.

WINE This simple dish suggests a smoky, fruity and round Pinot Gris from Alsace. Try the 1997 Domaine Schlumberger or the 1999 Trimbach Reserve.

Veal Croquettes with Marsala
4 SERVINGS ●

1 pound ground veal
1 small McIntosh apple—peeled, cored and cut into ¼-inch dice
⅓ cup walnuts, coarsely chopped
1 ounce Bel Paese or Taleggio cheese, cut into ¼-inch dice (about ¼ cup)
1 large egg, lightly beaten
2 tablespoons dry bread crumbs
4 sage leaves, chopped
Salt and freshly ground white pepper
All-purpose flour, for dredging
2 tablespoons unsalted butter
2 tablespoons extra-virgin olive oil
⅓ cup sweet Marsala wine

1. In a bowl, combine the veal, apple, walnuts, cheese, egg, bread crumbs and sage. Season with salt and white pepper and mix with your hands until combined. Shape into 12 croquettes about 2 inches long and 1 inch thick.

2. Spread some flour on a plate. Roll the croquettes in the flour, tapping off any excess. In a large skillet, melt the butter in the olive oil until shimmering. Add the croquettes and cook over moderate heat until browned, 2 to 3 minutes per side. Transfer the croquettes to paper towels to drain.

3. Add the Marsala to the skillet and cook over moderately high heat for 2 minutes, scraping up any browned bits from the bottom of the pan. Arrange the croquettes on 4 plates, spoon the sauce on top and serve at once.
—*Clifford A. Wright*

9 beef lamb game

Beef and Scallop Stir-Fry

4 SERVINGS ●●

- ¼ cup chicken stock
- 3 tablespoons soy sauce
- 2 tablespoons rice vinegar
- 2 teaspoons cornstarch
- 1 teaspoon sugar
- ½ teaspoon crushed red pepper
- 4 tablespoons vegetable oil
- 4 garlic cloves, minced
- 10 ounces beef tenderloin, cut into ¾-inch dice
- 10 ounces sea scallops, patted dry
- 1 large red bell pepper, cut into ½-inch dice
- 1 cup white corn kernels
- 6 scallions, cut into 1-inch lengths
- ¼ cup chopped basil

1. In a small bowl, combine the stock with the soy sauce, vinegar, cornstarch, sugar and crushed red pepper.

2. Set a nonstick wok over high heat until very hot. Add 2 tablespoons of vegetable oil and swirl to coat the wok. Add half the minced garlic and stir-fry for 30 seconds. Add the diced beef and scallops and stir-fry until the meat is no longer pink, 3 minutes. Transfer to a plate.

3. Add the remaining 2 tablespoons of vegetable oil to the wok and swirl to coat. Add the remaining half of the minced garlic and stir-fry for 30 seconds. Add the diced bell pepper, corn and scallions and stir-fry until crisp-tender, 2 to 3 minutes. Stir the sauce mixture and add to the wok. Stir-fry until the sauce thickens, about 2 minutes. Return the beef and scallops to the wok, stir to coat, then stir in the chopped basil. Transfer to a platter and serve. —*Susanna Foo*

SERVE WITH Steamed rice.

Beef Tenderloin with Shallot Marmalade

4 SERVINGS

- 1 tablespoon duck fat or unsalted butter
- 2 pounds beef short ribs, fat trimmed
- 5 garlic cloves, unpeeled
- 4 shallots, thickly sliced, plus 1 pound shallots, thinly sliced
- 2 quarts chicken stock or canned low-sodium broth or water

Salt

- 6 tablespoons unsalted butter
- 2 cups dry white wine

Freshly ground pepper

- 4 large shiitake mushroom caps, cut into ½-inch-wide strips

One 1½-pound trimmed beef tenderloin, tied

- 16 pitted Calamata olives
- 16 unsalted pistachios

1. In a large saucepan, melt the duck fat. Add the short ribs and cook over moderate heat until browned all over, about 10 minutes; discard the fat. Add the garlic and the 4 thickly sliced shallots and cook, stirring, until lightly browned, about 5 minutes. Add 1 quart of stock and simmer over low heat until reduced by half, about 1 hour. Add the remaining 1 quart of stock and simmer until reduced to 1½ cups, about 2 hours. Strain, skim the fat and season with salt.

2. In another large saucepan, melt 2 tablespoons of the butter. Add the 1 pound of thinly sliced shallots and cook over low heat, stirring occasionally, until softened, about 8 minutes. Season with salt, add the wine and cook until the shallots are meltingly tender and the liquid is absorbed, about 1 hour. Season the marmalade with pepper.

3. Preheat the oven to 350°. In a large ovenproof skillet, melt 1 tablespoon of the butter. Add the mushrooms, season with salt and pepper, cover and cook over low heat until nicely browned,

Beef Tenderloin with Shallot Marmalade

about 4 minutes. Transfer the mushrooms to a plate; wipe out the skillet.

4. Using a paring knife, make 4 dozen incisions all over the tenderloin about ½ inch apart. Push an olive, pistachio or mushroom strip into each incision, alternating the flavorings. Using cotton string, tie the tenderloin at 2-inch intervals.

5. Melt the remaining 3 tablespoons of butter in the skillet. Season the beef with salt and sear on 3 sides over moderately high heat until browned, about 9 minutes. Turn the roast uncooked side down, transfer the skillet to the oven and roast for 10 minutes. Baste the tenderloin with the pan juices and cook for about 6 minutes longer, or until an instant-read thermometer inserted in the center registers 120° for rare. Transfer the roast to a cutting board and season with pepper. Cover loosely with foil and let stand for 10 minutes. Discard the fat from the skillet.

6. Rewarm the shallot marmalade and beef jus. Add 1 cup of the jus to the skillet and bring to a boil, scraping up the browned bits. Pour the remaining jus into a gravy boat. Strain the pan juices into the gravy boat.

7. Slice the roast ½ inch thick. Mound a little shallot marmalade in the center of each plate and arrange 3 slices of the beef alongside the marmalade. Spoon a little beef jus onto the beef and pass the remaining jus separately.
—*Laurent Gras*

MAKE AHEAD The beef jus and shallot marmalade can be refrigerated for up to 1 day. Discard any fat from the jus before proceeding.

WINE The beef's intense flavors will find echoes in the fruit and olive character of Cabernet-based wines. Pick a medium-bodied, value-priced example with good fruit, such as the 1996 Château d'Armailhac or the 1997 Château Bernadotte, both from Bordeaux.

Grilled Strip Steaks with Pepper Relish

4 SERVINGS ●

- 3 tablespoons extra-virgin olive oil
- 1 large yellow bell pepper, finely chopped
- 1 medium shallot, minced
- 1 large garlic clove, minced

Salt and freshly ground pepper

- ½ cup jarred roasted red peppers, drained and chopped
- 1 jalapeño, seeded and minced
- 1 tablespoon sherry vinegar
- 2 teaspoons finely chopped oregano
- 3 tablespoons sliced almonds

Four 10-ounce strip steaks, ¾ inch thick

1. In a large skillet, heat 2 tablespoons of the olive oil until shimmering. Add the yellow pepper, shallot and garlic and season with salt and pepper. Cook over moderately low heat, stirring frequently, until just beginning to brown, about 7 minutes. Add the roasted peppers, jalapeño and vinegar. Cover and cook over low heat until the vegetables are very tender, about 10 minutes. Stir in the oregano.

2. Meanwhile, in a small skillet, toast the almonds over moderately high heat, stirring constantly, until golden, about 3 minutes. Transfer to a plate to cool.

3. Light a grill or heat a cast-iron grill pan over moderately high heat. Rub the steaks with the remaining 1 tablespoon of olive oil and season with salt and pepper. Grill the steaks for about 5 minutes per side for medium rare. Remove from the heat and let stand for 5 minutes, then transfer to plates. Spoon the pepper relish on top of the steaks, sprinkle with the toasted almonds and serve. —*Melissa Clark*

Grilled Texas T-Bone Steaks with Charred Onion Rings

4 SERVINGS

The true secret to grilling the perfect steak is choosing the right cut. You can't beat a T-bone, which is actually two steaks in one: a flavorful New York strip and a meltingly tender piece of filet mignon. A T-bone can also handle the assertively spicy rub used here.

- 2 cups mesquite or hickory chips
- 4 garlic cloves, coarsely chopped

Grilled Texas T-Bone Steaks with Charred Onion Rings

Kosher salt

Four 1-pound T-bone steaks, about
   1¼ inches thick

2 tablespoons ancho chile powder

1 teaspoon ground cumin

1 teaspoon dried oregano

1 teaspoon freshly ground pepper

2 tablespoons Tabasco sauce

2 tablespoons Worcestershire
   sauce

2 large sweet onions, such as
   Vidalia or Walla Walla, each cut
   crosswise into four 1-inch slices

2 tablespoons pure olive oil

Vegetable oil, for the grill

Lime wedges, for serving

1. Soak the mesquite chips in water for 30 minutes and drain. On a cutting board, sprinkle the garlic with a pinch of kosher salt and crush with the side of a knife until a smooth paste forms.

2. Lay the steaks in a large, shallow baking dish. Rub both sides of the steaks with the garlic paste. In a small bowl, combine the chile powder with 2 teaspoons of salt, the cumin, oregano and pepper. Sprinkle half of the rub on both sides of the steaks.

3. In another small bowl, combine the Tabasco with the Worcestershire sauce and spoon over the steaks; then pat the liquid into the spice rub so it

forms a paste. Refrigerate the steaks for 30 minutes or for up to 4 hours.

4. Light a grill. Thread the onion slices onto skewers and brush with the olive oil, then sprinkle both sides with the remaining spice rub.

5. If using charcoal, scatter the wood chips over the coals. If using a gas grill, place the chips in the smoker box or on a 12-inch square of foil; fold the foil into a 6-inch square and poke 12 holes in the top. Place the package near the flames and heat until smoking. Lightly brush the grate with vegetable oil.

6. Set the seasoned steaks on the grill and cook them over a medium-hot fire

THE ELEMENTS OF GRILLING Use this chart to match the meat, fish or vegetable you want to grill with the ideal method, seasoning and accompaniment. For instructions on grilling methods, see p. 237.

	THE METHOD	SEASON WITH	SERVE WITH
flank steak	direct grilling	garlic, ginger and soy sauce	grilled onions or scallions, steamed brown rice
beef ribs	indirect grilling	salt, pepper and Chinese five-spice powder	hoisin barbecue sauce and a slaw of bok choy, rice vinegar and black mustard seeds
beef brisket	indirect grilling	a Texas spice rub of paprika, chili powder, cumin, oregano, salt and pepper	slices of white bread and hot, not-too-sweet barbecue sauce
veal chops	direct grilling	a marinade of rosemary, garlic, lemon and olive oil	arugula with grilled bell pepper salad and grilled mushrooms
pork chops	direct grilling	oregano and garlic	buttered orzo and Greek salad
pork shoulder	indirect grilling	salt, pepper, paprika and sugar; baste with North Carolina vinegar sauce	North Carolina vinegar sauce, a hamburger bun and vinegared coleslaw
sausages	direct grilling after simmering briefly in beer	nothing	mustard and sauerkraut
fish fillets	direct grilling in a fish basket or on a fish grate	a marinade of olive oil, garlic, lemon and dill	grilled garlic bread or pita bread, grilled zucchini
shrimp	direct grilling	Cajun spices and hot sauce	red beans and rice
clams and oysters	direct grilling just until shells open	nothing	wasabi whipped cream, green salad and crusty bread
asparagus, okra and other long, skinny vegetables	direct grilling on a vegetable grate	sesame oil, salt and pepper	Chinese mustard aioli

for 4 to 6 minutes per side for medium rare. Grill the onion slices until they are tender and nicely charred, about 6 minutes per side. Transfer the steaks to plates and serve with the onion rings and lime wedges.

—*Steven Raichlen*

WINE An inexpensive juicy Shiraz or Zinfandel with bright berry and spice flavors, not too much oak and low alcohol will stand up to the spicy, smoky flavors of the steak. Try the 1998 Peachy Canyon Zinfandel Incredible Red or the 1999 McPherson South Eastern Australia Shiraz.

Asian Spiced Beef Jerky

MAKES ABOUT ½ POUND ●

- 1 teaspoon coriander seeds
- 5 allspice berries
- ½ cinnamon stick, crushed
- 2 teaspoons crushed red pepper
- ½ cup soy sauce
- ¼ cup granulated sugar
- ¼ cup packed dark brown sugar
- 2 tablespoons balsamic vinegar
- 1 tablespoon Worcestershire sauce
- ½ teaspoon salt
- 3 large garlic cloves, minced
- 2 teaspoons finely grated ginger
- 1 teaspoon Asian sesame oil

One 1-pound sirloin steak, about 1 inch thick, sliced lengthwise with the grain ⅛ inch thick

1. In a small skillet, toast the coriander seeds, allspice berries and crushed cinnamon stick over moderate heat, shaking the pan frequently, until fragrant, about 2 minutes. Transfer the spices to a plate and let cool. Transfer to a spice grinder and grind to a powder.

2. Add the crushed red pepper to the skillet and toast over moderate heat, stirring, for 20 seconds. Scrape the toasted red pepper onto a plate to cool.

3. In a medium saucepan, combine the soy sauce with the granulated sugar, dark brown sugar, balsamic vinegar,

three ways to use your grill

1. Direct grilling means cooking food right over the fire. There's no better way to grill things that are relatively thin and tender: steaks, burgers, sliced vegetables, fish fillets. Generally, direct grilling is done over medium-high or high heat.

2. Three-zone grilling is a more sophisticated form of direct grilling, useful for regulating the heat on a charcoal grill. Rake half the hot coals into a double layer at one side of the grill to make a high-heat zone. Rake the remaining coals into a single layer in the grill's center; this is the moderate-heat zone. Leave a portion of the grill without any coals at all for cooking over low heat (or for stopping something from burning).

3. Indirect grilling turns your grill into a sort of barbecue pit or outdoor oven. Use it to cook tougher or larger cuts of meat or whole birds—racks of ribs, beef briskets, legs of lamb—when direct grilling would burn the exterior before the center gets hot.

For a **charcoal grill,** rake the hot coals into two piles at opposite sides of the grill. Place a foil drip pan between them. If you're using wood chips for extra smoke, toss them on the coals. Install the grate and place the food in the center, over the drip pan. Cover the grill and adjust the vents to obtain a temperature of 325° to 350°. (Use an oven thermometer if your grill doesn't have its own.) After an hour or so, add 12 fresh coals to each side, leaving the grill uncovered until the coals light.

For a **two-burner gas grill,** preheat one burner to high and place the food above the other. For a **three- or four-burner gas grill,** light the outside burners and cook the food in the center. If the grill has a smoker box, put wood chips in it. If not, wrap them loosely in foil, poke holes in the top and place the package above one burner.

Worcestershire sauce and salt and cook over low heat, stirring to dissolve the sugars. Stir in the ground spices, crushed red pepper, garlic, ginger and sesame oil. Transfer the seasoning sauce to a medium bowl and let cool.

4. Preheat the oven to 225°. Line 2 large, rimmed baking sheets with foil and set a wire rack in each one. Add the sliced sirloin to the seasoning sauce and toss to coat the slices. Spread the sliced meat on the racks in a single layer. Using a pastry brush, dab the meat with some of solids from the seasoning sauce. Bake the meat on the lower and middle racks of the oven for 2 hours, or until dry but slightly pliable; switch the pans halfway through the cooking time. Let the beef jerky cool for 20 minutes.

—*Grace Parisi*

MAKE AHEAD The beef jerky can be refrigerated in an airtight container for up to 2 weeks.

Stir-Fried Sirloin with Ginger and Bok Choy

4 SERVINGS ●

- 2 tablespoons soy sauce
- 1 tablespoon dry vermouth
- 1 tablespoon cornstarch
- 1½ teaspoons sugar
- 1 pound sirloin steak, sliced across the grain ⅛ inch thick
- 2 tablespoons canola oil
- 2 large garlic cloves, very finely chopped
- 1 tablespoon finely chopped fresh ginger
- 1 large jalapeño, seeded and julienned
- 1½ pounds bok choy, cut into 1-inch pieces

Salt and freshly ground pepper

- 3 tablespoons chicken stock, canned low-sodium broth or water
- ¼ teaspoon Asian sesame oil

1. In a medium bowl, whisk the soy sauce with the vermouth, cornstarch and sugar. Add the sliced sirloin and toss well to coat.

2. Heat 1 tablespoon of the oil in a large skillet until almost smoking. Add half of the garlic, ginger and jalapeño and stir-fry over high heat until fragrant, about 30 seconds. Add half of the sliced sirloin and stir-fry until browned in spots, about 2 minutes. Transfer the meat to a plate. Return the skillet to high heat and repeat with the remaining oil, garlic, ginger, jalapeño and beef.

3. Add the bok choy to the skillet, season with salt and pepper and cook over high heat, stirring, until crisp-tender, about 4 minutes. Return the meat and any accumulated juices to the skillet. Add the stock and bring to a boil. Stir in the sesame oil and serve.

—*Grace Parisi*

SERVE WITH Steamed jasmine rice.

Grilled Sirloin with Shallot Soy Sauce

Grilled Sirloin with Shallot Soy Sauce

4 SERVINGS

The combination of soy and butter might seem odd, but it's no silly fusion invention. Rather, it's a superb blend. The base for the sauce needs to be refrigerated overnight to develop its flavor fully, so plan accordingly.

- 1 cup regular or low-sodium soy sauce
- ½ cup rice vinegar
- 3 garlic cloves, thinly sliced
- 2 shallots, thinly sliced
- 1 tablespoon honey
- ½ tablespoon black peppercorns
- ¼ cup fresh lime juice
- 6 tablespoons unsalted butter

Freshly ground pepper

- 1½ pounds mixed mushrooms—such as creminis, oysters and stemmed shiitakes—cut into ½-inch dice
- 1 tablespoon minced fresh ginger
- 2 tablespoons finely chopped chives

Salt

Four ½-inch-thick boneless sirloin steaks (about 6 ounces each)

- 2 tablespoons vegetable oil

1. In a small saucepan, combine the soy sauce with the vinegar, garlic, shallots, honey and peppercorns and simmer over moderate heat until the sauce is reduced by one-third, about 15 minutes. Remove from the heat and let cool to room temperature, then cover and refrigerate overnight.

2. Strain the sauce into another small saucepan and add the lime juice, 4 tablespoons of the butter and 1 teaspoon of ground pepper. Simmer the sauce over moderate heat for 2 minutes, then remove the pan from the heat and keep the sauce warm.

3. In a large skillet, melt the remaining 2 tablespoons of butter over moderately high heat. When the foam subsides, add the mushrooms and ginger and cook, stirring occasionally, until browned and almost tender, about 10 minutes. Remove the skillet from the heat, stir in the chives and season with salt and pepper.

4. Season the steaks with salt and pepper. Heat the oil in another large skillet. Add the steaks and cook over high heat until browned, about 2 minutes per side for medium-rare meat. Spoon 2 tablespoons of sauce onto each of 4 plates, set a steak on top and cover with the mushrooms. Pass the remaining sauce at the table.

—*Jean-Georges Vongerichten*

WINE The slight sweetness of the fresh ginger coupled with the earthy flavors of the mushrooms and sirloin tune the choice to a Cabernet or Merlot. Choose a wine that is fruity and not too tannic, such as the 1996 Rodney Strong Northern Sonoma Reserve Cabernet Sauvignon from northern California or the 1997 L'Ecole No. 41 Columbia Valley Merlot from Washington State.

Sirloin Steak with Radish Relish

4 SERVINGS

Although the minced relish looks delicate, it has a peppery, spicy punch. You can use a rib-eye steak of similar weight and thickness in place of the sirloin.

- 3 tablespoons soy sauce
- 1½ tablespoons rice vinegar
- 1 teaspoon Asian sesame oil
- One 2-pound sirloin steak, cut 1½ inches thick
- ¼ teaspoon cayenne pepper
- 3 tablespoons vegetable oil
- Salt
- 2 large red radishes, finely diced
- 1 small zucchini—halved lengthwise, seeded and finely diced
- 1 fresh red cayenne chile, seeded and finely diced
- 1 tablespoon pure olive oil

1. In a large, shallow baking dish, combine the soy sauce, vinegar and sesame oil. Add the steak, turn to coat and let stand at room temperature for 2 hours or refrigerate for up to 4 hours; turn often.

2. Meanwhile, in a small skillet, toast the cayenne pepper over moderate heat until fragrant, about 10 seconds. Scrape the cayenne into a small bowl and add the vegetable oil and a pinch of salt. Let stand at room temperature for at least 2 hours.

3. In a bowl, combine the diced radishes, zucchini and fresh cayenne chile. Cover and refrigerate for up to 4 hours.

4. Preheat the oven to 400°. In a large ovenproof skillet, heat the olive oil until almost smoking. Remove the steak from the marinade, season with salt and sear over moderately high heat until deeply browned on the bottom, about 4 minutes. Turn it over and roast in the oven for about 10 minutes, or until an instant-read thermometer inserted in the center registers 120°. Transfer the steak to a carving board and let rest for 10 minutes.

5. To serve, carve the steak on the diagonal into ¼-inch-thick slices and arrange on 4 plates. Garnish the beef with the radish relish, drizzle with the cayenne oil and serve.

—*FOOD & WINE Test Kitchen*

WINE Zinfandel and Cabernet Sauvignon are both possibilities here. The heat from the relish along with the slow burn of the cayenne oil and, of course, the succulence of the beef are all complemented by the strong fruitiness of the 1999 Howell Mountain Vineyards Zinfandel and the 1997 Dunn Vineyards Cabernet Sauvignon.

BACK: **Beef Tapa with Garlic Rice**
FRONT: **Eggplant Curry (p. 294)**

Beef Tapa with Garlic Rice

4 SERVINGS

An easy way to get uniform, paper-thin steak slices is to cut the meat a little thicker than called for and then flatten the slices with a meat pounder.

- 1½ **pounds rib-eye steak**
- 1¼ **teaspoons sugar**
- ¾ **teaspoon salt**
- ½ **teaspoon cayenne pepper**
- ¼ **teaspoon freshly ground black pepper**
- 3 **tablespoons fresh lime juice**
- **Vegetable oil, for brushing**
- **Garlic Rice (recipe follows), for serving**

1. Slice the steak across the grain ¼ inch thick; pound the slices ⅛ inch thick.

2. In a bowl, combine the sugar, salt, cayenne and black pepper. Brush both sides of the beef slices with the lime juice and sprinkle with the spices. Stack the slices and marinate in the refrigerator overnight.

3. Preheat a heavy cast-iron skillet. Brush the pan with a light coat of oil, add the steak in a single layer and cook in batches over high heat until medium rare and slightly charred, about 30 seconds per side. Serve at once with Garlic Rice.

—*Jennifer Aranas*

GARLIC RICE

4 SERVINGS ●

- 2 tablespoons Asian sesame oil
- 1 tablespoon minced garlic
- 4 cups cooked long-grain rice

Salt and freshly ground pepper

- 3 tablespoons chopped cilantro

Heat the oil in a large skillet. Add the garlic and cook over low heat until fragrant, about 3 minutes. Add the rice, stirring, until combined. Season with salt and pepper. Transfer to a bowl, sprinkle with the cilantro and serve.

—*J.A.*

Seared Rib Steak with Arugula

2 SERVINGS ●●

- ½ cup plus 1 tablespoon extra-virgin olive oil
- ¼ cup chopped rosemary
- 3 tablespoons balsamic vinegar

Salt and freshly ground pepper

One 1-pound prime rib-eye steak, about 1¼ inches thick, fat trimmed

- 6 ounces arugula, large stems discarded

Lemon wedges, for serving

1. Preheat the oven to 400°. In a small saucepan, combine ½ cup of the olive oil with the chopped rosemary and bring to a simmer over moderate heat. Remove from the heat and let stand for 10 minutes. Strain the oil through a fine sieve and let cool completely; reserve ½ teaspoon of the rosemary. Whisk the balsamic vinegar into the oil and season with salt and pepper.

2. In a medium ovenproof skillet, heat the remaining 1 tablespoon of olive oil until shimmering. Season the steak with salt and pepper and cook over high heat until well browned on the bottom, about 3 minutes. Turn the steak, transfer the skillet to the oven and roast for about 8 minutes for medium-rare meat. Transfer the steak to a carving board and let rest for 5 minutes.

3. Toss the arugula with 1 tablespoon of the rosemary vinaigrette and mound the salad on 2 dinner plates. Thinly slice the steak crosswise and arrange it over the arugula. Sprinkle each serving with ¼ teaspoon of rosemary and then drizzle with 1 teaspoon of the rosemary vinaigrette. Refrigerate the remaining vinaigrette for another use. Serve with lemon wedges.

—*Michael Romano*

MAKE AHEAD The vinaigrette can be refrigerated overnight. Bring to room temperature before using.

Vodka-Marinated Rib Roast

12 SERVINGS

Great roast beef starts with the best dry-aged and well-marbled loin roast you can find. The vodka marinade tenderizes the meat, while salting it before cooking develops flavor and a crust. The roasting method here is to begin at a high temperature to sear the exterior, then turn the temperature down to produce a succulent interior.

One 11- to 12-pound prime rib roast (5 ribs), chine bone removed

- 12 bay leaves
- ½ cup vodka
- 3 tablespoons kosher salt
- 1 tablespoon freshly ground pepper

Seared Rib Steak with Arugula, with Crab and Endive Salad with Creamy Cognac Dressing (p. 75)

Vodka-Marinated Rib Roast, with Vegetable Ragout with Fresh Herbs (p. 291)

1. Set the roast in a large roasting pan, fat side up. Using a sharp knife, make 12 shallow slits in the fat and insert the bay leaves. Rub the vodka, salt and pepper all over the roast and let stand at room temperature for 2 hours.

2. Preheat the oven to 425°. Roast the meat in the lower third of the oven for 30 minutes. Reduce the oven temperature to 325° and continue to roast for about 1¾ hours longer, or until an instant-read thermometer inserted in the thickest part registers 120° for rare to medium-rare meat. Transfer the roast to a carving board, cover loosely with foil and let rest for 30 minutes.

3. Set the roast on its side and run a long, sharp knife between the bones and the meat; remove the bones. Turn the roast right side up. Carve the roast into thick slices and transfer to plates. Pour any carving juices over the meat and serve at once.   —*Jeremiah Tower*

WINE A powerful, complex Barolo will stand up to the richness of the beef. Tower favors a mature example from Italian producer Bruno Giacosa, such as the 1997 Barolo Falletto or the 1997 Barolo Le Rocche de Falletto. For a less expensive alternative, turn to the 1993 Barolo Vigna Rionda Massolino.

M E N U

HORS D'OEUVRE
smoky chickpea dip (p. 14)

2000 GRANT BURGE KRAFT
SAUVIGNON BLANC

MAIN COURSE
garlicky eggplant and pepper
soup with mint (p. 91)

grilled rib-eye steaks with
caper and bread crumb salsa

two-bean and beet salad
with feta (p. 71)

arugula, fresh corn
and tomato salad (p. 60)

1998 KENDALL-JACKSON GRAND
RESERVE ZINFANDEL

DESSERT
peach and blackberry
cobbler (p. 363)

1996 CHÂTEAU DOISY-VÉDRINES
SAUTERNES

M E N U

FIRST COURSE
smoked sturgeon with deviled eggs
and basil-rose mayonnaise (p. 51)

1998 FRANÇOIS COTAT SANCERRE LA GRANDE CÔTE

SOUP
winter squash soup with porcini cream (p. 98)

MAIN COURSE
vodka-marinated rib roast
vegetable ragout with fresh herbs (p. 291)
jerusalem artichoke gratin with lentils (p. 298)

1997 BRUNO GIACOSA BAROLO FALLETTO

CHEESE COURSE
double-baked three-cheese soufflés (p. 35)

1998 E. GUIGAL CONDRIEU

DESSERT
pear, pear, pear (p. 372)

lemon cornmeal cakes with
lapsang souchong chocolate sauce (p. 330)

1998 M. CHAPOUTIER MUSCAT DE BEAUMES-DE-VENISE

Grilled Rib-Eye Steaks with Caper and Bread Crumb Salsa

8 SERVINGS

The crisp bread crumb topping sops up the delicious steak juices. Sprinkle any extra over the Arugula, Fresh Corn and Tomato Salad on page 60.

Six 1-inch-thick rib-eye steaks
    (about ¾ pound each)
¾ cup extra-virgin
    olive oil
Salt and coarsely ground
    pepper
One 1½-pound plain focaccia,
    cut into ½-inch pieces
½ cup minced shallots
¼ cup red wine vinegar
¼ cup drained small capers
2 tablespoons minced thyme
Vegetable oil, for the grill

1. On a large baking sheet, brush the rib-eye steaks on both sides with 2 tablespoons of the olive oil and season with ½ tablespoon each of salt and coarsely ground pepper. Let the steaks stand at room temperature for 2 hours.

2. Meanwhile, preheat the oven to 350°. Working in batches, pulse the focaccia in a food processor until it is chopped into coarse crumbs. Transfer the crumbs to a large bowl and toss with 2 tablespoons of the extra-virgin olive oil. Spread the bread crumbs on a large rimmed baking sheet and bake them for about 30 minutes, turning and stirring occasionally, until the crumbs are dry and golden. Let cool.

3. In a large bowl, mix the shallots with the vinegar and let stand for 15 minutes. Add the capers and thyme, then slowly whisk in the remaining ½ cup of olive oil until blended. Add the bread crumbs, season with salt and pepper and toss well.

4. Light a grill or preheat a cast-iron grill pan. Lightly brush the grate or grill pan with vegetable oil. Grill the steaks over a medium-hot fire until they are deeply browned on both sides, about

LEFT TO RIGHT: **Two-Bean and Beet Salad with Feta** (p. 71); **Grilled Rib-Eye Steaks with Caper and Bread Crumb Salsa; Arugula, Fresh Corn and Tomato Salad** (p. 60)

6 minutes for medium rare. Transfer the steaks to a cutting board and let rest for 10 minutes. Thickly slice the steaks across the grain and arrange on a platter. Spoon half of the bread crumb salsa over the meat and pass the rest at the table.—*Randy Windham*

MAKE AHEAD The bread crumbs and vinaigrette for the salsa can be made early in the day and tossed together just before serving.

WINE A rustic, medium-bodied Zinfandel with berry flavors and good acidity will complement the smoky grilled steaks and their tangy bread crumb salsa. Look for a lively, balanced and ready-to-drink bottling, such as the 1999 Beaulieu Vineyard or the 1998 Kendall-Jackson Grand Reserve, both from California.

Pan-Crusted Rib Steaks with Shallot Confiture

4 SERVINGS

Two 2-inch-thick beef rib steaks
    on the bone, trimmed
    (3½ pounds total)
Kosher salt and freshly ground pepper
  4 tablespoons
    unsalted butter
  1 pound shallots, peeled and
    quartered lengthwise
  2 tablespoons sugar
  1 bay leaf
  3 tablespoons crème de cassis
  ⅓ cup plus 2 tablespoons
    red wine vinegar
  ½ cup dry red wine
  4 thyme sprigs
  ½ cup beef or chicken stock or
    low-sodium broth
  2 tablespoons minced parsley

1. Season the steaks with kosher salt and freshly ground pepper and let stand at room temperature for 1 hour before cooking.

2. In a large skillet, melt 3 tablespoons of the butter over moderate heat. Add the shallots and sugar and season with salt and pepper. Cover and cook, stirring occasionally, for 5 minutes. Uncover, add the bay leaf and cook over low heat, stirring occasionally, until the shallots are soft, 25 to 30 minutes. Stir in the crème de cassis and ⅓ cup of the vinegar and cook, stirring, until the liquid is syrupy, 10 to 15 minutes. Remove from the heat and discard the bay leaf. Season with salt and pepper.

3. Heat a large cast-iron skillet over moderate heat for 5 minutes. Pat the steaks dry and season lightly with more salt. Add the steaks to the pan and cook over high heat for 2 minutes. Turn and cook for 2 minutes more. Continue turning and cooking for 2 minutes per side, discarding the fat, until an instant-read thermometer inserted in the center of a steak registers 135° for medium rare. Transfer the steaks to a warmed platter and cover loosely with foil.

4. Discard all of the fat in the skillet. Add the wine, thyme and the remaining 2 tablespoons of vinegar and cook, scraping up any browned bits from the bottom, until the pan is nearly dry, about 4 minutes. Add the stock and bring to a boil. Remove from the heat and remove the thyme. Whisk in the parsley and the remaining tablespoon of butter and season with salt and pepper. Slice the meat off the bone and serve with the pan sauce and shallot confiture.   —*Joshua Eisen*

MAKE AHEAD The shallot confiture can be refrigerated for 3 days.

WINE Pair the rib steaks with the 1998 Château Lagrange or the 1997 Dry Creek Vineyard Reserve Cabernet Sauvignon.

Spice-Rubbed Steaks with Spinach

4 SERVINGS ●

 1¼ teaspoons cayenne pepper
  1 teaspoon ground coriander
  1 teaspoon ground cumin
  1 teaspoon fennel seeds,
    lightly crushed
  1 teaspoon sweet paprika
  ½ teaspoon ground
    cardamom
Salt and freshly ground pepper
  4 Delmonico or boneless rib-eye
    steaks (about 2¼ pounds total),
    pounded ½ inch thick
  3 tablespoons unsalted butter
  2 tablespoons extra-virgin olive oil
  2 large garlic cloves, finely chopped
 10 ounces baby spinach

1. In a small bowl, combine 1 teaspoon of the cayenne pepper with the coriander, cumin, crushed fennel seeds, sweet paprika, cardamom,

Spice-Rubbed Steaks with Spinach

1½ teaspoons of salt and 1½ teaspoons of pepper. Sprinkle the spice mixture on both sides of the steaks, patting it onto the meat.

2. In a large, heavy skillet, melt 2 tablespoons of the unsalted butter in 1 tablespoon of the olive oil. Add the chopped garlic and the remaining ¼ teaspoon of cayenne pepper and cook the garlic over moderate heat, stirring, for 2 minutes. Add the baby spinach to the skillet and cook, turning, until the spinach is wilted, about 5 minutes. Season the spinach with salt and pepper. Transfer the spinach to a serving platter and keep warm.

3. Wipe out the skillet and melt the remaining 1 tablespoon of butter in the remaining 1 tablespoon of olive oil. Add the Delmonico steaks to the skillet and cook them over high heat for about 3 minutes per side for medium rare. Set the steaks on the wilted spinach and serve at once.

—*Clifford A. Wright*

Boiled Beef with Horseradish Sauce

6 SERVINGS ●

For this dish, use the tri-tip, or sirloin tip, a richly marbled triangular piece of meat. Any leftover beef is delicious in sandwiches.

- 1 pound marrow bones (in 3-inch lengths)
- 2 quarts water
- 2 medium onions, halved
- 2 large carrots, cut into 2-inch pieces
- 1 small celery root (½ pound), peeled and halved
- 4 pounds tri-tip or triangle beef roast
- 6 black peppercorns
- 6 coriander seeds
- 1 bay leaf
- 1 beef bouillon cube

Salt and freshly ground pepper

- 1 large leek, halved lengthwise
- ½ cup minced chives

Horseradish Sauce (recipe follows)

1. Soak the marrow bones in cold water in the refrigerator for 1 hour. Drain. Push the marrow out of each bone in 1 piece and cut it into ½-inch slices. Refrigerate the slices in a bowl of ice water.

2. In a large stockpot or enameled cast-iron casserole, combine the marrow bones with the 2 quarts of water, the halved onions, carrots and celery root and bring to a boil. Add the meat and return to a boil. Skim the surface. Add the black peppercorns, coriander seeds, bay leaf and bouillon cube and season with salt and pepper. Simmer over low heat, skimming occasionally, until the meat is very tender, about 2½ hours.

3. Transfer the meat to a shallow bowl, cover and let it rest for 30 minutes. Add the halved leek to the stockpot and simmer until tender, about 25 minutes. Add the marrow slices and simmer until translucent, about 4 minutes. Season the broth with salt and pepper.

4. To serve, slice the meat ⅓ inch thick and arrange on a large, warmed platter. Set the marrow slices on the meat and surround with the leeks, carrots and celery root. Ladle some of the broth over the meat and vegetables and sprinkle the chives on top. Serve at once, with the Horseradish Sauce.

—*Wolfgang Puck*

MAKE AHEAD The boiled beef can be prepared through Step 3 and then refrigerated overnight. Reheat the beef gently.

WINE A fairly powerful, dry, spicy white or a spicy, fruity red best matches the pungent horseradish in the sauce accompanying the boiled beef. For a white, consider the difficult-to-find 2000 Bründlmayer Grüner Veltliner Berg-Vogelsang from Austria, or the 1999 Lucien Albrecht Gewurztraminer d'Alsace. For an Austrian red, try the 2000 Glatzer Zweigelt Riedencuvée.

HORSERADISH SAUCE

MAKES ABOUT 2½ CUPS ● ●

- 2½ cups chicken or beef broth, preferably homemade
- 1 large kaiser roll (3 ounces), crust removed, center cut into ½-inch dice (about 2 cups)
- ½ cup crème fraîche
- ¼ cup plus 2 tablespoons drained prepared horseradish

Salt and freshly ground pepper

In a saucepan, pour the broth over the bread and simmer over moderate heat, mashing with a fork, until a thick sauce forms, about 3 minutes. Add the crème fraîche; simmer for 5 minutes. Just before serving, stir in the horseradish and season with salt and pepper. Serve hot. —*W.P.*

MAKE AHEAD The sauce can be refrigerated overnight. Reheat gently.

Beef Daube Arlésienne

4 SERVINGS ●

This dish comes from Arles, the small Provençal town Vincent van Gogh made famous. It's a beef stew with small potatoes, pearl onions and baby carrots, flavored with white wine, herbes de Provence, olives and capers. At the end, it's thickened with a minced mixture of bread, hazelnuts, parsley and garlic.

Shoulder-blade steaks (sometimes called top-blade, under-blade or flat-iron-blade steaks) are ideal because they are very lean except for a strip of nerve tissue in the center that becomes gelatinous as it cooks and keeps the meat moist and flavorful. Shank meat and chuck steaks, cut in large pieces, are good, readily available substitutes.

- 8 small red potatoes (1 pound), peeled
- 2½ cups water
- 1 cup pearl onions or 8 small boiling onions, peeled
- 16 baby carrots, peeled
- 2 tablespoons virgin olive oil

2 pounds boneless beef shoulder-
    blade steaks, cut in half
Salt and freshly ground pepper
1 medium onion, finely chopped
1 cup dry white wine
1 teaspoon herbes de Provence
2 tablespoons hazelnuts
One ¾-inch slice country bread
    (1 ounce), toasted and cut into
    1-inch pieces
½ cup flat-leaf parsley leaves
2 garlic cloves
¼ cup Niçoise olives, pitted
2 tablespoons drained capers
1 medium tomato, seeded
    and diced

I. In a medium saucepan, cover the potatoes with the water and bring to a boil over high heat. Reduce the heat to low, cover tightly and cook for 15 minutes. Add the peeled pearl onions and carrots, cover and cook until tender, 5 to 8 minutes. Drain the vegetables, reserving the cooking liquid.

2. Heat the olive oil in a medium enameled cast-iron casserole. Season the steaks with salt and pepper. Add half of the meat to the casserole and cook over moderately high heat, turning once, until well browned, about 10 minutes; transfer to a plate. Repeat with the remaining meat.

3. Return all of the meat to the casserole. Add the onion and cook for 2 minutes, stirring occasionally. Stir in the reserved vegetable cooking liquid, the wine and the herbes de Provence. Season lightly with salt and pepper and bring to a boil. Cover tightly, reduce the heat to very low and simmer until the beef is tender, 2 to 2½ hours.

4. Preheat the oven to 400°. Spread the hazelnuts in a pie plate and roast in the oven for 10 minutes, or until lightly toasted. Transfer the hazelnuts to a plate and let cool completely. In a food processor, combine the hazelnuts with the toast, parsley and garlic and process until finely chopped.

Beef Daube Arlésienne

5. Stir the roasted hazelnut mixture and the cooked vegetables into the daube. Cover the casserole and simmer gently for 5 minutes. Stir in the olives, capers and tomato and cook for 1 minute longer. Season the stew with salt and pepper and serve.

—*Jacques Pépin*

MAKE AHEAD The Beef Daube Arlésienne can be prepared through Step 4 and refrigerated overnight. Bring the stew to a simmer before proceeding with the recipe.

WINE Serve a dry but fruity rosé from the south of France to perfectly complement this typical Provençal stew. A Bandol, such as the 1999 Domaine Tempier, made from the region's Mourvèdre grapes, would fill the bill. Or, if you prefer a red, try a hearty Rhône Côte-Rôtie, such as the 1997 Jamet, or a Crozes-Hermitage, such as the 1997 Paul Jaboulet-Aîné Domaine de Thalabert, also from the Rhône.

Beef Goulash with Spaetzle

6 SERVINGS ●

For optimum flavor, use the freshest possible paprika.

- 1 tablespoon caraway seeds
- 2 tablespoons extra-virgin olive oil
- 2 large onions, thinly sliced
- 1 tablespoon sugar
- 3 garlic cloves, minced
- 3 tablespoons sweet Hungarian paprika
- 1 teaspoon hot Hungarian paprika
- 2 tablespoons minced marjoram
- 1 teaspoon minced thyme
- 1 bay leaf
- 3 tablespoons tomato paste
- 4 cups chicken stock or canned low-sodium broth
- 2½ pounds trimmed boneless chuck, cut into 2-inch pieces

Salt and freshly ground pepper

Spaetzle (recipe follows)

1. In a small skillet, toast the caraway seeds over moderate heat until darkened and fragrant, about 1 minute. Transfer the caraway seeds to a spice grinder and let cool completely, then grind to a powder.

2. Heat the extra-virgin olive oil in a large enameled cast-iron casserole. Add the sliced onions and sugar and cook over moderate heat, stirring occasionally, until the onions are evenly browned, about 20 minutes. Add the

Beef Goulash with Spaetzle

minced garlic and ground caraway to the casserole and cook, stirring, for 1 minute. Add the sweet paprika, hot paprika, marjoram, thyme and bay leaf and cook, stirring, until fragrant, about 2 minutes. Stir in the tomato paste and then the chicken stock or broth. Add the meat, season with salt and freshly ground pepper and simmer until the meat is very tender, about 2 hours. Skim off the fat, season the goulash with salt and pepper and serve with the Spaetzle.

—Wolfgang Puck

MAKE AHEAD The goulash can be refrigerated for up to 2 days.

SPAETZLE

6 SERVINGS

- 4 large egg yolks
- 1 large egg
- 1¾ cups milk
- 3½ cups all-purpose flour

Salt and freshly ground pepper

- ¼ teaspoon freshly grated nutmeg
- ¼ cup peanut oil
- 2 tablespoons unsalted butter
- 1 tablespoon minced parsley

1. In a small bowl, whisk the egg yolks with the whole egg and milk. In a large bowl, mix the flour with 1 teaspoon of salt, ¼ teaspoon of pepper and the nutmeg. Add the egg mixture and stir just until blended; do not overmix. Cover the batter and refrigerate for at least 1 and up to 4 hours.

2. Bring a large pot of salted water to a boil. Using a rubber spatula and working over the pot, push the batter into the boiling water through a colander with large holes, stopping once or twice to stir the water. Cook until the spaetzle are tender, about 4 minutes; drain.

3. In a large skillet, heat the peanut oil until shimmering. Add the spaetzle and cook over moderately high heat, without stirring, until they are beginning to brown on the bottom, about 3

minutes. Add the butter and cook, stirring occasionally, until golden brown, about 2 minutes longer. Season with salt and pepper, sprinkle with the parsley and serve. *—W.P.*

Seared Steak Tartare Burgers on Caesar Salad

4 SERVINGS ●

It's the pungent flavorings—capers, horseradish, parsley and onion, which are typically stirred into steak tartare—that give these burgers their name.

- 1 tablespoon unsalted butter
- ¼ pound baguette, crust removed, bread cut into ½-inch dice (1 cup)
- 1 large egg
- 10 anchovy fillets
- 2 tablespoons fresh lemon juice
- 1 tablespoon red wine vinegar
- 1 small garlic clove
- 1 tablespoon plus 1 teaspoon Dijon mustard
- 1 tablespoon Worcestershire sauce
- ⅓ cup extra-virgin olive oil

Salt and freshly ground pepper

- ¼ red onion, coarsely chopped (¼ cup)
- 2 tablespoons capers, drained
- 2 tablespoons coarsely chopped flat-leaf parsley
- 1 tablespoon prepared horseradish
- ¾ teaspoon hot sauce
- 1 pound ground lean top round or sirloin
- 2 teaspoons canola oil
- ½ pound romaine lettuce, torn into bite-size pieces (8 cups)

1. Melt the butter in a large skillet. When the foam subsides, add the diced baguette in an even layer. Cook over moderate heat until browned on the bottom, about 3 minutes. Stir and cook until evenly browned and crisp, about 2 minutes longer. Transfer to a plate.

2. Cook the egg in boiling water for 2½ minutes; drain, then scoop the egg out of the shell into a blender. Add 6 of the anchovies, the lemon juice,

vinegar, garlic, 1 teaspoon of mustard and 1 teaspoon of the Worcestershire sauce. Slowly add the olive oil and blend at medium-low speed until it is incorporated and the mixture is creamy. Pour the dressing into a small bowl and season with salt and pepper.

3. In a food processor, finely chop the 4 remaining anchovies with the onion, capers, parsley and horseradish. Transfer to a large mixing bowl. Add the remaining 1 tablespoon of mustard, 2 teaspoons of Worcestershire sauce, the hot sauce and ground beef and mix well. Form the meat into 12 patties and season them with salt and pepper.

4. Heat 1 teaspoon of the canola oil in a large, heavy skillet. Add 6 of the burgers and cook over high heat for about 1 minute on each side for rare, and about 30 seconds longer on each side for medium rare. Transfer to a plate. Repeat with the remaining 1 teaspoon of canola oil and 6 burgers.

5. In a large bowl, combine the lettuce with ½ cup of the anchovy dressing and the croutons and toss to coat. Mound the salad on plates and set 3 burgers on each salad. Drizzle the remaining dressing over the salads and serve. *—Michael Roberts*

MAKE AHEAD The dressing can be refrigerated for 2 days.

Herbed Meatballs with Garlicky Yogurt

4 SERVINGS ●

- ¾ pound ground pork
- ¾ pound ground beef or lamb
- ¼ cup freshly grated Pecorino Romano
- 3 tablespoons finely chopped mint
- 3 tablespoons finely chopped dill

Salt and freshly ground pepper

- 1 tablespoon vegetable oil
- 1 cup full-fat plain yogurt, at room temperature
- 1 small garlic clove, very finely chopped

ı. In a medium bowl, combine the pork, lamb, Pecorino, mint and dill with ½ teaspoon of salt and ¼ teaspoon of pepper. Mix with your hands until combined, then shape into 1-inch balls.

2. Heat the oil in a large, heavy skillet. Add the meatballs and cook over moderate heat, turning occasionally, until browned and firm, about 15 minutes.

3. Mix the yogurt and garlic, season with salt and pepper and spoon onto a serving platter. Top with the meatballs and serve immediately.

—*Clifford A. Wright*

Kefta with Two Sauces

4 SERVINGS ●

Kefta are Middle Eastern ground meat patties. Here they make a speedy meal.

1½ **pounds ground beef or lamb**
 4 **teaspoons ground cumin**
 ¼ **cup chopped flat-leaf parsley**
 1 **teaspoon salt**
 ½ **teaspoon freshly ground pepper**
Pinch of cinnamon
 1 **medium onion, coarsely grated**
 1 **tablespoon unsalted butter**
 2 **garlic cloves, minced**
 1 **cup full-fat plain yogurt**
 1 **cup tomato sauce**
Pinch of cayenne pepper
 2 **tablespoons vegetable oil**
 4 **large pitas, warmed**
 and quartered

ı. In a bowl, combine the meat with 2 teaspoons of cumin and the parsley, salt, pepper and cinnamon. Squeeze any excess liquid from the grated onion; add to the meat. Mix well. Form the meat into eight ½-inch-thick oval patties.

2. Melt the butter in a small skillet. Add the garlic and cook over moderate heat until fragrant but not browned, about 1 minute. Transfer to a small bowl and whisk in the yogurt. Season with salt and pepper. In the same skillet, warm the tomato sauce over moderate heat and stir in the cayenne and the remaining 2 teaspoons of cumin.

3. In a nonstick skillet, heat the oil until shimmering. Add the kefta and cook over moderate heat, turning the meat patties occasionally, until they are cooked through, about 10 minutes.

4. Place the pitas on 4 plates and top with the kefta. Spoon some tomato and yogurt sauce over the kefta and serve, passing the remaining sauce at the table. —*Joyce Goldstein*

Kefta with Two Sauces

VARIETAL	CHARACTERISTICS	DISHES
riesling	light- to medium-bodied; fruity, silky, floral, mineral, with refreshing acidity	sushi, oily fish, pork or poultry in butter or cream sauces
sauvignon blanc	light- to medium-bodied; herbal, fruity, aroma of fresh-cut grass	anything herbal or vegetal; light fish, veal or chicken dishes; goat cheese; vinegary foods
chardonnay	medium- to full-bodied; broad range of styles from lean and mineral-tasting to rich, fruity and oaky	simple chicken, veal or fish dishes with lighter wines; foods in rich sauces with bigger wines
pinot noir	light- to medium-bodied; earthy, hint of herbs, aromas of red fruit, game, licorice	roasted wild birds, veal, poultry, pork, seared salmon, mushrooms
sangiovese	medium- to full-bodied; acidic and tannic; aromas of black cherries, pine and leather	pizza or pasta with lighter wines; roasted or grilled poultry or steak with bigger wines
tempranillo	medium- to full-bodied; acidic and tannic; fruity and spicy	roasted or grilled lamb or pork; spicy foods; tapas such as cured ham, chorizo or roasted peppers
cabernet sauvignon	medium- to full-bodied; tannic; aromas of black currants, cedar and green bell pepper	roasted or grilled beef or lamb; sharp, hard cheeses with young wines; milder cheeses with older wines
syrah	medium- to full-bodied; tannic; aromas of ripe olives, rich fruit, exotic spices, earthy herbs	hearty, rustic stews, such as duck, lamb or beef; strong cheeses; spicy foods

Sautéed Calf's Liver with Onions, Lemon and Sage

4 SERVINGS ●

Calf's liver deserves a comeback.

½ **cup extra-virgin olive oil**

3 **medium red onions, halved lengthwise and sliced ¼ inch thick**

¾ **cup all-purpose flour**

Salt and freshly ground pepper

1½ **pounds calf's liver, sliced ⅓ inch thick**

1 **cup chicken stock or canned low-sodium broth**

8 **sage leaves**

2 **tablespoons fresh lemon juice**

Lemon wedges, for serving

I. In a large, heavy saucepan, heat ¼ cup of the olive oil until shimmering. Add the onions and cook over moderate heat until softened and lightly browned, about 10 minutes.

2. In a large pie plate, season the flour with salt and pepper. Dredge the liver in the flour, shaking off any excess. In a large skillet, heat the remaining ¼ cup of oil until shimmering. Add the liver and cook, turning once, until browned and just cooked through, about 5 minutes. Transfer to a platter, cover loosely with foil and keep warm.

3. Pour off any excess oil from the skillet. Add the chicken stock and boil until reduced by half, about 5 minutes. Add the onions, sage and lemon juice and cook for 2 minutes; season with salt and pepper. Spoon the onion-and-lemon sauce over the liver and serve with lemon wedges.

—*Joyce Goldstein*

Herb-Marinated Rack of Lamb

4 SERVINGS

30 **thyme sprigs, lightly crushed**

15 **mint sprigs, lightly crushed**

8 **rosemary sprigs, lightly crushed**

¼ **cup extra-virgin olive oil**

4 **large garlic cloves, crushed**

3 **tablespoons fresh lemon juice**

½ **teaspoon sweet paprika**

Fine sea salt and freshly ground pepper

2 **racks of lamb (about 1½ pounds each), chine bones removed, racks Frenched (see Note)**

Kosher salt

I. In a large, sturdy, resealable plastic bag, combine the thyme, mint, rosemary, olive oil, garlic, lemon juice, paprika, ¾ teaspoon of sea salt and ½ teaspoon of pepper. Add the lamb and press out the air. Seal the bag. Refrigerate overnight or for up to 3 days. Let the lamb stand at room temperature for 1 hour before cooking.

2. Preheat the oven to 450°. Spread a ¼-inch layer of kosher salt in a roasting pan just large enough to hold the lamb. Remove the lamb from the marinade and scrape off the herbs and garlic; pat dry. Season with salt and pepper. Set the lamb, meaty side up, on a rack in the prepared pan and roast for 25 minutes for medium rare, or until an instant-read thermometer inserted in the center of the meat registers 135°. Transfer the lamb to a carving board, cover loosely with foil and let stand for 10 minutes. Carve the racks into chops and serve.

—*Joshua Eisen*

NOTE To French lamb bones, scrape or cut the fat and meat from the bones that project from the chops. Or ask

Herb-Marinated Rack of Lamb

your butcher to French the lamb bones.
WINE Either the 1994 Cune Imperial
Gran Reserva Rioja or the 1998 Clos
du Bois Tempranillo would make an
excellent accompaniment to the marinated rack of lamb.

Rack of Lamb with Fig-Port Sauce

4 SERVINGS ●

Two 1¼-pound racks of lamb,
    bones Frenched (See Note,
    previous recipe)
  2 tablespoons pure olive oil
Salt and freshly ground pepper
  1 tablespoon minced rosemary
  1 tablespoon minced thyme
  1 cup tawny port
  8 fresh Mission figs, halved
    (or dried figs, quartered)
  ¾ cup chicken stock or canned
    low-sodium broth
  1 teaspoon balsamic vinegar

I. Preheat the oven to 450°. Rub the
lamb with 1 tablespoon of the olive oil.
Season with salt and pepper and rub
with rosemary and thyme.

2. Heat the remaining olive oil in a
medium ovenproof skillet. Add the
racks of lamb, fat-side down, and cook
over high heat until browned, about 5
minutes. Turn the racks and cook until
lightly browned, about 1 minute. Add
½ cup of the port. Transfer the skillet
to the oven and roast the lamb for 18
minutes, or until an instant-read thermometer registers 125° for medium-
rare meat.

3. Transfer the racks to a carving
board; cover loosely with foil. Add the
remaining ½ cup of port and the figs to
the skillet. Bring to a simmer, scraping
up the browned bits from the bottom
of the pan. Add the stock and vinegar
and simmer the sauce over moderately high heat until thickened, about 3
minutes. Season the figs and sauce
with salt and pepper. Serve the racks
of lamb with the figs and sauce.

—*Alison Attenborough*

SERVE WITH Mashed turnips.
VARIATION Use four 14-ounce lamb
shoulder chops instead of the racks
and preheat the oven to 400°. Follow
Step 1. In Step 2, brown the chops
over moderately high heat, about 4
minutes per side, then roast for 20
minutes. Transfer the chops to a platter instead of a cutting board and proceed with Step 3.
WINE Cabernet is lamb's classic partner, but the sweet figs in this port
sauce make a delicious, jammy Zinfandel an even better choice.

Moroccan-Style Lamb Chops

4 SERVINGS ●

  1 medium onion, quartered
  2 garlic cloves, quartered
  3 tablespoons unsalted butter
  ¾ teaspoon cinnamon
  ¼ teaspoon ground ginger
  ¼ teaspoon cayenne pepper
  2 cups tomato sauce
  2 tablespoons honey
Salt and freshly ground pepper
  8 lamb loin chops, cut 1 inch thick
  ¼ cup extra-virgin olive oil
  2 tablespoons chopped cilantro

I. In a food processor, pulse the onion
and garlic until minced. Melt the butter in a medium saucepan. Add the
onion and garlic and cook over moderate heat until softened, about 7 minutes. Add the cinnamon, ginger and
cayenne and cook, stirring, for 2 minutes. Stir in the tomato sauce and
honey and simmer over low heat until
the sauce thickens slightly, about 5
minutes. Season with salt and pepper.

2. Season the lamb chops with salt
and pepper. In a large skillet, heat 2
tablespoons of the olive oil until shimmering. Add 4 of the lamb chops and
cook over moderate heat, turning
once, until they are browned and
almost cooked through, about 8 minutes; keep warm. Repeat with the
remaining 2 tablespoons of olive oil
and 4 lamb chops.

3. Pour off the fat from the skillet. Add
the tomato sauce and bring to a simmer over moderate heat. Add the lamb
chops and simmer until cooked
through, about 2 minutes. Transfer the
lamb to plates, spoon the tomato
sauce on top and garnish with the
cilantro.   —*Joyce Goldstein*
SERVE WITH Couscous or potatoes.

Sesame Lamb Chops with Potato and Green Bean Salad

4 SERVINGS ●

  ¼ cup soy sauce
  3 tablespoons Asian sesame oil
  2 tablespoons rice vinegar
  1 teaspoon finely grated ginger
  1 small garlic clove, minced
  ½ teaspoon honey
Four 6-ounce lamb loin chops, cut
    1½ inches thick
  3 tablespoons finely chopped basil
  2 tablespoons extra-virgin olive oil
  ½ pound fingerling or new potatoes,
    quartered if large
  ¾ pound thin green beans, trimmed

I. In a small bowl, whisk the soy sauce
with the sesame oil, vinegar, ginger,
garlic and honey. Pour half the mixture
into a small baking dish, add the chops
and turn to coat. Let stand for 10 minutes, turning once. Add the basil and
olive oil to the remaining marinade.

2. Light a grill or preheat the broiler. In
a large saucepan of boiling salted
water, cook the potatoes until tender,
about 10 minutes. Using a slotted
spoon, transfer the boiled potatoes to
a bowl. Add the beans to the boiling
water and cook until crisp-tender,
about 3 minutes; drain and pat dry.
Add the beans and the soy-basil dressing to the potatoes and toss. Cover
with foil and keep warm.

3. Remove the chops from the marinade and pat dry. Grill over moderate
heat for 4 to 5 minutes per side for
medium rare. Transfer the chops to
plates, add the potato and bean salad
and serve.   —*Melissa Clark*

Rack of Lamb with Fig-Port Sauce

Honey-Herb-Crusted Lamb Chops with Cipolline Onions

4 SERVINGS

- 8 loin lamb chops (6 to 7 ounces each)

Salt and freshly ground pepper

- 1½ tablespoons pure olive oil
- ½ pound cipolline onions, blanched and peeled
- 2 cups water
- 1 cup garlic shoots or scallion greens, cut into ½-inch lengths
- 1 tablespoon honey
- 1 tablespoon Dijon mustard
- ½ tablespoon minced flat-leaf parsley
- ½ teaspoon minced tarragon
- ¼ teaspoon minced thyme
- ¼ teaspoon minced rosemary

ı. Preheat the oven to 400°. Season the lamb chops with salt and pepper. Heat 1 tablespoon of the olive oil in a large skillet. When the oil is almost smoking, add 4 of the chops and brown on both sides over moderately high heat, about 3 minutes per side. Transfer the chops to a rimmed baking sheet and repeat with the remaining ½ tablespoon of oil and the remaining chops.

2. Add the onions to the skillet and cook over moderately high heat until browned, about 2 minutes per side. Add 1½ cups of the water, cover and simmer over low heat until the onions are tender, about 8 minutes. Add the garlic shoots, cover and cook for 3 minutes. Season with salt and pepper, cover and remove from the heat.

3. In a small bowl, mix the honey with the mustard, parsley, tarragon, thyme and rosemary. Brush the honey mustard on the chops and roast them for 7 minutes, or until an instant-read thermometer inserted in the center of a chop registers 125° for medium-rare meat. Transfer the chops to a warm platter and cover loosely with foil.

4. Set the baking sheet over 2 burners on moderate heat. Add the remaining ½ cup of water and bring to a boil, scraping up the browned bits from the bottom of the baking sheet. Add the pan juices to the onions and reheat them. Set the lamb chops on plates and serve with the onions and pan juices. —*Eberhard Müller*

MAKE AHEAD The honey-herb mixture can be refrigerated overnight.

Grilled Lamb Chops with Blackberry Relish

4 SERVINGS ●

In Scotland berries and lamb are classic partners, but this sweet-tart relish is also great with grilled pork, duck, beef or venison.

- 2 cups blackberries
- 2 tablespoons sugar
- 1 tablespoon chopped mint
- 1 tablespoon drained prepared horseradish
- 1 tablespoon fresh lime juice
- 1 tablespoon extra-virgin olive oil, plus more for brushing

Salt and freshly ground pepper

Eight 4- to 5-ounce loin lamb chops (1 inch thick), trimmed

ı. In a medium saucepan, cook the blackberries with the sugar over moderately high heat until they are softened but still hold their shape, about 5 minutes. Transfer to a bowl and stir in the mint, horseradish, lime juice and the 1 tablespoon of olive oil. Season with salt and pepper and let cool.

2. Light a grill or preheat a grill pan. Brush the lamb chops with olive oil and season with salt and pepper. Grill over a medium-hot fire until medium rare, about 2 minutes per side. Serve with the blackberry relish. —*Bobby Flay*

MAKE AHEAD The blackberry relish can be refrigerated for 2 days. Let return to room temperature before serving.

SERVE WITH Boiled potatoes with parsley.

WINE An intense Merlot or Rhône-blend Cabernet Sauvignon with hints of fruit will stand up to the pungent lamb and echo the fruit in the tart blackberry relish. Try the 1998 Benziger Merlot from Sonoma or the 1998 Château-Fortia Châteauneuf-du-Pape from France.

Grilled Lamb Chops with Blackberry Relish

WEDDING MENU

HORS D'OEUVRES

fava bean crostini (p. 14)

warm white bean bruschetta (p. 15)

FIRST COURSE

baby lettuce and herb salad with shallot vinaigrette (p. 57)

NONVINTAGE VEUVE CLICQUOT CHAMPAGNE

MAIN COURSE

braised lamb with syrah jus

morel and sweet pea risotto (p. 309)

1998 QUPÉ BIEN NACIDO HILLSIDE ESTATE SYRAH

DESSERT

chocolate wedding cake with chocolate-hazelnut filling (p. 334)

Lamb Chops with Lavender Salt

4 SERVINGS ●

1 tablespoon dried lavender
   flowers (see Note)

Coarse sea salt

1 tablespoon olive oil

3 garlic cloves, halved

Eight 4- to 5-ounce lamb
   rib chops (1 inch thick)

Freshly ground pepper

1. In a spice grinder, pulse the dried lavender flowers until finely ground. Transfer the ground flowers to a small bowl and toss with 1 tablespoon of coarse sea salt.

2. Heat the olive oil in a large skillet. Add the halved garlic cloves and cook over moderately high heat until golden, about 2 minutes. Discard the cooked garlic cloves. Season the lamb chops with salt and pepper, add them to the skillet and cook them until they are browned outside and medium rare within, about 5 minutes per side. Transfer the lamb chops to plates and serve the lavender salt on the side.

—*Joanne Weir*

ONE SERVING Calories 260 kcal, Total Fat 15.9 gm, Saturated Fat 5 gm, Protein 27 gm, Carbohydrates 0 gm

NOTE Lavender flowers are available from Dean & DeLuca (877-826-9246; www.deandeluca.com).

Lamb Steaks with Shallot-Anchovy Relish

4 SERVINGS ●

5 tablespoons extra-virgin olive oil

4 large shallots, thinly sliced

¼ cup coarsely chopped
   flat-leaf parsley

3 large anchovy fillets, minced

1 teaspoon coriander
   seeds, crushed

1 teaspoon minced rosemary

Salt and freshly ground pepper

Four bone-in lamb leg steaks, about
   ½ inch thick (6 to 7 ounces each)

1. Heat 1 tablespoon of the olive oil in a large skillet. Add the shallots and cook over high heat, stirring, until just softened, about 1 minute; transfer to a small bowl. Stir in 3 tablespoons of the olive oil and the parsley, anchovies, coriander and rosemary. Season the shallot relish with salt and pepper.

2. In the same skillet, heat the remaining 1 tablespoon of olive oil. Season the lamb with salt and pepper. When the oil is almost smoking, add the lamb and cook over high heat until well browned on the bottom, about 3 minutes. Turn the steaks and cook just until medium rare, about 1 minute longer. Transfer the steaks to a platter, top with the shallot relish and serve.

—*Marcia Kiesel*

Braised Lamb with Syrah Jus

12 SERVINGS ●

This is a version of osso buco with lamb shanks (off the bone) in place of veal.

Twelve 1-pound lamb shanks

Salt and freshly ground pepper

6 tablespoons olive oil

5 medium carrots, coarsely
   chopped

4 celery ribs, coarsely chopped

3 medium onions, coarsely
   chopped

2 tablespoons tomato paste

1 bottle (750 ml) Syrah or other
   hearty red wine

2 bay leaves

10 whole black peppercorns

8 cups chicken stock or canned
   low-sodium broth

2 cups (packed) flat-leaf parsley
   leaves, finely chopped

4 teaspoons finely grated
   lemon zest

6 garlic cloves, minced

Morel and Sweet Pea Risotto (p. 309),
   for serving

1. Preheat the oven to 300°. Season the lamb shanks with salt and pepper. Heat ¼ cup of the olive oil in a large enameled cast-iron casserole. Working in batches, cook the lamb shanks over moderate heat, turning often, until well browned on all sides, about 12 minutes; transfer to a platter.

2. Pour off any fat from the casserole and add the remaining 2 tablespoons of olive oil. Add the carrots, celery and onions and cook over moderate heat until the vegetables start to brown, about 8 minutes. Stir in the tomato paste, then add the wine, scraping up the browned bits from the bottom. Stir in the bay leaves and peppercorns. Return the lamb shanks to the casserole and add the stock. Bring to a boil, cover and bake the shanks in the oven for about 3 hours, or until the meat is very tender.

3. Transfer the lamb shanks to the platter and remove the meat from the bones. Put the meat in a bowl and cover with a damp towel. Strain the sauce into a large saucepan, pressing on the vegetables to extract as much liquid as possible. Boil the sauce over high heat until it is thick enough to coat the back of a spoon, about 25 minutes; season with salt and pepper. Return the lamb to the sauce and rewarm over moderate heat.

4. In a small bowl, mix the parsley with the lemon zest and garlic. Spoon the lamb stew over the Morel and Sweet Pea Risotto, sprinkle with the gremolata and serve.   —*Brandon Miller*

MAKE AHEAD The stew can be prepared through Step 3 and refrigerated for 2 days. Reheat gently.

Moroccan-Style Lamb Shanks

4 SERVINGS ●

- ¼ cup extra-virgin olive oil
- 4 meaty lamb shanks (about 1¼ pounds each)
- Salt and freshly ground pepper
- 1 large onion, finely chopped
- 2 carrots, finely chopped
- 2 large garlic cloves, minced
- 1 teaspoon ground cumin
- ½ teaspoon ground coriander
- ½ teaspoon ground cinnamon
- ¼ teaspoon ground allspice
- ¼ teaspoon freshly grated nutmeg
- 2 tablespoons tomato paste
- 1 teaspoon harissa or other chile paste
- 1 cup dry red wine
- One 28-ounce can whole peeled tomatoes, drained and coarsely chopped
- 2 cups chicken stock or canned low-sodium broth
- ¼ cup slivered almonds, chopped
- 2 tablespoons finely chopped mint
- 2 tablespoons chopped cilantro
- 2 tablespoons unsalted butter
- 1 large shallot, minced
- One 10-ounce box instant couscous
- 1 cup water
- ¼ cup dried currants

Grilled Lamb and Red Onion Skewer

I. Preheat the oven to 325°. In a large enameled cast-iron casserole, heat 2 tablespoons of the oil. Season the shanks with salt and pepper. Add them to the casserole, 2 at a time, and cook over moderately high heat until browned all over, about 12 minutes. Transfer to a plate and wipe out the casserole.

2. Heat the remaining 2 tablespoons of olive oil in the casserole. Add the onion, carrots and garlic and cook over moderate heat, stirring, until lightly browned, about 5 minutes. Add the cumin, coriander, cinnamon, allspice and nutmeg and cook, stirring until lightly toasted, about 1 minute. Add the tomato paste and harissa and cook over moderately high heat, stirring, until lightly browned, about 2 minutes. Stir in the wine and boil until reduced to a thick syrup, about 4 minutes.

3. Add the tomatoes and 1 cup of the chicken stock to the casserole. Season with salt and pepper and bring to a boil. Nestle the lamb shanks in the liquid. Cover tightly and braise in the oven for about 3 hours, basting occasionally, until the meat is almost falling off the bone. Transfer the shanks to a platter and cover with foil. Leave the oven on.

4. Spread the almonds in a pie pan in an even layer and toast for about 10 minutes, or until golden.

5. Strain the sauce into a bowl, pressing on the vegetables; skim any fat. Return the sauce to the casserole and boil over high heat until reduced to 1 cup, about 10 minutes. Return the vegetables and lamb to the sauce and keep warm.

6. In a small bowl, mix the mint with the cilantro and almonds and season lightly with salt and pepper.

7. Melt the butter in a medium saucepan. Add the shallot and cook over moderately high heat until softened, about 2 minutes. Stir in the couscous and cook until lightly browned, 2 to 3 minutes. Add the remaining 1 cup of chicken stock, the water and ¼ teaspoon of salt and bring to a boil.

Remove from the heat and add the currants. Cover and let stand for 10 minutes. Fluff with a fork and stir in half of the herb-almond mixture.

8. Mound the couscous in the center of a large platter. Arrange the lamb shanks around the couscous and spoon the sauce on top. Sprinkle with the remaining herb-almond mixture and serve. —*FOOD & WINE Test Kitchen*

MAKE AHEAD The lamb shanks can be refrigerated for up to 3 days. Rewarm gently.

WINE The warm spices, the luscious braised lamb and the sweet toasted almonds are all a great match for the hit of fruit in the 1999 Howell Mountain Vineyards Zinfandels—Old Vines, the Beatty Ranch and the Black Sears.

Grilled Lamb and Red Onion Skewers

4 SERVINGS ●

1¼ pounds boneless leg of lamb, trimmed and cut into 1-inch cubes
5 tablespoons extra-virgin olive oil
Salt and freshly ground pepper
1 small red onion, cut into 1-inch pieces
1 garlic clove, minced
1 tablespoon balsamic vinegar
2 medium beefsteak tomatoes, cut into wedges
1 tablespoon finely chopped basil
Four 1-inch slices of peasant bread
¼ cup black olive tapenade

1. Light a grill or preheat a large cast-iron grill pan. In a medium bowl, toss the lamb with 1 tablespoon of the olive oil and season with salt and pepper. Alternate the lamb on four 12-inch skewers with pieces of red onion.

2. In another bowl, combine the garlic with the balsamic vinegar and 3 tablespoons of the olive oil. Add the tomatoes and basil, season with salt and pepper and toss well.

3. Brush the bread on both sides with the remaining 1 tablespoon of oil.

Grill, turning once, until toasted, about 2 minutes per side. Spread about 2 teaspoons of the tapenade on each toast. Grill the lamb until browned all over, 7 to 8 minutes for medium-rare meat. Spread the remaining tapenade on the lamb.

4. Spoon the tomato salad onto large plates. Add a lamb skewer and a tapenade toast to each and serve.
—*Ruth Van Waerebeek*

WINE The rich lamb will stand up to and mellow a Cabernet Sauvignon's tannin. Opt for the bargain 1999 Alamos Bodegas Esmeralda Mendoza or the 2000 Domaine Chandon Terrazas de los Andes Mendoza Reserva, both from Argentina.

Turkish Shish Kebabs with Garlicky Tahini

4 SERVINGS

Here is a "divide and conquer" approach to shish kebabs: Grill the meat and vegetables on separate skewers to allow foods with different cooking times to reach the perfect degree of doneness.

6 garlic cloves, crushed
3 tablespoons extra-virgin olive oil, plus more for brushing
3 tablespoons fresh lemon juice
1 teaspoon kosher salt
1 teaspoon freshly ground pepper
1 teaspoon dried mint
1 teaspoon dried oregano
1½ pounds trimmed boneless leg of lamb, cut into 1½-inch cubes
1 small bunch of fresh mint
1 large red onion, cut into 2-inch pieces
1 large yellow bell pepper, cut into 2-inch pieces
1 large green bell pepper, cut into 2-inch pieces
Vegetable oil, for the grill
Garlicky Tahini (recipe follows)
Lemon wedges and pita bread, for serving

1. In a large bowl, combine the garlic with the 3 tablespoons of olive oil, the lemon juice, salt, pepper, dried mint and oregano. Add the lamb, toss to coat and refrigerate for at least 1 hour or for up to 3 hours.

2. Thread the lamb onto skewers, placing 1 fresh mint leaf between the pieces of meat. Skewer alternate pieces of onion and bell pepper and brush lightly with olive oil.

3. Light a grill. Lightly brush the grate with vegetable oil and grill the lamb and vegetables over a medium-hot fire, turning frequently, until the lamb is medium, about 6 minutes, and the vegetables are tender and lightly charred, about 8 minutes. Let the kebabs stand for 2 minutes, then serve with the Garlicky Tahini, lemon wedges and pita bread.
—*Steven Raichlen*

WINE The berrylike fruit of a young, robust Zinfandel has an affinity with grilled lamb, especially when the dish includes pungent garlic and herbs. Consider the 1997 Fetzer Home Ranch, or a Zinfandel blend, the 1998 Laurel Glen Reds.

GARLICKY TAHINI
MAKES ABOUT 1⅓ CUP ●●●

Cooks throughout the Middle and Near East serve this creamy, garlicky condiment as a sauce for grilled lamb. It is also wonderful with chicken or swordfish.

5 garlic cloves, coarsely chopped
⅓ cup tahini
⅓ cup fresh lemon juice
⅓ cup extra-virgin olive oil
⅓ cup water
1 teaspoon salt
½ teaspoon freshly ground pepper
1 tablespoon coarsely chopped flat-leaf parsley

In a blender, puree the garlic with the tahini, lemon juice, olive oil, water, salt and pepper until smooth. If the sauce

appears thick, add a little more water. Scrape the sauce into a bowl, sprinkle with the parsley and serve. —*S.R.*
MAKE AHEAD The Garlicky Tahini can be refrigerated for 1 week. Bring to room temperature and stir before serving.

Butterflied Leg of Lamb with Pineapple-Ginger Glaze

4 SERVINGS
Butterflying a leg of lamb—cutting it almost in half through the side and removing the bone—turns a large roast into a broad, flat steak that's thin enough to grill directly over the fire.

One 3-pound butterflied leg of lamb
One 3-inch piece of ginger, 1 inch thinly slivered, 2 inches chopped
6 garlic cloves, 2 thinly sliced, 4 coarsely chopped
4 scallions, white parts chopped, green parts minced
Two 3-inch strips of lemon zest
1 cup ginger beer
½ cup pineapple juice
⅓ cup soy sauce
3 tablespoons Asian sesame oil
2 tablespoons fresh lemon juice
½ teaspoon freshly ground pepper
Vegetable oil, for the grill

I. Using the tip of a paring knife, make 1-inch-deep incisions all over the lamb, spacing them 1 inch apart. Insert the slivered ginger in half of the incisions and the sliced garlic in the other half. Spread the lamb in a shallow glass or ceramic baking dish.
2. In a blender, combine the chopped ginger and garlic with the scallion whites and lemon zest and chop. Add the ginger beer, pineapple juice, soy sauce, sesame oil, lemon juice and pepper and puree. Pour the marinade over the lamb and refrigerate for at least 4 hours or overnight, turning twice.

Turkish Shish Kebabs with Garlicky Tahini

3. Light a grill. Transfer the lamb to a platter. Strain the marinade into a medium saucepan and boil it over high heat until reduced to ½ cup, about 10 minutes. Remove the glaze from the heat.

4. Lightly brush the grate with vegetable oil. Grill the lamb over a medium-hot fire for 8 to 10 minutes per side for medium rare and 10 to 12 minutes per side for medium. During the last 3 minutes of cooking, baste both sides of the lamb with the glaze.

5. Transfer the lamb to a cutting board; let stand for 3 minutes. Slice thinly on the diagonal and arrange on a platter. Drizzle the lamb with the remaining glaze, sprinkle with the scallion greens and serve. *—Steven Raichlen*

WINE The best match for the sweet-spicy marinade is a medium-bodied but intense and fruity Pinot Noir with smoky overtones. Look for the 1998 Argyle Pinot Noir Willamette Valley Nuthouse from Oregon or the 1999 Pipers Brook Vineyard Estate Pinot Noir Tasmania from Australia.

dinner party game plan

The dinner party menu (above right) can be prepared from start to finish in less than four hours. To save time, consider a store-bought appetizer and dessert.

1. Marinate the lamb. **2.** Stuff and wrap the dates. **3.** Roast the onions. **4.** Cut up the root vegetables and toss with the oil and seasonings. **5.** Make the vinaigrette. **6.** Start roasting the lamb. **7.** When the onions are finished, roast the root vegetables. **8.** Prepare the bananas and caramel sauce. **9.** Slice the avocados. **10.** Roast the dates. **11.** Make the cherry sauce for the lamb. **12.** Add the cheese to the vegetables and roast. **13.** Twenty minutes before dessert, bake the bananas, then serve warm.

Leg of Lamb with Dried-Cherry Sauce

8 SERVINGS, PLUS LEFTOVERS

- 6 **ounces basil, leaves only (4 cups)**
- ¼ **cup extra-virgin olive oil**
- ¼ **cup coarsely ground black pepper**

One 6-pound boneless leg of lamb, trimmed of excess fat and tied

- 1 **cup dried sour cherries (¼ pound)**

Boiling water

Kosher salt and freshly ground black pepper

- ½ **cup dry red wine**
- ¼ **cup balsamic vinegar**
- 1 **cup rich beef stock or veal demiglace (see Note)**
- 1 **tablespoon unsalted butter**

Caramelized Red Onions (recipe follows), for serving

1. In a food processor, pulse the basil leaves just until coarsely chopped. Add the extra-virgin olive oil and the coarsely ground black pepper and pulse just until a coarse paste forms. Rub the basil paste all over the lamb and set the roast on a rack set in a roasting pan. Let the roast stand at room temperature for 45 minutes to marinate. After 30 minutes, preheat the oven to 400°.

2. Meanwhile, in a small heatproof bowl, cover the dried cherries with boiling water and let stand until plump, about 30 minutes. Drain.

3. Season the lamb with salt and pepper. Roast the lamb on the bottom shelf of the oven for 30 minutes. Reduce the oven temperature to 350° and roast the lamb for 1½ hours longer, or until an instant-read thermometer inserted in the thickest part of the roast reads 125°.

4. Transfer the roasted lamb to a carving board, cover the roast loosely with foil and let stand for 15 minutes.

5. Meanwhile, spoon off the fat from the roasting pan and set the pan over

DINNER PARTY MENU

HORS D'OEUVRES

crispy bacon-wrapped stuffed dates (p. 20)

pecorino cheese and sliced pears

CRICKET BALL APERITIF (P. 397)

MAIN COURSE

leg of lamb with dried-cherry sauce

caramelized red onions (p. 261)

root vegetables with gorgonzola (p. 307)

sliced avocados with black-olive vinaigrette (p. 71)

1995 ALFREDO PRUNOTTO BAROLO

DESSERT

bananas with caramel and honey-roasted nuts (p. 377)

2 burners. Add the red wine and balsamic vinegar and bring to a boil over high heat, scraping up any browned bits from the bottom of the pan with a wooden spoon. Simmer until the liquid is reduced by half, about 5 minutes, then strain the liquid into a small saucepan. Add the beef stock and cook over moderately high heat until reduced to ¾ cup, about 15 minutes. Add the reconstituted cherries and the butter, season the dried-cherry sauce with salt and pepper and keep warm.

6. Remove the strings from the lamb roast and cut it into thin slices. Arrange the meat on a platter and surround it with the Caramelized Red Onions. Pour the dried-cherry sauce into a bowl and pass at the table.

—Jimmy Bradley

NOTE Veal demiglace is available at specialty food shops and can be mail-ordered from Williams-Sonoma (877-812-6235; www.williams-sonoma.com).

MAKE AHEAD The roasted lamb can be prepared through Step 1 and then

Leg of Lamb with Dried-Cherry Sauce, with Caramelized Red Onions

refrigerated overnight. Bring to room temperature before proceeding.

WINE A lively, intense Pinot Noir with dried-cherry-fruit nuances, such as the 1997 Lynmar Russian River Valley Quail Hill Vineyard, will echo the lamb's dried-cherry sauce. Alternatively, you could choose an intense Barolo with hints of earth and cherry, such as the 1995 Alfredo Prunotto.

CARAMELIZED RED ONIONS

8 SERVINGS

  4 medium red onions (2 pounds), sliced crosswise 1½ inches thick
  2 tablespoons extra-virgin olive oil
Salt and freshly ground pepper

Preheat the oven to 400°. Spread the onions in a baking dish. Drizzle with the oil and season with salt and pepper. Roast the onions on the top shelf of the oven for about 50 minutes, or until they are tender and caramelized; turn the onions halfway through roasting. Serve hot or at room temperature.
—J.B.

Auberge Ravoux's Braised Leg of Lamb

4 SERVINGS ●

In this recipe, the leg of lamb marinates overnight in wine with aromatics before it is braised in the oven for three hours.

One 3-pound boneless leg of lamb roast from the hip end, tied
  1 carrot, coarsely chopped
  1 onion, coarsely chopped
  1 celery rib, coarsely chopped
  1 head of garlic, cut in half crosswise
  3 thyme sprigs
  3 bay leaves
  1 tablespoon crushed black peppercorns
  1 bottle (750 ml) dry white wine
  2 tablespoons peanut oil
Salt and freshly ground pepper
  2 pounds meaty lamb bones
Water
Chopped chives, for garnish

I. Put the leg of lamb in a bowl just large enough to hold it. Add the carrot, onion, celery, garlic, thyme sprigs, bay leaves and crushed peppercorns. Pour the wine over the lamb. Cover with plastic wrap and refrigerate overnight.
2. Remove the lamb from the marinade and pat dry. Strain the marinade in a colander set over a bowl; reserve the liquid and vegetables separately.
3. Preheat the oven to 300°. In a large skillet, heat the oil until shimmering. Season the lamb with salt and pepper and brown on all sides over moderately high heat. Transfer to a medium enameled cast-iron casserole.

4. Add the bones to the skillet; cook over moderate heat until browned all over. Transfer to the casserole. Pour off all but ½ tablespoon of the fat from the skillet. Add the reserved vegetables and cook over moderate heat, stirring, until browned, about 5 minutes. Add the vegetables to the casserole. Pour the reserved marinade into the skillet and boil, scraping up the browned bits from the bottom of the pan. Pour the marinade into the casserole. Add just enough water to cover the meat and bring to a boil. Cover and braise in the oven for 2½ to 3 hours or until the lamb is very tender. ▸

Auberge Ravoux's Braised Leg of Lamb

5. Transfer the lamb to a carving board and cover loosely with foil. Strain the braising liquid and skim the fat from the surface. Pour the liquid back into the casserole and boil over high heat until reduced to 2 cups, about 15 minutes. Season with salt and pepper.

6. Carve the lamb into thick slices and transfer to a deep platter. Pour some of the braising liquid over the meat and garnish with chives; pass the remainder at the table. —*Van Gogh's Table*

MAKE AHEAD The recipe can be prepared 2 days ahead through Step 4. Reheat gently before proceeding.

SERVE WITH Potatoes with Smoky Bacon (p. 306).

WINE A rich Syrah-based red with smoky overtones and plenty of fruit will contrast with the succulent lamb and echo the smoky bacon in the potatoes. Look for a medium-bodied St-Joseph from the Rhône Valley, such as the 1999 Jean-Luc Colombo or the 1999 Domaine Courbis.

Cumin-Ancho Lamb Burritos
4 SERVINGS ●

- 1 tablespoon vegetable oil
- ¾ pound ground lamb
- 1½ teaspoons ground cumin
- 1½ teaspoons unsweetened cocoa powder
- 1½ teaspoons ancho chile powder
- ¼ teaspoon crushed red pepper
- ½ small red onion, finely chopped
- Salt and freshly ground pepper
- 1 cup canned refried beans
- Four 12-inch flour tortillas
- 6 ounces grated Monterey Jack (2 cups)
- 1 medium tomato, coarsely chopped
- 1 cup cilantro leaves
- ½ cup jarred salsa
- 1 cup sour cream, for serving

1. Preheat the oven to 450°. Heat the oil in a large skillet. Add the ground lamb, cumin, cocoa, chile powder and crushed red pepper and cook over

moderate heat, stirring to break up the lamb, until the meat is cooked through, about 6 minutes. Stir in the onion, season with salt and pepper and transfer the lamb to a bowl. Add the beans to the skillet and cook over moderate heat until they are hot.

2. Lay the tortillas on a work surface and spoon one-quarter of the ground lamb in a band across the center of each tortilla, leaving a 2-inch border on either side. Top each with one-quarter of the refried beans, cheese, chopped tomato, cilantro and salsa and roll up the tortillas, folding in the ends as you go. Put the rolled tortillas in a large baking dish and bake them for about 10 minutes, or until hot and bubbling. Serve the burritos at once, passing the sour cream at the table.

—*Michael Roberts*

Bacon-Wrapped Rack of Venison
4 SERVINGS

There's one rule for venison: It should be served rare and hot. The dish can also be made with a boneless loin; the roasting time will be slightly shorter. Regardless of what cut you use, the meat needs to marinate in garlic and olive oil overnight, so plan accordingly.

- One 1½-pound rack of venison
- 4 garlic cloves, smashed
- ¼ cup extra-virgin olive oil
- Salt and freshly ground pepper
- ½ cup plus 2 tablespoons coarsely chopped cilantro
- 6 thin slices of smoky bacon (3 ounces)
- ½ cup chicken stock or canned low-sodium broth
- 1 tablespoon unsalted butter
- Kale with Garlic and Oven-Roasted Parsnips (p. 287)

1. Set the venison in a glass or ceramic baking dish and rub with the smashed garlic. Pour the olive oil over the meat. Cover and refrigerate overnight.

2. Transfer the venison to a plate; discard the garlic and reserve the oil. In a

large ovenproof skillet, heat 1 tablespoon of the reserved oil until shimmering. Season the venison with salt and pepper and cook over moderately high heat until browned all over, about 3 minutes per side. Transfer to a plate to cool. Wipe out the skillet.

3. Press ½ cup of the chopped cilantro onto the meaty top of the venison. Wrap the bacon around the meat, between the rib bones, overlapping slightly. Using cotton string, tie up the rack at ½-inch intervals to secure the bacon. Let stand at room temperature for up to 2 hours.

4. Preheat the oven to 400°. Heat 1 tablespoon of the reserved oil in the skillet until shimmering. Set the venison in the skillet, bacon side down, and cook over moderate heat, turning, until browned all over, about 10 minutes. Turn the rack bacon side up and roast in the oven for about 20 minutes, or until an instant-read thermometer inserted in the center of the meat registers 115° to 120°. Transfer the venison to a carving board, cover loosely with foil and let rest for 5 minutes.

5. Pour off the fat from the skillet. Add the chicken stock and boil, scraping up any browned bits from the bottom of the skillet, until reduced to ¼ cup, about 2 minutes. Remove from the heat and whisk in the butter. Add the remaining 2 tablespoons of cilantro.

6. Carve the venison into 4 thick chops and transfer to plates. Spoon the pan sauce over the chops, mound the Kale with Garlic and Oven-Roasted Parsnips alongside and serve.

—*FOOD & WINE Test Kitchen*

MAKE AHEAD The venison can be prepared through Step 3 and refrigerated for 6 hours; bring to room temperature before cooking.

WINE The 1999 Howell Mountain Vineyards Old Vines Zinfandel and the 1997 Dunn Vineyards Cabernet Sauvignon are lush enough to complement the heartiness of the venison.

Bacon-Wrapped Rack of Venison (p. 262),
with Kale with Garlic and Oven-Roasted
Parsnips (p. 287)

10 breads sandwiches pizzas

Popovers

MAKES 6 GIANT POPOVERS OR
2 DOZEN MINI POPOVERS

- 1 cup milk
- 1 cup all-purpose flour
- ½ teaspoon salt
- 3 large eggs, beaten
- 1 tablespoon unsalted
  butter, melted

1. Preheat the oven to 450°. Generously butter a popover pan or 2 mini-muffin pans. In a medium bowl, whisk the milk with the flour and salt; there will be some lumps. Add the eggs and butter and whisk just until blended.

2. Heat the prepared pan or pans in the oven until the butter is sizzling, about 1 minute. Carefully spoon the popover batter into the pan or pans: Fill the popover pan two-thirds full for giant popovers or fill the mini-muffin pans three-quarters full for mini popovers. Bake the popovers for 15 minutes without opening the oven, then lower the temperature to 350° and bake the minis 15 minutes longer, or the giants 20 minutes longer. Transfer the popovers to a baking sheet, poke a small hole in the tops with a toothpick and then dry them out in the oven for another 10 minutes. Serve the popovers warm. —*Grace Parisi*
SERVE WITH Shrimp salad or sweet butter and jam.

Moroccan Chickpea Flat Breads

MAKES SIXTEEN 6-INCH LOAVES ● ●
These flat breads are very quick to make as they need to rise only once. They're great for dipping in spreads and for stuffing with salads, salsas and grilled meat.

- 1 tablespoon cumin seeds
- 1 tablespoon coriander seeds
- 2 cups plus 2 tablespoons
  warm water
- 2 tablespoons honey
- 3 envelopes dry active yeast
  (2 tablespoons and 1 teaspoon)
- 7½ cups bread flour, plus more
  for dusting
- One 15-ounce can chickpeas—
  drained, rinsed and
  coarsely mashed
- 1½ tablespoons salt

1. In a small skillet, toast the cumin and coriander seeds over moderately high heat until fragrant, shaking the pan frequently, about 2 minutes. Transfer the spices to a spice grinder and let cool, then grind coarsely.

2. In a small bowl, mix the warm water with the honey and yeast and let stand until foamy, about 10 minutes. Put the 7½ cups of flour in a large bowl and stir in the chickpeas, spices and salt. Make a well in the center of the flour and add the yeast mixture. Using a wooden spoon, stir the mixture until the dough becomes very stiff.

3. Scrape the dough out onto a lightly floured work surface and knead until silky and smooth, about 5 minutes, adding more flour as necessary to prevent sticking. Form the dough into a ball and return it to the bowl. Cover with plastic wrap and let stand in a warm spot until doubled in bulk, about 1 hour.

4. Preheat the oven to 450°. Punch down the dough and divide it into 16 equal pieces. Shape each piece into a round ball and let rest on a lightly floured work surface for 15 minutes.

5. Roll out each piece of dough to an irregular 6-inch oval. Working quickly, set 4 of the flat breads directly on the rack in the upper third of the oven and bake for about 10 minutes, or until golden and puffed, like pita. Using tongs, transfer the baked loaves to a rack to cool. Let the oven return to

Popovers

450° before baking the remaining flat breads. Serve warm. —*Jamie Oliver*
MAKE AHEAD The flat breads can be stored in a sturdy plastic bag at room temperature for 2 days or frozen for 1 month. Reheat before serving.

Angel Biscuits

MAKES ABOUT 40 BISCUITS ●

Southerners might recognize these light and buttery rolls as Bride's Biscuits, named for their popularity with novice cooks because of their foolproof use of two leavening agents. This dough is refrigerated overnight, so plan accordingly.

- 2¼ teaspoons active dry yeast (1 envelope)
- ¼ cup plus 1 pinch of sugar
- 2 tablespoons lukewarm water
- 5 cups self-rising all-purpose flour
- 1 cup cold solid vegetable shortening, cut into small pieces
- 2 cups buttermilk
- 6 tablespoons unsalted butter, melted

1. In a small bowl, dissolve the yeast and the pinch of sugar in the lukewarm water and let stand for 5 minutes, or until foamy. Meanwhile, in a large bowl, mix the flour with the remaining ¼ cup of sugar. Using a pastry blender or 2 knives, cut in the shortening until the mixture resembles small peas. Add the yeast and buttermilk and stir until the dough just comes together.

2. Turn the dough out onto a lightly floured work surface and knead 5 times; the dough should have a soft, moist texture. Return the dough to a clean bowl and cover with plastic wrap. Refrigerate the dough overnight.

3. Transfer the chilled dough to a lightly floured surface and knead 10 times. Roll out the dough to a 16-inch round ⅓ inch thick. Using a 2¼-inch biscuit cutter, stamp out biscuits as close together as possible. Gather the dough scraps, knead 3 times and

reroll, then stamp out more biscuits as close together as possible from the rerolled dough. Discard the remaining scraps.

4. Lightly butter 2 large baking sheets. Brush the tops of the biscuits with the melted butter. Fold the biscuits in half, then brush the unbuttered sides with the remaining melted butter and place on the prepared baking sheets. Cover loosely with plastic wrap and let the biscuits rise in a draft-free place for 2 hours.

5. Preheat the oven to 400°. Bake the biscuits for about 15 minutes, or until browned on the bottom and light golden on top. Serve warm.—*Scott Howell*
MAKE AHEAD The biscuit dough can be refrigerated for up to 2 days. The unrisen biscuits can be frozen on a baking sheet, then transferred to a resealable freezer bag and kept frozen for up to 1 week. Return the biscuits to room temperature, let them rise, then bake.

Bacon Biscuits with Roasted Apple Butter

MAKES ABOUT 20 BISCUITS

- 10 thin slices of smoked bacon (about 5 ounces)
- 3 cups all-purpose flour
- 1½ teaspoons kosher salt
- 1½ teaspoons baking powder
- ¾ teaspoon baking soda
- 1½ cups heavy cream
  Roasted Apple Butter (recipe follows)

1. In a large skillet, cook the bacon over moderate heat until crisp, about 8 minutes. Drain on paper towels, then finely chop. Pour the bacon fat into a small bowl and let cool; refrigerate until solid.

2. Preheat the oven to 400°. In a bowl, whisk the flour with the salt, baking powder and baking soda. Add 5 tablespoons of the cold bacon fat. Use your fingers to gently blend it with the flour until the mixture resembles coarse meal. Stir in the cream and chopped

bacon until a loose dough forms. Scrape onto a lightly floured surface and knead gently until smooth.

3. Roll out the dough to a 10-by-12-inch rectangle about ½ inch thick. Cut into 2¼-inch squares and transfer to an ungreased baking sheet. Bake the biscuits for 22 minutes, or until golden. Let cool slightly on a wire rack and serve with Roasted Apple Butter.

—*Marcia Kiesel*

ROASTED APPLE BUTTER

MAKES ABOUT 3 CUPS ●●

- 2¾ pounds McIntosh apples (about 8)—peeled, quartered and cored
- 2 cups unsweetened apple juice

1. Preheat the oven to 450°. Arrange the apples in a large roasting pan. Pour the apple juice over the apples and bake for 30 minutes, or until tender and browned. Lower the oven to 350°.

2. Using a fork or potato masher, thoroughly mash the apples in the roasting pan. Bake the apple puree, stirring occasionally, for 1½ to 1¾ hours, or until very thick and deeply browned. Scrape into a bowl and let cool. Serve at room temperature or chilled.—*M.K.*
MAKE AHEAD The apple butter can be refrigerated for up to 3 days.

Nana's Skillet Corn Bread

MAKES ONE 9-INCH CORN BREAD ●

- 1¼ cups coarse stone-ground yellow cornmeal
- ¾ cup all-purpose flour
- 2 tablespoons sugar
- 2 teaspoons baking powder
- ¼ teaspoon baking soda
- 1¼ teaspoons salt
- 2 large eggs, lightly beaten
- ⅔ cup milk
- ⅔ cup buttermilk
- 1 tablespoon unsalted butter, melted
- 2 tablespoons rendered bacon fat

1. Preheat the oven to 425°. Heat a 9-inch cast-iron skillet in the oven for 5 minutes. Meanwhile, in a medium bowl, whisk the cornmeal with the flour, sugar, baking powder, baking soda and salt. Stir in the lightly beaten eggs, milk and buttermilk until blended, then stir in the melted butter.

2. Pour the bacon fat into the hot skillet and swirl it around until the skillet is evenly greased. Pour the batter into the skillet and bake for 20 minutes, or until the corn bread is golden brown and a toothpick inserted in the center comes out clean. Let cool in the skillet for 5 minutes, then turn the corn bread out on a cutting board. Cut the corn bread into wedges and serve warm.

—Scott Howell

MAKE AHEAD The corn bread can be baked earlier in the day and reheated in a 350° oven.

Parmesan-Herb Cloverleaf Rolls

MAKES 1½ DOZEN ROLLS ●

The unbaked rolls need to be refrigerated overnight, so plan accordingly.

- 1½ cups milk
- 11 tablespoons unsalted butter
- 2 tablespoons sugar
- 1 envelope active dry yeast
- 4 cups all-purpose flour, plus more for dusting
- 1½ teaspoons salt
- ½ cup packed freshly grated Parmesan
- 2 tablespoons finely chopped flat-leaf parsley
- 1 teaspoon finely chopped thyme
- 1 teaspoon finely chopped rosemary

1. In a medium saucepan, heat the milk with 3 tablespoons of the butter and the sugar just until the butter melts. Transfer to a large bowl and let cool slightly. Stir in the yeast and let stand until dissolved, about 5 minutes. Add the 4 cups of flour and the salt and stir to form a soft, sticky dough.

2. Turn the dough out onto a lightly floured surface and knead until silky, about 4 minutes. Transfer the dough to a lightly oiled bowl, cover with plastic wrap and let rise in a warm spot until doubled in bulk, about 1 hour.

3. In a small shallow bowl, mix the cheese with the parsley, thyme and rosemary. Melt the remaining 8 tablespoons of butter in a small saucepan.

4. Lightly butter 18 of the cups in 2 or more nonstick muffin pans. Punch down the dough and divide it into 3 equal pieces. Working with 1 piece of dough at a time and keeping the rest covered, roll the piece of dough into a 1-inch-thick rope, then cut the rope into 18 equal pieces; roll each piece into a ball. Dip half of each ball into the melted butter and then into the herb-cheese mixture and arrange 3 balls in each prepared muffin cup, coated sides touching in the center. Repeat with the remaining dough and topping. Brush the tops of the rolls with the remaining melted butter. Cover the muffin pans with plastic wrap and refrigerate overnight.

5. Loosely re-drape the plastic wrap over the muffin tins. Let the rolls rise in a warm spot until they are about 1 inch above the cup rims, about 2 hours.

6. Preheat the oven to 425°. Bake the rolls in the lower and middle thirds of the oven for about 15 minutes, or until golden and sizzling; shift the pans halfway through from top to bottom and back to front for even browning. Turn the rolls out onto a rack and let cool slightly before serving.

—Grace Parisi

MAKE AHEAD The rolls can be baked earlier in the day and reheated.

Wild Mushroom Stuffing

12 SERVINGS

- One 2-pound loaf of peasant bread, crusts trimmed, bread cut into 1½-inch cubes
- ⅓ cup extra-virgin olive oil
- Salt and freshly ground pepper
- ½ cup dried porcini mushrooms (1 ounce)
- 1 cup boiling water
- 1½ cups hazelnuts (about 6 ounces)
- 2 sticks (½ pound) unsalted butter
- 1 medium onion, chopped
- 2 celery ribs, finely chopped
- 2 large shallots, minced
- 2 pounds mixed wild mushrooms, tough stems trimmed and the rest finely chopped
- 3 cups Rich Turkey Stock (p. 203)
- 1 cup dried cranberries (4 ounces)
- ¼ cup chopped parsley
- 1 tablespoon chopped thyme
- 2 teaspoons chopped sage

1. Preheat the oven to 375°. Butter 2 large baking dishes. On 2 large rimmed baking sheets, toss the bread cubes with the olive oil and season with salt and pepper. Bake for about 20 minutes, or until golden. Let cool. Reduce the oven temperature to 350°.

2. In a heatproof bowl, soak the dried porcini in the boiling water until softened, about 20 minutes. Rub the porcini to remove any grit, then remove them from the water and coarsely chop. Slowly pour the soaking liquid into a small saucepan, leaving behind any grit. Boil the liquid over high heat until reduced to ¼ cup, about 5 minutes.

3. Spread the hazelnuts on a rimmed baking sheet and toast for 12 minutes, or until richly browned. Transfer to a kitchen towel and let cool completely. Rub the hazelnuts in the towel to remove their skins. Coarsely chop the hazelnuts.

4. Melt 4 tablespoons of butter in a large skillet. Add the onion and celery and cook over moderately low heat until softened, about 10 minutes. Scrape the mixture into a very large bowl. In the skillet, melt the remaining 1½ sticks of butter over moderately high heat. Add the shallots and cook, stirring, until softened, about 3 minutes. Add the fresh mushrooms, porcini and reduced soaking liquid and

Parmesan-Herb Cloverleaf Rolls

season with salt and pepper. Cook over high heat until the liquid evaporates, about 15 minutes. Add the mushrooms to the onion mixture in the bowl, along with the toasted bread, turkey stock, chopped hazelnuts, dried cranberries, parsley, thyme and sage. Toss well and season with salt and pepper.

5. Spread the stuffing in the prepared baking dishes and cover with foil. Bake for about 30 minutes, or until heated through. Uncover and bake until crusty, about 25 minutes longer.

—*Tom Douglas*

MAKE AHEAD The unbaked stuffing can be refrigerated overnight; bake it slightly longer than called for if chilled.

Sourdough Rye Stuffing with Ham and Cheese

10 SERVINGS ●

One 1½-pound loaf of sourdough rye
   bread, cut into ½-inch cubes
1½ sticks (6 ounces) unsalted butter,
   4 tablespoons melted
¼ cup plus 2 tablespoons freshly
   grated Parmesan
1 large onion, coarsely chopped
6 medium scallions,
   coarsely chopped
2 celery ribs, finely chopped
½ pound ground country ham
   (see Note) or minced prosciutto
2 large McIntosh apples, cored and
   cut into 1-inch dice
1 tablespoon minced thyme
Salt and freshly ground pepper
4 cups chicken stock or canned
   low-sodium broth
2 large eggs

1. Preheat the oven to 350°. In a very large bowl, toss the the bread cubes with the 4 tablespoons of melted butter, then spread on 3 large baking sheets. Sprinkle with the grated Parmesan and bake for 15 to 20 minutes, or until browned and crisp. Let cool. Return the bread to the bowl. Leave the oven on.

2. Melt the remaining 1 stick of butter in a large skillet. Add the chopped onion, scallions and celery and cook over moderately low heat, stirring, until softened, about 12 minutes. Add the ground ham or minced prosciutto and cook over moderately high heat, stirring, until golden, about 4 minutes. Stir in the diced apples and minced thyme and let cool.

3. Scrape the ham and apple mixture over the toasted bread cubes and toss to coat; season with salt and pepper. In a large bowl, whisk the stock with the eggs and pour over the stuffing; mix thoroughly.

4. Butter 2 large, shallow baking dishes and divide the stuffing between them. Cover with foil and bake until heated through, about 25 minutes. Uncover and bake until browned and crisp, about 15 minutes. Serve at once.   —*Marcia Kiesel*

NOTE Ground cooked country ham is available from Meacham Country Hams (www.meachamhams.com; 800-552-3190). The prosciutto can be finely ground in a food processor.

MAKE AHEAD The Sourdough Rye Stuffing with Ham and Cheese can be refrigerated overnight. Bring to room temperature before baking.

Corn Bread, Chorizo and Collard Stuffing

10 SERVINGS ●

CORN BREAD

2 tablespoons vegetable oil
2½ cups stone-ground
   white cornmeal
2½ cups all-purpose flour
¼ cup sugar
1 tablespoon plus 1 teaspoon
   baking powder
1 teaspoon salt
¾ teaspoon baking soda
3 cups buttermilk
2 extra-large eggs
1½ sticks (6 ounces) unsalted
   butter, melted

STUFFING

2 pounds collard greens, large
   stems discarded
4 tablespoons unsalted butter
1 pound chorizo, coarsely chopped
1 large onion, coarsely chopped
3 celery ribs, finely chopped
Salt and freshly ground pepper
4 large eggs
2½ cups chicken or turkey stock or
   canned low-sodium broth

1. **MAKE THE CORN BREAD:** Preheat the oven to 425°. Pour the oil into a 9-by-13-inch baking dish and heat in the oven. In a large bowl, whisk the cornmeal with the flour, sugar, baking powder, salt and baking soda. In another bowl, whisk the buttermilk with the eggs. Pour the buttermilk mixture into the dry ingredients, add the melted butter and stir with a wooden spoon until just blended; do not overmix.

2. Remove the baking dish from the oven and swirl to coat with the oil. Scrape the batter into the hot dish and bake for 25 minutes, or until springy and a cake tester inserted in the center comes out clean. Transfer to a rack and let cool. Turn the oven down to 375°. Crumble the corn bread into small chunks and spread on 2 large baking sheets. Bake the corn bread for 15 to 20 minutes, stirring occasionally, or until dry and golden. Leave the oven on.

3. **MAKE THE STUFFING:** In a large pot of boiling salted water, cook the collard greens until just tender, about 5 minutes. Drain and let cool slightly. Squeeze dry and coarsely chop.

4. Melt the butter in a large skillet. Add the chorizo and cook over moderately low heat for 5 minutes. Add the onion and celery and cook, stirring, until softened, about 10 minutes. Stir in the collards and remove from the heat. Let cool completely.

5. Scrape the crumbled corn bread into a very large bowl and add the collard mixture. Season with salt and pepper. In a bowl, whisk the eggs with the stock and pour over the stuffing; mix well.

6. Butter 2 large, shallow baking dishes and divide the stuffing between them. Cover and bake at 375° for about 25 minutes, or until heated through. Uncover and bake for about 10 minutes longer, or until browned. Serve hot.   —*Marcia Kiesel*

MAKE AHEAD The corn bread can be frozen for up to 1 month. The stuffing can be assembled and refrigerated overnight. Bring to room temperature before baking.

Cranberry-Walnut Scones

MAKES 8 SCONES ●●

1⅓ cups cake flour

3 tablespoons sugar

2 teaspoons baking powder

⅛ teaspoon salt

3 tablespoons cold unsalted butter, cut into small pieces

½ cup cranberries, chopped

¼ cup finely chopped walnuts

⅓ cup buttermilk

½ teaspoon pure vanilla extract

I. Preheat the oven to 425° and line a baking sheet with wax paper. In a medium bowl, mix the flour with the sugar, baking powder and salt. Using a pastry blender or 2 knives, cut in the butter until the mixture resembles fine crumbs. Stir in the cranberries and walnuts.

2. In a small bowl, mix the buttermilk with the vanilla extract. Add the wet ingredients to the dry ingredients and stir with a fork just until the dough comes together. Do not overmix. Turn the dough out onto a lightly floured surface and knead twice. Pat the dough into a round and cut into 8 wedges. With lightly floured hands, pat the wedges into ½-inch-thick rounds. Set the dough rounds on the prepared baking sheet and bake for 12 to 14 minutes, or until the scones are puffed

and pale golden. Transfer the scones to a rack and cool before serving.

—*Suki Hertz*

ONE SCONE Calories 156 kcal, Total Fat 7.1 gm, Saturated Fat 2.9 gm

Lemon—Poppy Seed Angel Muffins

MAKES 12 MUFFINS ●

MUFFINS

⅔ cup all-purpose flour

½ cup confectioners' sugar

½ cup granulated sugar

1 tablespoon poppy seeds

½ teaspoon finely grated lemon zest

8 large egg whites, at room temperature

¼ teaspoon salt

GLAZE

½ cup confectioners' sugar

1 tablespoon unsalted butter, softened

1 tablespoon low-fat milk

½ teaspoon pure vanilla extract

½ teaspoon poppy seeds

I. MAKE THE MUFFINS: Preheat the oven to 400°. Lightly spray a standard-size 12-cup muffin pan with vegetable cooking spray and line the cups with paper or foil liners.

2. In a bowl, sift the flour with the confectioners' sugar and granulated sugar. Stir in the poppy seeds and lemon zest.

3. In a large bowl, using an electric mixer, beat the egg whites with the salt at high speed until stiff peaks form. Using a large rubber spatula, fold the dry ingredients into the wet ingredients in 3 batches.

4. Spoon the batter into the prepared muffin cups and bake for 15 minutes, or until the muffins are golden and firm to the touch. Transfer the pan to a wire rack and leave the muffins in the pan to cool completely. Run the tip of a small knife around the muffins to loosen them, if necessary, then unmold them.

5. MAKE THE GLAZE: In a small bowl, beat the confectioners' sugar with the butter, milk and vanilla until smooth. Spread the glaze evenly over the tops of the muffins and sprinkle with the poppy seeds. Let the glaze set completely before serving.

—*Diana Sturgis*

ONE MUFFIN Calories 121 kcal, Total Fat 1.5 gm, Saturated Fat 0.7 gm, Protein 3 gm, Carbohydrates 24 gm

Cranberry Muffins with Walnut Crumb Topping

MAKES 12 MUFFINS ●

CRUMB TOPPING

¼ cup walnut pieces

½ cup all-purpose flour

2 tablespoons granulated sugar

2 tablespoons light brown sugar

¼ teaspoon baking powder

Pinch of salt

2½ tablespoons unsalted butter, melted

MUFFINS

2 cups all-purpose flour

½ cup plus 1½ tablespoons granulated sugar

2 teaspoons baking powder

½ teaspoon baking soda

Pinch of salt

1 cup plain low-fat yogurt

1 large egg, lightly beaten

1 stick (4 ounces) unsalted butter, melted and cooled

1½ cups fresh or frozen cranberries

GLAZE

1 cup confectioners' sugar

1½ tablespoons water

I. Preheat the oven to 425°. Lightly grease the cups and top of a 12-cup nonstick muffin pan.

2. MAKE THE CRUMB TOPPING: In a pie plate, toast the walnuts for 5 minutes, or until browned and fragrant; cool. In a large bowl, mix the flour with the sugars, baking powder and salt. Stir in the butter, then add the walnuts and pinch the topping mixture into clumps.

Cranberry Muffins with
Walnut Crumb Topping

3. MAKE THE MUFFINS: In a medium bowl, mix the flour with ½ cup of sugar, baking powder, baking soda and salt. In another bowl, mix the yogurt with the egg and butter; stir in the dry ingredients. Toss the cranberries with the remaining 1½ tablespoons of sugar and fold into the muffin batter.

4. Spoon the batter into the muffin cups and cover with the crumb topping. Gently press the topping onto the muffins so it adheres. Bake for 20 minutes, or until the muffins are golden and a toothpick inserted in the center comes out clean. Let the muffins cool in the pan for 5 minutes, then transfer to a rack set over a baking sheet.

5. MAKE THE GLAZE: In a medium bowl, mix the confectioners' sugar with the water until smooth and barely runny. Drizzle the glaze over the warm muffins and let it set. Serve the muffins warm or at room temperature.

—*Grace Parisi*

Squash-Cardamom Tea Bread

8 SERVINGS ●●

- 2 cups all-purpose flour
- 2 tablespoons cornstarch
- 1 teaspoon baking soda
- 1 teaspoon ground cardamom
- 1 teaspoon ground ginger
- ½ teaspoon cinnamon
- ½ teaspoon salt
- 4 tablespoons unsalted butter, at room temperature
- 1 cup sugar
- 3 large eggs
- 1 teaspoon pure vanilla extract
- 1 cup Simple Squash Puree (p. 95)
- ¼ cup buttermilk

1. Preheat the oven to 350°. Coat a 9-by-5-inch loaf pan with cooking spray. Sift the flour, cornstarch, baking soda, cardamom, ginger, cinnamon and salt.

2. Using an electric mixer, beat the butter at high speed until fluffy. Gradually beat in the sugar. Add the eggs,

1 at a time, beating between additions. Beat in the vanilla. At low speed, beat in the flour mixture, alternating with the Squash Puree and buttermilk. Scrape the batter into the prepared pan and smooth the top. Bake for 55 minutes, or until a toothpick comes out clean. Let the cake cool in the pan for 15 minutes. Turn it out onto a rack, then invert and let cool completely.

—*Suki Hertz*

ONE SERVING Calories 298 kcal, Total Fat 7.9 gm, Saturated Fat 4.2 gm

Herb and Ginger Sandwiches

MAKES 12 TEA SANDWICHES ●●

To add substance to these delicate open-faced sandwiches, you can add thin slices of smoked salmon or tuna.

- ¼ cup light cream cheese, softened
- 1 teaspoon finely grated fresh ginger
- ½ teaspoon fresh lime juice
- Salt
- 1 tablespoon minced tarragon
- 1 tablespoon finely chopped chives
- 2 tablespoons chopped parsley
- 12 thin diagonal slices of baguette
- 24 to 36 paper-thin slices of European seedless cucumber

1. In a small bowl, mix the light cream cheese with the ginger, lime juice and salt. Cover and refrigerate.

2. In a bowl, mix the tarragon with the chives and parsley. Spread each baguette slice with 1 teaspoon of the cheese and top with 1 teaspoon of the herbs. Cover with the cucumber slices and serve. —*Sally Schneider*

THREE SANDWICHES Calories 99 kcal, Total Fat 4 gm, Saturated Fat 2.2 gm

MAKE AHEAD These sandwiches can be refrigerated for up to 1 hour.

Roasted Portobello and Vegetable Club Sandwiches

4 SERVINGS ●●

- 2 large portobello mushroom caps
- ¼ cup pure olive oil
- Salt and freshly ground black pepper
- ½ cup mayonnaise
- 2 tablespoons Dijon mustard
- 2 tablespoons fresh lemon juice
- ⅛ teaspoon cayenne pepper
- 12 slices of whole-grain bread, lightly toasted
- 1 avocado, sliced ¼ inch thick
- 3 ounces shredded Gruyère
- 1 cup packed arugula leaves
- 1 small European cucumber, very thinly sliced crosswise
- 2 cups packed alfalfa sprouts

1. Preheat the oven to 400°. Place the mushrooms on a rimmed baking

Roasted Portobello and Vegetable Club Sandwiches

sheet. Brush both sides of the mushrooms with the olive oil and season generously with salt and pepper. Roast the mushrooms for 15 minutes, or until tender and browned. Let cool, then thinly slice.

2. In a bowl, blend the mayonnaise, mustard, lemon juice and cayenne. Season this aioli with salt and black pepper.

3. Lay 4 slices of the toast on a work surface and spread them with aioli. Top with the sliced avocado and the shredded Gruyère. Spread 4 slices of toast on both sides with aioli and set on the sandwiches. Top with the arugula, cucumber, sliced portobellos and sprouts. Cover with the remaining toast, cut the sandwiches in half and serve. —*Tom Valenti*

Grilled Chile-Cheese Toasts

4 SERVINGS ●

Fresh spices and jalapeños add a twist to these open-faced grilled cheese sandwiches. Serve them with a mixed green salad for a satisfying lunch.

- 1 pound whole milk mozzarella, shredded
- ½ cup finely chopped onion
- 1 medium tomato, finely chopped and drained on paper towels

Grilled Chile-Cheese Toasts

Two-Cheese Croque-Monsieurs

- 2 jalapeños, seeded and finely chopped
- ½ cup chopped cilantro
- ½ cup mayonnaise
- ½ teaspoon cayenne pepper
- Salt and freshly ground black pepper
- Twelve ½-inch-thick slices of hearty whole wheat bread

1. Preheat the broiler. In a large bowl, mash together all of the ingredients except the bread.

2. Arrange the bread slices on a baking sheet and toast them until lightly browned. Let cool slightly, then turn the toasts over and spread the mozzarella cheese mixture on top. Broil for 3 to 5 minutes, until melted and lightly browned. Serve hot. —*Suvir Saran*

Two-Cheese Croque-Monsieurs

6 SERVINGS ●

- Twelve ½-inch-thick slices of dense peasant or sourdough bread
- 6 ounces thinly sliced Gruyère
- 1 pound thinly sliced baked smoked ham
- 12 arugula leaves, stemmed

- 1 cup shredded sharp English Cheddar (6 ounces)
- 3 large eggs, beaten
- 1 tablespoon water
- 1 tablespoon finely chopped flat-leaf parsley
- ½ teaspoon finely chopped tarragon
- ½ teaspoon finely chopped thyme
- 2 tablespoons unsalted butter
- Whole grain mustard, for serving

1. Top half of the bread slices with the Gruyère and ham. Trim the overhang and add to the sandwiches. Top with the arugula and Cheddar.

2. In a bowl, beat the eggs with the water. Dip 1 side of the remaining bread slices into the egg; top the sandwiches with the bread, egg side up, and sprinkle with the parsley, tarragon and thyme.

3. Melt 1 tablespoon of the butter on a cast-iron griddle. Add the sandwiches, egg side up, and cook over moderately low heat until golden on the bottom, about 4 minutes; transfer to a work surface. Melt the remaining 1 tablespoon of butter on the griddle. Return the sandwiches to the griddle, egg side down. Cook, pressing lightly with a spatula, until golden and the cheese is melted, 3 to 4 minutes longer. Cut the sandwiches in half and serve with mustard. —*William Sherer*

WINE With its silky texture, vibrant fruit and easy tannins, the 1999 Edmunds St. John Rocks and Gravel Grenache, Mourvèdre and Syrah blend from California is a lovely match for the Two-Cheese Croque Monsieurs. Its toastiness matches the smoky flavor of the ham, and its peppery, lavender tones echo the Provençal herbs.

Chicken, Avocado and Tomato Wraps

6 SERVINGS

Here, thin sheets of soft lavash, which crisp up nicely on the grill, are layered with chicken, cheese, avocados, chard, tomatoes and seasoned yogurt. The yogurt needs to drain overnight, so plan accordingly.

Two ½-pound skinless, boneless
    chicken breast halves, pounded
    ¼ inch thick
  2 tablespoons extra-virgin olive oil,
    plus more for brushing
Salt and freshly ground pepper
Vegetable oil, for the grill
  ½ pound Swiss chard leaves or
    spinach leaves
  2 cups whole milk yogurt,
    drained overnight
  2 large garlic cloves, minced
Four 9-by-10-inch sheets of lavash
  6 ounces Monterey Jack, thinly sliced
  2 avocados, cut crosswise into
    ¼-inch slices
  1 tablespoon plus 1 teaspoon
    fresh lemon juice
Hot sauce
  2 large yellow tomatoes, sliced
    ¼ inch thick

Chicken, Avocado and Tomato Wraps

1. Light a grill or preheat a grill pan. Brush the chicken breasts with olive oil and season with salt and pepper. Lightly brush the grate or grill pan with vegetable oil and cook the chicken over a hot fire until browned and just cooked through, about 3 minutes per side. Transfer to a plate and let cool to room temperature.

2. In a medium saucepan of boiling water, blanch the chard leaves for 1½ minutes; blanch the spinach for 30 seconds. Drain well. Let cool slightly, then squeeze dry and coarsely chop. In a large bowl, mix the chard with the 2 tablespoons of olive oil and season with salt. Stir in the drained yogurt and the garlic and season with salt and pepper.

3. For each wrap, arrange 2 sheets of lavash on a work surface, overlapping the short sides by 5 inches. Tuck half of the cheese slices under the overlapping flap to within ½ inch of the edge. Spread half of the avocado slices on top of the overlapping flap and sprinkle with half of the lemon juice; season generously with salt, pepper and hot sauce. Top with half of the tomato slices and season with salt and pepper. For each wrap, fold 1 of the flaps of lavash over the tomatoes and spread half of the chard on the lavash. Top with a chicken breast, trimming it to fit. Fold the second lavash flap over the chicken. Repeat to assemble the second sandwich. Tightly wrap the sandwiches in foil and refrigerate until firm or for up to 4 hours.

4. Light a grill. Unwrap the sandwiches and brush both sides with olive oil. Lightly brush the grate with vegetable oil. Grill the sandwiches over a low fire, cheese side down, for about 4 minutes, or until the cheese melts and the lavash is crisp. Using 2 large spatulas, carefully flip the sandwiches and grill for 5 minutes longer, or until they are heated through and very crisp.

Transfer to a cutting board. Using a serrated knife, cut each sandwich crosswise into thirds and serve.

—*Marcia Kiesel*

BEER An ice-cold, very dry pilsner-style beer, such as Pilsner Urquell or Grolsch, will pair well with the tangy, spicy flavors of this sandwich.

Smoked Turkey and Arugula Quesadillas

4 SERVINGS ●

Vegetable oil, for brushing
Four 10-inch flour tortillas
½ **pound pepper Jack, shredded or thinly sliced**
¾ **pound thinly sliced smoked turkey**
1 **tablespoon extra-virgin olive oil**
2 **teaspoons fresh lime juice**
1 **teaspoon sour cream, plus more for serving**
¾ **pound arugula, thick stems discarded**
2 **plum tomatoes—halved, seeded and diced**
Salt and freshly ground pepper
Hot sauce and lime wedges, for serving

1. Preheat the oven to 450°. Lightly brush 2 large baking sheets with vegetable oil and heat in the oven for 5 minutes. Lightly oil 1 side of each tortilla and place them oiled side down on the baking sheet. Layer the cheese and turkey on the tortillas and bake until the cheese is melted and the bottoms of the tortillas are golden, 4 to 5 minutes.

2. Meanwhile, in a large bowl, mix the olive oil with the lime juice and sour cream. Add the arugula and tomatoes, season with salt and pepper and toss well. Transfer the tortillas to a work surface, top with the arugula salad and fold in half to close. Cut each quesadilla into 3 wedges and serve right away with sour cream, hot sauce and lime wedges on the side.

—*Grace Parisi*

Grilled Pork Tenderloin on Cornmeal-Cheddar Biscuits with Spiced Ketchup

10 SERVINGS ●●●
The marinade here also works well with beef, lamb, chicken and fish.

1½ **teaspoons coriander seeds**
1½ **teaspoons cumin seeds**
¾ **teaspoon fennel seeds**
1 **cup cilantro**
1 **cup extra-virgin olive oil**
1 **medium onion, quartered**
½ **cup mint leaves**
1 **tablespoon fresh orange juice**
1 **teaspoon finely grated orange zest**
5 **pounds whole pork tenderloins**
Freshly ground pepper
Salt
Vegetable oil, for the grill
Cornmeal-Cheddar Biscuits and Spiced Tomato Ketchup (recipes follow), for serving

1. In a small skillet, lightly toast the coriander, cumin and fennel seeds over moderate heat until fragrant, about 2 minutes. Transfer to a plate and let cool. In a spice or coffee grinder, grind the seeds to a fine powder.

2. In a blender, combine the cilantro with the olive oil, onion, mint, orange juice and zest; puree until smooth. Scrape the marinade into a large glass baking dish. Stir in the ground spices. Season the pork with pepper and add to the marinade; turn to coat. Refrigerate for 2 to 4 hours, turning occasionally.

3. Light a grill or preheat a grill pan. Remove the pork from the marinade and scrape off any excess. Season generously with salt and pepper. Lightly brush the grate with vegetable oil. Grill the tenderloins over a medium-hot fire or in the grill pan, turning occasionally, for 20 to 25 minutes, or until an instant-read thermometer inserted in the thickest part registers 140° for medium.

4. Transfer the tenderloins to a cutting

Grilled Pork Tenderloin on
Cornmeal-Cheddar Biscuits
with Spiced Ketchup

board and let them rest for 5 minutes. Cut the meat into ¼-inch-thick slices. Split the Cornmeal-Cheddar Biscuits, spread with Spiced Tomato Ketchup and make sandwiches with the pork.

—*Danielle Custer*

MAKE AHEAD The grilled pork can be refrigerated for 2 days; let it return to room temperature before serving.

WINE A simple, fresh, fruity-spicy and versatile Pinot Noir from Oregon will perfectly complement the smoky pork tenderloin and the spicy-sweet tomato ketchup. Two excellent choices are the inexpensive 1997 King Estate and the 1998 Benton-Lane.

CORNMEAL-CHEDDAR BISCUITS

MAKES TWENTY 2½-INCH
BISCUITS ● ● ●

- 3 cups all-purpose flour
- 4 ounces extra-sharp Cheddar, shredded (1½ cups)
- ¾ cup stone-ground cornmeal
- 2 tablespoons sugar
- 1½ tablespoons chopped thyme
- 1 tablespoon baking powder
- 1¼ teaspoons salt
- ¾ teaspoon baking soda
- 1 stick (4 ounces) cold unsalted butter, cut into tablespoons
- 1½ cups buttermilk
- 2 large egg yolks

1. Preheat the oven to 400°. In a bowl, using a fork, stir the flour, cheese, cornmeal, sugar, thyme, baking powder, salt and baking soda. Using a pastry blender or 2 knives, cut in the butter until the mixture resembles coarse meal.

2. In a small bowl, whisk the buttermilk with the egg yolks. Add the liquid ingredients to the dry ingredients and stir with a fork until a dough forms.

3. Turn the dough out onto a lightly floured surface and pat it into a ½-inch-thick disk. Using a 2½-inch round biscuit cutter, cut out as many biscuits as possible. Transfer the biscuits to a baking sheet. Gather the dough and repeat, handling the dough as little as possible.

4. Bake the biscuits in the upper and lower thirds of the oven for 18 minutes, or until golden; switch the pans halfway through baking. Transfer the biscuits to racks and let cool slightly and serve. —*D.C.*

SPICED TOMATO KETCHUP

MAKES ABOUT 1½ CUPS ● ● ●

- 2 pounds plum tomatoes, coarsely chopped
- ¾ cup plus 2 tablespoons sugar
- ¼ cup water
- Two 1-inch strips of lemon zest
- ¼ teaspoon ground allspice
- ¼ teaspoon cinnamon
- Salt and freshly ground pepper

1. In a medium saucepan, combine the chopped tomatoes with the sugar, water, lemon zest, allspice and cinnamon and bring to a boil over high heat, stirring occasionally. Reduce the heat to moderately low and simmer briskly, stirring occasionally, until the ketchup has thickened and reduced to 1½ cups, about 25 minutes.

2. Remove the lemon zest. Pass the ketchup through a coarse strainer, pressing on the solids; discard the solids. Let cool to room temperature and season with salt and pepper.

—*D.C.*

MAKE AHEAD The ketchup can be refrigerated for up to 5 days.

Inside-Out Roquefort Cheeseburgers

4 SERVINGS

Although cooking hamburgers to at least 160°—or medium doneness—prevents food-borne illnesses, it robs the meat of its juiciness. A delicious solution to this problem is to tuck a disk of ultra-rich Roquefort butter into the center of each burger. The butter melts as the burger grills, basting it from within. Another key to a really great burger is to handle the meat as little as possible.

- 2 ounces Roquefort, softened
- 4 tablespoons unsalted butter, softened
- 1½ pounds ground sirloin
- Four ½-inch-thick slices of sweet onion, such as Vidalia
- Four ½-inch-thick beefsteak tomato slices
- 2 tablespoons extra-virgin olive oil
- Salt and freshly ground pepper
- Vegetable oil, for the grill
- 4 kaiser rolls, split
- 4 ounces arugula

1. In a small bowl, blend the Roquefort with the butter. Scrape the butter onto

Inside-Out Roquefort Cheeseburger

Grilled Flank Steak Sandwiches

plastic wrap and roll into a 4-inch cylinder. Refrigerate the Roquefort butter until firm, about 1 hour. Slice the butter into 4 disks.

2. Gently shape the ground sirloin into 4 thick patties. Using your thumb, make a depression in the center of each patty and fill with a disk of Roquefort butter. Fold the meat over to encase the butter completely and gently pat the burger into a plump, round patty.

3. Light a grill. Thread each onion slice onto a skewer. Brush the onion and tomato slices with 1 tablespoon of olive oil and season with salt and pepper. Lightly brush the grate with vegetable oil. Grill the onions over a medium-hot fire until charred and tender, about 5 minutes per side. Grill the tomato slices until charred, about 1 minute per side.

4. Season the burgers with salt and pepper and grill over a medium-hot fire until browned and cooked through, about 6 minutes per side. Transfer to a platter and let stand for 2 minutes. Brush the cut sides of the rolls with the remaining 1 tablespoon of olive oil and grill until lightly browned, about 10 seconds. Set the burgers on the rolls, top with the onion, tomato and arugula and serve. —*Steven Raichlen*
MAKE AHEAD The Roquefort butter can be refrigerated for 2 days or frozen for 1 month. The uncooked burgers can

be refrigerated for up to 6 hours.
WINE Balance the intense flavor and richness of the Roquefort butter filling with a smoky, fruity, inexpensive Cabernet Sauvignon. Try the 1998 Viñas del Vero Somontano from Spain or the bargain 1999 De Martino from Chile.

Grilled Flank Steak Sandwiches
8 SERVINGS ●

One 1¾-pound flank steak
  1 tablespoon Dijon mustard
  ¼ cup dry red wine
  ¼ cup pure olive oil
  4 large garlic cloves
  ½ teaspoon finely chopped thyme
  ½ cup mayonnaise
  1 teaspoon fresh lemon juice
Salt and freshly ground pepper
  8 rosemary focaccia or other rolls, split
  ½ pound sliced imported provolone or Fontina
  8 lettuce leaves

1. Brush the flank steak on both sides with the Dijon mustard. Put the steak in a sturdy resealable plastic bag and add the red wine. Seal the bag, pressing out any air, and refrigerate overnight. Drain the steak, pat dry and bring to room temperature before grilling.

2. Meanwhile, in a small saucepan, combine the olive oil and garlic cloves

and cook over low heat until the garlic is golden and soft, about 15 minutes. Using a slotted spoon, transfer the garlic to a small bowl; reserve the garlic oil. Add the thyme to the garlic and mash to a paste. Stir in the mayonnaise and lemon juice and season with salt and pepper.

3. Light a charcoal grill or preheat a cast-iron grill pan. Brush the steak with the reserved garlic oil, season liberally with salt and pepper and grill over moderate heat for about 15 minutes, turning once, for medium-rare meat. Transfer the steak to a cutting board to rest for 5 minutes. Thinly slice the meat across the grain on the diagonal.

4. Spread the garlic mayonnaise on the rolls and top with the flank steak, cheese and lettuce. Cut the sandwiches in half and serve. —*Michael Kramer*
MAKE AHEAD The sandwiches can be made 6 hours ahead.

Hot Strip Steak Sandwiches
6 SERVINGS

A good-quality beef or veal demiglace is the key to this flavorful steak sandwich.
  1 cup Pinot Noir
  ½ cup beef or veal demiglace (see Note)
  1 cup Niçoise olives, pitted
Salt and freshly ground pepper
  ¼ cup extra-virgin olive oil
  1 large Spanish onion, thinly sliced lengthwise
  1 large red bell pepper, cored and thinly sliced lengthwise
  1 large green bell pepper, cored and thinly sliced lengthwise
  2 pounds strip steak, sliced ⅛ inch thick across the grain
  2 large baguettes, cut in half
  4 cups baby spinach (5 ounces)

1. In a medium saucepan, boil the wine until reduced to ⅓ cup. Add the demiglace and cook until reduced to ½ cup, about 10 minutes longer;

PICNIC MENU

marinated portobellos with olives and goat cheese (p. 299)
japanese coleslaw with sesame seeds (p. 65)
chilled asparagus with crab vinaigrette (p. 38)
lobster salad with potatoes, corn and tomatoes (p. 39)
grilled vegetable salad with pesto dressing (p. 70)
grilled flank steak sandwiches
south carolina peach and blueberry tartlets (p. 338)

1999 BERINGER NAPA VALLEY SAUVIGNON BLANC
1996 RUFFINO CHIANTI CLASSICO SANTEDAME

remove from the heat. Add the olives and season with salt and pepper. Cover and keep warm.

2. In a large cast-iron skillet, heat 1 tablespoon of the olive oil until almost smoking. Add the onion and cook over moderate heat, stirring frequently, until softened and browned, about 10 minutes. Transfer the onion to a bowl. Add another tablespoon of the olive oil to the skillet along with the bell peppers and cook over moderate heat, stirring frequently, until softened and browned, about 10 minutes. Add the peppers to the onion and season with salt and pepper.

3. Wipe out the skillet. Heat another tablespoon of the olive oil over high heat until shimmering. Season one-third of the steak slices with salt and pepper and add them to the skillet in a

Hot Strip Steak Sandwich

single layer without crowding. Cook until browned on the bottoms, about 30 seconds. Flip the steak slices and cook for about 20 seconds longer for medium; transfer the meat to a plate and keep warm. Heat the remaining 1 tablespoon of olive oil in the skillet, season and cook the remaining steak in 2 batches.

4. Arrange the seared steak slices on the bottom halves of the baguettes and drizzle any accumulated juices on the cut sides of the top halves. Top the steak with the onion and peppers, the spinach and the wine and olive sauce. Close the baguettes, cut each in thirds and serve. —*Rajat Parr*

NOTE Beef and veal demiglace are available at specialty food shops.

WINE A steak sandwich is obviously meaty, but this one's not too heavy. That's why it pairs well with a wine like the medium-bodied 1998 Cayuse Walla Walla Valley Syrah from Washington State. The Syrah's fruit also goes beautifully with the steak sandwich's Pinot Noir sauce.

Seared Beef Tenderloin and Avocado Sandwiches

4 SERVINGS ●

This sandwich is popular in Chile, where it is known as *churrasco*. It combines spicy seared beef, a smooth avocado spread and a vibrant tomato salad.

- 1 medium tomato, finely chopped
- 1 tablespoon finely chopped cilantro
- 1 small garlic clove, minced
- 1 small jalapeño, seeded and minced
- 3 tablespoons canola oil

Salt and freshly ground pepper

- 1 ripe Hass avocado, peeled
- 1 pound beef tenderloin, sliced ½ inch thick and pounded to a ¼-inch thickness
- 4 soft rolls, split
- ¼ cup mayonnaise

1. In a medium bowl, toss the tomato with the cilantro, garlic, jalapeño and 1 tablespoon of the canola oil. Season with salt and pepper. In another bowl, mash the avocado and season with salt and pepper.

2. In a large, heavy skillet, heat 1 tablespoon of the oil until shimmering. Season the meat with salt and pepper and add half to the skillet. Cook over high heat until the meat is browned around the edges but still pink in the center, about 1½ minutes. Turn and cook for 1 minute longer for medium. Transfer the meat to a large plate. Repeat with the remaining half of the meat and 1 tablespoon of oil.

3. Spread the avocado on the bottom halves of the rolls and the mayonnaise on the top halves. Arrange the meat on the avocado, top with the tomatoes and drizzle with the tomato and meat juices. Set the tops on the sandwiches and serve immediately.

—*Ruth Van Waerebeek*

WINE A fruity, rustic red with lots of flavor and good acidity, such as a Zinfandel, best complements this spicy beef and creamy avocado sandwich. Two good examples: the 1999 Cline California and the 1999 Montevina Amador County.

Summer Tomato Pissaladière

8 SERVINGS ●

The traditional Provençal onion pizza, pissaladière, is a jumping-off point for this tomato tart. The base is pastry dough instead of pizza dough, and it is topped with chopped onions, garlic and zucchini and a layer of sliced tomatoes and halved cherry tomatoes. The classic garnish of anchovy fillets decorates the tart.

PASTRY DOUGH

- 2 cups all-purpose flour
- ¼ teaspoon salt
- 1 stick cold unsalted butter, cut into small pieces
- 2 large eggs, beaten

TOPPING

- 2 garlic cloves, minced
- 1 small onion, finely chopped
- 1 small zucchini, cut into ¼-inch dice

Salt and freshly ground pepper

- 2 pounds assorted medium to large tomatoes, sliced ¼ inch thick
- ½ pound red cherry tomatoes, halved
- 1 tablespoon herbes de Provence

One 3-ounce jar of anchovy fillets, drained

- ¼ cup freshly grated Parmesan

Extra-virgin olive oil, for drizzling

I. MAKE THE PASTRY DOUGH: In a food processor, pulse the flour with salt. Add the butter and pulse until the mixture resembles coarse meal. Add the eggs and pulse until the dough looks like wet sand. Transfer the dough to a work surface and pack it into a ball. Using the palm of your hand, flatten into a disk, wrap in plastic and refrigerate until chilled, about 2 hours.

2. Preheat the oven to 375°. On a lightly floured work surface, roll out the dough to a 13-by-16-inch rectangle about ¼ inch thick. Fold the dough in half and, using 2 large spatulas, transfer the dough to a large baking sheet, then unfold it. Refrigerate the dough until firm, about 15 minutes.

3. ASSEMBLE THE TART: Fold up the edges of the dough to make a 12-by-15-inch rectangle. Scatter the garlic, onion and zucchini on the dough and season with salt and pepper. Arrange the tomato slices in slightly overlapping rows inside the rim of dough. Fill in any gaps with the cherry tomatoes. Season with the herbes de Provence and salt and pepper. Decorate with the anchovy fillets. Sprinkle the Parmesan over the tart and drizzle with olive oil.

4. Bake the tart in the upper third of the oven for 30 minutes. Move the baking sheet to the lowest oven rack and bake for 25 to 30 minutes longer, or until the crust is crisp and browned and the cheese is lightly browned. Let the pissaladière cool for about 5 minutes, then cut it into 4-inch squares. Serve the tomato tart warm or at room temperature.

—*Stéphane Garnier*

MAKE AHEAD The dough can be refrigerated overnight or frozen for 2 weeks.

WINE A fresh-tasting Sauvignon Blanc with high acidity will balance the saltiness of the anchovies and match the tanginess of the tomatoes in the pissaladière. Look for an example from the Loire Valley, such as the citrusy, herbal 1999 Domaine Sautereau Sancerre or the richer 1998 Pascal Jolivet Pouilly-Fumé La Grande Cuvée.

Two-Potato Pizza with Olives and Garlic

4 TO 6 SERVINGS

This pizza is true comfort food: Carbohydrates—in ample supply in potatoes and pizza dough—raise serotonin levels in the brain, thus alleviating stress and anxiety.

- 1 pound pizza dough, at room temperature

All-purpose flour, for dusting

- ¼ cup plus 2½ tablespoons extra-virgin olive oil
- 1 large sweet potato (1 pound), peeled and cut into ½-inch dice
- 1 large Yukon Gold potato (¾ pound), peeled and cut into ½-inch dice
- 5 large garlic cloves, halved lengthwise

Three 6-inch rosemary sprigs

- 1 cup green and black brine-cured olives (6 ounces), such as Picholine, Calamata and Gaeta, pitted
- 1 scallion, white and light green parts, thinly sliced

Coarse sea salt

Pinch of crushed red pepper

I. Preheat the oven to 500°. Preheat a pizza stone or oil a large baking sheet.

2. On a floured surface, roll or stretch the dough to an 8-inch round; let stand for 10 minutes. Roll or stretch the dough to a 13-inch round. Transfer to a floured pizza peel or rimless cookie sheet.

3. Heat ¼ cup of the olive oil in a large nonstick skillet until shimmering. Add all of the diced potatoes and cook over moderately high heat, turning occasionally, until barely tender, about 10 minutes. Add the garlic and rosemary and cook, shaking the skillet, until the garlic is golden and the potatoes are golden brown, about 10 minutes longer.

4. Remove the rosemary sprigs and garlic. Pick off the rosemary leaves and add to the potatoes. Transfer the garlic to a mini food processor. Add the olives and scallion and pulse until finely chopped. Scrape the mixture into the skillet, toss with the potatoes and season with sea salt and crushed red pepper.

5. Transfer half of the potatoes to a bowl and mash coarsely. Spread the mashed potatoes all over the pizza dough, leaving a 1-inch border. Top with the remaining potatoes and brush the crust with ½ tablespoon of the olive oil.

6. Slide the pizza onto the hot stone or oiled baking sheet and bake for 10 minutes on the stone or 16 minutes on the sheet. The pizza is done when the crust is golden brown. Transfer to a rack to cool slightly. Drizzle the remaining 2 tablespoons of oil on the pizza and sprinkle with salt. Cut into wedges and serve. —*Grace Parisi*

WINE The slightly bitter and briny flavors of the tapenade should be contrasted with a refreshing, low-alcohol Riesling or a fruity red. Two good choices are the 1998 Hugel Alsace Jubilee Riesling and the 1995 Bolla Le Poiane Valpolicella Classico.

11 vegetables

the good fat

Olive oil is fat, right? So what makes it so good for you? That's easy. Olive oil is monounsaturated, making it a good fat—a fat that wipes out the wrong kind of cholesterol (LDL) and cheers on the good kind (HDL). There's also evidence that olive oil helps prevent the mental decline that can come with age. Another good thing: Because extra-virgin olive oil isn't refined, it retains antioxidants that help protect you against many different kinds of cancer. This doesn't mean that you should add olive oil to a diet that already has plenty of fat in it; the healthy approach is to substitute olive oil for other fats.

Tuscan-Style Sautéed Spinach

6 SERVINGS ● ●

One of the best and simplest ways to prepare greens is to boil or steam them until almost cooked, then sauté them in olive oil with garlic.

- 2 pounds baby spinach
- ½ cup water
- 3 tablespoons extra-virgin olive oil
- 1 large garlic clove, minced

Pinch of crushed red pepper

Salt

- 1 tablespoon fresh lemon juice

1. In a large pot, combine the spinach with the water and bring to a boil. Cover and cook over moderately low heat until just wilted, about 10 minutes. Drain the spinach, pressing out as much water as possible; chop coarsely.

2. Heat the olive oil in a large skillet. Add the garlic and cook over moderately low heat until softened and lightly browned, about 2 minutes. Add the spinach, crushed red pepper and a generous pinch of salt and cook, tossing until heated through, about 3 minutes. Add the lemon juice and serve.

—*Nancy Harmon Jenkins*

ONE SERVING Calories 76 kcal, Total Fat 7.2 gm, Saturated Fat 0.9 gm, Protein 4 gm, Carbohydrates 1 gm

MAKE AHEAD The recipe can be prepared through Step 1 and refrigerated overnight.

Spinach with Porcini and Rosemary

8 SERVINGS ● ●

Dried porcini and fresh rosemary contribute an intensely woodsy and aromatic character to this side dish.

- 1 cup dried porcini (½ ounce)
- 1 cup boiling water
- 4 tablespoons unsalted butter
- 2 large garlic cloves, minced
- 1 tablespoon finely chopped rosemary
- 4½ pounds spinach, large stems discarded

Salt and freshly ground pepper

1. Soak the porcini in the boiling water until softened, about 20 minutes. Drain the porcini, reserving the liquid separately. Rinse the mushrooms to remove any grit, then coarsely chop.

2. Melt the butter in a large, deep skillet. Add the porcini and garlic and cook over moderate heat until golden, about 3 minutes. Add the rosemary and cook for 1 minute. Pour in half of the porcini soaking liquid and simmer until reduced to 2 tablespoons, about 5 minutes. Add the spinach, 1 large handful at a time, tossing and letting it wilt slightly before adding more. Cook over moderate heat, stirring, until tender but still bright green, about 4 minutes. Season with salt and pepper and serve.

—*Jamie Oliver*

Baby Spinach and Garlic Bread Pudding

4 SERVINGS

This bread pudding is almost like a tart, with the croutons acting as a crunchy crust. Tender baby spinach in the filling turns incredibly silky when cooked.

- 2 tablespoons unsalted butter
- 15 ounces baby spinach, stems removed
- 2 tablespoons water
- 1 small garlic clove, minced

Kosher salt and freshly ground pepper

- ¼ pound French baguette, crusts removed, bread cut into ¼-inch dice (1 cup)
- 2 large eggs
- ¾ cup heavy cream

Pinch of freshly grated nutmeg

1. Preheat the oven to 325°. Butter a 6-cup soufflé dish or other deep baking dish. In a large skillet, melt ½ tablespoon of butter over moderately high heat. Add the spinach, water and garlic, season with salt and pepper and stir a few times. Cover and cook the spinach until it wilts, about 2 minutes.

2. Set a colander over a bowl and drain the spinach; press very lightly on the spinach to extract ¼ cup of liquid. Spread out the spinach on a rimmed baking sheet to cool.

3. Heat the remaining 1½ tablespoons of butter in a large skillet. Add the diced bread and cook over moderate heat until browned on the bottom, about 3 minutes. Stir and continue to cook until the croutons are crisp all over, about 2 minutes longer. Transfer the croutons to a plate to cool.

4. In a bowl, whisk the eggs with the cream, reserved spinach cooking liquid, ½ teaspoon of salt, ⅛ teaspoon of pepper and the nutmeg. Stir in the spinach and pour the mixture into the prepared soufflé dish. Spread the fried croutons evenly over the top.

5. Set the soufflé dish in a roasting pan and pour enough hot water into the pan to reach one-third of the way up the side of the soufflé dish. Bake the bread pudding for 35 to 40 minutes, or until set. Let the pudding cool slightly, then serve directly from the soufflé dish or invert it onto a platter and serve.

—*Eberhard Müller*

The Baby Spinach and Garlic Bread Pudding can be prepared in advance through Step 3. Refrigerate the spinach, and store the croutons in an airtight container, overnight.

Sautéed Mixed Greens with Olives and Ricotta Salata

4 SERVINGS ●

    5 tablespoons extra-virgin olive oil
    2 tablespoons pine nuts
    4 garlic cloves, thinly sliced
    1 pound kale, large stems
      discarded, leaves rinsed and
      cut into 1-inch pieces
Salt
    1 head of escarole (about 1 pound),
      cored and cut into 3-inch pieces
    1 pound spinach, stemmed
    ¼ cup pitted Calamata olives,
      coarsely chopped
    1 tablespoon drained capers
Freshly ground pepper
    3 ounces ricotta salata or feta,
      cut into small dice (¾ cup)
    1 tablespoon fresh lemon juice

I. Heat 3 tablespoons of the olive oil in a very large skillet. Add the pine nuts and cook over moderate heat, stirring,

Sautéed Mixed Greens with Olives and Ricotta Salata

until golden, about 3 minutes. Add the garlic and cook until golden, about 2 minutes longer.
2. Add the kale and season with salt. Cook over low heat, stirring often, until softened, about 10 minutes. Add the escarole, season with salt and cook, stirring often, until just tender, about 5 minutes longer. Stir in the spinach and cook until wilted, about 3 minutes. Stir in the remaining 2 tablespoons of olive oil, the olives and capers and season with salt and pepper. Fold in the cheese, add the lemon juice and serve.   —*Stephanie Lyness*

Brown Butter Kale

12 SERVINGS ●

    4 pounds kale, large
      stems discarded
    1½ sticks (6 ounces) unsalted butter
Salt and freshly ground pepper
Lemon wedges, for serving

I. In a large pot of boiling salted water, cook the kale until tender, about 5 minutes. Drain and let cool slightly. Squeeze dry and coarsely chop.
2. In a large, heavy casserole, cook the butter over moderately high heat until browned and nutty smelling, about 7 minutes. Add the kale and stir to coat with the butter. Season with salt and pepper. Transfer to a bowl and serve with lemon wedges.   —*Tom Douglas*
The recipe can be prepared through Step 1 and refrigerated for 1 day. Steam the kale to reheat.

Kale with Garlic and Oven-Roasted Parsnips

4 SERVINGS ●●

    1¼ pounds parsnips, peeled and cut
       into 2-by-½-inch sticks
    5 tablespoons extra-virgin olive oil
Salt and freshly ground pepper
    2 pounds kale, stems discarded
    4 garlic cloves, thinly sliced
    8 large scallions, cut into
      ½-inch lengths

I. Preheat the oven to 400°. Spread the parsnips on a large, rimmed baking sheet and toss with 2 tablespoons of the extra-virgin olive oil. Season with salt and pepper and roast in the bottom third of the oven for about 25 minutes, or until lightly browned on the bottom and tender.
2. Meanwhile, bring a large pot of water to a boil. Add salt and then the stemmed kale and cook until just tender, about 5 minutes. Drain and then squeeze out the excess water. Coarsely chop the kale.
3. Heat the remaining 3 tablespoons of olive oil in a large skillet. Add the garlic and cook over moderate heat until golden, about 2 minutes. Add the scallions and cook over moderate heat, stirring, until softened, about 2 minutes. Add the kale, season with salt and pepper and cook, stirring, until heated through, about 3 minutes.
4. Add the parsnips to the kale, warm through over moderate heat and serve.   —*FOOD & WINE Test Kitchen*
The Kale with Garlic and Oven-Roasted Parsnips can be prepared through Step 2 and refrigerated overnight. Let return to room temperature before finishing.

Swiss Chard with Chickpeas and Feta

4 TO 6 SERVINGS ●●

    ¼ cup extra-virgin olive oil
    3 pounds Swiss chard,
      stems discarded, leaves
      rinsed but not dried
    4 scallions, white and light green
      parts only, thinly sliced
    ¼ cup chopped dill
    2 garlic cloves, minced
One 19-ounce can of chickpeas,
      drained and rinsed
Salt and freshly ground pepper
    3 ounces feta cheese, crumbled

I. Preheat the oven to 400°. Coat an 8-inch-square nonreactive baking dish with 1 tablespoon of the olive oil.   ▸

2. Put the chard in a large pot, cover and cook over high heat, stirring occasionally, until wilted, about 4 minutes. Drain and rinse under cold water; squeeze dry and coarsely chop. In a medium bowl, toss the chard with the remaining 3 tablespoons of olive oil, scallions, dill, garlic and chickpeas. Season with salt and pepper.

3. Spoon the mixture into the prepared baking dish. Sprinkle the feta on top and push the cheese into the greens. Bake for 15 to 20 minutes, until sizzling hot. Serve immediately.

—*Clifford A. Wright*

Creamed Collard Greens with Parmesan Crumbs

12 SERVINGS ●

Bake the greens in individual dishes for a more sophisticated presentation.

- 2 **cups water**
- 4 **ounces smoky bacon, sliced crosswise into ¼-inch strips**
- 8 **pounds collard greens, stems and tough inner ribs discarded**
- 2 **large onions, chopped**
- ¾ **cup coarse dry bread crumbs**
- ¼ **cup plus 2 tablespoons freshly grated Parmesan**
- 1 **tablespoon minced parsley**
- 1 **teaspoon minced sage**
- 1 **garlic clove, minced**
- 1 **tablespoon extra-virgin olive oil**
- 2 **cups heavy cream**

Salt and freshly ground pepper

- 3 **large eggs, lightly beaten**

1. In a large stockpot, add the water and bacon and bring to a boil. Add the collard greens by handfuls, stirring until each batch is wilted before adding more. Bring to a boil and add the onions. Cover and simmer over moderate heat until the collards are very tender, about 40 minutes. Remove from the heat and let cool, then squeeze the collards almost dry and coarsely chop them.

2. Meanwhile, in a food processor, combine the bread crumbs with the Parmesan, parsley, sage, garlic and olive oil. Pulse until just blended.

3. Preheat the oven to 350°. Generously butter a shallow 4-quart casserole. In a large bowl, mix the collards with the cream and season with salt and pepper. Stir in the eggs until blended and spread the collards in the prepared casserole. Cover with foil and bake for 30 minutes.

4. Sprinkle the Parmesan crumbs over the collards and bake for about 20 minutes longer, or until the crumb topping is golden. Preheat the broiler and broil the collards 10 inches from the heat until the bread crumb topping is golden brown and crisp. Serve hot.

—*Scott Howell*

MAKE AHEAD The recipe can be prepared through Step 3 and refrigerated overnight. Bring to room temperature before proceeding.

Sautéed Endives with Apples and Currants

6 SERVINGS ●

- 3 **pounds Belgian endives (about 8)—halved, cored and sliced lengthwise into thin strips**
- 2 **medium tart apples, such as Granny Smith—peeled, cored and cut into thin julienne strips**
- 3 **tablespoons dried currants or coarsely chopped dark raisins**
- 3 **tablespoons confectioners' sugar**
- 2 **tablespoons fresh lemon juice**

Salt and freshly ground pepper

- 4 **tablespoons walnut oil**

In a large bowl, toss the endives with the apples and currants. Add the sugar and lemon juice, season with salt and pepper and toss well. Heat 1 tablespoon of the walnut oil in each of 2 large skillets. Add one-quarter of the endives to each skillet and cook over high heat, stirring constantly, until browned, about 5 minutes. Transfer to a large platter. Repeat with the remaining walnut oil and endives. Serve warm.

—*Ruth Van Waerebeek*

Asparagus with Butter and Parsley

4 SERVINGS ●

Look for fresh, green asparagus with firm, smooth stalks and tightly closed tips. To make the entire spear edible, peel the asparagus stalks to remove all of the fibrous skin. Begin peeling one to two inches below the tip. Once all of the spears have been peeled, cut off and discard the fibrous ends.

- 2 **dozen medium green asparagus, peeled and trimmed**
- ⅓ **cup water**
- ½ **teaspoon salt**
- 4 **tablespoons unsalted butter, cut into pieces**
- ¼ **cup finely chopped parsley**

Cut the asparagus spears on the diagonal into 1-inch lengths and put them in a medium skillet. Add the water and salt, cover and bring to a vigorous boil over high heat; boil for 1½ minutes. Uncover the skillet and add the butter and chopped parsley. Bring the water back to a strong boil, shaking the skillet constantly. Boil the asparagus for 20 to 30 seconds longer, or just until the sauce thickens and becomes foamy. Pour the cooked asparagus into a bowl and serve immediately.

—*Jacques Pépin*

Stir-Fried Asparagus

4 SERVINGS ●

- 2 **tablespoons vegetable oil**
- 1 **pound thin asparagus, cut into ⅓-inch lengths**
- 1 **large garlic clove, minced**
- 1 **teaspoon Asian sesame oil**
- ½ **teaspoon finely grated lemon zest**

Salt and freshly ground pepper

Heat the vegetable oil in a large skillet. Add the asparagus and stir-fry over moderately high heat until softened, about 5 minutes. Add the minced garlic, sesame oil and lemon zest, season with salt and freshly ground pepper and stir-fry for 2 minutes. Serve hot.

—*Alex Lee*

Asparagus and Oyster Mushroom Fricassee

Asparagus and Oyster Mushroom Fricassee

4 SERVINGS ●

2 pounds asparagus, cut on the diagonal into 1½-inch lengths

2 tablespoons unsalted butter

1½ pounds oyster mushrooms, large stems discarded, large caps halved

Salt and freshly ground pepper

1 shallot, minced

¼ cup dry white wine, such as Riesling

½ cup chicken stock or canned low-sodium broth

¾ cup heavy cream

1 tablespoon coarsely chopped flat-leaf parsley

1 tablespoon minced chives

1 tablespoon coarsely chopped chervil or 1 teaspoon minced tarragon

ı. In a medium saucepan of boiling salted water, blanch the asparagus until bright green, about 2 minutes. Drain, refresh in a bowl of ice water; drain again.

2. Melt the butter in a large skillet. Add the mushrooms in an even layer, season with salt and pepper and cook over moderate heat until browned on the bottom, about 3 minutes. Stir the mushrooms and cook until tender, about 4 minutes longer.

Add the shallot and cook, stirring, until lightly browned, about 3 minutes. Add the wine and cook until evaporated, about 30 seconds. Add the chicken stock and asparagus and simmer until the liquid has reduced to 2 tablespoons, about 2 minutes. Stir in the heavy cream and simmer over low heat until slightly thickened, about 5 minutes. Season with salt and pepper, stir in the parsley, chives and chervil and serve at once. —*Eberhard Müller*

Zucchini Baked in Parchment

4 SERVINGS ●

This recipe relies entirely on the freshness of the zucchini. Try it when you have homegrown or farmers' market produce.

4 small zucchini (6 to 7 ounces each)

4 large lemon thyme or thyme sprigs

4 fresh bay leaves

¼ cup extra-virgin olive oil

Sea salt and freshly ground pepper

ı. Preheat the oven to 375°. Set 4 foot-long sheets of parchment paper on a work surface. Put a zucchini, a lemon thyme sprig and a bay leaf in the center of each. Drizzle each zucchini with 1 tablespoon of olive oil and season with salt and pepper. Fold the paper in half over the zucchini, then fold up the 3 open sides, leaving a ½-inch border around the zucchini; staple each side once or twice to seal.

2. Set the packets on a baking sheet and bake for 45 minutes, or until the zucchini is very tender. Transfer the packets to dinner plates, open carefully and serve at once. —*Guy Martin*

Grilled Vegetables with Green Goddess Dressing

6 SERVINGS ●●

Slicing the fennel and cauliflower straight through the core keeps the slices intact during grilling and makes for a dramatic presentation.

1 cup extra-virgin olive oil

½ cup finely chopped basil

Salt and freshly ground pepper

6 Asian eggplants (about 2 pounds), sliced lengthwise ½ inch thick

6 portobello mushrooms, stems removed

2 fennel bulbs, stalks and feathery fronds discarded, bulbs sliced lengthwise ½ inch thick through the core

2 medium zucchini, sliced lengthwise ½ inch thick

2 medium yellow squash, sliced lengthwise ½ inch thick

1 medium cauliflower, core trimmed, head sliced lengthwise ½ inch thick

2 large red bell peppers, cored and quartered

Green Goddess Dressing (recipe follows)

ı. Light a grill. In a medium bowl, mix the olive oil with the basil and season generously with salt and pepper. Brush the basil oil on the vegetables. When the fire is medium-hot, arrange the eggplant slices on the hottest area of the grill and surround with the portobellos and sliced fennel. Grill, basting often with the oil and turning once, until the vegetables are nicely charred and almost tender, about 6 minutes for the eggplant and 10 minutes for the portobellos and fennel. Transfer the vegetables to a platter and cover loosely with foil.

2. Put the zucchini and yellow squash on the hottest part of the grill and surround them with the cauliflower and red bell peppers. Grill, basting often with the basil oil and turning once, until the vegetables are nicely charred and almost tender, 1 to 2 minutes for the zucchini, 6 minutes for the bell peppers and 10 minutes for the cauliflower. Add the vegetables to the platter and serve with the Green Goddess Dressing. —*Todd English* ▶

vegetables

MAKE AHEAD The grilled vegetables can be kept at room temperature for 2 hours.

WINE A fresh, citrusy white is the perfect foil for the smoky grilled flavors of the vegetables and will echo the tanginess of the sour cream dressing. Turn to a juicy, zesty Pinot Grigio, such as the 1998 Livon Collio or the 1998 Polencic Collio.

GREEN GODDESS DRESSING
MAKES 1¼ CUPS ●●●

- ½ cup coarsely chopped flat-leaf parsley
- 6 anchovy fillets, finely chopped
- 2 garlic cloves, finely chopped
- 2 tablespoons minced tarragon
- ½ cup sour cream
- ½ cup mayonnaise
- 2 tablespoons fresh lemon juice

Salt and freshly ground pepper

In a mini food processor, combine the parsley, anchovies, garlic and tarragon and process to a fine paste. Blend in the sour cream, mayonnaise and lemon juice. Scrape the dressing into a bowl and season with salt and pepper. Refrigerate until serving time.

—*T.E.*

MAKE AHEAD The dressing can be refrigerated for up to 3 days.

Grilled Vegetables with Green Goddess Dressing

Summer Vegetable Packs with Toasted Pecan Butter

Summer Vegetable Packs with Toasted Pecan Butter

MAKES 6 PACKS ●●

Here's a novel way to steam summer vegetables: Bundle them together in banana leaves, which impart a gentle aroma, and throw them on the grill for a few minutes. You can substitute 12-inch squares of foil for the leaves; just fold them around the vegetables to form neat packages. Crimp the sides to seal and make handles.

- ¼ cup plus 2 tablespoons pecans
- 3 tablespoons unsalted butter, softened

Salt

- 2 zucchini (about 4 ounces each), sliced crosswise ⅓ inch thick
- 2 large beefsteak tomatoes, each cut into 12 wedges
- 1 yellow squash (about 4 ounces), sliced crosswise ⅓ inch thick
- 1 small onion, thinly sliced
- ½ pound thin wax beans or green beans, cut into 2-inch lengths
- ½ cup corn kernels
- 6 ounces Swiss chard, stalks discarded, leaves cut into wide ribbons (about 2 packed cups)

Six 2-by-1-foot pieces of frozen banana leaf, thawed (see Note)
- 12 bacon slices, cut in half crosswise

Extra-virgin olive oil, for drizzling
Freshly ground pepper
Vegetable oil, for the grill

1. Preheat the oven to 350°. Spread the pecans in a pie plate and bake for 8 minutes, or until lightly toasted. Transfer to a plate, let cool completely, then chop. In a bowl, mix the pecans with the butter. Season generously with salt.

2. Light a grill. In a large bowl, gently toss the vegetables. Spread the banana leaves on a work surface. Lay 4 pieces of bacon side by side in the center of the bottom half of each leaf. Spread the vegetables over the bacon and drizzle with olive oil. Season with salt and pepper. Fold the top half of each leaf over the vegetables, then tuck the sides underneath to seal. Tie the packs with kitchen string to secure.

3. Lightly brush the grate with vegetable oil. Grill the packs, bacon side down, over a medium-hot fire until you hear the juices bubble steadily, about

15 minutes. Transfer the packs to plates. Untie the packs, top the vegetables with the toasted pecan butter and serve. —*Marcia Kiesel*

NOTE Whole banana leaves are available frozen at Latin markets and can be cut to the desired size. Wipe with a damp cloth before using.

MAKE AHEAD The pecan butter can be refrigerated for 2 days or frozen for 1 week. The assembled vegetable packs can be refrigerated overnight.

Vegetable Ragout with Fresh Herbs

12 SERVINGS ●

- 6 cups water
- 1 tarragon sprig, plus 1 teaspoon minced tarragon
- 1 thyme sprig

Kosher salt

- 1 pound pearl onions, peeled
- 3 medium carrots, peeled and cut into 2-by-⅓-inch sticks
- 1 pound haricots verts or thin green beans
- 6 small zucchini, halved lengthwise
- 1 red bell pepper, cut into 2-by-⅓-inch strips
- 1 yellow bell pepper, cut into 2-by-⅓-inch strips
- 1 stick (4 ounces) cold unsalted butter, cut into tablespoons
- 2 tablespoons chopped flat-leaf parsley
- 2 tablespoons minced chives
- 1 large garlic clove, minced

Freshly ground pepper

I. Preheat the oven to 300°. In a medium enameled cast-iron casserole, bring the water to a boil with the tarragon and thyme sprigs and 1 teaspoon of salt.

2. Add the peeled pearl onions to the casserole, cover and simmer over low heat until tender, about 8 minutes. Using a slotted spoon, transfer the onions to a large shallow baking dish. Add the carrot sticks to the simmering water, cover and cook until tender, about 8 minutes. Transfer the carrots to the shallow dish. Repeat with the haricots verts (about 4 minutes), followed by the zucchini halves (about 3 minutes) and, finally, the red and yellow pepper strips (about 3 minutes). Cover the vegetables with foil and keep them warm in the oven.

3. Boil the vegetable cooking liquid over high heat until reduced to 1 cup, about 5 minutes. Remove from the heat and whisk in the butter, 1 tablespoon at a time. Stir in the minced tarragon, parsley, chives and garlic. Season with salt and pepper. Pour the sauce over the vegetables, toss gently and serve. —*Jeremiah Tower*

Green Beans with Cremini Mushroom Sauce

10 SERVINGS ●

- 1 pound shallots, thinly sliced
- ⅓ cup plus 3 tablespoons all-purpose flour

Vegetable oil, for frying

Salt

- 2½ pounds green beans
- 2 tablespoons unsalted butter
- 1 medium onion, thinly sliced
- ½ teaspoon paprika

Pinch of cayenne pepper

Freshly ground pepper

- 1 pound cremini mushrooms, stems discarded, caps thinly sliced
- 2 cups chicken stock or canned low-sodium broth
- ½ cup crème fraîche
- 2 tablespoons fresh lemon juice

I. On a large, rimmed baking sheet, toss the shallots with ⅓ cup of the flour; shake off any excess flour. In a large, deep skillet, heat 1 inch of oil until shimmering. Add the shallots in 2 batches and fry over moderate heat until very crisp, about 3 minutes. Using a slotted spoon, transfer to paper towels, then sprinkle with salt. ▶

Vegetable Ragout with Fresh Herbs

Green Beans with Cremini Mushroom Sauce

2. In a large pot of boiling salted water, cook the green beans until just tender, about 5 minutes. Drain and refresh under cold running water; drain and pat dry.

3. Melt the butter in a large enameled cast-iron casserole. Add the sliced onion and cook over low heat, stirring occasionally, until softened, about 5 minutes. Add the paprika, cayenne pepper and a large pinch of black pepper; cook for 1 minute, stirring. Add the cremini mushrooms, cover and cook over moderate heat until softened, about 5 minutes. Uncover and cook, stirring, until the mushrooms are browned, about 5 minutes longer. Stir in the remaining 3 tablespoons of flour and gradually stir in the chicken stock until smooth.

4. Simmer the mushroom sauce over low heat, stirring, until thickened, about 5 minutes. Stir in the crème fraîche, lemon juice and beans. Cover and simmer, stirring occasionally, until the beans are heated through, about 5 minutes. Season with salt and pepper and transfer to a large glass or ceramic baking dish.

5. Preheat the oven to 400°. Cover the casserole with foil and bake until bubbling, about 20 minutes. Uncover, scatter the shallots on top and serve.
—Marcia Kiesel

MAKE AHEAD The assembled green bean casserole can be refrigerated overnight. Let return to room temperature before baking. The fried shallots can be kept overnight in an airtight container. Recrisp in a 350° oven and let cool.

FAVORITE VEGETABLE VARIETIES

enchantment tomatoes	Egg-shaped, amazingly uniform three-inch ovals (look like plum tomatoes, but aren't). Very productive over much of the summer. So sweet—great for slicing and eating.
freckles lettuce	Delicious—and a real visual standout. Also called Troutback because its chartreuse leaves are speckled with wine-red spots. Austrian heirloom variety.
asparagus beans	Asiatic pole beans. Very pale green beans with a rosy tip that grow to a foot long or more. Also called Yard Longs. Taste slightly like asparagus, hence the name.
joseph's coat amaranth	South American heirloom that has a walnutlike flavor. Striking magenta and gold leaves can be eaten raw in salads or steamed like spinach.
blue solaise leeks	Impressively large blue stalks with elegantly symmetrical, straplike leaves. French heirloom variety. These plants produce from May to September.
imperial star artichokes	The king of vegetable plants in terms of physical presence, growing to five feet or more. Like their cousins the cardoons, they're often seen in decorative garden borders.
kwintus beans	Succulent, flat pole beans that can grow to an inch wide and eight inches long. Unlike other beans, these remain sweet and tasty no matter how long they stay on the vine.
rat-tail radishes	Green, tapering pods on long, arching stalks. Pick pods when young and eat raw, or add to a stir-fry for a hot, radishy bite. Pods later bloom with delicate white flowers. South Asian heirloom.
malabar spinach	A "false spinach" grown in the tropics. Succulent, crinkly green leaves on vibrant red climbing vines. Sometimes called Land Kelp because it tastes slightly like seaweed.
blue curled scotch kale	Deeply ruffled, blue-green leaves that, when picked young, can be used in salads. But they taste even better after a touch of frost, when everything else has stopped producing. Mature leaves can be steamed like collard greens.

Kwintus Beans with Marjoram, Walnuts and Bacon

6 SERVINGS ●●

Flat, yellow Kwintus beans are similar in shape and texture to Romano beans. Their succulent texture pairs well with crisp bacon and crunchy walnuts.

1½ pounds Kwintus beans
6 strips of bacon
1 garlic clove, sliced
1 tablespoon marjoram, chopped
Coarsely ground pepper
½ cup walnuts, chopped

1. In a large skillet, steam the beans in ½ inch of water until crisp-tender, about 5 minutes. Drain and refresh under cold water; pat thoroughly dry.

2. In the same skillet, cook the bacon over moderately high heat until crisp; drain well and crumble. Add the garlic to the drippings in the skillet and cook until golden, about 1 minute. Add the beans and half of the marjoram, season generously with pepper and toss until hot. Transfer the beans to a platter. Garnish with the walnuts, bacon and the remaining marjoram and serve.
—Jack Staub

Kwintus Beans with Marjoram, Walnuts and Bacon

Roasted Cherry Peppers with Balsamic Vinegar

6 SERVINGS ● ●

These tender sweet-and-tart peppers make a great accompaniment to almost any kind of grilled meat or thick fish fillets. The peppers can be served whole, stems and all.

¼ cup balsamic vinegar

¼ cup cider vinegar

¼ cup extra-virgin olive oil

3 tablespoons fresh lemon juice

2 garlic cloves, minced

Salt and freshly ground pepper

2 pounds red and yellow sweet cherry peppers or baby bell peppers

About ¼ cup water

6 chive flowers, torn

1. Preheat the oven to 425°. In a small bowl, whisk the balsamic and cider vinegars with the olive oil, lemon juice and minced garlic. Season the dressing with salt and pepper.

2. Arrange the peppers in a large baking dish, pour the dressing on top and toss to coat. Bake for about 30 minutes, or until barely tender. Add ¼ cup of water and bake for about 20 minutes longer, or until the peppers are tender and blackened in spots; add more water to the pan if it dries out.

3. Transfer the peppers to a large platter and pour the pan juices over them. Just before serving, sprinkle with the chive flowers. Serve warm or at room temperature. —*Ilene Rosen*

MAKE AHEAD The baked peppers can be refrigerated for up to 2 days. Let return to room temperature before serving.

Indian-Style Red Velvet Okra and Tomatillos

6 SERVINGS ● ●

Red Velvet okra is spectacular with its crimson stems and pods and gorgeous yellow blossoms.

3 tablespoons vegetable oil

½ cup coarsely chopped onion

2 teaspoons ground turmeric

¾ pound Red Velvet okra, sliced crosswise ½ inch thick

1 pound tomatillos—husked, washed and quartered

2 large plum tomatoes, chopped

1 jalapeño, seeded and minced

1 tablespoon grated fresh ginger

¼ cup water

Salt

¼ cup coarsely chopped cilantro

Heat the oil in a medium skillet. Add the onion and turmeric and cook over moderate heat for 3 minutes. Add the okra and tomatillos and cook over moderately high heat, stirring, until browned and beginning to soften, about 5 minutes. Stir in the tomatoes, jalapeño, ginger and water, season with salt and simmer over low heat until the okra is tender and most of the liquid has evaporated. Add the cilantro and serve. —*Jack Staub*

Tahini-Glazed Eggplant

4 SERVINGS ●

2 large, slender eggplants (about 2½ pounds total), peeled and sliced lengthwise 1¼ inches thick

¼ cup plus 1 tablespoon extra-virgin olive oil

Salt and freshly ground pepper

½ cup tahini, at room temperature

1 tablespoon honey

2 teaspoons fresh lemon juice

1 large garlic clove, minced

Lemon wedges, for serving

1. Preheat the oven to 500°. Brush the eggplant slices with ¼ cup of the extra-virgin olive oil and arrange them on a large, rimmed baking sheet. Season the eggplant slices with salt and pepper and roast them on the bottom shelf of the oven for about 15 minutes, until they are tender and browned on the bottom.

2. Meanwhile, in a small bowl, whisk the tahini with the honey, lemon juice, minced garlic and the remaining 1 tablespoon of olive oil. Season with salt and pepper.

3. Preheat the broiler. Flip the eggplant slices so the browned side is up and spread them with an even layer of the tahini mixture. Broil the eggplant, rotating the pan as necessary, until the tahini sauce is browned. Serve at once with lemon wedges.   —Marcia Kiesel

Eggplant Curry

4 SERVINGS ●

Commercial curry powder can be substituted for the version used here. To mellow its raw flavor, toast the curry in a dry skillet until it's fragrant.

 2 tablespoons pure olive oil
 1 medium tomato, chopped
 1 garlic clove, minced
 1 teaspoon minced fresh ginger
 1 tablespoon Rambutan Curry
    Paste (recipe follows)
1½ pounds eggplant, cut into
    1-inch dice
 2 cups vegetable or chicken stock
    or canned low-sodium broth
Salt and freshly ground pepper

1. Heat the oil in a large saucepan. Add the tomato, garlic and ginger and cook over moderate heat, stirring, for 3 minutes. Add the curry and cook, stirring, until fragrant, about 2 minutes. Stir in the eggplant. Add the stock and bring to a boil. Add a pinch each of salt and pepper, cover and simmer over low heat, stirring occasionally, until the eggplant is tender, about 8 minutes.

2. Using a slotted spoon, transfer the eggplant to a bowl. Boil the cooking liquid over high heat until reduced to ½ cup, about 3 minutes. Return the eggplant to the pan and reheat it. Season with salt and pepper and serve.

—Jennifer Aranas

RAMBUTAN CURRY PASTE

MAKES ABOUT ¼ CUP ● ●

This complex curry blend is also a great seasoning for chicken, shrimp, dumpling fillings and stir-fry sauces.

 1 tablespoon crushed red pepper
1½ teaspoons ground coriander
 1 teaspoon ground cumin
 1 teaspoon sweet paprika
 ½ teaspoon freshly ground pepper
 ½ teaspoon ground turmeric
 ½ teaspoon ground cloves
 ½ teaspoon cinnamon
 1 tablespoon chopped cilantro
 ½ tablespoon chopped garlic
 1 teaspoon finely grated lime zest
 1 teaspoon chopped lemongrass
 ½ teaspoon salt
 ¼ teaspoon shrimp paste

1. In a small skillet, combine the crushed red pepper with the coriander, cumin, paprika, pepper, turmeric, cloves and cinnamon. Toast over moderate heat until fragrant, about 30 seconds. Transfer to a plate and let cool.

2. In a mortar, pound the cilantro, garlic, lime zest and lemongrass until a puree forms. Stir in the toasted spices, salt and shrimp paste. Scrape into a jar, cover and refrigerate.   —J.A.

MAKE AHEAD The curry paste can be stored in an airtight container and refrigerated for 1 week.

Osterei Eggplant and Cherry Tomatoes with Gorgonzola

6 SERVINGS ●

Osterei eggplants resemble large eggs.

 7 tablespoons olive oil
 2 garlic cloves, finely chopped
 ¾ pound Osterei eggplants,
    cut into ¾-inch dice

 ⅓ cup coarsely chopped basil
Salt and freshly ground pepper
 2 tablespoons balsamic vinegar
 3 cups Sungold cherry
    tomatoes, halved
 ½ cup crumbled Gorgonzola

1. Heat 3 tablespoons of the olive oil in a large skillet. Add the garlic and cook over moderate heat until softened, about 1 minute. Add the eggplants and 2 tablespoons of the basil and season with salt and pepper. Cook over moderately high heat until browned, 6 to 8 minutes. Cover and cook over very low heat, stirring, until the eggplants are tender, about 3 minutes longer. Remove from the heat and let cool.

2. In a medium bowl, whisk the vinegar with the remaining 4 tablespoons of olive oil. Add the eggplants, tomatoes, cheese and the remaining basil, season with salt and pepper, toss and serve.   —Jack Staub

Heirloom Tomato and Eggplant Gratin

8 SERVINGS ● ●

This recipe is served family style in one large gratin dish. For a more elegant presentation, assemble the gratin in individual dishes.

 ¼ cup extra-virgin olive oil
1½ pounds tomatoes, sliced
    ½ inch thick
 1 pound baby Italian eggplants,
    peeled and sliced into rounds
    ¼ to ⅓ inch thick
 4 thyme sprigs
Sea salt and freshly ground pepper
 ¼ pound goat cheese, coarsely
    crumbled (1 cup)

1. Preheat the oven to 425°. Brush a large oval baking dish with 1 tablespoon of olive oil. Arrange the tomato and eggplant slices in a single layer of overlapping concentric circles. Scatter the thyme sprigs on top and season with salt and pepper. Drizzle the remaining 3 tablespoons of olive oil over the top. Cover with foil and bake

**Heirloom Tomato and
Eggplant Gratin**

Heat the olive oil in a large, deep skillet. Add the onion and cook over moderate heat until softened, about 5 minutes. Add the garlic and cook for 1 minute. Reduce the heat to moderately low and add the tomatoes, eggplant, zucchini, bell pepper and bay leaf. Season with salt and pepper, cover and cook, stirring occasionally, until the vegetables are very tender, about 1 hour. Discard the bay leaf and serve warm or at room temperature.

—*Jean Calviac*

MAKE AHEAD The ratatouille can be refrigerated for 3 days.

WINE Look for a clean, crisp white to contrast with the sharp eggplant and sweet onions. Inexpensive, citrusy dry examples from the Côtes de Gascogne, such as the 1999 Domaine de Pouy or the 1999 Domaine du Tariquet Sauvignon, are excellent choices.

Giambotta with Fried Eggs

6 SERVINGS ●

Giambotta means "mixture" or "big mess." This dish is usually made with peppers, tomatoes and eggplant, all cooked together in one pot.

- ¼ cup extra-virgin olive oil
- 2 Italian frying peppers, seeded and thinly sliced
- 2 medium zucchini, thinly sliced
- 2 medium tomatoes, chopped
- 1 medium eggplant (¾ pound), peeled and cut into ½-inch dice
- 1 medium red bell pepper, cut into ½-inch dice
- 1 medium onion, coarsely chopped
- ¼ pound mushrooms, thinly sliced

Salt and freshly ground pepper

Six 4-inch squares of focaccia, cut 1 inch thick

- 6 large eggs

I. Heat 2 tablespoons of the olive oil in a large skillet. Add all of the vegetables, cover and cook over moderately low heat, stirring occasionally, until tender, about 8 minutes. Uncover and simmer over moderately high heat

for about 30 minutes, or until the eggplant is barely tender and the tomatoes have exuded their juices.

2. Uncover the gratin and bake for about 25 minutes longer, or until the juices have evaporated and the vegetables are very tender. Sprinkle the goat cheese on top and bake for about 10 minutes, or until lightly browned. Serve warm or at room temperature.

—*Stéphane Garnier*

MAKE AHEAD The gratin can be refrigerated for 2 days. Reheat, top with the cheese and bake 10 minutes just before serving.

Easy Ratatouille

4 SERVINGS ● ●

- 3 tablespoons extra-virgin olive oil
- 1 medium onion, thinly sliced
- 1 garlic clove, coarsely chopped
- 2 large tomatoes (about 1 pound), halved and sliced ½ inch thick
- 1 medium eggplant (1 pound), cut into 1-inch dice
- ½ pound zucchini, sliced crosswise 1 inch thick
- 1 medium red bell pepper, cut into 1-inch pieces
- 1 bay leaf

Salt and freshly ground pepper

until all the liquid has evaporated, about 3 minutes. Season with salt and pepper; keep warm.

2. Using a 2-inch round biscuit cutter, cut a hole in the center of each piece of focaccia. In each of 2 large skillets, heat 1 tablespoon of the oil. Add 3 pieces of focaccia to each skillet. Cook over moderately high heat until browned on the bottom, 1 minute. Reduce the heat to low, flip the bread and crack an egg into each hole. Cook over low heat until the eggs reach the desired doneness, 3 to 5 minutes. Transfer to plates and serve the giambotta alongside. —*Don Pintabona*

WINE The acidic tomatoes and earthy mushrooms point to a simple, fruity-herbal and non-oaky Sauvignon Blanc. Two good examples: the 1999 Meridian California or the 2000 Taft Street Russian River Valley.

Warm Cauliflower Salad

6 SERVINGS ●●●

In the Andean region of Ecuador, salad often means hearty vegetables cooked with onions, potatoes and cheese. This lighter version—minus the cheese and potatoes—can also be made with broccoli rabe or cabbage.

- 3 tablespoons Annatto Oil (recipe follows)
- 7 garlic cloves, minced
- 1 medium onion, finely chopped
- 1 teaspoon ground cumin
- 1 teaspoon salt

Freshly ground pepper

One 3-pound cauliflower, cut into 1-inch florets

1½ cups water

Ají (p. 319), for serving

Sherry vinegar, for drizzling

1. Heat the Annatto Oil in a large saucepan. Add the garlic and cook

Warm Cauliflower Salad

over moderate heat until golden, about 1 minute. Add the onion and cook, stirring frequently, until softened, about 4 minutes. Add the cumin, salt and pepper and stir in the cauliflower until coated. Add the water, cover and simmer over low heat until the cauliflower is tender, about 7 minutes.

2. Using a slotted spoon, transfer the cauliflower to a serving bowl. Simmer the cauliflower cooking liquid until reduced to ½ cup, about 4 minutes. Pour the liquid over the cauliflower and toss. Serve warm or at room temperature, with Ají, and sherry vinegar for drizzling. —*Maricel Presilla*

ONE SERVING Calories 99 kcal, Total Fat 7.1 gm, Saturated Fat 0.9 gm, Protein 2 gm, Carbohydrates 8 gm

MAKE AHEAD The cauliflower salad can be refrigerated overnight. Bring to room temperature before serving.

Giambotta with Fried Egg

ANNATTO OIL

MAKES ABOUT 1 CUP ●●

Tiny and virtually flavorless, annatto seeds, also known as achiote seeds, are commonly used throughout Latin America to add a distinctive reddish-yellow color to various sautéed foods. They are available at Latin markets and in the Latin section of some supermarkets.

- 1 cup corn oil
- ¼ cup annatto seeds

In a small saucepan, combine the corn oil with the annatto seeds and bring to a simmer over low heat. Remove the oil from the heat, cover the pan and let the oil cool completely. Strain the annatto-infused oil into a jar. —*M.P.*

MAKE AHEAD The Annatto Oil can be refrigerated in a tightly sealed jar for up to 2 months.

Duet of Cauliflower

4 SERVINGS

Jean-Anthelme Brillat-Savarin was a lawyer by training, a politician and a passionate gastronome at the time of the French Revolution. This dish combines two Brillat-Savarin recipes—a crispy gratinée and a creamy puree.

- 1¼ pounds cauliflower florets (from 1 small head), half the florets left whole, half sliced lengthwise ½ inch thick
- ½ cup heavy cream
- ½ cup milk
- 2 tablespoons crème fraîche
- Salt and freshly ground pepper
- 5 thin bacon strips (about 4 ounces)
- 1 tablespoon pure olive oil
- ¼ cup chicken stock or canned low-sodium broth
- ¼ cup shredded Gruyère
- 2 tablespoons freshly grated Parmesan

I. In a medium saucepan of boiling salted water, cook the whole cauliflower florets until almost tender, about 6 minutes; drain. Add the cream and milk to the parboiled florets and simmer over low heat until very tender, about 9 minutes. Strain, reserving the cooking liquid, and puree in a blender until smooth, adding enough cooking liquid to make a loose puree. Stir in the crème fraîche, season with salt and pepper and keep warm.

2. Preheat the broiler. In a skillet, cook the bacon until lightly crisp; drain on paper towels. Discard the fat and heat the oil. Add the sliced cauliflower and cook over low heat until almost tender and lightly browned on both sides, about 11 minutes. Spread half of the cauliflower slices in a shallow baking dish, cover with the bacon and top with the remaining cauliflower. Add the stock and sprinkle with the Gruyère and Parmesan. Broil for 2 minutes, or until bubbling. Serve the gratin with the puree. —*Laurent Gras*

Creamy Cauliflower Gratin with Whole Wheat Crumbs

10 SERVINGS ●

- Two 2½-pound heads of cauliflower, cut into 2-inch florets
- 2 tablespoons extra-virgin olive oil
- 3 garlic cloves, minced
- 4 anchovy fillets, mashed to a paste
- 6 medium scallions, thinly sliced
- 1 cup chicken stock or canned low-sodium broth
- 2 cups heavy cream
- 1½ cups fresh whole wheat bread crumbs
- 3 tablespoons freshly grated Parmesan
- 1 tablespoon unsalted butter, melted
- Salt and freshly ground pepper

I. Preheat the oven to 400°. In a large saucepan, steam the cauliflower until just tender, about 7 minutes; let cool slightly. Cut the cauliflower into 1-inch pieces and spread evenly in a 10-by-15-inch shallow baking dish.

2. Heat the olive oil in a large skillet. Add the garlic and anchovies and cook over low heat until fragrant, about 2 minutes. Add the scallions and cook, stirring, until softened, about 1 minute. Add the chicken stock and boil over moderately high heat until reduced by half, about 5 minutes. Add the cream and simmer over low heat until reduced to 1½ cups, about 4 minutes. Pour the cream over the cauliflower.

3. In a bowl, toss the bread crumbs with the cheese and melted butter. Season with salt and pepper and sprinkle over the cauliflower. Bake in the upper third of the oven for about 20 minutes, or until bubbling and golden. Let stand for up to 20 minutes before serving. —*Marcia Kiesel*

MAKE AHEAD The recipe can be prepared through Step 2 and refrigerated overnight. Bring to room temperature before proceeding.

Parmesan-and-Sausage Stuffed Roasted Fennel

10 SERVINGS ●

- 5 large fennel bulbs, trimmed
- 6 tablespoons extra-virgin olive oil
- ½ pound Italian sausage, casings removed
- ½ small onion, finely chopped
- 2 garlic cloves, minced
- ¾ cup dry bread crumbs
- ¼ cup freshly grated Parmesan
- 2 tablespoons minced parsley
- Salt and freshly ground pepper
- ¼ cup chicken or turkey stock or canned low-sodium broth

I. In a saucepan, steam the fennel, root end up, until just tender, about 15 minutes. Let cool. Halve the bulbs lengthwise and remove the thickest part of the core.

2. Heat 2 tablespoons of the olive oil in a large skillet. Add the sausage, breaking it up with a wooden spoon, and cook over moderately high heat until no pink remains, about 5 minutes. Add the onion and garlic. Cook, stirring occasionally, until the onion is softened and the sausage is browned, about 5 minutes. Stir in the bread crumbs. Let cool. Stir in the cheese and parsley; season with salt and pepper.

3. Preheat the oven to 425°. Oil a large glass baking dish; pour in the stock. Working over the skillet, press two-thirds of the filling into the fennel layers. Arrange the fennel in the baking dish, cut side up, and top with the remaining filling. Tilt the fennel up slightly and drizzle ¼ cup of olive oil over and between the layers. Cover loosely with foil and bake for 20 minutes, or until the fennel is very tender. Uncover and bake for 10 to 15 minutes longer, or until the liquid in the dish has evaporated and the fennel begins to brown on the bottom.

4. Position an oven rack 10 inches from the heat and preheat the broiler. Broil the fennel until the topping is browned, about 5 minutes. Serve hot.

—*Grace Parisi*

MAKE AHEAD The recipe can be prepared through Step 3 early in the day. Rewarm and broil before serving.

Carrot Osso Buco

4 SERVINGS ●

In this recipe, a favorite Italian specialty—braised veal shanks with tomatoes and onions—is transformed by replacing the meat with carrots.

- 4 tablespoons unsalted butter
- 1½ pounds medium carrots
- 1 medium onion, halved lengthwise and thinly sliced crosswise
- 1 celery rib, finely chopped
- 1 garlic clove, smashed
- ½ pound tomatoes—peeled, seeded and chopped

Bouquet garni made with 6 parsley sprigs, 3 thyme sprigs and 1 bay leaf, tied with kitchen string

One ½-inch-thick orange slice, halved

Sea salt and freshly ground pepper

- 1 tablespoon coarsely chopped flat-leaf parsley

1. Melt the butter in a large skillet. Add the carrots and cook over moderate heat, turning frequently, until lightly browned, about 15 minutes. Transfer the carrots to a plate.

2. Add the onion, celery and garlic to the skillet and cook over moderate heat for 3 minutes. Add the tomatoes, bouquet garni and orange slice, season with salt and pepper; cook for 2 minutes. Nestle the carrots in the sauce. Cover and cook over low heat, turning occasionally, until very tender but not falling apart, about 1 hour. Discard the bouquet garni. Sprinkle the carrots with parsley and serve warm or at room temperature.   —*Guy Martin*

MAKE AHEAD The carrots can be refrigerated for 2 days.

Jerusalem Artichoke Gratin with Lentils

12 SERVINGS ●

The unique ingredients and hauntingly complex flavors of this gratin make it a standout.

- 2 cups French green lentils (¾ pound)

Salt

- ½ cup hazelnuts
- 1 lemon, halved
- 4 pounds large Jerusalem artichokes
- 2½ cups heavy cream
- 1 tablespoon finely grated lemon zest
- 1 tablespoon minced garlic

Freshly ground pepper

- 2 cups fresh bread crumbs
- 4 tablespoons unsalted butter, melted
- ¼ cup chopped flat-leaf parsley

1. In a medium saucepan, cover the lentils with water and bring to a boil. Cover partially and cook over low heat for 20 minutes, stirring occasionally. Add ½ teaspoon of salt and cook until tender, about 5 minutes longer. Drain the lentils and spread them on a large baking sheet to cool.

2. Preheat the oven to 350°. Spread the hazelnuts in a pie plate and bake for 10 minutes, or until they are lightly toasted. Transfer the toasted hazelnuts to a kitchen towel and let cool. Vigorously rub the nuts in the towel to remove the skins, then finely chop them.

3. Squeeze the lemon juice into a large bowl of cold water and add the lemon. Peel the Jerusalem artichokes and drop them into the acidulated water. Using a mandoline, slice the Jerusalem artichokes crosswise ⅛ inch thick. In a large pot of boiling salted water, cook the slices until crisp-tender, about 8 minutes. Drain the artichoke slices thoroughly and transfer to a large bowl. Add the lentils, hazelnuts, cream, lemon zest and garlic, season with salt and pepper; toss gently. Transfer to a 10-by-15-inch glass baking dish.

4. In a medium bowl, toss the bread crumbs with the melted butter and scatter over the gratin. Bake for 30 minutes, or until the gratin is bubbling and golden brown. Let stand at room temperature for 15 minutes, then sprinkle with the parsley and serve.

—*Jeremiah Tower*

MAKE AHEAD The gratin can be prepared through Step 3 and refrigerated overnight. Bring to room temperature before baking.

Sweet-and-Sour Beets

12 SERVINGS ● ● ●

- 1½ cups fresh orange juice
- 1½ cups water
- ¼ cup plus 2 tablespoons packed light brown sugar
- ¼ cup cider vinegar
- 1 teaspoon finely grated orange zest
- 3 pounds beets—peeled, halved and thinly sliced
- 1½ teaspoons cornstarch dissolved in 2 tablespoons water

Salt and freshly ground pepper

In a large saucepan, combine the orange juice, water, brown sugar, vinegar and orange zest and boil, stirring, until the sugar dissolves. Add the beets, cover and cook over moderately low heat until tender, about 20 minutes. Stir in the cornstarch mixture and simmer until thickened and glossy, about 2 minutes. Season with salt and pepper and serve.

—*Tom Douglas*

MAKE AHEAD The beets can be refrigerated overnight. Reheat gently to keep the cornstarch from over-thickening.

Shallot-Stuffed Mushrooms

4 SERVINGS ●

These small stuffed mushrooms, suffused with intense, woodsy flavor, are a perfect vegetarian finger food.

- 6 tablespoons unsalted butter
- 1 shallot, minced

Sea salt

- 1 pound medium white mushrooms, stems finely chopped, caps reserved separately
- ⅓ cup heavy cream
- 2 teaspoons fresh lemon juice
- ¼ cup water
- 1 tablespoon minced chives

I. Melt 4 tablespoons of the butter in a medium skillet. Add the minced shallot and a pinch of salt, cover and cook over low heat until softened, about 2 minutes. Add the chopped stems and cook over moderately low heat until the liquid has evaporated but the mushrooms are still white, about 5 minutes. Add the cream and lemon juice, cover partially and cook over moderate heat until slightly thickened, about 5 minutes.

2. Pour the water into a large skillet. Add the remaining 2 tablespoons of butter and a generous pinch of salt and bring to a boil. Add the mushroom caps, stemmed side up, cover and cook over moderate heat until tender,

about 5 minutes. Uncover and cook, stirring occasionally, until the liquid has evaporated and the caps are browned, about 5 minutes longer. Turn the caps stemmed side down to drain any remaining liquid.

3. Transfer the caps to a platter and spoon in the filling. Scatter the chives on top. Serve warm or at room temperature. —*Guy Savoy*

MAKE AHEAD The stuffed mushrooms can stand at room temperature for 4 hours.

Mushrooms with Toasted Hazelnuts

4 SERVINGS ●

- 3 tablespoons hazelnuts
- 4 tablespoons unsalted butter
- 2 pounds mixed mushrooms, such as chanterelle, oyster and hen-of-the-woods, cut into bite-size pieces

Salt and freshly ground pepper

- 1 teaspoon hazelnut oil
- 1½ tablespoons minced chives

I. Preheat the oven to 350°. Toast the hazelnuts in a pie plate in the oven for 10 minutes, or until browned. Transfer to a kitchen towel and rub the nuts together to rub off the skins, then finely chop.

2. In a large skillet, melt the butter over moderately high heat. Add the mushrooms, season with salt and pepper and cook, tossing, until their liquid evaporates, 5 to 8 minutes. Reduce the heat to moderate and cook, stirring, until lightly browned, about 4 minutes. Transfer the mushrooms to a platter. Drizzle with the hazelnut oil and sprinkle with the chopped hazelnuts. Garnish with the chives and serve. —*Van Gogh's Table*

Marinated Portobellos with Olives and Goat Cheese

8 SERVINGS ●●

Shiitakes, cremini and even white mushrooms would all make great substitutes for the portobello mushrooms.

Marinated Portobellos with Olives and Goat Cheese

- 8 portobello mushrooms (about 2 pounds), stems discarded
- ½ cup extra-virgin olive oil
- ¼ cup plus 1 tablespoon balsamic vinegar

Salt and freshly ground pepper

- 1 cup green olives, preferably Picholine (about 6 ounces)
- ½ tablespoon herbes de Provence

One 5-ounce log of fresh goat cheese, crumbled

I. Light a charcoal grill or preheat the broiler and position a rack 6 inches from the heat. Using a spoon, scrape out the brown gills from the mushrooms. Set the mushrooms, top side up, on a large baking sheet and brush with ¼ cup of the olive oil. Drizzle 1 tablespoon of the balsamic vinegar over the mushrooms and season with salt and pepper. Grill or broil for about

25 minutes, turning the mushrooms frequently, or until they are tender and browned. Transfer the mushrooms to a bowl and let cool.

2. Meanwhile, in a shallow bowl, toss the olives with the herbes de Provence and the remaining ¼ cup of olive oil and ¼ cup of balsamic vinegar. Add the mushrooms and turn to coat. Just before serving, sprinkle the goat cheese on top and season with salt and pepper.

—*Michael Kramer*

MAKE AHEAD The mushroom salad can be refrigerated for 4 days. Bring it to room temperature and add the goat cheese before serving.

wines for vegetables

The current enthusiasm for vegetables demands a whole new look at the wine cellar. Here are some rules for choosing wines to go with vegetables.

Select vegetal wines. All the flavors that can be found in vegetables can also be found in certain kinds of wine—flavors of grass, herbs, even green beans. Try Riesling, Pinot Gris and Pinot Blanc from Alsace and, from the Loire, Chenin Blanc and Sauvignon Blanc.

Match flavors. Remember that wines with some acidity, such as Sauvignon Blanc or a Mondeuse from Savoie, can stand up to tomatoes. Sweetish wines are great with carrots and onions. Big, dry Chardonnays, white Rhônes and Pinot Gris from Alsace go well with earthy mushrooms.

Avoid oaky or tannic wines. These qualities overwhelm the delicate floral components, earthy tones and fruity flavors in vegetables.

Make the vegetables more wine-friendly. Add ingredients such as cheese, nuts and cream to vegetables that are difficult to pair with wines, such as artichokes, asparagus and salad greens, especially bitter ones like arugula.

Smoky Grilled Corn with Parmesan Butter

4 SERVINGS ●

Many cooks debate whether it's better to grill corn with the husks on or off. This recipe supports the husk-off approach. Exposing the kernels to the fire gives corn a richer, smokier flavor, and the pulled-back husks provide great no-mess handles.

- 6 tablespoons unsalted butter, softened
- ½ cup freshly grated Parmesan (2 ounces)
- 1 garlic clove, minced

Salt and freshly ground pepper

- 4 ears of corn

Vegetable oil, for the grill

I. Light a grill. In a bowl, mix the butter with the Parmesan and garlic. Season with salt and pepper.

2. Strip the husks from each ear of corn and remove the silks. Using kitchen string, tie the husks together at the end of each ear to form a handle.

3. Lightly brush the grate of the grill with vegetable oil. Grill the corn over a medium-hot fire, turning, until partially cooked, about 5 minutes. Brush the corn with the Parmesan butter and continue grilling, turning frequently and brushing with more butter, until deeply browned and tender, about 5 minutes longer. Serve at once with the remaining Parmesan butter.

—*Steven Raichlen*

MAKE AHEAD The Parmesan butter can be refrigerated for 5 days.

Crisp and Spicy Corn on the Cob

6 SERVINGS ●

Here, a spicy mayo is slathered on corn on the cob, which is then coated with bread crumbs and baked until crisp.

- ½ cup mayonnaise
- 2 tablespoons fresh lemon juice
- 2 large scallions, green part only, minced
- 1 jalapeño, seeded and minced

Salt and freshly ground pepper

- 4 cups fresh white bread crumbs
- 6 ears of corn, shucked

Smoky Grilled Corn with Parmesan Butter

Preheat the oven to 375°. In a bowl, mix the mayonnaise with the lemon juice, scallions and jalapeño and season with salt and pepper. Spread the bread crumbs on a rimmed platter. Generously brush each ear of corn with the mayonnaise mixture and roll in the bread crumbs to coat. Put the corn on a large, rimmed baking sheet and bake for about 35 minutes, or until browned and crisp. Serve at once.

—*Todd English*

Spicy Scalloped Rutabagas with Parsley

10 SERVINGS ●

- 5 pounds rutabagas, peeled and sliced ⅛ inch thick
- ½ pound flat-leaf parsley, large stems discarded
- 3 tablespoons unsalted butter
- 4 shallots, thinly sliced
- 2 large jalapeños, seeded and thinly sliced
- 2 large garlic cloves, minced

Salt and freshly ground pepper

- 1 cup chicken stock or canned low-sodium broth
- 2 cups heavy cream
- ¼ cup freshly grated Parmesan

1. In a large pot of boiling salted water, cook the rutabagas until crisp-tender, about 5 minutes. Using a slotted spoon, transfer the rutabagas to a large baking sheet and let cool. Add the parsley to the boiling water and cook until tender, about 4 minutes. Drain and let cool slightly. Squeeze dry and coarsely chop.

2. Melt the butter in a large skillet. Add the shallots, jalapeños and garlic. Season lightly with salt and pepper and cook over low heat, stirring occasionally, until softened, about 10 minutes. Add the stock and cook over moderately high heat until reduced by half, about 5 minutes. Add the cream and simmer over low heat until reduced by one-third, about 8 minutes. Stir in the parsley and simmer until thickened,

about 4 minutes. Season generously with salt and pepper.

3. Preheat the oven to 400°. Butter a 10-by-15-inch glass baking dish. Arrange half of the rutabaga slices in the dish. Season with salt and pepper. Using a slotted spoon, cover the rutabagas with the parsley and pour half of the cream over the parsley. Top with the remaining rutabagas and pour the remaining cream over them; press gently to even out the slices. Cover with foil and bake for about 1 hour, or until bubbling.

4. Position an oven rack 6 inches from the heat and preheat the broiler. Sprinkle the Parmesan over the rutabagas and broil, rotating the dish as necessary, until browned, about 2 minutes. Let cool for at least 15 minutes before serving.

—*Marcia Kiesel*

MAKE AHEAD The scalloped rutabagas can be assembled and refrigerated overnight. Bring the dish to room temperature before baking.

Acorn Squash and White Beans with Autumn Pistou

Acorn Squash and White Beans with Autumn Pistou

4 SERVINGS ●

Acorn squash is so often simply halved and baked. This recipe gives the gourd a more sophisticated treatment.

- 1½ cups dried white beans, soaked overnight and drained
- 6 small garlic cloves, plus ½ teaspoon minced garlic
- 4 carrots, cut into 1-inch lengths
- 2 celery ribs, halved crosswise
- 3 large leeks, white parts halved lengthwise, 1 leek green reserved
- 1 bay leaf

Salt and freshly ground pepper

- 2 parsnips, quartered lengthwise
- 7 tablespoons extra-virgin olive oil

Two 2¼-pound acorn squash, halved lengthwise and seeded

- 1 cup packed flat-leaf parsley
- 4 teaspoons rosemary leaves
- 1 tablespoon thyme leaves

1. In a large saucepan, combine the white beans with 3 garlic cloves,

12 potatoes
grains

Tangy Hot Potato Salad

4 SERVINGS ●

- ¾ cup dry white wine
- ¼ cup white vinegar
- 3 tablespoons unsalted butter
- 1 medium shallot, finely chopped
- 1½ pounds baby red new potatoes, scrubbed and quartered
- 2 tablespoons water

Salt and freshly ground pepper

- 2 tablespoons coarsely chopped tarragon leaves

In a medium saucepan, combine the wine with the vinegar, butter, shallot, potatoes and water and bring to a boil. Cover and cook over moderately high heat, stirring occasionally, until the potatoes are tender, about 15 minutes. Transfer to a bowl and season with salt and pepper. Toss with the tarragon and serve. —*Kate Heddings*

Braised Potatoes with Fresh Bay Leaves

4 SERVINGS ●

These potatoes go with just about everything, from simple roast salmon or chicken to any kind of stew.

- 1½ pounds small Yukon Gold potatoes (about 3 ounces each)
- ¼ cup water
- 4 fresh bay leaves
- 3 garlic cloves, unpeeled
- 1 teaspoon extra-virgin olive oil

Coarse sea salt

In an enameled cast-iron casserole or saucepan just large enough to hold the potatoes in 1 layer, put the potatoes, water, bay leaves, garlic, oil and ¾ teaspoon of salt. Cover and cook over low heat, stirring occasionally, until the potatoes are tender, 25 to 40 minutes, depending on size. Check the water during cooking and add a little more if the casserole is dry. Transfer the potatoes to a bowl and serve, passing more salt at the table. —*Patricia Wells*
ONE SERVING Calories 148 kcal, Total Fat 1.3 gm, Saturated Fat 0.2 gm, Protein 3 gm, Carbohydrates 32 gm

Potatoes with Saffron and Lemon

4 SERVINGS ●

Large pinch of saffron threads, finely crushed

- ¾ cup hot water
- ¼ cup fresh lemon juice
- ¼ cup minced shallots
- ¾ teaspoon salt

Pinch of sugar

- 5 teaspoons extra-virgin olive oil
- 2 pounds medium Yukon Gold potatoes, peeled and quartered
- 1 bay leaf

Freshly ground pepper

1. Preheat the oven to 375°. In a large bowl, mix the crushed saffron with the hot water and let stand for 10 minutes. Add the fresh lemon juice, minced shallots, salt, sugar and 3 teaspoons of the extra-virgin olive oil. Add the quartered potatoes and bay leaf and toss to coat.

2. Transfer the potatoes and their liquid to a flameproof roasting pan; bake for 1 hour, turning occasionally, until tender. Set the roasting pan over moderately high heat and cook to evaporate any pan juices, about 2 minutes. Drizzle the remaining 2 teaspoons of oil over the potatoes, season with pepper and toss. Roast the potatoes for 15 minutes longer, or until lightly browned. Serve at once.

—*Sally Schneider*

ONE SERVING Calories 237 kcal, Total Fat 5.9 gm, Saturated Fat 0.8 gm

Greek Fries

8 SERVINGS

- 4 pounds medium baking potatoes, peeled and cut into 3-by-½-inch sticks

Pure olive oil, for deep-frying

Salt

Verjus, for sprinkling

1. Soak the potato sticks in a large bowl of salted cold water for 1 hour.

2. Preheat the oven to 325°. Line a large, rimmed baking sheet with paper towels. In a large cast-iron skillet, heat ½ inch of olive oil to 375°. Drain the potatoes and pat dry. Working in batches, fry the potatoes until golden and crisp, 8 minutes per batch. Using a slotted spoon, transfer the fries to the paper towels to drain. Transfer the fries to a baking sheet and keep warm in the oven while you fry the rest; add more oil to the skillet as needed.

3. Heap the fries on a large platter and sprinkle lightly with salt and verjus. Serve right away. —*Cary Gott*

Potatoes with Smoky Bacon

4 SERVINGS

- 1½ pounds all-purpose potatoes
- 6 ounces double-smoked slab bacon, cut into ⅓-inch dice
- 1 tablespoon minced chives

Coarse sea salt

1. In a medium saucepan, steam the potatoes until just tender, about 25 minutes, and then drain. Peel and halve the potatoes, then slice them ⅓ inch thick.

2. Preheat the oven to 450°. In a medium skillet, cook the bacon over low heat until most of the fat has been rendered, about 8 minutes. Scrape the bacon and the fat onto a large, rimmed baking sheet. Add the potatoes and toss gently to coat. Spread the potatoes in a single layer and bake for about 15 minutes, or until browned on the bottom and crisp. Transfer the potatoes to a bowl. Sprinkle with the chives, season with salt and serve.

—*Van Gogh's Table*

Yukon Potato Whip

12 SERVINGS

- 6 pounds large Yukon Gold potatoes, peeled and quartered

Salt

- 2 sticks (½ pound) unsalted butter, at room temperature
- 2 tablespoons finely chopped garlic
- 1½ cups heavy cream

1 cup freshly grated
Parmesan (3 ounces)
¾ cup sour cream
Freshly ground pepper

1. In a large pot, cover the potatoes with cold water and bring to a boil. Add salt and cook until tender, about 30 minutes. Drain and return to the pot. Shake over high heat until the potatoes are dry, about 1 minute.

2. Meanwhile, melt the butter in a large saucepan. Add the garlic and cook over moderately low heat until fragrant but not browned, just 4 minutes. Add the cream and bring to a simmer; keep warm. In a large bowl, mash the potatoes until smooth. Blend in the garlic cream, Parmesan and sour cream and season with salt and pepper. Serve piping hot. —*Tom Douglas*

Buttermilk Mashed Potatoes

6 SERVINGS ●

What pasta is to Italy, potatoes are to Belgium. This version of mashed potatoes mixed with other vegetables, called *stoemp,* is deeply rooted in traditional peasant cooking.

2 pounds baking potatoes, peeled and cut into ½-inch dice
1 firm medium celery root (about 1 pound), peeled and cut into ½-inch dice
Salt
2 tablespoons unsalted butter
4 small leeks, white and light green parts, sliced crosswise ½ inch thick
½ cup heavy cream
Freshly ground pepper
1 cup buttermilk
¼ teaspoon freshly grated nutmeg

1. In a large saucepan, cover the potatoes and celery root with water, add a pinch of salt and bring to a boil. Simmer over moderate heat until the vegetables are tender, 35 to 40 minutes. Drain the vegetables and return them to the pan.

2. Meanwhile, melt the butter in a

small saucepan. Add the leeks, cover and cook over moderate heat for 5 minutes. Add the cream, season with salt and pepper and simmer, uncovered, until the leeks are tender, about 7 minutes. In another small saucepan, gently heat the buttermilk; do not boil or it will curdle.

3. Coarsely mash the potatoes and celery root. Stir in the hot buttermilk and then the creamed leeks. Season with salt, pepper and nutmeg and serve. —*Ruth Van Waerebeek*

Potato and Kohlrabi Gratin

4 SERVINGS

3 ounces sliced bacon, cut crosswise into thin strips
2 cups heavy cream
2 tablespoons crème fraîche or sour cream
½ garlic clove, minced
½ teaspoon minced thyme
Salt and freshly ground pepper
4 large Yukon Gold potatoes (2 pounds), peeled
2 medium kohlrabi (6 ounces each), peeled

1. Preheat the oven to 300°. Butter a 9-by-13-inch glass baking dish. In a small skillet, cook the bacon over moderate heat, stirring, until barely crisp, about 4 minutes. Drain on paper towels, then transfer to a large bowl. Stir in the heavy cream, crème fraîche, garlic and thyme. Season the cream mixture generously with salt and pepper.

2. Thinly slice the potatoes and kohlrabi using a mandoline, then add to the cream and toss to mix. Spread the potatoes, kohlrabi and cream in an even layer in the prepared baking dish and bake for 15 minutes. Increase the oven temperature to 325° and bake for about 1 hour and 15 minutes longer, or until the potatoes are tender and the top is browned. Let the gratin stand for 10 minutes before serving. —*Eberhard Müller*

Root Vegetables with Gorgonzola

8 SERVINGS ●

1 medium rutabaga (1½ pounds), cut into 1-inch dice
2 pounds Yukon Gold potatoes, peeled and halved
1 large fennel bulb—halved, cored and cut into 1½-inch pieces
8 fresh thyme sprigs
2 tablespoons extra-virgin olive oil
Salt and freshly ground pepper
¼ cup balsamic vinegar
6 ounces Gorgonzola, crumbled

1. Preheat the oven to 350°. In a roasting pan, toss the rutabaga, potatoes, fennel, thyme and oil; season with salt and pepper. Roast for 1 hour and 40 minutes, or until tender. Discard the thyme.

2. In a small skillet, boil the vinegar until reduced to 2 tablespoons, about 5 minutes.

3. Sprinkle the cheese over the root vegetables and roast until melted. Drizzle with the balsamic glaze and serve. —*Jimmy Bradley*

MAKE AHEAD The Root Vegetables with Gorgonzola can be prepared through Step 2 up to 6 hours ahead. Reheat the vegetables before roasting with the cheese.

Sweet Potato Gratin with Prunes

12 SERVINGS ●

Using sweet potatoes instead of white ones puts a Southern spin on this French-inspired gratin. It's an ideal addition to a holiday feast.

2 tablespoons unsalted butter
1½ pounds medium leeks, white and tender green parts, halved lengthwise and thinly sliced crosswise
2 tablespoons chopped thyme
Salt and freshly ground pepper
2 cups heavy cream
½ pound plump pitted prunes
6 pounds sweet potatoes

1. Preheat the oven to 350°. Butter a 4-quart glass or ceramic baking dish. Melt the butter in a large saucepan. Add the sliced leeks and chopped thyme and season with salt and pepper. Cover and cook over moderate heat until the leeks soften, about 5 minutes. Uncover and cook until any liquid has evaporated. Add the heavy cream and bring to a boil, then remove from the heat.

2. Spread the prunes between sheets of plastic wrap and use a rolling pin or meat pounder to flatten them to a ¼-inch thickness. Peel the sweet potatoes and slice them ⅛ inch thick. Strain the cooked leeks, reserving the cream.

3. In a large bowl, toss three-fourths of the sliced sweet potatoes with the leeks and prunes and season with salt and pepper. Spread the sweet potatoes in the prepared baking dish and arrange the remaining sweet potato slices on top in a decorative pattern. Pour the reserved leek cream evenly over the sweet potatoes.

4. Cover the sweet potatoes with buttered parchment paper and then foil and bake for 45 minutes. Uncover, press the sweet potato layers down slightly and bake the gratin, uncovered, for 45 minutes longer, or until the sweet potatoes are tender, bubbling and golden brown.

—*Scott Howell*

MAKE AHEAD The sweet potato gratin can be prepared through Step 3 and refrigerated overnight. Bring to room temperature before baking.

Glazed Sweet Potatoes with Curried Onions

10 SERVINGS ● ●

- 5 pounds sweet potatoes, peeled and cut into 1-inch dice
- 4 tablespoons unsalted butter
- 3 tablespoons vegetable oil
- 2 large red onions, thinly sliced
- 1½ to 2 tablespoons curry powder

- 1½ cups fresh carrot juice (see Note)
- 1 tablespoon fresh lemon juice
- Salt and freshly ground pepper

1. In a very large saucepan, steam the sweet potatoes just until tender, about 12 minutes. Spread the steamed sweet potatoes in a large shallow baking dish and let cool slightly.

2. In a large skillet, melt the butter in the vegetable oil. Add the sliced red onions and cook over low heat, stirring occasionally, until softened, about 8 minutes. Add the curry powder and cook, stirring, until fragrant, about 4 minutes longer. Add the carrot juice and simmer until slightly thickened, about 3 minutes. Add the lemon juice and season with salt and pepper. Pour the curried onions over the cooked sweet potatoes.

3. Preheat the oven to 425°. Bake the sweet potatoes in the upper third of the oven until hot, about 25 minutes, then serve. —*Marcia Kiesel*

NOTE Fresh carrot juice is available in health food markets and some large supermarkets.

MAKE AHEAD The Glazed Sweet Potatoes with Curried Onions can be prepared through Step 2 and then refrigerated overnight. Bring to room temperature before baking.

Three Onion Risotto

8 SERVINGS ●

- 2 medium leeks, white and tender green parts only, halved lengthwise and rinsed thoroughly
- 6 cups water
- Salt
- 3 tablespoons unsalted butter
- 1 large sweet onion, such as Vidalia, minced
- 1½ cups medium-grain Italian rice, such as Arborio (10 ounces)
- ½ cup dry white wine
- ½ cup freshly grated Parmesan
- Freshly ground pepper
- 2 tablespoons snipped chives

1. Re-form the washed leeks and tie the 2 of them together with kitchen twine. In a medium saucepan, bring the water to a boil and add a small handful of salt. Put the tied leeks into the boiling water, cover and cook until tender, about 8 minutes. Transfer to a plate to cool slightly; reserve the leek broth and keep warm. Untie the leeks and cut into thin strips.

2. Melt the butter in a large saucepan. Add the minced onion and cook over low heat, stirring occasionally, until softened, about 7 minutes. Add the rice and stir until evenly coated with butter, about 2 minutes. Add the white wine and simmer over moderate heat, stirring, until almost evaporated, about 3 minutes.

3. Add 1 cup of the reserved leek broth to the rice and cook, stirring constantly, until the liquid has been absorbed by the rice. Continue to add 4 more cups of the leek broth to the rice, 1 cup at a time, stirring, until the liquid has been absorbed by the rice, before adding more. When the rice is almost tender, after about 16 minutes, remove it from the heat and cover for up to 1 hour.

4. To reheat, bring the remaining 1 cup of leek broth to a boil in a small pan. Bring the risotto to a bare simmer over moderately high heat. Add the leeks and stir the risotto with a large spatula until smooth. Add the hot leek broth and stir until the risotto is creamy, about 3 minutes. Stir in the Parmesan and season with salt and pepper to taste. Put the risotto on individual plates, sprinkle each serving with the chives and serve immediately .

—*Kevin Taylor*

MAKE AHEAD The Three Onion Risotto can be made up to 1 hour ahead of time. Keep all the components—the risotto, the leeks and the leek broth—at room temperature. Then reheat, as directed in Step 4, just before serving.

Morel and Sweet Pea Risotto

al dente, about 30 minutes total. Remove the risotto from the heat. Stir in the Parmigiano-Reggiano and season with salt and pepper. Top with the goat cheese and the parsley, if desired, just before serving.

—Brandon Miller

WINE The earthy morels and nutty and tangy cheeses in the risotto find echoes in the elegant and fruity 1999 Morgan Monterey Chardonnay from California.

Risotto with Bitter Greens and Goat Gouda Cheese

4 SERVINGS

Unlike Gouda made from cow's milk, goat's-milk Gouda has a wonderful peppery flavor that cuts some of this risotto's richness. The best brands are Arina, Benning and Darcy.

- 2 tablespoons extra-virgin olive oil
- 1 pound red Swiss chard, stems trimmed and finely chopped, leaves coarsely chopped
- 1 garlic clove, minced

Salt and freshly ground pepper

- 6 cups chicken stock or canned low-sodium broth
- 1 small onion, finely chopped
- 1½ cups Arborio rice
- 6 ounces Gouda, preferably made from goat's milk, shredded
- 1 tablespoon unsalted butter

1. In a large, deep skillet, heat 1 tablespoon of the olive oil until shimmering. Add the chopped chard stems and cook over moderately high heat, stirring frequently, until crisp-tender, about 4 minutes. Add the garlic and cook until fragrant, about 1 minute. Add the chard leaves and cook, tossing, until wilted, about 3 minutes. Drain the chard and transfer to a bowl. Season with salt and pepper. Wipe out the skillet.

2. In a saucepan, bring the chicken stock to a simmer. Heat the remaining 1 tablespoon of oil in the skillet until shimmering. Add the chopped onion

Morel and Sweet Pea Risotto

12 SERVINGS

- 1 cup dried morels (1 ounce) or ½ pound fresh morels, lightly rinsed

Boiling water

- 6 tablespoons unsalted butter

Salt and freshly ground pepper

- 10 cups chicken stock or canned low-sodium broth
- 1 large onion, finely chopped
- 3 cups Italian rice for risotto, preferably carnaroli
- 2 teaspoons coarsely chopped fresh thyme
- 1 tablespoon finely chopped fresh sage
- 1½ cups dry white wine
- 2 cups fresh or thawed frozen peas
- 1 cup freshly grated Parmigiano-Reggiano
- 7 ounces fresh goat cheese, crumbled
- 1 tablespoon coarsely chopped fresh parsley (optional)

1. In a heatproof bowl, cover the dried morels with boiling water and soak until softened, about 20 minutes. Rub the morels to loosen any grit, then lift them out; discard the soaking liquid.

2. In a medium skillet, melt 2 tablespoons of the butter over moderate heat. Add the fresh or soaked morels, season with salt and pepper and cook for 2 minutes.

3. In a large saucepan, bring the stock to a simmer; keep warm over low heat. In another large saucepan, melt the remaining 4 tablespoons of butter over moderate heat. Add the onion and cook, stirring occasionally, until translucent, about 8 minutes. Stir in the rice until the grains are evenly coated with butter, then add the thyme, sage and wine and cook, stirring, until the wine is absorbed, about 2 minutes longer.

4. Add 1 cup of the hot stock to the rice and stir over moderately high heat until it has been absorbed, about 3 minutes. Continue to cook the risotto, adding 1 cup of stock at a time and stirring constantly until it is absorbed before adding more. Stir in the morels and peas. The risotto is done when it is creamy and porridgelike and the rice is

and cook over moderate heat, stirring frequently, until softened, about 7 minutes. Add the rice and cook, stirring until the rice is coated with olive oil, about 2 minutes. Add 1 cup of the hot stock and cook, stirring frequently, until the rice has absorbed most of the stock, about 3 minutes. Continue to cook the risotto, adding 1 cup of stock at a time and stirring constantly between additions until the stock is absorbed. The risotto is done when it is creamy and the rice grains are just tender, about 20 minutes.

3. Remove the risotto from the heat and stir in the cheese, butter and cooked chard. Season with salt and pepper and serve at once.

—*Grace Parisi*

WINE A rich Chianti Classico will echo the creamy texture of the Gouda and soften the sharpness of the greens. Try one from the 1998 vintage, such as the Fontodi or the Vignamaggio.

Risotto with Bitter Greens and Goat Gouda Cheese

Hazelnut-Cranberry Wild Rice

4 SERVINGS ●

- 1 cup wild rice
- 8 cups cold water
- Salt
- 1 bunch of scallions, white and light green parts, thinly sliced (½ cup)
- ⅓ cup hazelnuts—lightly toasted, skinned and coarsely chopped
- ¼ cup dried cranberries
- Freshly ground pepper

1. In a large saucepan, cover the rice with the water, add 1 teaspoon of salt and bring to a boil. Cover and simmer over moderately low heat until the wild rice is tender but still chewy, about 1 hour. Drain the wild rice well.

2. Toss the wild rice with the scallions, hazelnuts and cranberries. Season with salt and pepper and serve.

—*Ann Chantal Altman*

ONE SERVING Calories 241 kcal, Total Fat 7.2 gm, Saturated Fat 0.5 gm, Protein 8 gm, Carbohydrates 39 gm

SERVE WITH Turkey Scaloppine (p. 201) or Pork and Winter Squash Stew (p. 220).

Middle Eastern Phyllo Rice Torte

8 SERVINGS ● ●

This is a vegetarian take on a festive traditional Moroccan dish called *bisteeya,* or pigeon pie. Here, an elaborate phyllo shell is filled with spices, dried fruit, almonds and, in place of meat, the wild rice blend from Lundberg Family Farms (available at supermarkets and health food stores). You can substitute a combination of half wild and half brown rice.

- Olive oil spray
- 1½ cups wild-rice blend, rinsed well (10 ounces)
- 3 cups water
- 3 plum tomatoes, halved and seeded
- 4 portobello mushrooms, stems discarded (¾ pound)
- Salt and freshly ground pepper

Middle Eastern Phyllo Rice Torte

2 tablespoons extra-virgin olive oil

2 medium sweet onions, such as Oso Sweet, thinly sliced

Pinch of cinnamon

2 teaspoons garam masala

¼ cup golden raisins

¼ cup chopped dried apricots

¼ cup finely chopped flat-leaf parsley

10 sheets phyllo dough, plus extra in case of tearing (½ pound), thawed if frozen

4 large eggs, beaten

¼ cup almonds, toasted and coarsely chopped

1. Preheat the oven to 350°. Spray a 9-inch springform cake pan generously with olive oil. In a medium saucepan, cover the rice with the water and bring to a boil. Cover and cook over low heat until the rice is barely tender and just cooked through, about 30 minutes. Drain well.

2. On a large nonstick baking sheet, arrange the tomatoes, cut side down, and the portobellos, stemmed side down. Season the tomatoes and mushrooms generously with salt and pepper and bake until tender, about 30 minutes. When the vegetables are cool enough to handle, peel the tomatoes and thinly slice the mushrooms.

3. Heat the olive oil in a medium enameled cast-iron casserole. Add the onions, cover and cook over low heat, stirring occasionally, until softened, about 10 minutes. Uncover and cook over moderately high heat, stirring frequently, until the onions are browned, about 10 minutes longer. Add the cinnamon and garam masala and cook, stirring, until fragrant, about 2 minutes. Remove from the heat. Add the cooked rice, raisins and dried apricots and season with salt and pepper. Stir in half of the sliced portobellos and 1 tablespoon of the chopped parsley.

4. Layer 5 sheets of the phyllo dough on a work surface, turning each successive one a quarter turn so that the stack forms a large round. Spray the top layer with olive oil and sprinkle with 1 tablespoon of the parsley. Repeat with the 5 remaining phyllo sheets, spraying the last sheet with olive oil. Fit the phyllo stack into the prepared cake pan, pressing it into the corners. Scatter 1 tablespoon of the parsley over the bottom. Gently pack the rice mixture into the cake pan and smooth the surface with the back of a spoon. Top the rice mixture with the remaining portobellos and the tomatoes. Pour the beaten eggs evenly over the tomatoes. Sprinkle the torte with the chopped almonds and the remaining 1 tablespoon of chopped parsley. Using kitchen scissors or a sharp knife, trim the phyllo overhang to about ¼ inch.

5. Bake the rice torte on the bottom rack of the oven for about 1 hour, or until the phyllo is deep golden and the filling is set in the middle. Let the rice torte cool in the pan for 10 minutes, then carefully remove the ring and slide the torte onto a large serving plate. Cut into wedges and serve.

—*Toni Robertson*

ONE SERVING Calories 345 kcal, Total Fat 10.5 gm, Saturated Fat 1.9 gm, Protein 12 gm, Carbohydrates 52 gm

MAKE AHEAD The torte can stand at room temperature for up to 4 hours. Serve warm or at room temperature.

WINE The berry-fruit flavors of a ripe, robust Zinfandel are very well suited to the sweet, slightly acidic and nutty notes in this torte. Two delicious examples from Sonoma are the 1997 Ravenswood Dry Creek Valley Teldeschi Vineyard and the 1997 St. Francis Sonoma County Old Vines.

Three-Grain Pilaf with Olives

8 SERVINGS ●

- ½ cup dried red beans (4 ounces), soaked overnight and drained
- 2 bay leaves
- 1 thyme sprig, plus 1 teaspoon fresh thyme leaves
- 2 garlic cloves, 1 minced and 1 left whole
- 1 tablespoon extra-virgin olive oil
- 1 cup short-grain brown rice (3½ ounces)
- ½ cup pearl barley (3½ ounces)
- ½ cup whole wheat berries or farro (3½ ounces)
- 1 cup finely chopped onion
- 2 plum tomatoes (½ pound), seeded and coarsely chopped
- ½ cup pitted green olives (2 ounces), coarsely chopped
- 3½ cups defatted canned low-sodium chicken broth
- 2 scallions, thinly sliced
- 1 tablespoon unsalted butter

Hot sauce, for serving (optional)

1. In a medium saucepan, cover the soaked beans with 2 inches of water. Add 1 bay leaf, the thyme sprig and the whole garlic clove and bring to a boil. Cook over moderate heat until the beans are barely tender, about 20 minutes. Drain the beans and discard the bay leaf, thyme sprig and garlic.

2. Preheat the oven to 350°. Heat the olive oil in a medium enameled cast-iron casserole. Add the rice, pearl barley and wheat berries or farro and cook over moderately high heat, stirring constantly, until lightly browned, about 10 minutes. Add the onion, minced garlic and thyme leaves and cook, stirring, until the onion is softened, about 5 minutes. Stir in the chopped tomatoes, pitted olives, red beans, chicken broth and the remaining bay leaf and bring to a simmer over moderately high heat.

3. Cover the casserole and bake for 50 minutes, or until the liquid is absorbed and the grains are tender but still slightly chewy. Let the pilaf stand for 10 minutes, then remove the bay leaf. Stir in the scallions and butter and serve with hot sauce, if desired.

—*Grace Parisi*

ONE SERVING Calories 282 kcal, Total Fat 5.7 gm, Saturated Fat 1.4 gm, Protein 9.4 gm, Carbohydrates 49.4 gm

Farro with Shiitake Mushrooms

2 SERVINGS ●

- 1½ tablespoons unsalted butter
- ½ small onion, minced
- ¾ cup farro
- 1 thyme sprig
- 1¼ cups water

Salt and freshly ground pepper

- 2½ ounces finely diced shiitake mushroom caps (1 cup)

1. Melt half of the butter in a skillet. Add the onion and cook over moderately low heat, stirring frequently, until softened, about 8 minutes. Add the farro and thyme and cook, stirring occasionally, until the farro is lightly toasted, about 3 minutes. Add the water and a pinch each of salt and pepper. Bring to a simmer, cover and cook over low heat until the water is absorbed and the farro is al dente, about 30 minutes. Discard the thyme.

2. Meanwhile, melt the remaining ¾ tablespoon of butter in a medium skillet. Add the mushrooms and cook over moderate heat, stirring frequently, until softened, about 5 minutes. Add the mushrooms to the farro, season with salt and pepper and serve.

—*Dan Barber*

MAKE AHEAD The Farro with Shiitake Mushrooms can be refrigerated overnight; gently reheat with ½ cup of water before serving.

Tabbouleh with Mint, Cilantro and Chives

4 SERVINGS ● ●

- 1 garlic clove, coarsely chopped

Kosher salt

- 1 cup chicken stock or canned low-sodium broth
- 1 cup water
- 1 small shallot, minced
- 1 thyme sprig
- 1½ cups coarse bulgur wheat (½ pound)
- ¼ cup fresh lemon juice
- 2 tablespoons extra-virgin olive oil
- 2 tablespoons minced chives
- 2 tablespoons minced mint
- 2 tablespoons minced cilantro

Freshly ground pepper

1. On a work surface, using the side of a knife, mash the garlic with 1 teaspoon of salt to make a paste.

2. In a small saucepan, combine the stock with the water, shallot, thyme and garlic paste and bring to a boil.

3. Put the bulgur in a heatproof bowl and pour the seasoned stock over it. Stir, cover and let stand until the bulgur has absorbed all of the liquid and is tender, about 40 minutes. Discard the thyme sprig and stir in the lemon juice, olive oil, chives, mint and cilantro. Season with salt and pepper and serve at room temperature or chilled.

—*Eberhard Müller*

ONE SERVING Calories 291 kcal, Total Fat 8.8 gm, Saturated Fat 1.4 gm, Protein 10 gm, Carbohydrates 47 gm

MAKE AHEAD The tabbouleh can be refrigerated for 4 hours.

Andean Quinoa Salad

4 SERVINGS ● ● ●

- 1 cup quinoa (about 7 ounces)
- 2 cups water

Salt

- ¼ cup vegetable oil
- 2 tablespoons fresh lime juice
- ¾ cup finely diced bell peppers, preferably a mix of green, red and yellow

½ medium cucumber—peeled, seeded and finely diced

2 tablespoons finely chopped mint

1 tablespoon minced jalapeño

1 scallion, minced

Freshly ground pepper

1. In a medium bowl, rinse the quinoa under cold running water for 2 minutes; drain. Transfer the quinoa to a medium saucepan, add the water and ½ teaspoon of salt and bring to a boil. Cover and cook over low heat until the water is absorbed and the quinoa is tender, about 17 minutes. Spread the quinoa on a baking sheet and let cool completely.

2. In a medium bowl, mix together the vegetable oil and lime juice. Add the diced bell peppers, diced cucumber, chopped mint, minced jalapeño, scallion and quinoa and toss. Season the salad with salt and pepper and serve at room temperature or chilled.

—*Ruth Van Waerebeek*

MAKE AHEAD The quinoa salad can be refrigerated for up to 4 hours before serving.

Grilled Polenta

4 SERVINGS ●●

1 cup medium-coarse or coarse organic stone-ground cornmeal (4½ ounces)

3½ cups water

1½ tablespoons unsalted butter

Kosher salt and freshly ground pepper

Olive oil, for brushing

1. Preheat the oven to 350°. Grease an 8-inch-wide heavy, ovenproof saucepan. Add the cornmeal, water, 1 tablespoon of the butter and 1½ teaspoons of salt and stir well. Bake the polenta uncovered for 45 minutes. Stir the polenta and bake for 25 minutes longer.

2. Remove the polenta from the oven. Stir in the remaining ½ tablespoon of butter and season with salt and pepper. Let stand for 5 minutes. Pour the polenta into an 8-by-4-inch loaf pan and let cool. Cover and refrigerate until firm.

3. Light a fire or heat a grill pan. Unmold the polenta onto a work surface and cut the loaf crosswise into 8 slices. Lightly brush the slices with olive oil and grill over low heat to crisp slowly, turning once, about 15 minutes per side. Transfer the polenta to a platter and serve. —*Paula Wolfert*

MAKE AHEAD The polenta can be prepared through Step 2 and refrigerated for up to 4 days.

Polenta with Mushroom-Roquefort Sauce

4 SERVINGS ●●

You can use sturdy wild or cultivated mushrooms—such as creminis, portobellos, shiitakes and chanterelles—in place of the white ones here.

3 tablespoons unsalted butter

¾ pound small white mushrooms, quartered

1 shallot, minced

Salt and freshly ground pepper

½ cup dry white wine

¾ cup heavy cream

½ cup crumbled Roquefort (about 2 ounces)

¼ teaspoon finely chopped rosemary

2 cups milk

2 cups water

1 cup instant polenta

1 tablespoon coarsely chopped flat-leaf parsley

1. Melt 1½ tablespoons of the butter in a large, deep skillet. Add the mushroom quarters and minced shallot, season with salt and pepper and cook over moderately high heat, stirring frequently, until the mushrooms are softened and golden, 6 to 7 minutes. Add the wine and simmer until reduced to 2 tablespoons, about 5 minutes. Add the cream, crumbled Roquefort and rosemary and simmer over moderately low heat until slightly thickened, about 7 minutes. Season the mushroom sauce with salt and pepper and keep warm.

2. Meanwhile, in a medium saucepan, combine the milk with the water, the remaining 1½ tablespoons of butter and 1 teaspoon of salt and bring to a gentle boil. Add the polenta in a thin stream, whisking constantly. Reduce the heat to moderate and cook, stirring with a wooden spoon, until the polenta is tender and pulls away from the side of the pan, about 10 minutes.

3. Spoon the polenta into deep bowls and spoon the mushroom sauce on top. Sprinkle with the parsley and serve immediately.

—*Ruth Van Waerebeek*

MAKE AHEAD The mushroom sauce can be refrigerated overnight. Rewarm before serving, adding a little water if necessary.

WINE The salty, tangy blue cheese and creamy polenta in this flavorful dish call for a rich, fruity red. Try a Portuguese bottling, such as the 1997 Sogrape Tinta Roriz Dao Quinta dos Carvalhais or the 1998 Ramos-Pinto Douro Duas Quintas.

13 sauces
condiments

Zesty Lemon Dressing

MAKES ½ CUP ● ● ●

- ¼ cup extra-virgin olive oil
- 3 tablespoons fresh lemon juice
- 1 tablespoon boiling water
- 1 teaspoon grated lemon zest

Salt and freshly ground pepper

Combine the olive oil, lemon juice, boiling water, lemon zest and salt and pepper in a jar and shake to emulsify.

—*Suki Hertz*

ONE TABLESPOON Calories 61 kcal, Total Fat 6.8 gm, Saturated Fat 0.9 gm

SALAD MATCH Romaine or other crisp lettuce.

Lemon-Thyme Vinaigrette

MAKES ½ CUP ● ● ●

- ¼ cup aged balsamic vinegar
- 2 tablespoons extra-virgin olive oil
- 2 teaspoons minced thyme
- ½ teaspoon pure lemon oil

Salt and freshly ground pepper

Combine the balsamic vinegar, olive oil, thyme, lemon oil and salt and pepper in a jar and shake to emulsify.

—*Suki Hertz*

ONE TABLESPOON Calories 38 kcal, Total Fat 3.7 gm, Saturated Fat 0.5 gm

SALAD MATCH Dandelion greens, red orach or romaine lettuce.

Pomegranate Vinaigrette

MAKES ½ CUP ● ● ●

- ¼ cup pomegranate or raspberry vinegar
- ¼ cup extra-virgin olive oil
- 2 teaspoons minced shallot
- 1 teaspoon grainy mustard

Salt and freshly ground pepper

Combine the vinegar, oil, shallot, mustard and salt and pepper in a jar and shake to emulsify. —*Suki Hertz*

ONE TABLESPOON Calories 62 kcal, Total Fat 6.8 gm, Saturated Fat 0.9 gm

SALAD MATCH Red Russian kale, yellow chard or leaf lettuce.

Verjus Vinaigrette

MAKES ½ CUP ● ● ●

Verjus is the juice of wine grapes. It's popular with chefs because, unlike vinegar, its flavor doesn't conflict with wine.

- ⅓ cup verjus
- 3 tablespoons grapeseed oil
- 1 scallion, minced
- 1½ teaspoons finely chopped dill
- 1 teaspoon Dijon mustard

Salt and freshly ground pepper

Combine all of the ingredients in a jar and shake to emulsify. —*Suki Hertz*

ONE TABLESPOON Calories 53 kcal, Total Fat 5.2 gm, Saturated Fat 0.5 gm

SALAD MATCH Pea shoots or mixed greens.

Carrot-Ginger Dressing

MAKES ¾ CUP ● ● ●

- ¼ cup minced shallot
- ¼ cup finely shredded carrot
- 2 tablespoons fresh lemon juice
- 2 tablespoons mirin
- 2 tablespoons rice vinegar
- 1 tablespoon soy sauce
- 2 teaspoons grated peeled fresh ginger
- 1 teaspoon Asian sesame oil

In a blender, puree all of the ingredients until smooth. —*Suki Hertz*

ONE TABLESPOON Calories 17 kcal, Total Fat 0.4 gm, Saturated Fat 0.1 gm

SALAD MATCH Tatsoi or mizuna.

Orange-Miso Vinaigrette

MAKES ABOUT ¼ CUP ● ● ●

Sweet white miso makes an excellent thickener for Western-style vinaigrettes, so you can use much less oil. In addition to serving this dressing on salad greens, try it on cooked green beans and raw vegetable salads such as shaved fresh fennel and celery root. This recipe can easily be doubled.

- 2 tablespoons fresh orange juice
- 1 tablespoon aged sherry vinegar

american miso

Japan isn't the only place that makes miso. Using traditional Japanese methods, Massachusetts-based **South River Miso Company** produces 11 kinds of miso, including golden millet, chickpea, adzuki bean and an intriguing dandelion-leek variety (413-369-4057; www.southrivermiso.com). **Great Eastern Sun** in North Carolina was one of the first to produce miso in the U.S. It sells nine varieties, including one made from corn (800-334-5809; www.great-eastern-sun.com). These misos are not as widely distributed as the Japanese brands sold at every Asian market and health-food store, but they're worth seeking out. Whatever miso you choose, you can store it in the refrigerator in a tightly sealed container for several months.

- 2 teaspoons sweet white (shiro) miso
- ½ teaspoon minced shallot
- 1 tablespoon walnut oil

Freshly ground pepper

In a small bowl, whisk the orange juice with the vinegar, miso and shallot until smooth. Whisk in the walnut oil and season with pepper. —*Sally Schneider*

ONE TABLESPOON Calories 40 kcal, Total Fat 3.5 gm, Saturated Fat 0.3 gm, Protein 0 gm, Carbohydrates 2 gm

MAKE AHEAD The vinaigrette can be refrigerated in a glass jar for 3 days.

Creamy Herb Dressing

MAKES 1 CUP ● ● ●

This delicious dressing has practically no fat.

- ¼ pound silken tofu (2-inch cube)
- ¼ cup watercress leaves
- ¼ cup mixed herbs, such as basil, parsley and dill
- 1 scallion, cut into 1-inch lengths
- 2 tablespoons white wine vinegar

1 tablespoon fresh lemon juice
1 tablespoon water
1 teaspoon Dijon mustard
Salt

In a blender, puree all of the ingredients until smooth. —*Suki Hertz*

ONE TABLESPOON Calories 5 kcal, Total Fat 0.2 gm, Saturated Fat 0 gm

SALAD MATCH Romaine or other crisp lettuce.

Tangy Buttermilk Dressing

MAKES ¾ CUP ● ● ●

½ cup buttermilk
2 ounces goat cheese
¼ teaspoon grated lemon zest
¼ teaspoon finely chopped thyme
Salt and freshly ground pepper

In a blender, pulse all of the ingredients until mixed but not smooth.
—*Suki Hertz*

ONE TABLESPOON Calories 17 kcal, Total Fat 1.1 gm, Saturated Fat 0.8 gm

SALAD MATCH Romaine or other crisp lettuce.

speedy asian sauces

Keep Asian condiments in your pantry so that you can make quick sauces and marinades.

BBQ sauce In a small bowl, mix ½ cup soy sauce with ¼ cup hoisin sauce, ¼ cup ketchup and 1 tablespoon honey. Brush liberally on pork or chicken during and after grilling.

Dipping sauce In a small bowl, mix ¼ cup soy sauce with 1 tablespoon sugar and the juice of ½ lemon. Stir in chili oil to taste. Serve with steamed fresh vegetables.

30-minute marinade In a bowl, mix ¼ cup of vegetable oil, 3 tablespoons of oyster sauce, 3 chopped scallions, 1 minced garlic clove and 1 tablespoon of peeled and minced fresh ginger. Pour over steaks and marinate for 30 minutes.
—*Alex Lee*

White Almond Romesco

MAKES FOUR 4-OUNCE JARS ● ● ●

This sauce is delicious as a dip for raw vegetables or pita crisps. It can also be spread on turkey or chicken sandwiches, or used as a topping for poached chicken or pan-fried fish. Or whisk it with lemon juice for a salad dressing.

1 cup milk
6 large garlic cloves
½ cup whole blanched almonds (2½ ounces)
½ cup pine nuts (2 ounces)
1 bay leaf
1½ teaspoons crushed red pepper
Salt
¼ cup extra-virgin olive oil
One 3-ounce piece of baguette, crusts removed, bread cut into ½-inch dice
½ teaspoon cumin seeds
½ teaspoon coriander seeds
1 teaspoon honey
¼ cup rice vinegar

1. In a medium saucepan, combine the milk with the garlic cloves, almonds, pine nuts, bay leaf, crushed red pepper and a pinch of salt. Cover and cook over low heat until the garlic is slightly tender, about 10 minutes. Discard the bay leaf.

2. In a medium skillet, heat 2 tablespoons of the olive oil. Add the diced bread and cook over moderately low heat, stirring occasionally, until golden, about 4 minutes. Add the cumin and coriander seeds and cook until fragrant, about 1 minute.

3. In a small bowl, dissolve the honey in the rice vinegar. Transfer to a blender; add the milk mixture and the diced bread. Add the remaining 2 tablespoons of olive oil and blend until smooth. Scrape the sauce into a medium bowl and season with salt. Transfer the romesco sauce to jars and refrigerate. —*Marcia Kiesel*

MAKE AHEAD The sauce can be refrigerated for 1 month.

Madeira Sauce

MAKES 1 CUP ● ● ●

All the elements in this sauce play off each other: Madeira is sweet with a woody earthiness; ginger adds a floral quality; and the acidic rice vinegar offsets the sweetness of the sugar. Use the sauce to marinate salmon or swordfish or to glaze poached fish or scallops. Or toss it with steamed bok choy, napa cabbage and mustard greens, or seaweed salad.

1 cup unseasoned rice vinegar
½ cup Madeira
½ cup soy sauce
½ cup sugar
½ cup minced peeled fresh ginger

In a medium saucepan, combine the the unseasoned rice vinegar with the Madeira, soy sauce, sugar and all but 1 tablespoon of the ginger. Simmer the sauce over moderate heat until it is reduced to 1 cup, about 15 minutes. Let the sauce cool to room temperature, then stir in the remaining tablespoon of minced ginger. —*Gray Kunz*

MAKE AHEAD The sauce can be refrigerated for up to 1 week.

Ancho and Chipotle Mole

MAKES ABOUT SIX 4-OUNCE JARS ● ●

The rich flavors of this mole are perfect with steak, pork, shrimp or beans. The sauce can also be simmered with chicken or turkey for a mole stew.

2 large ancho chiles
2 dried chipotle chiles
1½ cups boiling water
2 red bell peppers
2 whole cloves
1½ teaspoons cumin seeds
1 cinnamon stick, broken
3 tablespoons sunflower seeds
2 tablespoons extra-virgin olive oil
10 garlic cloves, thinly sliced
2 tablespoons tomato paste
2½ ounces bittersweet chocolate, coarsely chopped
Salt

1. In a bowl, cover the anchos and chipotles with the boiling water. Let soak for 30 minutes, until softened. Drain, reserving the liquid. Discard the stems, cores and seeds; coarsely chop the chiles.

2. Preheat the broiler or light a gas flame. Char the bell peppers for 10 minutes, turning occasionally, until charred all over. Transfer to a medium bowl, cover with plastic and let steam for 5 minutes. Peel the peppers and discard the skin, stems and seeds, then coarsely chop.

3. In a small dry skillet, toast the cloves, cumin and cinnamon stick over moderately low heat until darkened and fragrant, 1½ minutes. Let cool. Grind to a powder in a spice grinder. Transfer to a plate. Add the sunflower seeds to the skillet and toast, shaking the pan a few times, about 3 minutes. Let cool. Transfer the seeds to the grinder; finely grind.

4. Heat the oil in a medium skillet. Add the garlic and cook over low heat until golden, about 3 minutes. Add the tomato paste and cook, stirring, until glossy, about 2 minutes. Remove from the heat and stir in the chocolate until melted.

5. In a blender, combine the chiles and their soaking liquid with the bell peppers, the ground spices, the ground sunflower seeds and the garlic mixture and blend until smooth. Scrape the mole into a large bowl and season with salt. Transfer the sauce to jars and refrigerate.   —*Marcia Kiesel*

MAKE AHEAD The Ancho and Chipotle Mole can be refrigerated for 3 weeks.

Coconut-Lime Sauce

MAKES ABOUT FIVE 4-OUNCE JARS ●●
Serve this sauce with sautéed shrimp or chicken, grilled pork chops, lamb kabobs or grilled salmon. It can also be tossed with steamed rice, rice noodles or thin pasta.

- 2   limes, zest finely grated
- ¼   cup vegetable oil
- ¼   cup curry powder
- ¼   cup sugar
- 8   large scallions, white and light green parts only, finely chopped
- 4   cups unsweetened coconut milk

Salt

1. Using a sharp knife, peel the limes, removing all of the bitter white pith. Working over a bowl, cut in between the membranes to release the sections into the bowl. Finely chop the sections.

2. Heat the oil in a large saucepan. Add the curry powder and stir over low heat until fragrant, about 5 minutes. Add the chopped lime and lime zest and cook over moderately high heat until the juices have evaporated, about 5 minutes. Add the sugar and stir until melted. Add the scallions and cook, stirring, for 2 minutes. Add the coconut milk and boil over moderately high heat, stirring often, until reduced to 2½ cups, about 15 minutes. Let cool, then season with salt. Transfer to jars and refrigerate.   —*Marcia Kiesel*

MAKE AHEAD The sauce can be refrigerated for 1 month.

Ginger-Carrot Sauce

MAKES THREE 4-OUNCE JARS ●●●
A sweet and spicy sauce like this is perfect with boiled shrimp, steamed edamame or vegetable tempura.

- 1   large carrot, peeled and thinly sliced

One 3-inch piece of fresh ginger, chopped, plus 1 teaspoon finely grated fresh ginger

- 1   cup fresh carrot juice
- 2   tablespoons sugar
- 1   tablespoon water
- 2   tablespoons mustard powder
- ¼   teaspoon Asian sesame oil

Salt

1. In a saucepan, steam the carrot until tender, about 8 minutes. Let cool.

2. In a food processor or blender, pulse the chopped ginger until minced. Scrape into a small sieve set over a medium bowl and press to extract the juice; discard the solids. Stir the carrot juice into the ginger juice.

3. In a small saucepan, combine the sugar and water and bring to a boil. Remove from the heat and whisk to dissolve the sugar. Let cool. Whisk in the mustard powder, then cover and let stand for 5 minutes. Whisk in some of the carrot-ginger juice to loosen. Transfer the mixture to a blender. Add the remaining carrot-ginger juice and steamed carrot and puree. Transfer the sauce to a bowl. Stir in the grated ginger and sesame oil and season with salt. Transfer the sauce to jars and refrigerate.   —*Marcia Kiesel*

MAKE AHEAD The sauce can be refrigerated for 1 month.

Wasabi-Beet Sauce

MAKES SIX 4-OUNCE JARS ●●
Serve this sauce with boiled beef, pot roast, shrimp, mackerel, chicken, gefilte fish or grilled swordfish.

- 2   pounds medium beets
- 1   cup fresh orange juice
- 2   tablespoons sugar
- 3   tablespoons wasabi powder
- 1   teaspoon finely grated orange zest

Salt

1. Preheat the oven to 350°. Put the beets in a baking dish, cover with foil and bake for about 1 hour, or until tender. When cool enough to handle, peel the beets and cut into wedges.

2. In a small saucepan, boil the orange juice until reduced by half, about 8 minutes. Add the sugar and simmer for 2 minutes. Remove from the heat and let cool slightly. Whisk in the wasabi powder, cover the pan and let stand for 5 minutes.

3. In a blender, combine the beets and orange juice mixture and blend until

smooth. Transfer the sauce to a bowl, stir in the zest and season with salt. Transfer to jars and refrigerate.

—*Marcia Kiesel*

MAKE AHEAD The sauce can be refrigerated for 1 month.

Jalapeño-Garlic Sauce

MAKES ABOUT FOUR 4-OUNCE JARS ● ● ●

This sauce is great with steak, but it can also be used as a topping for nachos, tacos, quesadillas and burritos. Alternatively, rub it under chicken breast skin before roasting.

Vegetable oil, for brushing
20 garlic cloves, unpeeled
12 medium jalapeños
½ cup extra-virgin olive oil
¼ cup plus 2 tablespoons fresh lime juice
2 cups chopped cilantro leaves
Pinch of sugar
Salt

1. Brush two 9- or 10-inch cast-iron skillets with oil. Add half of the garlic and jalapeños to each. Cover and cook over low heat, turning the jalapeños occasionally, until they are blistered all over and the garlic is softened, about 15 minutes. Transfer to a plate to cool. Peel the jalapeños and discard the stems, seeds and cores. Peel the garlic cloves.

2. Transfer the jalapeños and garlic to a blender and add the olive oil, lime juice and cilantro. Blend until smooth. Scrape the sauce into a bowl, stir in the sugar and season with salt. Transfer the sauce to jars and refrigerate.

—*Marcia Kiesel*

MAKE AHEAD The sauce can be refrigerated for 1 month.

Trinidadian Pepper Sauce

MAKES EIGHT 4-OUNCE JARS ● ● ●

7 habanero or Scotch bonnet chiles
15 garlic cloves, coarsely chopped
15 scallions, cut into 1-inch pieces
1 large carrot, coarsely chopped

1 cup water
¾ cup distilled white vinegar
½ cup yellow mustard
⅔ cup chopped cilantro leaves
2 tablespoons thyme leaves
2 tablespoons fresh lime juice
Salt

1. In a small saucepan of boiling water, blanch the chiles for 1 minute. Drain and let cool. Discard the stems.

2. In a blender or food processor, pulse the chiles with the garlic, scallions, carrot and water until finely chopped. Add the vinegar, mustard, cilantro, thyme and lime juice and pulse just until combined. Season with salt. Transfer the sauce to jars and refrigerate.

—*Grace Parisi*

MAKE AHEAD The sauce can be refrigerated for 1 year.

Smashed Zucchini with Garlic, Chiles and Mint

MAKES ABOUT 4 CUPS ● ●

This spread is fantastic with toasted flat breads (such as the Moroccan Chickpea Flat Breads on p. 266) or over pasta. You can also mix it with ricotta as a filling for ravioli.

¼ cup plus 2 tablespoons extra-virgin olive oil
2 large garlic cloves, minced
2 dried red chiles, stemmed and chopped
8 small zucchini (2½ pounds), 4 thinly sliced and 4 thickly sliced
Salt and freshly ground pepper
3 tablespoons finely chopped mint
2 tablespoons fresh lemon juice

1. Heat ¼ cup of the olive oil in a large saucepan. Add the minced garlic and chopped chiles and cook over moderately high heat, stirring, until the garlic is golden, about 2 minutes. Add all the zucchini slices, cover and cook over moderately low heat, stirring frequently, until very tender and chunky, about 40 minutes.

2. Using a wooden spoon, break up any large pieces of zucchini. Season with salt and pepper and stir in the remaining 2 tablespoons of olive oil. Transfer to a bowl and stir in the mint and lemon juice. Serve the zucchini warm or at room temperature.

—*Jamie Oliver*

MAKE AHEAD The zucchini can be refrigerated for 2 days. Bring to room temperature and stir in the mint and lemon juice just before serving.

Lime Cream

MAKES 2 CUPS ●

Lime cream is a wonderful tart filling. It's also great on pound cake or pancakes.

1 cup sugar
½ tablespoon finely grated lime zest
½ cup of fresh lime juice
4 large eggs
1 large egg yolk
6 tablespoons cold unsalted butter, cut into tablespoons

1. In a bowl, rub the sugar with the lime zest using your hands.

2. In a nonreactive medium saucepan, whisk the lime juice with the eggs, egg yolk and lime sugar until well blended. Add the butter and whisk over moderate heat until small bubbles appear around the sides. Immediately remove from the heat and strain the lime cream through a fine sieve into a bowl.

3. Press a piece of plastic wrap directly on the surface of the lime cream and let cool completely, then refrigerate until chilled.

—*Maury Rubin*

MAKE AHEAD The cream can be refrigerated for up to 2 weeks.

Ají

MAKES ABOUT 1½ CUPS ● ●

Found on every table in Ecuador, ají, which can mean either hot sauce or hot pepper, is an all-purpose condiment. Some versions are smooth purees that look like Tabasco sauce, while this chunky onion ají is more like a relish. The ají is refrigerated overnight before serving, so plan accordingly.

- 2 medium red onions, very thinly sliced on a mandoline
- Salt
- 1½ cups boiling water
- 1 medium tomato, seeded and finely chopped
- 2 fresh cayenne or serrano chiles, seeded and minced
- ½ cup fresh lime juice
- 2 tablespoons minced cilantro
- Freshly ground pepper

I. In a medium heatproof bowl, toss the sliced onions with 1 tablespoon of salt; let stand for 5 minutes. Add the boiling water; let stand for 10 minutes. Drain the onions, rinse under cold water and pat dry.

2. Wipe out the bowl with paper towels and return the onions to it. Stir in the tomato, chiles, lime juice and cilantro and season with salt and pepper. Cover with plastic wrap and refrigerate overnight. Serve at room temperature.

—*Maricel Presilla*

MAKE AHEAD The ají can be refrigerated for up to 1 week.

Bright Lights Swiss Chard Relish

6 SERVINGS ●●●

This unusual relish highlights the multicolored stems of this leafy green, which is also known as Rainbow chard.

- 2 tablespoons olive oil
- 1 garlic clove, minced
- 1½ pounds Bright Lights chard, leaves reserved for another use, stems cut into ¼-inch dice (2 cups)
- ½ cup finely chopped sweet onion, such as Vidalia
- Salt and freshly ground pepper
- ½ cup golden raisins
- 3 tablespoons cider vinegar
- 1 tablespoon honey
- ¼ cup chopped mint

I. Heat the olive oil in a large skillet. Add the garlic and cook over moderate heat until softened. Add the chard stems and onion, season with salt and pepper and cook until the onion softens, about 4 minutes.

2. Stir in the raisins, vinegar, honey and half of the mint. Cover and cook until the chard is crisp-tender, about 1 minute longer. Transfer to a bowl and let cool before mixing in the remaining mint. —*Jack Staub*

Salsa with Tequila-Soaked Currants

MAKES ABOUT 8 CUPS ●●

The unusual addition of sweet currants tempers the heat from the jalapeños.

- ¼ cup tequila
- ½ cup dried currants
- 2 chayotes (1 pound total)—halved lengthwise, pitted and cut into ¼-inch dice
- 2 pints cherry tomatoes, coarsely chopped
- 1 medium red onion, minced
- 3 garlic cloves, minced
- 3 jalapeños, seeded and minced
- ½ cup coarsely chopped cilantro
- Salt and freshly ground pepper

I. In a small saucepan, bring the tequila to a simmer. Remove from the heat, add the currants and let soak for 10 minutes; drain. In a medium saucepan of boiling salted water, blanch the chayotes for 1 minute; drain and let cool.

2. In a medium bowl, toss the chayotes, tequila-soaked currants, tomatoes, onion, garlic, jalapeños and cilantro. Season the salsa liberally with salt and pepper and serve.

—*Marcia Kiesel*

ONE SERVING Calories 39 kcal, Total Fat 0.3 gm, Saturated Fat 0 gm, Protein 1 gm, Carbohydrates 8 gm

MAKE AHEAD The unseasoned salsa can be refrigerated for up to 1 day. Bring the salsa to room temperature and season with salt and pepper to taste just before serving.

Fried Capers

MAKES ABOUT ½ CUP ●

- ⅓ cup salt-packed capers (see Note)
- ¼ cup pure olive oil

I. Soak the capers in 2 cups of cold water for 1 hour. Drain, rinse and pat thoroughly dry.

2. In a small skillet, heat the oil until shimmering. Add the capers and cook over moderately high heat, stirring occasionally, until lightly browned and frizzled, about 2 minutes. Drain on paper towels and serve immediately.

—*Peggy Knickerbocker*

NOTE Salt-packed capers are available at specialty food shops.

SERVE WITH Baked potatoes or pasta.

Amalou

MAKES ABOUT ½ CUP ●●

- ¼ pound blanched almonds
- ¼ cup argan oil
- 2 tablespoons honey
- ¼ teaspoon salt

Preheat the oven to 350°. Spread the almonds on a baking sheet and toast for 8 minutes, or until browned. Let the almonds cool. In a food processor or blender, combine the almonds with the argan oil, honey and salt and blend to a paste. Serve as a spread for toast or flat bread. —*Paula Wolfert*

NOTE Store argan oil in the refrigerator; bring to room temperature before use.

Grapefruit-Ginger Chutney

MAKES ABOUT 1 CUP ●●●●

The honey's floral quality helps balance the tanginess of the grapefruit and the spiciness of the chile so they don't overwhelm what they are served with. The chutney is delicious with grilled pork loin chops, duck or smoked turkey, as well as with salmon fillets or steaks and swordfish steaks.

- 4 small grapefruits
- 1 cup fresh grapefruit juice
- 3 tablespoons wildflower honey

Grapefruit-Ginger Chutney

1 tablespoon sugar

½ small dried
red chile, crushed

1½ tablespoons minced
fresh ginger

1 tablespoon fresh lemon juice

Zest of ½ medium orange,
finely julienned

1 tablespoon black onion seeds
or mustard seeds (optional)

Kosher salt and freshly ground
white pepper

ɪ. Using a sharp paring knife, carefully peel the grapefruits, removing all the bitter white pith. Working over a medium glass or stainless steel bowl, cut in between the membranes to release the grapefruit sections into the bowl. Discard any seeds.

2. In a medium stainless steel saucepan, combine the grapefruit sections with the grapefruit juice, wildflower honey, sugar and dried red chile and simmer over moderate heat until thickened, about 20 minutes. Remove the chutney from the heat and stir in the minced ginger, lemon juice, orange zest and onion seeds. Season with salt and white pepper. —*Gray Kunz*

MAKE AHEAD The grapefruit-ginger chutney can be refrigerated for up to 1 week in an airtight container.

Cran-Pineapple Chutney

MAKES SEVEN 4-OUNCE JARS ● ●
A versatile chutney like this makes an ideal condiment to serve with pork, ham, lamb or seafood.

1 peeled and cored golden
pineapple (about 1½ pounds),
cut into ½-inch pieces (4 cups)

1 small sweet onion, such as
Vidalia or Maui, finely chopped

1 small green bell pepper,
finely chopped

½ cup sugar

⅓ cup cider vinegar

12 cardamom pods,
lightly crushed

2 tablespoons finely chopped
crystallized ginger

1 cup fresh or thawed
frozen cranberries

Salt

In a large saucepan, combine the pineapple with the onion, bell pepper, sugar, vinegar, cardamom and ginger and let stand at room temperature for 1 hour, stirring occasionally. Bring to a boil over high heat, stirring occasionally. Add the cranberries and cook over moderately low heat until the pineapple is translucent and the cranberries have popped, about 40 minutes. Season with salt; let cool. Transfer to jars and refrigerate.
—*Grace Parisi*

MAKE AHEAD The chutney can be refrigerated for 1 month.

Cranberry-Ginger Chutney

MAKES ABOUT 5 CUPS ● ● ●

1½ cups sugar

1 cup Champagne or white
wine vinegar

1 cup fresh orange juice

¼ cup finely julienned peeled
fresh ginger

1 tablespoon finely grated
orange zest

1 medium shallot, minced

1 cinnamon stick

½ teaspoon salt

Two 12-ounce bags of cranberries

1 teaspoon vegetable oil

1 tablespoon plus 1 teaspoon
mustard seeds

ɪ. In a large saucepan, combine the sugar with the vinegar, juice, ginger, zest, shallot, cinnamon stick and salt. Bring to a boil over high heat, stirring, until the sugar dissolves and the syrup is slightly thickened, about 7 minutes. Add the cranberries and boil until they burst, about 10 minutes. Remove the chutney from the heat.

2. Heat the oil in a small skillet. Add the mustard seeds and cook over moderately high heat until toasted, about 1½ minutes. Stir the mustard seeds and oil into the cranberry chutney and let cool. Discard the cinnamon stick. Serve the cranberry chutney at room temperature or chilled. —*Tom Douglas*

MAKE AHEAD The chutney can be refrigerated for 1 week.

Green-Tomato Jam

MAKES 3 CUPS ●
It may seem weird, but this is delicious on ice cream. Raspberries and grapes make a nice garnish.

1½ pounds firm green tomatoes,
cored and finely chopped

2 cups sugar

½ lemon, scrubbed and
thickly sliced

ɪ. Spread half of the tomatoes in a large saucepan. Cover with ⅔ cup of sugar, the lemon slices and another ⅔ cup of sugar. Spread the remaining half of the tomatoes and ⅔ cup of sugar on top. Let stand without stirring until most of the sugar has dissolved, about 1 hour.

2. Stir the tomatoes. Bring to a boil over moderate heat, stirring frequently. Reduce the heat to moderately low and cook, stirring occasionally, until the jam cooks down to 3 cups, about 1 hour. Let cool, then discard the lemon slices. —*Stéphane Garnier*

14

cakes
pies
cookies

Homey Pear Cake

Little Pistachio and Almond Cakes

MAKES 12 INDIVIDUAL CAKES ●●

These moist, chewy cakes are flavored with lemon zest and kirsch or framboise, which gives them a delicate floral fragrance. They are delicious with fresh fruit—tropical fruits or citrus in the winter and fresh berries or cherries in the summer. Be sure to have your equipment ready and all of the ingredients measured out before you start mixing up the batter; you'll need to work quickly once you've beaten the eggs so they don't deflate.

1½ teaspoons unsalted butter

2 tablespoons all-purpose flour, plus more for dusting

¾ cup shelled unsalted pistachios (3½ ounces)

½ cup sliced or slivered blanched almonds (2 ounces)

½ teaspoon baking powder

3 large eggs, separated, at room temperature

½ cup plus 2 tablespoons sugar

¼ teaspoon salt

2 teaspoons finely grated lemon zest

1½ tablespoons kirsch

¼ teaspoon cream of tartar

2 teaspoons confectioners' sugar, for dusting

I. Preheat the oven to 325°. In a small saucepan, cook the butter over low heat until it is lightly browned and smells like roasted nuts. Remove from the heat and brush a 12-cup muffin pan with the butter. Spoon a little flour into each cup and tap the pan in all directions to lightly coat the cups, then turn the pan over and tap out the excess.

2. Spread the pistachios in a pie plate and roast for about 5 minutes, until dry and fragrant. Transfer to a plate to cool. Turn the oven up to 350°. Spread the almonds in the pie plate and roast for 4 to 5 minutes, until golden and fragrant. Transfer to the plate to cool.

3. In a food processor, combine the cooled nuts with the 2 tablespoons of flour and the baking powder and process to a fine meal. In a small bowl, using an electric mixer, beat the egg yolks with ½ cup of the sugar and ⅛ teaspoon of the salt at high speed until thick and pale, 4 minutes. Add the lemon zest and kirsch and beat for 2 minutes longer. Wash and dry the beaters.

4. In a clean medium bowl, beat the egg whites with the cream of tartar and the remaining ⅛ teaspoon of salt until soft peaks form. Gradually beat in the remaining 2 tablespoons of sugar until stiff peaks form. Using a large rubber spatula, scrape the beaten whites into the beaten yolk mixture and fold together 4 times. Sprinkle the ground nut meal on top and fold it in.

5. Scrape the batter into the prepared muffin cups and smooth the surfaces. Bake the cakes in the middle of the oven for about 15 minutes, or until a tester inserted in the center of a cake comes out clean. Transfer the cakes to a rack and let cool in the pan for at least 10 minutes. Run a blunt knife around the cakes and pry them out of the cups. Let cool completely. Sift confectioners' sugar over the cakes before serving. —*Sally Schneider*

ONE SERVING Calories 158 kcal, Total Fat 8.6 gm, Saturated Fat 1.4 gm

MAKE AHEAD These cakes are best the day they are baked, but they can be wrapped well in plastic and stored for 3 days or frozen for 2 weeks.

Grandmother's Apple Cake

MAKES ONE 9-INCH CAKE ●

2 tablespoons unsalted butter

2 large baking apples, such as Golden Delicious or Rome— peeled, cored and coarsely chopped

1½ tablespoons Calvados

1½ teaspoons cinnamon

1¼ cups sugar

⅔ cup plain yogurt

¾ cup vegetable oil

3 large eggs at room temperature, lightly beaten

2 cups all-purpose flour

1 teaspoon baking soda

1. Preheat the oven to 350°. Generously grease a 9-inch round pan.

2. In a medium skillet, melt the butter over moderate heat. Add the apples and cook, tossing occasionally, until lightly browned all over, about 5 minutes. Stir in the Calvados, cinnamon and 1 tablespoon of the sugar and remove the skillet from the heat.

3. In a large bowl, mix the yogurt with the remaining sugar until completely smooth. Mix in the oil and eggs, then mix in the flour and baking soda. Stir in the apples. Scrape the batter into the prepared pan, spreading it evenly. Bake for 50 minutes, or until the cake is set and a toothpick inserted in the center comes out clean. Transfer the pan to a rack and let the cake cool completely before unmolding.

—*Van Gogh's Table*

MAKE AHEAD The cake can be covered and kept overnight.

SERVE WITH Whipped cream.

Homey Pear Cake

MAKES ONE 8-INCH CAKE ●

This pear cake made with slices of juicy fruit gets its warm, slightly nutty flavor and rich texture from almond paste. Apples can be substituted for the pears.

- 2 cups plus 1 tablespoon all-purpose flour
- ¾ cup plus 2 tablespoons granulated sugar
- 2 tablespoons light brown sugar
- 1 teaspoon baking powder
- ¼ teaspoon salt
- 1 stick plus 2 tablespoons (5 ounces) unsalted butter, softened
- 1 large egg, lightly beaten
- ½ cup almond paste
- 2 tablespoons fresh lemon juice
- 1 teaspoon cinnamon
- 2 pounds firm but ripe pears—peeled, cored and thinly sliced

Vanilla ice cream or crème fraîche, for serving

1. Preheat the oven to 350°. Butter an 8-inch square baking dish.

2. In a food processor, pulse 2 cups of the flour with ¾ cup of the granulated sugar, the light brown sugar, baking powder and salt. Add the softened butter and pulse until the mixture resembles coarse meal. Add the egg and pulse just until combined. Turn the dough out onto a work surface and knead several times. Divide the dough roughly in half; leave 1 piece slightly larger. Flatten the dough into disks, wrap in plastic and refrigerate for 20 minutes.

3. Wipe out the food processor. Add the almond paste, lemon juice, cinnamon and the remaining 2 tablespoons of granulated sugar and 1 tablespoon of flour; process until smooth. Scrape into a bowl and gently stir in the pear slices.

4. On an unfloured work surface, roll out the larger piece of dough to an 11-inch square. Fit the dough into the baking dish, pressing it three-quarters of the way up the side. Spoon the pear filling into the cake pan in an even layer. Roll out the remaining dough to an 8½-inch square. Set the dough on top of the pears and press the rim to seal. Bake for 55 minutes, or until golden.

5. Transfer the cake to a rack and let cool for at least 6 hours, or preferably overnight. Cut into squares and serve with vanilla ice cream or crème fraîche. —*Don Pintabona*

MAKE AHEAD The cake can be kept at room temperature for 2 days.

SERVE WITH Dried pears.

WINE A late-harvest Riesling will echo the sweet succulence of the pears and blend with the cake's toasty almond flavor. Look for a reasonably priced example, such as the 1999 Mount Horrocks Cordon Cut from Australia or the 1999 Konrad & Conrad Marlborough Noble Late Harvest Sigria from New Zealand.

Sponge Cake with Lemon Zest and Raspberries

MAKES ONE 10-INCH CAKE ●●

Using fruity extra-virgin olive oil in place of butter cuts the cholesterol and produces a light and flavorful sponge cake.

- 1¾ cups all-purpose flour
- 1 teaspoon baking powder
- ½ teaspoon baking soda

Pinch of salt

- ¼ cup extra-virgin olive oil
- 3 tablespoons milk

Finely grated zest of 1 lemon, plus 1 tablespoon fresh lemon juice

- 1 cup sugar
- 4 large eggs
- 2 cups individually quick-frozen raspberries (6 ounces)

1. Preheat the oven to 350°. Lightly grease and flour a 10-inch round cake pan, tapping out any excess flour.

2. In a bowl, whisk the flour with the baking powder, baking soda and salt. In a small pitcher, mix the olive oil with the milk and lemon juice.

3. In a large bowl, using an electric mixer, blend the sugar with the lemon zest. Add the eggs, 1 at a time, and beat at medium speed until thick and pale, about 3 minutes. Beat in the dry ingredients, alternating with the olive oil mixture until the batter is smooth.

4. Pour the batter into the prepared pan and scatter the raspberries on top. Bake for about 40 minutes, or until the cake is golden and a toothpick inserted in the center comes out with a few moist crumbs attached. Invert the cake onto a wire rack, turn it right side up and let cool completely. Cut the cake into wedges and serve.

—*Toni Robertson*

ONE SERVING Calories 309 kcal, Total Fat 9.9 gm, Saturated Fat 1.9 gm, Protein 6 gm, Carbohydrates 49 gm

MAKE AHEAD The cake can be stored at room temperature for 3 days.

WINE Serve an off-dry sparkling wine that is slightly sweeter than this delightful, not-so-sweet sponge cake. Look for the 1995 Schramsberg Vineyards Demi-Sec Napa Valley or the bargain 1999 Vietti Cascinetta Moscato from Italy.

Oat Cake with Warm Mixed-Berry Compote

MAKES ONE 9-INCH CAKE ●

A staple of the Scottish diet, rolled oats add a pleasant nutty flavor to cakes, biscuits, cookies and other simple desserts. For a lovely, dense and moist texture, use regular rolled oats rather than the instant or quick-cooking kind.

 1   cup rolled oats
1¼   cups boiling water
1½   cups all-purpose flour
 1   teaspoon baking soda
 1   teaspoon cinnamon
 ¼   teaspoon freshly grated nutmeg
 ¼   teaspoon salt
 1   stick (4 ounces) unsalted butter, softened
 1   cup packed light brown sugar
 ½   cup granulated sugar
 2   large eggs
 1   teaspoon pure vanilla extract
Warm Mixed-Berry Compote (recipe follows)
Clotted cream, for serving (see Note)

1. Preheat the oven to 350°. Butter and flour a 9-inch-square cake pan. In a heatproof bowl, soak the rolled oats in the boiling water for 20 minutes. Drain well.

2. In a medium bowl, sift the flour with the baking soda, cinnamon, nutmeg and salt. In a large bowl, using a hand-held electric mixer, beat the softened butter until creamy. Add the light brown and granulated sugars and beat the mixture until light and fluffy. Beat in the eggs, 1 at a time, then beat in the vanilla extract. Add the soaked oats and beat at medium speed just until combined. At low speed, beat in the dry ingredients.

3. Scrape the batter into the prepared pan and bake the cake in the middle of the oven for 40 minutes, or until a toothpick inserted in the center comes out clean. Let the cake cool in the pan for 10 minutes. Turn the cake out onto a wire rack, then invert it and let cool completely.

4. Cut the oat cake into squares and serve with the Warm Mixed-Berry Compote and clotted cream.

—*Bobby Flay*

NOTE Clotted cream is available at specialty food stores and on-line from www.thebritishshoppe.com.

WARM MIXED-BERRY COMPOTE

MAKES ABOUT 3 CUPS ● ● ●

1½   cups fresh orange juice
 3   tablespoons mild honey
 1   large vanilla bean, split
1½   cups blueberries
1½   cups blackberries
1½   cups raspberries
 1   tablespoon cornstarch dissolved in 1½ tablespoons water

In a medium saucepan, combine the orange juice with the honey. Scrape the seeds from the vanilla bean into the saucepan and add the bean. Bring to a boil over moderate heat, stirring to dissolve the honey, about 2 minutes. Add the blueberries and blackberries and cook just until softened, about 2 minutes. Gently fold in the raspberries. Stir the cornstarch slurry and add it to the saucepan. Simmer the compote until thickened and glossy, about 2 minutes. Discard the vanilla bean. Serve warm.   —*B.F.*

MAKE AHEAD The compote can be refrigerated overnight. Reheat gently before serving.

Gingerbread with Pears

MAKES ONE 9-BY-12-INCH CAKE ●

2½   cups all-purpose flour
 1   tablespoon ground ginger
1½   teaspoons baking soda
 1   teaspoon cinnamon
 ½   teaspoon salt
 ¼   teaspoon ground cloves
 1   large egg
 1   large egg white
 ½   cup packed brown sugar
 1   cup unsulphured molasses
 ⅓   cup low-fat buttermilk or plain nonfat yogurt
 ¼   cup canola oil
 1   ripe Bartlett pear—peeled, cored and cut into ½-inch dice

1. Preheat the oven to 325°. Spray a 9-by-2-inch baking pan with vegetable oil cooking spray. In a bowl, whisk the flour with the ginger, baking soda, cinnamon, salt and cloves.

Oat Cake with Warm Mixed-Berry Compote

2. In a medium bowl, beat the egg and egg white with the brown sugar until creamy. Beat in the molasses, the buttermilk or yogurt and the canola oil. Pour the mixture over the dry ingredients and stir until blended. Fold in the diced pear.

3. Pour the batter into the prepared pan and bake for 45 minutes, or until a toothpick inserted in the center of the gingerbread comes out clean. Transfer to a rack to cool before serving.

—*Diana Sturgis*

ONE SERVING Calories 261 kcal, Total Fat 5.4 gm, Saturated Fat 0.6 gm, Protein 4 gm, Carbohydrates 50 gm

Pumpkin Gingerbread Upside-Down Cake

MAKES ONE 10-INCH CAKE ●

One 2½-pound sugar pumpkin or other winter squash—halved, seeded, cut into ½-inch wedges and peeled

3   sticks (¾ pound) unsalted butter, 2 sticks melted and cooled slightly

1   cup packed light brown sugar

½   cup coarsely chopped pecans (about 2 ounces)

3   Medjool dates (about 2 ounces), pitted and julienned

2½ cups all-purpose flour

2   teaspoons baking soda

1   teaspoon salt

1   teaspoon cinnamon

¼   teaspoon freshly grated nutmeg

1   cup hot strong coffee

½   cup molasses

2   teaspoons finely grated peeled fresh ginger

2   large eggs

1   cup granulated sugar

Sweetened whipped cream, for serving

1. Preheat the oven to 375°. Butter a 10-by-2-inch round cake pan and line the bottom with parchment paper. Wrap a 2-inch-tall foil collar around the cake pan and tape closed. Secure the collar with kitchen string. Lightly butter the foil collar.

2. Lightly butter a large baking sheet. Arrange the pumpkin wedges on the sheet and bake them for about 20 minutes, or until tender when pierced with the tip of a knife. Reduce the oven temperature to 350°.

3. In a small saucepan, melt the solid stick of butter with the light brown sugar. Pour the mixture into the cake pan and sprinkle with the chopped pecans. Arrange the pumpkin slices in the pan in a decorative pattern, overlapping them if necessary. Tuck in the dates.

4. In a medium bowl, whisk the flour with the baking soda, salt, cinnamon and nutmeg. In another bowl, whisk the hot coffee with the molasses and ginger. In a large bowl, whisk the eggs with the granulated sugar and the remaining 2 sticks of melted butter until smooth. Add the dry ingredients in 2 batches, alternating with the coffee mixture and beating with a wooden spoon until smooth. Pour the batter over the pumpkin slices in the prepared cake pan.

5. Bake for about 1 hour and 20 minutes, or until a toothpick inserted in the center of the cake comes out clean. Loosely cover the cake with foil if the top browns too quickly.

6. Let the cake cool in the pan for 10 minutes. Remove the foil collar. Run a thin knife around the cake to loosen it. Cover with an inverted plate and turn the cake out onto the plate; remove the pan. Carefully peel off the parchment paper and replace any pumpkin, pecans or dates stuck to the paper. Let the cake cool completely before slicing. Serve with sweetened whipped cream.

—*Tom Douglas*

MAKE AHEAD The cake can be made up to 6 hours ahead.

WINE Look for a rich, sweet dessert wine with enough acidity to keep the intense sweetness of the cake from being cloying. Try a honeyed ice wine, such as the 1998 Covey Run Chenin Blanc Yakima Valley from Washington State or the 1999 Bonny Doon Muscat Vin de Glacière from California.

Banana Cakes with Rum Sauce

MAKES 6 INDIVIDUAL CAKES CAKES

6½ tablespoons unsalted butter, softened

½   cup self-rising flour

1   teaspoon baking soda

⅔   cup light brown or turbinado sugar

2   large eggs

3   large ripe bananas, mashed (1⅓ cups)

Banana Cake with Rum Sauce

one-fourth of the whipped cream and top with the remaining layer, cut side down. Spread the top and sides of the cake with the remaining whipped cream and refrigerate for up to 2 hours.

6. Just before serving, sprinkle the Coffee Toffee Crunch on top of the cake and press it onto the sides and serve.
—Vickie Gott

MAKE AHEAD The unfrosted cake can be stored in an airtight container for 1 day.

COFFEE TOFFEE CRUNCH
MAKES ABOUT 1½ CUPS ●

Vegetable oil

½ **cup sugar**

2 **tablespoons light corn syrup**

2 **tablespoons strong brewed coffee**

½ **teaspoon baking soda, sifted**

Brush a large baking sheet with oil. In a small, heavy saucepan, combine the sugar, corn syrup and coffee. Bring to

Lemon Cornmeal Cake with Lapsang Souchong Chocolate Sauce

a boil, stirring just until the sugar dissolves. Cook over moderately high heat, stirring occasionally, until the syrup registers 290° on a candy thermometer, about 7 minutes. Carefully stir in the baking soda until completely blended. Immediately pour the toffee onto the prepared baking sheet. Let cool until brittle, about 1 hour, then crack into ½-inch pieces. *—V.G.*

MAKE AHEAD The coffee toffee crunch can be stored in an airtight container for 1 week.

Lemon Cornmeal Cakes with Lapsang Souchong Chocolate Sauce

MAKES 12 INDIVIDUAL CAKES ●

This dessert is all about a startling combination of flavors—apricots, smoky Lapsang souchong tea, chocolate, maraschino liqueur and cream. Every element of this dessert can be made in advance.

2 **cups cake flour**

1 **cup fine stone-ground yellow cornmeal**

½ **teaspoon baking soda**

½ **teaspoon salt**

4 **sticks (1 pound) unsalted butter, softened**

2 **cups sugar**

8 **large eggs, separated**

1 **cup sour cream**

1 **teaspoon finely grated lemon zest**

1 **teaspoon pure vanilla extract**

Maraschino Crème Anglaise (recipe follows)

Lapsang Souchong Chocolate Sauce (recipe follows)

Apricots in Armagnac Syrup (recipe follows)

I. Preheat the oven to 350°. Butter twelve 1-cup muffin tins and dust with cornmeal. In a medium bowl, sift the flour with the cornmeal, baking soda and salt. In a standing mixer with a paddle attachment, beat the butter at medium speed with all but 1 tablespoon of the sugar until light and fluffy,

about 10 minutes. Beat in the 8 egg yolks, 1 at a time. Then beat in the sour cream, lemon zest and vanilla. Using a rubber spatula, fold in the dry ingredients.

2. In a large stainless steel bowl, beat the 8 egg whites with a pinch of salt until almost firm. Add the remaining 1 tablespoon of sugar and beat until firm and glossy. Fold one-fourth of the beaten whites into the cake batter, then fold in the remaining egg whites. Spoon the batter into the prepared muffin tins.

3. Bake the cakes for about 30 minutes, or until golden brown and a toothpick inserted in the center comes out clean. Set the pan or pans on a wire rack and let the cakes cool for 5 minutes. Run a knife around the edges, then invert the cakes onto the rack and let cool completely.

4. To serve, spoon about 2½ tablespoons of Maraschino Crème Anglaise onto 12 dessert plates and drizzle each with ¼ cup of the Lapsang Souchong Chocolate Sauce. Set a cornmeal cake in the center and top with the Apricots in Armagnac Syrup. *—Jeremiah Tower*

MAKE AHEAD The cakes can be wrapped in plastic and stored at room temperature overnight or frozen for up to 2 weeks.

WINE Only a rich, fragrant Muscat de Beaumes-de-Venise will complement the intense range of flavors, from zesty lemon and sweet apricot to smoky bittersweet chocolate. Two good examples are the 1998 Paul Jaboulet Aîné and the 1998 M. Chapoutier.

MARASCHINO CRÈME ANGLAISE
MAKES ABOUT 2 CUPS ●●

2 **cups milk**

3 **large egg yolks**

2 **large eggs**

½ **cup sugar**

Pinch of salt

1 **tablespoon maraschino liqueur**

1 **teaspoon pure vanilla extract**

I. Scald the milk in a medium saucepan. In a medium heatproof bowl, whisk the egg yolks with the eggs, sugar and salt. Slowly whisk in half of the hot milk, then whisk in the remaining milk. Return the mixture to the saucepan and cook over low heat, whisking constantly, until the custard is thick enough to coat the back of a wooden spoon, about 6 minutes.

2. Strain the custard through a fine sieve and let cool completely. Stir in the maraschino liqueur and vanilla and refrigerate until chilled.   —*J.T.*

MAKE AHEAD The custard can be refrigerated for up to 2 days. Bring to room temperature before serving.

LAPSANG SOUCHONG CHOCOLATE SAUCE
MAKES ABOUT 3 CUPS ●

- 2 cups heavy cream
- 1 tablespoon Lapsang souchong tea leaves
- ¾ pound bittersweet chocolate, coarsely chopped

Salt

Scald the cream in a medium saucepan. Remove from the heat and stir in the tea. Cover and let stand for 1 hour. Strain through a fine sieve set over a clean saucepan and bring to a simmer over moderate heat. Remove from the heat and stir in the chocolate and a pinch of salt. Whisk until smooth. Let cool slightly. The sauce should be thick but pourable.   —*J.T.*

MAKE AHEAD The sauce can be stored overnight at room temperature.

APRICOTS IN ARMAGNAC SYRUP
MAKES 2 TO 3 CUPS ●●
Some swear no apricots are better than the glacéed ones from Australia.

- 1 cup Armagnac
- 12 glacéed apricots, preferably Australian
- ¼ cup sugar
- 1 tablespoon pomegranate juice (optional)

I. Preheat the oven to 300°. Heat the Armagnac in a small saucepan. Arrange the apricots in a glass baking dish and pour the Armagnac over them. Cover with foil and bake for 15 minutes.

2. Drain the hot Armagnac into a large skillet and carefully ignite it. When the flames die down, add the sugar and simmer over moderately high heat until thickened, about 5 minutes. Add the pomegranate juice and the apricots and simmer over low heat, turning them twice, until the syrup is reduced to about ⅓ cup, about 3 minutes; let cool. Thickly slice the apricots; store in the syrup.   —*J.T.*

MAKE AHEAD The apricots can be kept at room temperature for 2 days.

Silky Chocolate Cake
MAKES ONE 8-INCH CAKE ●
Before the vogue for molten chocolate cakes, these desserts were cooked all the way through yet remained silky.

- 2 sticks plus 2 tablespoons (9 ounces) unsalted butter, cut into tablespoons
- 1 cup granulated sugar
- ½ cup water
- ½ pound bittersweet chocolate, coarsely chopped
- ½ cup all-purpose flour
- 3 large eggs, beaten

Confectioners' sugar, for dusting

I. Preheat the oven to 350°. Wrap the outside of an 8-by-3-inch round springform pan in heavy-duty foil, then generously butter the inside of the pan. Set the springform in a small roasting pan.

2. In a saucepan, combine the butter with the granulated sugar and water and bring to a boil over moderate heat, stirring. Remove from the heat. Add the chocolate and stir until smooth; let cool.

3. In a medium bowl, whisk the flour with the eggs until blended. Add to the chocolate batter and whisk until smooth. Pour the batter into the prepared springform pan. Pour enough hot water into the roasting pan to reach halfway up the side of the springform. Bake the cake in the oven for about 1 hour and 15 minutes, or until the top is crusty and a cake tester inserted in the center of the cake comes out with a few moist crumbs attached. Let the cake cool in the springform on a rack for 20 minutes. Remove the foil and the side of the pan and let the cake cool completely. Dust the cake with confectioners' sugar just before serving.

—*Murielle Andraud*

MAKE AHEAD The cake can be prepared 6 hours ahead.

WINE A sweet red wine with intense ripe plum and raisin flavors, from Maury or Banyuls in the south of France, best complements the rich chocolate flavor and smooth texture of this cake. If you can't find the 1980 Mas Amiel Maury, two other great bottlings are the 1998 Mas Amiel Maury and the 1997 Casa Blanca Banyuls.

Wolfgang's Sacher Torte
MAKES ONE 9-INCH TORTE ●
CAKE

- 6 ounces bittersweet chocolate, finely chopped
- 6 tablespoons unsalted butter
- 4 large eggs, separated
- ½ cup sugar
- ⅓ cup all-purpose flour
- 1 large egg white
- ¼ teaspoon salt
- ½ cup apricot preserves
- 1½ teaspoons apricot brandy

GLAZE

- 6 ounces bittersweet chocolate, finely chopped
- 2 tablespoons unsalted butter
- ¼ cup heavy cream

I. MAKE THE CAKE: Preheat the oven to 350°. Butter and flour a 9-inch round cake pan. In a small stainless steel bowl set over a small saucepan of simmering water, melt the chocolate with the butter, stirring constantly. Remove the bowl from the heat and let cool.

2. In a medium bowl, using a handheld electric mixer, beat the 4 egg yolks with 3 tablespoons of the sugar until light, about 5 minutes. Beat in the melted chocolate, then gently fold in the flour.

3. In another large bowl, using clean beaters, beat the 5 egg whites with the salt until soft peaks form. Add the remaining 5 tablespoons of sugar and beat until firm and glossy. Fold one-third of the beaten whites into the chocolate mixture to lighten it, then fold in the remaining whites until incorporated. Scrape the batter into the prepared pan and bake for 40 minutes, or until a cake tester inserted in the center comes out clean. Transfer to a rack to cool.

4. Puree the apricot preserves in a food processor, then blend in the brandy.

5. MAKE THE GLAZE: In a small stainless steel bowl set over a small saucepan of simmering water, melt

the chocolate with the butter. In another small saucepan, bring the cream to a boil. Stir it into the melted chocolate and let the shiny glaze cool until warm.

6. Run a thin knife around the edge of the cake to loosen it. Turn the cake out onto a cake rack set over a baking sheet; let cool. Using a serrated knife, cut the cake in half horizontally. Spread the apricot preserves evenly over one of the cut sides and set the second layer on top. Slowly and evenly pour the chocolate glaze over the cake, using a metal offset spatula to spread it evenly over the top and around the sides; any excess glaze will drip into the pan below. With a large, wide spatula, transfer the glazed cake to a platter and refrigerate to firm the chocolate glaze, about 30 minutes. Cut the cake with a warmed knife.

—*Wolfgang Puck*

MAKE AHEAD The glazed cake can be refrigerated for up to 5 days.
SERVE WITH Whipped cream.
COFFEE Instead of wine, serve this world-famous Austrian chocolate cake with a strong Viennese coffee topped with plenty of whipped cream.

Classic Devil's Food Cake

MAKES ONE 9-INCH LAYER CAKE ●
This divine, cocoa-rich cake with bittersweet chocolate frosting is a great make-ahead dessert because it is even better the day after it is baked.

CAKE
1½ **cups cake flour**
⅔ **cup unsweetened
    cocoa powder**
1½ **teaspoons baking soda**
½ **teaspoon salt**
1 **stick (4 ounces) unsalted butter,
    at room temperature**
1½ **cups sugar**
2 **large eggs, at room temperature**
1 **teaspoon pure vanilla extract**
1 **cup buttermilk or sour cream,
    at room temperature**

FROSTING
10 **ounces bittersweet or semisweet
    chocolate, coarsely chopped**
½ **cup water**
1 **stick (4 ounces) cold unsalted
    butter, cut into tablespoons**

I. MAKE THE CAKE: Preheat the oven to 350°. Butter two 9-by-2-inch round cake pans; line the bottoms with parchment paper. Butter the paper.

2. In a bowl, sift the cake flour with the cocoa powder, baking soda and salt. In a large bowl, beat the butter with the sugar until light and fluffy. Beat in the eggs, 1 at a time, then beat in the vanilla extract. Stir in half of the dry ingredients, then the buttermilk or sour cream. Stir in the remaining dry ingredients until just blended. Do not overmix.

3. Scrape the batter into the prepared cake pans and smooth the surfaces. Bake the cakes for 25 minutes, or until a toothpick inserted in the centers comes out clean. Transfer the pans to a wire rack and let cool for 10 minutes, then turn out the cakes and let them cool completely.

4. MAKE THE FROSTING: In a medium heatproof bowl set in a saucepan filled with 1 inch of simmering water, melt the chopped bittersweet or semisweet chocolate in the ½ cup of water; stir until smooth. Remove the bowl from the saucepan and stir in the butter, 1 tablespoon at a time, until blended. Let the mixture cool for about 10 minutes. Using an electric mixer, beat the frosting at high speed until light and fluffy, about 5 minutes.

5. Peel the parchment off the cakes and discard. Set 1 cake layer on a plate and spread about ¾ cup of the frosting on top. Top with the second cake layer. Spread the remaining frosting all over the top and sides of the cake. Cut the cake into wedges and serve.

—*David Lebovitz*

Wolfgang's Sacher Torte

Classic Devil's Food Cake

Deep Dark Chocolate Coconut Cake

MAKES 1 BUNDT CAKE

Feeling blue? Have a slice of this cake. The chocolate and yogurt it's made with can supposedly boost levels of the feel-good brain chemical tyrosine.

CAKE

One 7-ounce bag of sweetened
    shredded coconut (2 cups),
    finely chopped
½ cup sweetened condensed milk
1 large egg white
2 cups all-purpose flour
½ cup unsweetened cocoa powder
2 teaspoons baking powder
Scant ½ teaspoon baking soda
Scant ½ teaspoon salt
1½ sticks (6 ounces) unsalted
    butter, softened
1 cup plus 2 tablespoons sugar
3 large eggs
3 ounces bittersweet or semisweet
    chocolate, melted and cooled
2¼ teaspoons pure vanilla extract
1½ cups plain nonfat yogurt

GLAZE

½ cup sugar
¼ cup water
1 tablespoon unsweetened
    cocoa powder
½ teaspoon pure vanilla extract

1. MAKE THE CAKE: Preheat the oven to 350°. Butter and flour an 8-cup Bundt pan. In a small bowl, mix the coconut with the condensed milk and egg white. Transfer the mixture to a large sheet of plastic wrap. Using your hands, roll it into an 18-inch rope. Wrap and refrigerate until slightly firm, at least 20 minutes.

2. In another small bowl, sift the flour with the cocoa, baking powder, baking soda and salt. In a large bowl, using an electric mixer, beat the butter until creamy. Add the sugar and beat until light and fluffy. Add the eggs, 1 at a time, beating well after each addition. Add the melted chocolate and the vanilla and beat until the batter is smooth. Beat in the dry ingredients in 3 batches, alternating with the yogurt.

3. Scrape the batter into the prepared pan and smooth the surface. Unwrap the coconut rope and join the ends to form a circle. Lay the rope on the batter, centering it in the pan. Press the coconut into the batter until it is submerged 1 inch. Bake the cake for 1 hour, or until a toothpick inserted in the center comes out clean. Let cool in the pan for 10 minutes, then invert onto a rack to cool completely.

4. MAKE THE GLAZE: In a medium saucepan, combine the sugar and water and bring to a boil; stir to dissolve the sugar. Whisk in the cocoa and vanilla and let cool. Brush a thin layer of the glaze over the cake and let dry slightly. Repeat 3 more times, letting the glaze dry slightly before brushing the cake again. Refrigerate until the glaze is set and slightly cracked before serving. —*Grace Parisi*

Chocolate-Hazelnut Wedding Cake

10 TO 12 SERVINGS ●

This tiered cake is a serious undertaking: you will need corrugated cardboard, plastic straws, small and large offset spatulas, a pastry bag fitted with a ½-inch star tip and a lazy Susan.

CAKE

3 cups sifted cake flour
1 cup unsweetened cocoa powder
2 teaspoons baking soda
½ teaspoon salt
2½ sticks (10 ounces) unsalted
    butter, at room temperature
2 cups sugar
4 teaspoons pure vanilla extract
4 large eggs, at room temperature
2 cups buttermilk

FILLING

½ pound semisweet chocolate,
    finely chopped
1 cup heavy cream
5 tablespoons hazelnut liqueur
Vanilla Buttercream (recipe follows)

1. MAKE THE CAKE: Preheat the oven to 325°. Lightly butter a 15-by-17-inch jelly-roll pan with 1-inch sides. Line the bottom with parchment or wax paper; butter the paper. Dust the pan with flour, tapping out any excess.

2. In a medium bowl, sift the flour with the cocoa powder, baking soda and salt. In a large bowl, using an electric mixer, beat the butter at medium speed until creamy. Add the sugar and vanilla and beat until fluffy. Add the eggs, 1 at a time, beating well after each addition. Scrape down the side and bottom of the bowl. At low speed, beat in the dry ingredients in 3 batches, alternating with the buttermilk.

3. Pour the batter into the prepared pan and smooth the surface. Bake the cake in the middle of the oven for about 35 minutes, or until a toothpick inserted in the center comes out clean. Let the cake cool completely in the pan. Refrigerate until chilled, about 2 hours.

4. MAKE THE FILLING: Heat the chocolate in a microwave oven until nearly melted. Let stand for 1 minute, then stir until smooth. Whisk in the heavy cream and 2 tablespoons of the hazelnut liqueur. Refrigerate the chocolate filling, stirring occasionally, until slightly firm, about 2 hours.

5. Run the tip of a paring knife around the side of the cake. Set a large cookie sheet or cutting board on top and flip. Remove the pan and peel the paper off the cake. Using a 6-inch corrugated cardboard round as a template, cut out three 6-inch cake rounds as close together as possible. Using a 4-inch round cardboard template, cut out 2 rounds of cake; using a 2-inch template, cut out 2 rounds from the remaining cake.

6. Using an electric mixer, beat the chocolate filling until slightly pale and stiff, about 1 minute. Set one 6-inch cake round on a 6½-inch cardboard round and brush lightly with some of

Chocolate-Hazelnut
Wedding Cake

the hazelnut liqueur. Spread ¼ cup of the chocolate filling on the top and cover with another 6-inch cake round. Brush with hazelnut liqueur and spread another ¼ cup of the chocolate filling on top. Cover with the last 6-inch cake round; set aside.

7. Set one 4-inch cake round on the 4-inch cardboard template and brush with hazelnut liqueur. Spread 3 tablespoons of the chocolate filling on the top and cover with the second 4-inch cake round; set aside. Set one 2-inch cake round on the 2-inch template and brush with hazelnut liqueur. Spread 2 tablespoons of the chocolate filling on top and cover with the second 2-inch cake round. Refrigerate all 3 layer cakes until thoroughly chilled, at least 2 hours.

8. Fill a pastry bag fitted with a ½-inch star tip with 1 cup of the Vanilla Buttercream. Pipe a small dollop of buttercream into the center of a lazy Susan and anchor the 6-inch layer cake on it. Pipe the buttercream around the cake to fill any gaps between the layers. Using a large offset spatula, spread a very thin layer of buttercream over the entire cake. Carefully lift the cake off the lazy Susan and refrigerate to set the frosting, about 10 minutes. Fill in between the layers and frost the 4-inch and 2-inch layer cakes.

9. Return the 6-inch cake to the lazy Susan and frost with 1 cup of the buttercream. Run a large offset spatula under hot water, wipe it dry and use it to spread the frosting on the side of the cake in a smooth, even layer. Insert a plastic straw in the center of the cake and trim the straw flush with the cake. Refrigerate until chilled, at least 2 hours. Frost the 4-inch cake with buttercream. Insert a plastic straw in the center, leaving it protruding. Refrigerate until firm. Frost the 2-inch layer cake with buttercream and refrigerate until chilled.

10. Transfer the 6-inch cake to a cake plate. Center the 4-inch cake on top, using the straw to help maneuver the cake. Trim the straw flush with the cake. Center the 2-inch cake on top. Fill the pastry bag with the remaining buttercream and pipe a decorative border around the base of each tier, covering the cardboard. Refrigerate the assembled cake until firm. Let the cake stand at room temperature for at least 1 hour before serving.

—Sam Godfrey

MAKE AHEAD The finished cake can be refrigerated for 3 days. Chill completely and cover loosely with plastic wrap. Remove the plastic wrap while the cake is still cold.

VANILLA BUTTERCREAM

MAKES ABOUT 3½ CUPS ●

This buttercream is made with a cooked meringue, which calls for heating the sugar with egg whites before beating.

- ¾ cup egg whites (about 6 large whites)
- 1½ cups sugar
- 1½ teaspoons pure vanilla extract
- 3 sticks (¾ pound) unsalted butter, cut into tablespoons and softened

1. In a double boiler, beat the egg whites with the sugar over simmering water until the sugar has dissolved and the whites reach 160° on a candy thermometer, about 7 minutes.

2. Pour the egg whites into the bowl of a standing electric mixer fitted with the whisk and beat at medium speed until stiff, glossy and cool. Beat in the vanilla extract. At medium-low speed, beat in the softened butter, a few tablespoons at a time; continue beating until the buttercream is fluffy yet firm. *—S.G.*

MAKE AHEAD The vanilla buttercream can be refrigerated for 2 days. Bring to room temperature before using.

Chocolate Cheesecake Cupcakes

MAKES 20 CUPCAKES ●●

These chocolatey, creamy cupcakes are also known as black bottoms.

FILLING

- ½ pound cream cheese, at room temperature
- ⅓ cup sugar
- 1 large egg
- ⅛ teaspoon salt
- 1 cup mini chocolate chips (8 ounces)

BATTER

- 1¼ cups all-purpose flour
- 1 cup sugar
- ¼ cup unsweetened cocoa powder
- 1 teaspoon baking soda

Salt

- 1 cup water
- ⅓ cup canola oil
- 1 large egg
- 1 teaspoon pure vanilla extract
- 1 teaspoon white vinegar

TOPPING

- ½ cup blanched sliced almonds
- ⅓ cup sugar

1. Preheat the oven to 350°. Line 20 muffin-pan cups with foil liners.

2. MAKE THE FILLING: In a bowl, using an electric mixer, beat the cream cheese with the sugar, egg and salt until smooth. Stir in the chocolate chips.

3. MAKE THE BATTER: In a large bowl, whisk the flour with the sugar, cocoa, baking soda and a pinch of salt. In a small bowl, whisk the water with the oil, egg, vanilla and vinegar. At low speed, beat the liquid ingredients into the dry ingredients until a smooth batter forms.

4. Spoon the batter into the prepared muffin cups to fill them halfway. Spoon a heaping tablespoon of the cream cheese filling into the center of each cupcake, then sprinkle the almonds and sugar on top.

5. Bake the cupcakes in the upper and lower thirds of the oven for 25 to 30 minutes, or until puffed and springy to the touch. Switch the pans halfway through baking. Unmold the cupcakes; let cool on racks before serving.

—*Danielle Custer*

MAKE AHEAD The baked cupcakes can be frozen for up to 5 days.

Creamy Vanilla Cheesecake with Lavender Syrup

MAKES ONE 9-INCH CAKE ●

CRUST

-   1 cup all-purpose flour
-   2 tablespoons sugar
-   6 tablespoons cold unsalted butter, cut into pieces
-   1 large egg
-   ½ teaspoon pure vanilla extract

FILLING

-   1 pound cream cheese, softened
-   1½ cups mascarpone (¾ pound), at room temperature
-   ⅔ cup sugar
-   2 teaspoons pure vanilla extract
-   Seeds from ½ vanilla bean
-   5 large eggs, at room temperature
-   Lavender Syrup (recipe follows)
-   Hazelnut Tuiles (p. 347), optional

I. MAKE THE CRUST: In a food processor, pulse the flour with the sugar. Add the butter and pulse until the mixture resembles coarse meal. Beat the egg with the vanilla and add to the processor; pulse just until the dough begins to come together.

2. Scrape the dough out onto a work surface and knead briefly. Pat into a disk, wrap in plastic and refrigerate until chilled, about 1 hour or overnight.

3. Preheat the oven to 350°. On a lightly floured work surface, roll out the dough to an 11-inch round. Fit the dough into a 9-inch springform pan, gently pressing it into the bottom of the pan and 1 inch up the sides without stretching. Prick all over with a fork and freeze until firm, about 10 minutes. Bake the crust for about 15 minutes, or until golden brown. Transfer to a rack to cool.

4. MAKE THE FILLING: Reduce the oven temperature to 325°. In a large bowl, using an electric mixer, beat the cream cheese with the mascarpone and sugar at moderately high speed until light and fluffy, about 5 minutes. Add the vanilla extract and the seeds from the vanilla bean and beat until blended. Add the eggs, 1 at a time, beating well after each addition.

5. Pour the mixture on top of the cooked crust in the springform pan and bake in the center of the oven for about 45 minutes, or until lightly browned on top and still slightly jiggly in the center. Transfer the cheesecake to a rack and let cool completely, then cover with plastic wrap and refrigerate overnight.

6. Run a thin knife around the edge of the cheesecake to loosen it, then remove the side of the pan. Cut the cake into wedges and serve with the Lavender Syrup and Hazelnut Tuiles.

—*Glenn Monk*

MAKE AHEAD The baked crust can be stored in an airtight container for 2 days. The cheesecake can be refrigerated for 2 days.

WINE The light, delicate cheesecake will find an unusually subtle complement in ice wine; the 1995 Gray Monk Ehrenfelser is a fabulous example.

LAVENDER SYRUP

MAKES ABOUT ½ CUP ● ●

-   ¼ cup organic dried lavender flowers
-   ½ cup plus 3 tablespoons water
-   ½ cup sugar

I. In a small saucepan, cover the lavender flowers with ½ cup of the water and bring to a boil. Simmer over moderately high heat for 3 minutes. Cover, remove from the heat and let stand for 20 minutes. Strain and discard the flowers.

2. In a small saucepan, combine the sugar with the remaining 3 tablespoons of water and bring to a boil

over moderate heat, stirring once or twice to dissolve the sugar. Continue to simmer the syrup, undistributed, until it reaches 280° on a candy thermometer (soft ball stage), about 4 minutes. Slowly and carefully pour in the strained lavender water, stirring constantly over moderate heat until smooth. Let the lavender syrup cool to room temperature, transfer to a small pitcher and serve.   —*G.M.*

MAKE AHEAD The syrup can be refrigerated for 3 days. Bring to room temperature before serving.

Big-Hair Raspberry Tarts

MAKES 12 INDIVIDUAL TARTS

-   2 sticks (½ pound) unsalted butter, softened
-   2 cups granulated sugar
-   2 cups all-purpose flour
-   ⅛ teaspoon salt
-   ¾ cup seedless raspberry jam
-   8 large egg whites
-   Confectioners' sugar, for dusting

I. Preheat the oven to 350°. Line a 9-by-13-inch baking pan with foil, leaving 4 inches of overhang at the ends.

2. In a medium bowl, using an electric mixer, beat the softened butter with ½ cup of the granulated sugar at high speed until fluffy, 3 to 5 minutes. Reduce the mixer speed to low, add the flour and salt and beat just until blended, 2 to 3 minutes. Press the dough into the baking pan in an even layer. Score the dough lengthwise into thirds, then score crosswise 4 times to make 12 squares. Bake the shortbread for 20 to 25 minutes, or until lightly browned. Transfer the pan to a rack and let the shortbread cool completely, about 1 hour.

3. Lift the shortbread out of the pan. Spread the jam evenly over the shortbread. Using a serrated knife, cut the shortbread into 12 squares following the score lines. Transfer the shortbread squares to a large baking sheet.

4. In a large stainless steel bowl set

over a pan of simmering water, stir the egg whites with the remaining 1½ cups of granulated sugar until the sugar dissolves, about 1 minute. Remove the bowl from the heat. Using an electric mixer, beat the whites at medium speed until frothy. Increase the speed to high and beat until a stiff, glossy meringue forms, about 5 minutes longer.

5. Spoon ½ cup of the meringue onto each of the squares. Using the back of a spoon, pull up the meringue to form high spikes. Bake for 20 to 25 minutes, or until the meringue is golden brown. Let cool for 10 minutes on the baking sheet on a rack, then transfer the tarts to the rack and let cool completely. Sift confectioners' sugar over the tops before serving.

—*Rebecca Rather*

South Carolina Peach and Blueberry Tartlets

MAKES 8 INDIVIDUAL TARTS ●

These crunchy mini tarts (there's cornmeal in the pastry) are great at a picnic because they're served whole, so they don't need to be cut and they can be eaten with fingers.

 1 cup all-purpose flour
 ¼ cup fine yellow cornmeal
 ¼ cup plus 2 tablespoons sugar
Pinch of salt
 7 tablespoons unsalted butter, diced and chilled
 ¼ cup ice water
 4 medium peaches, peeled and cut into ½-inch chunks
 ½ cup blueberries

1. In a medium bowl, combine the flour with the cornmeal, 2 tablespoons of the sugar and the salt. Add the butter and, using a pastry blender, 2 knives or your fingers, work it into the flour until the mixture resembles coarse meal. Add the ice water and stir just until a dough forms. Gather the dough together and knead 2 or 3 times.

2. Roll the dough into a fat log and cut it into 8 equal pieces. On a lightly floured surface, flatten each piece of dough into a 2-inch disk. Wrap each disk in plastic and refrigerate for at least 30 minutes or overnight.

3. Preheat the oven to 350°. Line a large baking sheet with parchment paper. On a lightly floured surface, roll each disk of dough out to a 6-inch round. In a medium bowl, toss the peaches with the blueberries and the remaining ¼ cup of sugar. Spoon the fruit onto the dough and fold up the sides, overlapping and crimping as you go. Transfer the tartlets to the baking sheet and bake for 50 minutes, or until the crust is golden and crisp and the fruit is bubbling. Let cool.

—*Michael Kramer*

MAKE AHEAD The tartlets can be stored in an airtight container at room temperature for 6 hours.

Big-Hair Raspberry Tart

South Carolina Peach and Blueberry Tartlets

Apple Galette

MAKES ONE 10-INCH GALETTE ●

Galette Dough (recipe follows)

- 2 tablespoons finely chopped candied orange peel (see Note)
- 3 large Golden Delicious apples (about 1¾ pounds)—peeled, quartered, cored and thinly sliced crosswise
- 3 tablespoons unsalted butter, melted and cooled
- 3 tablespoons sugar
- 1 tablespoon honey, warmed

I. Preheat the oven to 400°. Line a large rimless baking sheet with parchment paper. On a lightly floured surface, roll out the galette dough to a 14-inch round. Transfer the dough to the baking sheet. Sprinkle 1 tablespoon of the candied orange peel over the dough and spread the sliced apples on top, leaving a 2-inch border all around. Fold up the edges of the dough, overlapping and crimping as you go. Brush the apples and crust with the melted butter. Sprinkle half of the sugar on the apples and half on the dough.

2. Bake the galette in the lower third of the oven for 55 minutes, or until the pastry is crisp and the apples are tender. Slide the galette onto a wire rack and sprinkle the remaining candied orange peel over the apples. Let cool. Drizzle the galette with the warm honey, cut into wedges and serve.

—*Chez Panisse, Berkeley, California*
NOTE Candied orange peel is available at specialty food shops and some candy stores, or use strips of peel from a jar of orange marmalade.
SERVE WITH Crème fraîche, vanilla ice cream or whipped cream.

GALETTE DOUGH

MAKES ENOUGH DOUGH FOR
ONE 10-INCH GALETTE

This pastry dough is best made by hand, but it can also be started in a food processor.

- 1 cup all-purpose flour
- ½ teaspoon sugar

Pinch of salt

- 6 tablespoons cold unsalted butter, cut into ½-inch pieces
- ¼ cup ice water

In a bowl, mix the flour with the sugar and salt. Using a pastry blender or your fingers, cut in half of the butter until the mixture resembles coarse meal. Cut in the remaining butter until the largest pieces are the size of lima beans. Drizzle the water over the dough and stir until moistened. Gather up the dough and knead it 2 or 3 times. Flatten the dough into a disk, wrap in plastic and refrigerate for at least 30 minutes. —*Chez Panisse*

Caramelized Apple-Pecan Pie with Calvados

MAKES TWO 9-INCH PIES ●

- 2 cups pecans (about ½ pound)
- 1½ sticks unsalted butter (6 ounces), 1 stick melted and cooled
- ¼ cup sugar
- 4 large Granny Smith apples— peeled, cored and cut into ½-inch dice
- 2 tablespoons Calvados or other apple brandy
- 1½ cups packed light brown sugar
- 1½ cups light corn syrup
- 2 tablespoons all-purpose flour
- 6 large eggs, lightly beaten
- 1 tablespoon pure vanilla extract

Pâte Brisée Pie Shells (recipe follows)

I. Preheat the oven to 350°. Spread the pecans on a rimmed baking sheet and bake for 7 minutes, or until lightly toasted. Transfer the toasted nuts to a plate and let cool. Reduce the oven temperature to 325°.

2. In a large nonstick skillet, melt 4 tablespoons of the butter with the sugar over high heat. Add the apples and cook, stirring frequently, until browned, 12 to 14 minutes. Add the Calvados and cook until evaporated. Let cool.

3. In a large bowl, combine the brown sugar with the corn syrup, flour and the cooled melted butter and beat until smooth. Beat in the eggs and vanilla.

4. Spoon the caramelized apples into the Pâte Brisée Pie Shells and pour the custard on top. Scatter the pecans on the custard, lightly pressing them in. Bake in the lower third of the oven for about 1 hour, or until the crusts are golden and the custard is set. Cover the crusts loosely with foil if they brown too quickly. Let the pies cool on a wire rack before cutting into wedges.

—*Grace Parisi*
MAKE AHEAD The pies can be refrigerated overnight. Bring to room temperature before serving.
SERVE WITH Whipped cream.

PÂTE BRISÉE PIE SHELLS

MAKES TWO 9-INCH PIE SHELLS ●

- 2 cups all-purpose flour
- 1 teaspoon sugar
- ¼ teaspoon salt
- 10 tablespoons cold unsalted butter, cut into 1-inch pieces
- 1 large egg yolk mixed with ¼ cup ice water

I. In a food processor, pulse the flour with the sugar and salt. Add the butter and pulse until the mixture resembles coarse meal. Add the egg yolk and pulse until a crumbly dough forms.

2. Turn the dough out onto a lightly floured surface; knead 3 times until it just comes together. Pat the dough into two disks. Wrap in plastic and refrigerate for at least 30 minutes or overnight.

3. On a lightly floured work surface, roll each disk out to a 12-inch round. Fit each round into a 9-inch glass pie plate. Trim the overhang to 1 inch and fold the edge under, then crimp decoratively. Refrigerate until firm. —*G.P.*
MAKE AHEAD The dough can be frozen for 1 month. The pie shells can be refrigerated overnight.

Rustic Pear and Hazelnut Crostata

MAKES ONE 12-INCH CROSTATA ●

- 1 cup hazelnuts (4½ ounces)
- 2 cups plus 2 tablespoons all-purpose flour
- ¼ cup plus 3 tablespoons sugar
- ¼ teaspoon salt
- 1½ sticks cold unsalted butter, cut into tablespoons
- 1 large egg, separated
- ¼ cup ice water
- 6 firm, ripe pears, such as Bartlett or Anjou—peeled, halved, cored and cut lengthwise into ¼-inch wedges
- 2 tablespoons apple jelly, melted

I. Preheat the oven to 350°. Spread the hazelnuts in a pie plate. Bake for 12 to 14 minutes, or until lightly toasted. Transfer to a kitchen towel and let cool completely, then rub the nuts together vigorously to remove the skins.

2. In a food processor, pulse half of the hazelnuts until finely chopped. Add 2 cups of the flour, 3 tablespoons of the sugar and the salt and process until the nuts are finely ground. Add all but 2 tablespoons of the butter and pulse until the mixture resembles coarse meal. Whisk the egg yolk into the ice water, add to the processor and pulse until the pastry comes together. Turn the pastry out onto a lightly floured surface and pat it into a 1-inch-thick disk. Wrap in plastic and refrigerate for at least 1 hour.

3. In a food processor, combine the remaining half of the hazelnuts with the remaining 2 tablespoons of flour and ¼ cup of sugar and process until finely ground. Add the remaining 2 tablespoons of butter and the egg white and process until the filling is smooth and creamy.

4. On a work surface, slightly overlap two 18-inch-long sheets of wax paper. Lightly flour the pastry disk and set it in the center of the wax paper. Roll out the pastry to a 16-inch round. Gently flip the pastry onto a parchment-lined baking sheet and peel off the wax paper.

5. Spread the hazelnut filling over the pastry to within 2 inches of the edge. Arrange the pear wedges over the filling in concentric circles, overlapping the wedges slightly. Fold the edge of the pastry up and over the pears, crimping decoratively. Refrigerate the assembled crostata for 15 minutes before baking.

6. Preheat the oven to 375°. Bake the crostata in the center of the oven for 1½ hours, or until the pears are tender and the crust is golden. Preheat the broiler. Cover the crostata crust with strips of foil and broil until the pears are browned in spots, 2 to 3 minutes. Slide the crostata with the parchment paper onto a rack to cool. Brush the pears and crust with the melted apple jelly and let cool to room temperature. Cut into wedges and serve.

—Grace Parisi

MAKE AHEAD The hazelnut pastry can be refrigerated for up to 3 days. The crostata can be baked earlier in the day.

SERVE WITH Crème fraîche or whipped cream.

Lemon Marshmallow Pie

MAKES ONE 9-INCH PIE

This playful rendition of lemon meringue pie has an intensely tangy lemon filling topped by a spongy cloud of firm marshmallow instead of soft meringue. Be sure to save the egg whites you don't use in the filling for the topping. You'll need a candy thermometer to make this pie.

CRUST

- 1¼ cups graham cracker crumbs (about 10 whole crackers)
- 4 tablespoons unsalted butter, melted
- 2 tablespoons sugar

FILLING

- ⅔ cup fresh lemon juice, strained
- ½ cup plus 2 tablespoons sugar
- 3 large eggs
- 2 large egg yolks
- 1 teaspoon finely grated lemon zest
- 6 tablespoons unsalted butter, cut into ½-inch pieces

TOPPING

Water
- 2½ teaspoons unflavored gelatin
- ½ cup sugar
- ⅓ cup light corn syrup
- 3 large egg whites at room temperature
- 1½ teaspoons pure vanilla extract

I. MAKE THE CRUST: Preheat the oven to 375°. In a bowl, stir the graham cracker crumbs with the butter and sugar. Evenly press the crumbs over the bottom and up the sides of a 9-inch pie plate. Bake for 8 minutes, or until firm and golden. Transfer to a rack and let cool. Leave the oven on.

2. MAKE THE FILLING: In a stainless steel saucepan, whisk the lemon juice with the sugar, whole eggs, egg yolks and lemon zest. Add the butter and cook over moderate heat, whisking constantly, until the filling thickens and nearly comes to a boil, about 4 minutes. Pour into the cooled crust and bake for about 8 minutes, or until just set. Transfer the pie to a rack and let cool. Turn the oven up to 450°.

3. MAKE THE TOPPING: In a small bowl, mix ¼ cup of cold water with the gelatin and let stand until the gelatin softens, at least 5 minutes. In a small saucepan fitted with a candy thermometer, combine the sugar with the corn syrup and ⅓ cup of water and bring the mixture to a boil over moderately high heat.

4. In a standing mixer fitted with a whisk, begin beating the egg whites at medium speed when the candy thermometer in the sugar syrup reads 210°. When the syrup reaches 245°, gradually beat it into the whites at

Lemon Marshmallow Pie

Flemish Sugar Tart

medium speed. Scrape the gelatin into the warm saucepan and stir until melted, then drizzle it into the whites. Add the vanilla and beat at high speed until soft peaks form, about 3 minutes.

5. Using a spatula, spread the marshmallow topping over the lemon filling, making decorative swirls. Bake in the top third of the oven for 4 minutes, or until the marshmallow topping is golden brown. Transfer the pie to a rack and let cool to room temperature. Use a sharp knife, dipping it into hot water between slices, to cut the pie into wedges. —*David Lebovitz*

MAKE AHEAD The pie can be prepared through Step 2 and refrigerated overnight.

WINE The pie's tart filling and super-sweet topping call for a fresh, sweet sparkling Italian Asti; the wine's fruitiness goes well with the citrus flavor while its bubbles are a good contrast to the creamy filling and spongy topping. Fine examples: the Nonvintage Banfi and Zonin and the opulent 1998 Contratto Asti De Miranda Metodo Classico.

Flemish Sugar Tart

MAKES ONE 10-INCH TART

This homey custard tart redolent of cinnamon and brown sugar tastes best when it's still warm from the oven. Have the filling ready and the dough pressed in the pan, but assemble and bake the tart shortly before serving.

PASTRY

- ¼ cup milk, warmed to 100° (slightly warm to the touch)
- 1½ teaspoons active dry yeast
- 1½ cups unbleached all-purpose flour
- 1 tablespoon granulated sugar
- ¾ teaspoon cinnamon

Pinch of salt

- 1 large egg, beaten
- 4 tablespoons unsalted butter, softened

FILLING

- ½ cup heavy cream

- 2 large eggs
- 1 teaspoon pure vanilla extract
- 1 cup packed dark brown sugar
- 4 tablespoons unsalted butter, melted and slightly cooled

Confectioners' sugar, for dusting

- 1 pint blueberries, strawberries, currants or cape gooseberries, for serving

Unsweetened whipped cream, for serving

1. MAKE THE PASTRY: In a small bowl, combine the milk with the yeast. Sift the flour with the sugar, cinnamon and salt into a medium bowl. Make a well in the center of the flour mixture and add the milk mixture, egg and butter. Using your fingers, gradually work the flour into the ingredients in the well. Knead the dough until the pastry comes together. Pat the pastry into a ball and transfer it to a lightly oiled medium bowl. Cover with plastic wrap and let the pastry rise in a warm place until doubled in bulk, about 1 hour.

2. On a lightly floured work surface, roll out the pastry to a 12-inch round about ¼ inch thick. Fit the pastry into a 10-inch tart pan with a removable bottom and trim the overhang. Cover the tart shell with plastic wrap and let rise in a warm place for 10 to 20 minutes before filling.

3. MAKE THE FILLING: Preheat the oven to 375°. In a medium bowl, mix the cream with the eggs and vanilla. Whisk in the brown sugar and butter until smooth. Pour the filling into the tart shell and bake for 10 minutes. Reduce the oven temperature to 350° and bake the tart for about 20 minutes longer, or until the custard is completely set. Transfer to a rack to cool. Sift confectioners' sugar over the tart and serve warm or at room temperature with berries and whipped cream.
—*Ruth Van Waerebeek*

BEER A raspberry-flavored beer, such as a Boon Framboise, would complement this tart perfectly.

Chocolate Clementine Tart with Macadamia Nut Crust

MAKES ONE 10½-INCH TART ●

This citrus tart's rich ganache filling and buttery macadamia crust make it particularly decadent. If you like, almonds, hazelnuts or walnuts can be substituted for the macadamia nuts in the crust.

CRUST

- ½ cup roasted salted macadamia nuts (3 ounces)
- ¼ cup sugar
- 1½ cups all-purpose flour
- 6 tablespoons unsalted butter, cut into pieces and chilled
- 1 large egg yolk mixed with 1 tablespoon water

FILLING

- 5 clementines (preferably organic), scrubbed and thinly sliced crosswise, ends discarded
- ½ cup fresh orange juice
- 1 tablespoon Grand Marnier
- ¼ cup plus 1½ tablespoons sugar
- 10 ounces bittersweet or semisweet chocolate, coarsely chopped
- ¾ cup plus 2 tablespoons heavy cream

1. MAKE THE CRUST: Preheat the oven to 375°. In a food processor, finely chop the macadamia nuts with the sugar. Add the flour and process until the nuts are finely ground. Add the pieces of butter and pulse until the mixture resembles coarse meal. Sprinkle the egg yolk mixture over the dry ingredients in the processor and pulse until the dough just comes together to form a dough.

2. Press the macadamia nut dough evenly into a 10½-inch fluted tart pan with a removable bottom. Line the dough with parchment or wax paper and fill it with pie weights or dried beans to keep it from shrinking. Bake the crust for 30 minutes, or until it's slightly dry to the touch. Remove the parchment and weights and bake the crust for about 15 minutes longer, or until golden. Transfer the baked crust to a wire rack and allow it to cool completely. Reduce the oven temperature to 325°.

3. MAKE THE FILLING: Arrange the clementine slices in overlapping rows in a 9-inch-square glass, ceramic or stainless steel baking dish. Pour the fresh orange juice and the Grand Marnier over the clementines and sprinkle with 1½ tablespoons of the sugar. Cover loosely with foil and bake for 1 hour, or until several of the clementine rinds are tender when pierced.

4. Increase the oven temperature to 375°. Remove the aluminum foil and sprinkle the clementines evenly with the remaining ¼ cup of sugar. Continue to bake, uncovered, for 30 minutes, or until the liquid is syrupy and the

clementines are glazed. Let them cool completely.

5. Meanwhile, put the chopped chocolate in a medium heatproof bowl. In a small saucepan, bring the cream just to a boil. Pour the hot cream over the chocolate in the bowl and let stand for 5 minutes. Stir until smooth. Let the ganache cool for 10 minutes, then pour it into the crust, smoothing the surface with a spatula. Refrigerate the tart for 20 minutes, until the ganache is firm to the touch.

6. Arrange the clementine slices over the ganache in overlapping concentric circles. Spoon any remaining syrup over the clementines and serve.

—*Regan Daley*

MAKE AHEAD The tart can be prepared through Step 5 and refrigerated overnight. Bring the tart and clementines to room temperature before assembling.

Milk Chocolate Banana Pie

MAKES ONE 9-INCH PIE ●●

CRUST

- ¼ cup hazelnuts
- 1 stick unsalted butter, softened
- ⅓ cup sugar
- 1 large egg yolk
- ½ teaspoon pure vanilla extract
- 1 cup plus 3 tablespoons all-purpose flour

Pinch of salt

FILLING

- 1 cup heavy cream
- 3 large egg yolks
- ¾ pound milk chocolate, chopped
- 2 tablespoons unsalted butter
- 1 teaspoon pure vanilla extract
- 2 large bananas, sliced ¼ inch thick
- 1 tablespoon sugar
- 1 tablespoon dark rum

1. MAKE THE CRUST: Preheat the oven to 350°. Spread the hazelnuts in a pie plate and toast for 12 minutes, or until fragrant and blistered. Rub the nuts in a kitchen towel to remove the skins. Finely grind the nuts in a food processor.

2. Wipe out the processor. Add the butter and sugar and process until fluffy. Add the egg yolk and vanilla and process until just blended. Add the flour, salt and the ground hazelnuts and pulse until a crumbly dough forms.

3. Scrape the dough into a large disk, then press the dough into a 9-inch fluted tart pan with a removable bottom. Line the dough with plastic wrap and press evenly into the pan. Freeze until firm, about 10 minutes.

4. Discard the plastic and press a piece of well-buttered foil directly onto the dough. Fill the foil with pie weights or dried beans and bake for 30 minutes, or until the shell is golden around the edge. Remove the foil and weights and bake for 15 minutes longer, or until golden all over. Let the pie shell cool on a wire rack.

5. MAKE THE FILLING: In a medium saucepan, bring the cream to a

Chocolate Clementine Tart with Macadamia Nut Crust

boil. Remove from the heat. In a medium bowl, whisk half of the warm cream with the egg yolks. Return the cream to the saucepan and whisk constantly over moderately low heat until an instant-read thermometer registers 160°. Remove from the heat and immediately stir in the chocolate, butter and vanilla and whisk the mixture until smooth. Let the filling cool to room temperature.

6. In a medium bowl, toss the bananas with the sugar and rum. Arrange the bananas in a single overlapping layer in the tart shell and spoon the chocolate cream on top. Smooth the surface with a warmed offset spatula. Chill the tart until firm before serving.

—*Will Packwood*

MAKE AHEAD The pie can be made several hours before serving.

SERVE WITH Whipped cream.

dessert and wine pairing 101

Choose a wine that's sweeter than the dessert. An extremely sugary dessert makes even a rich wine taste thin, sharp and hard.

Pair the dessert with a wine of similar intensity. A powerful wine will overwhelm a delicate dessert; a rich and intensely flavored dessert will overwhelm a light, delicate wine.

Pick a wine that echoes the dessert's flavors. Tropical fruits, peaches and apricots are a good match for late-harvest Riesling; hazelnuts, almonds and ginger go nicely with sherry and tawny port; dried fruits and coffee are delicious with ruby port; chocolate is wonderful with sweet rich red wines such as ruby port or Banyuls. Creamy custards, lemon soufflés and berry tarts pair well with Sauternes.

Steer clear of desserts that feature sour fresh citrus. The acidity strips away any wine's flavor.

Lemon Coconut Bars
MAKES ABOUT 2 DOZEN BARS ●

CRUST

    3 cups all-purpose flour
    ¾ cup confectioners' sugar
    2 tablespoons finely grated
       lemon zest
    2 sticks plus 2 tablespoons
       unsalted butter, softened

TOPPING

    8 large eggs, beaten
 2½ cups sugar
    ¼ cup all-purpose flour
    2 teaspoons baking powder
Pinch of salt
    ¾ cup plus 2 tablespoons fresh
       lemon juice
 1½ cups shredded sweetened
       coconut

I. MAKE THE CRUST: Preheat the oven to 350°. In a food processor, pulse the flour with the confectioners' sugar and lemon zest. Add the butter and process just until a dough forms. Press the dough evenly into a 12-by-17-inch jelly-roll pan. Bake for about 30 minutes, until golden.

2. MAKE THE TOPPING: In a large bowl, using a handheld electric mixer, beat the eggs with the sugar, flour, baking powder and salt at medium speed. Add the lemon juice and half of the coconut and pour over the crust. Sprinkle the remaining coconut on top and bake for 35 to 40 minutes, or until the topping is golden brown and set. Let cool completely. Cut into 3-by-2-inch bars, arrange on a platter and serve.

—*Vickie Gott*

MAKE AHEAD The bars can be wrapped in plastic and refrigerated for 1 week or frozen for 1 month.

Marble Fudge Brownies
MAKES 6 BROWNIES ●●●

These brownies are swirled with a cream cheese batter and baked in individual tart pans. They're simple enough for every day but also pretty enough for a dinner party.

Milk Chocolate Banana Pie

Unsweetened cocoa, for dusting
 1½ sticks (6 ounces) unsalted butter,
       cut into tablespoons
    6 ounces semisweet chocolate,
       coarsely chopped (¼ cup)
    3 large eggs
 1½ cups sugar
    ¾ cup all-purpose flour
Pinch of salt
 1½ cups cream cheese
       (12 ounces), softened
    3 large egg yolks
    ¾ teaspoon pure vanilla extract
Sweetened whipped cream,
       for serving

I. Preheat the oven to 325°. Lightly butter six 4-by-1¼-inch round fluted tartlet pans with removable bottoms. Dust the molds with unsweetened cocoa powder, tapping out any excess cocoa.

2. In a small saucepan, melt the butter and chocolate over low heat. Remove the melted chocolate from the heat and let cool slightly. In a large bowl, whisk the eggs with 1 cup of the sugar until blended. Add the melted chocolate and stir in the flour and salt. Pour the batter into the tart pans.

3. In another large bowl, beat the cream cheese with the remaining ½ cup of sugar until smooth. Add the egg yolks and vanilla and beat until smooth. Spoon half of the cream cheese batter over the chocolate batter in each tart pan. Using a fork, decoratively swirl the batters together in 3 strokes.

4. Bake the brownies for about 35 minutes, or until lightly browned and slightly puffed, but not completely set in the center. Let cool on a wire rack for 15 minutes before unmolding. Serve warm with whipped cream.

—*Michael Romano*

MAKE AHEAD The brownies can be tightly wrapped in plastic and refrigerated for 2 days. Reheat at a low temperature.

Marble Fudge Brownie

Caramel Pecan Brownies

MAKES ONE 9-BY-13-INCH PAN OF BROWNIES ●

- 2 sticks (½ pound) unsalted butter, cut into small pieces
- ½ pound bittersweet chocolate, coarsely chopped
- 1½ cups sugar
- 4 large eggs, lightly beaten
- 1¼ cups all-purpose flour
- 1 tablespoon vanilla extract
- One 14-ounce package individually wrapped caramels, unwrapped
- ⅓ cup heavy cream
- 1½ cups pecans, coarsely chopped (5½ ounces)
- 1 cup semisweet chocolate chips (6 ounces)

1. Preheat the oven to 350°. Line a 9-by-13-inch baking pan with foil, leaving 4 inches of overhang at the ends. Lightly grease the foil.

2. In a medium saucepan, stir the butter with the chopped bittersweet chocolate over low heat until melted and smooth. Transfer to a large bowl. Add the sugar and eggs and whisk the mixture until it is smooth and glossy. Whisk in the flour and vanilla until smooth. Spread half of the brownie batter into the baking pan and bake for 30 to 35 minutes, or until firm. Transfer the pan to a rack and let the brownies cool slightly.

3. Meanwhile, in a large saucepan, stir the caramels with the cream over low heat until smooth. Stir in half of the pecans. Spread the caramel evenly over the brownies, then spread the remaining brownie batter on top. Sprinkle the remaining pecans and the chocolate chips over the top and bake for about 45 minutes, or until firm. Let cool completely in the pan. Turn the brownies out onto a work surface, remove the foil and cut into squares.

—*Rebecca Rather*

MAKE AHEAD The brownies can be stored in an airtight container for up to 1 week.

Gascon Walnut Bars

MAKES ABOUT 32 BARS ●

These moist and chewy bars are topped with a creamy walnut frosting.

- 2 cups walnut halves (½ pound)
- 1 cup granulated sugar
- Salt
- 1 stick (4 ounces) unsalted butter, softened
- 4 large eggs, separated
- 1 cup confectioners' sugar

1. Preheat the oven to 350°. Butter an 8-inch-square baking pan and line the bottom with wax paper or parchment. In a food processor, finely grind 1 cup of the walnuts with ¼ cup of the granulated sugar and ½ teaspoon of salt.

2. In a medium bowl, using an electric mixer, beat 4 tablespoons of the butter with the remaining ¾ cup of granulated sugar until pale and fluffy. Beat in the egg yolks, 1 at a time, making sure each is incorporated before adding the next. Stir in the ground walnuts.

3. Beat the egg whites with a pinch of salt until stiff peaks form. Gently fold the beaten whites into the walnut batter, then pour into the prepared pan. Tilt the pan to distribute the batter evenly. Bake for about 40 minutes, or until the cake is set and begins to pull away from the side of the pan. Transfer to a rack and let cool for 10 minutes. Run a knife around the side of the pan and turn the cake out onto a serving plate to cool completely.

4. In a food processor, pulse the remaining 1 cup of walnuts with the confectioners' sugar until finely ground. Add the remaining 4 tablespoons of butter and pulse until creamy. Spread the frosting evenly over the cake. Using the edge of a tablespoon, make a decorative pattern in the frosting. Cut the cake into 1-by-2-inch bars and serve. —*Jean Calviac*

WINE An Armagnac's hints of walnut and dark toffee will echo the same flavors in this cake; try a Larressingle XO Grand Réserve.

Gascon Walnut Bar

Mocha Meringues

MAKES ABOUT 1½ DOZEN
MERINGUES ●

⅓ cup confectioners' sugar
2 tablespoons unsweetened
cocoa powder
1 tablespoon finely ground
coffee beans
2 large egg whites
¼ cup granulated sugar
1 ounce chocolate-covered
espresso beans

I. Preheat the oven to 250°. Line a
baking sheet with parchment paper. In
a small bowl, whisk the confectioners'
sugar with the cocoa and coffee.
2. In a medium bowl, beat the egg
whites at high speed until frothy. Add
1 tablespoon of the granulated sugar
and beat for 30 seconds; gradually
beat in the remaining 3 tablespoons of
sugar until the meringue is thick and
glossy, about 2 minutes longer. Fold in
the cocoa mixture in 2 batches.
3. Mound scant tablespoons of the
meringue 1 inch apart on the prepared
baking sheet and top each one with
an espresso bean. Bake the meringues
for 1 hour, or until set and dry. Let the
meringues cool completely on the
sheet before serving. —*Diana Sturgis*

ONE MERINGUE Calories 24 kcal,
Total Fat 0.1 gm, Saturated Fat 0.1 gm,
Protein 1 gm, Carbohydrates 6 gm

Orange Cinnamon Tuiles

MAKES ABOUT 2 DOZEN TUILES ●
This citrusy version of a classic French
tuile is the perfect accompaniment to
ice cream or sorbet. To prevent the
batter for these crisp and delicate
cookies from curdling, be sure to use
soft butter.

1½ tablespoons finely grated
orange or lemon zest
7 tablespoons sugar
4 tablespoons unsalted
butter, softened
2 large egg whites, at
room temperature
⅓ cup all-purpose flour
¾ teaspoon cinnamon
¼ teaspoon pure almond extract

I. Preheat the oven to 375°. Butter 2
large baking sheets. In a food processor, pulse the grated orange or lemon
zest with the sugar. Add the softened
butter and room-temperature egg
whites and process until smooth. Add
the flour, cinnamon and pure almond
extract and pulse just until blended; do
not overmix.
2. To form each cookie, drop 2 level
teaspoons of batter 4 inches apart on
the prepared baking sheets. Using a
small spatula or the back of a spoon,
spread the batter evenly into 4-inch
rounds.
3. Bake the tuiles for about 7 minutes,
or until golden; shift the pans halfway
through baking for even browning. Let
the tuiles firm up on the baking sheets
for 30 seconds, then use a metal spatula to transfer them quickly to a rack;
alternatively, drape them over a rolling
pin or glasses and let cool completely.
Repeat with the remaining batter.
—*David Lebovitz*

MAKE AHEAD The tuiles can be
stored in an airtight container for up to
3 days. Recrisp them in a 350° oven,
then drape over a rolling pin or glasses
to cool completely.

WINE Echo the orange flavors in
these cookies with a sweet orange
muscat from California. Quady Winery
makes two: The low-alcohol Electra
and the richer, pricier Essensia.

Hazelnut Tuiles

MAKES ABOUT 2 DOZEN TUILES ● ●
1 cup hazelnuts (4 ounces)
2 extra-large egg whites
⅓ cup sugar
1 tablespoon all-purpose flour
1 tablespoon roasted hazelnut oil

I. Preheat the oven to 375°. In a pie
plate, toast the hazelnuts for about 10
minutes, or until they are fragrant and
browned. Transfer the hot nuts to a
kitchen towel and rub them together
to remove the skins. Let the nuts cool
completely, then finely grind them in a
food processor.
2. In a medium bowl, beat the egg
whites until frothy. Stir in the sugar,

Orange Cinnamon Tuiles

flour, hazelnut oil and the ground hazelnuts.

3. Line 2 baking sheets with parchment paper. Scoop rounded teaspoons of the tuile batter onto the prepared baking sheets, spacing the spoonfuls of dough 4 inches apart. Using an offset spatula, spread the batter into very thin 3-inch rounds.

4. Bake the tuiles for about 4 minutes, or until browned around the edges. While the tuiles are still hot, use a metal spatula to lift them from the parchment paper and gently drape them over a rolling pin to give them a nice shape. If the tuiles harden on the baking sheet, return the pan to the oven for 30 seconds to reheat the tuiles until they become pliable again. Repeat with the remaining batter.

—Glenn Monk

Orange and Polenta Biscuits

MAKES ABOUT 6 DOZEN BISCUITS ●

Polenta, or cornmeal, gives these simple cookies a fantastic crunch. They are great with ice cream, fruit salads and compotes or just a good strong cup of coffee.

- 1½ **cups medium non-instant polenta or yellow cornmeal**
- 1½ **sticks (6 ounces) chilled unsalted butter**
- ¾ **cup sugar**
- ⅔ **cup all-purpose flour**
- 2 **tablespoons finely grated orange zest**

Pinch of salt

- 2 **large eggs**

1. In a food processor, combine the polenta or cornmeal with the chilled butter, sugar, flour, grated orange zest and pinch of salt and pulse until the mixture resembles coarse meal. Add the eggs and pulse the mixture just until the dough comes together. Transfer the cookie dough to a bowl and refrigerate until it is slightly firm, about 1 hour.

Orange and Polenta Biscuits, with Chocolate Pot (p. 385)

2. Preheat the oven to 375°. Line several baking sheets with parchment paper. Drop slightly rounded teaspoons of the cookie dough onto the prepared baking sheets, spacing the spoonfuls of dough about 2 inches apart. Bake the cookies for 15 minutes, or until golden around the edges and on the bottoms. Let the cookies cool on the sheets for 5 minutes, then transfer them to wire racks to cool completely. *—Jamie Oliver*

MAKE AHEAD The Orange and Polenta Biscuits can be stored in an airtight container for 1 week or frozen for 1 month.

Cranberry-Almond Biscotti

MAKES ABOUT 2 DOZEN BISCOTTI ● ●

If you don't drink coffee after dinner, try dunking these in Fernet-Branca.

- 1¾ **cups all-purpose flour**
- 1½ **teaspoons baking powder**
- ¼ **teaspoon salt**
- 2 **large eggs**
- ¾ **cup sugar**
- 3 **tablespoons unsalted butter, melted and cooled**
- ¼ **teaspoon almond extract**
- 1 **cup dried cranberries**
- ½ **cup almonds, coarsely chopped (2½ ounces)**

ı. Preheat the oven to 350°. Line a large baking sheet with parchment paper. In a bowl, whisk the flour with the baking powder and salt.

2. In a medium bowl, beat the eggs with the sugar at medium speed until pale and creamy, about 3 minutes. Beat in the butter and almond extract. Pour the egg mixture over the dry ingredients and stir until combined. Stir in the dried cranberries and almonds.

3. Using lightly floured hands, shape the dough into 2 slightly flattened 10-inch logs on the prepared baking sheet. Bake for 30 minutes, or until golden. Let the logs cool slightly.

4. Using a sharp serrated knife, slice the logs ½ inch thick on the diagonal. Arrange the slices on the baking sheet cut sides up and bake for about 10 minutes, or until the biscotti are lightly browned and crisp. Let cool completely before serving. —*Diana Sturgis*
ONE BISCOTTI Calories 111 kcal, Total Fat 3.5 gm, Saturated Fat 1.2 gm, Protein 2 gm, Carbohydrates 18 gm

Chocolate-Nut Biscotti
MAKES ABOUT 3½ DOZEN
BISCOTTI ●
Crisp triple chocolate biscotti are ideal for dipping into coffee.

- ⅔ **cup whole almonds or pistachios (3 ounces)**
- ¾ **cup plus 2 tablespoons all-purpose flour**
- 3½ **ounces milk chocolate, chopped**
- ½ **cup sugar**
- ¼ **cup plus 2 tablespoons unsweetened cocoa powder**
- **Pinch of salt**
- 2 **large eggs at room temperature, lightly beaten**
- 1 **teaspoon pure vanilla extract**
- 1 **large egg white, beaten**
- 1 **pound semisweet or bittersweet chocolate, tempered (see Tempering Chocolate, at right)**

ı. Preheat the oven to 300°. Spread the nuts in a pie plate and toast them in the oven until golden brown, about 20 minutes. Transfer the nuts to a plate and let them cool completely. Raise the oven temperature to 350°.

tempering chocolate
Tempering melted chocolate ensures that it will set up firmly with a glossy sheen. Any leftover chocolate can be tempered again later.

1. Chop 1 pound of room temperature chocolate into ½-inch pieces.
2. Put ⅔ of the chocolate in a glass bowl. Microwave at medium-high power for 30-second periods, stirring with a rubber spatula in the intervals, until ¾ of the chocolate is melted, about 1½ minutes.
3. Stir the chocolate until completely melted, then scrape it into a clean, dry, room-temperature bowl. Measure the temperature of the chocolate with an instant-read thermometer; it should be between 100° and 115°F. Add the remaining chocolate in large handfuls, stirring constantly until the chocolate is at 88°. If the chocolate becomes too cool, melt a few more tablespoons of chopped chocolate and stir them in to raise the temperature.
4. Dip the tip of a knife in the chocolate; the chocolate on the knife should begin to set within 1 minute. Use at once.

2. In a food processor, combine the flour with the milk chocolate and process until the mixture resembles coarse meal. Add the sugar, cocoa powder and salt and pulse to mix. Add the beaten whole eggs and the vanilla and process until a dough forms. Transfer the dough to a lightly floured surface and knead in the toasted nuts.

3. Divide the dough in half. On a lightly floured work surface, roll each piece of dough into a foot-long log. Transfer the logs to a baking sheet lined with parchment paper or foil and flatten them slightly. Lightly brush the logs with the beaten egg white and bake for about 30 minutes, or until firm to the touch and slightly cracked. Remove the logs from the oven and let cool for

Chocolate-Nut Biscotti

1 minute. Turn the oven down to 325°.

4. Transfer the hot logs to a work surface. Using a serrated bread knife or a sharp chef's knife, slice the logs ⅓ to ½ inch thick on the diagonal. Arrange the slices upright on the baking sheet and bake for about 5 minutes, or until dry. Transfer the biscotti to a wire rack and let cool completely.

5. Line a baking sheet with wax paper. Dip half of a cookie into the tempered chocolate, letting the excess drip back into the bowl, and set the cookie on the wax paper, cut side down. Repeat with the remaining cookies. Let stand in a cool, dry place until set.

—*Jacques Torres*

MAKE AHEAD The Chocolate-Nut Biscotti can be stored in an airtight container for up to 3 weeks before dipping.

Snow-Tipped Sand Tarts

MAKES ABOUT 6 DOZEN TARTS

For these cookies and the Shortbread Stars that follow, if you don't have a sturdy handheld mixer, you'll need to prepare the recipe in two batches or use a standing electric mixer.

- 4 sticks (1 pound) unsalted butter, softened
- 1⅓ cups confectioners' sugar, plus more for dusting
- 2 tablespoons pure almond extract
- 4 cups all-purpose flour
- 2 cups finely chopped pistachios (½ pound)

I. Preheat the oven to 325°. Line 2 large cookie sheets with parchment paper.

2. In a large bowl, using an electric mixer, beat the butter, sugar and almond extract until smooth. Gradually add the flour until fully incorporated, then beat in the pistachios.

3. Roll tablespoons of the dough into rounds and transfer to the prepared cookie sheets. Bake for about 20 minutes, or until lightly browned. Let the cookies cool on the baking sheets for

15 to 20 minutes. Carefully transfer to racks and let cool completely. Use a small sieve to dust confectioners' sugar over the cookies.

—*Rebecca Rather*

NOTE For a decorative look, shape the dough into crescents and bake, then dip the tips of the cookies in melted white chocolate and finely chopped pistachios.

Shortbread Stars

MAKES ABOUT 4 DOZEN 3-INCH COOKIES ●

This tender, buttery shortbread can be cut in any festive shape and even used to adorn the Christmas tree.

- 4 cups all-purpose flour
- 1 teaspoon baking powder
- ⅛ teaspoon salt
- 4 sticks (1 pound) unsalted butter, softened
- 1½ cups confectioners' sugar
- 1 tablespoon pure vanilla extract
- 1 tablespoon finely grated lemon zest

Milk Glaze (recipe follows)

I. In a medium bowl, whisk the flour with the baking powder and salt. In a large bowl, using an electric mixer, beat the softened butter with the confectioners' sugar until light and fluffy, about 3 minutes. Beat in the vanilla extract and grated lemon zest. Add the dry ingredients and beat the mixture at low speed until a smooth dough forms. Shape the dough into a ball and knead it 2 or 3 times. Divide the dough in half and flatten into disks. Wrap the shortbread dough in plastic and refrigerate until firm, at least 2 hours or overnight.

2. Preheat the oven to 350°. Line several cookie sheets with parchment paper. Remove the dough from the refrigerator and let the dough stand at room temperature for 15 minutes before rolling out.

3. Roll 1 disk of dough between 2 sheets of wax paper ¼ inch thick.

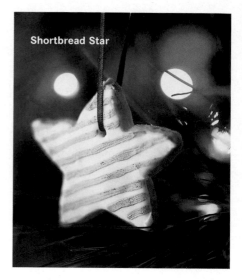

Shortbread Star

Refrigerate the rolled-out dough until firm, about 10 minutes. Dip a star-shaped cookie cutter in flour and stamp out cookies as close together as possible. Using a metal spatula, transfer the cookies to the prepared cookie sheets.

4. Bake the cookies for 16 to 20 minutes, or until lightly browned around the edges. Let the cookies cool on the sheets for 2 minutes, then transfer them to racks to cool completely. Repeat with the remaining dough. Gather any scraps, knead briefly and refrigerate before re-rolling. Brush the shortbreads with Milk Glaze and let dry completely, at least 3 hours, before serving or storing.

—*Rebecca Rather*

MAKE AHEAD The shortbread cookies can be stored in airtight containers for 2 weeks.

MILK GLAZE

MAKES ¾ CUP ●

This glaze can be tinted lightly with food coloring if desired.

- 2 cups confectioners' sugar

About ¼ cup milk

Put the confectioners' sugar in a bowl and gradually whisk in the milk, adding just enough to make a thick glaze.

—*R.R.*

Gingersnaps

MAKES ABOUT 4 DOZEN COOKIES ●

- 2 cups all-purpose flour
- 2 teaspoons baking soda
- 1 teaspoon ground ginger
- 1 teaspoon ground cinnamon
- ½ teaspoon ground cloves
- ¼ teaspoon salt
- ¾ cup solid vegetable shortening
- 1 cup sugar, plus more for rolling
- ¼ cup unsulphured molasses
- 1 large egg, lightly beaten

1. Preheat the oven to 350°. In a bowl, whisk the flour with the baking soda, ginger, cinnamon, cloves and salt.

2. In a large bowl, using a handheld electric mixer, beat the shortening with the 1 cup of sugar at medium speed until light and fluffy, about 2 minutes. Beat in the molasses, then beat in the egg. Add the dry ingredients and beat at low speed until blended.

3. Roll level tablespoons of the dough into balls and roll the balls in sugar. Arrange the balls 1 inch apart on 2 large ungreased baking sheets. Bake on the lower and middle racks of the oven for about 15 minutes, or until the tops are cracked; shift the pans from top to bottom and front to back halfway through baking. Transfer to wire racks to cool.   —*Cary Gott*

MAKE AHEAD The cookies can be stored in an airtight container for 1 week.

Gingerbread Cookies

MAKES ABOUT 4 DOZEN 3-INCH
COOKIES ●

- 1 cup sugar
- ½ cup molasses
- ½ cup water
- 1 tablespoon ground ginger
- 2 teaspoons cinnamon
- 1 teaspoon ground cloves
- 2 sticks (½ pound) unsalted butter
- 4 cups all-purpose flour
- 1½ teaspoons baking soda
- ¼ teaspoon salt

1. In a large saucepan, combine the sugar with the molasses, water, ginger, cinnamon and cloves. Bring to a boil, stirring until the sugar dissolves. Remove the pan from the heat. Add the butter and stir occasionally until melted. Let cool for 15 minutes.

2. In a large bowl, whisk the flour with the baking soda and salt. Add to the saucepan and mix with a wooden spoon until completely blended. Spoon the dough into a large resealable plastic bag, flatten and seal. Refrigerate until the dough is firm and cold, at least 6 hours or overnight.

3. Preheat the oven to 375°. Cut the dough into quarters. Work with 1 piece of dough at a time and keep the rest chilled. On a lightly floured surface, roll out the dough ⅜ inch thick. Dip 3-inch cutters in flour and stamp out cookies as close together as possible. Transfer the cookies to ungreased cookie sheets and bake for 10 to 12 minutes, or until risen, firm and dry. Let the cookies cool on the sheets for 5 minutes before transferring them to racks to cool completely.

4. Repeat with the remaining pieces of dough. Gather any scraps, knead briefly and refrigerate before re-rolling.
        —*Rebecca Rather*

MAKE AHEAD The cookies can be stored in an airtight container for 2 weeks.

Cranberry-Orange Florentines

MAKES ABOUT 3 DOZEN
FLORENTINES ●

- 2 cups slivered almonds (½ pound)
- 1 stick (4 ounces) unsalted butter
- 1 cup sugar
- ½ cup dried cranberries
- ½ cup golden raisins
- 1 tablespoon finely grated orange zest
- ½ cup Lyle's Golden Syrup or light corn syrup (see Note)
- ¾ cup all-purpose flour
- 4 ounces white chocolate

1. Preheat the oven to 350°. Line several large cookie sheets with parchment paper. Spread the almonds on a rimmed baking sheet and toast for about 7 minutes. Let cool. In a food processor, finely grind ½ cup of the almonds.

2. Melt the butter in a medium saucepan. Remove from the heat and stir in the sugar until thoroughly blended, then stir in the cranberries, raisins and orange zest. Add the syrup and stir to combine. Beat in the flour and ground and slivered almonds.

3. Roll tablespoons of the mixture into balls. Arrange the balls on the prepared cookie sheets, spacing them about 4 inches apart. Bake the florentines for about 15 minutes, or until lacy and deep golden. Let the florentines cool on the sheets for 10 minutes to firm up. Using a metal spatula, transfer them to wire racks to cool completely. Repeat with the remaining mixture.

4. In the top of a double boiler set over simmering water, melt the white chocolate, stirring, until smooth. Remove the pan from the heat and let the chocolate cool slightly, stirring from time to time. Using a fork, drizzle the cookies with the melted white chocolate. Let stand until completely set before serving or storing them.
        —*Rebecca Rather*

NOTE English Lyle's Golden Syrup is worth seeking out at specialty shops for its distinctive caramel flavor.

MAKE AHEAD The cookies can be stored in an airtight container between sheets of wax paper for 2 weeks.

Triple-Threat Chocolate Cookies

MAKES ABOUT 3½ DOZEN
COOKIES ●

- 1 cup pecan halves (3 ounces)
- 1 cup walnut halves (3 ounces)
- ½ pound bittersweet or semisweet chocolate, coarsely chopped
- 3 ounces unsweetened chocolate, coarsely chopped

6 tablespoons unsalted butter

3 large eggs

1 cup sugar

2 ½ teaspoons pure vanilla extract

⅓ cup all-purpose flour

¼ teaspoon baking powder

¼ teaspoon salt

1 ½ cups semisweet chocolate chips (9 ounces)

1. Preheat the oven to 350°. Line several cookie sheets with parchment paper. Spread the pecan and walnut halves on a rimmed baking sheet and bake in the preheated oven for about 8 minutes, or until lightly browned and fragrant. Let cool completely, then coarsely chop the nuts.

2. In a saucepan, melt the bittersweet and unsweetened chopped chocolate with the butter over low heat, stirring constantly. Remove from the heat and let cool.

3. In a medium bowl, using a standing or handheld electric mixer, beat the eggs and sugar until they're fluffy. Add

Chocolate Cornflake Clusters

Triple-Threat Chocolate Cookies, with Snow-Tipped Sand Tarts (p. 350)

the vanilla extract and melted chocolate and beat until thick and glossy. In a small bowl, whisk the flour with the baking powder and salt; add to the chocolate mixture and beat until blended. Fold in the nuts and semisweet chocolate chips. Let the dough rest for 20 minutes.

4. Scoop up 2 tablespoons of the dough and place it in a mound on one of the prepared cookie sheets. Continue mounding the batter, placing the cookies 3 inches apart. Lightly moisten your hands and flatten the mounds slightly. Bake for 12 to 15 minutes, or until the cookies are slightly firm and the tops are cracked and glossy. Slide the paper onto racks and let the cookies cool for 10 minutes. Remove the

cookies from the paper and let cool completely on the racks. Repeat with the remaining cookie dough, reusing the parchment paper.

—Rebecca Rather

MAKE AHEAD The Triple-Threat Chocolate Cookies can be stored in an airtight container for up to 2 weeks.

Chocolate Cornflake Clusters

MAKES ABOUT 4 DOZEN CLUSTERS ● ●

Crispness is all-important in these simple sweets, so be sure to start with a fresh box of cornflakes.

4 cups cornflakes

1 pound semisweet or bittersweet chocolate, tempered (see Tempering Chocolate, p. 349)

1. Line a large baking sheet with wax paper. Put the cornflakes in a large bowl and pour half of the tempered chocolate over them. Using a rubber spatula, quickly fold the cornflakes into the chocolate until they're evenly coated; add the remaining chocolate and fold gently until all of the cornflakes are generously coated with chocolate.

2. Working quickly and using a teaspoon, scoop the chocolate-covered cornflakes onto the prepared baking sheet and shape them into free-form clusters with a second teaspoon. Let cool at room temperature until set.

—*Jacques Torres*

MAKE AHEAD The Chocolate Cornflake Clusters can be stored in an airtight container at cool room temperature for up to 2 weeks, if you can resist eating them.

WINE When matching chocolate with wine, it is essential for the wine to be sweeter than the chocolate. The rich, fruity sweetness of a late-bottled vintage port makes it the perfect partner for the bittersweet chocolate used in the recipe here. Two ports that fit the bill: the 1994 Osborne and the 1994 Graham's.

Butterscotch Chocolate Sandwich Cookies

MAKES ABOUT 2 DOZEN LARGE SANDWICH COOKIES ●

A rich butterscotch frosting flavored with a touch of bourbon makes these an adult treat.

COOKIES

2¼ cups all-purpose flour
¾ cup unsweetened cocoa powder
½ teaspoon baking powder
½ teaspoon baking soda
½ teaspoon salt
2 sticks (½ pound) unsalted butter, softened
1 cup sugar
1 large egg, lightly beaten
2 teaspoons pure vanilla extract

FILLING

¾ cup packed dark brown sugar
¼ cup plus 2 tablespoons heavy cream
1 stick (4 ounces) unsalted butter
1½ cups confectioners' sugar
1 tablespoon bourbon

1. MAKE THE COOKIES: In a large bowl, whisk the flour with the cocoa, baking powder, baking soda and salt. In a standing electric mixer fitted with the paddle, cream the butter with the sugar until fluffy. Add the egg and vanilla and beat until blended. ▸

Butterscotch Chocolate Sandwich Cookie, stacked with chocolate chip cookies

Beat in the dry ingredients at low speed. Scrape out the dough and pat it into two 6-inch disks. Wrap the dough in plastic and refrigerate for 30 minutes, or until chilled.

2. Preheat the oven to 350°. Let the dough soften at room temperature for 15 minutes. On a lightly floured surface, roll out 1 disk of dough to a scant ¼-inch thickness. Using a floured 3-inch round or square cookie cutter, cut out as many cookies as possible and transfer them to 2 large ungreased baking sheets. Gather the scraps, press them together and chill briefly until firm enough to roll. Roll out the scraps and cut out more cookies.

3. Bake the cookies on the lower and middle racks of the oven for 12 minutes, or until they have puffed and the tops look dry. Let cool for 5 minutes on the sheets, then transfer the cookies to a wire rack to cool completely. Repeat with the second disk of cookie dough.

4. MAKE THE FILLING: In a medium saucepan, combine the brown sugar with the cream and 4 tablespoons of the butter and bring to a boil. Cook over moderately high heat, stirring, until syrupy, about 2 minutes. Remove from the heat and let cool until thickened and barely warm to the touch, about 15 minutes. Transfer to a medium bowl and beat in the remaining 4 tablespoons of butter, the confectioners' sugar and the bourbon until the filling is fluffy.

5. Arrange half of the cookies on a work surface, tops down. Scoop 1 tablespoon of the butterscotch filling into the center and cover with the remaining cookies, tops up; press gently to form sandwiches. Transfer the cookies to a platter and serve.

—*Grace Parisi*

MAKE AHEAD The Butterscotch Chocolate Sandwich Cookies can be stored in an airtight container for up to 1 week.

Chocolate-Marshmallow Sandwiches

MAKES 20 SANDWICH COOKIES ● ●
To make this grown-up version of Moon Pies, you will need a standing electric mixer and a candy thermometer.

COOKIES

3½ cups all-purpose flour
1¼ cups whole wheat flour
1½ teaspoons salt
¾ teaspoon baking soda
2½ sticks (10 ounces) unsalted butter, softened
⅔ cup confectioners' sugar
⅓ cup granulated sugar
1 large egg, beaten
¼ cup honey
1 tablespoon heavy cream

FILLING AND TOPPING

1¾ cups warm water
3 envelopes of unflavored powdered gelatin
3 cups sugar
1½ cups light corn syrup
6 large egg whites
¼ teaspoon cream of tartar
¼ teaspoon salt
3 ounces unsweetened chocolate—coarsely chopped, melted and cooled
1 tablespoon pure vanilla extract
Cornstarch, for dipping
1 pound milk chocolate—coarsely chopped, melted and cooled slightly
3 ounces white chocolate—coarsely chopped, melted and cooled slightly
3 ounces semisweet chocolate—coarsely chopped, melted and cooled slightly

I. MAKE THE COOKIES: In a large bowl, combine the all-purpose flour, whole wheat flour, salt and baking soda. In a standing mixer fitted with the paddle, beat the butter with the confectioners' sugar and granulated sugar until light and fluffy. Beat in the egg, followed by the honey and cream.

Gradually beat in the flour mixture until a dry dough forms. Pat the cookie dough into 2 disks, wrap them in plastic and refrigerate until chilled, about 30 minutes.

2. Preheat the oven to 350°. On a lightly floured work surface, roll out 1 disk of dough ¼ inch thick. Using a 3-inch round biscuit cutter, cut out 20 rounds. Place the rounds on 2 large cookie sheets and bake for 8 minutes. Turn the cookies over and bake for about 5 minutes longer, or until lightly browned. Transfer the cookies to a rack to cool. Repeat with the second disk of dough.

3. MAKE THE FILLING AND TOPPING: Pour ¾ cup of the water into a small saucepan and sprinkle the gelatin evenly over the surface. Let stand until the gelatin softens, then heat the water over moderate heat just until the gelatin dissolves completely. Keep warm.

4. Meanwhile, in a medium saucepan, combine 2½ cups of the sugar with the corn syrup and the remaining 1 cup of water and bring to a boil, stirring, until the sugar dissolves. Reduce the heat to moderate and simmer until the syrup reaches 240° on a candy thermometer, about 20 minutes. Carefully stir in the warm gelatin mixture.

5. In a standing mixer fitted with the whisk, beat the egg whites with the cream of tartar and salt until soft peaks form. With the machine on, gradually add the remaining ½ cup of sugar and beat until stiff peaks form. Beating constantly, slowly pour the hot sugar syrup down the side of the bowl and beat the meringue until it is thick and almost cool, about 8 minutes.

6. Meanwhile, lightly oil a 12-by-18-inch rimmed baking sheet or jelly-roll pan. When the meringue is almost cool, beat in the melted unsweetened chocolate and the vanilla. Pour the marshmallow filling into the prepared pan and smooth the surface with a

**Chocolate-Marshmallow
Sandwiches**

large offset spatula. Let the marsh-mallow firm up at room temperature, at least 4 hours or overnight.

7. Dip a 3-inch round biscuit cutter in cornstarch and cut out 20 marshmal-low rounds as close together as possi-ble. Arrange half of the cookies, face down, on a work surface. Spoon a scant teaspoon of the milk chocolate in the center of each cookie and set a marshmallow round on top. Spoon

another scant teaspoon of the milk chocolate in the center of each marsh-mallow and cover with the remaining cookies, face up. Refrigerate the cook-ies until the chocolate hardens, about 5 minutes.

8. Line 2 large baking sheets with wax paper. Dip the top of each sandwich into the milk chocolate, letting any excess drip back into the bowl. Set the sandwiches on the baking sheet,

chocolate side down. Spread the remaining milk chocolate over the sandwiches, coating them completely. Using a small spoon, drizzle the white and semisweet chocolates over the sandwiches and refrigerate until set.

—*Todd English*

MAKE AHEAD The Chocolate-Marshmallow Sandwiches can be stored in an airtight container for up to 3 days.

15 fruit desserts

Sweet Risotto Fritters with
Strawberry-Rhubarb Compote

Sweet Risotto Fritters with Strawberry-Rhubarb Compote

6 SERVINGS

These fritters taste like sophisticated doughnuts.

- 1 tablespoon extra-virgin olive oil
- ¾ cup arborio rice
- ¼ cup orange Muscat or late-harvest Riesling

Pinch of freshly grated nutmeg

Pinch of cinnamon

- 2½ cups whole milk
- 3 tablespoons granulated sugar
- ½ teaspoon pure vanilla extract

Finely grated zest of 1 orange

- 1 large egg, lightly beaten
- 7 tablespoons all-purpose flour
- ½ teaspoon baking powder
- 2 large egg whites

Peanut oil, for frying

Confectioners' sugar, for dusting

Strawberry-Rhubarb Compote (recipe follows)

1. Heat the olive oil in a heavy, medium saucepan. Add the rice and stir over moderate heat until coated with the oil. Add the orange muscat and cook, stirring, until it is completely absorbed. Add the nutmeg, cinnamon and ½ cup of the milk and cook, stirring constantly, until the milk is completely absorbed. Continue adding milk, ½ cup at a time, stirring constantly and waiting until it is absorbed before adding more. Cook until the risotto is creamy and porridgelike and the grains of rice are just tender. Stir in the sugar, vanilla and orange zest and transfer the rice to a bowl. Let cool slightly, stir in the beaten egg, then stir in the flour and baking powder.

2. In a medium bowl, beat the egg whites until stiff peaks form. Stir half of the beaten egg whites into the risotto, then fold in the rest.

3. In a large, heavy saucepan, heat 2 inches of peanut oil to 350°. Position a wire rack on a baking sheet and cover the rack with paper towels. Scoop rounded tablespoons of the rice into the hot oil without crowding and fry until golden brown all over, about 4 minutes. Using a slotted spoon, transfer the fritters to the rack to drain. Repeat to make the remaining fritters. Sprinkle with confectioners' sugar and serve warm, with the Strawberry-Rhubarb Compote. —*Melissa Kelly*

STRAWBERRY-RHUBARB COMPOTE

MAKES ABOUT 3½ CUPS ●

- 1 pint strawberries, hulled and quartered lengthwise
- 1 pound rhubarb, stalks only, cut into ½-inch pieces
- 1 cup sugar
- 1 vanilla bean, split lengthwise, seeds scraped
- 1 tablespoon fresh lemon juice

Combine all of the ingredients in a medium saucepan and bring to a boil over moderately high heat. Reduce the heat to moderately low and simmer for 10 minutes. Remove the vanilla bean and serve warm. —*M.K.*

MAKE AHEAD The compote can be refrigerated for 4 days.

Vanilla Pain Perdu

4 SERVINGS ●

Made with brioche, strawberries and almonds, this is an easy French dessert.

STRAWBERRIES

- ¼ teaspoon finely grated lime zest
- 1 tablespoon sugar
- 1 tablespoon fresh lime juice
- 1 pint strawberries, hulled, berries halved if large

PAIN PERDU

- 2 large eggs
- 2 tablespoons sugar
- 2 teaspoons pure vanilla extract

Pinch of salt

- ¾ cup milk

Four ¾-inch-thick slices of brioche or challah

- ½ cup blanched whole almonds (2 ounces), coarsely chopped
- 2 tablespoons unsalted butter

Whipped cream, for serving (optional)

Vanilla Pain Perdu

1. PREPARE THE STRAWBERRIES: In a medium bowl, rub the grated lime zest into the sugar. Stir in the lime juice and strawberries and let stand for 10 minutes, stirring occasionally.

2. MAKE THE PAIN PERDU: In a shallow dish large enough to hold the brioche in a single layer, whisk together the eggs, sugar, vanilla and salt, then whisk in the milk. Add the brioche to the dish and turn to coat, then let the brioche soak for 10 minutes.

3. Place the almonds in a shallow bowl. Melt the butter in a large non-stick skillet. Dip 1 side of each slice of brioche into the almonds and add to the skillet, nut side down. Cook over moderate heat until the almonds are golden brown, about 3 minutes. Flip the brioche slices and cook until browned on the second side, about 3 minutes longer. Transfer the pain perdu to 4 plates, spoon the strawberries on top and serve. Pass the whipped cream at the table.

—*Alex Lee*

Mixed Berry Mosaic

Strawberry Granité

4 SERVINGS ●●

½ pound strawberries, hulled
and halved

2 cups bottled still spring water

⅓ cup sugar

¼ teaspoon finely grated
lemon zest

1. Put the strawberries in a blender. In a small saucepan, combine the water with the sugar and cook over moderate heat, stirring occasionally, until the sugar dissolves. Pour the hot syrup over the strawberries and add the lemon zest. Blend to a smooth puree.
2. Pass the puree through a fine strainer into a large glass baking dish. Place in the freezer. Stir the puree every 20 minutes with a fork, until fine frozen shards have formed. Alternatively, freeze the puree overnight and let stand at room temperature for 5 minutes, then crush with a potato masher until it resembles coarse ice. Serve the granité in chilled glasses or cups.

—*Eberhard Müller*

ONE SERVING Calories 78 kcal, Total Fat 0.2 gm, Saturated Fat 0 gm, Protein 0 gm, Carbohydrates 20 gm

MAKE AHEAD The granité can be frozen for 2 days.

Summer Berries with Goat Cheese Cream

4 SERVINGS ●●●

⅓ cup granulated sugar

⅓ cup water

1 pound mixed summer berries (about 4 cups), strawberries thickly sliced if large

1 teaspoon fresh lemon juice

½ pound chilled fresh goat cheese

¾ cup heavy cream

3 tablespoons confectioners' sugar

½ teaspoon pure vanilla extract

1. In a medium skillet, stir the granulated sugar and water over moderately high heat until the sugar dissolves. Add the mixed berries and lemon juice and cook, gently stirring occasionally, until the berries are heated through and begin to release their juices, about 2 minutes. Drain the berries and return the juices to the skillet. Cook the juices until reduced by half. Let the syrup cool slightly, then gently fold it into the berries. Refrigerate until chilled, about 20 minutes.
2. Meanwhile, in a food processor, puree the cheese, cream, confectioners' sugar and vanilla. Scrape into a bowl, cover and refrigerate until ready to serve.
3. Serve the summer berries in bowls topped with the goat cheese cream.

—*Michael Leviton*

Mixed Berry Mosaic

8 SERVINGS ●●

This colorful mosaic of seasonal berries suspended in a glistening Moscato d'Asti jelly is fragrant and refreshing. The aspic needs to set for six hours or overnight, so be sure to plan accordingly.

2½ cups Moscato d'Asti

½ cup water

Four 3-inch strips of orange zest

Four 3-inch strips of lemon zest

2½ teaspoons unflavored powdered gelatin

1 cup blueberries

1 cup raspberries

32 small strawberries, hulled and quartered

1. In a medium saucepan, mix the Moscato with the water and orange and lemon zests and bring to a simmer. Cover, then remove from the heat and let steep for 10 minutes. Strain and let the infused Moscato cool down to warm.
2. Pour 1 cup of the infused Moscato into a small saucepan, sprinkle the gelatin on top and let stand until softened. Set the saucepan over moderate heat and stir until the gelatin has completely dissolved, about 2 minutes; do not let the Moscato get too hot. Stir the dissolved gelatin mixture into the remaining Moscato and let cool.
3. Set eight ½- to ⅔-cup glass bowls on a baking sheet. Ladle 2 tablespoons of the Moscato into each bowl and refrigerate until set, about 1 hour. Layer the berries in the bowls, starting with the blueberries, then ladle the remaining Moscato over the berries. Refrigerate until firm, 6 hours or overnight.
4. Pour boiling hot water into a wide bowl and carefully dip each glass bowl into the hot water for about 10 seconds to loosen the aspic. Invert the aspics onto dessert plates and serve.

—*Massimo Bottura*

ONE SERVING Calories 97 kcal, Total Fat 0.3 gm, Saturated Fat 0 gm, Protein 1 gm, Carbohydrates 12 gm

MAKE AHEAD The aspics can be refrigerated for 2 days.

WINE A sweet, fruity Moscato like the one used in this dessert is the best choice here. Try the 1998 Maculan Moscato Veneto Dindarello or a sparkling Moscato d'Asti, such as the 1999 Coppo.

Kemptville Blueberry Bread Pudding

4 SERVINGS

2 cups milk

1 teaspoon pure vanilla extract

1 day-old baguette (1 pound), cut into 2-inch chunks

2 large eggs

1 cup sugar

1 cup blueberries

2 ounces white chocolate, broken into 1-inch chunks (optional)

1½ teaspoons unsalted butter, softened

1. Preheat the oven to 375°. Butter a 9-inch-square glass or ceramic baking dish. In a large bowl, whisk the milk with the vanilla. Add the bread, submerge it in the milk and let stand for 5 minutes.
2. In a bowl, whisk the eggs and sugar

**Kemptville Blueberry
Bread Pudding**

until pale and fluffy. Add to the soaked bread and stir; fold in the blueberries. Transfer to the prepared baking dish and poke the chocolate halfway into the pudding. Dot the pudding with the butter and bake for 45 minutes, or until the pudding is browned and crisp. Let the pudding stand for 10 minutes before serving.

—*Charles Leary and Vaughn Perret*

Raspberry Custard Tart

MAKES ONE 10-INCH TART ●

SAUCE

½ **pint fresh raspberries**

1 **cup sugar**

¼ **cup water**

1 **tablespoon unsalted butter**

⅛ **teaspoon salt**

PASTRY

1⅓ **cups all-purpose flour**

¼ **cup sugar**

¼ **teaspoon salt**

1 **stick cold unsalted butter**

2 **tablespoons heavy cream**

1 **large egg yolk**

1½ **tablespoons fresh lemon juice**

1 **teaspoon finely grated
lemon zest**

FILLING

1 **pint raspberries, plus more
for serving**

1½ **cups heavy cream**

4 **large egg yolks**

¼ **cup sugar**

1 **vanilla bean, split and scraped**

1. MAKE THE SAUCE: Puree the raspberries in a food processor or blender. Strain the puree through a fine sieve set over a medium bowl and discard the solids. In a small, heavy saucepan, bring the sugar and water to a boil. Cook over moderately high heat, without stirring, until a medium-amber caramel forms, about 6 minutes. Reduce the heat to low and carefully stir in the raspberry puree until smooth. Stir in the butter, then remove from the heat and stir in the salt. Let the raspberry sauce cool completely.

2. MAKE THE PASTRY: In a food processor, pulse the flour with the sugar and salt. Cut the butter into 8 pieces and add to the flour; pulse until the mixture resembles coarse meal. In a small bowl, whisk the cream with the egg yolk, lemon juice and zest. Add to the flour mixture and process just until large clumps of dough form. Pat the dough into a disk, wrap in plastic and chill until firm, about 30 minutes.

3. On a lightly floured surface, roll the dough ⅛ inch thick and fit in a 10-inch fluted tart pan with a removable bottom. Freeze 15 minutes, or until firm.

4. Preheat the oven to 350°. Line the dough with foil and fill with pie weights or dried beans. Bake the tart shell for 25 minutes, then remove the foil and weights and bake for 5 minutes longer, or until the pastry is lightly browned on the bottom. Cover the shell loosely with foil if the sides begin to brown too quickly. Let cool completely on a rack.

5. PREPARE THE FILLING: Arrange the raspberries in concentric circles over the bottom of the tart shell. In a small bowl, whisk the cream with the egg yolks, sugar and scraped vanilla seeds. Pour the custard into the tart shell. Bake in the middle of the oven for 50 to 55 minutes, or until the custard is set. Let the tart cool on a wire rack for at least 30 minutes. Serve with fresh raspberries and the raspberry-caramel sauce.

—*Nancy Silverton*

MAKE AHEAD The raspberry-caramel sauce can be refrigerated for 2 weeks. Bring to room temperature before serving.

Raspberry Custard Tart

Amaretti-Stuffed Figs with Raspberry Sauce

6 SERVINGS ●

Fresh figs and balsamic vinegar are classic partners. That's why the filling here is moistened with a little balsamic vinegar, a tiny bit of which is also drizzled on top of the grilled figs before serving. Authentic aged balsamic vinegar, made in Italy, is called Aceto Balsamico Tradizionale. It's relatively expensive, but well worth the cost.

- 1 cup raspberries
- 2 tablespoons plus 1½ teaspoons sugar, plus more for sprinkling
- ¼ cup mascarpone, softened
- ¼ teaspoon pure vanilla extract
- 6 amaretti cookies (about 1 ounce), coarsely crumbled
- 3 teaspoons unsalted butter, softened
- 1½ teaspoons aged balsamic vinegar, plus more for drizzling
- 6 large fresh green figs, stemmed
- 12 large fresh corn husks

1. In a food processor, puree the raspberries with 2 tablespoons of the sugar. Strain the raspberry sauce through a fine sieve. In a small bowl, blend the mascarpone with the remaining 1½ teaspoons of sugar and the vanilla. In another small bowl, combine the amaretti cookies with the butter and 1½ teaspoons of balsamic vinegar.

2. Set the figs on a work surface, stemmed side up. Using a paring knife, quarter them vertically, keeping 1 inch of the bottoms intact. Open the figs slightly and lightly sprinkle them with sugar. Spoon the amaretti cookie crumbs into the figs and press them lightly to close.

3. Spread 6 corn husks on a work surface and set a fig, stemmed side up, 2 inches from the base of each husk. Top each fig with a second husk to enclose it completely. Tie the corn husks together tightly at each end with kitchen string.

4. Light a grill or preheat a grill pan. Grill the figs over a low fire, turning them every 2 minutes, until they are tender and the filling is bubbling, about 8 minutes total. Transfer the corn husks to plates and untie the packages. Discard the husks. Open the figs slightly and top each with a rounded teaspoon of the sweetened mascarpone. Lightly drizzle the figs with the raspberry sauce and balsamic vinegar and serve. —*Marcia Kiesel*

MAKE AHEAD The raspberry sauce, sweetened mascarpone and stuffed figs can be refrigerated overnight.

Nectarine and Raspberry Grunt with Cinnamon Basil

4 SERVINGS ● ●

- 3 plums, thinly sliced
- 2 nectarines, thinly sliced
- 1½ cups raspberries (¾ pint)
- ⅓ cup water
- 1 tablespoon fresh lemon juice
- 2 teaspoons cornstarch
- 6 tablespoons granulated sugar
- ¾ cup all-purpose flour
- ¾ teaspoon baking powder
- ¼ teaspoon baking soda
- ½ cup buttermilk
- 1½ tablespoons butter, melted
- 1 tablespoon light brown sugar
- ¼ cup shredded cinnamon basil

1. In a 9-inch cast-iron skillet, combine the plums, nectarines, raspberries, water, lemon juice, cornstarch and 5 tablespoons of the granulated sugar.

2. In a bowl, blend the flour with the baking powder, baking soda and the remaining 1 tablespoon of granulated sugar. Stir in the buttermilk and melted butter.

3. Bring the fruit to a boil. Reduce the heat to low. Drop the batter by tablespoons on the bubbling fruit. Sprinkle the brown sugar over the batter. Cover tightly and simmer for 13 minutes.

Remove from the heat, uncover and let cool to warm or room temperature. Garnish with the cinnamon basil and serve. —*Suki Hertz*

ONE SERVING Calories 362 kcal, Total Fat 6.6 mg, Saturated Fat 2.8 mg

Peach and Blackberry Cobbler

8 SERVINGS

You can bake the cobbler in individual ramekins for a more elegant touch.

PASTRY
- 2½ cups all-purpose flour
- ¾ teaspoon salt
- ½ cup plus 2 tablespoons cold solid vegetable shortening
- ½ cup ice water

FILLING
- 1 cup sugar, plus more for sprinkling
- ¼ cup cornstarch
- 5½ pounds ripe peaches— peeled, pitted and cut into ½-inch wedges
- 3 cups blackberries
- ¼ cup plus 1 tablespoon fresh lemon juice
- 2 tablespoons unsalted butter, cut into small pieces
- 2 tablespoons half-and-half, for brushing

1. MAKE THE PASTRY: In a food processor, pulse the flour with the salt. Add the vegetable shortening and pulse until the mixture resembles coarse meal. Add the ice water to the mixture all at once and pulse just until the pastry comes together. Scrape the pastry out onto a lightly floured work surface and pat the pastry into an 8-inch square. Wrap the pastry square in plastic and refrigerate until it is firm, at least 30 minutes or overnight.

2. MAKE THE FILLING: In a small bowl, mix the 1 cup of sugar with the cornstarch. In a large bowl, gently toss the peaches with the blackberries. Add the sugar-and-cornstarch mixture and lemon juice to the mixed fruit and

fruit desserts

gently toss the fruit again. Spoon the fruit into a 3-quart shallow glass or ceramic baking dish and scatter the pieces of unsalted butter over the top of the fruit filling.

3. Position racks in the middle and lower third of the oven and preheat the oven to 425°. Line a large rimmed baking sheet with aluminum foil. On a lightly floured work surface, roll out the cobbler pastry until it is 2 inches larger than the baking dish on all sides and about ⅛ inch thick.

4. ASSEMBLE THE COBBLER: Drape the cobbler pastry over the baking dish and trim the overhang to 1 inch. Fold the overhang under itself and press it lightly onto the rim of the baking dish; crimp the pastry edge decoratively. Brush the pastry with the half-and-half and sprinkle it with 1 tablespoon of sugar. Using a paring knife, make 6 small slits in the pastry crust to allow steam to escape.

5. Slide the aluminum foil–covered baking sheet onto the lower oven rack and bake the peach and berry cobbler on the middle oven rack for 50 minutes, or until the pastry is crisp and golden brown and the fruit filling is bubbling. Transfer the cobbler to a wire rack and let it cool for at least 1 hour or for up to 4 hours.

—*Randy Windham*

MAKE AHEAD The cobbler pastry can be tightly wrapped in plastic before rolling out and refrigerated overnight or frozen for 2 weeks.

SERVE WITH Crème fraîche, sweetened whipped cream flavored with vanilla or vanilla ice cream.

WINE The sweet peaches and tart blackberries in this fruit cobbler call for a sweet wine with citrusy acidity. Two good possibilities include a lemony Sauternes, such as the 1996 Château Doisy-Védrines from France, or the delicious Muscat-based Bonny Doon Vineyard Muscat Vin de Glacière from California.

Vanilla-Roasted Peaches

4 SERVINGS ●

- 1 cup sugar
- ⅓ cup water
- 1 vanilla bean, split lengthwise, seeds scraped and reserved
- ½ cinnamon stick

Pinch of salt

- 8 small ripe peaches, halved and pitted

Vanilla ice cream or coconut sorbet, for serving

Preheat the oven to 400°. In a small saucepan, combine the sugar with the water, vanilla bean and scrapings, cinnamon stick and salt. Cook over moderate heat, stirring frequently, until the sugar dissolves. Pour the syrup into a large baking dish. Arrange the peaches in the syrup, cut side up, and bake for 30 minutes, basting frequently. Spoon the peaches and syrup into bowls and serve warm with ice cream.

—*Melissa Clark*

Yellow Fruit Salad with Ginger-Thyme Syrup

6 SERVINGS ●

You will need a candy thermometer to make the Ginger-Thyme Syrup.

- 1 cup superfine sugar
- ½ cup water

Three ¼-inch-thick slices of fresh ginger

- 1 large thyme sprig
- 2 large egg whites, at room temperature
- ½ teaspoon pure vanilla extract
- 1 large ripe mango, peeled and thinly sliced
- 2 peaches, peeled and thinly sliced
- 1 golden plum, thinly sliced

1. Preheat the oven to 225°. In a heavy saucepan, bring the sugar, water, ginger and thyme to a boil, stirring until the sugar dissolves. Lower the heat and simmer the syrup for 10 minutes. Strain ½ cup of the syrup into a bowl and let cool.

Peach and Blackberry Cobbler

2. Boil the remaining syrup over high heat until it reaches 230° on a candy thermometer, about 5 minutes. Discard the ginger and thyme.

3. In a bowl, beat the egg whites at medium speed until soft peaks form. At high speed, slowly beat in the hot syrup. Add the vanilla and beat until the meringue is stiff, glossy and at room temperature.

4. Line 2 baking sheets with parchment paper. Fit a pastry bag with a ⁵⁄₁₆-inch round tip (#3). Add one-third of the meringue at a time and pipe it out onto the prepared baking sheets in 5-inch-long straight or squiggly lines about ½ inch apart.

5. Bake the meringues for about 1½ hours, or until dry to the touch. Turn off the oven and leave the meringues in for 1 hour; they should be completely crisp and dry. Let cool on the baking sheets.

6. Fold the sliced fruit into the reserved cool syrup. Let stand for 20 minutes. Spoon the fruit and syrup into bowls and serve with the meringues.

—*Grace Parisi*

Yellow Fruit Salad with Ginger-Thyme Syrup

Skillet Soufflés with Plum Compote

6 SERVINGS

The batter for *Kaiserschmarren,* this Viennese dessert, is light and delicate, but that doesn't mean these soufflés are challenging to make: They taste good whether they turn out soft in the middle or cooked to a crisp. The sugar sprinkled in the skillets helps the soufflés rise.

    3 tablespoons golden raisins
    ½ cup sugar
    2 large eggs, separated
    ½ cup crème fraîche
    2 tablespoons dark rum
    3 tablespoons all-purpose
       flour, sifted
    4 large egg whites
Confectioners' sugar, for dusting
Plum Compote (recipe follows)

1. Preheat the oven to 425°. In a small saucepan, cover the raisins with water and bring to a boil; set aside until softened, about 10 minutes. Drain the raisins and pat dry.

2. Butter two 8-inch ovenproof skillets and sprinkle each with 1 tablespoon of the sugar; shake to coat the bottoms and sides. In a medium bowl, using a handheld electric mixer, beat the 2 egg yolks with ¼ cup of the sugar until thick and pale, about 5 minutes. Beat in the crème fraîche and then the dark rum. Fold in the flour and softened raisins.

3. In a large stainless steel bowl, beat the 6 egg whites until soft peaks form. Add the remaining 2 tablespoons of sugar and beat until firm and glossy. Fold the egg whites into the egg yolk mixture. Pour the soufflé batter into the skillets and bake in the center of the oven for 12 minutes, or until the soufflés have risen and are golden brown.

4. Spoon the soufflés onto 6 plates and dust with confectioners' sugar. Serve at once with the Plum Compote.

—*Wolfgang Puck*

WINE A lusciously rich late-harvest wine with good acidity will complement this light soufflé while adding a refreshing citrusy note. Try the 1998 Joseph Phelps Johannisberg Riesling Select Late Harvest Anderson Valley from California. ▶

fruit desserts

PLUM COMPOTE

6 SERVINGS ● ● ●

- 1 cup sugar
- ½ cup water
- 9 red plums, halved and pitted
- 1 tablespoon fresh lemon juice

In a large saucepan, combine the sugar and water and bring to a boil. Add the plums, cover and simmer over low heat, turning the plums once, until they are tender but still hold their shape, about 10 minutes. Stir in the lemon juice and serve warm or at room temperature. —*W.P.*

MAKE AHEAD The compote can be refrigerated for up to 2 days.

Five-Spice Melons

4 SERVINGS ● ● ●

These sweet-and-spicy melons make a wonderful and unexpected dessert.

- ¼ teaspoon Szechuan peppercorns
- ¼ teaspoon pink peppercorns
- ¼ teaspoon white peppercorns
- ¼ teaspoon black peppercorns
- ¼ teaspoon whole allspice

Two 2-pound ripe cantaloupes, halved crosswise and seeded

Mint sprigs, for garnish (optional)

1. Combine the pink, white and black peppercorns with the allspice in a spice grinder or a mortar and finely grind them.

2. Using a melon baller, scoop out the melon flesh without cutting through the rind. Replace the flesh in the shells and sprinkle each with about ¼ teaspoon of the spice mix. Garnish with mint sprigs and serve. —*Jean Calviac*

MAKE AHEAD You can scoop out the melon flesh two hours ahead. Drain and return to shells just before serving.

WINE A tart Jurançon from the Pyrenees foothills will mirror the melons' flavor and contrast with their sweetness. Consider the 1998 Château Jolys or the 1997 Domaine Bru-Baché.

Yin-Yang Melon Soup

4 SERVINGS ● ●

This dessert is a pairing of orange- and green-melon soups. Serving the soups together in one bowl is especially colorful, but each can stand alone.

- 1 pound peeled green melon, such as honeydew, cut into 1-inch dice (3 cups)
- ¼ cup mint leaves
- ¼ cup fresh lime juice
- 2 tablespoons sugar
- 1 pound peeled orange melon, such as cantaloupe, cut into 1-inch dice (3 cups)
- 3 tablespoons fresh lemon juice

1. In a food processor or blender, puree the green melon with the mint, lime juice and 1 tablespoon of the sugar. Pour into a pitcher and refrigerate until chilled, about 1 hour.

2. Rinse out the blender. Add the orange melon, lemon juice and the remaining 1 tablespoon of sugar and puree. Pour into a pitcher and refrigerate until chilled, about 1 hour.

3. At the same time, pour both soups from opposite sides into shallow bowls, taking care to keep them from mixing, and serve. —*Suki Hertz*

ONE SERVING Calories 110 kcal, Total Fat 0.3 gm, Saturated Fat 0.1 gm

MAKE AHEAD The soups can be refrigerated overnight.

Skillet Soufflés with Plum Compote

Simple Melon Sorbets

4 SERVINGS ●●

¾ cup water

1¼ cups sugar

1 pound peeled green melon, such as honeydew, cut into 1-inch dice (3 cups)

2 tablespoons melon liqueur

½ cup fresh orange juice

1 pound peeled orange melon, such as cantaloupe, cut into 1-inch dice (3 cups)

1½ pounds peeled seedless watermelon

Mint sprigs, for garnish (optional)

1. In a small saucepan, combine the water with ¾ cup of the sugar and cook over moderate heat, stirring, until the sugar dissolves. Cool completely.

2. In a blender or food processor, puree the green melon with the sugar syrup and melon liqueur. Freeze the puree in an ice cream maker according to the manufacturer's instructions. Pack the sorbet into a plastic container, press plastic wrap directly on the sorbet, cover and freeze.

3. Rinse out the blender. In a small saucepan, combine the orange juice with the remaining ½ cup of sugar and cook over moderate heat, stirring, until the sugar dissolves. Let cool completely. In the blender, puree the orange melon with the orange syrup. Freeze the puree in an ice cream maker according to the manufacturer's instructions. Pack the sorbet into another plastic container, press plastic wrap directly on the sorbet, cover and freeze.

4. Using a large melon baller or a small ice cream scoop, make 8 balls of watermelon. Freeze for 20 minutes.

5. Put 2 watermelon balls in each of 4 large margarita or parfait glasses. Scoop 2 balls of each sorbet into each glass, garnish with mint and serve.

—*Suki Hertz*

ONE SERVING Calories 413 kcal, Total Fat 1.1 gm, Saturated Fat 0.2 gm

Five-Spice Melon

melon news

Next to the honeydew and cantaloupe in the produce aisle, you may see these unfamiliar melon and watermelon varieties: **Charentais** A very pretty melon—small and striated, with dense, satiny orange flesh and a flowery aroma. This melon was originally from France but is now grown here too. **Cavaillon** Also from France, this small fruit with its gray-green rind and blue-green stripes has deep-salmon flesh. Its intense sweetness and honey-citrus flavor make it arguably the world's best melon. **Galia** Dense, white-green flesh with a honeyed flavor and spicy aroma; originally from Israel. **Orange honeydew** Combines the best of honeydew and cantaloupe—the flesh has the texture and color of a cantaloupe but tastes like a honeydew. **Sharlyn** White-green flesh tinted coral near the seeds, with a creamy texture and a hint of vanilla in the flavor. **Watermelon** The new ones are yellow, orange, even white inside.

Watermelon and Mascarpone Parfaits

10 SERVINGS ● ●

It is important to assemble the watermelon and mascarpone parfaits just before serving, so be sure to plan accordingly.

5 ½ cups diced (1 inch) watermelon
1 teaspoon finely grated lime zest
3 tablespoons minced mint, plus whole mint leaves for garnish
1 ¼ cups mascarpone (about 9 ½ ounces), at room temperature
¾ cup heavy cream
3 tablespoons sugar
1 tablespoon plus 1 teaspoon fresh lime juice
1 ¼ teaspoons pure vanilla extract
Lime slices, for garnish

1. In a bowl, combine the watermelon, lime zest and minced mint. Refrigerate until chilled.

2. In a bowl, combine the mascarpone, cream, sugar, lime juice and vanilla. Using an electric mixer, beat at low speed until fluffy. Do not overbeat.

3. Spoon one-third of the watermelon into Champagne flutes or wineglasses and top with half of the mascarpone cream. Add another layer of watermelon and mascarpone cream. Top with a final layer of watermelon, garnish with mint leaves and lime slices and serve.   —*Danielle Custer*

MAKE AHEAD The mascarpone cream can be refrigerated for 1 day.

Striped Purple Grape and Panna Cotta Parfait

6 SERVINGS ●

This dessert contrasts sweet, tart grape jelly with smooth, creamy buttermilk panna cotta. The differing textures play off each other beautifully, and both melt in your mouth.

3 cups unsweetened Concord grape juice
2 ¾ teaspoons unflavored gelatin
1 cup plus 2 tablespoons heavy cream
3 tablespoons superfine sugar
Four 1-inch strips of lemon zest
1 cup plus 2 tablespoons buttermilk
Amaretti cookies, for serving (optional)

1. In a medium saucepan, boil the grape juice over moderately high heat until reduced by half; let cool. Transfer ¼ cup of the juice to a small skillet. Sprinkle 1 ½ teaspoons of the gelatin over the grape juice and let stand until softened, about 10 minutes. Warm the mixture over low heat, stirring once or twice until dissolved. Let cool, then stir the mixture back into the remaining cooled grape juice; reserve ¾ cup of the grape gelatin and carefully pour

Watermelon and Mascarpone Parfaits

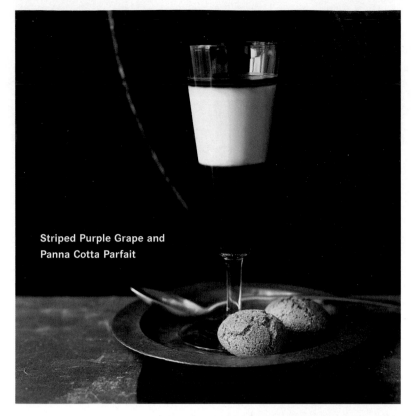

Striped Purple Grape and
Panna Cotta Parfait

Baked Almond-Stuffed Apples

4 SERVINGS ●

    3   tablespoons slivered
        blanched almonds,
        lightly toasted
One 2.3-ounce box of amaretti,
        finely crumbled
    ⅓   cup dried currants
    2   tablespoons dark brown sugar
    ½   teaspoon cinnamon
Finely grated zest of 1 lemon
    2   tablespoons unsalted
        butter, softened
    4   Fuji apples (about
        7 ounces each)
    1   cup apple juice
    2   tablespoons dark rum

1. Preheat the oven to 375°. In a medium bowl, mix the almonds with the amaretti crumbs, currants, brown sugar, cinnamon and lemon zest. Add

the rest into 6 Champagne flutes. Refrigerate the flutes until the grape gelatin is chilled and set, at least 2 hours.

2. In a medium saucepan, combine the heavy cream, sugar and lemon zest and bring to a simmer. Let cool, then discard the lemon zest. Pour ¼ cup of the cream mixture into a small skillet and sprinkle the remaining 1¼ teaspoons of gelatin on top. Let stand until the gelatin is softened, about 10 minutes. Warm the gelatin mixture over low heat until dissolved, then stir it into the remaining cream mixture along with the buttermilk; let cool completely.

3. Carefully pour the buttermilk panna cotta into the Champagne flutes and chill until set, about 2 hours. If necessary, rewarm the remaining grape gelatin over low heat until it's just pourable; pour a thin layer over the panna cotta in each flute. Refrigerate until set. Serve the parfaits with amaretti.   —*Grace Parisi*

MAKE AHEAD The parfaits can be refrigerated for up to 2 days.

Baked Almond-Stuffed Apple

the butter and mix with your fingers until the filling resembles coarse meal.

2. Using a sharp knife, cut a ¼-inch-thick slice from the top and bottom of each apple. Working from the stem end and using a melon baller, apple corer or sharp knife, remove the interior core and seeds to within ½ inch of the bottom. Using a paring or channeling knife, score the apple skin lengthwise at 1½-inch intervals. Arrange the apples so they don't touch in an 8-inch square baking dish and spoon the filling into them, mounding any remaining filling on top. Pour the apple juice and rum around the apples.

3. Bake the apples for 20 minutes. Cover loosely with foil and bake for 45 to 50 minutes longer, or until the apples are very soft. Transfer the apples to plates with a spatula. Spoon the pan juices on top and serve.

—*Ann Chantal Altman*

ONE SERVING Calories 339 kcal, Total Fat 10.7 gm, Saturated Fat 4.1 gm, Protein 3 gm, Carbohydrates 59 gm

Winter Apple Gratin

4 SERVINGS ●●

- 2 teaspoons unsalted butter
- 4 large Fuji or Jonagold apples— peeled, cored and cut into eighths
- 1 tablespoon light brown sugar
- 3 large egg yolks
- 3 tablespoons granulated sugar
- 2 tablespoons applejack or other brandy

Yogurt Sorbet (recipe follows)

1. Preheat the broiler. Melt the butter in a large skillet. Add the apple wedges in a single layer and sprinkle them with the brown sugar. Cook over moderate heat, stirring a few times, until lightly browned on both sides, about 8 minutes. Cover and cook over low heat until tender, about 5 minutes. Uncover and cook over high heat until the juices evaporate and the apples are

Winter Apple Gratin

glazed, about 3 minutes. Spread the apples in a single layer in a 10-inch glass pie plate or in 4 individual gratin dishes.

2. In a small, heavy saucepan, whisk the egg yolks with the granulated sugar and applejack. Cook over low heat, whisking constantly until thickened, about 2 minutes; do not boil. Pour the custard over the apples and broil until it is lightly browned on top and set, about 2 minutes. Serve hot, with the Yogurt Sorbet.—*Patricia Wells*

ONE SERVING Calories 211 kcal, Total Fat 6.4 gm, Saturated Fat 2.5 gm, Protein 2 gm, Carbohydrates 36 gm

WINE Search for a sweet or semisweet white wine, such as a young Sauternes or an Anjou Coteaux de la Loire.

YOGURT SORBET

MAKES 1 QUART ●●

- 3 large egg whites
- ⅔ cup sugar
- 3 cups plain nonfat yogurt

1. In a medium bowl, using a handheld electric mixer, beat the egg whites until frothy. Slowly add the sugar and beat at high speed until the egg whites hold stiff, shiny peaks, about 4 minutes.

2. In another bowl, whisk the yogurt until smooth. Fold in the egg whites. Transfer the mixture to an ice cream machine and freeze according to the manufacturer's instructions. —*P.W.*

ONE-HALF CUP Calories 120 kcal, Total Fat 0.2 gm, Saturated Fat 0.1 gm, Protein 7 gm, Carbohydrates 23 gm

MAKE AHEAD The yogurt sorbet can be frozen for 2 days.

Baked Apple Dumplings with Cherry Butter and Apple Brandy Sauce

12 SERVINGS ●

- ½ cup dried tart cherries
- 1 cup hot water
- 1 stick (4 ounces) unsalted butter, softened
- ⅓ cup light brown sugar

Six 6-ounce Granny Smith apples, peeled and halved lengthwise

Pastry (recipe follows)

- 1 large egg yolk beaten with 1 tablespoon heavy cream
- ¼ cup granulated sugar
- 2 teaspoons cinnamon

Apple Brandy Sauce (recipe follows), for serving

Baked Apple Dumplings
with Cherry Butter and
Apple Brandy Sauce

1. In a small bowl, soak the dried cherries in the hot water until plumped, about 20 minutes. Drain the cherries and squeeze dry. In a mini food processor, pulse the cherries with the butter and light brown sugar until finely chopped. Scrape the cherry butter into a small bowl and refrigerate until the butter is slightly firm.

2. Preheat the oven to 400°. Line a large baking sheet with parchment paper. Using a melon baller, scoop out the core of each apple half. Fill the cores with the cherry butter.

3. Working with 4 at a time, lightly brush the pastry squares with water. For each dumpling, set an apple half, cut side down, in the center of a square. Bring the corners of the pastry up and over the apple, overlapping them; press lightly to seal. Transfer the dumpling to the prepared baking sheet. Brush the pastry leaves with water and press 1 on the top of each dumpling.

4. Brush the dumplings with the egg wash. Mix the granulated sugar with the cinnamon and sprinkle 1 teaspoon over each dumpling. Bake for about 40 minutes, or until the pastry is golden and the apples are tender. Serve with Apple Brandy Sauce. —*Tom Douglas*
MAKE AHEAD The apple dumplings can be prepared through Step 3 and refrigerated overnight.

PASTRY
MAKES TWELVE 6-INCH SQUARES
AND TWELVE LEAVES ●
- 3¾ cups all-purpose flour
- 1½ tablespoons sugar
- 1½ teaspoons kosher salt
- 3 sticks (¾ pound) unsalted butter, cut into 1-inch pieces
- 1 cup ice water

1. In a food processor, pulse the flour with the sugar and salt. Add half of the butter and pulse until the mixture resembles coarse meal. Add the remaining butter and pulse until the mixture resembles small peas. Transfer the mixture to a bowl, add the water and stir just until a dough forms. Knead several times just until the pastry comes together, then form into 3 disks. Refrigerate until chilled.

2. On a lightly floured surface, roll each disk out to a 12- to 13-inch square ⅛ inch thick. Trim the pastry to even 12-inch squares, then cut each square into quarters, forming four 6-inch squares. Make a cut in each corner of each pastry square, extending halfway to the center. Reroll the pastry scraps. Using a leaf-shaped cookie cutter, stamp out 12 large pastry leaves; score decoratively. —*T.D.*
MAKE AHEAD The pastry squares and leaves can be stacked between sheets of wax paper and refrigerated for 3 days or frozen for 1 month.

APPLE BRANDY SAUCE
MAKES ABOUT 1½ CUPS ● ●
- 2 sticks (½ pound) unsalted butter, at room temperature
- 2 cups confectioners' sugar
- 3 tablespoons apple brandy

In a medium bowl, beat the butter until creamy. Gradually add the confectioners' sugar and beat at low speed until blended. Add the brandy and beat at medium speed until light and fluffy. Serve at room temperature. —*T.D.*
MAKE AHEAD The apple brandy sauce can be kept at room temperature for 2 days or refrigerated for 5 days. Bring to room temperature before serving.

Pear, Pear, Pear
12 SERVINGS ●
- 6 ripe Comice or Bartlett pears
- 2 tablespoons fresh lemon juice
- ½ cup pear eau-de-vie
- Salt
- 1½ cups sugar
- 1½ cups water
- ½ cup fresh or unsweetened frozen raspberries
- 1½ pints pear sorbet
- ½ cup julienned organic rose petals, for garnish

1. Peel the pears and brush them with the lemon juice; reserve the peels. Quarter and core the pears, then slice them lengthwise ⅛ inch thick. Transfer to a large, shallow dish. Sprinkle ¼ cup of the pear eau-de-vie over the pears and add a pinch of salt. Cover and refrigerate for at least 30 minutes or for up to 2 hours.

2. Meanwhile, in a medium saucepan, combine the sugar with the water and simmer over moderate heat until the sugar dissolves. Add the reserved pear peels, cover partially and simmer over low heat for 15 minutes. Strain the syrup and refrigerate until chilled.

3. Using a wooden spoon, press the raspberries through a fine sieve set over a bowl. Reserve the raspberry puree.

4. Scoop ¼ cup of the pear sorbet into each of 12 shallow bowls. Spoon the chilled pears and pear syrup around the sorbet. Pour the remaining ¼ cup of eau-de-vie over the pears and dot each serving with 2 teaspoons of the raspberry puree. Garnish with the rose petals and serve. —*Jeremiah Tower*

Pear Soufflés
2 SERVINGS ●
- 1 cup dry white wine
- 1 cup water
- ½ cup sugar
- 2 large ripe Bartlett pears—peeled, halved and cored
- 2 large egg yolks
- 3 tablespoons egg whites (see Note)

1. Preheat the oven to 375°. Butter two 1-cup ramekins and dust them lightly with sugar. In a medium stainless-steel saucepan, combine the white wine, water and sugar and bring to a boil; stir to dissolve the sugar. Add the pears and simmer over low heat until very tender, about 7 minutes.

Transfer the pears to a food processor and puree until smooth. Boil the pear cooking liquid over high heat until it is reduced to ⅓ cup, about 20 minutes. Let the pear syrup cool completely.

2. Meanwhile, in a small saucepan, cook the pear puree over moderately low heat, stirring often until reduced to ½ cup, about 15 minutes. Transfer the puree to a medium bowl.

3. In a small stainless-steel bowl, whisk the egg yolks with 1 tablespoon of the reduced pear syrup. Set the bowl over a small saucepan filled with 1-inch of gently simmering water and whisk constantly until the egg yolks thicken, about 2 minutes. Scrape the egg yolks into the pear puree and stir to blend.

4. In a medium stainless-steel bowl, beat the egg whites until firm peaks form. Add 1 tablespoon of the reduced pear syrup and beat the egg whites until glossy; refrigerate the remaining pear syrup for another use. Using a large rubber spatula, fold one-third of the beaten whites into the pear puree mixture to loosen it, then fold in the remaining beaten egg whites just until blended.

Poached Pear with Fragrant Cream

Pear Soufflé

5. Spoon the soufflé mixture into the prepared ramekins. Bake the soufflés in the center of the oven for about 20 minutes, or until golden and well risen. Serve the soufflés at once.

—*Galen Zamarra*

N O T E Egg whites are easier to measure after they have been lightly beaten.

MAKE AHEAD The pear syrup and pear puree can be prepared in advance and refrigerated separately overnight.

Poached Pears with Fragrant Cream

4 SERVINGS

- 4 **cups water**
- ¾ **cup sugar**
- 2 **whole cloves, broken, plus a pinch of coarsely ground cloves**
- 1½ **cinnamon sticks, plus a pinch of coarsely ground cinnamon**
- 1½ **teaspoons white peppercorns, lightly cracked**
- 1 **star anise pod, broken into pieces**
- 4 **ripe but firm pears, such as Bosc, peeled, stems left intact**
- 4 **tablespoons unsalted butter**
- ½ **cup crème fraîche**
- 1 **tablespoon fresh lemon juice**

1. In a medium saucepan, combine the water, sugar, broken cloves, cinnamon sticks, peppercorns and star anise and bring to a boil. Add the pears and cover them with a small pot lid to keep them submerged. Cook over moderate heat until tender, about 15 minutes. Transfer the pears to a plate to cool. Pick out any spices that are embedded in the pears. Cut a thin slice off the bottoms so the pears stand upright.

2. Boil the poaching liquid until reduced to ½ cup, about 50 minutes. Strain the syrup into a medium skillet and add the butter. Cook over moderate heat, stirring occasionally, until thickened, about 5 minutes. Stir in the crème fraîche, lemon juice and ground cloves and cinnamon. Add the pears and turn to coat with sauce. Set the pears on plates, spoon the sauce around them and serve warm.

—*Jean-Georges Vongerichten*

WINE With its intense aromatics and higher alcohol, a Muscat de Beaumes-de-Venise from southern France will stand up to the buttery sweetness of the pears and spiced cream here. Look for the 1999 Paul Jaboulet Aîné or the 1998 M. Chapoutier.

Roasted Pear and Fig Compote

4 SERVINGS ● ●

    4   ripe but firm Bartlett pears
    ½   cup granulated sugar
    ½   cup apple juice
    1   tablespoon unsalted butter
    ½   teaspoon cinnamon
    ¼   teaspoon allspice
    6   dried figs, quartered lengthwise
    8   ounces plain low-fat yogurt
    1   teaspoon pure vanilla extract
    1½ tablespoons superfine sugar

1. Preheat the oven to 425°. Halve the pears lengthwise and core them, then cut each half lengthwise into 3 wedges.

2. In a large nonstick ovenproof skillet, cook the granulated sugar, apple juice and butter over moderate heat until the butter melts. Stir in the cinnamon and allspice. Stir in the pears and figs and cook for 5 minutes.

3. Transfer the compote to the oven and roast for 25 minutes, or until the fruit is tender.

4. In a small bowl, whisk the yogurt with the vanilla and superfine sugar. Spoon the compote on plates. Serve warm or at room temperature with the yogurt sauce.   —*Ann Chantal Altman*

ONE SERVING Calories 350 kcal, Total Fat 5 gm, Saturated Fat 2.6 gm, Protein 5 gm, Carbohydrates 77 gm

Passion Fruit Pavlova

6 SERVINGS ●

Pavlova, a classic Australian dessert named after the Russian ballerina Anna Pavlova, is a crisp meringue shell topped with whipped cream and, often, passion fruit.

    3   large egg whites, at room
        temperature
    ¾   cup superfine sugar
    1½ teaspoons fresh lemon juice
    1½ teaspoons sifted cornstarch
    1   teaspoon pure vanilla extract
    ¾   cup heavy cream
    2   tablespoons confectioners' sugar

    1   large ripe mango, peeled and cut
        into ½-inch dice
    1   papaya—peeled, seeded and cut
        into ½-inch dice
    4   fresh passion fruits (see Note),
        halved crosswise and seeds and
        pulp scooped out

1. Preheat the oven to 325°. Line a baking sheet with parchment paper or foil. In a large bowl, beat the egg whites at medium speed until soft peaks form. Beat in the superfine sugar, 1 tablespoon at a time, beating at high speed for about 15 seconds between additions. Continue beating at high speed until the meringue is stiff and glossy. Beat in the lemon juice, cornstarch and vanilla. Spoon the meringue into 6 mounds on the prepared baking sheet. Using the back of a tablespoon, make a well in each meringue.

2. Bake the meringues in the center of the oven for 5 minutes, until slightly dry to the touch and just set. Reduce the oven temperature to 225° and bake the meringues for 1 hour longer. Turn the oven off and leave the meringues in the warm oven with the door closed for 1 hour. The meringues should be crisp and snowy white on the outside and slightly chewy within.

3. Using a handheld mixer, beat the heavy cream at moderately high speed until soft peaks form. Add the confectioners' sugar and beat until thoroughly combined. Set the meringues on dessert plates and top them with whipped cream. Spoon the mango and papaya on top, garnish with the passion fruit and serve.

—*Andrew Evans*

ONE SERVING Calories 279 kcal, Total Fat 11.3 gm, Saturated Fat 7 gm, Protein 3 gm, Carbohydrates 43 gm

NOTE When shopping for passion fruit, look for ones that are heavy and deep purple, with wrinkled skin. They can be stored in the refrigerator for up to 5 days.

MAKE AHEAD The meringues for the Passion Fruit Pavlova can be stored in an airtight container for up to 3 days if the weather is clear and dry.

Floating Island with Coconut Milk and Mango Chutney

4 SERVINGS

    ¼   cup large pearl tapioca
        (not instant)
    1½ cups milk
    1   mango—peeled, pitted and
        cut into ½-inch dice
    1   tablespoon water
    ½   vanilla bean, split lengthwise
    1   cup plus 1 tablespoon sugar
    3   tablespoons fresh lime juice
    1½ teaspoons finely grated
        lime zest
  One 13½-ounce can unsweetened
        coconut milk
    ½   teaspoon salt
    4   large egg whites

1. Preheat the oven to 225°. Soak the tapioca in ½ cup of milk for 1 hour. Lightly butter four 6-ounce ramekins.

2. In a small saucepan, combine the diced mango with the water, vanilla bean and 1 tablespoon of the sugar. Simmer over low heat, stirring occasionally, until the mango softens, about 5 minutes. Remove the pan from the heat. Remove the vanilla bean from the saucepan and stir in the lime juice and zest.

3. In a medium saucepan, combine the tapioca and any of its soaking milk with the remaining 1 cup of milk. Simmer over low heat, stirring occasionally, until the tapioca is tender but still chewy, 30 to 35 minutes.

4. In a small saucepan, whisk the coconut milk with ⅓ cup of the sugar and the salt and bring to a boil over moderate heat. Transfer to a medium bowl. Stir in the tapioca and chill in the refrigerator or quick-chill by setting the bowl in a larger bowl of ice water.

5. In a stainless-steel bowl, whisk the egg whites with the remaining ⅔ cup of sugar. Set the bowl over but not in a medium pan of simmering water and whisk constantly until the whites are slightly warmer than body temperature, about 100° on a candy thermometer. Remove the bowl from the water and beat the egg whites at high speed until very stiff and glossy, about 3 minutes.

6. Spoon the meringue into the buttered ramekins. Tap the ramekins against the work surface to settle the meringue. Run your thumb around the rim to create a small ridge between the rim and the meringue. Set the ramekins in a small roasting pan and pour in enough hot water to reach halfway up the sides of the ramekins. Cover the pan loosely with foil and bake for about 25 minutes, or until the meringues are barely set. Transfer the ramekins to a rack.

7. Spoon the coconut-tapioca sauce into 4 shallow bowls. Run a knife around the meringues and invert 1 into the center of each bowl. Using a tablespoon, scoop a small "cap" from the center of each meringue, fill the meringue with the mango chutney and replace the "cap." Serve the desserts immediately.

—*Jean-Georges Vongerichten*

Moroccan Citrus Fruit Salad

4 SERVINGS ●●

Orange-flower water and cinnamon give this citrus fruit salad a Moroccan accent.

    4 navel oranges (see Note)
    2 pink grapefruits
2½ cups fresh orange juice
    3 tablespoons orange-flower water
    2 tablespoons honey
    1 vanilla bean, halved lengthwise, seeds scraped and reserved
    ½ teaspoon cinnamon
Small mint leaves, for garnish

I. Using a sharp knife, peel the oranges and grapefruits, removing all of the bitter white pith. Cut in between

the membranes to release the sections into a bowl. Squeeze the juice from the citrus membranes into another bowl.

2. Add the orange juice, orange-flower water, honey, vanilla bean seeds and cinnamon to the bowl of juice and whisk to mix. Strain the flavored juice over the fruit and refrigerate for at least 2 hours or overnight. Spoon the fruit salad into glasses or bowls, garnish with mint leaves and serve.

—*Eberhard Müller*

ONE SERVING Calories 204 kcal, Total Fat 0.6 gm, Saturated Fat 0.1 gm, Protein 3 gm, Carbohydrates 51 gm
NOTE Choose citrus fruits that are heavy for their size.

Roast Pineapple Splits with Macadamia Brittle

8 SERVINGS

CARAMEL SAUCE

    1 cup sugar
    ¼ cup water
    1 tablespoon light corn syrup
    1 teaspoon fresh lemon juice
    1 cup heavy cream
    1 tablespoon unsalted butter

PINEAPPLE SPLIT

    2 peeled and cored 4-pound golden pineapples, each cut crosswise into eight ½-inch rings
    1 cup unsweetened pineapple juice
    ⅔ cup sugar
Vanilla ice cream and Macadamia Brittle (recipe follows), for serving

I. MAKE THE CARAMEL SAUCE: In a heavy, medium saucepan, combine the sugar, water, corn syrup and lemon juice and bring to a boil. Stir the mixture once and simmer over moderate heat until a light amber caramel forms, about 8 minutes. Remove from the heat and carefully stir in the cream and butter. Return the sauce to high heat and stir constantly until smooth and glossy, about 1 minute. Remove from the heat. Rewarm before serving.

Roast Pineapple Split with Macadamia Brittle

2. MAKE THE PINEAPPLE SPLITS: Preheat the oven to 400°. Arrange the pineapple rings on 2 large, rimmed baking sheets. Pour the pineapple juice over them and sprinkle with the sugar. Bake the pineapple rings for 1 hour, or until dark brown on both sides; turn the rings and rotate the baking sheets every 20 minutes for even browning. Let the rings cool on the baking sheets. ▶

3. To serve, arrange 2 halved pineapple rings in each of 8 tall glasses or serving bowls and top with scoops of vanilla ice cream. Drizzle with the caramel sauce and garnish with the Macadamia Brittle. —*Kevin Taylor*

MAKE AHEAD The pineapple can be roasted early in the day and warmed in a hot oven before serving. The caramel sauce can be refrigerated for up to 3 days.

WINE Two organic wines—the 1997 Lolonis Eugenia Late Harvest Sauvignon Blanc and the 1998 Günter Wittmann Westhofener Steingrube Albalonga Beerenauslese Riesling—have just the right mix of sweetness and acidity to showcase this decadent dessert.

MACADAMIA BRITTLE

MAKES ONE 13-BY-10-INCH SHEET OF BRITTLE ●

To cool the brittle quickly, place it in the freezer until it hardens.

- 1½ **cups macadamia nuts (7 ounces)**
- ½ **cup sugar**
- ⅓ **cup honey**
- 2 **tablespoons unsalted butter**

1. Preheat the oven to 350°. Spread the macadamia nuts on a 13-by-10-inch rimmed baking sheet and bake for 5 minutes, or until lightly toasted. Transfer the nuts to a plate; let cool and coarsely chop.

2. Wipe off the rimmed baking sheet and coat it lightly with vegetable oil. In a medium saucepan, combine the sugar, honey and butter and boil the mixture over moderately high heat until a candy thermometer inserted in the syrup registers 290°, about 7 minutes. Stir in the chopped macadamia nuts and scrape the mixture onto the prepared baking sheet; spread in an even layer. Let cool completely, then break the brittle into large pieces.
—*K.T.*

MAKE AHEAD The brittle can be frozen for 1 week.

Banana-Chocolate Spring Rolls

MAKES 8 SPRING ROLLS ●

These dessert spring rolls were inspired by Filipino *turon,* which are often filled with bananas and jackfruit. The chocolate in this recipe is a distinctly American twist.

- 2 **medium bananas**
- Eight 7½**-inch-square spring-roll wrappers**
- 1 **egg white, lightly beaten**
- 32 **semisweet chocolate chips**
- 8 **teaspoons shredded sweetened coconut**
- **Vegetable oil, for frying**
- **Confectioners' sugar and cocoa, for dusting**

1. Cut each banana in half lengthwise and halve each piece crosswise. Work with 1 wrapper at a time; cover the rest with a damp paper towel. Lay 1 wrapper on a work surface and lightly brush the edge with beaten egg white. Place a banana quarter 2 inches from the bottom of the wrapper and top it with 4 chocolate chips and 1 teaspoon of coconut. Fold the bottom edge over the filling and roll up 1 complete turn. Fold in the sides and continue rolling to form a tight cylinder. Repeat with the remaining ingredients.

2. In a medium saucepan, heat 2 inches of vegetable oil to 350°. Add 2 spring rolls at a time and fry until golden brown, about 1 minute per side. Drain on paper towels. Dust the spring rolls with the sugar and cocoa and serve. —*Jennifer Aranas*

Caramelized Banana Split

6 SERVINGS

- 1 **pint strawberries, hulled**
- ¼ **cup superfine sugar**
- ½ **cup turbinado sugar or granulated brown sugar**
- 6 **firm, ripe bananas, halved lengthwise**

FOR SERVING

- 1 **pint vanilla ice cream**
- 1 **pint chocolate ice cream**
- 1 **pint strawberry ice cream**
- **Pineapple Penuche Sauce (recipe follows)**
- **Chocolate Fudge Sauce (recipe follows)**
- **Chopped unsalted pistachios**
- **Sweetened whipped cream**
- **Brandied cherries**

1. In a blender, puree the strawberries with the superfine sugar. Strain the sauce and refrigerate until chilled.

2. Preheat the broiler. Grind the turbinado sugar in a blender; transfer to a plate. Dip the cut side of the bananas in the sugar and arrange them, sugared side up, on a baking sheet. Broil the bananas as close to the heat source as possible for 2 to 3 minutes, or until caramelized.

3. Place 2 caramelized banana halves in each of 6 oval bowls and add 1 scoop each of vanilla, chocolate and strawberry ice cream. Pass the sauces and the toppings at the table.
—*George Morrone*

WINE Blandy's 10-year-old Madeira is remarkable all by itself, thanks to its richness and low acidity; it's also one of the few dessert wines that goes well with ice cream. Its sweet and chocolate malt–like flavors are superb with the banana splits, no matter what sauces you spoon on top.

PINEAPPLE PENUCHE SAUCE

MAKES 1¾ CUPS ● ●

This sauce was inspired by the creamy candy penuche, which gets its name from the Mexican term for brown sugar.

- 1½ **cups sugar**
- ¾ **cup water**
- 1 **cup heavy cream, warmed**
- 3 **tablespoons unsalted butter**
- 3 **tablespoons dark rum**
- ¼ **cup finely diced fresh pineapple**

In a heavy, medium saucepan, simmer the sugar and water over high heat, stirring gently, until the sugar dissolves. Lower the heat to moderate and simmer undisturbed until a deep amber caramel forms, about 12 minutes. Remove from the heat. Gradually stir in the cream. Stir in the butter and rum. Transfer the sauce to a bowl and let cool. Stir in the pineapple and serve. —G.M.

MAKE AHEAD The sauce can be refrigerated for 2 weeks. Stir in the pineapple just before serving.

CHOCOLATE FUDGE SAUCE

MAKES ¾ CUP ●●

½ cup water

¼ cup sugar

½ cup unsweetened cocoa powder

½ cup light corn syrup

½ pound bittersweet or semisweet chocolate, finely chopped

In a saucepan, combine the water with the sugar, cocoa, corn syrup and chopped chocolate. Bring just to a boil over moderate heat, stirring constantly, to melt the chocolate. Strain the fudge sauce into a bowl and serve warm. —G.M.

MAKE AHEAD The chocolate sauce can be refrigerated for 2 weeks.

Bananas with Caramel and Honey-Roasted Nuts

8 SERVINGS ●

8 just-ripe bananas, peeled and halved lengthwise

1 cup dark brown sugar

6 tablespoons unsalted butter

1 tablespoon boiling water

Vanilla ice cream, for serving

½ cup roasted nuts, preferably honey-roasted, for serving

1. Preheat the oven to 400°. In a large, shallow baking dish, arrange the halved bananas, cut side up.

2. In a medium saucepan, combine the sugar and butter and cook over moderate heat, stirring, until just melted. Raise the heat to moderately high, add the boiling water and boil for 3 minutes. Pour the caramel sauce over the bananas.

3. Bake the bananas for 15 minutes, or until golden and the caramel is bubbling. Serve the bananas warm with the ice cream and pass the nuts at the table. —Jimmy Bradley

MAKE AHEAD The banana halves and caramel sauce can be prepared through Step 2 in advance and then kept at room temperature for up to 3 hours.

Bananas with Caramel and Honey-Roasted Nuts

16 other desserts

Crème Caramel

Crème Caramel

6 SERVINGS ●

With heavy cream, whole milk and eggs, this may just be the richest crème caramel ever.

1⅓ cups sugar
¼ cup water
2 cups heavy cream
1¼ cups whole milk
1 vanilla bean, split and scraped
2 large eggs
2 large egg yolks

1. Preheat the oven to 350°. Set six 6-ounce ramekins in a small roasting pan.
2. In a medium saucepan, combine 1 cup of the sugar with the water and bring to a boil over moderate heat, stirring, until the sugar dissolves. Cook, swirling the pan occasionally, until the syrup turns a deep amber, about 6 minutes longer. Carefully pour the hot caramel into the ramekins, tilting them to coat the bottoms evenly. Let cool.
3. In a medium saucepan, combine the cream with the milk and vanilla seeds. Cook over moderate heat, stirring occasionally, until bubbles appear around the edge. Remove from the heat and let stand for 5 minutes.
4. In a medium bowl, whisk the eggs with the egg yolks and the remaining ⅓ cup of sugar. Gradually whisk in the hot cream. Strain the custard and ladle it into the ramekins.
5. Pour enough hot water into the roasting pan to reach halfway up the sides of the ramekins. Bake for about 40 minutes, or until the custards are set but still wobbly. Remove the ramekins from the water bath and let cool completely on a rack, then refrigerate until chilled, for at least 6 hours or for 3 days.
6. To unmold, run a thin knife around the edges of the custards. Set a small plate on top of each and invert. Serve cold or at room temperature.
—Murielle Andraud

WINE A honeylike wine from Sauternes will echo the creamy texture of this custard. Look for the garagiste 1990, 1995 or 1998 Château d'Arche Sauternes, or try the more available 1996 Château Tirecul La Gravière Monbazillac.

Citrus Crema Catalana

2 SERVINGS ●

The silky texture of this crème brûlée is irresistible.

1½ tablespoons light brown sugar
¾ cup whole milk
¼ cup heavy cream
2 tablespoons sugar
Zest of ½ lemon or lime
Zest of ½ orange
1 cinnamon stick
2 large egg yolks

1. Preheat the oven to 300°. Sift the light brown sugar into a small baking dish or a pie plate. Bake the sugar for about 18 minutes, or until dry. Transfer the sugar to a plate and set aside. Keep the oven on.
2. In a saucepan, combine the milk with the cream, sugar, citrus zests and cinnamon stick and bring to a simmer over moderate heat. Remove the saucepan from the heat.
3. In a medium bowl, lightly beat the egg yolks. Whisk in ½ cup of the infused milk, then whisk the yolk mixture into the remaining infused milk in the saucepan. Strain the custard and pour it into two ¾- or 1-cup ramekins.
4. Set the ramekins in a small baking dish and add enough hot water to the dish to reach halfway up the sides of the ramekins. Bake for about 45 minutes, or until the custards are barely set. Remove the ramekins from the baking dish, let the custards cool slightly and cover them loosely with foil. Refrigerate the custards until chilled, at least 2 hours.
5. Preheat the broiler. Set the ramekins in a shallow baking dish packed with ice. Sprinkle the baked brown sugar evenly over the custards and broil them 4 inches from the heat until they are golden brown, about 15 seconds; shift the baking dish for even browning. Serve the custards at once.
—Alex Urena

MAKE AHEAD The custards can be prepared through Step 4, tightly wrapped in plastic and refrigerated for 2 days.

Creamy Butterscotch Pudding with Chocolate Scribbles

6 SERVINGS ●

This creamy pudding can be served in wineglasses for an elegant touch or in custard cups for a homey feel. Don't hesitate to chill the puddings uncovered; some think the skin that forms on the top is the best part.

2 cups whole milk
3 tablespoons cornstarch
¾ cup plus 2 tablespoons packed dark brown sugar
2 large eggs
½ teaspoon salt
1 cup heavy cream
4 tablespoons unsalted butter
1 tablespoon Scotch whisky
6 ounces bittersweet chocolate, finely chopped
Sweetened whipped cream, for serving

Citrus Crema Catalana

**Creamy Butterscotch Pudding
with Chocolate Scribbles**

1. In a medium bowl, whisk ½ cup of milk with the cornstarch. Whisk in the sugar, eggs and salt. In a large saucepan, cook the remaining 1½ cups of milk with the cream over moderate heat until a skin forms on the surface, about 4 minutes.

2. Gradually whisk one-half of the warm cream into the pudding mixture; pour the mixture into the saucepan and cook over moderately low heat, whisking constantly, until the pudding thickens and just begins to boil, about 5 minutes. Remove from the heat and whisk in the butter and Scotch. Spoon the pudding into six 6-ounce custard cups or glasses and refrigerate until set, at least 4 hours.

3. Meanwhile, line a baking sheet with parchment paper. In a small heatproof bowl set in a saucepan filled with 1 inch of gently simmering water, melt half of the chocolate. Add the remaining chocolate and remove the bowl from the saucepan; stir until smooth. Let stand until cool to the touch.

4. Spoon the chocolate into a small, sturdy resealable plastic bag and squeeze the chocolate into 1 corner. Then, using scissors, cut off the very tip of the corner of the bag (where the chocolate is). Drizzle the chocolate onto the prepared baking sheet in 6 tightly woven scribbles. Let stand at room temperature or refrigerate until set, about 30 minutes.

5. Carefully peel the paper off the scribbles and stick 1 in each pudding. Garnish with a dollop of whipped cream and serve.   —*David Lebovitz*

MAKE AHEAD The pudding can be refrigerated for 3 days. The scribbles can be layered with wax paper and refrigerated for 2 days.

WINE Highlight the buttery toffee flavors of this silky pudding with a sweet and smooth cream oloroso sherry, such as the Nonvintage Emilio Lustau Rare Cream Solera Reserva or the Nonvintage Sandeman Royal Corregidor.

Candied Winter Squash Parfaits with Chocolate

10 SERVINGS ●

Pumpkin pie in a glass: a creamy squash custard with chocolate crumbs and candied diced squash.

One 2¼-pound butternut squash, peeled and cut into ½-inch dice
2 tablespoons unsalted butter
¾ cup plus 2 tablespoons sugar
1 teaspoon finely grated fresh ginger
6 large egg yolks
3 tablespoons cornstarch
3 cups milk
2 teaspoons pure vanilla extract
1½ cups heavy cream
One 9-ounce package of chocolate wafers, finely crushed

1. In a large saucepan, steam the squash until barely tender, about 7 minutes. Let cool slightly and pat dry. In a large nonstick skillet, melt the butter with ¼ cup of the sugar. Add the squash and cook over moderately high heat, stirring occasionally, until golden, about 12 minutes. Add the grated ginger and cook, stirring, for 1 minute.

Transfer two-thirds of the candied squash to a food processor and puree until smooth.

2. In a medium saucepan, whisk the egg yolks with the remaining ½ cup plus 2 tablespoons sugar and cook over low heat, stirring constantly, until warmed through, about 1 minute. Stir the cornstarch into the milk, then whisk the mixture into the saucepan and bring to a boil over moderate heat, whisking constantly. Cook until thickened, about 7 minutes; the custard should have the consistency of thin sour cream. Whisk in the squash puree and vanilla. Strain through a fine-mesh sieve and let cool.

3. In a medium bowl, using an electric mixer, beat the cream until almost firm. Fold the cream into the cooled custard.

4. Spoon 1½ tablespoons of the cookie crumbs into each of ten 6-ounce glasses. Top with ⅓ cup of the custard and gently tap each glass to form even layers. Repeat with another 1½ tablespoons of the cookie crumbs and a large dollop of custard. Cover the

Candied Winter Squash Parfait with Chocolate

glasses with plastic wrap and refrigerate until the crumbs soften, at least 5 hours. Reserve the cookie crumb and candied squash garnishes at room temperature.

5. Sprinkle the candied squash on top of each parfait. Garnish with the remaining cookie crumbs and serve.

—*Grace Parisi*

MAKE AHEAD The parfaits and candied squash can be refrigerated separately for up to 3 days.

Vanilla Cream Profiteroles with Chocolate Sauce

6 SERVINGS

- 1 cup milk
- 3 tablespoons unsalted butter
- ¼ teaspoon sugar
- ⅛ teaspoon salt
- 1 cup all-purpose flour, sifted
- 4 large eggs

Egg wash made with 1 large egg yolk mixed with 1 tablespoon water

Light Pastry Cream (recipe follows)

Confectioners' sugar, for dusting

Chocolate Sauce (recipe follows)

1. Preheat the oven to 425°. Line a large baking sheet with parchment paper.

2. In a medium saucepan, combine the milk with the butter, sugar and salt and bring to a boil over moderately high heat. Remove from the heat, add the flour all at once and stir the mixture vigorously with a wooden spoon until a stiff dough forms. Return the saucepan to moderate heat and stir the dough until it pulls away from the side of the pan, about 30 seconds. Continue to cook the dough, stirring constantly, until the bottom of the pan is lightly coated with a floury film, about 2 minutes longer.

3. Transfer the dough to a large bowl. Add 1 of the eggs and stir vigorously with a wooden spoon until it is fully incorporated; the dough will separate into curdlike lumps at first, but it will come together in a smooth mass as

you stir. Add the remaining 3 eggs, 1 at a time, beating the dough vigorously until it is smooth between additions.

4. Spoon the warm choux pastry into a large pastry bag fitted with a ½-inch plain or star tip. Pipe the choux pastry out onto the prepared baking sheet in tablespoon-size mounds, leaving about 1 inch between them. Using a brush, dab the tops of the mounds with the egg wash to smooth them out.

5. Bake the choux pastry for about 30 minutes, or until puffed and golden. Turn the oven off. Prop the door open with a wooden spoon and let the puffs dry out in the cooling oven for about 30 minutes. Transfer the baking sheet to a rack and let the puffs cool completely.

6. Using a small knife, split each puff horizontally, one-third from the top. Spoon or pipe the Light Pastry Cream into the bottoms of the puffs and replace the tops. Sift confectioners' sugar over the profiteroles. Spoon the Chocolate Sauce onto plates, arrange the profiteroles on the sauce and serve.

—*Jacques Pépin*

Vanilla Cream Profiteroles with Chocolate Sauce

MAKE AHEAD The baked puffs can be kept at room temperature for 2 days or frozen for 1 month; recrisp before filling.

LIGHT PASTRY CREAM

MAKES ABOUT 2¼ CUPS ●

- 1¼ cups milk
- 4 large egg yolks
- 6 tablespoons sugar
- 1 teaspoon pure vanilla extract
- 2 tablespoons cornstarch
- 1 tablespoon unsalted butter
- ⅔ cup cold heavy cream

1. Bring the milk to a boil in a medium saucepan. In a medium bowl, whisk the egg yolks with the sugar and vanilla until pale and slightly thickened. Whisk in the cornstarch until smooth, then gradually whisk in the hot milk in a thin, steady stream. Transfer the pastry cream to the saucepan and bring to a boil over moderate heat; boil until thickened, whisking constantly, about 1 minute. Stir in the butter.

2. Scrape the pastry cream into a medium bowl. Press a sheet of plastic wrap directly onto the surface and refrigerate until firm, at least 1 hour.

3. In a medium bowl, beat the cream until stiff. Stir one-third of the whipped cream into the pastry cream, then fold in the remaining whipped cream.

—*J.P.*

MAKE AHEAD The pastry cream can be prepared through Step 2 up to 3 days ahead.

CHOCOLATE SAUCE

MAKES ABOUT 2½ CUPS ●●

- ½ **pound semisweet or bittersweet chocolate, coarsely chopped**
- 2 **cups milk**
- 3 **tablespoons sugar**
- 3 **large egg yolks**

1. In a medium saucepan, combine the chocolate with the milk and sugar and bring to a boil over moderate heat, stirring constantly until smooth.

2. In a medium bowl, whisk the egg yolks until smooth. Add the boiling chocolate sauce in a very thin stream, whisking constantly. Strain the chocolate sauce through a fine sieve and let cool before serving. —*J.P.*

MAKE AHEAD The chocolate sauce can be refrigerated for 2 days. Rewarm gently before serving, if desired.

profiterole tips

Refrigerate choux pastry for up to 3 days before baking; rub the surface with unsalted butter and cover tightly with plastic wrap.

Form the profiteroles with a tablespoon if you don't have a pastry bag, or transfer the choux pastry to a sturdy plastic bag, snip off a corner and pipe the dough onto the baking sheet.

Always use an egg wash. It gives the profiteroles a nice round shape and a lovely sheen.

Leave the profiteroles in the cooling oven for at least 30 minutes to dry them out and keep them from collapsing.

Chocolate Pots

8 SERVINGS ●●

This dessert is silky and rich—so rich, in fact, that it's best in small portions. Chocolate Pots are ideal for dinner parties, as you can make them ahead and keep them in the refrigerator.

- 2 **cups heavy cream**
- ¾ **pound semisweet or bittersweet chocolate, at room temperature, coarsely chopped**
- 4 **large egg yolks**
- 3 **tablespoons dark rum**
- 3 **tablespoons unsalted butter**

1. In a medium saucepan, heat the cream until bubbles appear around the edge. Remove the pan from the heat, add the chocolate and let stand for 1 minute, then stir until smooth.

2. Whisk the egg yolks in a small bowl, then whisk in ½ cup of the hot chocolate cream. Scrape this mixture into the saucepan and whisk constantly until smooth. Stir in the rum and butter. Pour the custard into eight ½-cup ramekins or espresso cups and refrigerate until chilled, at least 4 hours.

—*Jamie Oliver*

MAKE AHEAD The Chocolate Pots can be refrigerated overnight.

SERVE WITH Orange and Polenta Biscuits (p. 348) and lightly sweetened whipped cream.

Ginger Puddings with Bittersweet Chocolate Sauce and Ginger Caramel Crunch

MAKES 6 PUDDINGS ●

In England, cooks steam their Christmas pudding. But these individual ginger puddings are baked instead, then capped with warm Bittersweet Chocolate Sauce and delicious Ginger Caramel Crunch.

- ¼ **cup all-purpose flour**
- 2 **teaspoons ground ginger**
- ½ **teaspoon baking powder**
- ¼ **teaspoon salt**
- ¼ **cup finely chopped crystallized ginger (2 ounces)**

- 3 **large eggs, at room temperature**
- 3 **large egg yolks, at room temperature**
- ½ **cup sugar**
- ⅓ **cup unsulphured molasses**
- 1 **teaspoon finely grated lemon zest**
- 6 **tablespoons unsalted butter, melted and cooled slightly**

Bittersweet Chocolate Sauce (recipe follows)

Ginger Caramel Crunch (recipe follows)

1. Preheat the oven to 400°. Butter and flour six ½-cup ramekins. Tap out all of the excess flour and set the ramekins on a heavy, rimmed baking sheet.

2. In a small bowl, whisk the flour with the ground ginger, baking powder and salt. Stir in the chopped crystallized ginger.

3. In a medium bowl, whisk the whole eggs and egg yolks with the sugar, molasses and grated lemon zest. Add the butter and whisk until smooth. Gently fold in the dry ingredients. Pour the batter into the prepared ramekins and bake for about 20 minutes, or until the puddings have risen and a toothpick inserted in the center of one comes out with a few moist crumbs attached. Let the puddings cool for 10 minutes.

4. Carefully run a thin knife around the edge of each ramekin to loosen the ginger pudding, then cover with a dessert plate and carefully turn over to unmold the pudding. Repeat with the remaining puddings. Drizzle the puddings with the Bittersweet Chocolate Sauce, garnish with the Ginger Caramel Crunch and serve.

—*Nick Malgieri*

MAKE AHEAD The baked ginger puddings can be refrigerated overnight. Bring the puddings to room temperature before rewarming them, loosely covered with foil, in a 300° oven for 10 minutes.   ▶

other desserts

BITTERSWEET CHOCOLATE SAUCE

MAKES 2½ CUPS ● ●

- 1   cup heavy cream
- ⅓   cup sugar
- ⅓   cup light corn syrup
- ¾   pound bittersweet or semisweet chocolate, chopped
- 2   teaspoons pure vanilla extract

Pinch of salt

In a medium saucepan, combine the heavy cream with the sugar and corn syrup and cook over low heat, stirring, just until the sugar dissolves. Bring to a boil, then remove from the heat. Add the chocolate and let stand for 3 minutes. Add the vanilla and salt and stir the sauce until smooth.   —N.M.

MAKE AHEAD The chocolate sauce can be refrigerated for 3 weeks. Rewarm before serving.

GINGER CARAMEL CRUNCH

MAKES ABOUT 1½ CUPS ● ●

- ½   teaspoon ground ginger
- ½   teaspoon baking soda
- ½   cup sugar
- 1½   tablespoons light corn syrup
- 2   tablespoons water
- ½   cup toasted pecan pieces

1. Line a large baking sheet with aluminum foil and butter the foil well. Sift the ginger with the baking soda into a small bowl.

2. In a heavy, medium saucepan, combine the sugar with the corn syrup and water and cook over moderate heat, stirring, just until the sugar dissolves. Bring to a boil and cook over moderate heat until the syrup is a pale honey color and registers 310° (hard-crack stage) on a candy thermometer. Remove the syrup from the heat. Using a long-handled wooden spoon, stir in the nuts, then carefully stir in the ginger mixture. Immediately pour the caramel onto the prepared baking sheet and spread the nuts. Let cool completely; crack into long shards.   —N.M.

Peanut Butter Cups

MAKE AHEAD The Ginger Caramel Crunch can be stored in an airtight container for 3 days.

Peanut Butter Cups

MAKES 12 CUPS ●

You will need twelve 5-ounce paper cups to make these oversize candies.

- 1   pound semisweet or bittersweet chocolate, tempered (see Tempering Chocolate, p. 349)
- 6   ounces semisweet or bittersweet chocolate, coarsely chopped
- 2   cups smooth peanut butter

1. Using scissors, cut the paper cups to a 1½-inch height. Line a baking sheet with wax paper and set a wire rack on top. Working with 1 paper cup at a time and using a spoon, fill the cup with tempered chocolate, hold the cup upside down, tap gently and let the excess chocolate drip back into the bowl. Scrape the rim of the cup against the rim of the bowl to make a neat edge and place the cup upside down on the rack. Repeat to make 11 more chocolate cups. Let the cups stand for at least 5 minutes to firm up.

2. Using a sharp knife, scrape the chocolate cup rims to make clean, straight edges; this will also make the cups easier to unmold. Turn the cups right side up and refrigerate for 10 minutes. Carefully peel the paper off the chocolate cups. Set the cups right side up on a platter and store in a cool place.

3. In a medium stainless-steel bowl set over a pan of barely simmering water, melt the chopped chocolate, stirring occasionally. Remove the bowl from the pan, wipe the bottom dry and stir the chocolate until smooth. Let cool to warm room temperature. Add the peanut butter and stir with a wooden spoon until thoroughly blended.

4. Spoon the peanut butter and chocolate filling into a sturdy resealable plastic bag and press it to one side at the bottom of the bag. Snip off the tip of one corner. Pipe the peanut butter and chocolate filling into the chocolate cups until it almost reaches the rims. Tap the filled cups very lightly against the platter to release any air bubbles. Let the peanut butter cups stand in a cool, dry place for about 1 hour, or until set. The filling will be soft and creamy, but it will still hold its shape.

—Jacques Torres

MAKE AHEAD The peanut butter cups can be refrigerated in an airtight container for up to 1 week, but the chocolate cups may develop some white streaks on the outside.
SERVE WITH Cold sweetened whipped cream.

Chocolate Soufflé Sundae
MAKES ONE 9-INCH SOUFFLÉ

- 6 ounces bittersweet or semisweet chocolate, coarsely chopped
- 6 tablespoons unsalted butter, cut into pieces
- 4 large eggs at room temperature, 3 separated
- ⅔ cup sugar
- 1 teaspoon pure vanilla extract
- 1½ pints premium-quality vanilla ice cream
- Caramel Sauce (recipe follows)
- Bittersweet Chocolate Sauce (recipe follows)

1. Preheat the oven to 350°. In a medium bowl, melt the chopped bittersweet or semisweet chocolate in a microwave oven at medium-high speed, stirring at 30-second intervals until smooth. Whisk in the butter until fully incorporated; let the mixture cool slightly.

2. In a large bowl, whisk the 3 egg yolks with the whole egg and ⅓ cup of the sugar until thoroughly blended. Add the melted chocolate and vanilla extract and whisk the mixture until smooth.

3. In a medium bowl, beat the 3 egg whites with an electric mixer until soft peaks form. Add the remaining ⅓ cup of sugar, 1 tablespoon at a time, beating for 10 seconds between additions. Continue beating at medium-high speed until the whites are firm and glossy. Whisk one-quarter of the meringue into the chocolate mixture until well blended. Gently fold the remaining meringue into the chocolate mixture just until no white streaks remain.

4. Scrape the chocolate soufflé mixture into an ungreased 9-inch glass pie plate. Gently shake the pie plate to smooth the surface and bake for about 35 minutes, or until the soufflé is cracked and no longer wobbles. Transfer the soufflé to a wire rack to cool.

5. Meanwhile, line a large plate with plastic wrap and freeze until well chilled. Scoop ice cream balls onto the chilled plate and freeze them. If necessary, soften the ice cream in the refrigerator for 15 minutes before scooping.

6. Set the vanilla ice cream balls on the soufflé, mounding them in the center. Drizzle with ¼ cup each of Caramel Sauce and Chocolate Sauce, cut into wedges and serve right away. Pass the remaining sauce at the table.
—*Peggy Cullen*

MAKE AHEAD The chocolate soufflé crust can be baked up to 1 day ahead; cover with plastic wrap and let stand at room temperature.

CARAMEL SAUCE
MAKES ½ CUP ●●

- ½ cup heavy cream
- ½ cup sugar
- 2 tablespoons water
- 1 teaspoon pure vanilla extract

In a small saucepan, heat the cream just until small bubbles appear around the edge. In a medium saucepan, cook the sugar with the water over high heat until the sugar is dissolved, washing down the side of the pan with a wet pastry brush. Continue cooking, without stirring, until a light honey–colored caramel forms, about 5 minutes. Remove from the heat and carefully stir in the scalded cream. Let cool for 1 minute, then stir in the vanilla. Serve the sauce warm. —*P.C.*

MAKE AHEAD The caramel sauce can be refrigerated in an airtight container for up to 1 week.

BITTERSWEET CHOCOLATE SAUCE
MAKES ¾ CUP ●●

- ½ cup heavy cream
- 4 ounces bittersweet chocolate, coarsely chopped
- 1 teaspoon pure vanilla extract

In a medium saucepan, heat the cream just until small bubbles appear around the edge. Remove from the heat, add the chopped chocolate and let stand for 1 minute. Add the vanilla and stir until smooth; serve warm.

MAKE AHEAD The chocolate sauce can be refrigerated in an airtight container for up to 1 week. —*P.C.*

Chocolate Soufflé Sundae

other desserts

Yogurt Sorbet

MAKES 1 QUART ● ●

- 3 large egg whites
- ⅔ cup sugar
- 3 cups plain nonfat yogurt

1. In a medium bowl, using a handheld electric mixer, beat the egg whites until frothy. Slowly add the sugar and beat at high speed until the egg whites hold stiff, shiny peaks, about 4 minutes.

2. In another bowl, whisk the yogurt until smooth. Fold in the egg whites. Transfer the mixture to an ice cream machine and freeze according to the manufacturer's instructions.

—*Patricia Wells*

ONE-HALF CUP Calories 120 kcal, Total Fat 0.2 gm, Saturated Fat 0.1 gm, Protein 7 gm, Carbohydrates 23 gm

MAKE AHEAD The yogurt sorbet can be frozen for 2 days.

Mini Ice Cream Cone Trio

6 SERVINGS

These crisp tuile cones in three flavors are somewhat fragile, so it's best to fill them with slightly softened ice cream.

- 2 large egg whites
- 6 tablespoons sugar
- 5 tablespoons unsalted butter, melted and cooled
- ¼ teaspoon pure vanilla extract
- ⅓ cup all-purpose flour
- ½ tablespoon finely chopped candied ginger
- ⅛ teaspoon ground ginger
- 1 tablespoon unsweetened cocoa powder
- 1 tablespoon finely grated unsweetened coconut

Pinch of salt

- 1 tablespoon chopped toasted pistachios

Scant ⅛ teaspoon pure almond extract

Ice cream

1. Preheat the oven to 350°. Lightly butter a baking sheet. In a bowl, beat the egg whites with the sugar, butter and vanilla. Add the flour and beat with a wooden spoon until smooth.

2. Divide the batter among 3 bowls. Stir the candied and ground ginger into the first bowl, the cocoa powder, coconut and salt into the second, and the pistachios and almond extract into the third.

3. Scoop 6 slightly rounded teaspoons of tuile batter onto the prepared baking sheet, spacing them about 4 inches apart. Using your index finger or the back of a spoon, spread the batter into 3-inch rounds. Bake the tuiles in the middle of the oven for about 9 minutes, or until light golden all over. Working quickly, remove the tuiles from the baking sheet with a small offset spatula and roll them around a large pastry tip to form cones; make sure the points are tightly rolled. The cones will crisp as they cool. If they firm up too fast, return them to the oven for 30 seconds to soften. Repeat with the remaining batter to make 12 more cones, cleaning and re-buttering the baking sheet between batches.

4. Top each cone with a small scoop of ice cream and serve at once.

—*Grace Parisi*

Berry Lollipops

MAKES ABOUT 2 DOZEN
LOLLIPOPS ● ●

Lollipop sticks are sold at supermarkets and at baking supply shops. If unavailable, substitute wooden skewers; cut off the tips before using. You will need a candy thermometer to make this recipe.

Vegetable oil, for brushing

- 1 cup sugar
- ½ cup water
- ⅓ cup light corn syrup
- ¼ cup cranraspberry concentrate
- 4 drops red food coloring

Twenty-four 6-inch lollipop sticks

1. Brush 2 flat baking sheets with oil. Fill a pie plate with 1 inch of cold water.

2. In a small, heavy saucepan, put the sugar, water and corn syrup and bring to a boil, stirring just until the sugar dissolves. Boil over high heat, without stirring, until the syrup reaches 280° on a candy thermometer, about 20 minutes. Add the cranraspberry concentrate and food coloring and cook over moderately high heat until the syrup reaches 300°. Briefly dip the saucepan in the cold water to stop the cooking.

3. Once the bubbling subsides, carefully spoon 6 scant tablespoons of syrup about 2 inches apart on 1 of the prepared baking sheets. Working quickly, place a stick in each of the lollipops, turning it to cover with syrup. Continue to form the lollipops, 6 at a time, until both baking sheets are full. If the syrup in the saucepan becomes too thick, melt it over low heat. Let the lollipops harden, then wrap in plastic.

—*Grace Parisi*

MAKE AHEAD The wrapped lollipops can be stored flat in an airtight container in a cool, dry place for 1 month.

VARIATION To make citrus lollipops, replace the cranraspberry concentrate and red food coloring with the juice and zest of 1 lemon or lime and 4 drops of green food coloring. Stir in the zest just before spooning out the lollipops.

Turtledoves

MAKES ABOUT 4 DOZEN
CARAMELS ●

You will need a candy thermometer to make this recipe.

- 1½ cups shelled pistachios or pecans (about ½ pound)
- 1½ cups heavy cream
- 1 cup sugar
- ⅔ cup light corn syrup
- 2 tablespoons unsalted butter
- 3 tablespoons water
- 1 cup dried sour cherries
- 1 pound bittersweet or semisweet chocolate, chopped

1. Preheat the oven to 350°. Spread

the pistachios on a rimmed baking sheet and toast for about 7 minutes, or until fragrant. Let cool.

2. Line 2 large baking sheets with parchment paper and place them in the freezer. In a heavy, medium saucepan, combine the heavy cream with the sugar, light corn syrup and butter and bring to a boil. Stir just until the sugar dissolves. Cook over moderately low heat, without stirring, until the caramel reaches 240° to 244° on a candy thermometer; this can take up to 45 minutes.

3. Fill the sink with 1 inch of cold water. Add the 3 tablespoons of water to the caramel and boil over high heat for 5 minutes, stirring occasionally. Briefly dip the saucepan in the cold water to stop the cooking, then let the caramel cool to 200°.

4. Stir the pistachios and dried cherries into the caramel. Spoon scant tablespoons of the caramel onto the chilled baking sheets and let cool completely, at least 1 hour.

5. In a microwave, in a medium bowl, melt three-quarters of the chocolate. Stir in the remaining chocolate until melted. Dip the bottom of each caramel into the chocolate and return to the baking sheets. Refrigerate for 10 minutes to set the chocolate.

—*Grace Parisi*

MAKE AHEAD The caramels can be stored at room temperature in a cool, dry place for up to 1 month.

Marbled Black-and-White Truffles

MAKES ABOUT 3 DOZEN TRUFFLES ●

- 7 ounces white chocolate, chopped
- 2 tablespoons unsalted butter, cut into 8 equal pieces
- 4½ tablespoons heavy cream
- ½ pound bittersweet chocolate, chopped
- 1 teaspoon light corn syrup

White sprinkles, for topping

1. Melt the white chocolate in a glass bowl in a microwave oven. Stir in 6 pieces of the butter until melted, then stir in 2½ tablespoons of the heavy cream. Scrape the white chocolate ganache into a clean bowl and let cool.

2. Put one-fourth of the bittersweet chocolate in a small bowl. In a small saucepan, combine the remaining butter and heavy cream with the corn syrup and bring to a boil. Pour the cream over the chocolate and let stand for 2 minutes, then whisk until smooth. Let the ganache cool to room temperature.

3. Swirl the two ganaches with a knife and refrigerate until firm. Scoop scant teaspoons of the ganache onto a baking sheet and chill for 15 minutes. Roll each truffle into a ball and chill until firm.

4. Melt two-thirds of the remaining bittersweet chocolate in a microwave oven. Scrape the chocolate into a clean bowl and stir in the remaining chopped chocolate until smooth. Using a fork, dip the truffles into the melted chocolate to coat and set them on the baking sheet. Top with sprinkles and refrigerate until firm or for up to 1 week.

—*Wai Chu*

Rose Water Marshmallows

8 SERVINGS ●

You need a candy thermometer to make these marshmallows.

- ½ **cup cornstarch**
- ½ **cup confectioners' sugar**
- 2 **tablespoons unflavored gelatin**
- 1½ **cups water**
- 1 **cup granulated sugar**
- ⅓ **cup light corn syrup**
- 5 **large egg whites, at room temperature**
- 3 **tablespoons rose water**
- 2 **teaspoons pure vanilla extract**

1. Generously butter a 9-by-13-inch cake pan. Sift the cornstarch with the confectioners' sugar and set half aside. Add the remaining mixture to

the pan and shake to coat; tap the excess out onto wax paper and sift it back into the pan.

2. In a small bowl, soften the gelatin in ½ cup of the water. In a medium saucepan, boil the remaining 1 cup of water with the sugar and corn syrup until the syrup reaches 245° on a candy thermometer; remove from the heat. Add the gelatin mixture and stir until dissolved.

3. In a standing mixer, beat the egg whites until soft peaks form. At medium speed, beat in the hot syrup in a thin stream. Increase the speed to medium-high and beat until cooled to room temperature, about 10 minutes. Beat in the rose water and vanilla. Spread the marshmallow in the prepared pan and let stand until set, at least 2 hours.

4. Run a thin knife around the marshmallow. Generously sift some of the reserved cornstarch mixture on top. Cover with a cutting board and invert, then tap on the pan to release the marshmallow. Using a moistened sharp knife, cut the marshmallow into 1-inch pieces. Cover a large board with wax paper and dust with more cornstarch. Coat each marshmallow with the cornstarch, then transfer to wax paper to set.

—*Jean-Georges Vongerichten*

Candied Rose Petals

MAKES ABOUT 2 DOZEN CANDIED PETALS ●●

- 2 **organic roses, petals removed**
- 1 **large egg white, lightly beaten**
- ½ **cup sugar**

Line a baking sheet with wax paper. Brush both sides of each rose petal with the beaten egg white and dip in the sugar. Let dry on the wax paper.

—*Jean-Georges Vongerichten*

17 beverages

Lemony Fresh Herb Cooler

pomegranates & health

Like grapes, pomegranates contain polyphenols, which are particularly potent **antioxidants** that protect against heart disease. According to Adel Kader, a professor of pomology (fruit growing) at the University of California–Davis, a glass of pomegranate juice has two to three times the antioxidant potency of an equal serving of red wine. Should you drink a glass of pomegranate juice every day? It certainly wouldn't hurt, because in addition to the polyphenols, pomegranates contain, on average, 9 milligrams of **vitamin C**—nearly 16 percent of the RDA—and are an excellent source of **potassium**. Eat the seeds from a whole pomegranate instead and you will get all these benefits plus a healthy dose—more than 5 grams—of **fiber**. Also, pomegranates are low in calories: An entire fruit has only about 105.

Lemony Fresh Herb Coolers

MAKES ABOUT 8 DRINKS ● ●

The combination of fresh basil, mint, cilantro and tarragon makes a deliciously refreshing drink.

2 cups water
½ cup sugar
2 cups (packed) basil leaves
   and small sprigs
1 cup (packed) cilantro leaves
   and small sprigs
1 cup (packed) mint leaves
   and small sprigs
2 tablespoons tarragon leaves
2 teaspoons finely grated
   lemon zest
1 tablespoon fresh lemon juice
Cold club soda
Lemon twists and mint sprigs,
   for garnish

1. In a medium saucepan, combine the water and sugar and bring to a boil, stirring with a wooden spoon until the sugar dissolves. Reduce the heat to moderate and simmer for 5 minutes; let the sugar syrup cool.

2. In a blender or food processor, combine the sugar syrup with the basil, cilantro, mint, tarragon, lemon zest and lemon juice and puree. Let the mixture stand for 1 hour, then strain it through a coarse sieve, pressing on the solids with the back of a spoon to extract as much liquid as possible.

3. For each drink, pour ¼ cup of the fresh herb syrup over cracked ice and fill with club soda. Garnish the drinks with a lemon twist and mint sprigs and serve. —*Marcia Kiesel*

VARIATION To make a cocktail, add half a shot of vodka and half a shot of rum to each drink.

MAKE AHEAD The herb syrup can be refrigerated overnight.

Plum-Blueberry Spritzers

MAKES ABOUT 8 DRINKS ●

In a drink flavored with blueberries and plums, bay leaves make an unusual (and welcome) appearance.

5 cups water
1 cup fresh ripe blueberries
3 ripe black plums, pitted and
   cut into eighths
8 fresh or dried bay leaves,
   plus extra for garnish
¼ cup plus 2 tablespoons sugar
8 cups cold club soda, for serving

1. Bring the water to a boil in a medium saucepan. Add the blueberries, plums, 8 bay leaves and sugar, cover and boil over high heat, stirring, until

the juice is reduced to about 3 cups and the plums are tender, about 20 minutes. Strain the mixture though a fine sieve, pressing lightly with a spatula to extract the juice; reserve the bay leaves. Return the juice to the pan, add the reserved bay leaves and simmer over moderate heat until reduced to 2 cups, about 10 minutes. Discard the bay leaves; let the syrup cool.

2. For each drink, gently whisk ¼ cup of the plum-blueberry syrup into 1 cup of cold club soda, pour into a glass, garnish with a bay leaf or 2 and serve.

—*Marcia Kiesel*

VARIATION Pour 2 tablespoons of the berry syrup into a Champagne flute and top with Champagne.

MAKE AHEAD The syrup can be refrigerated for 1 week.

Plum-Blueberry Spritzer

Steaming Hot Mulled Pomegranate Punch

MAKES 4 DRINKS ●●

Pomegranates, limes and star fruit brighten the flavor of this warming winter drink.

- 2 limes
- 2½ cups fresh apple cider
- 1 cup pomegranate juice
- 1 cinnamon stick
- 4 whole cloves
- ½ teaspoon allspice berries
- 1 cup sparkling cider
- 4 slices of star fruit (carambola)
- 1 tablespoon plus 1 teaspoon pomegranate seeds

1. Juice 1 of the limes; this should yield you 2 tablespoons of juice. Cut 4 slices from the second lime and reserve the remainder of the lime for another use.

2. In a medium saucepan, combine the fresh apple cider with the pomegranate juice, cinnamon stick, cloves and allspice berries and simmer over low heat for 10 minutes. Strain the punch and stir in the lime juice and sparkling cider. Pour the punch into heatproof glasses, float the slices of lime and star fruit and the pomegranate seeds in the punch and serve immediately.

—*Suki Hertz*

ONE SERVING Calories 133 kcal, Total Fat 0.8 gm, Saturated Fat 0 gm

Melonade

MAKES 4 DRINKS ●●●

This light and refreshing drink tastes like a cross between a smoothie and a lemonade. Use very ripe melon.

- 2 tablespoons water
- 2 tablespoons sugar
- 1¼ pounds peeled green melon, such as honeydew, cut into 1-inch dice (4 cups)
- ½ cup fresh lemon juice
- ¼ cup tightly packed mint leaves

Seltzer

Mint sprigs and lemon slices, for garnish

melons & health

Melons and watermelons are primarily carbohydrates and water, but eat a slice and you'll get significant amounts of **soluble fiber, folic acid, vitamin A** and **vitamin C.** The orange-fleshed melons are especially good sources of vitamin A. Cantaloupe in particular is a vitamin powerhouse: A quarter melon has as much C as an orange (lighter-fleshed and green-fleshed melons have about half as much). As for watermelons, they deliver a cancer-fighting substance called **lycopene.** Plus all melons and watermelons are low in calories (1 cup of diced honeydew has just 60 calories) and virtually fat free.

1. In a small saucepan, combine the water with the sugar and cook over moderate heat, stirring, until the sugar dissolves. Let cool completely.

2. In a blender or food processor, puree the melon with the lemon juice, mint and sugar syrup. Fill 4 large glasses with ice and pour in the melon puree. Top with seltzer, garnish with mint and lemon slices and serve.

—*Suki Hertz*

ONE SERVING Calories 77 kcal, Total Fat 0.2 gm, Saturated Fat 0.1 gm

Banana Smoothies

MAKES 2 SMOOTHIES ●●

In just a bit more time than it takes to prepare cereal, you can make this healthy, delicious breakfast shake.

- 2 ripe bananas, cut into 1-inch chunks
- ½ cup plain yogurt
- 1 cup fresh orange juice
- 2 tablespoons honey
- 2 tablespoons wheat germ
- 2 cups crushed ice

Combine the bananas with the yogurt, orange juice, honey, wheat germ and crushed ice in a blender. Blend at high speed until smooth and frothy. Adjust the sweetness with more honey or orange juice and serve immediately.

—*Jean-Georges Vongerichten*

ONE SERVING Calories 290 kcal, Total Fat 3.4 gm, Saturated Fat 1.5 gm, Protein 6 gm, Carbohydrates 63 gm

Spiced Honey Iced Tea

MAKES ABOUT 8 DRINKS ●

This exotically spiced iced tea was inspired by Indian chai, which is a blend of tea, milk and ground spices—cardamom, cinnamon, cloves and ginger. The tea has to steep overnight, so plan accordingly.

- 1 quart water
- 8 Earl Grey tea bags
- 8 cinnamon sticks, broken into pieces
- 8 cardamom pods, crushed
- 2 tablespoons coriander seeds, crushed
- 2 teaspoons anise seeds, crushed
- 2 teaspoons allspice berries, crushed
- ½ to 1 teaspoon black peppercorns, crushed
- 3 tablespoons honey

Lime wedges, thinly sliced oranges and cinnamon sticks, for garnish

I. Bring the water to a boil in a medium saucepan. Add the tea bags, remove from the heat and let steep for 20 minutes; discard the tea bags. Reheat the tea and pour it into a heat-proof bowl. Add all of the spices, cover and let steep overnight.

2. Strain the tea into a medium saucepan. Reheat the tea and stir in the honey; let cool. For each drink, pour the spiced tea over cracked ice. Garnish with a lime wedge, an orange slice and a cinnamon stick and serve.

—*Marcia Kiesel*

VARIATION Add a shot of Mount Gay rum to each drink.

MAKE AHEAD The strained and sweetened spiced tea can be refrigerated for 3 days.

Black Cherry Iced Tea

MAKES 2½ QUARTS ● ● ●

- 2½ quarts water
- 1 pound fresh black cherries, pitted, or two 10-ounce bags frozen pitted black cherries, thawed
- 1¼ cups sugar
- ¼ cup fresh lemon juice
- 3 whole star anise
- ½ vanilla bean, split and scraped, seeds reserved
- 16 green-tea bags

Mint sprigs, for serving

I. Bring the water to a boil in a large saucepan. Add the black cherries, sugar, lemon juice, star anise and the vanilla bean with its seeds. Simmer the cherries over low heat for 15 minutes, crushing them against the side of the pan with a wooden spoon. Remove the cherries from the heat, cover and let stand for 1 hour.

2. Strain the cherry juice through a fine sieve into a clean saucepan, pressing on the solids. Discard the solids. Bring the cherry juice to a boil over moderate heat. Remove from the heat, add the tea bags and let steep for 5 minutes. Discard the tea bags and let cool to room temperature. Transfer the cherry tea to a large pitcher and refrigerate until chilled or for up to 2 days. Serve the tea over ice, garnished with mint sprigs.

—*Danielle Custer*

Black Cherry Iced Tea

Minty Lemongrass Orange Tea

MAKES ABOUT 5 CUPS OF LOOSE TEA ● ●

Dried rose hips are available from Aphrodisia at 212-989-6440 or on-line from Arts, Crafts, Gifts and More at www.artscraftsgifts.com. This recipe takes a minimum of five days to prepare, so plan accordingly .

Peels of 3 large oranges (preferably Temples) torn into 3- to 4-inch-long strips, white pith removed with a small knife
1¼ pounds lemongrass, bottom half cut off and frozen for another use
2 bunches of spearmint (about 6 ounces), leaves removed
2 ounces dried rose hips

I. Spread the orange peels, lemongrass and spearmint on racks or screens set over baking sheets. Set in a dry, dark place until dried but not brittle, 5 to 10 days, depending on the humidity.

2. Using scissors, cut the orange peels and lemongrass into 1-inch pieces and place in a large bowl. Lightly crush the spearmint leaves and add to the bowl along with the rose hips; toss gently. Pack the tea in small tins.

3. When ready to make the tea, steep about 1 tablespoon of the dried mixture per cup of boiling hot water for 3 to 5 minutes before straining into a cup or mug.

—*Marcia Kiesel*

MAKE AHEAD The tea can be kept in airtight tins for up to 3 months.

Frothy Vanilla Milk

MAKES 4 DRINKS ●

- 1 quart whole milk
- 2 tablespoons granulated sugar
- 2 tablespoons light brown sugar
- 1½ vanilla beans, split and seeds scraped

Sweetened whipped cream and freshly grated nutmeg, for serving

I. In a large saucepan, combine the milk with the granulated and brown sugars and vanilla seeds and beans

mixture and the salt and cook over moderate heat, whisking constantly, until the hot chocolate is thickened, about 5 minutes. Serve at once.

—Maricel Presilla

NOTE Toasted whole barley is available at Korean markets.

Sucker Punch

MAKES 6 DRINKS ●

- ⅛ **cup cassis (black currant syrup)**
- ¼ **cup fresh lemon juice**
- ¾ **cup vodka**
- 1¼ **cups cold ginger ale**

Combine the cassis, lemon juice and vodka in an ice-filled glass. Stir well. Add the ginger ale, stir gently and serve. —Pete Wells

Three-Pepper Bloody Mary

MAKES 4 DRINKS (ABOUT 4 CUPS) ●●

- 1 **cup vodka**
- ¼ **cup finely chopped onion**
- 1 **small garlic clove, smashed**
- 1 **small jalapeño, seeded and coarsely chopped**
- 1 **tablespoon fresh lemon juice**
- 1 **teaspoon hot sauce, preferably habanero**
- 2½ **cups tomato juice**
- 4 **teaspoons prepared horseradish**
- 1 **teaspoon celery salt**
- ½ **teaspoon freshly ground pepper**

Lime wedges and celery ribs, for serving

In a blender, combine the vodka with the onion, garlic, jalapeño, lemon juice and hot sauce and puree until smooth. Add the tomato juice, horseradish, celery salt and pepper and blend. Strain into tall glasses over ice and serve with lime wedges and celery ribs.

—Grace Parisi

VARIATION Make a Tailgate Bloody Hot by heating 2½ cups Three-Pepper Bloody Mary with ½ cup vodka (instead of the 1 cup suggested above) and ½ cup beef broth. Serve the drink hot, with celery.

Hot Chocolate with Máchica

and bring to a simmer. Cover and set aside for 30 minutes to infuse.

2. Discard the vanilla beans. Rewarm the milk over moderate heat, whisking vigorously, until frothy and warm. Serve in mugs, with a generous dollop of whipped cream and a sprinkling of nutmeg. —Rebecca Rather

Hot Chocolate with Máchica

MAKES 6 DRINKS ●

Máchica is a sweetened, spiced grain blend that Ecuadorans use to enrich the texture and flavor of drinks. This cooking technique was brought by Spanish colonists to Ecuador from Mexico, where corn is used instead of barley.

- ½ **cup toasted whole barley (see Note)**
- 3 **tablespoons dark brown sugar**
- 2 **teaspoons ground cinnamon**
- 6 **cups whole milk**
- 6 **ounces bittersweet chocolate, finely chopped**

Pinch of salt

1. In a spice or coffee grinder, grind the toasted barley to a fine powder. In a small bowl, mix the barley powder with the brown sugar and ground cinnamon.

2. In a medium saucepan, bring the milk to a boil, then remove it from the heat. Add the chopped bittersweet chocolate to the hot milk and whisk until it is melted. Whisk in the barley

Venetian Lemon Shake

The Bantamweight

MAKES 1 DRINK ●

- ¼ cup orange-flavored vodka
- 3 tablespoons fresh orange juice
- 1 teaspoon fresh lime juice
- 1 teaspoon Cointreau

Pour the ingredients over ice in a cocktail shaker. Shake violently; strain into a chilled martini glass. —*Pete Wells*

Venetian Lemon Shake

MAKES 4 DRINKS ●

- 1½ cups vanilla ice cream
- 1 cup lemon sorbet
- ½ cup fresh lemon juice
- ⅓ cup vodka
- ¼ cup Prosecco or Champagne

Grated zest from 1 lemon (optional)

Combine all of the ingredients except the lemon zest in a blender and blend until creamy. Pour into glasses, garnish with the zest if you like and serve immediately. —*Joanne Weir*

Reverse Martini

MAKES 1 DRINK ●

- 2 tablespoons gin
- 6 tablespoons dry vermouth
- 1 strip of lemon zest

Pour the gin and vermouth over ice in a shaker. Stir 40 times; strain into a chilled cocktail glass. Twist the lemon zest over the drink and drop it in. —*Pete Wells*

Juicy Margarita

MAKES 4 DRINKS (ABOUT 3½ CUPS) ●●

- 1 cup tequila (preferably 100% blue agave)
- ½ cup Cointreau
- 1¼ cups fresh lime juice
- ¼ cup fresh lemon juice
- ¼ cup fresh orange juice
- ¼ cup superfine sugar
- 4 teaspoons honey, warmed

Combine all of the ingredients in a large pitcher and stir to dissolve the sugar. Refrigerate until chilled or serve immediately over cracked ice.

—*Grace Parisi*

VARIATION Make a Margarita Rickey by mixing 2 cups Juicy Margarita (without the tequila and Cointreau) with ¾ cup gin and ½ cup club soda. Serve over ice.

Iced Teaquila

MAKES 6 DRINKS ●●●

- ½ cup sugar
- ¼ cup water
- 3 tablespoons fresh lemon juice
- 1½ cups guava nectar (see Note)
- 1 cup brewed Earl Grey tea
- ¾ cup silver tequila

Lemon twists, for serving

1. In a small saucepan, combine the sugar and water and bring to a simmer over moderately high heat, stirring to dissolve the sugar. Remove the sugar syrup from the heat and let cool to room temperature. Stir in the lemon juice.

2. In a large pitcher, combine the lemon syrup with the guava nectar, Earl Grey tea and tequila. Pour the teaquila into tall glasses over ice and garnish each with a lemon twist.

—*Todd English*

NOTE Guava nectar is available in the Latin section of many supermarkets and at health food stores.

MAKE AHEAD The teaquila can be refrigerated overnight.

Blueberry Mojito

MAKES 1 DRINK ●

- ½ cup plus 2 tablespoons blueberries
- 1½ tablespoons superfine sugar
- 2 lime wedges
- 2 large mint leaves

Club soda or seltzer

- ½ cup crushed ice
- 3 tablespoons (1½ ounces) white rum

1. In a cocktail shaker, lightly muddle ½ cup of blueberries with the sugar, lime wedges, mint and a small splash of club soda. Add the ice and rum and shake.

2. Spoon the remaining 2 tablespoons of blueberries into a tall glass and pour in the mojito. Top with a small splash of club soda and serve.

—*David Matthew Fickes*

Telluride Mojito

MAKES 4 DRINKS (ABOUT 3½ CUPS) ●

- 16 small fresh mint sprigs, plus 4 more for garnish
- ¼ cup plus 2 tablespoons superfine sugar
- ½ cup fresh lime juice
- ¾ cup white or gold rum
- 8 dashes bitters
- 2 cups club soda

1. In a bowl, using a wooden spoon, crush the mint with the sugar until the mint is coarsely chopped and the sugar is pale green. Add the lime juice, rum and bitters and stir to dissolve the sugar.

2. Strain the mixture through a coarse strainer into a small pitcher. Pour into tall glasses over ice and top each drink with ½ cup of the club soda. Garnish with mint sprigs and serve.

—*Grace Parisi*

VARIATION Make a Colorado Dark-n-Stormy by mixing 1 cup Telluride Mojito (without the rum and soda) with ¾ cup dark rum and 2 cups ginger beer. Serve over ice.

Lillet Fizz

MAKES 1 DRINK ●

¼ cup Lillet Blanc
½ teaspoon Cointreau
2 tablespoons seltzer
1 strip of orange zest

Pour the Lillet, Cointreau and seltzer over ice in a shaker. Shake, then strain into a chilled cocktail glass. Twist the strip of orange zest over the drink and drop it in.
—*Pete Wells*

Cricket Ball Aperitif

MAKES 8 DRINKS ●

¼ cup water
¼ cup sugar
¾ cup Lillet Rouge (6 ounces)
   Bitters
1 bottle (750 ml) chilled
   demi-sec Champagne
8 lemon twists

1. In a small saucepan, combine the water with the sugar; bring to a simmer over moderately low heat. Cook, stirring until the sugar dissolves; let the syrup cool.

2. In a pitcher, combine the Lillet with the syrup and 8 dashes of bitters. Refrigerate until chilled. Pour the mixture into 8 Champagne flutes and fill with Champagne. Garnish with the lemon twists.
—*Jimmy Bradley*

Sushi Bar Cocktail

MAKES 1 DRINK ●

1 cucumber, peeled and sliced
3 tablespoons sake
1 teaspoon liquid from a jar
   of pickled ginger
½ teaspoon fresh lime juice
   Pinch each of salt and superfine
   sugar

Blueberry Mojito

In a blender or food processor, puree the cucumber with 2 tablespoons of water. Strain 3 tablespoons of the cucumber juice over ice in a shaker. Add the other ingredients and shake. Strain into a chilled cocktail glass.
—*Pete Wells*

Spanish Sangrita

MAKES 1 DRINK ●

¼ cup fino sherry
3 tablespoons tomato juice
2 tablespoons fresh orange juice
1 teaspoon fresh lime juice

Pour the all the ingredients over ice in a shaker; shake vigorously. Strain into a chilled cocktail glass. —*Pete Wells*

Any Port in a Storm Cocktail

MAKES 1 DRINK ●

¼ cup ruby port
2 tablespoons pineapple juice
½ teaspoon fresh lemon juice
1 fresh mint sprig

Pour the port, pineapple juice and lemon juice over ice in a shaker; shake vigorously. Strain into a chilled cocktail glass and garnish with the mint.
—*Pete Wells*

Iced Teaquila

index

Page numbers in **boldface** indicate photographs.

index

index

index

index

index

index

index

index

index

index

index

index

index

index

contributors

Jody Adams was named one of FOOD & WINE's Best New Chefs in 1993. She is the executive chef and partner at Rialto in Cambridge, Massachusetts, and Red Clay in Chestnut Hill, Massachusetts, and a partner at blu in Boston.

Engin Akin is a radio talk-show host, cookbook author and Turkish food expert. She lives in Istanbul.

Ann Chantal Altman is the chef for the executive dining room at Vivendi Universal in New York City.

Murielle Andraud is the owner, with her husband, Jean-Luc Thunevin, of Château de Valandraud, a vineyard in St-Émilion, France.

Jennifer Aranas is the chef and co-owner with her husband, Cesar Cassillas, of Rambutan in Chicago.

Alison Attenborough is a food stylist in New York City.

Generoso Bahena is the chef and owner of three Mexican restaurants in Chicago: Chilpancingo, Ixcapuzalco and Generoso's Bar and Grill.

Dan Barber is the chef and owner of Blue Hill Restaurant and Dan Barber Catering, Inc., both in New York City.

Lily Barberio is an assistant editor at FOOD & WINE Magazine.

Peter Birmingham is the sommelier at the restaurant Elisabeth Daniel in San Francisco.

Jean-François Bonnet is the pastry chef at the restaurant Cello in New York City.

Massimo Bottura is the chef and owner of La Francescana in Modena, Italy.

Jimmy Bradley is the chef and owner of The Red Cat and the Harrison, both in New York City.

Terrance Brennan, a 1995 FOOD & WINE Best New Chef, is the chef and owner of the restaurants Picholine and Artisanal in New York City.

Jean Calviac is co-owner of Castelnau des Fieumarcon, a privately owned 13th-century-village-turned-hotel in southwest France. He is also joint owner of France's largest organic-seed source, La Ferme de Sainte-Marthe.

Mike Chelini is the winemaker at Stony Hill Vineyards in St. Helena, California.

Wai Chu, chocolatier, is the owner of El Eden Chocolates, which specializes in handcrafted truffles, in New York City.

Melissa Clark, a freelance writer and *New York Times* contributor, is coauthor, with pastry chef Claudia Fleming, of *The Last Course.*

Michael Cordúa was named one of FOOD & WINE's Best New Chefs in 1994. He is now chef and owner of three restaurants in Houston: Churrascos, Amazón Grill and Américas.

Kelly Courtney was named one of FOOD & WINE's Best New Chefs in 2001. She is the executive chef and owner of Mod in Chicago.

Peggy Cullen, author of *Got Milk? The Cookie Book* (Chronicle Books), is a baker and candy maker.

Danielle Custer was named one of FOOD & WINE's Best New Chefs in 1998. She is the chef at 727 Pine in Seattle.

Regan Daley, a former pastry chef, is the author of *In the Sweet Kitchen* (Artisan). She lives in Toronto.

Daniel DeLong is the chef-partner at Manka's Inverness Lodge in Inverness, California.

Tom Douglas is the chef and owner of Palace Kitchen, Dahlia Lounge and Etta's Seafood, all in Seattle. He wrote *Tom Douglas' Seattle Kitchen* (Morrow), chosen by FOOD & WINE as one of the Best Cookbooks of 2000.

Wylie Dufresne was named one of FOOD & WINE's Best New Chefs in 2001. He is the executive chef at 71 Clinton Fresh Food in New York City.

Joshua Eisen is a former chef and restaurant wine director turned writer. He lives in New York City.

Todd English is the executive chef and owner of 16 restaurants across the United States. He is the author of *The Olives Table, The Figs Table* and *The Olives Dessert Table* (all Simon & Schuster), each of which was recognized by FOOD & WINE as among the Best Cookbooks published in their respective years. He was named one of FOOD & WINE's Best New Chefs in 1990.

Andrew Evans is the chef and owner, with his wife, Liz, of the Inn at Easton in Easton, Maryland.

David Matthew Fickes is the chef at Mojo in Los Angeles.

Bobby Flay is the executive chef at the New York City restaurants Mesa Grill and Bolo. He is the host of two Food Network shows—*Hot Off the Grill with Bobby Flay* and *Food Nation*—and the author of numerous cookbooks.

Susanna Foo, a 1989 FOOD & WINE Best New Chef, is the owner and executive chef at the restaurant Susanna Foo in Philadelphia.

Pierre Gagnaire is the chef and owner of the restaurant Pierre Gagnaire in Paris.

Sandro Gamba was named one of FOOD & WINE's Best New Chefs in 2001. He is the executive chef at NoMI in Chicago.

Stéphane Garnier is the head chef at the Château de la Bourdaisière, a 16th-century estate in Montlouis-sur-Loire, near Tours, France.

George Germon was named one of FOOD & WINE's Best New Chefs in 1988. He is the chef and owner, with Johanne Killeen, of Al Forno in Providence, Rhode Island.

Sam Godfrey is the owner of Perfect Endings bakery in California's San Francisco Bay Area.

Joyce Goldstein is a cookbook author and restaurant consultant. Her most recent cookbook is *Enoteca: Simple, Delicious Recipes in the Italian Wine Bar Tradition* (Chronicle Books).

Cary Gott is a fourth-generation winemaker and founder of Montevina winery (now owned by the Trinchero family) in Amador County, California. He lives with his wife, Vickie Gott, in St. Helena, California.

contributors

Duncan and Joel Gott are brothers and co-owners of Taylor's Automatic Refresher, a 1950s-style drive-in restaurant in St. Helena, California, and of Palisades Market in Calistoga, California. Joel also heads Joel Gott Wines.

Vickie Gott is a "damn fine" home cook. She lives in St. Helena, California.

Laurent Gras was formerly the chef at the Waldorf-Astoria's Peacock Alley in New York City.

Gabrielle Hamilton is the chef and owner of Prune in New York City.

Kate Heddings is a senior food editor at FOOD & WINE Magazine.

Suki Hertz is a chef, food stylist and nutritionist.

Gerald Hirigoyen, chef and co-owner of Fringale and Pastis restaurants in San Francisco, was named one of FOOD & WINE's Best New Chefs in 1994. He is the author of *Bistro* (Sunset) and, with his wife, Cameron, *The Basque Kitchen* (HarperCollins).

Scott Howell is the chef and owner of Nana's in Durham, North Carolina.

Nancy Harmon Jenkins lives much of the year in Cortona, Italy. Her latest cookbook, *Flavors of Tuscany* (Broadway Books), was named one of FOOD & WINE's Best Cookbooks of 1998. She is working on a book about key Mediterranean ingredients.

Melissa Kelly is the chef and owner of Primo in Rockland, Maine.

Emmanuel Kemiji is the owner and winemaker at Miura Vineyards and Candela Cellars, both in Santa Rosa, California. He is a wine consultant for the Ritz-Carlton hotel company.

Marcia Kiesel is the test kitchen supervisor at FOOD & WINE and co-author of *Simple Art of Vietnamese Cooking* (Simon & Schuster).

Johanne Killeen was named one of FOOD & WINE's Best New Chefs in 1988. She is the chef and owner, with George Germon, of Al Forno in Providence, Rhode Island.

Peggy Knickerbocker is a food writer and cooking teacher based in San Francisco. She is the author of *Olive Oil: From Tree to Table* (Chronicle) and coauthor of *Rose Pistola: A North Beach Cookbook* (Broadway Books), recognized by FOOD & WINE as one of the Best Cookbooks of 1999.

Michael Kramer is the chef at McCrady's in Charleston, South Carolina.

Gray Kunz is the author, with Peter Kaminsky, of *The Elements of Taste* (Little Brown and Company). Formerly the executive chef at New York City's Lespinasse, he was recognized by FOOD & WINE as one of the Best New Chefs of 1993.

Charles Leary is a co-owner of Trout Point Lodge and Trout Point Cooking School in Kemptville, Nova Scotia.

David Lebovitz is a pastry consultant, instructor and cookbook author. His 12 years of work in the pastry kitchen at Chez Panisse in Berkeley, California, gave rise to many of the recipes in his book *Room For Dessert* (HarperCollins), recognized by FOOD & WINE as one of the Best Cookbooks of 1999.

Alex Lee is the executive chef at the restaurant Daniel in New York City.

Michael Leviton was named one of FOOD & WINE's Best New Chefs in 2000. He is the chef and co-owner of Lumière in West Newton, Massachusetts.

Randy Lewis was named one of FOOD & WINE's Best New Chefs in 2001. He was formerly the chef-owner at Indigo in New Orleans.

Anita Lo was named one of FOOD & WINE's Best New Chefs in 2001. She is the co-owner and executive chef at Annisa in New York City.

Barbara Lynch is the executive chef and owner of No. 9 Park in Boston. She was named one of FOOD & WINE's Best New Chefs in 1996.

Stephanie Lyness is a cookbook author and editor. She is collaborating with Suvir Saran on a book about Indian home cooking.

Nick Malgieri is the director of pastry and baking at the Institute of Culinary Education in New York City. His books *Chocolate* and *Cookies Unlimited* (both HarperCollins) were recognized by FOOD & WINE as among the Best Cookbooks published in their respective years.

Guy Martin is executive chef at the restaurant Le Grand Véfour in Paris. His latest cookbook is *Cuisiner les Fromages* (Éditions du Chêne).

Frank Mendoza is the executive chef at Chicago's W Hotel.

Rene Michelena was named one of FOOD & WINE's Best New Chefs in 1998. He is the chef at Centro in Boston.

Brandon Miller is the chef at Stoke's Restaurant & Bar in Monterey, California.

Glenn Monk is co-owner of Beyond Hospitality Resources, a restaurant and hotel consulting firm in Vancouver, British Columbia.

George Morrone, formerly the chef at the restaurant Fifth Floor, is the executive chef at the newly opened Redwood Park. Both restaurants are in San Francisco.

Eberhard Müller, formerly the chef at Lutèce, is now the executive chef at Bayard's in New York City and the owner, with his wife, Paulette Satur, of Satur Farms on the North Fork of Long Island.

Tamara Murphy was named one of FOOD & WINE's Best New Chefs in 1994. She is the executive chef and owner at Brasa in Seattle.

Carrie Nahabedian is the chef and co-owner of the restaurant Naha in Chicago.

Jamie Oliver is the chef at Monte's Restaurant in London. He hosts the Food TV cooking show *The Naked Chef* and is author of a cookbook by the same name. His latest cookbook, *The Naked Chef Takes Off,* is published by Hyperion.

Will Packwood was named one of FOOD & WINE's Best New Chefs in 2001. He is the executive chef at Emilia's in Austin, Texas.

Grace Parisi, senior test kitchen associate at FOOD & WINE, is the author of *Summer/Winter Pasta* (William Morrow).

contributors

Rajat Parr is the sommelier at the restaurant Fifth Floor in San Francisco.

Jacques Pépin, master chef, TV personality, food columnist, cooking teacher and contributing editor to FOOD & WINE, is the author of numerous books and is co-host, with his daughter, Claudine, of the PBS television series *Jacques Pépin Celebrates*. A companion cookbook is published by Alfred A. Knopf. His books *Jacques Pépin's Kitchen: Encore with Claudine* (Bay Books and Tapes, Inc.) and, written with Julia Child, *Julia and Jacques Cooking at Home* (Knopf) were honored by FOOD & WINE as among the Best Cookbooks of the Year in 1999 and 2000, respectively.

Vaughn Perret is a co-owner of Trout Point Lodge and Trout Point Cooking School in Kemptville, Nova Scotia.

Don Pintabona is the chef at Tribeca Grill in New York City and author of *The Tribeca Grill Cookbook* (Villard Books).

Debra Ponzek is the executive chef at Aux Delices in Greenwich, Connecticut. Named one of FOOD & WINE's Best New Chefs in 1989, she is the author of *French Food, American Accent: Debra Ponzek's Spirited Cuisine* (Clarkson Potter).

Maricel Presilla is the chef and co-owner of the restaurant Zafra in Hoboken, New Jersey. Her new book is *The New Taste of Chocolate: A Cultural & Natural History of Cacao with Recipes* (Ten Speed Press).

Wolfgang Puck, instrumental in popularizing so-called California cuisine and renowned for his gourmet pizza, is the chef and owner of numerous restaurants throughout the world, including Spago Beverly Hills, voted Best Restaurant by FOOD & WINE readers in 2000. He hosts the Food TV show *Wolfgang Puck.*

Steven Raichlen is the author of 22 books, including the IACP/Julia Child Award–winning *Barbecue! Bible* (Workman), which was also honored by FOOD & WINE as one of the Best Cookbooks of 1999; the James Beard Award–winning *Healthy Jewish Cooking* (Viking); and, most recently, *How to Grill* (Workman). He is currently working on a book on regional American barbecue called *America on Fire.*

Rebecca Rather is the owner of the Rather Sweet Bakery & Café in Fredericksburg, Texas. She is the author of the forthcoming cookbook *The Pastry Queen*.

Christina Reid-Orchid is the chef and owner of Christina's on Orcas Island in Washington State.

E. Michael Reidt was named one of FOOD & WINE's Best New Chefs in 2001. He is the chef at Wish in South Beach, Florida.

Melissa Roberts is a freelance cook and food stylist in New York City.

Michael Roberts is a chef, restaurant consultant and food writer. His latest cookbook is *Parisian Home Cooking* (William Morrow).

Toni Robertson is the executive chef at the Sonoma Mission Inn & Spa in Sonoma, California.

Michael Romano is the chef and partner at New York City's Union Square Café. His new book, co-authored with Danny Meyer, *Second Helpings from Union Square Café,* is published by HarperCollins. He was named one of FOOD & WINE's Best New Chefs in 1991.

Ilene Rosen is the savory chef at the City Bakery in New York City.

Maury Rubin is the pastry chef and owner of City Bakery in New York City.

Frank Ruta was named one of FOOD & WINE's Best New Chefs in 2001. He is the owner and executive chef of Palena in Washington, D.C.

Suvir Saran is a cooking teacher and restaurant consultant. He is collaborating with Stephanie Lyness on a book about Indian home cooking.

Guy Savoy is the chef and owner of the restaurant Guy Savoy in Paris.

Sally Schneider is a contributing editor to FOOD & WINE Magazine. She is the author of *A New Way to Cook* (Artisan).

William Sherer is the wine director at Aqua, Pisces and Charles Nob Hill, all in San Francisco.

Jane Sigal is a senior food editor at FOOD & WINE and the author of *Backroad Bistros, Farmhouse Fare* (Doubleday) and *Normandy Gastronomique* (Abbeville).

Nancy Silverton is the author of *Nancy Silverton's Pastries from the La Brea Bakery,* honored by FOOD & WINE as one of the Best Cookbooks of 2000. Pastry chef and owner of La Brea Bakery and Campanile, both in Los Angeles, she was named one of FOOD & WINE's Best New Chefs in 1990.

Jack Staub is the co-owner of Hortulus Farm, featuring 100 varieties of heirloom vegetables, in Bucks County, Pennsylvania.

Craig Stoll was named one of FOOD & WINE's Best New Chefs in 2001. He is the executive chef and proprietor of Delfina in San Francisco.

Larry Stone is the wine director and a partner at Rubicon in San Francisco.

Diana Sturgis is the comfort food columnist at *Friends Magazine* and a frequent contributor to FOOD & WINE. She teaches in the Health and Nutrition Sciences department at City University of New York.

Johnathan Sundstrom was named one of FOOD & WINE's Best New Chefs in 2001. He is the executive chef at Earth & Ocean in Seattle.

Kevin Taylor is the executive chef and owner of the restaurants Dandelion in Boulder, Colorado; Restaurant Kevin Taylor and Jou Jou, both located in Denver's Teatro Hotel; and Palettes at the Denver Art Museum.

Jacques Torres, former executive pastry chef at Le Cirque 2000, recently opened his own chocolate factory, Jacques Torres Chocolate, in Brooklyn. He is the author of two cookbooks: *Dessert Circus* and *Dessert Circus at Home,* both recognized by FOOD & WINE as among the Best Cookbooks of 1998 and 1999, respectively.

Jeremiah Tower is a chef and the former owner of acclaimed San Francisco Bay Area restaurants Chez Panisse and Stars, among others. His latest cookbook is a revised edition of *Jeremiah Tower's New American Classics* (Abrams).

Rori Trovato is a chef and food stylist based in New York City.

Alex Urena is the chef at Marseille in New York City.

Tom Valenti, a 1990 FOOD & WINE Best New Chef, is the executive chef at Ouest in New York City.

contributors

Ruth Van Waerebeek is the author of *Everybody Eats Well in Belgium* and *The Chilean Kitchen*. She divides her time between New York City and her guesthouse in the foothills of the Chilean Andes Mountains.

Lance Dean Velasquez was named one of FOOD & WINE's Best New Chefs in 1996. He is the executive chef at Johnfrank in San Francisco.

Marc Vetri was named one of FOOD & WINE's Best New Chefs in 1999. He is the chef and owner of Vetri in Philadelphia.

Jean-Georges Vongerichten is chef and co-owner of the New York City restaurants Jo Jo, Mercer Kitchen, Jean Georges and Vong (which also has locations in Chicago, London and Hong Kong), as well as Prime Steakhouse in Las Vegas and Dune in the Bahamas. He is co-author of *Jean-Georges: Cooking at Home with a Four-Star Chef* (Broadway Books), named one of FOOD & WINE's Best Cookbooks of 1998. His newest cookbooks are *Simple to Spectacular* (Broadway Books) and *Simple Cuisine* (Macmillan).

Joanne Weir, a San Francisco cooking teacher, hosts the television show *Weir Cooking in the Wine Country*. Her newest book is *Joanne Weir's More Cooking in the Wine Country* (Simon & Schuster).

Patricia Wells, a Paris-based writer and food critic, is the author of the forthcoming *The Paris Cookbook* (HarperCollins).

Pete Wells, formerly a senior editor at FOOD & WINE Magazine, is an editor at *Details Magazine*.

Randy Windham is the chef at Cafe Monk in San Francisco.

Paula Wolfert is the author of six cookbooks, most recently *Mediterranean Grains and Greens* (HarperCollins), honored by FOOD & WINE as the Best Cookbook of 1998. She is currently at work on *Mediterranean Cooking—Slow and Easy*.

Arnold Eric Wong is the executive chef at Bacar Restaurant and Wine Salon and EOS Restaurant and Wine Bar, both in San Francisco.

Clifford A. Wright, winner of the 2000 James Beard Cookbook of the Year, is author of the recently published *Mediterranean Vegetables* (Harvard Common Press).

Galen Zamarra was formerly the chef at New York City's Bouley Bakery.

Special thanks to the following restaurants and institutions for their contributions to this book:

Chez Panisse, Berkeley, California
Hacienda Zuleta, Ecuador
Institute of Culinary Education, New York City

Jamie Oliver's recipes are adapted from *The Naked Chef Takes Off* by Jamie Oliver. Copyright ©2000 Jamie Oliver Ltd. Reprinted by permission of Hyperion. All rights reserved.

Gray Kunz's recipes are adapted from *The Elements of Taste* by Gray Kunz and Peter Kaminsky. Copyright ©2001 by Gray Kunz and Peter Kaminsky. Reprinted by permission of Little, Brown and Company (Inc.). All rights reserved.

The Van Gogh's Table recipes are adapted from *Van Gogh's Table*. Copyright ©2001 by Dominique-Charles Janssens. Reprinted by permission of Artisan, a division of Workman Publishing Co., Inc., New York. All rights reserved.

photo credits

Antonis Achilleos: 38 (bottom), 42, 61 (right), 130, 187 (left), 256; Cedric Angeles: 143; Quentin Bacon: 101, 161 (left), 167, 197, 207, 370; James Baigrie: 12 (bottom), 18, 38 (top), 40, 45 (left), 47 (top), 65 (right), 68 (left), 69, 70, 74, 76, 79, 85 (both), 171 (both), 184, 187 (right), 188, 194, 246, 260, 266, 273, 277, 280, 299, 321, 338 (both), 350, 352 (left), 353, 368, 377, 394, 396; Edmund Barr: 322 (WayneThiebaud); Mirjam Bleeker: 23, 108, 191 (left), 342; Luis Bruno: 11, 21, 24, 105, 124 (top), 126 (top), 155; Paul Costello: 61 (left), 63, 146, 152, 289, 349, 352 (right), 359, 386; Beatriz Da Costa: 10, 41 (top), 93, 106, 120 (left), 159, 198 (left), 201, 251, 272, 296 (right), 384, 395; Reed Davis: 15 (top), 71, 90 (right), 243, 364; Brian Doben: 5 (top left), 6, 8, 30, 41 (bottom), 183, 264, 329, 390; Jim Franco: 114, 115, 181 (top right); Andrew French: 7 (left), 231, 240, 346, 373 (bottom), 381; Dana Gallagher: 179 (bottom), 378, 392, 393; Fran Gealer: 73, 136, 311; Noah Greenberg: 176 (Patrick Martins); Ethan Hill: 356 (Ming Fay); Matthew Hranek: 2 (Isaac Mizrahi); Lisa Hubbard: 103, 119, 148 (top), 160, 181 (bottom right); Richard Gerhard Jung: 29, 37, 39, 49, 52, 72 (bottom), 80, 100 (bottom), 113, 120 (right), 128, 132, 139, 145, 148 (bottom), 151, 168, 172 (top right), 178, 181 (left), 192, 211, 274 (bottom), 287, 290 (bottom), 345, 355, 362 (bottom), 365, 369 (bottom), 397 (bottom); Keller & Keller: 122, 123, 134; John Kernick: 44, 48 (right), 65 (left), 72 (top), 97, 147 (right), 164, 172 (bottom right), 179 (top), 196, 254, 326, 373 (top); Rick Lew: 216, 304 (Gabrielle Hamilton), 327; Lisa Linder: 5 (top right), 82, 99, 170, 208 (Claude Steger), 228, 380; Maura McEvoy: 19 (left), 36 (left), 56, 68 (right), 77, 84, 98, 163, 191 (right), 203, 224, 232, 238, 241, 291 (top), 330, 362 (top), 371; William Meppem: 19 (right), 28 (bottom), 32, 36 (right), 43, 78, 86, 117 (left), 118, 124 (bottom), 125, 154, 198 (right), 199, 218, 219, 221, 225, 235, 253, 258, 263, 269, 274 (top), 275, 279, 282, 290 (top), 291 (bottom), 296 (left), 300, 301, 324, 344, 383; Mark Molloy: 247, 261, 332, 366; Amy Neunsinger: 5 (bottom), 397 (top); Victoria Pearson: 15 (bottom), 47 (bottom), 89, 161 (right), 309, 335, 375; Personal Collection of Jacques Pépin: 54 (Jacques Pépin); David Prince: 302, 303; Maria Robledo: 35, 48 (left), 87, 126 (bottom), 147 (left); Zubin Shroff: 16, 17, 25; Evan Sklar: 121, 129, 229, 230, 244; Hugh Stewart: 22, 26 (Jamie Oliver), 110 (Jamie Oliver), 124 (center), 213, 348; Petrina Tinslay: 90 (left), 185 (right), 284 (Stéphane Garnier), 295, 347 (top), 367; Richard Warren: 58, 293; Simon Watson: 28 (top), 59, 92, 96, 215, 314 (Teresa Chang), 360; Wendell T. Webber: 109, 117 (right), 193, 249; Michael Weschler: 234; Anna Williams: 12 (top), 33, 45 (right), 67, 100 (top), 127, 157, 169, 172 (left), 174, 185 (left), 239, 310, 333, 341, 347 (bottom), 358, 369 (top), 382, 387; Susan Yohann: 7 (right); Roy Zipstein: 140

AND PLEASE NOTE

Our annual FOOD & WINE collections are identified by the year in which each is released, rather than by the year in which the magazine issues were published. Hence this year's book, published in January of 2002, is titled *FOOD & WINE Magazine's 2002 Cookbook* and is a compilation of the recipes from the 2001 magazines.

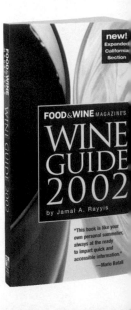